ALL
GOD'S
DANGERS

ALL
GOD'S
DANGERS

The Life of Nate Shaw

THEODORE
ROSENGARTEN

VINTAGE BOOKS
A DIVISION OF RANDOM HOUSE
NEW YORK

First Vintage Books Edition, February 1984
Copyright © 1974 by Theodore Rosengarten
and the Estate of Ned Cobb
All rights reserved under International and
Pan-American Copyright Conventions. Published in
the United States by Random House, Inc., New York,
and simultaneously in Canada by Random House of
Canada Limited, Toronto. Originally published by
Alfred A. Knopf, Inc. in 1974.

Library of Congress Cataloging in Publication Data
Shaw, Nate.
All God's dangers.
1. Shaw, Nate.
2. Share-cropping—History.
3. Afro-Americans—Alabama—Biography.
I. Rosengarten, Theodore.
II. Title.
HD1478.U6S5 1984   976.1′46′0924 [B]   83-19828
ISBN 0-394-72245-0

Manufactured in the United States of America
9876543
Cover photograph of Nate Shaw (Ned Cobb) in 1907

To Clyde and Anne

Whosoever is fearful and afraid, let him return
and depart early from mount Gilead.

JUDGES 7:3

CONTENTS

Lower Half of Tukabahchee County, Alabama

◯ County Seat
🏠 Towns and Settlements
⛪ Churches
⚰ Cemeteries
+++ Railroads
— Roads

Beaufort

Crane's Ford

Newcastle

Somerset

New Morning Church

Gem Stone

Lavender's bridge

Sylvan Grove Baptist Church

Chapel Ridge

COUNTY LINE

Sitimachas Creek

Tukabahchee River

Pottstown

Manassas Church

Elam Baptist Church

Pottstown Baptist Church

Sharon's Crossing

Holiness Church

Coalhouse hill

Highgate

Zion Baptist Church

Pilgrims' Rest Cemetery

Tukabahchee City

Teaks' Church

Two Forks

Jerusalem Cemetery

Litabixee

Beanville

Tucker's Crossing

Calusa

Ore City

Apafalya

East Calusa

Sinking Creek

State Street

COUNTY LINE

0   1   2   3   4   5
miles

PREFACE

This big book is the autobiography of an illiterate man. It is the story of a black tenant farmer from east-central Alabama who grew up in the society of former slaves and slaveholders and reached maturity during the advent of segregation law. For years he labored "under many rulins, just like the other Negro, that I knowed was injurious to man and displeasin to God and still I had to fall back." One morning in December, 1932, Nate Shaw faced a crowd of deputy sheriffs sent to confiscate a neighbor's livestock. He knew they would be after his, next. Burdened by the indignities he had suffered in the past and awed by the prospect of overturning "this southern way of life," Shaw stood his ground.

I met Nate Shaw in January, 1969. He had just turned eighty-four years old. I had come to Tukabahchee County with a friend who was investigating a defunct organization called the Alabama Share-croppers Union. We had learned that a survivor was living near Pottstown, some twenty miles south of the county seat, where we'd been sifting through trial dossiers and newspaper files in the court-house basement. One icy morning we set out to find him.

The road from Beaufort to Pottstown rolls and winds through piney woods country. Nate Shaw lives just below the foothills where

the lowlands begin. We hunted for his house along the asphalt by-
roads until we came across a mailbox with the name Shaw in bold
letters. A woman stepped out onto the porch of a tin-roofed cabin
and, seeing us hesitate, called us to come in.

Her name is Winnie Shaw and she is the wife of Nate's half-
brother TJ. She is a spare-built, walnut-colored woman with wide-
set eyes and a girlish face. She said she was seventy-three years
old but she looked much younger. We were already into the front
room of her house before we introduced ourselves. We explained
that we were students from Massachusetts and that we'd come to
Alabama to study this union.

TJ walked in. He had been overhauling one of his machines—
winter work—when he heard our car drive up in his yard. Winnie
told him, "They want to see Nate." TJ walked out again and across
the road to Nate's house. TJ completely filled the doorway walking in
and out. He is six and a half feet tall when he stands straight. But
sixty-five seasons of picking cotton have given him a stoop from
the hips, so that standing still he resembles a man leaning on a
long-handled hoe.

He came back with Nate, who had been feeding his mule—one
of the last mules in the settlement. Nate is six inches shorter than
TJ and a shade lighter, though both are dark men. He is trim and
square-shouldered; he has a small, fine head and high Indian
cheekbones and brow. We shook hands and he announced that he
was always glad to welcome "his people." He knew why we had
come by our appearance: young, white, polite, frightened, northern.
People who looked like us had worked on voter registration drives,
marched in Selma and Montgomery, rode those freedom buses
across the Mason-Dixon line. He had seen "us" on television and
it didn't surprise him to see us now because this was his movement
and he knew a lot about it; he had been active in it before we were
born. Raising his right hand to God, he swore there was no "get-back"
in him: he was standing where he stood in '32.

Nate took off his hat and sat down with us by the fireplace.
We asked him right off why he joined the union. He didn't respond
directly; rather, he "interpreted" the question and began, "I was
haulin a load of hay out of Apafalya one day—" and continued un-
interrupted for eight hours. He recounted dealings with landlords,
bankers, fertilizer agents, mule traders, gin operators, sheriffs, and

judges—stories of the social relations of the cotton system. By evening, the fire had risen and died and risen again and our question was answered.

TJ turned on the electric light, a single high-watt bulb suspended in the center of the room. We talked some more with the Shaws about how we planned to use the information Nate had just given us. They were glad to help us, they said, and if our "report" reached other people who found their lives instructive, they would be gratified. We thanked them for being so kind and for taking us into their confidence and, promising to return, we left.

Driving north, we felt something slipping out of our grasp. We could remember the details of Nate's stories but no reconstruction could capture the power of his performance. His stories built upon one another so that the sequence expressed the sense of a man "becoming." Although Nate Shaw and the Sharecroppers Union had intersected only for a moment, everything that came before had prepared him for it. Nate had apparently put his whole life into stories and what he told us was just one chapter.

We had come to study a union, and we had stumbled on a storyteller. Nate must have told his stories—at least the ones we heard—many times before. TJ and Winnie, who listened as closely as we did, would stir whenever he digressed and remind him where his story was going. Nate would roll his tongue over the lone yellow spearlike tooth at the corner of his mouth and say, "I'm comin to that, I just have to tell this first."

OVER the next two years I visited the Shaws twice. Each time I met other members of the family who, if more wary of my intentions, were no less hospitable. In particular, I struck up a friendship with Vernon Shaw, Nate's second son. Vernon is the last of nine brothers and sisters still farming. He has a sixty-acre place of his own on which he raises beef cattle and corn to feed his hogs. In addition, he farms a big crop of cotton on rented land. It was he who stepped into his father's shoes when Nate went to prison and stuck by his mother and the younger children for twelve years until Nate returned. His brothers and sisters look to him as the immediate link with the old family and the soil.

Four of Nate's children live in Alabama, three within shouting distance—Rachel, the second child and oldest girl, called "Sister"; Garvan, the eighth child and youngest boy; and Vernon. Calvin Thomas, the first child and oldest son, lives about twenty miles away. Five children live out of state—Francis, the third son, in Philadelphia; Mattie Jane, the second daughter, in Brooklyn, New York; Eugene, the fourth son, in Middletown, Ohio; Leah Ann, the third daughter, and Rosa Louise, the fourth daughter and youngest child, both in Chattanooga, Tennessee.

Each time I visited Nate Shaw, he told me a little more about them: how they support themselves, how they hold their heads up in the world. Shaw prides himself on the social standing of his children. They are upright and industrious, following the education they received in his home. But his chief fascination is with their deeper "natures," for which he doesn't hold himself accountable. "There's my Vernon," he would say, or "There's my Francis," and leap into some childhood incident that showed their natures to him and distinguished them from their brothers and sisters.

Shaw revealed less about his first wife, Hannah. He praised her for her strengths and virtues and chided himself for not having acknowledged her sufficiently during her life. His remarks were brief and I had no cause to press him at the time. Later I learned from him and his children what a great-hearted woman she was.

Nothing so aroused Shaw as his recollections of his father. Shaw is still in conflict with a man who was a boy during President Lincoln's administration. While it is not unusual for a child to have unresolved feelings about a parent, it is disarming to see a struggle so open and honest. Shaw demonstrates that a person is, at every moment, everything he always was; his current role can eclipse his past but not deny it. Shaw remains his father's child though he is in his eighties and his father has been dead over forty years.

In March, 1971, I went back to Alabama with a proposal to record Shaw's life. He agreed that the experience would be good for both of us and the results might prove useful to people interested in the history of his region, class, and race. To appreciate his part in that history it is helpful to know something about his setting.

East of the Black Belt and south of the Appalachians the Alabama countryside descends slowly to a plain. Young piney woods stretch methodically between pastures and farms. Off both sides of the roads derelict chimneys stand like watchkeepers on the sites of tenant farmer shacks. These are the tangible signs of the tenant system's collapse.

Upland, the population is predominantly white and poor. Lumber camps and textile mills offer the steadiest employment in the region. Some small farms produce cotton for the mills, and fruit—mostly peaches—for roadside and out-of-state markets. But the soil is not particularly suited to cotton and the fruit is vulnerable to the great rains and late frosts that distress hill country agriculture.

The people of the lowlands still grow cotton, along with corn, sugar cane, peanuts, watermelons, and other table foods. The land is smooth and fit for extensive cultivation. This was plantation country and the population today is largely black. After the Civil War, owners of the plantations divided their lands into tenant plots. To their surprise and uneasiness, poor whites came down from the hills to compete with the freed slaves for land. For about twenty-five years, or until the 1890's, whites and blacks worked adjacent farms as sharecroppers and tenants. Then, hoping to counter falling cotton prices by exploiting a more submissive class, landlords pushed the poor whites back into the hills and filled their places with blacks.

Cotton prices reached new highs during the First World War, but farmers at the bottom of the tenant system shared little in the profits; for the system that encumbered them with mandatory debts also deprived them of authority to sell their crops. Thus, poor black farmers lived under the twin yoke of race oppression and economic peonage. Taking advantage of new openings in wartime industry, many fled to the cities. This great movement north intensified during the early years of the boll weevil's devastation through about 1920, and again during the Great Depression and the Second World War. The migration continues at a regular pace today.

Nate Shaw stayed in Alabama because he believed his labor gave him a claim to the land. He watched his neighbors pick up and leave but "*that* never come in my mind." Though he loathed his situation, he thought, "Somehow, some way, I'd overcome it. . . . I was determined to try."

I was hoping Shaw's autobiography would be a first installment in an intensive study of the family. I had no idea what shape it would take, or if I would have the means to do it, or if the children would cooperate. I did know that the Shaw family's experience was typical of many southern black families: the voyage from farm to factory, from country to city, from south to north. These relocations had profound effects on family life, class situation, and consciousness. There was much here to lure the historian.

I returned in June with a hundred pages of questions to ask Shaw. It became clear during our first session that I'd never get to a fraction of them. It would have taken years; moreover, my prepared questions distracted Shaw from his course. Since it was my aim to preserve his stories, I learned how to listen and not to resist his method of withholding facts for the sake of suspense. Everything came out in time, everything.

We would sit under the eave of his tool shed and talk for two to six hours per session. Shaw would whittle or make baskets as he spoke. He would quarter and peel a six-foot section of a young trunk, weave the strips into the desired shape, then put a handle on it. A large laundry basket would take him half a day to make, working steadily with wood cut the day before.

When it rained we would move our chairs inside the shed. There, in near dark, cramped among baskets, broken-bottomed chairs, sacks of feed and fertilizer, worn harnesses and tools, Shaw enacted his most fiery stories. I am thankful for all the rain we had, for it moved us to a natural theater and pounded the tin roof like a delirious crowd inciting an actor to the peak of his energy.

To start, I asked Shaw if he knew how he got his name. This tapped an important source of his earliest knowledge—the stories of old people. Shaw announced a ground rule for himself: he would always distinguish between what was told for the truth and what was told to entertain, between direct experience and hearsay. He went on to recollect the content and flavor of his childhood. In sum, he described how a black boy growing up in rural Alabama at the turn of the century acquired a practical education. At the death of his mother and his first barefoot days behind a plow—events separated by two months—he learned what sort of hard life lay ahead.

Beginning with his recollections of the first time his father hired him out to work for a white man, in 1904, Shaw recalled events and relationships according to the year, as though he had kept a mental journal. Thus we would spend one session covering 1904 and 1905, pick up at 1906 and so on. Once he married and left his father's house and had his own crop, each harvest completed both his work cycle and the perimeter of his experiences for that year.

For each place he farmed I asked about the quality and extent of the land, changes in the technology of farming, the size of his crops and the prices they brought him, his contracts and relationships with white people at every stage of the crop, the growth of his family and the division of labor within it, and how he felt about all that. Shaw told me how he moved from farm to farm seeking good land and the freedom to work it to its potential. By raising all his foodstuffs and hauling lumber while his older boys worked the farm, he became self-sufficient. At every step along the way he faced a challenge to his independence. Landlords tried to swindle him, merchants turned him out, neighbors despised his success. In spite of their schemes and in spite of the perils inherent to cotton farming, he prevailed.

When we came up to the crucial events of the thirties the sessions turned into heated dialogues. I pressed Shaw for his motivations and challenged him to justify himself. Here, I want to make my sympathies clear. Nate Shaw was—and is—a hero to me. I think he did the right thing when he joined the Sharecroppers Union and fought off the deputy sheriffs, though, of course, I had nothing to lose by his actions. My questions must unavoidably have expressed this judgment but they did not, I believe, change the substance of his responses.

Our sessions dealing with the prison years were more even-tempered, just as Shaw had had to keep cool to live out his sentence. I asked him about conditions at each of the three prison camps in which he served. He answered with stories about his work life and his relations with prison officials and fellow convicts. During these years, his wife Hannah and son Vernon presided over his family and property. His mules died, his automobile ran down, but he forced himself not to think about it.

Shaw was fifty-nine years old when he came home from prison. The years following his release were the most painful for him to talk about. For in his struggle to reclaim a portion of his former status he faced insuperable barriers—his age, poverty, and obsolete skills. Again, my questions pursued him from farm to farm. I asked about the issues foremost in his mind—his new relationships with his children and, after the death of Hannah, with his second wife, Josie; the social and economic changes that directly affected him, his family, and his race; and still, his stand that morning in December, 1932, against the forces of injustice.

After sixty hours spread over sixteen sessions we completed the first round. Shaw had given me the outlines of his life and many representative stories. I hadn't asked the questions I'd come with and I had to choose between doing that and going over the same ground with a finer-toothed comb. Shaw wanted to add details and whole stories he had remembered after we passed their places in the narrative. Taking his lead and working from notes I had written while playing back the tapes, we began again. We lasted fifteen more sessions and another sixty hours. As our talks drew to a close the sessions grew longer. The initiative was his. Our work strengthened him and sustained his belief that his struggles had been worth the effort, although he had only his recollections to show for them. These filled his days with a reality more powerful than the present.

AFTER working with Shaw I began making the rounds of his children. They had, of course, their own views of what he had done. They knew I had been attracted to him because of his connection with the Sharecroppers Union, and while they acknowledged his courage they were invariably critical of his stand. For they had lost their father for twelve years and watched the task of raising a large family during hard times take its physical toll on their mother.

The ambition that drove Shaw to prosperity also led him to his "trouble." Rosa Louise, his youngest daughter, calls his drive "the white man in him." She means that her father demanded as much for himself and his family as the white man demanded for his own, and when he got it he wouldn't let it go without a fight.

Shaw was, without question, a hard worker and a great provider, unrivaled in his settlement. One could be guilty, however, in the eyes of the settlement and before God, of excessive zeal in the pursuit of a good life and excessive pride in attaining it. Righteousness consisted in not having so much that it hurt to lose it. This notion appears to cater to landlords, merchants, bankers, and furnishing agents by discouraging resistance or ambition on the part of their farmer-debtors. But people who lived by it achieved a measure of autonomy. Shaw describes his brother Peter as a man with just this spirit in him: "He made up his mind that he weren't goin to have anything and after that, why, nothin could hurt him." Two of Peter's sons who migrated to Detroit after the Second World War say that their father decided he never would own an automobile, an electric stove, or other trappings. He could have raised larger crops than he did, on larger debts, but he chose to live plainly, avoid commercial contact with white people, and not work himself to death. Under a system that deprived farmers of sovereignty over their crops and severely limited their social and political liberties, such self-restraint was one way a man could control the course of his own life.

Nate Shaw's spirit led him on a different course. To his children he felt obliged to leave an inheritance—mules, tools, wagons, etc.—that they could use to earn a living. And to his race he wanted to set an example. He was, for instance, one of the first black farmers to buy an automobile. "There's a heap of my race," he says, "didn't believe their color should have a car, believed what the white man wanted em to believe." Shaw's defiance peaked in the face of imminent foreclosure. When he walked out on his "mission" he had no definite plan for a new world; he just couldn't endure the old order.

Was this an impulsive act of bravery? Did Shaw miscalculate the support his union could deliver? Did he know that organizers of the union belonged to the Communist Party? And if he did know, did it matter to him? There are no easy answers. Shaw admits he learned little about the origins of the union. He was less concerned with where it came from than with its spirit, which he recognized as his own. Nor were the details of its program essential, for he knew that even the most meager demand black tenant farmers could make undermined the white man's prerogative upon which the whole system rested.

While Shaw occupies the foreground of his stage he makes no claim for the uniqueness of his struggle. On the contrary, he is careful to stress the social position each actor represents. The opposition between him and his landlord, for example, which culminates in the confrontation with the deputies, is historically significant because it is common.

WHEN Shaw came home from prison many people he had known were gone. Some were living in the north, some in nearby counties, and some had died. There were other important changes. The federal government had stepped into agriculture and guaranteed small farmers, even sharecroppers, the right to sell their own cotton. Local textile mills had begun hiring blacks for the most menial jobs, thereby opening an alternative to the farm. Farming itself had become more complex and prohibitive to an uneducated man: you had to fill out forms and participate in government programs; to ensure an adequate yield you had to buy imported seeds, new fertilizers, insect poisons, and weed killers; tractors, too, were coming into style.

Nate Shaw was a mule farmer in a tractor world. The most meaningful and exciting episode of his life was behind him. It had given him a standard to judge human conduct; it put all of his skirmishes in perspective. But history seemed to have made a great leap over the twelve years he spent in prison. His recollections of his heroism and the events that led up to it belonged to a vanished reality. When he spoke about the past, his own sons shied away from the implications: "Some of em that don't like the standard I proved in these union affairs tells me I talk too much."

Seeking a better judgment from God and his race, and aiming to leave his trace on the world, Shaw proceeded to narrate the "life" of a black tenant farmer. The result is an intimate portrait that reproduces the tempo of a life unfolding. Shaw has the storyteller's gift to suspend his age while reciting. Thus his childhood stories ring with the astonishment and romance of a boy discovering the universe. Similarly, stories of his old age are tinged by the bittersweet feelings of a passionate man who has lost his illusions.

Nate Shaw belongs to the tradition of farmer-storytellers. These people appear in all civilizations and are only beginning to disappear in the most advanced ones. Their survival is bound up with the fate of communities of small farmers. When these communities disperse and farms become larger, fewer in number, and owned more and more by absentee investors, the sources of story material and audiences dry up.

But the decline of storytelling is more complicated than this. It has to do with the passing of craft activities, like basketmaking, which generate the rhythms at which stories flow; with the appeal of competing voices of culture, such as television; and with the unfortunate popular assumption that history is something that takes place in books and books are to be read in school.

What happens to the history of a people not accustomed to writing things down? To whom poverty and illiteracy make wills, diaries, and letters superfluous? Birth and death certificates, tax receipts—these occasional records punctuate but do not describe everyday life. In this setting, Nate Shaw is a precious resource. For his stories are grounded in the ordinary occurrences of the tenant farmer's world. Furthermore, they display as few records could an awesome intellectual life.

Shaw's working years span approximately the same years as the Snopes family odyssey in William Faulkner's trilogy. Shaw's narrative complements the social history contained in the Mississippi writer's work. Faulkner writes about the white south; Shaw speaks about the black. Both focus on the impact of history on the family. Faulkner, heir to a line of southern statesmen, pursues the decay and decline of white landed families and the rise of their former tenants. Nate Shaw records the progress of a black tenant family through three generations.

Both are steeped in genealogies. With the rigor of an Old Testament scribe, Shaw names the parents and foreparents of many of his characters. In fact, he names over four hundred people. Shaw creates a human topography through which he travels with the assurance of a man who knows the forest because he witnessed the planting of the trees. The act of recalling names is also a demonstration of how long he has been living in one place. Thus, his family chronicles express both the bonds among people and a man's attachment to the land.

IN editing the transcripts of our recordings I sometimes had to choose among multiple versions of the same story; other times, I combined parts of one version with another for the sake of clarity and completeness. Stories that seemed remote from Shaw's personal development I left out entirely. By giving precedence to stories with historical interest or literary merit I trust I haven't misrepresented him.

Besides this hazardous selection process, my editing consisted of arranging Shaw's stories in a way that does justice both to their occurrence in time and his sequence of recollection. I tried, within the limits of a general chronology, to preserve the affinities between stories. For memory recalls kindred events and people and is not constrained by the calendar.

I have not reproduced a southern or black dialect because I did not hear it. I did hear the English language as I know it, spoken with regional inflection and grammar. In the case of present participles and other words ending in "ing," the common idiom usually drops the "g," such as in "meetin" for meeting, "haulin" for hauling, etc. Where the "g" is pronounced, often for exclamatory effect, I have kept it.

Shaw's vocabulary is remarkably broad and inventive, enriched here and there by words not found in the dictionary. The meanings of these words are usually clear from their contexts. In some cases I have offered definitions.

As a measure of protection and privacy I have had to change the names of all the people and most of the places in the narrative. In devising aliases I tried to be faithful to the sources, sounds, and meanings of the original names. Generally, where blacks and whites shared the same surnames or first names, they share aliases here.

There is something lost and something gained in the transformation of these oral stories to written literature. Their publication marks the end of a long process of creation and re-creation and removes them from the orbit of the storyteller. His gestures, mimicries, and intonations—all the devices of his performance—are lost. No exclamation point can take the place of a thunderous slap on the knee. The stories, however, are saved, and Nate Shaw's "life" will get a hearing beyond his settlement and century.

IN producing this book I have been assisted by many friends. Dale Rosen has worked closely with me at every stage of its composition. Her courage launched the project and her energies assured its fulfillment.

I am grateful to Alex Keyssar, Margaret Levi, Nancy Hopkin, Kaethe Worthen, and Maurianne Adams for reading the manuscript with profound attention and criticizing the preface; to Frank Freidel for urging me to do it and having faith; to John Beecher for lead-ing the way almost forty years ago; to John Oliver for giving me a home in Tukabahchee County; to Tom Sisson and Johnny Sisson for their financial support and good cheer; to the Ford Foundation for a grant that enabled me to work steadily toward completing the project; to Charles Adams for his technical aid and patience; and to my editor, Ashbel Green, for his sympathy and suggestions on form.

Finally, only the gracious cooperation of Nate Shaw, his wife, his brothers and their wives, and all of their children makes this book possible. What follows is Nate Shaw's narrative alone. As a subsequent volume I hope to present the complementary statements of the other Shaws.

Theodore Rosengarten

Somerville, Massachusetts
October 1, 1973

YOUTH

M Y daddy had three brothers—Hubert, Bob, and Nate—and
I'm named after one of em. Now, that Hubert, he was a
over-average man. It didn't do no man no good to take a hold of
him, so my daddy said. Uncle Hubert didn't take shit from nobody,
colored or white. After my daddy got up to be a big boy he claimed
to remember his brother Hubert's transactions and he even told
how his brother talked: he talked in a dry, high-pitched voice. But
Uncle Hubert was a grown man, he was much of a man.

So one day, Uncle Hubert went up to a white man's house. I
reckon that was after the surrender; my daddy didn't tell me how
old *he* was when Uncle Hubert done that. And that white man had
a bad bulldog and Uncle Hubert knowed—my daddy said his
brother Hubert knowed that that was a bad dog. God knows I aint
tellin no part of a lie, *he* said it. But used to in them days, I think
a heap of this old back yonder stuff was lies, a heap of it. The old
folks told so many stories and they told so many funny stories. All
of it couldn't have been true, the way I estimates it. They'd tell
stories to have fun and folly and cause a big laugh. But they told
a heap that was definite and proved out to be true. If I tell any kind
of story that I think was just something told to entertain, I'll say,

"That's what I heard So-and-so say," and so on. But my daddy told this for the truth.

Uncle Hubert went up to a white man's house one day. The white man had a bad dog and Uncle Hubert knowed it. And the white man knew he had a bad dog. My daddy said the white man told him, "Come on in. The dog's wired up, I fenced him."

It wasn't a matter definitely understood if Uncle Hubert was askin the white man or the white man was askin him to come in his house. Told him, "Just unlock the latch to the gate and come in the yard," that's all.

Uncle Hubert looked at the dog and said, "You goin to keep that damn dog off me, aint ya?"

Told him, "O, yes, the dog aint goin to bother you. Just come on in, come on in."

Hubert unlatched the gate and walked in the yard. And soon as he done that, the dog run up to grab him. The white man had done walked out there to guard the dog off of him. And when the dog runned up to grab Uncle Hubert, he just jumped behind that white man, picked him up by his waist and commenced a slingin him at the dog, fightin the dog with the man. And said, he beat that dog so with that man, one of the man's shoes flew off. Uncle Hubert just knocked that dog down goin and a comin until he knocked one of the white man's shoes off—and hurt the white man a little someway. He whipped that dog down, cleaned that dog up with his master's legs and feet. Then he put the white man down, the white man told him, "I'm goin to have you arrested, I'm goin to have you arrested."

Uncle Hubert said, "Have me arrested. I told you to keep that damn dog off me. You knowed he'd eat me up. I told you to keep him off me."

He just stepped on out the gate, he was a over-average man. And they never did meet up no crowd that'd whip up on Uncle Hubert. He left this country before I was born. I heard my daddy say many a time, "I don't know what become of my brother Hubert and my brother Nate." They left this country and gone; Uncle Bob left too, but he come back and died. When I got big enough to know anything he was livin out between here and Apafalya in the neighborhood of Litabixee. When Uncle Bob taken sick, got down on his bed, my daddy went over there several times and let me go with him—I was my daddy's first son—and eventually Uncle Bob died.

He had a wife, I've seen her people a number of times. She was a Millsaps, Eva Millsaps. And while Uncle Bob was alive and layin there sick, my daddy said Aunt Eva would tell Uncle Bob, "If you goin to die, die! Die! I can do better *d'rout* a man." She meant she could do better without a man, it was just her way of talkin: "I can do better *d'rout* a man."

Every child they had was older than I was, all Uncle Bob's children was older than me. Sim Shaw was the oldest boy he had to my knowin. Dill was the other one—them was the only two boys Uncle Bob had by Aunt Eva Millsaps. And the girls was named Hetty and Priscilla, but they called her Chick—that's two boys and two girls.

My daddy had a outside chap by one of Aunt Eva's daughters. Aunt Eva had this daughter before her and Uncle Bob married. So that was my daddy's half-niece—weren't no blood kin at all—that my daddy had a child by. His name was George and course, he went for a Shaw, George Shaw. And *he* lingered around and left this country. He traveled every whichaway some but he come back and he did little jobs for my daddy around our house. I've seed him many a time, talked with him. He was a darker shade boy than my wife, he weren't a real dark fellow. And he stayed near Uncle Bob's girls and boys just like a brother. Uncle Bob's wife, Aunt Eva, she kept George there with her children because that was her daughter's child.

HAYES SHAW was my daddy. He was just about my color or maybe a shade darker; he was dark. He was a kind of rawboned, slender man like I am. I never did know *his* daddy—he knowed who his daddy was, he claimed him but he died when my daddy was a young man, before I was born. But I knew his mother well. Her name was Cealy, that's what they called her; he called her Mammy. I've seed Grandma Cealy many a time. When I was a little old boy—I say little old boy, I was in my teens and had got big enough to travel on my own, I'd go up to Grandma Cealy's home way up yonder at a place they called Chapel Ridge beat, drivin a little old gray horse to a one-horse wagon, get her and bring her down to my daddy's home. She was about my color, his mother, Grandma Cealy. I was with her and around her from a chap up. Her second husband after my daddy's daddy—she had him after I got big enough to know anything and she had had him before then—was a old man by the name of Abner Todd. Old man Abner Todd was her husband when I come in this world.

My daddy trusted me to ride up in them hills after his mammy and I never had a wreck and hurt her. That horse never did show me no tricks with my grandmother. My daddy'd always tell me, "Nate, be careful now with your grandma, don't get her hurt." But the way it worked out there weren't no hurt to come; hauled her through them hills every time safe and sound.

At that time my daddy had bought a one-horse wagon from the Akers in Apafalya, iron-axle, nice little wagon. Hitch it to that little gray mare. His name was Silas and he was fractious. You had to treat him right, you didn't he'd play a trick on you. Played more tricks with my daddy than he ever played with me. My stepmother, TJ's mother, that was my daddy's wife at that time, she'd say, "Mr. Shaw"—she called him Mr. Shaw; his name was Hayes Shaw— "Mr. Shaw, why don't you let Nate handle that horse? He can get along with that horse better than you can. Every time you have anything to do with that horse you has a frolic with him and Nate never does have no frolic with him. He minds Nate just like a top. Let Nate drive that horse—"

My daddy didn't like for her to say that. He would holler at the horse and holler at my stepmother—that was his third wife, the first woman he married after he married my mother—and he'd be rough with that horse. If the horse looked like he didn't want to act to suit him, he'd strike him with the lines; Silas would show him another trick, give my daddy more trouble. Sometime he'd come to me in the field where I was plowin that horse, he'd catch hold of my plow and he wouldn't have that horse in charge ten minutes till that horse was tryin to get away from him, raisin the devil and would out-kick a dray mule if my daddy pushed on him. Silas was ill; it didn't do to play with him, just treat him nice like you treat a person. Silas had some sense somewhere someway, he didn't want you to mistreat him. Soon as my daddy would get him there was a frolic; soon as I'd go and take him over—quiet as a lamb. My stepmother looked into that, she talked to my daddy about it. But he was bull-headed: he wanted to boss and bulldoze his way through. Get mad sometime he go to squallin at that horse till it was a pity. Silas would resist him like the devil, too, but never did give me no trouble.

I hauled my grandmother more days than I can number. Drivin in them hills, from my daddy on this side of Sitimachas Creek clean on up in there, four, five miles all up in around Chapel Ridge. Silas never did break the gait I run him in.

And in her comins and spendin time with my daddy and her grandchildren, Grandma Cealy said many a time, tellin people who come in there while she was there, "Why, Hayes, that's my baby, that's my baby. He was fifteen years old when it surrendered."

Well, I didn't have no knowledge of what surrenderin was. But it come to me like this: that was in the days of freein the colored people. My daddy was fifteen years old, he come through fifteen years in slavery. And he worked for the Shaws, the Shaws was his masters, white people, and that's where our name comes from. All them slavery-time colored people went in the boss man's name and their children went in that name; didn't have a name of their own or any other name to give their children but the master's name.

But really, I was too little to *know* anything, only what I definitely heard em say and I never did hear nobody say what the surrender was. I just decided it was the beginnin of the days of freedom. "Hayes was fifteen years old when it surrendered." He was imprisoned in slavery for fifteen years—slavery were equal or worser than prison, but both of em bad and the poor colored man knows more about them two subjects than anybody.

The Bible says, "What has been will be again." And Grandma Cealy said a right smart about this: that that day was comin. Colored people once knowed what it was to live under freedom before they got over in this country, and they would know it again. That this very freedom movement that's on now would come. I heard them words and I was old enough to understand. And when I got to be a little old boy, when I got big enough to catch on to what people said, and even to the words of the old people, and the Bible, it was instilled in me many a time: the bottom rail will come to the top someday. I taken that to mean a change in the later years, durin of my lifetime maybe. I believe, if that day come, the poor generation on earth will banish away their toils and snares. But won't nobody do it for em but themselves. Take me, I'm a colored man, I've come in the knowledge of what it feels like to move out of this back yonder "ism"; and I'm confident all of my race will someday move out from under earthly bondage.

My grandmother and other people that I knowed grew up in slavery time, they wasn't satisfied with their freedom. They felt like motherless children—they wasn't satisfied but they had to live under the impression that they were. Had to act in a way just as though everything was all right. But they would open up every once in a while and talk about slavery time—they didn't know nothin about no freedom then, didn't know what it was but they wanted it. And when they got it they knew that what they got wasn't what they wanted, it wasn't freedom, really. Had to do whatever the white man directed em to do, couldn't voice their heart's desire. That was the way of life that I was born and raised into.

MY mother's name was Liza; she was Liza Culver. She was a deep yaller woman—her mother was a half-white woman. Her mother and daddy died before I was born—Grandpa Tom and Grandmother Jane Culver. My mother kept a lock of her mother's hair in a tin box about four inches long and near about the width of four fingers. My mother kept it as long as she lived. It was opened many a time and I seed the lock of hair in it—long, black hair, straight hair. My daddy said it was layin in that box growin, that hair growed— tellin what was told to me and accordin to my seein. Well, after my mother died, my daddy jumped up and married again and he done away with that lock of hair. I was absolutely sorry that it disappeared, I hated it. Because my mother had dearly kept that hair and therefore I felt strongly about it. I'd a held on to it knowin it was of my grandmother.

Grandpa Tom, who was due to be my granddad, it was said that he weren't my mother's daddy, said a Todd man, fellow by the name of Zeke Todd, was my granddaddy, my mother's daddy. But at the time my mother was born, her mother's husband was Tom Culver. My grandmother and granddaddy, Grandma Jane and Grandpa Tom, as I'd say, they was the mother and father of three girls—Liza Culver, Lydia Culver, and Virginia Culver—and eight boys, big healthy boys, all of em considered Grandpa Tom Culver's children. There was only one in the family I never did see and that was Uncle Hill Culver, one of the middle boys. He fell—that's the word we got—one Sunday, in Birmingham, he fell through the top of a three-story buildin to the floor of the first story and a scaffoldin fell behind him and busted his brains out. And that left seven boys.

And every one of them boys and every one of them girls looked like sisters and brothers. Looked like one man and one woman was the daddy and mother to all of em, regardless to what was said. Uncle Gates Culver, that was considered the oldest boy. I laughed and talked with Uncle Gates many a day; Uncle Sherman Culver, made a heavy, portly man; Uncle Jim Culver, smallest of the lot; Uncle John, made a big, heavy rascal; Uncle Grant Culver; Uncle Tom Culver; Uncle Junior Culver; Uncle Hill Culver. I've seed seven of them boys right with these eyes, before the death of em. Uncle John Culver was the baby. They appeared to be my uncles; they favored my mother, all those Culver boys and them Culver girls.

When my mother married my daddy, she taken them two baby boys at the death of *her* mother and raised em until they got to be grown men—Grandma Jane's two babies, the knee-baby, Uncle Sherman Culver, and the real baby, Uncle John Culver. Her other brothers and sisters was grown enough then, they could vouch for themselves, but the two little ones, my mother taken them in. I was a little fellow, I mean little, I weren't able to do nothin but eat and sleep when Uncle Sherman and Uncle John begin to board with us.

Good God, them two boys and my mother practically done all the field work. My mother especially done anything my daddy told her to do as far as cultivatin a crop out there—I seed her do it— that a man ought to done. She'd plow, she'd hoe; my daddy'd tell her, "Take that plow!" "Hoe!" And here's the way I seed her go many a day, and that was a every year's job for her. My daddy'd have his gun on his shoulder and be off on Sitimachas Creek swamps, huntin. And her and her little brothers would be in the field at work. She'd be out there with her dress rolled up nearly to her knees, just so she could have a clear stroke walkin. Pushed up and rolled up around her waist and a string tied around it and her dress would bunch up around her hips. She'd be in the field workin like a man, my daddy out in the woods somewhere huntin. Them boys would be plowin; if they was caught up with the plowin all three of em—my mother and her brothers—would be usin a hoe. My mother had to boss-instruct, she had to be a teacher to them boys, weren't nobody else there to teach em but her. She taught em how to plow, chop, work that crop every way—she raised em up in it. She was just a over-all leader for her two brothers. And when she taken down sick they was young men size but they were yet there. And they feared my daddy just like I had to fear him when I come along.

They called him Buddy and he was their brother-in-law. Uncle Sherman Culver and Uncle John Culver, my mother and daddy raised em right in the house with us. And when they got old enough to stand up and have man thoughts, they left.

I was nine years old when my mother died; I was too little to remember the date of the month but she died in August and I just lackin from the date she died up until the twenty-eighth day of December of bein nine years old. If I had a twenty-dollar bill this mornin for every time I seed my daddy beat up my mother and beat up my step-mother I wouldn't be settin here this mornin because I'd have up in the hundreds of dollars. Each one of them women—I didn't see no cause for it. I don't expect it ever come in my daddy's mind what his children thought about it or how they would remember him for it, but that was a poor example, to stamp and beat up children's mothers right before em.

I got wagon lines in my shed now, two-horse wagon lines; I used to drive my wagon with leather lines to hold them mules. The outside line catches one mule, outside her mouth to her bits; the other line catches the outside of the other mule's mouth—all them lines to them mules' mouths and a line from the one mule's mouth comes over and catches to the inside of the other mule's mouth and just so on. You pull on either one of them lines and you pull both mules thataway. Leather lines, the kind of lines my daddy kept up on a low loft in a old log barn. When he'd get unreasonably mad he'd jump up there and grab them lines out and double em up, or grab an old bull whip, had a staff bout a foot long, and he'd take up them lines or that bull whip and whip my mother down. He beat her scandalous. Jump up he would and grab the lines out of the loft, if them was the lines he wanted to whip her with; he'd double em twice, stand up before my mother's face and just strop her down.

She died with the dropsy. Swelled up all over her body; her feet and legs swelled to bust for several weeks before she died. She would just sit there in a rockin chair and her feet and legs swelled so bad until they shined. Well, the country wasn't full of doctors at that time but there was doctors and my daddy had a doctor to her. But he couldn't cure her. People come there givin advice and visitin, sittin with her, and they told my daddy to get some of these— there's a old bush and it gets to be a pretty good-sized tree, and it's called a holly-hoke. Has leaves on it and them leaves has got stickers all around em. And they told my daddy to get him a holly-hoke, tear a twig off bout two foot long—had them old sticker leaves on it— and whip her feet. She stood it; it hurt plenty, I reckon, but she stood it. And he'd squat down by her or sit down in a chair and whip her feet, whip em light, just enough for them old stickers on them leaves to prick her skin. And good God, the water would run out of her feet into little pools on the floor, and he'd put cloths down to catch the water. He'd sit there and whip her feet—that didn't do her no good under God's sun. And the doctor my daddy had come in to see her, white man by the name of Seth Ames—we chaps always called him Dr. Ames—he couldn't do her no good.

She died in August. They buried her over here at Elam Baptist Church. All right. My daddy was one of these kind—just tell the straight truth like it was—he liked other women while he kept him a wife. And when she died in August he got in a plumb hurry to marry again, and three weeks to Christmas that same year he was married again.

My mother was the mother for six children and before she died she lost two of em to my knowin. And that left her when she left this world, that left four children—my sister Sadie, my brother Peter, my brother Henry, and myself. Henry was the next child born after me, I was the oldest boy. My sister Sadie was older than I was and Peter was the baby of us all.

Henry died one year to the month after my mother died. My daddy didn't seem to grieve over my mother—of course, I was quite young and I couldn't estimate him then like I could when I got older, but I know he was right off huntin him another woman and went and married TJ's mother. And when Henry died the next August there was a grief among we children but my daddy and his new wife didn't take it hard at all, not a bit, nobody did but we children. The child, Henry, he seemed to grow considerably while he was sick. He stretched out and got tall and he would tell my daddy a heap of times, "Papa, I hear a roarin. There's somethin roarin in my head."

Don't know whether it was his imagination or it was true facts but that's what he said. "There's a roarin in my head. Roar like a train comin. Papa, don't you hear it?"

My daddy'd be sittin or standin by his bed. Said, "No, son, I don't hear it."

Henry said, "Hold your head down here close to me—" He
didn't realize that my daddy couldn't hear nothin through him. Just
said, "Well, there's somethin roarin in my head."

And my daddy had Dr. Seth Ames to treat Henry. He was a
nice, kind man, but as far as his practiceship, I don't know whether
he was on the dot or not. He told my daddy, "Hayes, I just can't
locate his complaint, I just can't do it. It seems to me like it's a case
of the St. Vitus Dance. It seems like the boy's worried with the St.
Vitus Dance."

Henry didn't live long after the doctor seed him; he went on
away from here. And a year to the month after my mother died, we
carried him to Elam Baptist Church over there by Apafalya and
buried him. Well, my sister lived—that didn't leave but three of us
then, me, my sister Sadie, and Peter. Sadie was three years older
than I was and she lived to marry and her and her husband had
three little boy children. He died and she married again, then she
died. She didn't live long after she married the second time. Well,
that didn't leave but two of us, me and Peter. No whole sister in the
world.

AFTER my mother died, my daddy married TJ's mother. She was a
Reed, Maggie Reed. And my daddy loved women, O God, he loved
women. Old man Jubal Reed's daughter and old lady Adeline—
used to be Adeline Milliken and after old man Jubal Reed married
her, him and her had one child and she went in the name of Maggie
Reed. And this old lady Adeline Reed, who was Adeline Milliken before Jubal Reed married her, she had had other men before him. I
knowed em: old man Coot Ramsey come in contact with her enough
to have four children and they all went under the Ramsey name—
Roland Ramsey, Reuben Ramsey, Waldo Ramsey, Hector Ramsey.
And the last time old lady Adeline—I don't say the first time and
the last time, I say this: when I come in the knowledge of that
family by my daddy marryin in it, she had married to a man by the
name of Jubal Reed. She weren't married to old man Coot Ramsey
—he just gettin children by this woman—and she went in the
name of Milliken, Adeline Milliken. And my daddy married in that
family to the only child that old lady Adeline Milliken and old man
Jubal Reed had—she went in the name of Reed, Maggie Reed. And
she was a half-sister to old man Waldo Ramsey; Adeline Milliken

was the mother for both of em. And I married Waldo Ramsey's daughter, in 1906, who was this old lady Adeline Milliken's grand-daughter. My daddy married Waldo Ramsey's half-sister, Maggie Reed. And I jumped up and married Waldo Ramsey's daughter. That made Maggie Reed, you might say, my wife's half-auntie, by Waldo bein Maggie's brother by the same woman. Well, that drawed me in to be my stepmother's brother's son-in-law—that's the way we mixed.

So my daddy married Maggie Reed and him and her was the father and mother of thirteen children—my old daddy was a rooster, he was a humdinger. Well, she lingered along and I don't remember what year she died, I was married and gone. Done become twenty-one years old. Well, she died. Got too hot and taken a bath one night, clipped out just like that. The night she died she'd put part of a day's work in the field. Went to the house out of the field and taken a bath. That prostrated her and she died. Well, that was my daddy's third wife gone. TJ's mother was a mighty good kind woman to we, my mother's children. She was a poor woman as usual amongst the colored race, but she was as good to us as she could be. And she was the mother of thirteen children for my daddy, two sets of twins. And today there aint but four livin out of all that number of children. Five of em died when they was little; lost all them twins. I was at home when the first child died and she was a good-sized little girl: her name was Patsey. Typhoid fever killed her. One of the sets of twins come into this world before Patsey died and one come after. But they was all behind TJ and all behind Lorna and if I don't make no mistakes they was all behind Judy. But the twins all died little. Today, out of them thirteen children, every one of em is dead except TJ, Bob, and Willis—them's boys —and Tessie, the only girl livin. Bob is in Detroit, last I heard of him; Tessie's in Birmingham; Willis is in Birmingham; and TJ, he's here.

I didn't know what it was to suffer for nothin while my mother lived. So far as somethin to eat, I didn't know what it was to go hungry in her lifetime. We killed plenty of meat in the fall; my daddy'd raise from three to four big hogs every year—that's all he done, raise meat to eat and what he didn't raise he got in the woods— and killed game. He killed game goin and a comin too. But after my mother died I knowed what it was to eat only dry bread or put it in water and mash it up. And just for a change in taste, I had a knack of mashin up a piece of old cornbread in water and sprinklin a little salt over it, and eat it. I knowed what it was to do that after my mother died. It really wasn't a change in my daddy; he was already providin only when it suited him. But my mother would take food from her own dinner and reserve it for her children. But after she died, if there was anything a little nourishin or tasty, I didn't get it and the rest of the children didn't get it—my daddy would eat it up. He'd sit down at the table with whatever he wanted to eat—fried eggs, fried ham, or anythin tasty like that. When my mother was livin, practically whatever my daddy et the whole family et. That was her way and she'd fight him to do it. But with my stepmother, TJ's mother, there come a new order. We had to eat what we could get then. We'd have enough to fill us but it wouldn't be nothin much but bread. If there was any fried ham or fried meat anyway it was strictly for my daddy. And she knowed, TJ's mother knowed how to feed him. He'd eat the best on the table and we children had to keep our hands out of the meat plate. After my daddy married TJ's mother I seed the change comin and I become used to all that. If there wasn't enough for the whole family to get some it was drawed up and set down to my daddy's plate.

Drink coffee? We didn't know what coffee was less'n we worked for Mr. So-and-so over yonder. Maybe Mr. So-and-so anywhere around that my daddy would put we children to chop cotton for, he'd give us a cup of coffee. TJ's mother have went and chopped cotton for white folks herself and usually she'd take me along. She'd cross the country sometime over a mile from home, carry Nate along with her. And some of the white people in them days was feedin you two meals, give you your breakfast and your dinner. And we had to put them full hours in the field at a low price. Give grown folks fifty cents a day to chop cotton; boy like me, anywhere from twenty-five to thirty-five cents, accordin to the size of you. Then you'd have to do good work and work regular. And my stepmother would carry me with her. My daddy wanted the few extra cents he could make off me and my stepmother wanted my company; but she also wanted to see me eat two good meals. Set down at the table at Mr. Curtis's place—that was Maynard Curtis's daddy, old man Jim Curtis, worked for him. Worked for Mr. Nelson Rivers, worked for a heap of different white people, and they'd feed us.

We'd go there and sit down at the table, eat breakfast; they'd be done et and got out to work. Mrs. Curtis or Mrs. Rivers would fix our breakfast, give us coffee to drink—there's so much I remember till I just can't breathe it.

We chaps just had to catch it as we could get it. Heap of times in the summer time I slept on a quilt spread down on the floor. And if I got up on a bed in the winter time, it'd be stuffed full of corn shucks or what hay I pulled out of the field; weren't a real mattress, just an old home-fixed thing I come up on. My daddy slept—him and his wives slept on the best store-bought bed they had available. He always had that for himself. When my mother died, at the time she died, and when I was born, she had good feather mattresses—feathers is soft, you know. And we children slept on the feather mattresses when my daddy'd let us but that weren't very often. These feather mattresses, my mother got em at the death of Grandma Jane.

MY daddy put me to plowin the first time at nine years old, right after my mother died. I remember the first plowin he put me to doin. She died in August and he put me to plowin in October, helpin him plow up sweet potatoes. He had two mules and he had me plowin one and him plowin the other. And the potatoes was very sorry that year—plowin em up for Mr. Shelton Clay, plowin up the white man's potatoes, hadn't been plowed up yet. And in them days the weather would be warm late on up until near Christmas. In October that year the weather was warm and the gnats was awful bad. And doggone it, the gnats looked like they would eat me up and I was just nine years old. So I would fight the gnats and my daddy got mad with me for that and he come to me and he picked me up by the arm and he held me up and he wore out a switch nearly on me, then dropped me back down. That was the first whippin he ever give me bout plowin. I just wasn't big enough for the job, that's the truth.

And that country where we was livin was rough and rocky. And he—my poor old daddy is dead and gone but I don't tell no lies on him—he put me to plowin a regular shift at twelve, thirteen years old. And I had to plow barefooted on that rocky country; anything liable to skin up my feet. And he'd go off, take his gun every mornin and hit the woods, practically every mornin, hit the woods and the swamps, huntin. And he was a marksman if there ever has been one. He'd go off with his gun and come back just loaded with game—shootin a old double barrel muzzle-loader too. You'd pour your powder in it and put you some paper in there and pack that powder tight. And he kept little sacks full of shot in his huntin pocket. Put that powder in the gun barrel, pack it down in there, then put his shot in there, charge of shot, push it down to that powder, just tamp it in place. You couldn't pack the shot in there; you could pack the powder close as you please, but when you put the shot in, pack it light. Then he'd pull them hammers back, take out his cap box, and set a little old cap on there—that's muzzle-loader style. Then he'd shoulder that double barrel muzzle-loader up. It was a long gun, too, longer than the average breech-loader.

And so he'd hunt and some mornins he'd tell his wife, my step-mother, "Give Nate his breakfast—" and he'd get his gun and step out the door, bolt across the woods, across the swamps, and he was gone. "Give Nate his breakfast and let him get to plowin quick as he can." And he'd go off and hunt until late time of day.

White people used to say—them Clays, we lived close to the Clay family: "Hayes sure is a hard worker," and laugh about it. "Hayes is a hard worker. But he's workin to keep from work." That was funny to me too, but it was all the truth.

I've known my daddy to kill more wild turkeys, wild ducks, and catch more fish in Sitimachas Creek up between Beaufort and Pottstown—we lived on the upper end of the creek close to Apafalya and Litabixee. And my daddy would catch fish, great God almighty. Catch em in baskets, two or three baskets; sometimes he'd catch more fish than the settlement could eat. And he'd get him some steel traps and go down to the creek—trap eels. Fish, eels, wild turkeys, wild ducks, possums, coons, beavers, squirrels, all such as that. But he wouldn't shoot a rabbit if it jumped up before him; just didn't fancy rabbits out of all the beasts of the forests and fields.

Sometimes he'd come back off his hunt and come across the field—he knowed where he said for me to plow. He'd expect to find me there and he'd find me there. I'd be plowin right along and the old mule I was plowin or old horse, whatever he had, he'd begin to throw up his head, turn around and look at me and kick at the plow—I knowed I was in for a whippin then. Because it didn't suit my daddy to have his mule actin up like that and his boy can't control him, and me barefooted too, just a little old boy plowin in that rough land. I'd go on plowin and my daddy'd just stand off in a row until I plowed up pretty close to him. He'd say, "Nate."

"Yes sir?"

"What sort of plowin is this you doin here? What sort of plowin is this you doin?"

He was like to blow me down. I'd tell him, "I's doin the best I can, Papa, I's doin the best I can."

Next word, "Drop them britches. Drop them britches."

He run around then to the old horse mule and begin to untie one of the lines from the bits.

"Drop them britches."

I'd be a little slow about it. He'd get that line out loose and sling it off the handle so I'd drop the loop, run it out the traces and swing it full loose and go to doublin it—double it once or twice, enough so it wouldn't worry him to beat me with. Then he'd walk up to me and if I weren't gettin out of my britches fast enough to suit him he'd grab me and snap my little old galluses down and drop my britches, stick my head between his legs—and when he got done with me that plow line was hot.

But I had to like him, had to like him. If he thought I got a little miffed about somethin or other, any way, if he thought my mind was runnin against what he wanted to do, right there was a beatin up. O, children when I come along come along the hard way. But I say after all that: a child aint got no business buckin his parents; parents aint got no business beatin a child.

One day my daddy had me plowin to a old steer, old oxen. He was off splittin rails for Mr. Jack Knowland and he had me in the field doin a man's work and I was a little old boy. And in them days, they didn't know what cuttin cotton stalks was. You'd take a stick and flail them cotton stalks down. Or else plow along and that single-tree would strip them old cotton stalks down, that averaged from three foot high to higher. My daddy was farmin, what little farmin he was havin carried on, by me. He put me out there to plowin in them cotton stalks and that single-tree flailin em down as that animal walked along. All of a sudden a stalk broke and flew back in my eye and knocked me out from between them plow handles—plowin under my daddy's administration. Knocked me down and when I got up I got up with my hands over that eye. It

just even hit that eye hard enough to bloodshot it through and
through. I lost my sight in that eye and I suffered seein a watery
gray for a week.

Well, soon as that happened, I had to go to the house and
carry that old steer out the field and put him up and carry my
daddy's dinner to him over on Mr. Knowland's place, which was
over a mile. I had to take my daddy's dinner to him and that eye
was just a lump of blood, just to look at it. I lingered with that bad
bloodshot eye—just nearly knocked it out. My stepmother bathed
it in salt water and cut me out a flap to wear over it, but I had to
go right along just the same; didn't stop work enough to tell it. I
felt that my daddy should have had more care and respect for me
than he did have. He oughta carried me to the doctor at the start.
He couldn't tell what damage was done to that eye. If I'd a lost it,
he'd a went on through life with his two eyes. He didn't see with
my eyes—and he never did carry me to no doctor. I had to linger
through my wound. It didn't stop me but it slowed me down some
on account of I was worried about it; didn't think about nothin else
but would I be a healthy boy with my own two eyes again. O, he
talked in a way that showed he had sympathy for me, but doin the
right thing, he never did do that.

She was really better to us than our daddy was, TJ's mother,
and there was four of us on her at the start. My daddy brought her
in over us as a stepmother and she was absolutely better to us than
our daddy was. But if my daddy was gone anywhere and anything
went disagreeable to her and she got up to whip us, I was up and
gone; didn't allow her to punish me. I was old enough to know
that she weren't my mother and I didn't recognize her as my
mother. You know, a child never recognizes a stepmother like he
do a mother. And that's why I showed her my heels; if I could get
out of her way and keep her from hittin me a lick, that's what I
done. I went out, my daddy'd be off somewhere at night, I done
things I know I shouldn't a done and she'd get at me to whip me—
outdoors I'd go and I'd sit around in the dark where she couldn't
find me until my daddy come in. Well, when he'd come in, he
would indulge me to a great extent, enough for me to know it. I
shoulda took my stepmother's whippins, for her sake, but I didn't
do it. After all outs and ins, I realize today she was better to we
children than my daddy was; she didn't butcher up with children.

He was just careless with us like a brute. One day he put me and my sister to cuttin cord wood for people to use in winter, cuttin mostly for the Clay family that lived down there close to us on Sitimachas Creek, run the big grist mill. My daddy had me and Sadie at that job. That was my tryin day. He kept us—he'd help us cut down the tree, maybe him and me and my sister, all three. And he'd always work me in a place in preference to my sister—she was about three years older than I was and I was past nine years old at that date—put us to helpin him cut cord wood for white people. Heavy job on kids, helpin pull a cross-cut saw. We practically sawed the most timber in wood lengths that my daddy cut up, me and Sadie did. And he had a ax—

So, one mornin in the woods, cut this wood in the winter, in the cold. There was two or three of the Clay family that my daddy always obligated himself to cut wood for em: Mr. Shelton Clay and old Mr. John Clay, Mr. Shelton's daddy. But not only for them; my daddy cut wood for anybody that wanted it. And he'd always tell we children, "When you get tired, stop and rest." Well, he lost his kind talk and kind acts that mornin. Had a big old oak log, big around as a man's waist, layin on the ground. We'd saw them big cuts, then split em up and stack em the cord-wood way. Sadie on one side and me on the other side, sawin. And he kept water there in the bucket where we could drink from when we wanted to. And if he figured in his way that one of us was gettin tired, whichever one of us it was, we both stopped then to rest, catch our wind. Sawin aint no easy job with a cross-cut saw; you must thoroughly have what it takes to pull that saw.

So, that mornin, unexpected, I seemed to get weak. My sister was older than I was and it didn't make no difference that she was a girl, she'd out-wind me sometimes. I got weak—and my daddy had a act, most of the time, he'd catch hold on my sister's side and spell her. I don't know what made him do it. I didn't feel that he had a right to do it except that she bein a girl—but he oughta looked at it more ways than that. He oughta knowed that sometimes I'd get tired as well as my sister, and me younger. And he was workin me at that time at things he always kept my sister back, just because I was a boy. So he grabbed that saw on her side; him on one side then, me on the other. And he set me down; he set me afire when he done it. When he grabbed the saw handle out of her hand —I was already tired, I had almost started to quit, but he walked up and grabbed her handle and had her to stand aside. And he commenced a snatchin that saw with all force that was needed to pull it and push it. He carried me a merry gait there a few minutes, and I'd already about lost my wind. I was fearful to stop after he grabbed the saw and I weakened down further when he hit a few licks with me. I slackened, I lost, I just about give out. He looked over that log at me, he seed plain somethin was goin to happen or had happened. He felt my pressure was weak, he felt it. But in place of stoppin, what did he do? Honest to my Savior, I held that against my daddy a long time, but finally I just outgrowed it and give it up. When he felt how that saw was goin and comin from my side, he raised up he did and squalled at me like I was a dog: "Saw on!"

Told me to saw on. I looked across the log and in a jiffy, backwards I went with my heels flew up. After he hollered, "Saw on," I hit one or two fast licks to all my power. I knowed what he'd do to me but there weren't nothin I could do at that period. He could-a killed me if he'd a wanted to. Weren't nothin for me to do but fall out. I fell out of there like a rabbit with my heels up, just layin backwards on the ground. All I could say as I begin to catch my breath, "Huyyyhh, huyyyhh, huyyyhh"—my eyes done watered— "huyyyhh, huyyyhh, cough, cough"—just about gone.

He told my sister, "Gimme that bucket of water, gimme that bucket of water."

He jumped at that bucket of water and commenced a wettin his hands and slappin it all over my face and head and all. I layin there, hollerin at him, "Huyyyhh, huyyyhh." Like to slay his boy that day, as sure as you born to die.

Some folks tell me, "Well, I'd just forget about it, I wouldn't hold it against my daddy." But my daddy was grown, he oughta knowed better. He couldn't use a child like he could use hisself. For several years after that I couldn't stand no cross-cut saw. How come it? The motion of a cross-cut saw across my breast—never has stood a cross-cut saw no more until this day. I been once killed nearly on it and I couldn't stand it no more, look to me in spite of redemption.

WHEN he weren't sawin wood, my daddy used to cut cross-ties for Mr. Joe Grimes. That was Mr. Clem Todd's son-in-law. Mr. Joe Grimes married one of Mr. Clem Todd's daughters. And we was livin at that time on Mr. Clem Todd's place. And right there we lived till I got nearly grown. And so, Mr. Joe Grimes, bein the son-in-law, he bought all of Mr. Todd's timber and had it cut up in cross-ties and he hired my daddy to cut em. My daddy cut cross-ties several years for the man. First ties my daddy learnt me how to cut, the way he learnt me, cuttin for Mr. Joe Grimes. Cuttin cross-ties is nasty for a man to do—with a broad ax and a club ax and a cross-cut saw. And my daddy couldn't have made much money at it, maybe fifteen or twenty cents a tie.

Cut down a big oak tree or a big hard pine, cut them ties out seven inches by nine inches by nine foot long. The railroad used to wouldn't buy ties if you cut the logs out, put em on carriages for the circle saw to saw em. Used to wouldn't have em that way; had to hew them ties with a broad ax and a club ax. I helped my daddy cut —O, it tested me; things my daddy learnt me, I've done em since then myself.

So one day we was in the woods cuttin cross-ties for Mr. Joe Grimes and him sellin em to the railroad and pocketin whatever money come of it. Weren't no trucks runnin then. You hauled your ties with a pair of good mules, hauled em to the railroad yard and stacked em. The railroad inspector from Atlanta, Georgia, would come and count them ties up. And one day—the road run along out yonder from where we was cuttin and me and my daddy wasn't far out from the road, under a hill, cuttin ties. Mr. Grimes had done been there that mornin, got a load of ties before we got there and carried em off to Apafalya and put em off on the right-of-way outside the railroad yard and stacked em, come right back to get another load. And me and my daddy was down under the hill there cuttin. I looked up—happened to look up and I seed Mr. Grimes comin back there for another load. My daddy didn't know Mr. Grimes was there. I wasn't expectin the white man myself but I *was* expectin to get a beatin. Mr. Grimes stopped up there, just jockeyin hisself, and my daddy was in a wrangle with me bout somethin or other bout them ties. And he just went out in the bushes and cut him a sweet-gum sprout bout as broad as my finger and as long as my arm. And he whipped me up scandalous down there, under that hill. Mr. Joe Grimes was up there on that road lookin down at us—my daddy still didn't know he was up there. After it was all over, Mr. Grimes left from his stoppin place and drove down the road a piece where he could turn off on a level with the road so he wouldn't have no steep grade to fight. Drove out, come

circlin around and on down to us on his wagon. Had done seed—
stood up there on the road and looked at my daddy beat me up. He
got down there and stopped his mules, looked at my daddy. He said,
"Hayes, what you beatin on your boy so bout this mornin?"

My daddy rattled off his excuses but it didn't do him no good.
There's some of these white people in this country done better
than others; they'd take up against the wrong thing. Especially with
me, I was a little old boy and I knowed I'd gived my daddy no
trouble.

And Mr. Grimes said, "Well, Hayes—" lookin right at my
daddy; I was standin right there—"Well, Hayes, that's your boy
but you beat him unmerciful. Hayes, don't ever let me see that no
more. If I catch you beatin him again like I stood up there on the
road and looked at you beat him, I'm goin to put the law on you.
He's your boy. He's your boy. But there's a law for the way you
beat him up."

My daddy drawed up and held his tongue. He just dropped
along and we cut ties for Mr. Grimes that year and the next year
too. Never did let Mr. Grimes see him beat me no more.

After Mr. Grimes went out of the business, cut all the ties he
could get out of that timber, I cut ties with my daddy for other white
men right on up close to grown. And my daddy had another boy by
a outside woman, and all the difference in my age and that boy's
age—I was born in December, 1885, and that boy was born in
March of the new year, 1886. He was about as big a boy as I was,
I was just from December to March over him. And bein his outside
boy my daddy had great sympathy for him. And this boy's mammy
washed all around for white folks and cooked for white folks and
all like that. Her name was Silvy Turpin, old lady Silvy Turpin. My
daddy went to her and got a young-un. Already had my mother in
a family way with me. So we two boys come along together close
in the settlement we always lived in till I got grown. So one day
we was cuttin ties for a white gentleman by the name of Jim Flint.
And this boy took a notion that he would follow my daddy around
in this tie cuttin. He didn't know nothin bout the job and my daddy
had stuck me in there bein that I was a chap by his wife—my
mother been dead since he learnt me to cut cross-ties, and he was
married to my stepmother at that time.

So this boy took a notion he wanted to go to the woods with
us. My daddy bein the daddy to him, he took him along. But the

boy wouldn't call him "daddy" and he was more like my daddy than I was. Went in the name of Willy Turpin, but he was really a Willy Shaw. My daddy wouldn't deny bein his daddy but he lived in a way that this boy never could walk out and boast on my daddy bein his daddy, and my daddy didn't boast bout him bein his child.

We went to the woods that day and went to cuttin. Twelve o'clock come and this boy didn't have no dinner with him. But my stepmother had fixed a dinner for my daddy and me. She always put my dinner in a different vessel than my daddy's. Got to the woods that day and Willy, he was there, helpin, but his mammy didn't fix him no dinner. I reckon she decided my daddy had plenty enough for him to let him eat with us. Place we called Cold Tree, in a big scope of woods cuttin ties for Mr. Jim Flint. Dinner time come, Willy didn't have no dinner. My daddy weren't goin to stand that. He took my vessel and gived Willy half of my dinner and then give him some out of his. Well, when I got done eatin—I was a big boy, right up close to fifteen years old, I wasn't satisfied. My daddy watched me and he knowed I weren't satisfied, and there was somethin or other said; Willy, I think, started it that day. My daddy said, "Nate's just mad cause you had to have part of his dinner."

And from one word to another—I didn't have enough to eat but I had to work just the same—my daddy jumped on me and whipped me up, right there in front of Willy Turpin. Well, Mr. Grimes weren't there that day; we was cuttin for a different white man. Mr. Grimes's timber was all hauled out; cuttin instead for Mr. Jim Flint. And my daddy jumped on me and whipped me up scandalous, harder than he ever done before because I had got up to be a older boy, I could take it. And I never did forget none of his treatments toward me. You forever remember the wrongs done to you as long as you live. But it's just like forgivin if you just go on in this world and don't worry bout it.

Now this is no lie of mine, these are the outside children that my daddy claimed. I seen some of em, two boys and a girl—that was my sister Stella, my brother Willy Turpin, and my brother George Shaw. This half-sister of mine, one of my mother's brothers married that gal; Uncle Jim Culver married her. Had several children and they was my half-nieces and -nephews on Sister Stella's side, and my full cousins by Uncle Jim.

This boy Will Turpin—went in the name of a Turpin—after he was told my daddy was his daddy he believed it. Old lady Silvy Turpin had been married and her first husband was named Asa Turpin; that throwed her to go in the name of Silvy Turpin. Old man Asa Turpin was the father of many a chap by old lady Silvy, but Will Turpin, her youngest son, he weren't one of em. We'd fight sometimes—he was my daddy's chap and my daddy always lived close to him and his mammy.

If my mother knowed about my daddy's carryin-ons she didn't make a fuss about it; she was a woman with good sense, she was a quiet-lifed woman. I think very well, accordin to my knowledge and understandin, all of my daddy's wives knowed he went with that Turpin woman. My stepmother, TJ's mother, knowed it.

Will Turpin, he was a Willy Shaw; Stella Crabb was a Stella Shaw; George Millsaps, by his mother's side, was a George Shaw. And my daddy had one, he often called his name, had a boy named Bud by some woman, I don't know who *she* was and I never seed *him*. That was four outside children and that bout gets all of em. My daddy was one of these—O, I knows too much, I knowed more than a child oughta knowed in them days. Never did know my daddy to boast about his outside children in front of his wives. He'd drop his head when they'd begin to shove them acts on him, he'd drop his head. My dear lovin mother never come up with such a thing as that against her as to have a young-un by a outside man; it never come up against TJ's mother to have a young-un by a outside man.

THIS boy that there weren't from December to March difference in our age—never did live in the house together but his mammy always lived close to my daddy. I never knew my daddy to give her very much but he might have made some money from his little jobs and divided it with her for that boy's sake. But my daddy kept me so straight I didn't have time to watch out for such as that.

Well, Willy's mammy sent him to school. He didn't have any finished learnin but he could read and write anything he wanted. But I couldn't do it. How come it? She sendin my daddy's child to school while he had me hard laborin all the time. I didn't never get out of the first reader; got no education to speak of. And another hurt addition to that: weren't no colored schools through here worth no count. You might find a school close to town somewhere that accommodated the colored and if you did you were doin well. But out in the country, even for such as Willy, weren't much school he could get.

Rocked along, rocked along, and these county headquarters that controlled the schools—they even done this when my children was goin to school. The white schools would all be floatin along, runnin on schedule; colored schools doin nothin, standin waitin for a chance to open. When the colored did start to school, we had to supplement the money the state give us with our own money. And durin of Willy Turpin's goin to school down through the years when my children was goin, they'd send out word from Beaufort, "Close the schools down. Money's out, money's out." Sometimes school wouldn't run over a month and a half or two months and they'd send out word from Beaufort, "Close the schools down, close the schools down. Money's out." Colored had to close their schools down, white folks' schools was runnin right on till May.

All right. Soon as our school closed down cotton would be ready to chop. We little colored children had to jump in the white man's field and work for what we could get, go choppin cotton, go to hoein; white folks' schools runnin right on and the white man's children goin to school while we workin in his field.

My daddy, when he had the opportunity, never did send me to school long enough to learn to read. If he sent his children he'd have to supplement the teacher's salary. But if he don't send his children, it don't cost him nothin and there's nothin said. But it wasn't entirely my daddy's fault that I didn't get a education and I don't believe either that the government was the cause of it. The money was just squandered and gone the other way. "Send the colored children to school till we say quit and when we say quit"— whoever it was sayin it in Beaufort—"quit!" Into the white man's field we'd have to go. None of my brothers and sisters, not one by name, got a good book learnin. And all I can do, I can put down on paper some little old figures but I can't add em up.

As a whole, if children got book learnin enough they'd jump off of this country; they don't want to plow, don't want no part of no sort of field work. That's the way it runs here. The biggest majority runs off to some place where they can get a public job.

I reckon my daddy was scared I'd leave him, so he held me down. Of course, I don't blame no man for not wantin his children to get away from around him but—there was a preacher used to come out of Tuskegee down there. His name, his initials was BB, BB Fletcher. He used to travel through right by our home when I was a boy. And he'd stop and visit with us on his way to Somerset, Alabama, to a colored church up there, they called New Mornin Church. He was the pastor of that church. One day he told my daddy, "Brother Shaw, give me that boy"—that was me—"give me that boy. I see somethin in him." I was standin there listenin. "Brother Shaw, give me that boy."

He wanted my daddy to give me up, let me get off to where I could get a better chance and have better treatment. Probably I would have let one of mine go off since I've looked through that thing as I have. Preacher Fletcher told my daddy, "Brother Shaw, let me have him, I see somethin in him. If you let me have him I'll let him learn any kind of trade he wants to learn, if you'll just give him to me."

There's a old word I used to hear my daddy speak: "That man just as well to been singin songs to a dead hog." Wasn't a way in the world that preacher could get me out of there. My daddy was dependin on me, education or no education, to work. Called me many a time, "Nate."

I'd say, "Sir?"

"Do so-and-so-and-so, do so-and-so-and-so."

That's what he wanted me for. He didn't know nothin but to work me. The way he acted showed he had a poor attitude to a education. And my dear mother, she died before I was nine years old; she didn't have no say. And my stepmother, she never did talk against my daddy and he asked her nothin about it. My daddy, what he took a notion to do, I had to fall in there and they had to fall in and do what he said do. And he never did look out for nothin that was good for the future; couldn't see ahead. The man just wasn't able that way.

My daddy was a free man but in his acts he was a slave. Didn't look ahead to profit hisself in nothin that he done. Is it or not a old slave act? Anything a man do in a slum way and don't care way,

I just lap it right back on slavery time days. It's that old back yonder "ism." Slavery just taught the colored man to take what come and live for today. And the colored man held his children back as he held hisself.

And I have heard my daddy describe how the colored people hurt themselves. I've heard my daddy say *hisself*—he seed the time he could have bought land around here in the piney woods for fifty cents a acre. For fifty cents a acre! And some few ones here and yonder about got em places, too. But my daddy didn't get nothin. The colored man lost—he dropped his candy right there. My daddy used to tell me when he was a young man he traveled all about the country after surrender; never did put hisself on a farm and settle down and go to work. Travelin around when he was a young man, before he married, through different parts of the southern states, makin good money. He'd come home—I heard him tell it and I heard my grandmother, his mother, tell it—come in many a time, walk in home to his mother—didn't have no daddy then—and turn first one pocket to her then another and just rake out money in her lap. Made it public workin, diggin ditches all around, clearin woods and swamps, every whichaway. Just rake out money from one pocket then the other into his mother's lap. Well, then he ought to been buyin some land when he could have got some cheap. But he was blindfolded; didn't look to the future. Just throwin his money in a dead hog's ass and takin shit. No fore-thought about it. He had got them old slavery thoughts in him, couldn't learn nothin from his experience. He had money but—whenever the colored man prospered too fast in this country under the old rulins, they worked every figure to cut you down, cut your britches off you. So, it might have been to his way of thinkin that it weren't no use in climbin too fast; weren't no use in climbin slow, neither, if they was goin to take everything you worked for when you got too high.

True, I seed my daddy cleaned up twice; everything he had they took away from him. Lloyd Albee done it once and after he took all my daddy had and put him in jail for selling mortgaged property, my daddy had to go up with Mr. Jasper Clay and lose a year's work. He moved right back down here after that and Mr. Clem Todd, the man whose place he was livin on before he traded with Mr. Albee, he took my daddy up and helped him to make another crop. And then my daddy decided he'd go to dealin with Mr. Akers in Apafalya, and that's twice he was cleaned up.

First time the white man stripped my daddy we was livin on Mr. Clem Todd's place and Mr. Lloyd Albee from Newcastle was furnishin him. And it was about ten or eleven miles my daddy had to travel to Mr. Albee to get what the man was furnishin. And my daddy had—when my mother died he had five or six head of cattle and he kept them cattle but Mr. Albee had a mortgage on all of em. Well, Mr. Albee wanted my daddy to move on his place. And in that, he was already controllin my daddy, had a mortgage on everything he had. Told my daddy—and I'll tell you what a trick that was; I was big enough to understand it thoroughly.

Old white gentleman by the name of Walker, lived way back down in the country, he come to my daddy and he wanted to buy one of them cows. My daddy went to Mr. Albee a few days later and asked Mr. Albee's release about sellin the cow before he sold it, knowin that Mr. Albee had a mortgage on em. He wanted to know could he sell a certain cow to Mr. Walker. Well, Mr. Albee give him a release to sell it. And when my daddy sold that cow, he carried the money to Mr. Albee and give it to him, as the man had a mortgage on the cow. Mr. Albee took the money and then turned around and sued my daddy for sellin mortgaged property. You see, here's the proposition—I understand a heap of things today more clear than I did in them days—if my daddy'd had the release in writin maybe he couldn't have been messed up that way. But he only had Mr. Albee's word, trustin him on it, and the man done him in.

So Mr. Albee jumped up and ordered my daddy to move over there close to Chapel Ridge on one of his places. My daddy told him—he was a pretty game old man still—he weren't goin to move over there, just weren't goin to do it, noway. Mr. Albee jumped up and sued my daddy then for sellin mortgaged property and put him in Beaufort jail. Well, he gived my daddy a release on that cow, told my daddy he could sell it and considered it done; he ought to have been honest enough to mark the cow's name off the book—he even had the names of the cows wrote on the mortgage. But he put my daddy in jail for sellin mortgaged property. Well, they smuggled the thing around and Mr. Jasper Clay, blood kin man to the Clays we lived close together with—these Clays over by us wanted my daddy to let Mr. Jasper Clay—he lived way up there at Gem Stone—get him out of jail. Well, my daddy agreed, not knowin definitely what he was agreein to. Mr. Jasper Clay went to Beaufort with a mind to buy my daddy out of jail. And when he got him out, he moved my daddy to Gem Stone then and put him to work on his place.

And Mr. Jasper Clay, it was known, had killed old man Henry Kirkland, the year before my daddy moved up there—shot the old man dead. He got on his horse one day and went over to where old man Henry Kirkland was livin, on one of his places, way up yonder in Crane's Ford beat. Old man Henry Kirkland had three boys and one daughter livin there with him and his wife. And this youngest boy of his had a pretty good book learnin—his name was Emmet—and he was keepin books, an account of everything his daddy got from Mr. Clay. Well, when it come time to settle, crops been gathered and come time to settle, Mr. Clay got on his horse and went over there. He had several mules and a saddle horse, he got on that horse and went over there to old man Henry Kirkland and got to talkin bout what he owed him and so on, *tellin* him what he owed him. Well, the old man knowed that his son had a statement too. But they didn't never go by nothin like that, nothin but what the white man might say accordin to his figures. No nigger would show anythin against em neither. But old man Henry Kirkland called Emmet's attention and told the boy to go in the house and get his figures and bring em out there to Mr. Clay. O, Mr. Clay didn't like that one bit. He flew in a passion—he toted his pistol all the time—he flew in a passion over that book business and throwed that pistol on old Uncle Henry and deadened him right there.

So, when he killed the old man on the spot, then he throwed his gun right on Emmet and shot Emmet through the lung someway, but Emmet got over it. That was old man Henry's baby boy— he married one of the Courteney girls after that, left here and went north with her. All them Kirkland boys left this country—and some of Henry's boys said when Mr. Clay shot their daddy, his horse reared up and almost threw him.

Well, they put Mr. Clay in jail but he didn't stay there very long. There was a company in Opelika that furnished Mr. Clay— he was a big man, big farmer—they furnished everything he needed for his hands and they had a mortgage on everything *he* had. Mr. Clay was a regular farmin man and they was holdin books against him for what he owed em—Davis and Podell, in Opelika. And when they put Mr. Clay in jail, here come Davis and Podell and got him out.

He lingered along, lingered along, and when my daddy got into it with Mr. Albee, Mr. Clay needed hands down at his place, so he went to Beaufort and bought my daddy out. But I have heard several of em say that it didn't cost Mr. Clay a penny; he just got him out. They runs a friendship business amongst the white race here. When he called on the jail and got my daddy out, then my daddy had to move up there on his place as a cropper, workin on halves. And when my daddy got up there he couldn't do nothin but what the man who so-called paid to get him out of jail said do.

Mr. Clay put my daddy to plowin with a squad of plow hands. He had one hand up there, colored, on his place and my daddy made the second colored fellow. George Porter and his mother and sisters—didn't one of them women have a man in that crowd—George Porter was old lady Nancy Porter's son, and they was workin there with Mr. Clay, old lady Nancy Porter's son and her daughters and also old lady Nancy herself was able to work. Put em all to work. And Mr. Clay's own boys was plowin on the premises. This crop over here went for my daddy's and over yonder was George Porter's and over yonder still was Mr. Clay's that was worked by his boys; but everybody floated through and through the field and kept up one big crop.

Mr. Clay was known—my daddy was scared, too—he was known to take it all, the whole crop. My daddy caught on to what was goin to happen. Mr. Clay didn't feed us on nothin but sorghum syrup and corn meal. I was big enough to work then, I was about fourteen years old and I made a hand choppin and hoein cotton. My daddy plowed, George Porter plowed, and Mr. Clay's two boys plowed, Floyd Clay and Matthew Clay. Mr. Clay had white and colored plowin together and he got it all. My daddy was sharp enough to catch on; he knowed he weren't goin to get nothin for his labor, just somethin to keep us alive while he was workin for nothin.

So my daddy looked for a way to get away from there. He knowed Mr. Clay done killed old man Henry Kirkland and shot old man Henry's youngest son. My daddy weren't lookin for that kind of trouble so he waited and he studied his points. He really was scared to ask the white man for anything, he plumb dreaded him. Mr. Clay would come to the field a many a time, sit down on a terrace and talk about killin old man Henry Kirkland—that worried Mr. Clay, seemed to eat away at his mind.

We moved up there in winter, started to work and worked until the crop was laid by. Then my daddy made Mr. Clay a offer. It was the best thing he could do because he weren't goin to get none of that crop nohow. My daddy was a basketmaker just like I am; he learnt me the trade, whipped me up about it too. So, he got on the good side of Mr. Clay and told him how many baskets he'd make for him to gather that crop—picked cotton in baskets in them days—how many baskets he'd make for him to get away from there if he could. In fact of the business, make him all the baskets he wanted if he'd just discharge him and let him move back down to where he come off of Mr. Todd's place. Mr. Clay accepted the offer. My daddy moved on out before the crop was gathered and he got down to where he wanted to be and he made so many baskets it was trouble to count em. And he carried em from down there on Siti-machas Creek up to Mr. Clay. Mr. Clay took em all but my daddy got away from there then.

So Mr. Clay got all my daddy's work that year for nothin and got the baskets too he needed to gather his crop. My daddy didn't get enough out of that crop to wrap his fingers around. But he got away from Mr. Clay and saved himself for the years to come by makin baskets for the man to gather his crop—the crop that my daddy helped to make but didn't get a bit of it.

Still and all we didn't go hungry because my daddy was a marksman: killed squirrels, possums, wild turkeys, catch fish and all. That was his job. I seed the day come and pass that he'd feed us just on his game. He wouldn't go out in the woods once a week without comin back with all the game he could tote.

NEXT cleanin up—Mr. Albee done come to the house and taken everything my daddy had in the way of stock and farm tools; taken my daddy's cows, his mule, harnesses, while my daddy was waitin in Beaufort jail for Mr. Jasper Clay to get him out. Moved away from Mr. Clay back down to Mr. Todd's place and scuffled around. Mr. Todd took my daddy up, furnished him land to work and helped him out, gived him the cost of a plow and money to buy a horse; my daddy worked that horse two years. And my daddy went—old man Clem Todd agreed for my daddy to get somebody else to furnish him but stay on his place. So my daddy went down there and got in with the Akers in Apafalya. And about the first or second year, Akers cleaned him up.

Ruel Akers' daddy was Dudley Akers. And Dudley Akers and his daddy, which was Ruel Akers' granddaddy, old Hy Akers—used to be a doctor accordin to the name they give him, Dr. Hy Akers—I know they didn't give my daddy a chance to redeem himself. They claimed they had a note against him and they took all he had. In those days, it was out of the knowledge of the colored man to understand that if you gived a man a note on everything you had, exactly how you was subject to the laws. Because the colored man wasn't educated to the laws for his use; they was a great, dark secret to him.

Akers took everything he had except goin in the house and gettin the house furnitures—they'd a got that if my stepmother had signed my daddy's note. Some of em ordered when they gived notes for furnishin, some of em wanted to go in the house and get that woman and have her sign it, too. Well, what was that for? I quickly learnt this: if you furnishes me any amount of money and I give you a note on what you want a note on as a security for the money you furnishin me, that aint enough to satisfy you, you want my wife to sign this note, too. And she come out and sign it—been that way ever since I was a little boy; have a Negro to sign a note, they goin to try to get that woman to stick her mark on that paper. That gets household, kitchen plunder and all. If I wanted supplies in the days I come along after I married my first wife, if I wanted to do any business with a white man for any part of furnishin, I didn't let her go on no notes; she stayed out of it because that would give em a chance to go in the house and get her stuff. O Lord, I have been through tribulations and trials in this world but nobody never has went in my house and got no house furnitures out of there.

The year them Akers cleaned up my daddy I begin to come in the knowledge of a crop. And I was plowin a little old gray horse —at that time it was the only horse or mule or anything my daddy had to plow. Mr. Clem Todd gived my daddy the money to buy that horse. And at the end of plowin, weren't plowin no more, them

Akers took that horse. They come out there—my daddy'd bought
a new one-horse wagon, little iron-axle wagon, good wagon; bought
it brand new from them Akers. They come out there and took that
horse and wagon and even went in the pen and got the fattenin
hog.

I watched em take it and I learnt right quick what it was all
about. Got all the cotton he made. But there was no corn for em
to get. That spring my daddy had as pretty a prospect for corn as
I ever seed. Corn was way up there, pretty, tall; I done the plowin
too. So that corn growed up there—and dry weather hit it. And
when it got to shootin, still stayed dry on that corn until the time
it oughta been made and the ears just standin off. Bless your soul,
it just continued dry and that corn come right on up there and
when it hit the key note that it oughta made a good crop of corn—
still dry, just stayed dry like a drought. There that corn stood with
nice shoots, done tasseled out—and didn't make enough corn to
pull. My daddy lost all his corn in the field—Akers lost it, them
Akers woulda got it all when they cleaned him out.

They could have, if they'd a done it, squared along with my
daddy and help him, if they wouldn't a helped him just a little bit.
Why, the next year was all right and he could have squared through
maybe and paid em. But they didn't give him no chance; they
grabbed what he had when he failed to come up with cotton enough
to pay em—dry weather parched that cotton crop to a great extent.
They took what cotton he made but there weren't no corn to take.
Took his horse and wagon, went in the pen and took his fattenin
hog, what meat my daddy was raisin for his family. I was big
enough and old enough to stretch my eyes at conditions and
abominate what I seed.

So I seed that twice: my daddy stripped of everything he had.
He moved off the Todd place, then just a little piece up the road on
the Wheeler place, and he never did prosper none after that.

HE wasn't a slave but he lived like one. Because he had to take
what the white people gived to get along. That much of slavery
ways was still hangin on. Accordin to slave days you wasn't allowed
the privilege to seek knowledge without the white man, master
man, allowin you. And that was the rule durin of my daddy's lifetime and up through my life, to be sure.

Of course, years ago I heard that President Lincoln freed the colored people; but it didn't amount to a hill of beans. And me, for myself, I was born in 1885, a very long time ago, and I know more about the happenins under this way of life than I can tell.

WHEN I was a little boy I watched em disfranchise the Negro from votin. I was old enough to look at folks and hear the talk. I didn't like it but nothin I could do. Over yonder in the settlement where my daddy lived at that time, they'd always go up here in Tuka-bahchee County to the Chapel Ridge beat, white and colored, to vote. What did I see and hear? Votin time come and I seen my daddy and plenty of other colored people from our settlement go on up to Chapel Ridge and vote. My daddy was a man that voted. The white man would let him vote, wanted him to vote. Some of em would travel around, workin for who they wanted and get the nigger's decision about who they was goin to vote for and they'd pay him in some way to vote for their pet man. I knowed and I thought at all times, it was only fair for a man, if he goin to vote to vote for who he wanted. But it never come to that; nigger didn't know the difference in one from the other. He was kept out of the knowledge of knowin so that he would *want* to sell his vote because that was the only advantage he could get from votin. White men traveled around, "Well, who you goin to vote for?" Sometimes, nigger would tell em he didn't know, he hadn't decided. How could he decide? They'd have the man for him to vote for. Give the nigger a middlin of meat, give him a barrel of flour—if they was able to give him that much, give him that to vote for who they wanted. Nigger would go ahead and vote. I *seed* that—whites buyin niggers' votes; give em a middlin of meat, shoulder of meat, sack of flour— flour was cheap them days; give em barrels of flour to vote their way. Nigger let himself be handicapped. If I'd a been a voter in them days they would have handicapped me because I wouldn't have knowed as much as I do now. And in that way my daddy was easily handicapped. In other words, it was just a thing to keep the nigger goin the white man's way. Let the nigger vote and turn the vote against the nigger, nigger doin it to hisself. Niggers just fell in there like pigs around their mammy suckin: votin the white man's way. Come time to vote, white man runnin all about the settlement buyin the niggers' votes. Give him meat, flour, sugar, coffee, anything the nigger wanted.

Then they disfranchised him, cut the nigger clean out from votin. The average nigger was votin the white man's way, especially if he lived on the white man's place. Combed in the niggers' votes like flies. Soon as enough of that was done they kicked the nigger out, deprived him of his rights, what that they had made a sham of while he had em. What was that, votin or not votin, either way under them conditions, but keepin the nigger under their thumbs? But takin the vote away was worse: if they couldn't just slave the nigger back like he used to be, it was pointin the nigger in that direction.

Never did hear my daddy say nothin bout losin the vote. But I believe with all my heart he knowed what it meant. He just as well —the way he handled hisself in this votin business and other colored handled themselves, they had to come under these southern rulins. They thought they did, and the white man said they did, and that's all there was to it. So he just stopped goin up to Chapel Ridge on votin day; stayed home or went out and done what he wanted to. But he didn't vote no more.

Who was behind that? I felt to an extent it was the rich white man and the poor white man, both of em, workin to take the vote away from the nigger—the big man and a heap of the little ones. The little ones thought they had a voice, but they only had a voice to this extent: they could speak against the nigger and the big man was happy for em to do it. But they didn't have no more voice than a cat against the big man of their own color.

As I growed to more knowledge I thought that was as bad a thing as ever happened—to disfranchise the nigger. Tellin him he didn't have a right to his thoughts. He just weren't counted to be no more than a dog.

I never voted: I was right there with my neck under the yoke like the rest of em. I wanted to vote, but I didn't want to vote if my vote weren't no good, weren't worth a doggone. What I goin to vote for? Just votin the other man's way, just like sugar in the bowl for him. I seed the nigger vote till he'd vote his head off—done him no good at all. It taken a enlightened day—today it's a new way as far as I can see. Nigger'll vote and if it come up any flaws in it the high authorities will take the matter over, straighten that thing out. They tell me now I can vote and I believe I could. But I been disencouraged so bad—I learnt too much about this votin after I growed up and begin to hear folks talk and seed how it was runnin regardless to how the cut went or come.

If anybody understood, had a education enough to understand that he had a right to vote, if a colored man was really eligible to vote, if he went on his way where his book learnin teached him what was right and what was wrong in the way of votin, or just if his experience teached him to vote for who he wanted to vote for—that kicked the nigger out of votin. White man revealed in that he was afraid the nigger was gettin to be too smart to just follow his way of votin like sheep.

Any way they could deprive a Negro was a celebration to em. "We just goin to pull the thing our way." They didn't definitely tell me—I was watchin and listenin. As the years come and go it leaves me with a better understandin of history.

II

1903, I worked up at an old water gin—that was the old Clay gin up on Sitimachas Creek right where I was born and raised. Gin brush fell on my forehead and knocked me as flat backwards on the floor as ever I was in my life. I was cleanin up the gins—Lord, it looked like it would kill me.

They had a gin house there and a sawmill and a grist mill, grind your own wheat. I've known wagon loads of wheat come out of the low country way back south up to Clay's mill. That was in the days when people raised wheat. I've cut many a grain—I never did raise no wheat but in my daddy's lifetime I et many a biscuit made from wheat grown here in this country. My daddy growed a little wheat; he was just a little hitter but I've known him to raise as high as twenty to thirty bushels of wheat. When I got old enough to marry, everybody practically had fell out with wheat. And then I was havin to work on halves for four years and didn't no white man want his niggers to fool with wheat—cotton brought the money; wheat was cheap.

There's a heap to a wheat crop; you got to know how to raise wheat and take care of it. And when it gets ready, when wheat gets ready to harvest, you couldn't fool around and cut it in your own

time, you had to obey that wheat. I've known my daddy to go out
in the field and cut wheat all day long for himself. And I've known
him to harvest many a wheat crop for other people and take me
with him to cut it. Wheat would get up waist high and he'd cut it
with a cradle—hand tool, wheat tool, oat tool. But wheat give out
in this country until there was none of it raised here when I begin
farmin for myself. People didn't have sufficient help to handle
wheat like it was due to be handled and owin to conditions they
learnt they could make more by foolin with cotton and not fool
with cotton and wheat both, but buy the flour they used in place of
growin the wheat.

It's been years and years since I seen a stalk of wheat grow.
And it grows just like oats. My daddy'd get out there with a old
grain cradle and sling it around, catch all he could hold his hand
around, cut it with that cradle, drop it in piles, knee-high—cuttin
wheat or oats. And he'd go back out there when it had laid on the
ground and dried—hot, fair weather calls for cuttin grain—gather
it up: go down, pick that wheat up enough to make a bundle, tie it
up, drop it down. When he got the field cut down and it all tied
up, if it looked like rain—wheat was a heap of trouble—cut all day
and it begin to look like rain, he'd have to shock that wheat in a
close shock; if he didn't and it rained on that cut crop, it'd ruin the
wheat and he done squandered his labor. You got to use special care
for a wheat crop. A oat crop too, if you want to feed your stock
on pure, cured-out oats. That consumed a whole lot of time. And
you take the average farmer, when the price of cotton fell, why, he
just quit foolin with wheat and oats altogether for cotton, cotton
and corn. Now, by God, they're leavin the corn off, right here in
this settlement.

FIRST time my daddy hired me out—he never did hire me out but
twice; he kept me right under his thumb until the year I was nineteen years old. 1904, he hired me out. He'd kept me around him all
the time until then but he thought he could help hisself more by
drawin on me. Well, he hired me out and he et up my wages as
fast as I worked. Truthful to God, I got one suit of clothes out of
my labor that year, store-bought Sunday suit of clothes and my
daddy collectin the balance of it. Well, that was just like slavery
with me. I thought I was a little too old to be treated that way.

Hired me to Mr. Jack Knowland, 1904. And I always—not boastin or braggin—but I always was a apt little kid, and I was willin. I knowed I had to be willin under my daddy. Mr Knowland had two more hands hired besides me—Tyler Fox, old lady Silvy Turpin's grandchild; we was born and raised up together. Old lady Silvy's oldest daughter, Inez Turpin, was Tyler's mother. And Luke Milliken—my stepmother was Luke Milliken's auntie. Mr. Knowland hired me from my daddy, hired Tyler Fox from his grandmother and hired Luke Milliken—Luke was older than we was, he was runnin his own business kind of, and he hired himself to Mr. Knowland. All three of we colored boys was there workin for the white man.

Mr. Knowland put me to plowin his buggy horse, Henry. And he was a hard road horse. You throwed a saddle on Henry and Henry would carry you anywhere you wanted to go. Hitch him to that Barnville buggy Mr. Knowland had and he was travelin sport. He could single-foot, pace, give you any sort of gait you wanted. Mr. Knowland would hitch him to the buggy, "Go along, Henry. Go along, sir." He gone! And he put me to plowin that horse.

Tyler Fox plowed a little old crooked-necked mule; his neck had been hurt when he was a colt but he was a thoroughgoin little old mule, he'd plow like a horse and quick, quick like a horse. His name was Tom and he'd a weighed about seven, eight hundred pounds. Tyler Fox plowed Tom. Luke Milliken plowed old Bob, big old bay horse woulda weighed between twelve hundred and fourteen hundred pounds. He was a kind of slow horse but Bob and that buggy horse I plowed done all the haulin on that place.

Many a mornin Mr. Knowland would come out of his house, fixed up nice, his coat on his arm, and he'd walk four and five miles any way he wanted to go, buyin cattle. He was a cow buyin man, he dealt with cows. And he'd take em when he had enough to suit him, fatten em up and huddle em in the road and put we boys to drivin em. Drive em way down to Tuskegee, through the low country and sell em at Tuskegee Normal School. He'd be drivin Bob and Henry to his wagon and when one boy got tired drivin them cows he could get up on the wagon and rest; and when he rested up there awhile, Mr. Knowland would have him to get back on the cow drivin job, followin that huddle of cattle into Tuskegee.

His wife's name was Lottie. I knowed who she was before Mr. Knowland married her. She was Mr. Sam Reed, in Apafalya, 's sister.

She was a Reed, Lottie Reed. Her and Mr. Knowland never did have
no children. He was a man that had right smart money but no
children. They moved to Apafalya after so many years and he
bought him a store and she died before he did. And after she died
he broke up storekeepin and commenced a travelin out in the country amongst his people.

So he found out I was apt and dutiful—and he'd dress, leave
home, off huntin cattle to buy, tell Miss Lottie before he left,
"Lottie—"

He was a white gentleman that when he'd tell you a thing he'd
say it a heap of times twice. He come by the field where we was
plowin before he left: "Nate, Nate, I told Lottie before I left the
house, that when a certain hour comes this evenin, for her to tap
the bell for you, and I thought I'd tell you, too. When you hear that
bell tap, you take Henry out of the field and hitch him to the
buggy and come after me."

When I heard that bell tone—had a big dinner bell they'd
ring—right there I stopped and taken Henry to the house. I'd pull
that Barnville buggy out from under the shed and hitch Henry to
it, then gone to pick up Mr. Knowland.

I was his foreman, in a way of speakin; he'd leave his farmin
all to me, see after it and keep it goin. I just saw that he was givin
me a responsibility he weren't givin the other boys. That was a
three-horse farm to look after too, and had more land than that
under cultivation. He had his sister livin there on his place and her
two daughters and one son and he give her a little crop. And when
he hired we three boys to plow we just plowed her crop and his'n
too. Of course, she paid him to have her plowin done. Her little
boy, Jeffers, he weren't big enough to plow. But her two girls was
old enough to receive boy company.

Nine dollars a month he gave my daddy. Nine dollars a month
for me. And he didn't give as much for them other boys as he give
for me because I was apt and he soon learnt he could trust his
business over to my hands.

Do you know what that white man done? I was just nineteen
years old. Knowed nothin bout haulin no logs, but he believed that
I could haul logs. He went to Tuskegee and bought six steers, six
head. And he bought a dray somewhere, a good dray. That gived
him steers for three yokes and a dray. Put a yoke to the wheel, put
a yoke to the lead, and add a yoke in between, two cows to the yoke.

That white man put me to haulin logs after the crop was laid by. "Nate, Nate, I want you to haul logs."

Well, I knowed nothin bout haulin logs, had never hauled no logs; but put me at anything, I made a success. One mornin I got out and he'd left home, went on off and left me to rule. I went to the lot—and them yokes was heavy. I called them cows together and I laid a yoke across two that I got in a pair, side by side; I laid that yoke across their neck and got that bore and stuck it up there and keyed it down until I yoked up six head. I set the biggest cows to the wheel and the next biggest in the swing and then the third yoke was the lead cows'. I went and picked up that dray tongue— it was heavy as the devil—and hitched them wheel cows up. Then I went and put a big chain in there to the end of that yoke and hitched them swing cows in there. Then I went back and got them lead cows and swung their chain to the swing cows' yoke. Mr. Knowland had me a big rawhide whip, handle bout as long as my hand. I called them cows—and I drove em bout a half a mile from Mr. Knowland's house and I hit a scope of woods on his place. I went down in there, cut me some skids to set side the wheels, dray wheels and back wheels. Cut notches in them skids and propped the wheels against em—I seed enough logs hauled to understand how to start. Take that big long chain, unwrap it where it's fastened to the hounds over the front wheels, straighten it out and lay it out there, stretch it out. Then get my can-hook and roll them logs up one by one. Get my lead steers, pull their chain back and hitch it to the log chain and drive them cows on out through the woods. That log is on the log chain and when the cows pull it up on that dray, it got to roll up and hit the dray almost square before I go back and get another. When I had em all snaked up and loaded I was ready to go to the sawmill.

Now at that time, Mr. Knowland was havin em hauled to the sawmill down on Sitimachas Creek, right next to Clay's mill, where I'd worked the year before. All them mills workin off that creek— gin house, grist mill, sawmill. Grist mill had separators would grind flour all sorts of ways. Gin house ginned folks' cotton—there's not one of them mills operatin today. Gone out of business, every one of em; left the country, I reckon. You can still find a trace of the buildins where there used to be a foundation. But the buildins is actually destroyed and it's like you lookin at a shadow.

I hauled logs for Mr. Knowland, drove his cows and his dray

up to that sawmill and dropped off my load. Then I drove em back to the woods as many trips as it taken to load up all the logs there was cut to be hauled that Mr. Knowland wanted to sell that day. So I learnt to haul logs under the white man's administration and it soon become known through all the country that I was a apt log haulin man.

1904, I nearly banged in Luke Milliken's head. I liked to kill Luke one night—that's true facts. Luke Milliken was a woman's son that was a half-sister to my stepmother, TJ's mother. And what it come up about that night, in a white man's house too—how come they was there in that white man's house? Luke's mammy was Jim Flint's—he weren't married, never had been married—Luke's mammy was his woman.

That year me and Tyler Fox and Luke Milliken all worked together every day. Eventually, at the period of time when me and Luke got into it, Luke had quit workin for Mr. Knowland. And durin of me and Tyler Fox goin home, averagely bout once a week, at night, we'd go by Mr. Flint's house. Luke's mammy's brother, half-brother, he lived there in part of the house with the white man; white man in one part, him in the other. And this here woman, Luke's mammy, her and Luke stayed in a little house out the edge of the yard. At night, nobody there, no tellin where they slept at, the way they runned it when night come.

So one night me and Tyler went by there goin home, and stopped. We walked in, as usual, and the fireplace to the white man's room was on the left side of the house as you walked in the door, and his bed was back there too. He was layin up there that night asleep when we walked in. Luke and his mammy and her half-brother, old man Frank Milliken—he weren't no old man, he was settle-aged, but he could get up and work, outwork a cooter, and he was a good cook, too; very often he helped fix old man Flint's meals, he was as good a cook as the woman was—and they all stayed there in a combined, jumbled up way.

So that night me and Tyler stopped there and walked in, and we all set there at the foot of Flint's bed, to the fire, and that white man asleep. Settin there, laughin and talkin as usual and after a while—Luke's mammy was sittin in a half-turned position toward the fire but back away from it. I was sittin close up to the fire with my head down. And I seed a great big old black long-legged spider run out from between that woman's feet and run across that fireplace into the far corner. Some of the rest of em discovered the spider at that time. I jumped up, not thinkin nothin, and I called Aunt Polly—that was her name, Polly—I said, "Aunt Polly, that spider come right out from between your feet."

She jumped up and looked at me, got mean about me sayin that. I was lookin at the spider when it runned out from between her feet, took off across the fireplace and went into that far corner. O, she got red hot about it, mad as the devil at me. All right. Luke set up there, her old boy, and he swelled up about it. And she just commenced a hollerin, "You're a liar, you're a liar. That spider didn't run out from about my feet."

Well, me a fool, just stuck to it. I knowed what I seed and I weren't goin to give back on it. Didn't make no difference how mad she was—I was nineteen years old then. But I didn't know my words had touched Luke that bad until I seed his act. He reached over there in the corner—he was sittin over there on the other side of the fireplace, and Tyler Fox sittin right about the center of the fireplace—and he got him a flat larded splinter bout two foot long and he stuck it in the ashes, turned it over and over, and just as soon as he done that it got hot and he beat the ashes off it and stuck it to the blaze. Whoop! Just like kerosene.

In this country, they used a larded limb, pine timber with fat on it, that if the fire ever got on it, it would burn till it burned clean up. He beat the ashes off it and stuck it in the fire—whoop! Then he jumped up, walked on out the house and here's the words he spoke: he was good and mad as the devil because he thought I'd insulted his mother, but it wasn't nothin to insult her about. God knows I never said a harmful word to the woman. He got heartily mad. He lit that splinter and walked out the door, right by old man Flint's bed, and he said, "Come on, Mama, come on, Mama, let's go to the house and go to bed."

She wouldn't pay no attention to him; she just kept gnarlin at me. Well, we set there a minute or two. I decided me and Tyler Fox just as well to go. I got up and told Tyler, "Let's go."

We went on out the house and Uncle Frank went out ahead of us. That old wench followed me to the door—I say wench, she weren't nothin but a outlaw—then on out the house. I didn't quit walkin till I stepped down on the last step—the house stood three or four steps high off the ground. I didn't have one more step to step or I'd a stepped right on the ground, clear away from the house. And as I done that, before I stopped, she come right up to the top of the steps, right behind me, standin over me, just raisin the devil. Luke was standin out there at the door of the house they stayed at, their home place where they was supposed to live. Standin there, fumblin around, and she had the door locked and he couldn't get in; he standin there waitin for her to bring the key out.

"Come on, Mama, and bring the key."

She didn't pay him a bit of attention; she just kept gnarlin at me. I reckon Luke was gettin madder and madder. All at once he just whirled away from the door, comin right straight to the doorsteps where we was; weren't sayin a word, comin right straight. Got about halfway to us, he laid his lamp-light on the ground, just kept a walkin. He walked up and I was standin there yet on that last step, next step would have been on the ground. And before I knowed anythin—he just never quit walkin till he walked right up to me and he runned his hand between my arm and my side—had a knife in his hand and he throwed it into the center of my back and split my coat—good coat—split it clean through to the linin, just a rake. And as God would have it, he never split the linin nowhere, just split the coat *to* the linin. I dropped my hands down good then and he just cuttin at me fast as a cat. Pulled his hand back—I discovered what he was tryin to do, tryin to cut my heart out. I closed my arms down and he hit me in the center of the back again and split that coat until it got to my arm and he raked on across that arm and split the sleeve and come on around and split the front of the coat. Good God almighty, what he do that for? Didn't touch the flesh noway.

So I discovered all that—whooooo, if I didn't jump, I jumped ever so high, jumped to runnin, goin around that house like a wounded fox. When I done that they decided I was cut heavily and I was runnin off—old lady Polly thought it and Uncle Frank and Tyler all thought it. But that weren't the commode. He'd done touched my blood through a mad spell and I was aimin to kill Luke Milliken then, God knows I didn't mean nothin but kill him.

Round the house I went, runned just like I was cut up and scared to death, but I was only mad. And believe me—the old place was rocky there and the rocks was what I was dearly after; I wanted to get me a couple, just a couple, and I was goin to run right back around there close enough to him to bust his brains out. I hunted for rocks around there several minutes, couldn't find the rock I wanted to save my life. Looked like God kept the rocks out of my hands, as rocky as that place was, I especially hunted rocks and couldn't find one. So I didn't know what to do. I just made up my mind right quick to go back around there and die with him, with my natural hands. Back around that house from behind it in the dark, around the corner I come. Just as I got to the corner I runned over a piece of four-inch sealin bout five foot long. I just swept it off the ground, gathered it runnin, looked like I never broke my gait. And he looked and seed me. His light was layin out there in the yard and he could see. And old man Frank Milliken and Tyler Fox and old lady Polly, all of em seed me comin in full force.

"Here come that sonofabitch, here come that sonofabitch. Come on, I'll meet you on halfway ground."

And when he met me there, got up in good reach of me, his body right next to mine, I whaled him right up a side of his head just as hard as I could hit. One piece of that plank flew off yonder way and another dropped right down at him and I had about two feet in my hand. God bless your soul, the ground caught him. I jumped right straddle of his body and stood there. By that time his old mammy let into hollerin and squallin—but I just stood there over him and if he'd a wiggled I'd a beat his brains out. Never moved, knocked him clean unconscious. He overcome it after a while—and his old mammy hollered when I hit him and stood over him and he wouldn't get up in a jiffy. I was bound to hit him a death lick in the head if he'd a ever moved. Still as a mouse, I seed there weren't no get-up to him, I dropped that piece and run off across the yard and I went around the north corner of the house where they slept and stopped. Looked backwards, peeped around; well, he weren't gettin up any. His old mammy squallin, "Whaaaaa-aaaaaooooooooo—" Lord, she was scared of his death, she was just scared to death.

"Done killed my child. Mr. Flint, that nasty stinkin nigger done killed my child."

What you reckon that white man done? He grabbed his double barrel breech-loader and runned out there in his draws, me peepin around the corner of that house lookin at him. I heard what was said.

"O, Mr. Flint, that nasty stinkin nigger come here to kill my child tonight; he come here to kill him."

Old Flint said, "Where is he? Where is he?"

He lookin, standin out there in his draws, me spyin round the corner of the house at him.

"Lord, Mr. Flint, he's gone, he's gone."

Tyler Fox was standin there, old man Frank Milliken—nobody didn't know where I was; they thought I'd gone. Standin there peepin round the corner of that house watchin Luke Milliken to see if he'd be able to get up. I was mad as a wet hen then. Old man Flint standin there, double barrel breech-loader in his hands, didn't have nothin on but his sleepers and them was his draws, two piece worth. Old Luke was still on the ground, too. My mind told me to hustle away from there. I runned to the other corner of the house and there was a hog pasture fence joined the corner, and I jumped that fence—when I done that, Tyler Fox found it out. He heard me runnin and he runned to the hog fence up there where it joined the yard, round the back of that house, and he jumped the fence too, and runned down across the hog pasture, leavin fast. He was gettin away from there because he thought I done killed Luke Milliken. And I whistled, called Tyler a low whistle and he heard me. He stopped when he detected who it was and I runned up to him.

"Fella, fella," he said, "you done killed him, you done killed him," just that way. And said, "You better be gettin away from here."

My first thought was this: O, he'll get up directly. I said, "I aint goin no damn where, Tyler."

He said, "If you leave, we'll leave together, we'll leave together."

He hadn't picked out no place nowhere, only just leave from here. And so, after I told Tyler I weren't goin no damn where, he kept insistin, "You better leave, you better leave."

Told him, "No, I aint goin no damn where. I'm goin up here in the pine thickets so I can hear what's said. I'm goin to set down here until I hear whether he ever get up or not."

So we went out there in the pine thickets after leavin the house, just a little piece above the hog pasture and set down. After awhile, Luke's mammy squalled out again. I decided that Luke must have asked about me—I knowed I hadn't killed him then—and I heard her holler this way:

"Lord, honey, that nasty stinkin nigger is gone."

He had to be alive to make her speak that way. He had to come to his senses enough to ask her a question. And she just told him directly, "Lord, that nasty stinkin nigger is gone. He come here tonight to kill you, he come here to kill you."

When she got done talkin I raised up. I said, "No, I aint gone no damn where. Here I am over in the pine thickets. Come over here, Luke, come over here."

O, she heard that; she hollered back, "You better get out from over there. Luke has got Mr. Flint's gun and he's goin to kill you."

I said, "Come on over here; here I am."

Egged him out three or four different times.

"Come on over here, I's over here in the pine thickets. I'm nowhere by the house."

After a while I heard the gun shoot. And when it shot, it shot over in the direction where we was; but the gun was throwed in the air, only shot it for a scare. Couldn't see us—and if a piece of shot had struck me, the devil in hell couldn't a kept me from killin him. Only reason I wouldn't a got him I'd a been tied down.

When that gun shot—BOOM—I heard somebody runnin, and I didn't know whether it was his mammy shot for a bluff, or Flint or Luke, but whoever shot that gun, when the report of that gun went off, I heard em just runnin up them steps goin back in the house.

Next mornin, I went right back through that yard. Didn't see Luke nowhere about the house. I wanted to get him, I wanted to beat him up still. I was liable to kill him if I'd a got my hands on him that mornin—the way he come at me with that knife and I hadn't said a cross word to him. I never used a cuss word in that old white man's house to nobody. And the thing worked out like it did, him tryin to cut my heart out.

So that next mornin I went right back to Mr. Knowland, me and Tyler Fox together. Walked through the yard, didn't see Luke around the house there nowhere. I knowed he generally fed old man Flint's mules—had two mules there. Fed em, seed after em—and as I walked on through the back yard, me and Tyler, we hit the road comin down on the west side of the house; hit the road at a old wagon shelter and the road run straight from there to where we was workin. And I looked way out there at a outer edge of a patch just on up the left side of the road and there was Luke comin out the lot gate with his feed basket. He seed me and stopped. I just went on out there to the gate where he was that mornin. He seed I was comin and he went anglin off to keep from meetin me. I walked up just about twenty yards from him. I said, "Luke, how come you treat me like you done last night? I hadn't done a thing to you. I just estimated you got hot as the devil with me off of what your mammy was sayin."

He said, "I didn't do nothin to you. You see here, look what a scar you put up aside of my head and I didn't do nothin to you."

I said, "You didn't try to cut my clothes off me? Luke, I'm goin to kill you."

That time I made a dash at him. God almighty, talk about runnin, he hauled ass. Well, I wouldn't run back in the yard at him, just let him go. I'd a fastened him that mornin; when I'd a got done with him he'd a been one beat up soul. He was a little older than I was but I was his match.

Me and Tyler went on then—Luke runned on in the white man's yard; I didn't attempt to follow him. Didn't have no fence around the yard at all to enclose the yard in, house in. Me and Tyler went on then to Mr. Knowland's. Flint had an old place went by the name of the Sutter place, small old plantation back beyond the creek. That mornin after we got to Mr. Knowland's, Mr. Knowland and his wife got on the buggy and left, went wherever they wanted to go. And up in the mornin a while, I looked down there through the grove and comin through there was Luke and his uncle, goin down on the Sutter place. Well, I stopped em out there in the grove in front of Mr. Knowland's house. And I just got dead at Luke's ass, just as hot at it as a dog would a rabbit. And he runned around hidin behind his uncle, old man Frank Milliken, tryin to keep from me. Well, old man Frank was a heavy-bodied man and that there Luke was just holdin to him to keep me off. And Uncle Frank was turnin, keepin up with him in a way to keep me from him. I seed that. Well, I wouldn't have no rally with him there before Uncle Frank. He just begged me to let Luke alone—never said a word out the way to me, just begged me to let him alone, let him go. I tried to grab him several times and every time I tried, Uncle Frank would protect him. Luke behind Uncle Frank and Uncle Frank floodin every way to keep me from Luke and Luke was doin all he could to keep out of my hands. I eventually let him alone, let him go on. Luke never did give me a minute's trouble after that. He wouldn't never give me a fair fight, and tell the truth, after he had cut my clothes thataway I didn't want no fair fight. I just cooled on him, paid him no attention. But he stayed scared of me and I had him in my power.

As I growed up in the world, I started off obeyin white folks' orders every way except white man come up to me and ask me, "What about So-and-so over yonder? What did he do? What did he say? What did he come over here for?" And all like that. I learnt years ago to keep my tongue still. But I also learnt to obey the white man. I aint quit that yet in some ways. My daddy told me, many a time, to obey the white man, do what he tell you to do and avoid trouble; and also, even my daddy's ways and actions told me that. My daddy stood back off of white folks considerably. First year he hired me out, I found out my daddy's weakness toward white folks. But it was just a matter he thought he had to go thataway; he was born and raised in slavery habits. He shunned white people, never did give a white man no trouble, not in my history. He'd make out like sometimes he told em this, that, and the other and he done this, that, and the other, but I never did see him do it.

Well, 1904, I heard him say one day, tell me— And old lady Silvy Turpin, that was one of my daddy's women—I'm goin to sweep the floor clean as I go—I was born up around old lady Silvy Turpin, Will Turpin's mammy. She had a mess of boys but she was only the mother of two girls, Inez and Martha. And this Aunt Inez was the mother of Tyler Fox. He was darker-skinned than I am and I know a colored man was his daddy. And Martha had a daughter named Lottie—a white man was Lottie's daddy. Hair hung off Lottie's head just like it hung off a white gal's head. Well, old lady Silvy raised up them two grandchildren, Tyler and Lottie. And Tyler went in the name of a Fox.

The year me and Tyler worked together, Mr. Knowland had a log house on his place he had built for colored folks, set about a quarter mile from the main house or a little further. And my daddy went together with old lady Silvy Turpin and put in bed clothes, put a bed in that house for us to sleep there on Mr. Knowland's place and gived us orders, told Mr. Knowland about it—we was to come home every night we wanted to, spend the night with our parents where they would keep a check on us. And every once in a while Tyler would go to his grandma's house and I'd go up to my daddy's house, spend the night. Next mornin we would get up— didn't live far apart; my daddy and old lady Silvy didn't live as far apart as from here to the crossroads out yonder. Of a mornin me and Tyler would get up and go back to Mr. Knowland, to our jobs—farmin, drivin cows. Mr. Knowland had us both hired by the month.

So one night we goes home. And my daddy lived about three quarters of a mile from old man Jim Flint, who Luke Milliken was the mainline nigger for. My daddy had some corn down on Siti-machas Creek, nice corn—old man Flint had a drove of cattle. I went home one night and I learnt that Jim Flint's cattle was breakin in that corn on the creek, eatin my daddy's corn up. My daddy set there in the house that night and we was talkin. He told me, "Son, old man Jim Flint's cows is just ruinin my corn down on Siti-machas."

Well, I knowed that white man was in the habit of lettin his stock destroy what folks had and there was nothin to it, especially if it was a nigger; and it had to be a Negro, didn't no white people live close to him.

Said, "Son, Jim Flint's cows is just ruinin my bottom of corn down on Sitimachas."

I said, "Do what, Papa?"

He said, "Yeah, just ruinin it."

I was close to grown. I set there and looked at him, studied over it.

I said, "Eatin up your corn on the creek!"

I was feelin my man, gettin up close to grown. If a young fellow ever take on and feel like he's a man, he'll start it close to the time when he's eighteen, nineteen years old. He'll begin to feel himself and I begin to feel myself too. That's no lie; and I always wanted to see the right thing done.

I said, "Well, he goin to keep them cows out of your corn and I don't mean maybe, he's goin to keep em out of there."

My daddy set and listened at me. He didn't know how I felt. I felt right then that I was a man and I begin to take on man ways, man acts, so far as right. I didn't want to impose on nobody; I was always taught by my daddy to treat people with care and respect, colored and white. And I had to treat the whites right; didn't, there was trouble. I wasn't sassy and impudent to nobody, but I done got to the wrong age on me then to feel like it was right for folks to run over me or run over my folks.

I said, "Yeah, I don't mean maybe. He goin to keep them cows out of your corn."

He looked at me, said, "Son, don't say nothin about it; might cause trouble."

When he said that word to me it touched me and touched me very deep. Man's stock eatin up his corn, destroyin his crop, and he wouldn't say nothin to him and didn't want me to say nothin.

I said, "In the mornin when I go back through his yard I'm goin to tell him what-and-what about that."

I meant—I might have been a little wrong, but it was wrong for him to let them stock eat up my daddy's crop of corn—I meant, sure enough, I was goin to approach the man with it if God give me a chance.

I walked through there that mornin, me and Tyler Fox; I stopped. And old lady Polly was in the house—the whole community knowed Flint was usin her for a wife, but niggers wouldn't meddle with it because they was scared. And I didn't meddle with it, I didn't care nothin about it; I didn't think it was right but then, I realized it was the wrong thing for me to busy myself about when it had been goin on ever since I was big enough to know anything. Paid no attention to it; weren't nothin to me, weren't hurtin me and weren't buildin me up noway.

So I stopped there like a man should do. I felt I was too far advanced to take what he was dishin out to my daddy and not holler about it. I stopped there and called for him. Old lady Polly poked her head out the kitchen window, said, "Mr. Flint aint here this mornin, he's gone. He left here bout daylight."

Then Uncle Frank, her half-brother and TJ's mother's half-brother, he spoke a word or two with me. I told old lady Polly to tell Mr. Flint when he come in—O, I done got raw about it, my daddy settin up lettin his cows eat and destroy his corn on the creek and wouldn't say nothin to him. Shit! Only reason I wouldn't a said somethin to him about it, God woulda paralyzed my tongue.

I said, "Well, you tell him when he comes home—" I spoke stout and strong—"You tell him when he come home that *I* said keep his cows out of my daddy's corn down on the creek yonder, and I don't mean *maybe*." I put it on her, said, "and tell him I don't mean *maybe*. Keep em out of my daddy's corn."

When he come back she told him every word I said and I reckon some more. He got hot as the devil about it but he wouldn't take no chances to see me. He went on to my daddy—no doubt he thought my daddy would whip me. But my daddy's time was out for whippin me then. Good God, and I was workin for Mr. Knowland, him drawin my wages just like I was a child. I beared him to do that, but time was drawin near he'd have to quit that too.

So Mr. Flint taken it on hisself and goes to see my daddy about it. And he preached his sermon to my daddy and in two or three nights I went back home, my daddy told me what the white man said. He jumped on me and boned me about it. I thought but little of him for bein that weak-kneed. I got home, first thing my daddy told me, "Son, I told you to not say nothin to Flint about his cows eatin up my corn. Now he's hot as the devil—" I set there and looked at my daddy— "Now you done went and told him what for, said somethin and he's raisin the devil about it. He come over here the other day since you been here and he told me I just 'ought to hear the words that big man Nate left at my house for me, and I'm goin to whip big man Nate's ass.' " Uh-oh, when he said that I had another thought— "He said he goin to whip your ass, 'big man Nate's ass. You just oughta heard how he talked and what sort of words he left at my house for me.' "

I quickly fell this way, humbled down like I was scared. I said, "Papa, what did you tell him?" Talkin just like a little old chap. "What did you tell him when he said he goin to whip my ass?"

"I never said nothin."

Right there gived me a hold of a weak spot in him. If a man had walked up to my face, I don't care who the devil it was, and talk about he goin to whip one of my boys' ass, I'd tell him, "I expect you better not do that," if nothin else. I looked right into that. My daddy weren't goin to take up for me and I was right. I admit I talked rough about it but you have to get rough in some cases; if you don't a person won't quit what he's doin against you.

So I said, "Well, I'm goin to tell you—" I changed my voice then; God in heaven is my true witness. I humble-talked him just to get his goods about how he felt toward me. Told me he didn't say nothin, just listened at the white man. And I thought he oughta told the white man, "Well, you better not try that." But no, in place of that he held his voice and let the man say what he pleased. Whoooooo, I liked to jump up out of the chair. I said, "I'm goin to tell you somethin, Papa—" I raised my voice; I weren't no chap, I didn't consider myself no chap. I said, "Let him jump on me whenever he pleases. I guarantee you won't nobody have to get him off. Just let him jump on me, let him do it. Don't you worry, let him jump on me. I'll guarantee you won't nobody have to get him off me."

I just kept goin backwards and forwards through that white man's yard; never would say nothin to me neither. I wanted him to say somethin but he never said "umph" about it. Well, it was a long grudge, lasted for seven long years and it worked out and stopped. He picked at me for seven long years, Flint did. So he got to where he wouldn't speak to me, have nothin to do with me, and it's very good he didn't, very good he didn't.

1905, my daddy took me back home. Mr. Knowland wanted me back but my daddy wouldn't let me go, took me back home. I told him when I got back home, I said, "Papa—"

I had never known my daddy to do nothin that profited him much and he eventually drifted me off to Mr. Knowland in 1904. Well, that ruint me to an extent because I learnt to see further under the white man than ever I seed before; I was trusted more. Mr. Knowland weren't home more than half of the time. Hit the road and leave me there with two other hired boys like myself, colored boys, and if anything needed to be done that he wanted done, he'd leave it in my hands. And that stuck me up and made me think a lot of myself. Things went absolutely straight under my administration. Just anything Mr. Knowland put me at I could do it and did do it. That year Mr. Knowland made twenty-five bales of cotton and corn to walk on. Well, that put my britches on, put me in the lights of what I could do. Mr. Knowland done trusted me and I found out what was in me—it was just revealed to me in the work I done. I begin to feel like I was becomin part of a man.

My daddy had nothin goin to learn me but plow a old mule or old horse, chop cotton, hard labor—cut cross-ties, split rails, and all. My daddy would do a little of everything and I had to go, too. But turn the business over in my hands like Mr. Knowland done, he never would do it. And I caught on like fire to whatever Mr. Knowland put me up to. Well, Mr. Knowland wanted me back in 1905 but my daddy wouldn't let him have me. I went on and stayed where my daddy put me; took me back to work for him so he could go on his way.

It was nothin I expected to get so much at Mr. Knowland's in the way of money, but I had more privileges and I could learn something. I told my daddy, 1905, said, "Papa—"

He didn't know what was in me but I was growin to knowledge every day. Had no book learnin to speak of but I got to where I thought I could do anything just as good as anybody else. I had a great conceit of myself since Mr. Knowland done turned me loose. I said, "Papa—"

I knowed I had never done nothin that was any value to me before I worked for that man, nothin but go day, come night, God send Sunday. I'd get a thing today and eat it up and I didn't know where anything was comin from tomorrow. I didn't like that old way no more. I told my daddy, him half workin, just puttin in half time in the field, grass eatin up his crop every year—most he ever made was six bales of cotton and I had to plow that cotton, corn too. He could have made more cotton if he'd a put his attention to farmin in place of huntin and messin around. And he didn't use much fertilize. But mostly he was slack when it come to hard work. If he'd a stretched himself out there and worked like his poor little son have had to work, he'd a made some. The year that the Akers cleaned him up and dry weather burnt his corn crop—looked over the field every day and that corn just went down to nothin. It sprout and shot and a few days after it shot it gone as far as it could go. Some of it fell into the dust, it was so weak it could hardly stand. Some of it stood up and died, dried up. Well, I looked into all that and seed there was a heap of it a man couldn't help, but a heap of it was on account of a man not workin it like it oughta been. That corn, we would have made it if it hadn't been for the dry weather. But there was so many other years the grass just et up his crops because they weren't half worked. I had all that stuck in me. I said, "Papa—" 1905 when he took me back from Mr. Knowland, "Papa —" I didn't sass him, I knowed better—"Papa, I done learnt something workin for Mr. Knowland. If you will turn your business over to my hands, I'll make you something."

I was a stuck up little colored boy. Looked at me and said, "Son, I'm goin to do that, I'll do that."

Show you where the disencouragement come. I said, "Now you get me what I ask for, turn the work over to me and turn them children over to me and let me work em."

Had nothin never been made much in his hands. If that aint the truth there aint no God. I puts a terrible distress behind my words because I know I'm right.

In a week's time after he promised to swing the business my way, one mornin I got out in the yard. We done all et breakfast. His children that was able to get out there and use a hoe from time to time, he'd let em do as they pleased, weren't sendin em to the field. As he fooled around hisself, he didn't send them. They'd loll around the house; consequently, there weren't much made. If you wanted a bulky crop you had to put your children to work. Had a crowd there big enough to chop cotton and hoe all day long; two or three of em, three or four of em, big enough to go to the field, my half-sisters and -brothers, TJ was in the crowd.

I got out in the yard and commenced a callin for em to come out. "Let's get in the field, children. It's time, it's time for us to go."

Oooooo, it just set fire to my daddy, looked like. He was snappish anyhow and he wanted to be the boss, but his bossin weren't accountin for nothin, that was his trouble. He heard me callin them children, he jumped up and come out to the door—I was callin in a loud voice too: "Come out, come out. Let's get in the field. Time we was in the field, hear?"

First one come to the door was him.

"Nate, Nate."

I said, "Sir."

"I want you to know I'm boss here. And if there's anything you want to do, you go on and do it. I'll tell these children what to do."

Lord, I just sunk down in mind.

"I'm boss here."

I said to myself, 'Went back on his word that quick, won't keep hisself under a muzzle; just actin triflin and parleyin off and comin up in the fall of the year with no crop.'

I shied my mouth and let the tail lead the head from that day. Fall come and it was about three or four bales of cotton made. Made a good corn crop but the corn happened to be down on the creek bottoms—and it made itself. Best land I ever worked in my life for corn. It'd make corn as close as one leg to the other from one to two ears average, just as sweet and full as you could imagine. My daddy always got a pretty good corn crop with no labor hardly. Plow that corn once, twice, and go on about his business. But corn weren't the money crop and he fell down on cotton.

Many a boy mighta left his daddy and gone on about his business. I known many a boy run away from his daddy in his teens of years. Hit the road and his daddy had to hunt him up. Wilson Rowe had a boy, his oldest, and they was livin right there in our settlement. This boy was at home, he weren't grown. And he had to milk cows for his mother—didn't have no girls in that crowd. He was a little older than me or just about my age. One Sunday evenin he took the milk buckets as was his duty and went to milk the cows and he got out there to the barn—I was well informed of it; his daddy hunted him like a dog huntin a rabbit and he told all the transactions—the boy went out to milk the cows as usual and he caught the drop on his mammy and daddy both; went out there and set the buckets down and gone! Wilson Rowe's oldest son. He weren't the only boy done his parents that way. And the old man hunted him, hunted him, and he found him way up there in a place they call Sylacauga, fifty miles north, and he forced the boy to come home. But my daddy stayed on my head and I knowed to obey him —and maybe well that I did. I didn't do nothin but he had to know what it was and where it was. He just stood over me in a position that I knowed better and knowed it was wrong to run away from him.

1905, he just disrecognized me, discounted me; wouldn't turn nothin over in my hands like Mr. Knowland did. Good God, my feathers fell then. I went through with him, I sulked and got down —but I worked. The crop had been laid by and we didn't have nothin to do but prepare a way to haul it. And my daddy didn't have no cotton bodies for his wagon. I jumped out of bed one mornin, got the hand-saw, hammer, nails—I got out there in the yard sawin planks and nailin em together, makin cotton bodies to put on the wagon and haul off what little cotton had been made. As a help to my daddy and as a addition to what had to be done, I was doin it.

At that period of time, Lorna, my half-sister by TJ's mother, and TJ, and two or three of the other girls was able to get out in the field and work. And while I was fixin them bodies up before we all had to go to pickin cotton—the old house we lived in there on the Wheeler place had long, wide-set doorsteps—Lorna or TJ, one of em come out there first and the other one followed. And come up a hank* between em—I was out there by the well knockin, nailin the cotton body planks. After a while, Lorna let in to cryin. She was older than TJ but she let in to cryin. Lorna was the first child in the family after my mother died and my daddy married again.

And they got to hankin around there so rampant—I just kept a nailin, payin no attention to em much; a cryin spell amongst children, I weren't interested in that but I did come interested in it. Soon as I looked around, my daddy run out the house and grabbed TJ—he was sittin up in the house and he come out there rough amongst em, bout that cryin, and he grabbed TJ up by the arm and held him up and laid a whippin on the child with a switch. He was already objectin to my work and now he was puttin down the ways of his little children. I didn't know how come the fracas had started between TJ and Lorna but the way he whipped TJ weren't called for by what had happened. So I stuck my mouth in there. Held TJ up by his arm and he was layin it on him, flailin him. And he cleaned up TJ to a farewell.

It attracted my attention enough—I was off there nailin right by that well, I looked over there by the doorsteps and seed him layin it on TJ. Lorna had done run in the house. When my daddy got done whippin TJ—I didn't say nothin to him while he was whippin him—he dropped him back down. I looked at my daddy, I said, "Papa, it weren't no use you whippin that child like you did—"

And he had a knack, when he'd get mad as the devil his neck veins would just stand up. And when I spoke he got mad as the devil with me. I stopped my work and gived him my opinion. TJ was only my little half-brother; but half-brother, whole-brother or what, he whipped him more than he needed to. My daddy looked at me and squalled, "Do you take it up? Do you take it up?"

Right at that pile of lumber I was workin at, there was a old oak board that been layin out there several days before it was ever moved, about three foot long and as wide as my hand. And when I spoke against him for whippin that boy he squalled at me until

---

* A disagreement; ruckus; frenzy.

his veins stuck up and his eyes turned red. And when he got done squallin at me and darin me to take it up, he jumped off of them steps, runned across the yard and grabbed that old oak board. I still aint moved, still aint moved. He was goin to play the devil with that board; come to me right at that well with that board drawed back full force. I aint said a word, I aint said nothin. And when he got to me he hit at me with that board, right against my left arm down on my wrist. I standin there lookin at him. And just before he hit me he checked hisself and he didn't hit me as hard as he looked like he was goin to hit me; and he come down on me, checkin on that board, lightly. And it just even knocked the grain off of my wrist, bruised the outside skin, left a print there. If he'd a hit me like he drawed back to hit me he'd a broke it.

I just stood there, let him hit me, didn't say a word. Dropped the board down, back in the house he went, said no more about it. He was my daddy and daddy to the children that all lived in that house. I didn't have long to go there, I knowed that. And I knowed from the past histories of his life that if I'd a hit him back when he hit me, or if I'd a runned into that house after him and knocked heads, he woulda taken it out on the little children, girls and boys. He oughta been ashamed of himself, and he was, maybe, by him pullin back on that board before he hit me. That was all my satisfaction that day. I weren't scared of him for my sake. And he knowed, I think, that I was just as strong as he was then. I just considered what to do for the best and indulged him.

III

I started to correspondin a girl in 1905. The woman that my daddy married after my mother died, this girl I was correspondin was my stepmother's brother's daughter, Hannah Ramsey. She lived at that time just about two miles due west of us.

I was entered into my twentieth year when I started correspondin her and we got engaged to marry that same year. I pulled off in 1906, the year that I become of age, and the day I stood beside that girl and married her I weren't a day over twenty-one, not a day over—and not under a day. And when she married me she lacked from the time we married in the Christmas until the twenty-seventh of February of bein nineteen years old.

I had a half-sister that tried to be by me just like a whole-sister: she didn't want me to marry this Ramsey girl. It was one of my daddy's outside chaps, but he was man enough that when her mother died—this half-sister's name was Stella and her mother come from the Crabb family—and when she died, my daddy decided he'd take Stella. She was small at the time. My daddy never did marry her mother; he just plugged into that Crabb family and got a young-un, was a girl. And at the death of her mother he decided he'd take Stella and put her at *his* mother's, and he done it.

This girl's grandmother on her mother's side was named Classey Crabb, that's what they called her. And they had a lawsuit over Stella. When they had the lawsuit, this old lady, Stella's grandmother, she couldn't defeat my daddy because he was the natural father for the girl, but she was there for the argument. They questioned her some—my daddy said the laws asked old Aunt Classey Crabb who was this child's daddy? She didn't understand what was goin on and also she was contrary about it—I can't blame the old lady, you know, because it was her granddaughter.

Here's the words my daddy told me. In law, in court, they asked old lady Classey Crabb who was this child's daddy? She said, "She aint got no daddy. She aint got no daddy. The Lord's her daddy."

Well, the Lord aint nobody's daddy. The Lord aint birthed nobody here on earth. Went on to tell em, "The Lord is her daddy, the only daddy she has."

Well, what could they make of them words in court? Kept foolin around there and arguin and all, and the court give Stella to my daddy. Her mother was dead and the old lady couldn't take care of her proper, so they give her to my daddy. He taken her and put her with his mother, old Grandma Cealy. He put her at Mammy's—that was before I was born, that's what he said. He put her at Mammy's, Mammy raised her. She got grown and married a uncle of mine, one of my mother's brothers. So, she was my half-sister by me and her havin the same daddy and she become my auntie by her bein married to my mother's brother. And before she died—they lived way up yonder in them hills between here and Beaufort, and before she died her and Uncle Jim moved down in this settle-ment—Uncle Jim Culver, she was Uncle Jim Culver's wife. And she'd visit my daddy and she called him "Pappy." And she called my daddy's mother "Mammy," what my daddy called her too. And she moved down on one of Akers' places from up there in the hills, and lived several years down here.

But first I knowed of them they was livin up yonder in them hills above Chapel Ridge beat. And when their first child come, my mother was willin and my daddy wanted to put me up there to rock the cradle for Sister Stella, with her daughter, first child; her name was Wanda. I stayed up there a couple of weeks, little old boy just big enough to rock a cradle good and hand anybody anything they needed. I took a notion I wanted to come home. I give em a big talk up there—every time they'd make me mad about something I'd about halfway sass em out. I wanted to come out from up there, I didn't want to be no cradle rocker. My mother and daddy found it out and they come up there and got me, brought me home. I'd come to know as much about my sister Stella and Uncle Jim practically as anybody knowed about one another as far as knowin em. I stayed with em bout two weeks—they was my mama's and papa's folks and I stayed where they put me until I got tired of it, then I hollered like the devil.

Some years after that, Sister Stella and Uncle Jim moved down here in the piney woods, smooth land country. And I kept visitin em all along—I liked em as folks regardless to bein blood kin. I'd go to their house, set down, laugh and talk, after I got to be a young man. I was at home anywhere I went amongst my mother's and daddy's folks.

Well, Sister Stella and Uncle Jim lived close to a fellow named John Ivey, and he had three girls. Sometimes I'd knock around there but I wouldn't have none of them girls, didn't need em. My brother, half-brother, Will Turpin, married one of em. He married Lula. And my sister Stella wanted me to have Alice. Shit! I always had a head of my own after I got up big enough to know myself. I was aimin to marry, and if I had my way, I'd marry Hannah Ramsey. Some pretty tough words come from Sister Stella's lips in regards to the matter.

This Ramsey girl that I was goin to see, that was my heart-throb and my choice for a wife. First time I went to see her at her house me and her got engaged—that's right. I knowed her; I'd played with her a little after my daddy married, at the death of my mother, this Ramsey girl's auntie. And she always—I watched Hannah, I always watched her; I liked her, I sure liked her and I come to love her. When she'd visit her Aunt Maggie, TJ's mother

—when she come to see her she was quiet, she was pretty. I'd look at her—I played with her some, a little bit, but very little. Sometimes my daddy'd hitch up the mule and buggy—he had a old mule or two and he kept a buggy for my stepmother to travel on and see her folks, sometimes through the week. I'd climb in there and go with her. My brothers and sisters would say, "Mama's goin to carry Nate with her." She'd carry me over to her brother, Waldo Ramsey, and I'd play with his children, Hannah amongst em. And that gal eventually hung me. I did not meddle this girl under God's sun or be fresh around her, but it come to me just as plain as day —I fell in love with her and by the time I begin to get about twenty years old, I wouldn't have no other.

I'd meet her at church—I was fast and flip but I tried to carry myself in a nice way. Meet that girl at Pottstown or Elam Church over yonder between here and Apafalya; sometime I'd see her in a crowd of girls. It was just so, I couldn't shun her. Many a time I'd go to Pottstown—that was their membership, old lady Molly Ramsey and old man Waldo Ramsey and two or three of their children at that time. Old man Waldo was a deacon at Pottstown Baptist Church.

So I'd be goin along to Elam Church sometimes and they had to go to a spring to get their water for the church; the spring was less'n a quarter of a mile from church, good spring of water. And I'd be there, maybe not long got there, or I'd be there a pretty good while before I'd see her. But if she was there I'd arrange it, just so arrange it, I'd take a notion I wanted a drink of water—and I never did prefer a crowd of boys hangin at me. There'd be some boys sometime go along with me but if I wanted to go over yonder to see a girl I didn't need nobody followin me up. Some of em might be rowdy and I never did live, God hears me speak it, a rowdy life. I'd start off to the spring from that church and I'd meet Hannah and maybe two or three more girls with her—done that two or three times, runned into her goin for water at a heap of these churches, other churches besides Elam and Pottstown. But over there at Elam especially or Pottstown—there's well water at Pottstown and been so for years before I got grown. Anyhow I could I'd meet up with her, look at her, howdy with her. And just as soon as I seed her, just as soon as I'd spy her in a crowd of girls, I'd reach up and touch my old hat and pull the brim down over my eyes. I weren't scared of her but I had never been correspondin her. And I'd go on, just keep a walkin and I'd meet em.

She'd ask me right off, "How is Aunt Maggie gettin along?" That was TJ's mother, her own dear auntie, her daddy's sister.

"How's Aunt Maggie and Uncle Hayes gettin along?"

I'd say, "Well, they just fine, all right, all of em well there."

She'd smile and wait for me to say somethin next. That stuck me up but I wouldn't run up to her and ask her for her company. I'd tell her what she asked me for in a nice way and just keep on goin toward the spring. Wouldn't stand around for no long talk. I'd just go on, maybe wouldn't see her no more that day.

It got to where, in all them rounds—I was up in the world big enough and old enough to correspond her and she was up there too. Of course, she wasn't as old as I was. But I just kept travelin along, run into her a heap of times. I'd speak to her nice and everything'd be all right. She was my very heart-throb for a girl. And I soon found out she felt the same by me.

So, rocked along, rocked along—1904, one Sunday I went up to Uncle Grant Culver's. I was workin for Mr. Knowland at that time. I went home, put on my best clothes, and went right back through there by Mr. Knowland. That was the straightest route up to my uncle. So I went back through there and one of Hannah's daddy's sisters lived on Mr. Knowland's place. Right up above Mr. Knowland's house was her house, old man Waldo Ramsey's sister's house. I stopped there that Sunday on my way to Uncle Grant. I was used to her and her children because I stayed right there on Mr. Knowland's premises and she lived in callin distance of his house. Looked in there and Hannah's mother, old lady Molly Ramsey, was there. She was a mulatto woman straight. White man was her daddy—that's where her girl got her color. I didn't know Aunt Molly's parents but I heard em say many a time who was her daddy. He was a doctor, to my understandin, lived at Pottstown. And he recognized her for his daughter and kept up with her after she was birthed. Old man Waldo Ramsey was as dark as I am, a little darker man than I am. But his wife was a half-white woman; her hair'd swing down her back, long black hair.

So I happened to walk on by there, I looked in and seed Hannah was there with her mother. I stopped—round there in the field every day of my life at that time, workin for Mr. Knowland by the month, and Hannah's auntie was workin for Mr. Knowland too. Her and her husband had been separated for several years. She went for a Milliken, Betsey Milliken, and his name was Lucky Oneal. He'd come there sometimes to visit—I'd see him—but they never did go back together.

Well, there I was, laughin and talkin with the girls and Hannah. Hannah wasn't old enough to marry at that time and I wasn't neither but we was gettin right on the border age, 1904. After a while I pulled on away like I was intendin to and went on up to my Uncle Grant Culver's.

And that was in time of plums, plums a plenty on the trees. We got some vessels after I got to Uncle Grant's and come down from his house on a ramble to the old Pollard place. Weren't nobody livin there at that time. Old man Amos Pollard and old lady Becky Pollard, I knowed em well, that was their old home place. But him and his wife had both died. I don't know what all the changes was but after they died a fellow by the name of Morris Wiley, white man, bought that place.

So that Sunday we got some vessels and went down on that vacant Pollard place to pick some plums, plum trees all around there loaded with plums. Me and Uncle Grant and his wife and one of their girls and their boy. Uncle Grant's wife was named Leafy MacFarland before he married her; then she become Aunt Leafy Culver.

We was down in the bushes pickin plums, there in the old growed-up plum orchard and I heard somebody talkin. Just kept a pickin plums—and there was a old rail fence come right up through that plum orchard. I had a idea who it was approachin—on their way home. I didn't say nothin, I didn't let it worry me. That Ramsey crowd had just left from down there on Mr. Knowland's place—Hannah and her mother and the other two small children, Mattie and little Waldo—down there on a visit, see how Aunt Betsey was gettin along. And it'd been maybe three hours since I left there. And here come Hannah and her mother and the little children—sisters Lena and Lily was married out at that time.

Hannah walked up to the fence and looked at me. She said, "Why, here is Mr. Shaw over here."

Her mother and all of em then looked and seed me. It was surprisin to em, no doubt, that I was out there, but thank God I was in a clean clear place, didn't catch me at no devilment. I was up in them bushes pickin plums. Weren't no other girls about there except my first cousin, Uncle Grant and Aunt Leafy's daughter.

Hannah said, "Why, Mr. Shaw appears to be caught up in a plum bush. He don't even come down and talk to us. Watch out for yourself, Mr. Shaw."

So I told her, yes, I would, and they went right on up the road, crossed and went right across the Pollard place to their place.

Well, all such as that was keepin me stuck up. I was comin to like her more every year of my life and she liked me. Kept on pickin plums and they went on home. Got done pickin plums and went back to Uncle Grant's house. I stayed over there till late hours, then went on back to my daddy's.

I lingered; I never did go to see that girl yet. I was gettin to be a man in them days but still I wouldn't lurch out and be too fast. But the kind of creature I am, when I take out at anything or want to do anything, I'll bust to do it.

1905, I was beginnin to pick up and spur my own horse then. One Sunday in October—I disremember whether it was the first Sunday, second Sunday, third Sunday, or the fourth Sunday, but it was October—I heard that this girl—I done waited as long as I could. I loved her, I loved her. I done got to where I couldn't stay away from her—I heard that she was goin down to the piney woods on a Saturday and spend the night, her and her baby sister Mattie, with her older sister and Malcolm Todd. Hannah's older sister was named Lily, Lily Ramsey, and she married Malcolm Todd. And I heard one day durin the week, 1905, in October, that them two youngest Ramsey gals was goin down there on a visit, goin on a Saturday and comin back on Sunday. It was about four miles from where my daddy was livin on the Wheeler place down there to where Sister Lily was livin, on Mr. Harry Black's place. I got right busy, prepared myself all week—that Sunday, cleaned up, fixed myself up, I got one of them old mules out the lot and hitched him to my daddy's buggy, pretty good buggy, and I took a drive.

I done stayed out of correspondin with that girl as long as I could. I drove down there that Sunday and when I drove up in the yard, she was the first one that I seed comin to the door. She said, "Mr. Shaw, what are you doin way down here?"

I said, "I'm just drivin around for a little enjoyment."

She said, "Well, get out and come in."

She called her brother-in-law "Brother." She said, "Brother and

Sister aint here"—that was Malcolm and Lily— "there ain't nobody here but me and Lena and Mattie. Come on in." Sister Lena stayed with Malcolm and Lily at that time; her and her husband was separated.

I went in and set down. She taken a chair and set down pretty close to me, reasonably close. We set there and talked a while.

She said, "Mr. Shaw, we are down here on a visit. Sister and Brother, they gone over to Teaks' Church to a sing. We was plannin and preparin to go down to Mr. Spivey's"—fellow by the name of Will Spivey, lived right below em—"we was plannin to walk down there this evenin. They goin to have a little singin down there."

I done got hot in the collar then. I was drivin in, too; goin to learn which way the world was goin or which way that girl was goin.

She said, "Would you wish to drive down to the singin?"

I said, "No, I wouldn't care to go down there right now. I just got here. You all can go down there if you like."

Right then Sister Lena begin talkin with me on some conversation, but Lena weren't on my mind a bit. Set there a few minutes and I said, "I'll probably come down there before I turn around and go back the other way. I may drive down."

Hannah said, "All right. If you decide, come on down. We goin down there now—" her and Mattie. You could see one house from the other; weren't a half-mile apart. I set there and talked with Lena again.

After a while I got up, walked out and untied my mule, throwed my tie halter in the buggy, crawled up there and drove straight down to Mr. Spivey's where Hannah was. I got down there and the house was full of gals. Whooooeeeee, when I drove up and stopped, a crowd of em come to the door, bulged up in the door. They come jumpin out that house then, into the yard, runnin in their long skirts. Hannah weren't sayin a word, only just laughin with the rest of em and laughin at what they said.

"What you doin way down here, Mr. Shaw? What you doin way down here? You way out of your country. Never seed you down here before. How come you down here?"

One of them gals spoke, said, "Hannah's here, that's the reason of it; don't you understand? Hannah's here. That's who he come down here after."

All of em run out to my buggy then and surrounded me, and

they commenced a chattin, talkin. I weren't sayin nothin, just lookin at em, laughin, humorin em in their talk. They just hit the very key note. Got high enough to go to jabbin with me—I was always a fellow that taken well amongst the girls. All I had to do was present myself. But there was one in the bunch that I liked better than I did the others; consequently, I didn't go no further with em than to treat em right, treat em with respect. I conducted myself well and I was just a young fellow. I was a popular young man—the girls would cut buttonholes over me—but I never thought I was more than I was. It was the easiest thing I ever done in my life, tamperin with women. I was a heavy hitter surely; I knowed I could hit heavy in any way I wanted to but I held myself back.

So, "Mr. Shaw, aint that how you come down here? Didn't you come down here to take Hannah home?"

O, they was hot at me. I looked straight at em, pulled myself up on the buggy seat, said, "If them buggy wheels turns over I'm goin to carry her home."

That's all I give em. Hannah smiled. I had never asked her *could* I carry her home, neither. I just told that drove of girls, "If them buggy wheels turns over I'm goin to carry her home this evenin." I didn't bite my tongue.

Well, when the crowd broke up, then I *asked* Hannah for the privilege of carryin her back home. She granted me the privilege. And when that buggy left there, she left on it with me. Drove back up to Malcolm Todd's and Lily's. She got her things together, what she had carried down there to spend the night in; nicely fixed em up and put em in the buggy. Luke Milliken happened to be down there that Sunday. He was a little kin to em and he brought Mattie home, the baby sister. So that give me and Hannah the buggy by ourselves.

That evenin, late, just before sundown I landed her home. And just before we got there we met her mother, walkin, at a fork in the road. She was on her way up to Uncle Price MacFarland's house. It set right up the road along the right hand side of the fork goin away from the Ramsey land. Takin a late evenin walk up there. Met her right at the fork and stopped the buggy. She walked up and looked in at Hannah said, "Sweet"—they called her "Sweet" —"who is this got you on the buggy? Who is this?" She smiled and laughed. "Who is this man?"

She liked me—her and old man Waldo Ramsey liked me for a young fellow; been knowin me from before I was nine years old. My mother died in August and three weeks to Christmas my daddy married old man Waldo's sister. And in the Christmas I become nine years old. So the Ramseys and the Shaws done been together, learnt about one another—names and families and so on. And I liked Hannah from a girl on up. I used to look at her when she was small—I was a small boy, too. Her little old cheeks would be just as red, just as red—her mother was a half-white woman.

So, her mother went on, "Well, Sweet, you all can go on to the house, you and your company."

I knowed I stood well with em because I always treated in growin up her mother and father nice as a little boy could treat old folks.

I drove on up to her house and helped Hannah out the buggy, went in and stayed there until just about first dark. Her mother come back home right quick, and old man Waldo was already there; but they didn't come into the room where we was. That was where my love was. I was highly appreciated by the old folks and I knowed it.

First dark I got up to go. Me and Hannah stood at the fireplace —weren't cold enough for no fire. The mantel board was reasonably low and we stood against it talkin. I hit her then, hit her a hard lick and this is the way I hit her. I done been granted the privilege to correspond her—that evenin when she allowed me to carry her home I asked her about it and she agreed. Got her home then, stayed until about first dark, I decided I'd better be pullin out. But before I did I just come out fair, didn't ask her in no roundabout way. I thought she had it in her for me; I knowed I had it in me for her. I said, talkin low, "Well, do you love me or think enough of me to live a married life with me?"

It stuck her. She smiled but she was slow to answer. She said, as a girl would, "Mr. Shaw, I'll talk with you further about that on your next trip."

I said, "Very well as far as talkin goes, we'll talk. But I wants to know now."

She hated to say it, she hated to say it, but she decided to make up her mind right there and answer my question.

She told me, "Yes, I love you. And I agree to marry you, live a married life with you."

I lingered along with her then; went a few times to see her. I had got up to twenty years old and come in the knowledge of so many different things; I'd come into the knowledge of women to an extent. Nature will teach you like it teaches a stallion to jump a fence; you aint goin to hold down. The thing for a boy to do when he gets old enough for his nature to begin to teach him, don't make a dog of himself. So, I was afraid my nature would take over me and I stayed away from Hannah to a great extent.

I corresponded her until Christmas, 1906. Anywhere she'd tell me she wanted to go, to meetin or just for a pleasure trip, I'd hire me a nice buggy and take the best mule in the lot—my daddy happened to have a old mule, called him Haggard. That old mule, you could take a straw and drive him to death. You better not touch old Haggard, slap him with the lines or either hit him with a straw —Haggard's gone. That scoundrel could trot like a horse. He was a slender-built, sorrel-colored mule.

1906, my daddy had me hired to Mr. Jim Barbour, but Saturday evenins I'd go around—and there was three fellows that had nice buggies: Mr. Stark, man that I lived with in the year of '23, he had a nice buggy and he was livin at that time on a place he had bought right on the road between Apafalya and my daddy. I'd stop there, hire Mr. Stark's buggy for Sunday use. If I didn't get it, Mr. Chester Allen lived right up above Mr. Stark; *he* had a nice buggy. I'd get Mr. Allen's. If I missed on any one of em, a young white fellow lived across Sitimachas Creek, just the other side of my daddy, by the name of Chester Edmonds. I could hire his buggy any time he weren't usin it. And out of the three of them buggies—all of em was nice buggies—one of em was goin to stand in the yard. And I'd hire that buggy for Sunday; go there Sunday mornin and get it. Sunday night, first part of the night, I'd drive the buggy back in there. Everybody'd be asleep—I wouldn't rouse em up. Drive up to the shed, take that buggy out, lay the harness off my mule, lay it in the foot of that buggy, pick up them shafts, and push that buggy back under the shed. That's just workin one mule to the buggy; if it's two, it'd be a pole—I never did carry Hannah nowhere with two mules. Just get old Haggard and put him between the shafts of some white man's buggy. Drive over to the Ramsey home on Sundays, Hannah would come out and invite me in. I'd get out the buggy, hitch my mule, walk in. The old folks, I'd just as soon talk to them as talk to their daughter. That's the way I conducted myself. Never did shine my eyes to old folks and ignore em. And they never turned me down for nothin.

Hannah would go on and get ready to go out with me. Sometimes before we'd leave she'd come in the room where I was settin, say, "Mr. Shaw, Mama wants to go with us this mornin. Would you carry her?"

I'd say, "Of course, I wouldn't miss it. Tell her to get ready."

They had—old man Waldo had a nice mule, long-legged scoundrel, and his wife was scared to ride behind him. Name of the mule was Prince. He'd run away with you if you let him. He weren't real bad about it but he'd do it. See anything in the road he didn't like he'd turn around. Old man Waldo was a good old man but he was *too* good in a way; he let that mule do him as he pleased a heap of times and in that the mule developed a mind of his own. Old lady Molly Ramsey didn't want to ride behind him, scared her. She'd jump out of that buggy when that mule started.

Hannah kept a comin to me that way. I'd just tell her, "Yes, why sure, your mother's plumb welcome to go with us anywhere she wants to go, if we go."

They had a nice Barnville buggy. Old man Waldo bought it second-handed from some Higgins fellow in here about Pottstown; was goin off to some sort of business or school and he sold his buggy to old man Waldo. Nice buggy, just wasn't a rubber tire buggy. And he had nice lap robes for buggy use, a summer robe, fall robe, winter robe. Old lady Molly Ramsey'd take the lap robe from their buggy and cover her and Hannah's lap with it. I'd take mine and fold it up and spread it across the buggy down in the foot. I'd set down straight, cross them lines on the dashboard, put my foot in the buggy stirrup, Hannah and her mother sittin on the seat of that hired buggy—didn't use their buggy, didn't use their mule. I hired a buggy and drove the best mule my daddy had. And that old Haggard would put you wherever you called. My daddy had one old yellow mule, called him Pomp. Old Pomp, he'd trot along for you but he didn't get up and get off down the road like old Haggard.

So I'd sit there and drive that mule to Pottstown or Elam or Bethany—there was three different churches I'd carry em to pretty regular. I had no kicks about the mother travelin with us; I weren't goin to do a thing but accommodate her if I could. I was already engaged to her daughter. I tried, and it was my full aim, to marry on my birthday. And one Sunday night along the last of December, 1906, my brother Peter carried me over to Hannah's from home. None of my folks didn't go but Peter. He went over and seed his brother married, right around my birthday, right *on* my birthday, or a day sooner or a day later.

Now my half-sister Stella knowed I was goin with this girl and she supposed I intended to marry her. And at that period of time her and Uncle Jim lived down in Akers' woods, they called it, smooth land country, easy to plow and work. Weren't like that up in them hills where they moved down from. So, one day in May, before I ever married Hannah, I had cause to be in that neighborhood and I met up with my half-sister.

Hannah had wrote me a letter and asked me would I take her to commencement at Tuskegee, school closin, for the ceremony. People from every whichaway come that day to Tuskegee Normal School, colored school, commencement. Crowd so thick you couldn't squeeze between em. So, she wrote me word that she would be at her sister's and I could come by there and pick her up, drive straight on in to Tuskegee. That commencement mornin, I hitched old Haggard to the buggy I'd rented and I dropped right down to her sister's. Got there and Lily, oldest sister in the bunch, told me, "She aint here, she was to come—"

I said, "I know she was to come because she told me on a letter that I should come here and pick her up."

She said, "Well, Sweet wrote me a letter since then and told me to tell you that she is sick and disabled to come."

Well, I had sense enough to know what that sickness was; women and girls has it every month until they changes lives, get too old for it. So, she didn't say that's what it was, but I had a idea.

I said, "All right then. I sure hate it that I can't meet Hannah here and take her on to commencement."

I just crawled back in that buggy right by myself and went on to Tuskegee. Enjoyed it very well that day but I didn't enjoy it as well as I would have if she'd a been with me. Had a big gatherin down there, big eats, hear the bands beatin and so on—just a real enjoyment.

I stayed there long as I cared to stay and that was the best part of the day. I fed my mule in due time and he was ready to leave when I was. Hitched him back to that hired buggy and pulled right back out the way I went in there and went on back by Malcolm Todd and Lily's. I got off there—and I had a gold ring on one of my fingers and I had on a pair of leather drivin gloves and when I got out the buggy I pulled one of them gloves off and I lost that gold ring. It weren't mine, it was my uncle's ring, Uncle Grant Culver's ring. He let me wear it some—he brought it to this country with him. Some of them boys went away from this country after the surrender and stayed off for years before they ever come back; nobody knowed where they was. I had two uncles done that—and they never did come back.

So I lost that ring in Lily's yard. Stopped my buggy, wrapped my lines around the whip in the stand, pulled that glove off and pulled the ring off with it. It was a little slack on that finger anyhow. When I got ready to get on that buggy and leave out I didn't know I'd lost that ring, didn't pay no attention to it until I got home to my daddy, way up yonder on Sitimachas Creek. And as God would have it, Lily's husband, Malcolm Todd found that ring in the yard. I got it—didn't keep it long, give it back to my uncle. If anybody else had found it—it was a gold ring—I'd a never seed it again.

I drove on up the road after I lost that ring—didn't know I'd lost it though. And Uncle Jim and Sister Stella was livin down there at that time, close to Hannah's people. And also, Charley Todd and his wife—she was a Marsh woman, Lucy Marsh. All that bunch come out together from up in them hills. And they all settled just a little piece above Malcolm's home. Well, my half-sister was visitin with Charley Todd and his wife. I stopped my mule and buggy in their yard, got out, went in the house. Happened Sister Stella was in there—I didn't know it when I walked in. We howdyed and talked right there in Charley Todd and Lucy's house. I never did set down, only went in there to pay a visit and say hello. While I was standin there, Sister spoke to me like this. I didn't say nothin to her about how come I was down in that part of the country—been down there at Malcolm Todd's to pick up Hannah and carry her to commencement; I didn't tell her nothin about that. But she boned me about Hannah. She said, "Brother"—she called me "Brother"—"I got a little talk for you."

I wanted to know what that little talk was. I insisted on it, told her, "All right, Sister, anything you got to say, I'll listen."

Right in front of Lucy Todd she told me—them was the only two in that room, Uncle Jim's wife, my half-sister, and Charley Todd's wife. She said, "What I want to talk with you concerns this girl you goin with. I want you to listen at me and understand me good. I'd rather you wouldn't marry that girl."

I reckon she gleaned the idea the way I was goin to see Hannah regular as I was goin to see her, and the news of it reached her, there must have been somethin behind it.

She said, "This girl that you correspondin, there's nothin I knows bad about her at all. She's a nice girl far as I ever heard of. There's nothin hurtin her morals and her ways, only what I wants to say to you: she looks like she's a sickly girl. I wouldn't wish for my brother to marry a girl of that type. She looks like she's terrible sickly. And if you marry her you might just marry a doctor's bill. Furthermore, she might not live out a married life with you. Now, if you'll consider, I know a man that's got three good healthy daughters—"

I said, "Well, listen, Sister. Stop and listen to me. I aint goin to marry for sure, I don't *know* that I'm goin to marry, I aint married so far. Many things could come up that could devoid my and her married life—but we aint married yet and I don't know, I couldn't say that we goin to ever marry at this present time. We got to get up to that yet."

The gal that *she* wanted me to have was Alice Ivey. Well, everybody's got a rather, but some folks carries their rathers too far.

I said, "Let me tell you, Sister, I aint goin to marry no man and no woman's daughter for her health. Health or unhealth, I won't stand back off the girl that I love."

I got mighty about it then. She seed it too. I stood there a few minutes and said, "You all be good, I got to go."

Nothin more said after that. Fellow by the name of Bull Tankard married Alice Ivey. I was there that night but I never would go in the house. I went there just to be goin somewhere. I didn't care nothin about the girl at all, weren't studyin her. I felt that way about it before that girl ever married Bull Tankard. Well, the night of their marriage I come out from Apafalya close to Zion Church where John Ivey lived with his family. But I didn't stay too long. My mind was runnin and my heart was on Hannah.

1906, my daddy jumped up smart and hired me to Mr. Jim Barbour. 1905, that fall, near Christmas, my daddy went to Apafalya one day—he was aimin to get shed of me again. Mr. Barbour wanted to hire me and my daddy made a trade with him. He come back home that night late, between sundown and dark when he got back. Talked with my stepmother awhile, then he called me.

That was after we had gathered the crop, cut wood for winter —he called me. And when he wanted me to do anythin accordin to his request, he'd call me "son."

"Son, Mr. Barbour out at Apafalya wants to hire a hand."

Come back home with that in him. He was already in business with Mr. Barbour and he found out Mr. Barbour wanted to hire a hand.

Said, "He done hired John Thomas and he wants another hand."

I was readin between the lines fast as he spoke. I knowed that he already done promised me to the man. I said, "When do he want a hand to start, if he hires one, Papa?"

"He wants him New Year's Day."

I set still, listenin. I started to tell him when he told me Mr. Barbour wanted another hand, I started to say, "O, Papa, why don't you"—that's just the way I determined it in my mind— "O, Papa, why don't you just tell me you done hired me to Mr. Barbour," but I wouldn't say that. I knowed he woulda flew hot as the devil. He were workin in a way and I seed it plain, to draw my last dollar until I was twenty-one years old. I seed it, I understood the hitch very well from all the back transactions, takin all my labor he could until I was grown.

Well, I set there but I wouldn't say nothin. I cut myself off; he kept talkin. In a few minutes he said, "He wants you. He wants you."

My mind told me, 'I expected that.' I had mapped that out on my own. I caught the meanin by askin him when did Mr. Barbour want the hand to start *regardless* to who he was—"New Year's Day." Told me Mr. Barbour had hired John Thomas. I knowed John Thomas well, me and John come along boys together but John was a little older than I was. Mr. Barbour hired John from his own self, he was grown. Didn't have to go to John's daddy to hire him.

Said, "He wants you. Would you work for him?"

"Yes, Papa, I'll work anywhere you put me, to help you."

If he seed fit, as he did do right on, to draw my labor until I was twenty-one years old, it was just his game. I was goin to give it to him. But I was thoroughly intendin, the day I become twenty-one years old, that was the crop right there. I taken that in mind when I was eighteen years old. That hit my mind and hit it very heavy, and the Lord blessed me to do it. I just definitely decided— good God, you couldn't tell me nothin bout my way of life, so far as bein under my daddy—I throwed up my hand before my Savior, I just wanted, I aimed with all of my thoughts, I studied this thing and made up my mind, that when I got to be twenty-one years old, on the very day I come of age, that'd be the last day I'd ever live under my daddy's charge. I wanted to stay with my daddy until the right time to leave, I wanted to do that—my Savior listenin at my heart. And I got a great thrill out of doin as my mind led me. I begin to feel my man, I begin to want to be a man of my own, get out there and do what would prosper me in life. Never did have a thought I wanted to gamble—win money—or be a thief. I was de- pendin on the twist of my own wrist. Never did have a doubt about it neither; always thought I could do a thing, anything, and I done it. But I never thought, never had no idea of becomin somethin I wasn't. I seed then too, when I walked out from under my daddy's administration, I couldn't do it. And I just rested right easy where I was and tried to make a support for my family.

So I went in there to work for Mr. Barbour; he lived just inside the Apafalya corporation. Walked in there on the mornin of the first day of January, 1906, and stuck right there until the third day of August. My daddy come around every week I stayed there, on a Saturday, drawin my labor. I didn't know if he was takin up money on his own self, on his note with Mr. Barbour, or if he was drawin cash on me.

I didn't get a suit of clothes that year and I didn't have nothin but passable clothes. Here's what I had: a coat of one grade of cloth and a pair of pants of another, mixed suit. That's all I had to wear the whole year round.

One day I walked up to Mr. Barbour—my daddy had no con- veniences for me to enjoy myself with my friend-girls, and him drawin on my labor now and could have got some on his own, but I knowed accordin to what Mr. Barbour told me, he was takin up on me and gettin by with that. So, one Saturday I walked up to Mr. Barbour, said, "Mr. Barbour, I wants a little money—" first time and the last time.

"You better be careful bout askin for money. Your daddy owes me more now than he'll ever pay me."

I had nothin to do with that. I knowed my daddy weren't drawin money on me for my gratification. He drawin it to keep up his family. I stood there and looked at Mr. Barbour.

"You better be careful bout these money matters. Your daddy owes me now more than he'll ever pay me."

I thought to myself, 'Let the devil come off. I's nearly grown and ought to be drawin my own money or be given part of it, anyway.'

"How much you want?"

I said, "I just want three dollars."

Give me the three dollars with his warnings. What did I want that three dollars for? I wanted that money to pay a white gentleman for the use of his buggy on a Sunday.

Mr. Barbour had right smart money; least he operated as if he did. He was a cotton seed buyer at that time and a fertilize agent, orderin fertilize in from plants and companies and sellin it out again. And as usual amongst these town-based dealers, he run a sizable plantation in the country.

When I first went to work for him, and me and John Thomas run together on New Year's mornin, right at that hour and period of time, Mr. Barbour was in Opelika; he done took off to Opelika that mornin. So I give in to his wife, Mrs. Gertie Barbour—they called her Miss Gertie—what I was there for and so on. And durin that day, Mr. Barbour called up home from Opelika and called for John Thomas—that was the man he picked. He knowed of John more so than he knowed of me. We was both there, fresh hands, come into his home to go to work. John Thomas's daddy lived on his place at that particular time, old man Obie Thomas. Just a place Mr. Barbour had rented for him, joinin Mr. Barbour's lot there in town. Mr. Barbour didn't own no big lot but he owned a pretty good outlet, maybe two or three acres. Mr. Barbour lived right down close to the highway and old man Obie Thomas lived right above him.

So John shot out to Opelika accordin to Mr. Barbour's word

and when he got there Mr. Barbour had him fitted up with what he had bought for John to bring back. Mr. Barbour hisself hit the train and come on in home. The railroad run right into Apafalya—them trains was hootin and railin around there every day the Lord sent, mainly railroad transportation in them days. And just before night —it wasn't supposed to be but twenty-one miles from Apafalya to Opelika—John drove in there with a young pair of mules that woulda weighed fully eleven hundred pounds apiece, to a big low-wheeled white hickory wagon. Tires on that wagon broad as my four fingers.

Next day Mr. Barbour had a job settin ready. Me and John had to take that wagon and a pair of mules and go to haulin cotton seed out of the cotton seed house where loads of cotton seed would come in, all that the people livin in the country could bring in and sell. Had scales right there at the seed house, weighed the seed and chunk it in the seed house. And if the seed house was full he'd send some of them wagonloads of cotton seed to the train depot and throw em in the carboxes. Or if he had a shipment to ship out at the present time, he'd have the man that's sellin him these cotton seeds to carry em on and load em in the carbox.

Mr. Barbour was one of two men in Apafalya buyin cotton seed. Mr. Lester Watson, he was the other big cotton seed buyer in them days. After people would have their cotton ginned and didn't sell the seed to the gin men, they loaded their seed up and brought em to the seed buyin man.

Just any hour that we got our job done, it was another one to do; and it was from cotton seed to guano, from guano to cotton seed. Guano come shipped in on trains from these foreign guano factories. Mr. Barbour would announce, "Boys, there's a carload of guano at the depot to be hauled off. I want you to get it quick as you can, let that carbox go."

That carbox had to be unloaded on the spot or else it stood there overtime and he had to pay rent on it. But if he moved it off in quick time and released the carbox, nothin to it but pay for shippin the fertilize in there. Sometimes part of that guano we'd haul right up to the cotton seed house if there was room to hold it and stack it there. Or he'd sell it directly off of that carbox. Then it was, "You boys carry so-many and so-many tons of guano to such-and-such a customer in the country." He'd tell us where to deliver it—to a white man that owned a big plantation or several plantations and rented em and divided em out amongst his hands, white hands and black hands, but mostly black.

Soon as spring of the year come, he begin lettin off guano; everybody'd got supplied. And he weren't the only guano man in Apafalya. They were fightin amongst each other "who should" and "who shant" sell in different territories. And they never would agree; it was just every man sellin all he could, the devil keepin score.

Soon as this guano business dropped off, Mr. Barbour had a plantation out in the country rented—it weren't his—went out and rented a place for us to farm for him. Every day we had to drive them mules to that big wagon on out there, carry our dinner along with us. Take them mules loose from the wagon and go to plowin. Kept us farmin—kept us busy from New Year's Day until he got through with us in August. No corn planted at all, he was strictly a cotton man. And also he had a farm right there at his house and John Thomas's daddy worked it with a horse. Me and John handled them big mules, tendin strictly to the country farm.

Time it come to make a crop, that other work had pulled me down. I was young, weren't grown quite, weren't used to heavy jobs every day. So I went to the doctor to see about my condition— weak, all out and down, weren't able to do the work that was put on me. Dr. Herman, in Apafalya, told me the mornin I went to him— he called me Tate; my name was Nate Shaw but he called me Tate. He never did say "Tate Shaw" but he called me Tate. He examined me, said, "Tate"—seemed to be a kind man, middle-aged —"Tate, you just about lost your nervous system—"

Well, I'd been handlin heavy stuff, big forks of cotton seed every day, from that to haulin guano and natural soda and all that mess. Them fertilize bags was two-hundred-pound bags, ought to been handled by two men, one on each end pickin it up. John Thomas—he was a young fellow too but he was a little older than I was, he was stouter-built than I was—he was used to that heavy work. He stood it better than I did. I give out at it. By spring of the year, crop time come, I weakened down.

Dr. Herman said, "Tate, you about lost your nervous system. You got to slow down, boy. I'll fix you some medicine that'll fix you up though. Do what I tell you to do and how I tell you, you'll be all right."

He fixed me up a bottle of liquid medicine—I don't know

what was in it—and he gived me orders to take it so many times a day. Picked me right up, got my nerves together, went on and done every job that was put on me.

Mr. Barbour had some old Boy Dixie plows, old-timey weak plows, wood beams. Good mule would snap the beam clear out of one. And he put us to plowin—now, them Oliver Goober plows come in several years after that Boy Dixie plow; Vulcan plow come in, too. Both of em was iron-beam plows, Vulcan number six, Oliver number seven—plows that stood up with big mules and cut deep. The points on them plows cut that many inches, accordin to the number of the plow: cut six inches, cut seven inches. That Boy Dixie run about five inches deep. But that Oliver Goober, when it come into this country, it didn't cut under seven inches; it was a seven-inch cutter. For my personal use, after I got old enough to run mule plows for myself, I never did run a Boy Dixie. You know, wood is never as strong as iron and a animal pullin against that beam, single-tree hung to the end of that beam, if it strike a severe stump or hang up on a root under the ground and that mule have good weight about him—POP—pull that Boy Dixie beam clean in two. But it couldn't do them iron beams that way; might break the frog in them Olivers, break the points, but never break that beam, that beam was substantial.

So at that period of time, 1906, them Boy Dixies was beginnin to go down and them iron-beam plows takin their place. But Mr. Barbour hadn't got a hold of them new plows yet. Put me and John Thomas to plowin them old Boy Dixies. And many a farmer had his crop all laid by by July, but Mr. Barbour didn't. It come a heavy wet spell that year and we couldn't plow at all. Soon as it quit rainin he got in a hurry and wouldn't wait for the ground to dry. Any time your crop of cotton sprouts, or your corn—when you get a stand of cotton all over your farm or a stand of corn, if you want to prosper and not defect it no way, you better keep your plow out the field when the ground's wet or you'll ruin your crop in its growth. Plow that land wet around that stuff you'll disturb the roots and the ground dries, it dries in a hard position. It injures your land to plow it wet, it injures your crop. You must cultivate your crop when the ground is dry. Pile up wet earth around the stalks, it dries and scalds em out. Tear up them roots and the sun run out behind it, that earth hardens away from the roots and there's no moisture can stay in there very long. And it dries out and crusts up around them roots, smothers them feed roots to that cotton or that corn—it's just a plumb killin and a disadvantage to your crop. For God's sake, don't plow it that way. Wait till the ground dries.

But he wouldn't wait. He was in a hurry. I don't know what old man Jim Barbour meant by havin me and John Thomas plow them Boy Dixies around that cotton with that wing settin to that row and just pilin up dirt to one side, then go to the other end and turn right around and that wing right to that row again. Makin a list around that cotton, coverin up the grass and vegetation around the stalks. If he'd a done it in dry weather it wouldn't have hurt at all. In a few days, by plowin that ground when it was wet—I could take up a handful of that dirt after we plowed it and squeeze it up tight to a ball in my hand, pitch it up and catch it and it wouldn't bust, too much water in it, it aint goin to bust, it'll hold. You hurtin that cotton, you hurtin that corn. He oughta made twenty bales of cotton off of that farm that year but when he wound up he didn't get but thirteen bales. I seed it gathered every day—I weren't workin for him durin pickin time, he'd turned me and John Thomas loose by then; but when I'd go to Apafalya to catch the train, in August, after I left him the third day of August and was goin to my job down between Stillwell and DeGrasse, at the sawmill, I seed his hands pick that crop and I heard em say what he made that year—nothin but thirteen bales of cotton when he oughta made at least twenty. His cotton done come up short and thin, pitiful plants. I seed it myself travelin backwards and forwards through the month of August.

Me and John knowed it would injure his crop to plow it like he told us, we had the experience of a crop—I was right at grown and John was older than I was. But it weren't no use to tell that white man nothin. He runnin his business and we had to do what he said do. He'd a told us, if we told him, "Mr. Barbour, that's ruinin your crop"—"Well, plow it, plow it." If he hire you to work, you just go on and work, that's all you can do. He tell you to plow it, or whatever he say do, and you workin by the day, just go on and do it, you hired to him and you might not be seein any of that money your labor is drawin. If he ruins his stuff, you aint to blame. It weren't none of my business: he put me out there to plow it and he oughta been capable of the knowledge to know hisself what to do in that situation. And if he didn't know he could have asked me.

But he didn't ask, didn't expect a nigger to have any idea about it one way or the other. He was a old white man. He had several children and they was grown. Some of em was in California at that time.

So, two or three days after we done that work, the cotton started to turn yellow; it went on down, yellowed up and throwed off the fruit, parched up considerably. And he made just thirteen bales of cotton off of that crop when he shoulda made twenty, the way he worked. He was a guano salesman and he'd just use any amount of guano he wanted to on his crop. He spoke these words: "Put it down, put it down"—that's guano—"if I don't make enough to pay for it, I've already got enough."

The way I was treated there, his wife had more dealins with me in some ways than he did. When I first went there, the mornin I walked in, Miss Gertie asked me had I et breakfast.

I said, "No ma'am, I haven't et."

She give me breakfast—I et three meals a day there, from the first day of January, 1906, up until the third day of August, and if I didn't it was because lunch was brought out in the field or because I was at home on Saturdays and Sundays.

The white lady didn't give me the same food to eat that they et, not all the way through. She fed me mostly on boiled grits and some sort of cornbread. And I et off a table out on the north veranda of the kitchen, up against a wall. I'd sit there and eat, rain or shine, cold or hot. And if it rained it just blowed in there over me. Sometime the wind shaked my back down, and when it weren't shakin me down, it was blowin the food off my plate. And she had a knack of feedin me on sour bread, sour biscuits; I couldn't hardly eat em to save my life. I wasn't used to eatin sour bread. At home and at Mr. Knowland's house I ate straight good biscuits, and at Mr. Knowland's I took my meals in the dinin room.

Sour biscuits, sour bread, that's what they fed me. I didn't like em noway. I told her, one mornin, "Miss Gertie, I can't eat your sour bread. I don't like it at all."

What the devil good did it do tellin the white lady that? Just kept pilin em up there for me, bout two good biscuits—no 'bout' to it, just two biscuits, fresh cooked biscuits for breakfast like they et themselves and all else they'd give me was sour biscuits, sour bread. And what reason they had to feed me that way I never learnt. I got so tired of that I partly lost my appetite. At dinner or night, if she had any cold biscuits left, she'd put em out for me. But my regular diet at breakfast was two good biscuits and three or four, maybe five, sour biscuits. No butter, not a bit, just plain biscuits. Piled them sour biscuits high on a plate and set em out there in spite of redemption; I couldn't stop her. And the way she acted when I told her, she let me know it weren't none of my business to try to stop her. All I could do was tell her in a nice, kind way that I didn't like sour bread. But she paid me no more attention than she paid to a bird eatin crumbs off the ground.

The mornin I wound up with Mr. Barbour, after me and John Thomas had completed what he told us to do—no kicks to come on it; we done followed his orders to the last notch—he sent me home just like I was a little boy. It was in the way he told me—John weren't there that mornin. He hadn't come down from his daddy's because he knowed we was wound up. But I had to be there. I stayed at Uncle Obie's: me and John slept on the bed together every night God sent from the first day of January, 1906, until the third day of August, except maybe I'd take a notion to run off and go over to Cousin Lark Shaw's and be with his folks, spend the night. But very few nights I missed stayin at Uncle Obie's. Cousin Lark was livin on Mr. Ruel Akers' place; it weren't over a mile. But I didn't go over there three times. I stayed with John Thomas. Mr. Barbour had me hired by the month and he had that place prepared up there for me to sleep at Uncle Obie's. It was part of the deal. And Uncle Obie was plowin a horse, durin the day, on a small farm under Mr. Barbour's jurisdiction.

Last day I worked for Mr. Barbour, the second day of August; the third day of August he told me, "Well, I'm through with you now. You can go home to your daddy."

I looked at him, said, "Yes sir."

Third day of August, and the twenty-eighth day of December comin I come grown, and he talkin to me that way. I felt that he taken me for less than I was—I thought little about that.

So, I took what they gived me until the last and I went on home. Walked up there that mornin, my daddy was settin out at the lot; old lot lay southward from the house. I left the road, comin in from Apafalya where he had put me at, I looked and there was my daddy sittin under a big oak tree, close to the lot fence. I seed he was makin a basket.

I said, "Good mornin, Papa."

"Good mornin, son."

I asked him how they all was, his wife and children. He said, "They's gettin along pretty well." He looked at me. "Well, you come in, did you?"

I said, "Yes, sir, I come in. Mr. Barbour got through with me and John Thomas both this mornin and turned us out."

I had been comin home every weekend; come home on Saturday nights and go back early Monday mornin. But I had wound up workin under Mr. Barbour and it was my duty to come home and present myself to my daddy.

After a while I asked him—I looked him over and looked around at the place and all, as a boy would do comin home—I said, "Papa, what are you doin now for a regular job?"

"Well, workin some white oak, son."

I seed he was workin white oak and that was his old trade. But the thing of it with me, from one word to another, I wanted to find out all the details. I didn't ask him in a tone that called for the answer he gived me. I wanted to know what he was doin for a *average* job. And the next word he said—I pleaded again—"Right now I'm workin some white oak. You can pitch in and help me if you want to."

Ooooooooo, just like he throwed a dipper of hot water in my face. I knowed the past life of that. When I made baskets or he made em, they was all his. He sold em and put the money in his pocket, gived me nothin. Well, I thought at all times, the older I got, he oughta pinched himself and gived me somethin for a encouragement. But he gived me nothin. His rule, the way he worked his business, he'd work me from Monday mornin till Friday night, and if the job was open and anyway I could keep on, I'd stay put. He'd collect the money and take off to town. But if I made baskets on Saturday I could have that. After he done worked me all week, maybe Saturday I didn't feel like doin nothin much but set about restin—had to work Saturday all day to get anything; then I didn't get much. And what hurt me so bad, he showed by his way of actin that he'd a took that if I weren't careful, what little I worked and made on Saturday.

He didn't understand what I was askin. All he could say, "I'm workin some white oak, son. You can fall in and help me if you want to." Well, I was too old for that. I done looked way down the road and up the road and his work led nowhere.

I said, "Papa, I don't want to make no baskets, work no white oak. A job makin me some money is what I want. I aint got nothin— money, clothes, or nothin decent. Papa, furthermore, I been obedi- ent to you. I've hit everywhere you wanted me to hit, up until this day. Now I'm only lackin from today until the twenty-eighth day of December of bein twenty-one years old. And I've got nothin. I've got nothin. And you aint got nothin to give me. I'm goin to try to hunt me a job and make what I can until another year. And then I'm goin to try to get me a little crop on halves with somebody and make somethin if I can. You've got nothin to give me to help me start off through life. It tells me that it's high time I was lookin ahead to try to help myself."

He takin it in, weren't sayin nothin.

"And I been obedient to you all of my days. Kept me workin under your administration and you collectin my labor. I've tried my best to give you satisfaction and help you up until now. And it leaves me today, after me bein hidden everywhere you put me— Papa, today I wound up on the last job you ever put me on and I got nothin out of it this year. And the way I see the business run, there's nothin to come. Soon I'll be thoroughly of age and I'll have to start from the stump. I aint got decent Sunday clothes; I aint got decent everyday clothes—I don't know what I'm goin to do. And I *may* marry"—I laid it to him—"accordin to my mind and notions now, I may marry"—I didn't tell him I had arrangements cut and dry to marry. I said, "I *may* marry, I don't know. But if I marry or aim to marry, I'll have to do somethin for myself then sure enough."

I was a poor young colored man but I had the strength of a man who comes to know himself, all in me from my toes to my head. I meant right and no wrong; I meant to get up and out of that old rut and act a man. I didn't want to marry no man and no woman's daughter, take her off and perish her to death because I couldn't support her, just an old hack through the world.

So I told my daddy, "I don't know as I'm goin to marry, but if I do marry it means somethin to me. And here I aint got a change of clothes in the world like I ought to have, and no money. I got to go to work, Papa."

He said, "Well, son, if you marry who would you marry?"

I jumped up this way: "I don't know that I'm goin to marry. There's so many things can come between a person and a marriage contract. But if I marry I want to be in better shape than I am now. And if I marry I'm goin to marry this girl that I'm correspondin."

White and black in the country knowed that.

I said, "If I marry and don't avoid it, it'll be to that girl I'm correspondin."

He dropped his head. "Well, son, that aint no more than I'm expectin."

I said, "You may well expect it because I've got a hope and I'm booked to go accordin to my word and the agreement between me and this girl. I'm goin to marry if God lets me."

I spilled all around the edges to him that mornin and let him know enough that he could estimate my complete intention if he cared to. I was a game peacock, uneducated boy that I was, and I had many things in my mind that was pointin to my advancement regardless of education. I'd been here long enough. I'd been trusted by people and I never had had no trouble and everybody seemed to think well of me.

I had done cut cross-ties many a day. My daddy learnt me how to cut ties and we cut ties until I wore out nearly. I said to him, "Papa, aint Uncle Grant Culver and Uncle Jim Culver my mother's brothers? And aint they cuttin ties across over here close to Sitimachas Creek on the old Sutter place for Mr. Jim Flint?"

He said, "Yeah, they over there cuttin ties."

I said, "Well, I believe I'll go there and join in with em, go to cuttin ties; see if I can come out at it any way to help me. Papa, where is your old tie tools?"—I knowed he had em—"Your mole and your measurin stick, your broad ax and your blacken line? Where is the tools you used to use back yonder year or two ago, two or three years ago?"

He said, "They down in the old shop house."

"Well, I'll get em out in the mornin and I'm goin over there where they cuttin ties, see what I can do."

Next mornin, my brother Peter went with me and got them tools out of that house and we shouldered em and walked a mile: short-cut saw, broad ax, and the balance of tools you need—wedges and so on. Down on Sitimachas Creek we walked, straight on to the Sutter place. Got down to where my uncles was workin and my brother helped me cut down two big post oak trees, big around as a tub. We had the cross-cut saw and everything we needed for the job. First we cut down somethin for em to fall on, ground cushion, then cut down the trees. I measured out two ties from each tree; measured seven inches across the ends of the trees and laid em off, true from one end to the other. Then we had to cut into them scores and slug em off. If they was big enough that I couldn't stand there flat-footed after I cracked them scores up, from the bottom to the top, I'd take my ax and throw it on a slant and give it a quick twist and knock them scores off of that log from one end to the other— if it's a good workin tree. Then get up there right close to my lines and chip it, owin to how much I lacked of knockin them scores off to the lines, just what it takes. Then get down beside that log and take that broad ax with a right-hand stroke and dress the side of that log, all the chips and all the frazzles off of it, and smooth that log up on each side. And if the tree would make two ties, I'd pull it out there and line it up and split it.

I worked that job from Tuesday mornin till Friday night—O, if it didn't burn me down standin on that log, glory! Hot work, heavy work, sweaty work. I decided I couldn't stand it. One of them two logs I never even shaped it off—gived it to my uncles to finish. I sawed one log down and cleaned it up to tie limit—that was about as far as I went. I got plumb disgusted. Sweatin to death, workin the devil out of me. Went home that Friday evenin, late; Saturday mornin I got up and give out, doin that heavy work. It was so hot it was a pity.

Saturday evenin I went out to Apafalya, met John Thomas. We runned together as we had been together all year. We howdyed with one another and John asked me, "Well, Nate, what are you doin now? What sort of job you followin?"

I said, "O, I'm tryin to cut ties, John, but it's too hot for me and I just about decided in my mind I ought to quit because it's killin me, sweatin me to death, heavy job, too. I wants to get me a job I can handle without draggin me down. What is you doin?"

He said, "I got a job. I went right on out from here last Monday after we left Mr. Barbour; I went right on and caught the train to Stillwell, got off and walked about four miles out in the country, toward DeGrasse, and I'm workin haulin logs there now. I'm just at home on a Saturday evenin. I'm right from Stillwell, out in the country between Stillwell and DeGrasse, haulin logs for a fellow by the name of Frank Sharp, white man, loggin his mill for him."

"Um-hmm."

"I wish, Nate, you was down there with me."

I said, "John, you reckon I could get a job down there?"

Said, "Yeah, you can get a job, you can get a job down there."

Pay was light in them days. I realized that but I knowed that I was a single man and just come in off the job where my daddy put me, and I was aimin to marry and I had to get up and help myself—that's what I figured.

I said, "All right, John, if you think I can get a job, I'm goin to meet you down there."

And he begged me this way: when I agreed to go back with him Monday mornin, he said, "Now Nate, I'm lookin for you to come to Apafalya Monday mornin and we'll get together and catch a train and go down there where I work. Nate, don't fool me, don't fool me—"

Well, me and John caught the train together that Monday mornin, went on to Stillwell. Of course, Stillwell weren't no more than the country, just two stores; but that was a train juncture place, depot there and all. Got down there, got off the train, took us till about one o'clock to walk out to the sawmill, four miles in the country. Got there, John decided that he was hungry and best for us to stop at the work shack and cook somethin to eat. We did so. We cooked us a great big old hoecake of biscuits—put plenty of lard in it, too. We et there and went on down to the sawmill; sawmill was just about a quarter mile from the shack. Mr. Frank Sharp was at the mill himself, the owner of the mill. He was haulin logs. John Thomas was a log hauler but Mr. Sharp hauled on Mondays till John would come in. John walked up to a four-mule dray, had four mules hitched to it. Mr. Sharp had just unloaded his logs and got off, standin around there now, bein the boss man. Him and John got off from me about fifteen feet, just got out from right under me to talk. But they kept their voices up loud enough for me to hear.

John said, "Mr. Sharp—" Mr. Frank, he called him, "Mr. Frank, I brought you a new man. He's a good hand, too."

John didn't know definitely all I could do. But he advised Mr. Sharp anyway in my favor. Well, I was a log hauler too. Learnt to haul logs for Mr. Jack Knowland; drove six head of steer to a wagon.

Mr. Sharp walked up to me, said, "Well, is you a man huntin a job?"

Told him, "Yes sir, I'd like to have a job, any job that you can give me that I can handle."

He said, "Well, what can you do?"

I said, "Well, I can do any job except pull that saw lever to saw lumber. I can't do that, don't know nothin about it. And firin that boiler settin right over here at your mill, I don't know nothin bout firin no boiler. But runnin that edger saw, haulin logs, or cuttin down logs to be hauled in, I can do all—I can do any one of them jobs you put me at. Sawin logs out in the woods, I can do that. Or I can haul logs into your mill here to be sawed. Or I can drive that edger; but I don't know nothin bout sawin lumber with the saw, that circle saw; I don't know nothin bout firin that boiler. Them is two things—I can do anything you want done at your mill except them two jobs."

He caught it, looked at me, said, "John—"

John answered him.

Said, "In the mornin, you help this man catch out them dray mules, all four of em and help him to hitch em up. Show him where each mule goes. Catch em out, gear em up, and get em ready to hitch em to the dray. When you do that, you get Brother Manny's mules"—that was his baby brother; both of em was grown men— "and hitch em to that low-wheel wagon."

It was a dray itself but it was a two-mule dray. Mr. Frank Sharp's brother, Manny Sharp, he had some interest in there somehow and he furnished a big pair of mules and they worked to that dray.

And said, "After you get him straightened out, you take Brother Manny's mules and hitch em to that low-wheel wagon that they belong to and you haul right on with it."

John done, next mornin, just like Mr. Sharp told him. And John hauled with me about two or three days and Mr. Sharp stopped John—I couldn't imagine how come he stopped John from helpin haul but one way: John just weren't needed in the haulin business. I was just throwin enough logs down to that mill to keep it runnin without John. Of course, Mr. Sharp might not have looked at it that way—but I gained the name of a good log hauler in full before I quit haulin logs. In three days' time or sooner, he stopped John and put Mr. Manny Sharp's mules, great big old mules—Jim was a fat gray mule, would have weighed around fourteen hundred pounds, he was all mule; and another big old black mule, called him Simon —great big elephant-lookin rascals.

I drove four mules to a four-mule dray: Rallie and Rollie was my wheel mules, Rollie was a mare mule and was my saddle mule on top of that; Pigeon and Queen, two black mules, was my lead mules. I took over them mules and started to haulin logs and in two or three days, not over three, Mr. Sharp stopped John complete; put him at the mill. Put Mr. Manny's team in the lot. And he had a road team too, to haul the lumber to the railroad every day. And sometime, his brother Manny's mules, if they was needed for the road, owin to how much lumber was called for, he'd put them mules on the road.

He was payin us by the week, but it was so much a day no matter how much or how little work you done. I was givin him full satisfaction. Must have undoubtedly been worth the money that I was earnin—they made more money off me than I made off myself.

All right. Come home every other week on the weekend. We shacked down there at the mill camp. I was way away from home— home was up here on the old Wheeler place where my daddy was livin. Well, I was buildin myself up to prove a man, workin down in the low country. The money I earned, I'd come home—I didn't *bring* it to my daddy but he got part of it. He'd put up a pitiful mouth; didn't just ask me how I wanted to give it to him, he'd always be in a tight someway, he needed money, he owed this and he owed that and he owed the other. I'd give him what he called for and sometime it was more and sometime it was less. And I'd give my stepmother, TJ's mother, a dollar every time I come home. I weren't there regular and she cookin and washin and ironin for me, but when I'd leave out from my daddy's house on Monday mornin, she'd see I had clean clothes—that was all she had to do for me. And I'd give her a dollar, I didn't miss givin her a dollar, just for a present. Gived my daddy more than that. I looked at it this way. If I gived my daddy more than one dollar, they was eatin it up, him and his wife and children was all eatin up everything I'd give him—if they didn't they should have been. So, thinkin that I was a support for his family, I gived him freely. And I gived his wife a dollar, hit or miss, just tryin to prove to her that I thought as much of her as I did, as a stepmother.

So, when I'd leave home Monday mornin to catch the train

in Apafalya, there was two or three of my daddy's girls, my half-sisters, that stayed there at that time, and they was there every night—that was Tessie and Amy. Both of em was grown-sized girls, they knowed what I was givin their mother. So they commenced a tellin me—I'm just cuttin loose all the strings—"Brother Nate"—they called me "Brother"; I was only their half-brother—"when you give Mama any money and you leave, Papa makes her give it to him."

O good God that just fired me up. I knowed my daddy was seein everything out of me he could and knowin too that he knowed I was givin her a little divvy. And he'd wait till I leave home, make her give it to him. I found it out—but I didn't stop givin her a dollar and I didn't say nothin to my daddy about it. As long as I worked at Stillwell on that job, kept givin my stepmother a dollar. I knowed it'd a been a devil of a twist-out. I was buckin up as a grown man then, I was paddlin my own boat and helpin him, and he takin that dollar I gived my stepmother and puttin it in his pocket—my poor daddy's dead and gone, but I should not hold up anybody in their wrong. She didn't tell me what she did with the money; she knowed at that time I mighta raised up at it and he'd a found out that I come in the knowledge—he'd a beat the fool out of some of em and made em tell who told it, he'd a beat em up unmerciful. So I just rested quiet about it on the outside. He mighta beat her up too, and she was a good woman, remarkably good to we motherless children.

ALL the work I done after Mr. Barbour let me go, except one week work tryin to cut cross-ties in the neighborhood of home—the balance of my time I put in right there at Sharp's sawmill, haulin logs for Mr. Frank Sharp. One day, I drove up to the mill with a load of logs, and I come to know anything, old man Jim Flint was pullin that lever to saw lumber. I looked at him—I didn't know he was down there. Well, didn't worry about it, weren't none of my business, I just tryin to keep myself clear. Found who was the sawyer—never did say nothin to me, no way, shape, form, or fashion.

So, I drove in there, had a load of logs; I unblocked the bolts into the bolsters, unchained the load, and doggone it, every one of them logs fell off of there. One, about the last log that fell off, it

run down on that log ramp towards the carriage leadin to the saw
—looma-looma-looma-looma-looma—got overbalanced and flew up,
one end dropped on the ground. Old man Flint was standin there
lookin at me. Mr. Sharp too, the boss man, owner of the mill, he
was standin there lookin at me. I didn't look around at that log, I
weren't studyin it. Plenty of hands there to ramp them logs and
straighten em out. Jumped on that dray and blocked up the corners
of my bolsters and wrapped my chain up, stuck my boom in the
hounds and crawled in the saddle, off I went.

Well, the boys at the sawmill, all of em knowed me, all of em
was from up there around Apafalya; they told me, some of em, that
old man Flint told Mr. Frank Sharp, "You oughta made that damn
nigger get that log up off the ground, you oughta made that damn
nigger get it up."

The boys heard him; I come back to the shack that night and
they told me. I said, "O, well, he don't like me nohow. He comes
from up yonder right at my home. Him and my daddy lives close
together—" I didn't tell em what it was all about. I said, "He don't
like me nohow, no wonder he said that. What did Mr. Sharp say?"

Said, "Mr. Sharp never said nothin that we could catch. He
didn't seem to take none of his talk bout that log at all."

Well, lingered along, lingered along, and right up close to
Christmas, Mr. Sharp paid off all of we boys and shut the mill down;
lumber was gettin *too* plentiful, more than he could sell, so he shut
the mill down. I went home; John Thomas went home; Flint quit
and he come on home, too.

A few days after that, Mr. Flint met me on the road one day—
and he had a brother, Warren Flint, had married a sister of Mr.
Sharp. Warren Flint stayed here in Calusa until he lost his first
wife; then he went out south from Calusa in there through Stillwell,
goin round amongst the women of that country. Well, he was a
settle-aged man and he got in touch with one of Mr. Sharp's sisters
and he married her. Durin the time when the sawmill was goin on
and I was there, Mr. Warren Flint, Mr. Sharp's brother-in-law,
which was old man Jim Flint's brother, he was livin there on Mr.
Sharp's place where his wife—Frank Sharp's sister—had a interest.
When old man Jim Flint come out from down there the last day on
the job, he left his watch with his brother. I seed his watch many
a time, seed him pull it out—it was a Elgin watch, expensive watch,
good watch.

Met me on the road and he said, "You goin back down to the sawmill to get the balance of your pay?"

Mr. Sharp had done paid me down to five dollars, owed me five dollars.

I told him, "Yes sir, I'm goin down there."

That's the first words he ever said to me after that cow trouble come up, first words.

He said, "I come off from down there and left my gold watch at my brother's. If you go back down there I'll pay half your railroad fare if you'll go up to my brother's"—I knowed em all—"and bring my watch back with you."

He talked just like he weren't goin back there for no cause no more. In other words, he wanted his watch and I was goin back down there. He knowed I was trustworthy. I didn't hold nothin in my heart against the man.

So I went back down there on a Thursday night. Mr. Sharp paid me but I couldn't get away. Had a call for a little lumber all of a sudden and he wanted me to haul logs Friday and Saturday till dinner. Well, I had a round trip ticket and due to come home Friday night, at least. I told him I couldn't stay and handle logs. He put in and begged me and he begged me clean out of the notion of leavin and got me to haul logs for him Friday and Saturday and paid me in full for the two days I worked and what balance I was due. Then I went up to Mr. Sharp's sister's house and got old man Flint's watch from Warren Flint. Put it in my pocket, took special care.

Luke Milliken, Flint's nigger, he was in Apafalya that Saturday evenin when I come in there on the train and we started out to the country together from town, home. I wouldn't let Luke have the watch until we come to the forks in the road and Luke due to turn off and go to Flint's where his mother was. I pulled the watch out of my pocket and give it to Luke, told him, "Take care of it now and give it to Mr. Flint."

A few days after that I stopped in Mr. Flint's yard. He come out the house and I asked him, "Did Luke bring your watch back safe and sound?"

Told me, "Yes, just like it always is, perfect all right."

Then I asked him to pay me fifty cents on my trip, half the fare to Stillwell. I was a poor boy, colored too, and I wanted the little money he'd promised me.

Told me, "Pay you nothin, pay you nothin."

Well, he chopped me down right there. What did that amount to? Just his old hatred, a old man's hatred. It burned in him a slow fire.

I pushed myself to save enough money off that Stillwell job to marry. When I went to Beaufort to get my license, I had eleven dollars and thirty-somethin cents in my pocket, and I wouldn't have had that if I'd a paid attention to my daddy.

Just before Christmas when we were supposed to marry, the girl asked me, "Have you ever said anything to Mama and Papa definite about my and your marriage? When it's comin off or anything about it at all?"

I said, "No, I haven't said anything about it."

She smiled and said, "When we get ready to marry, if you want to we'll just go off and marry."

I said, "Uh-uh, I wouldn't trick your mother and father like that, by no means. I mean to marry you, I mean for us to marry, but I'm goin to consult them in a nice way. They seems to recognize me in full as your company keeper. We've got along good up till now and I want to keep it that way."

One night me and her was settin in her livin room talkin, the subject come up again. I said, "Well, I'm goin to talk with your mama and papa some over my and your agreement."

Good God almighty, it looked like she would just faint away. But I got up and went to the room where her parents was and I consulted with em. I first spoke to her father, talked with him. He had no objections, said, "That's up to you all. You two must decide."

Then I approached her mother. She settin there listenin, didn't say nothin when I was talkin to him. Got into it then: how did I get into it when I approached her? He had gived me full satisfaction and then I asked her how did she feel about it? What were her desires? I got a big eye-sheddin off of them questions. She dropped her head in her lap and shed her tears over it. But when she got straightened out she agreed that it was the best thing for her daughter. That was her main girl. That was her foreman in the business. If the mother had got sick, Hannah would become the head woman in the house. She had a pretty good education and she transacted my business after me and her married. So, I got their consent;

everything was agreeable. Her mother just shed her tears because she hated to see her go.

I left home one Saturday evenin along the last of December and went over to Hannah's. We set down in a room by ourselves, as usual, and we talked. I told her, "Well, our marriage is near at hand. I got to go to Beaufort and get out a license. I don't know how I'll get there but I got to go, I'm goin to get there."

She said, "Yes, Mr. Shaw, you need a way to travel. Papa's goin to Beaufort Monday to pay his tax—" She'd found that out. He was goin to pay the tax on his land and any personal property he had such as cows, mules—"Papa's got to go on Monday, I'm sure; you can ride with him to Beaufort."

It suited me any way I could get there; if I could go with her father it was all right to me.

I said, "I'll speak to your father then. Monday's my day to go get the license bindin us to marry."

I talked with her awhile and went on in to her father and mother's room and I consulted with him. He said, "Yes, I'm goin to Beaufort and I'd appreciate your company."

Monday mornin I went over there after breakfast and he pulled his buggy out from under the shed, hitched his mule to it and me and him got in there and went on out to Beaufort, headquarters for Tukabahchee County. Got up there—weren't but twenty-somethin miles to Beaufort—and first thing I seed my daddy walkin the streets. I said to myself, 'He's up here to pay his tax'—he had a little old place to pay on at that time, forty acres—'and up here to get him some whiskey, too.'

Well, they went in to pay their tax at the same time, my daddy and the father of the girl I was goin to marry. I lingered along with em—they went before the tax assessor and the tax collector and paid their tax. I went straight on from there to the probate judge's office and get what I come for. They seed where I was headin—the girl's daddy definitely knowed. My daddy—I had never woke him up to my plot that mornin. My daddy had married old man Waldo Ramsey's sister after my mother died. So Hannah had become a family connection, but I knowed that didn't cut no figure with my daddy: him marryin her daddy's sister and me marryin the daughter.

So I walked on and they followed me, walkin along and talkin behind me as I went into the probate judge's office. The judge was sittin at his desk; I walked up to him and said, "Good mornin, Judge."

"Good mornin, young fella."

He smelt a mouse. Anybody that's on a job and used to young folks walkin up, chattin with him, he knows it's liable to be for some papers.

He said, "Well, young fella, what are you huntin this mornin?"

I said, "Judge, I'm huntin some papers."

I didn't tell him what kind of papers; he knowed, he knowed. He smiled and got up. "Well," he said, "about how old is this girl you're wantin papers for?"

I said, "Well, Judge, I'm twenty-one years old; I'm right near bout on the day of bein twenty-one. And as far as the girl's age, if that's anything to you, there stands her father right there—and there stands my father."

My daddy didn't say a word; he didn't grunt. The girl's daddy said, "Well, Judge, she's old enough to marry. If she desires a married life, that's just her affair."

That's all the judge wanted to know. My daddy was findin out for the first time what this was all about. Right there he learnt for sure I was goin to marry his wife's brother's daughter. He didn't reveal his feelins to nobody that mornin. I got the license I come to get, and me and the father of the girl I was goin to marry hit the road back to his house.

I married Hannah on a Sunday night in December, 1906. It weren't long until the preacher that married us got ready and left and the crowd broke. Well, we set around, laughin and talkin and at the usual time after the marriage, me and her went to bed in a room in her daddy's house right by ourselves. That night, that Sunday night I stood up and married her, I didn't know no more about bein with her in nature-course than I knowed about flying—it wouldn't have been no harm if I did. I meant to marry her and carry out the full obligation of my acts.

Next mornin we got up—she had a nice family of people and really, by all appearance, she had a shrewd woman for a mother. So she went in the dinin room to prepare breakfast, her mother did, and what did Hannah do? She got up out of the bed, bathed her face and hands and left me; went to help her mother cook breakfast. I went into the dinin room after her—her and her mother cooked breakfast and set the table, poured out coffee and got everything ready for the balance of the family. Got ready to call em in to breakfast. The table was set with plenty of biscuits, butter, coffee —that was the breakfast they fixed that mornin: good biscuits, good butter, good coffee. Just before her father come into the room I set down to the table. And about the time he come in and set down, a subject had come up between me and her mother—no argument, just a little fun. Well, the blessin hadn't been asked; waitin for all the incomers to arrive. And I had discovered that the coffee was sweetened—I wasn't used to drinkin coffee at home noway. My daddy always claimed that coffee griped his stomach and he wouldn't buy it; but it weren't the gripin of his stomach that stopped him—I caught it all—it was a matter of buyin coffee at the store.

I set there at the breakfast table and I said somethin against drinkin the coffee—I tasted the coffee and it was sweet and strange to my taste.

Her mother said, "Drink that coffee, son. Drink it."

So I let it out that I weren't used to settin at the table drinkin coffee.

She said, "Well, I know now that I have married my daughter to a poor boy that has hardly never had no coffee to drink at home. You just goin to have to be poor at the start of your marriage— but you goin to drink coffee. Drink it!"

She insisted on me to drink it. It wasn't a matter that I didn't want to drink the coffee, I just weren't used to it. I went on and drinked it.

DEEDS

I went over to my daddy's home after we were married to get my gun and my trunk and a little old yearlin that I had over there. I couldn't bring my yearlin and my trunk both at the same time, but I got my gun and my daddy give me a small ham of meat and one hen. I took my gun and my meat and my hen and got on my way back to my daddy-in-law's where my wife was.

All right. I walked through Mr. Flint's yard—I knowed he always kept a bunch of chickens and I thought I'd get me a rooster. My wife didn't and her people didn't have a rooster but they gived her a bunch of hens for her marriage and I got one hen at my daddy's and that was all hens and no rooster.

So I stopped and asked him did he have a rooster that he'd sell. First he told me, "No, I aint got nary one I'd sell."

I started on off and he says, "I might have one."

I stopped and asked him where was the rooster. He said, "On the yard somewhere."

I said, "Call him up and let me see him."

So he went and got the rooster—and my wife needed a rooster for her hens, six or seven hens now with the one my daddy gived me; and the rooster was suitable, nice rooster.

I said, "Well, Mr. Flint, I'll take your rooster. How much do you want for him?"

He said, "Forty cents."

I said, "I'll trade with you, Mr. Flint, but I can't afford to pay you right now. I'll take the rooster, if you'll agree to it, and pay you soon as I'm able."

I thought to myself, 'Well, I'll eventually do you just like you done me: I'll fail and refuse to pay you for the rooster just like you wouldn't pay me for bringin your watch home.'

Talked him out of the rooster and he followed me up several times and asked me for that forty cents. Wouldn't pay him nothin. So, fooled around there, kept a lingerin, and he asked me for that forty cents as much as three or four times. I never did have it to pay him.

So at last, one day, it worked out. I had stayed with Mr. Maynard Curtis two years and after that moved off down to Mr. Gus Ames toward Tuskegee and stayed with him two years. Last year I stayed down there I heard my grandmother was sick. Well, Uncle Frank Milliken, old lady Polly's half-brother, he was my wife's daddy's half-brother too, and he'd visit us down there. He called my wife "Hannie"—most people called her "Sweet," white and colored. And I was goin to see about my grandmother bein sick, Grandma Cealy, my daddy's mammy. Uncle Frank was visitin at our house that day and I told him, "Uncle Frank, I'm fixin to go up to see my grandmother, I heard she was sick. It's too wet to plow and I'm goin up there this evenin to see her. There aint nobody to be here but my wife and the two little tots"—that was Rachel and Calvin.

He said, "Well, Nate, if you got to go see about your grandmother, or want to go, I'll be here with Hannie and the children. Don't you worry, I'll stay right here with em until you come back."

He was her uncle and he done a uncle's duty.

So I went in the house that evenin, right after dinner, and I put me several shells in my pocket and reached and got my gun and unbreeched it and dropped it down in my buggy. I toted that gun all the way to Uncle Jim Culver's—that was my own dear mother's brother who married one of my outside sisters, Stella. Well, he was plowin in the field right beside the road and Grandma Cealy lived in the next house just below him. I set there and talked with him awhile, right beside the road. I got off my buggy and set down on a big high stump and set my gun up beside the stump—unbreeched, old single barrel breech-loader, broke down.

After awhile, talkin to my uncle, I looked down the road and seed a man comin up the road on a buggy. Way far as I could tell, it was a man drivin one horse to a buggy. Me and Uncle Jim was there talkin. He was sittin down against his plow and I was sittin on that stump. I said, "Who is that yonder comin up the road in that buggy, Uncle Jim?"

Said, "That's Jim Flint."

Flew in me like this: if he come up the road and see me he's goin to dun me again; and his old rule, the way he'd do it, hold out his hand. At that period of time it'd been six or seven years since me and him first got into it about his cows destroyin my daddy's corn, and he marked his time on it too.

When he got there and seed who it was sittin on that stump, he throwed his hand out, wanted that forty cents for that rooster. Stopped his horse and held his hand out thataway; aint said a word, aint got off the buggy, just stopped his horse and held out his hand.

I looked at him, said, "What do you mean holdin your hand out there to me?"

"You know. You know."

I said, "I don't owe you nothin"—I really owed him ten cents less than what he owed me, but I considered it equal. "I don't owe you nothin."

He said, "You know what you done. You know what you done. You just lied." Because I took his rooster, told him I'd pay him and didn't do it, that's what he was talkin about. "You just lied."

I jumped up, flew hot; I said, "Well, if there's any lyin been done, you told the first lie—" That was recallin to him when I went to Stillwell and got his watch; he'd promised to pay half my fare and when I asked him for it—"Pay you nothin."

So I told him, "I don't owe you nothin."

He got mad and doggone it he was fallin out of that buggy, comin at me in a jiffy. Uncle Jim was settin there lookin, listenin, sayin nothin; he wouldn't say a word. God almighty, when I accused old man Flint of tellin the first lie he fell out of that buggy and was dashin to me, his knife wide open. I jumped off the stump and grabbed my gun—it was already broke down; I give it a shake or two and dropped the barrel, changed ends and got the muzzle end in my hand and throwed that butt next to the stock back on my shoulder, runnin backwards while I was doin it, he steady comin on me. I commenced a cussin him and I said, "Come on. Come on."

He stopped.

I cussed him to everything I could think of and said, "Come on, I'll bust your damn brains out."

I commenced inchin toward him. God almighty, when he seed that he whirled and runned around the back of the buggy, gettin in on the far side. I wouldn't run after him. He jumped up in the buggy, grabbed them lines and started off. As he drove off he told me, "I'm goin to get you, I'm goin to get you if it takes ten years."

Well, it done been a seven-year period of time already, but he wanted to carry it on, he was goin to get me.

I said, "You won't have a damn bit better time to get me than you got right now. Now's the best damn time you'll ever have."

And I walked on out in the road, told him, "Stop! We'll settle it right now; just stop."

He just put that horse to trottin and down the road he had business. But before he runned off, when he jumped in the buggy he asked Uncle Jim, said, "Jim, you got a gun in the house? You got a gun in the house?"

Uncle Jim told him, "Yes, I got a gun in the house but you aint goin to get it."

He seed where Uncle Jim stood—well, he got gone, said he'd get me if it took him ten years.

That was in spring of the year. After crops was laid by I took a notion that I'd go down to my daddy down near the creek. So one day I rode my mule to Uncle Jim's—I was livin on Mr. Ames' place at the time—got up there and walked back down on the creek. And there's some crooked roads runs from where Uncle Jim was livin up in them hills to my daddy. And I walkin along in the road, didn't have nothin on my mind, and I got about halfway to my daddy's from Uncle Jim's and the road where I was walkin come to a place it curved to the left, and right there, at that point, that mornin, all at once I looked down the road ahead of me and who was comin around that curve? Old man Jim Flint! He looked and seed me; I looked and seed him. I just stuck to the road, never swayed from my course. Flint sort of dropped his head, never would look at me once he found out who I was. And right at that particular place there was some old blackjack trees standin beside the road and the big limbs wavin out over the road. And he got clean out to the edge of that road and got under them blackjack trees walkin, he had to tuck his head to go under. I stayed in the road where I was and he walked by to the left of me, his head stooped under them blackjack limbs. I kept my eyes sighted on him. I got about fifty feet from him, turned my head and looked back good at him— still walkin with his head down; couldn't hardly see his head rise above his shoulders. I just kept a walkin.

Went on, next news I heard he'd moved to his brother-in-law's, Billy Barr's, out there in Apafalya. Billy Barr had married his sister, one of the Flint girls, and old man Jim Flint moved out there and got in the house with them. Two years to the month after me and him got into it in front of my uncle, on my way to Grandma Cealy, he was dead.

MAYNARD CURTIS was old man Jim Curtis's son. And durin of my correspondin Waldo Ramsey's daughter I had to go right by Mr. Maynard Curtis's house any time I went to her house. Waldo Ramsey and Mr. Curtis owned land joinin—houses didn't set over two hundred yards apart. Mr. Curtis had known of me through I used to work for his daddy—choppin cotton, pullin fodder, strictly day labor. I was well known by Maynard Curtis. So he knowed who it was correspondin this girl that lived up the road from him.

Of course, quite naturally, Mr. Curtis owned both sides of the road there, right and left; that road come along and divided his plantation. Public road; and right up above his house a piece I'd turn to my right and go out to Hannah's house.

And so he caught on to me goin over there regular and he figured I was liable to marry over there and I believe he might have heard something about it. So, me and Mr. Curtis agreed—he got at me bout buildin me a house, before we married, and I traded with him and he went on and built it. But at the time we married, in the Christmas, he didn't have the house completed. My wife's daddy told me, "Nate, go ahead and make yourself at home until Mr. Curtis gets your house finished. Stay right here in the house with us; it won't cost you a thing."

We stayed there a month and a half, until some time in February. Old man Waldo Ramsey forbid me of buyin any groceries at all. He said, "We got plenty. Just make yourself at home, you and your wife, until your house gets done."

They had two underage children, a boy and a girl, called em little Waldo and Mattie, only boy they had and the baby girl—they was in the house with us, they wasn't grown. But the rest of em— her parents didn't have but five children—the two older girls was grown and married and out of the house at that time. Old man Waldo and old lady Molly Ramsey treated me as they did their own dear children. I called the old man "Pa" and I called his wife "Ma"; Ma and Pa and not for no hearsay, but to recognize em.

Mr. Curtis soon got the house done. Just a old plantation style house, built for colored folks, no special care took of how it was built. But it'd keep you out the rain, it'd keep you out the cold; just a old common-built house, board cabin. In them days they weren't buildin no houses for white men. It was a actual fact: the white folks mixin up and one livin on the other one's place, it was quickly becomin a thing of the past in this country. They wanted all colored people on their places and they built the house accordin to the man and because it was a nigger they just put up somethin to take care of him. And the white man would cut his britches off if the nigger fooled around in that house too much. Whenever a white man built a house for a colored man he just run it up right quick like a box. No seal in that house; just box it up with lumber, didn't never box it up with a tin roof. They'd put doors to the house and sometimes they'd stick a glass window in it, but mostly a wood window. Didn't put you behind no painted wood and glass, just built a house for you to move in then go to work.

So, Mr. Curtis built me a cheap house with wood windows and put a chimney to it. We moved in the house—and when we moved in I was ready to go to work with Mr. Curtis on halves, 1907. He put me on the sorriest land he had and he took all the best. Couldn't complain, no complainin come. I was the underdog and as a colored man I taken what he prepared for me and stuck out there with him; went on to the field and went to work. And when I went to work I worked the sorriest land he had—that was the whole proposition. Land so doggone thin—and what was said about the grade of land Mr. Curtis put me on to make a crop? People would laugh and talk: never knowed about or seed a crop growed on that grade of land. They'd say, "God, that land's so poor it won't sprout unknown peas."

He worked all the land out on front of his plantation. And at the time I moved there, there wasn't a full one-horse farm cleared up on the side he gave me to work. Some of it was timbered land; some of it was swamp land, disused land.

And he had a brother-in-law, Mr. Calvin Culpepper—Mr. Curtis married a Culpepper woman, Miss Beatrice Culpepper, Mr. Calvin Culpepper's sister, Mr. John Culpepper's children. Single man, Mr. Calvin moved out from up in them hills across Sitimachas when he become of age, down over there this side of Sitimachas with his sister and brother-in-law. Mr. Curtis rented him a small one-horse farm. And he had his own animal to plow—he had a gray mare and a buggy, was all I seed Mr. Calvin Culpepper had. And Miss Beatrice, his sister, washed and ironed and cooked for him, and he lived there that year, and also 1908, in the house. Just before I left there he married Mr. Avery Brown's daughter, Miss Ruth Brown. And I moved from there in the fall of 1908, to Mr. Gus Ames' place, and Mr. Calvin Culpepper remained right on there someways and he worked all the open land that I had worked, same sorry land, workin it with his brother-in-law.

Before I moved away from there I bought Mr. Calvin's buggy. I'd scuffled to save enough off my basketmaking to buy that buggy. And before I moved away from there I had that buggy some—I'd hitch Mr. Curtis's mule to it, the mule I plowed. He called the little old mule Nate. He had two mules, a mare mule and a horse mule, both of em was good mules. Mr. Curtis plowed the mare mule; her name was Clyde. Nate was a horse mule. And Mr. Curtis would tell me, if there was some place I wanted to go, "Nate, you drive the mule you plow."

So I'd hitch Nate up on Sundays and go visitin, hitch him up and go to church. Practically whenever I went to church, I'd take Nate and hitch him to Mr. Curtis's two-horse wagon, beside of my daddy-in-law's mule, and all of us would get on that wagon and go to church, come back, stop Mr. Curtis's wagon, me and my daddy-in-law would separate the mules and he'd carry his mule home and I'd leave Mr. Curtis's mule and wagon there. But if just me and my wife was goin somewhere, I'd drive Nate alone to the buggy I bought from Mr. Calvin Culpepper.

Moved away from there and I used the buggy right on with the mule I plowed of Mr. Ames, and her name was Sally; she was a young mule, youngest of a pair of mules Mr. Ames had when I moved on his place.

I moved away from Mr. Curtis because I seed I couldn't make nothin on that sorry land he gived me to work. That was one reason. But Mr. Curtis also done this—and that was a great disconsolation to me. I bought me a cow—I had a little old poor yearlin, bull yearlin, I paid for workin for Mr. Jack Knowland in 1904. I worked hard for the man—of course, Mr. Knowland didn't give me no hard time but it just meant *work* as I was hired to him. I tried my best to please him and nothin ever come between me and Mr. Knowland. So, my daddy come over there one day—and Mr. Knowland was a cow man. He was pickin up good cows, sorry cows, and all kinds nearly. And he had a heifer yearlin there, a Jersey heifer yearlin. My daddy wanted to buy a cow and Mr. Knowland sold him that heifer *and* her calf—Jersey heifer, crumple horn. He charged my daddy sixteen dollars and a half for the both of em. I worked there and paid for em; my daddy took the cow and her calf and carried em home. My daddy kept that cow and made a good cow out of her—she was a good-blooded heifer, Jersey milk type.

So, 1904, Mr. Knowland sold the heifer and her yearlin to my daddy; my daddy had me hired to Mr. Knowland by the month. 1905, Mr. Knowland wanted to hire me right on, my daddy wouldn't let me work for him, took me back home under his administration. I worked there, had tribulations and trials with my daddy that year but I stuck there. 1906, he hired me to Mr. Jim Barbour in Apafalya and just before he done that, he gived that cow to Mr. Barbour on a debt—at forty-five dollars on the debt. And kept that calf until the time I went off to Stillwell and got me a job at the sawmill and begin to come home with money in my pocket and he standin there with his hands open, ready for it, all he could get of it. And he told me one Saturday night when I come in off my job, "Son, I owe Mr. Roy Bacon in Apafalya—" givin him money and he wanted me to trace around and pay off his debts for him—"I owe Mr. Roy Bacon in Apafalya—" that's where he traded, at Mr. Roy Bacon's a whole lot and at Mr. Richard Tucker's, them was his two main places to trade. So, I was comin backwards and forwards every other week, givin him money; told me one Saturday night, "Son, I owe Mr. Roy Bacon in Apafalya five dollars and sixty cents and if you'll pay the debt for me, I'll give you Dolly's calf."

1906, and he'd paid Mr. Knowland for the cow and her calf both with my labor in 1904. I thought, when he done it—I didn't have no better sense than to think it—as close as I was to grown, I'd get a good part of that, maybe I might stand a chance to get the cow. Shit! Get nothin. Gived the cow to Mr. Jim Barbour on his debt. He still had that bull yearlin there but he hadn't growed worth a damn hardly. It was the heifer's first calf and as a rule, unless they're mighty well treated, a heifer's first calf don't grow good—knotty and small. If you just leave off a little of that care for your animal, he aint goin to prosper. That's what my daddy done. Didn't pay no attention to that calf, but he made a nice cow out of that cow. But he gived that cow away on his debt—that put the cow gone, out the way. He kept the little old bull yearlin there but he never did grow good; he never would amount to nothin.

That Monday mornin when I went to Apafalya to catch the train for Stillwell, first thing I done—I thought that was a dickens of a deal but I went right on just like I was due to do—paid my daddy's debt for five dollars and sixty cents. And in the end of the deal he gived me the yearlin. But I looked at it this way: done paid Mr. Knowland, worked hard and paid him for the cow and calf both and my daddy done sold the cow and I had to pay for the calf again. Calf weren't worth a bit more than what I paid neither.

Well, I took the calf when I married and carried her on to Mr. Curtis's place. I kept the calf a few months in Mr. Curtis's pasture —he let me pasture the calf. One day, in the fall of the year, I traded the yearlin—he done picked up but still he weren't nothin but a little knot—traded him to Mr. Carl Fagan for a nice heifer and she was with calf, 1907. Mr. Fagan lived at that time just about a mile west of Pottstown; he was a farmin man. I put a rope on that yearlin, not valuin the yearlin at all, and drove him over there. Mr. Fagan looked at him and told me he'd trade with me. I give him twelve dollars and a half, to boot, between that bull calf and that heifer. I'd call that reasonable. Taken that heifer home and in a few months she come in.

I made somethin out of that heifer, I improved her by takin care of her. She made me a milk cow that everybody that seed her wanted her if they had any use for a cow at all. Now I aint goin to lie: she was a mischievous heifer, she'd get out and ramble. She got out one day in Mr. Curtis's cotton—had his cotton growin right there close to his house and barn. She got out in his cotton and he was fractious as the devil. He runned out there and commenced chunkin rocks at the cow and he hit her on the bone of one of her front legs and he broke her down practically. The cow limped and hopped several weeks after that.

He told me, "Nate, I hated to do it, but through a mistake I throwed and hit her with a rock."

Well, the rock cut her hide and left a print. She hopped, she limped—I doctored her and eventually she got over it. 1908, I moved to Mr. Gus Ames', I carried that cow—that calf she had, I sold it; it was a bull calf, had no use for a bull calf at that present time.

I didn't make two good bales of cotton the first year I stayed with Mr. Curtis. Sorry land, scarce fertilize, Mr. Curtis not puttin out, riskin much on me and I a workin little old fool, too. I knowed how to plow—catch the mule out the lot, white man's mule, bridle him, go out there and set my plow the way I wanted—I knowed how to do it. Bout a bale and a half was what I made.

The second year he went out there and rented some piney wood land from Mr. Lemuel Tucker, sixteen acres bout a half mile from his plantation and he put me on it. Well, it was kind of thin but it was a king over Mr. Curtis's land. I worked it all in cotton; what little corn I had I planted on Mr. Curtis's place. Well, I made six pretty good bales of cotton out there for Mr. Curtis and myself. When I got done gatherin, wound up, by havin to buy a little stuff from Mr. Curtis at the start, in 1907—it sort of pulled the blinds over my eyes. It took all them six bales of cotton to pay Mr. Curtis. In the place of prosperin I was on a standstill. Second year I was married it took all I made on Mr. Tucker's place, by Mr. Curtis havin rented it from Mr. Tucker for me, to pay up 1908's debts and also 1907's debts—as I say, by me buyin a right smart to start me off to house-keepin, cleaned me. I had not a dollar left out of the cotton. And also, Mr. Curtis come in just before I moved off his place—I was determined to pay him and leave him straight; in fact, I reckon I just had to do it because he'd a requested it of me, movin from his place, clean up and leave myself clear of him.

Mr. Curtis had Mr. Buck Thompson to furnish me groceries. Mr. Curtis knowed all of what Mr. Thompson was lettin me have; kept a book on me. See, he was standin for everything Mr. Thompson gived me; he paid Mr. Thompson and I paid him—the deal worked that way—out of my crop. So he made somethin off my grocery bill besides gettin half my crop when the time come.

Took part of my corn to pay him. He come to my crib, him and

Mr. Calvin Culpepper come together to my crib and got my corn, so much of it. And what I had he got the best of it, to finish payin him on top of them six bales of cotton.

Then I moved to Mr. Gus Ames', 1908. Mr. Ames' land was a little better than Mr. Curtis's, but it was poor. Worked his pet land hisself and whatever he made off me, why, that was a bounty for him. I didn't make enough there to help me.

Hannah was dissatisfied at it, too. We talked it over and our talk was this: we knew that we weren't accumulatin nothin, but the farmin affairs was my business, I had to stand up to em as a man. And she didn't worry me bout how we was doin—she knowed it weren't my fault. We was just both dissatisfied. So, we taken it under consideration and went on and she was stickin right with me. She didn't work my heart out in the deal. I wanted to work in a way to please her and satisfy her. She had a book learnin, she was checkin with me at every stand. She was valuable to me and I knowed it. And I was eager to get in a position where I could take care of her and our children better than my daddy taken care of his wives and children.

Mr. Curtis and Mr. Ames both, they'd show me my land I had to work and furnish me—far as fertilize to work that crop, they'd furnish me what *they* wanted to; didn't leave it up to me. That's what hurt—they'd furnish me the amount of fertilize they wanted regardless to what I wanted. I quickly seed, startin off with Mr. Curtis in 1907, it weren't goin to be enough. First year I worked for him and the last year too he didn't allow me to use over twenty-two hundred pounds of guano—it come in two-hundred-pound sacks then—that's all he'd back me up for all the land I worked, cotton and corn. It was enough to start with but not enough to do any more. Really, I oughta been usin twice that amount. Told him, too, but he said, "Well, at the present time and system, Nate, you can't risk too much."

I knowed I oughta used more fertilize to make a better crop— if you puts nothin in you gets nothin, all the way through. It's non-sense what they gived me—Mr. Curtis and Mr. Ames, too—but I was a poor colored man, young man too, and I had to go by their orders. It wasn't that I was ignorant of what I had to do, just, "Can't take too much risk, can't take too much risk." Now if you got anything that's profitable to you and you want to keep it and prosper with that thing, whatever it is, however you look for your profit—say it's a animal; you're due to look for your profit by treatin him right, givin him plenty to eat so he'll grow and look like somethin. Or if you fertilize your crop right, if you go out there and work a row of cotton—that's evidence of proof—I have, in my farmin, missed fertilizin a row and it stayed under, too. Them other rows growed up over it and produced more. If you don't put down the fertilize that crop aint goin to prosper. But you had to do what the white man said, livin here in this country. And if you made enough to pay him, that was all he cared for; just make enough to pay him what you owed him and anything he made over that, why, he was collectin on his risk. In my condition, and the way I see it for everybody, if you don't make enough to have some left you aint done nothin, except givin the other fellow your labor. That crop out there goin to prosper enough for him to get his and get what I owe him; he's makin his profit but he aint goin to let me rise. If he'd treat me right and treat my crop right, I'd make more and he'd get more—and a heap of times he'd get it all! That white man gettin all he lookin for, all he put out in the spring, gettin it all back in the fall. But what am I gettin for my labor? I aint gettin nothin. I learnt that right quick: it's easy to understand if a man will look at it.

I worked four years on halves, two with Mr. Curtis. I was just able when I moved from his place to leave him paid. What did I have left? Nothin. Of course, if I'm left with nothin, no cash in my pocket, I can look back and say what I paid for I got. But what little I did get I had to work like the devil to get it. It didn't profit me nothin. What little stuff I bought to go in my house—it set in my house! What is that worth to me in my business out yonder? It aint prosperin me noway in my work. I'm losin out yonder to get a little in my house. Well, that's nothin; that aint to be considered. You want some cash above your debts; if you don't get it you lost, because you gived that man your labor and you can't get it back.

Now it's right for me to pay you for usin what's yours—your land, stock, plow tools, fertilize. But how much should I pay? The answer ought to be closely seeked. How much is a man due to pay out? Half his crop? A third part of his crop? And how much is he due to keep for hisself? You got a right to your part—rent; and I got a right to mine. But who's the man ought to decide how much? The one that owns the property or the one that works it?

Mr. Ames was a little better man than Mr. Curtis, and not sayin that altogether because he put me on better land—it weren't much better. I didn't just look at one angle or one point in the difference. I looked at it this way: Mr. Ames did put me on a little better land than Mr. Curtis, but I had to go by his orders, too. Well, that cut my britches; he didn't let me branch out like I wanted to. But I got along well with him. He never did cripple my cow and he never stood over me, tell me how to drive his mule of a Sunday—Mr. Curtis done that. When I'd go and get that plow mule to hitch him to the buggy that I bought from his brother-in-law, go where I wanted to, he'd tell me—well, I know that no man wants his stuff mistreated, but I never did treat his mules wrong; he had no cause to get at me about it. And I never was pleased to mistreat my mules after I got able to buy my own mules. Mr. Curtis laid his larceny to me: "Nate, when you get to where you goin, you'll be thar. Give the mule his time, give the mule his time."

Didn't want me to drive him out of a slow gait. His way of speakin was *"thar"*; he didn't say "be there," he'd say, "be *thar.*" That was his mule, it weren't mine, but he just disrecognized me, considered me not to know nothin. Know or not know I had to go by his orders to please him. He just considered me not to know nothin so he would have to tell me.

It's stamped in me, in my mind, the way I been treated, the way I have seed other colored people treated—couldn't never go by what you think or say, had to come up to the white man's orders. "You aint got sense enough to know this, you aint got sense enough to know that, you aint got sense enough to know nothin—just let me tell you how to do what I want you to do." Well, that's disrecognizin me, and then he slippin around to see that I doin like he say do, and if I don't he don't think it's on account of I got my own way of doin, but he calls it ignorant and disobeyin his orders. Just disrecognized, discounted in every walk of life. "Just do what I say, like I tell you. Don't boot me." Showin me plain he aint got no confidence in me. That's the way they worked it, and there's niggers in this country believed that shit. The only way you could gain any influence—he puts you out there, come along after a while and look over what you done—"O, it's done nice, it's done to suit me." Then he'll—some of em will do it—he'll give you praises, thisaway

he'll give it: "O, Nate, you is better than I thought, you all right."
And so on. Pleased at it, didn't know I could do it. I've studied and
studied these white men close. And I've studied em up to many and
many a thing that surprises me.

IT wasn't my first choice of a place to live when I moved to Mr.
Ames'. But I'd got turned down from where I wanted to go. I had
some kinfolks livin in the low part of the country down here; white
folks in Apafalya was dictatin over em. I went down there on a
visit one Sunday in 1908, and they was tellin me—they was livin
on smooth land, I liked the way they was makin crops and I told
em to speak up for me and tell the white gentleman that lived in
Apafalya that I'd like to live on one of his places down close by
where they was. Tell him that I'd love to get down there and get on
a farm where I could make a good livin and all—used to call that
section Akers' woods, piney woods country, had colored and white
livin down there.

George Hardy and Malcolm Todd was down there; Malcolm
married my wife's oldest sister and George married Malcolm's sister.
They was down there together, all connected, kind of kinfolks.
Those boys had good crops; we walked through the fields and looked
at the crops. They told me, "Nate, you a young fellow, you ought to
be down here workin."

Well, in fact, I look back over the past histories since then and
I reckon they didn't know exactly what they was talkin about. They
got holes in their boots before they left out from down there. Every
nigger, Akers shot him through the little end of the horn. George
Hardy, I knowed George when he was a young man and I was a
little boy; Malcolm Todd; Charley Todd; old lady Jennie Crisp, she
moved down there with Akers and raised up her family—that's four
colored families I knowed lived down in Akers' woods; every one
of em left out of there with nothin much.

But all the white people that moved in with Akers, if they
wasn't up at the start, well, they liked that smooth land country and
they stood on over there. If a white man moved on Akers' land he
was liable to stay for many years, and his children too, if there was
land enough for em to work. Some of em that started with nothin
has become wealthy. But all the niggers caught the devil down
there. Wiped out the niggers and gived the benefit of the land to

the whites. White man livin today on a part of that property. Luddie McClure—I know the family he married in—his daddy lived there before him, Barney McClure, and his daddy before him, the first Barney McClure. And that first McClure begin rentin from Ruel Akers in his lifetime and he didn't have a mule or a harness either to his name at the start. And by the time his son, the second Barney McClure, taken over the place, why, he had got up high in this world. I seed young Barney many a time; come by ridin his horse, horn hangin off his belt, gang of dogs followin him—fox hunter, fox hunter.

So me and my wife went down ‚to visit her kinfolks in Akers' woods one Sunday. I looked over the situation—they had good crops, the land was easy to work, and they recommended livin down there to a man that wanted to accumulate a little somethin. I told em, "See Mr. Ruel Akers and tell him I want to get me a home on his place, down here close to you all."

When they gived him my talk in regards I wanted to move on his place, here's what he told em—if I'm tellin a lie I hope I fall down a corpse after I tell it—he told em he didn't want nothin to do with nary a damn Shaw he ever saw.

How come he didn't want nothin to do with no damn Shaw? Well, I had a cousin that had lived on his place and bucked him some—Cousin Lark Shaw, durin of the time my daddy had me hired to Mr. Jim Barbour—wouldn't do just like Mr. Akers wanted him to do. And by God, that fall Mr. Akers took all he had, cleaned him up.

Mr. Akers bought Lark a pair of middlin-sized mules: weren't no big mules and weren't no little bitty mules, just middlin-sized mules big enough and good enough to work. Cousin Lark went in the name of buyin them mules—and a brand new wagon put up there for Cousin Lark. It was fully a two-horse farm on that place —went in the name of the Lee place and I don't know definitely whether Mr. Akers had bought that place or whether he just rented it for Cousin Lark, but Lark lived up there under his administration. And Akers was backin him up and furnishin him. Put him up there in a shape to rent and Lark moved down there from Somerset, Alabama, in 1906.

Lark was a member and he was a preacher, too—he weren't no ordained minister, but he preached up at New Mornin Baptist Church in his old home settlement near Somerset. And every Saturday he'd go up there to his church; sometime he'd hitch them mules to that wagon and the whole family would go, stay over until Sunday evenin. Some few times he wouldn't come out from there until Monday mornin.

Mr. Akers didn't like that. Man go to work for him he wanted to see him out in that field from Monday mornin until Saturday night. Lark'd be at conference and the white man wanted him at home diggin like a slave on Saturday too: that was his argument with him.

Lark made about fifteen bales of cotton that year on that man's place, and fall come he took everything he had. He charged Lark enough in the deal for what he was furnishin him—took all the cotton, mules back, wagon back, and everything. Just took all that to clear him. He didn't leave Lark with nothin—all through prejudice, the way he was treatin him.

So Cousin Lark moved on back up in them hills around Somerset, Alabama, after everything he had was took. Well, quite natural, he only asked that the man have the heart to give him justice and right. But a heap of things is a messed-up affair—he had to stand for it and just go on.

I seed how Akers was doin the colored people—it was the Akers family, same bunch, that cleaned my daddy up when I was a little old boy just learnin how to plow and make a crop—but that was the best, really, that we could do; we had to take a chance at somethin. And the land was rich, smooth land easy to plow, makin heavy crops. That was a big temptation for a young colored man, got big eyes and high hopes. Common sense oughta teached us that we'd go through the same chute, but you couldn't make a livin with common sense only—you had to have land.

WORKED with Mr. Gus Ames 1909 and 1910; never made over three bales of cotton nary year. And he bossed me bout how much fertilize to use and it never was sufficient. But I went on, I didn't say nothin. I would take my buggy, hitch my plow mule—mule belonged to him; it was his land and his personal property—and I'd go to Apafalya every Saturday I wanted or needed to and get groceries. He furnished me the money and I would take it and shop with the man of my choice. He didn't have no special place for me to trade.

Mr. Ames liked me and my wife, too. We was good people, he said. And he'd always tell me he had sympathy for the farmin class of people—he was a farmin man himself. And when crops was gathered, he traveled through different parts of the state as a gin reporter, takin up gin reports. Well, 1910, he didn't say nary a word to me that fall bout stayin with him the next year. I was aimin to move anyhow and I just kept my mouth shut. Went on, durin the time he was travelin about, and I rented me a little place back up there pretty close to the first man I lived with after I married; rented me twenty-two acres of land up there and a house on it. Went on back to Mr. Ames' place, finished gatherin my crop. Didn't make much corn, much peas, nor much cotton, but I had a little of all—he required me to plant it.

I'd watched and scuffled four years first one way then another —makin baskets, mostly, cuttin stove wood for people—until I could buy me a mule so I could rent me a little land and go to work and run my own affairs. Got my crop gathered, 1910, I went on and bought me a mule. Mule had a good deal of age on her but she was a stinkin good mule. I bought her from a white gentleman by the name of Ed Hardy; gived him a cash hundred dollars.

I had spoken to Mr. Charley Stokes about buyin a horse from him. I knowed the horse well—been watchin that horse for years. Mr. Lyman Carter, between here and Apafalya, he had owned the horse before I married even. Cream-colored mare, weighed somethin close to nine hundred, a thousand pounds, around in them weights. Mr. Carter raised several mule colts from her and they'd work anywhere you hitched em.

So, spring of the year, 1910, I found out Mr. Charley Stokes had got a hold of her—Mr. Carter had quit farmin and died. And I went over to see Mr. Stokes about the mare—I was aimin to buy me somethin that would plow, mule or horse, didn't make no difference, just let it be a reasonable price. I asked Mr. Stokes would he sell the mare. He said, "Yeah, I'll sell her."

I said, "All right. Sell her to me and don't back out. What do you want for her, Mr. Stokes?"

He said, "I want seventy-five dollars; it'll take seventy-five dollars to move her."

Well, I kept that in remembrance through that year, 1910. Got my crop gathered and just about ready to move, I went back to speak to Mr. Stokes about the mare. Told him, "Well, Mr. Stokes, you know I'm bargainin to buy that main mare from you and I got the money to pay you now." I had eighty dollars in my pocket. I said, "I'd like to have her this mornin. I've brought you your seventy-five dollars."

He looked at me, said, "Uh-uh, I couldn't take that for her. That mare is one of the best mares in this country."

Well, I knowed she was a good work horse; she had a little age on her but her age wouldn't hinder her from plowin. I said, "What do you want for her then?"

"Take a smooth hundred to move her."

I said, "Well, Mr. Stokes, you aint doin what you promised you'd do. You want a hundred for her now and you told me to start I could buy her this fall—I told you I was comin this fall for her if you kept her here. I got your money, seventy-five dollars, what you told me it would take."

"No, Shaw, I can't take that for her. That's one of the best mares in this country. She's got all sorts of gaits; she's got more gaits in her than any horse ever walked through a barn door."

I said to myself, 'I aint after her for her gaits, I'm after her for her to plow.'

So I said to him, "All right, Mr. Stokes. I can't give you a hundred dollars because I aint got but eighty dollars in my pocket. You'll have to knock off the price to near about your first quotation or I can't buy the mare."

I just put my foot in the road and I had heard that Mr. Ed Hardy was aimin to sell his oldest mule—he had a pair of good mules. I watched Mr. Ed Hardy's hands plow them mules for two years, the two years I stayed with Mr. Ames—Mr. Hardy's plantation was right joinin Mr. Ames'. His mules was named Lu and Cola. George Todd plowed Lu and Jake Upton plowed Cola, heavy-bodied mule. And I heard somebody say that Mr. Hardy said he was goin to sell that Lu mule. So I just walked right out of Mr. Stokes' yard and went on up to Mr. Hardy.

"Hello, Mr. Hardy."

"Hello, Nate."

I said, "Come out, Mr. Hardy, I want to talk with you a little, please, sir."

He come out, spoke a word or two to me.

I said, "Mr. Hardy, I heard some days ago that you said you was goin to sell that Lu mule of yours and get a younger mule, somethin to match your Cola mule."

He looked at me and said, "Yes, I did say that, Nate. I did put it out that I was goin to sell her. But I aint decided yet just definitely whether I'd sell her or not. I been studyin over it. Lu's a damn good mule. She's got a little age on her but she's a damn good mule. I couldn't tell you right now that I'd let her go or not, though I might, I might let her go if I get what I want for her."

I said, "What do you want for her, Mr. Hardy?"

"I wants a smooth hundred dollars for her. I wouldn't take ninety-nine dollars and ninety-nine cents for the mule."

I stood there and listened at him. I was willin to buy the mule at any reasonable price. I said, "Where is your mules, Mr. Hardy?"

He said, "They're out there in the barn."

I said, "Would you mind me lookin at Lu?"

"No, help yourself."

Me and him went out there to look. He had the mules in the stable, one in one stall, one in another, and a bar across the double doors. Walked in there; he said, "Come out of there Lu, you and Cola."

Just snapped at em thataway and they jumped out of there and by the way they moved you couldn't tell the old one from the young one, only by their size: Cola was a little heavier than Lu but Lu weighed all of a thousand pounds. Soon as they jumped out of the stable I followed Lu around, looked her over good. I said, "Mr. Hardy, you say you'll take a smooth hundred for her?"

"Yes, if you want her I'll let you have her for that."

I looked her over—just a doggone good mule, had some age on her; she had hit up there in her teens of years and she was good I reckoned for twenty-odd years, so she had maybe ten years of work left in her. I've seed a mule thirty-five years old, still was a good plowin mule; she just walked slow.

I said, "Well, Mr. Hardy, I aint got the money to pay you this mornin, but I'm goin to ask you one question: will you keep this mule here until Monday morning and give me a chance to bring you your money?"

He said, "Yeah, I'll keep her right here. I'll do that if it takes the hair off my head, I'll do it."

I said, "All right, Mr. Hardy. Look for me, I'll be back. If I don't come back and get this mule—I'm goin to definitely try."

Went right on home and told my wife: "Well, I went over to Mr. Stokes this mornin to buy that mare and he turned me down complete. Told me it would cost me a hundred dollars after promisin the mare this fall for seventy-five dollars. Went up to Mr. Hardy's place and I bought Mr. Hardy's mule fair and square for a hundred dollars. All I got to do is carry him the money. Now I lack twenty dollars of havin what I need. If I had that twenty dollars more I could go and bring that little mule home, bein it would belong to us. So I'm goin up to your father; I believe he'll let me have twenty dollars."

She said, "Yes, darlin, if Papa's got it you can get it." Because her mother and father thought the world—I found that out before I ever married their daughter. They'd take up with me and I showed my manners with the family after I started correspondin Hannah. I'd walk in there and nothin but care and respect would pass from me to them. I'd talk to her mother and father just as quick as I'd talk to her. Of course, I'd rather been alone in her company but they was her parents and they was to be respected.

It was drizzlin rain that Saturday mornin. I walked up about three miles to my daddy-in-law's house. And when I pulled on in there, old man Waldo Ramsey was out there in a oak grove in front of his house, cuttin wood.

I said, "Good mornin, Pa."

"Good mornin, Nate."

I said, "How are you all this mornin?"

"O, we doin fair, we're up and well. How is Sweet and the babies gettin along?"

I said, "They just all right, all right."

We talked a minute or two and I said, "Now, Pa, for my business up here, I thought I was buyin a mare from Mr. Charley Stokes last spring. And I went up there this morning and he done runned the price up to a hundred dollars. I just walked off from him and went up to Mr. Ed Hardy's and bought one of his mules at a hundred dollars. I didn't have—I bought it fair and square; all I got to do is carry him a hundred dollars there Monday mornin. And I lack twenty dollars of havin that hundred. I come up here to see if I could get it from you. I'm just obliged to hustle it up from somewhere."

He looked at me and said, "Well, Nate, you just obliged to have it then, you just obliged to have it."

He laid his tools down and walked on in the house; he come back out to where me and him was standin talkin and he laid a twenty-dollar bill in my hand.

I hit the road and come right straight back down to Mr. Hardy.

"Hello, Mr. Hardy."

"Hello, Nate."

"Well, Mr. Hardy, I come back to close the trade out and get my mule."

"Where'd you get the money that quick?"

I said, "I had to get it up—a man will get about, someway, if he has to. Now I got your price and I want the mule. I'm ready for her."

I paid him that smooth hundred dollars. He accepted it and said, "Well, let's go catch the mule."

I said, "No, Mr. Hardy, I ain't got no bridle. If you first let me have a bridle—I aint askin you to give me a bridle—"

"No, I couldn't give you a bridle, Nate. It's a brand new bridle and I'm goin to get me another mule—"

I said, "Just loan it to me till Monday. If you let me use it till Monday, that will give me a chance to go buy me a bridle."

He agreed. I went on and led that mule away from Mr. Hardy's lot right straight to Mr. Ames' premises. Mr. Ames had two boys and one girl there with him and Mrs. Ames. I passed their house and the boys was at the window. Boys yelled out, "What are you goin to do with Mr. Hardy's mule?"

I said, "She don't belong to Mr. Hardy no more. She belongs to me."

Led the mule on down to my house, down across the field and across a road. My wife come out the house and we put the mule in the barn, first mule we ever called our own. Next morning, Sunday mornin, I hitched that mule to the buggy, took my wife and two little chaps on it, went to her daddy's and mother's. I kept that mule —made the first crop with her, 1911, after I'd moved off of Mr. Ames' place and on to a twenty-two-acre farm, rentin. Got me a mule and gived up workin on halves.

Worked on halves with Mr. Curtis two years, 1907, 1908, and made nothin. Left him, worked on halves with Mr. Gus Ames two years, 1909, 1910, and made nothin there. 1911 I moved on to Mr.

Bill Reeve's wife's place, close to where I used to live when I first married. I commenced makin a heavier crop, makin a better crop, handlin my own affairs. Paid cash rent and made a profit from my farmin: I come up from the bottom then.

MY first child was born August twentieth, 1907, on the Curtis place —that was Calvin Thomas. I kept the dates for the first ones but after the work commenced a comin on substantially I quit checkin on dates. But I do know when the first two was born: Calvin and then come Rachel, August twenty-second, 1909. We was livin on the Ames place at the time. And it kept on till there was ten born into my home and nine of em livin today.

Hannah had a doctor to the births of all her children: Dr. Andrews, in his lifetime, and Dr. Collins, in his lifetime. For the oldest children, her mother come, but the doctor come too.

When Calvin was born, I went to Apafalya and got Dr. Andrews. Hannah was in labor and he come in before sundown Sunday evenin, stayed till nine or ten o'clock Monday mornin before that child was born. Stayed there all night long—it was a doctor's duty, you know. He set there patiently with her in the south room—we stayed in the south room of the house. And in the late hours of the night, Dr. Andrews went in the north room and lay down on the company bed. And he told me and her mother, if he was needed wake him at once. She was a long time bringin that baby into this world. Dr. Andrews said, "Generally it's that way. A woman is slow to deliver, on the average, her first child. She'll linger." And when sunup come, he got up off that bed and set by her through the end of her labor.

This midwife business was stylish then. Many a child born in this country, white and black, nothin but a midwife at the mother's bed. At my daddy's home, back yonder when I was born, it weren't much recognized but a midwife. And to the best of my knowledge there was more midwives had jobs around the birth of a chap than a doctor did. Well, durin of my first married life when my wife got around to havin babies, her mother would go there like hotcakes and I had confidence that she could take care of the proposition until the doctor could get there.

When that Vernon of mine was born, I was in the road b' a doctor—we was livin on the Reeve place, five miles fro

falya, where there was doctors. And I knowin too that when my
wife begin to complain I had to get up and get. So I got up that
mornin busy as a bee and as soon as she begin to cry out, touched
by labor at the birth of that child, and that was Vernon, I run out
and called Dr. Collins. And I found out that Dr. Collins was down
at Sam MacFarland's—he'd tarried there for some cause—just
about three miles from our house; that's where he answered at.
Told me he'd be there just as quick as he could. And I turned to go
back home from where I was, out on the Apafalya road, and when
I got there the baby was born and Dr. Collins was already there.
Told me the baby was born before *he* got there. My wife's mother
was with her, who I'd left by her bed when I run out to get the
doctor.

My wife's mother said, "Doctor, you haven't examined her."
He said, "Well, Aunt Molly, she's all right; I can see that."
But to please her and to please me he went in there and thoroughly examined her and he announced her to be all right, okay.
And he said, "Aunt Molly"—that's what they called old colored
women as a rule, "Aunt this" and "Aunt that"—"Aunt Molly, you just
as good as gold. If everybody handled cases like you handled your
daughter here, wouldn't nobody need a doctor at birth. I couldn't
a done no more."

Well, lingered along, lingered along from child to child and
doctors always gived us satisfaction. And Mother Ramsey was the
only midwife that I ever cared to have around my wife. I trusted
her accordin to what the doctor said himself. One time she taken
sick and my wife was due to have a baby—that was the next child
behind Mattie Jane. We was livin on the Bannister place at that
time and the doctors was scattered when I called for one. My wife
was a woman like this: after her first child, whenever she complained and laborin pains begin to hit her, it was *now*; she weren't
goin to linger, it was *now*. So, knowin that, I run around and struck
up with a old lady by the name of Prue Todd, old lady Prue Todd.
She was a midwife. Me runnin around to get a doctor and I couldn't
get connected with a doctor that day, hardly, noway, looked like.
Aunt Prue, she went on over there and stuck around. Well, after so
long I got a doctor but the baby was born, boy baby. My wife named
him after one of her brothers that her mother lost: named him John
Alton. And durin of his birth, my wife watched Aunt Prue and she
told me that the old lady done some things around her that she

didn't like—I weren't there to see it, out hustlin for a doctor. And Aunt Prue didn't cut the baby's navel string exactly right, and then she throwed the waste in the fire. That was somethin my wife never seen before. Well, in that, if you feel doubtful of a thing, heap of times it's just like you feel. And that baby never was healthy. It lived to be three months old; that's as long as it lived and it died.

HANNAH stayed off of her cookin job a month after each of her children was born. Her sisters stayed close to her and helped her— Mattie, the baby girl, she stayed especially close to her durin them times. And when Hannah did go back to workin, she didn't work in the field then. She didn't make no field hand—never did allow it. When my girl children got big enough to help in the house, they took over her work durin the birthin periods.

I was a poor colored man but I didn't work my wife in the field like a dog. Just as sure as God is settin in his restin place, I'd be in the field at work and my wife—I'd look around, see her comin out there with a hoe. I'd say, "What you comin out here for?"

"I thought I'd come out here and help you."

She was as industrious as the very devil—I aint goin to put her down, I'm goin to tell the truth, all my faults and failures if there's any—I was a fool kind of man over that gal. I loved her and she proved to be a wife to me. Anything that was done in the field—I done been out there a good while, maybe, and she at the house cookin and correctin the children or doin her other house duty, I didn't expect her to show herself in the field. She'd come out there —I'd be choppin cotton and just as quick as she could get things done at the house, here she come with a hoe on her shoulder. She couldn't stay in the field where I was and chop cotton all day, then go to the house and do her work. I considered I was the mainline man to look at conditions and try to keep up everything in the way of crops and stock and outside labor.

If she come to the field where I was and didn't have no hoe, what would she have in her hands? A waiter! Sometimes with somethin tasty to eat and somethin cold to drink. She'd be comin on with a waiter in her hands and wouldn't stop till she got to me. Tell me, "Darlin, I brought you a snack out here to eat, drink." Come to me, I'd be plowin over yonder and she could see me. It was level country enough for her to see me out in the field every place we lived: on the Curtis place, on the Ames place, on the Reeve place, on the Tucker place, on the Stark place, on the Pollard place—all of them places was open enough. Even after I was put in prison and come back home in '45, she had that same temper. She seed me over yonder plowin—she looked for me, she could see me.

She was industrious, she didn't mind work, she was born and raised workin in the field. When she was home with her mother and father she was a kind of foreman girl for the business. And she chopped cotton, picked cotton; she milked cows. When we married, that was all off: she milked no cows, I milked em. I wanted her to keep the bucket out of her hands all except to bring the milk in the house and strain it, prepare it for the family to drink and make butter. She worked at the house. Of course, she worked some in the field but she didn't make me no sort of regular hand in the field. When I married her I cut her loose from the field to a great extent. I didn't try to take her teetotally out, but the work she done in the field weren't enough to wear her down.

And I didn't allow her to go about washin for white folks. I didn't want any money comin into my house from that. My wife didn't wait on white folks for their dirty laundry. There was plenty of em would ask her and there'd be a answer ready for em.

In a year's time after I begin rentin on Mr. Reeve's place, she had a cotton patch of her own. She didn't work it—I worked it and I worked my crop too, and hired a little to help me. And when fall of the year come, I'd pick it every bit, chop it, pick it, take it to the gin and sell it and give her the money. Soon as the children got big enough to help me with it, they'd help me and her cotton was comin to her. We all of us worked it for her and gived her the money.

I worked that hundred-dollar mule on the Reeve place 1911, 1912, 1913 and I begin to rise up; I could help myself some. Bought my own guano, planted and worked what I wanted to—Mr. Bill Reeve, old white gentleman, the place belonged to his wife, Miss Hattie Lu. He furnished me all, the word is, all that the cat ever wanted to farm up there.

First year I farmed with him I made five heavy bales of cotton, more cotton than I'd made any place that I'd ever lived. Sold that cotton for better than ten cents a pound. It was dry that year but still I made them five bales and I made plenty of corn to feed my family and fatten my hogs. Scratched and made corn enough that I didn't have to buy none to feed that mule, and that mule stayed rollin fat. She was fat when I bought her from Mr. Hardy and I kept her fat as a pig. Miss Hattie Lu and Mr. Bill Reeve, they'd ride around on their wagon—they weren't bad to boss you, try to run over you, raise a fuss at you if they caught you sittin down—they'd come by the field, my farm, part of it run right along the public road. They'd see me plowin and stop, wait till I got to the road. I'd speak to em politely and they'd speak to me—there's some good white people in this country. Said, "Nate"—Miss Hattie Lu—"Nate, your mule sure is pretty and fat. You are just naturally a good stock-master."

I said, "Well, Miss Hattie Lu, I feed anything that's around me. Any animal I tries to take care of it."

"Yes," she said, "you know what it's worth to you."

First year there I made five bales of cotton. Second year, I made —I just kept a climbin, second year there I made six bales with that hundred-dollar mule; and corn, potatoes, vegetables of all kinds, peanuts, watermelons—didn't have to buy no foodstuffs to speak about. And I killed my meat every year. I was a good Charley-at-the-wheel at that. Third year I stayed there, good God, I made eight bales of cotton with that hundred-dollar mule. I was saving myself a little money at the end of each year, getting a footin to where I wouldn't have to ask nobody for nothin.

They didn't hold back on fertilize like other white people would do, didn't try to stick you by their judgment. You was handlin your own business when Miss Hattie Lu Reeve and Mr. Bill Reeve was furnishin you. Mr. Reeve laid me down a check any time I'd go up to his house—he was as fine a white man as there was in this country, appeared to be, proved out to be. He was a old gentleman with a lot of money and he married a young woman—I'd go there for a check, Mr. Reeve would say, "Come in, Shaw, have a seat."

I'd sit down.

"Well, Shaw, what are you lookin for this mornin?"

"I'm huntin a check, Mr. Reeve." Gived you nothin but a check.

"All right, Shaw. Hattie Lu! Hattie Lu! Here's Shaw in here wantin a check. Come in and fix it for him."

She'd come in. "Good mornin, Nate."

I'd say, "Good mornin, Miss Hattie Lu."

"You all right this mornin?"

Tell her, "Yes, I'm gettin along fine, I reckon. Glad to see you all are too."

She'd say, "Yes, well, Mr. Reeve, he's been a little poor along but he's gettin along all right now. Nate, what sort of check do you want? What do you want it for?"

Never called for no amount that she'd refuse me. First year I lived on Mr. Reeve's and his wife's place I had a mule and a good buggy and I borrowed money from Mr. Reeve to buy me a brand new one-horse wagon, Welbuilt wagon; I bought it from Mr. Sadler in Apafalya—that's who I done my wagon buyin from.

I went and put high bodies on that new one-horse wagon and hauled a bale of cotton at a load with that hundred-dollar mule; didn't have no hills to pull to get to the gin house from where I was livin. Some bales would weigh a little less than five hundred pounds, some would weigh a little more and she could pull it as easy as air because I was livin in level country and the gin was right convenient.

Well, I got tired of packin a heavy bale into a small wagon and havin one mule to pull it all by herself. Made my third crop there, 1913, and went out to Apafalya, bought me another mule, young mule just three years old, had never had the bridle on. Bought her out the drove; I gived Mr. Grimes at the Apafalya mule pen one hundred and eighty-five dollars for that mule, carried her home and put her in the lot with that hundred-dollar mule. Borrowed the money from Mr. Reeve—I knowed it was goin to get me deeper in debt, but I risked it—clear cash money so I knowed exactly how much I was receivin and how much interest he was makin off me. Give me a check and all I had to do was go to the bank and draw that money. No fancy figurin, "I'll let you have this now, that later, and you just pay me right along." A straight deal all the way.

Put her in the lot with the other mule, fed her, watered her from the well—well was close to the lot. I'd go to the house at dinner time and evenins too when I quit pickin cotton, I'd come in and that mule would be walkin around in that lot lookin with her head up.

My wife asked me one day, said, "Darlin, what you goin to do with a pair of mules and aint got a child big enough to hand you a glass of water?" Them's the words she spoke. And said, "You aint got no two-horse wagon; you got a one-horse wagon out there and just can work one mule to it. You got two mules now and aint got no way of hitchin both of em to it."

I said, "I'll handle em. If I can't have a two-horse wagon to hitch em both to, I'll plow em double; that's the main thing, plowin. I can take em out to the field and break my land double. Come to the wagon business I may have a pole put in front of that one-horse wagon and hitch em both to it."

My mind told me—I was talkin to her—my mind told me, 'That wagon too light; a one-horse wagon won't take a pair of mules, it's just too light.'

I went right on and studied every day, thought about it as best I could, what I'd do about havin two mules and only a one-horse wagon to hitch em to and that wouldn't take em.

One mornin I got up, told my wife, "Well, darlin, get breakfast ready quick as you can. I'm goin to hitch Lu to that one-horse wagon, who was bought to work her to it. And I'm goin to lead that other mule behind. I'm goin out to Apafalya and I'm goin to swap that one-horse wagon and get me a two-horse wagon."

I left off from home leadin that young mule—my wife had named her Mattie—had never been harnessed. Turned in my one-horse wagon—good one-horse wagon, the paint hadn't worn off it. I walked in Mr. Sadler's store that mornin; he looked me over, said, "Shaw, what'll you have?"

I said, "Well, Mr. Sadler, I come out here this mornin to make a wagon deal with you if I could. I want to swap you that one-horse wagon back that I bought from you for a two-horse wagon."

He said, "All right, Shaw, I'll go out and look. Where's your wagon at?"

I said, "It's right there in the back way."

He said, "I'll go out and look at it just as soon as I get through in my little office here."

He got up and come out there right soon enough and looked over my wagon. Tugged at it—that was one of the best grade wagons put out in them days, a Welbuilt wagon.

He said, "Tell you what I'll do. You let your harness go back with this one-horse wagon—" I'd got it all from him, wagon, harness, and a nice seat on that one-horse wagon and a little false bottom. He said, "You let your wagon stay just as it stands and your seat, let that stay: harness, wagon, and seat. I'll put you up a two-horse wagon and all that you aint got that you need with this two-horse wagon, I'll furnish that to you, thirty-five dollars to boot."

I made the trade right there. He went in then—I didn't have a thing for this young mule, even to a bridle. She had a halter on and I hitched a plow line to it and led her into Apafalya that mornin.

Well, I followed Mr. Sadler back on in the store. And he had a fellow clerkin in there for him by the name of Priestly. He told him, "Priestly, go out there and put Nate up a two-horse Welbuilt wagon."

Looked at me and said, "You'll help him, won't you?"

Told him, "Yes sir."

Went out there and me and Mr. Priestly got all the parts—it was all shipped in there loose: the bed, wheels, axles, and everything that go to the wagon. We got out there and put it up, put the tongue in it and got it ready for the road. Went back in the store, Mr. Priestly did—he was young, he wasn't a real young fellow; he was young but he wasn't as young as he had been—went back in there and Mr. Sadler got me up brand new breast chains for that wagon, double length breast chains; britchin—that was all that old mule needed, britchin to go on her hips and britchin to go on that young mule's hips; and lines, a good heavy set of lines, brand new; a collar, haines, and traces for that young mule—just fixed me up direct. Handed em over to me—all that for thirty-five dollars to boot. Of course, he didn't give me no backbends for plowin but he fitted me up with everything else.

There was a fellow out there by the name of Elihu Swift, colored fellow, helped me hitch them mules up that mornin. Worked with me at it on account of me havin that young mule. And when I got her hitched up, I twisted her nose to see if she weren't goin to take it; and Elihu held that twist on that mule for me to harness her. Then we backed her up to the tongue and I goes around and hitches the old mule up first and full. Told Elihu to hold that twist. I goes around there—Elihu holdin the twist on the young mule's nose—and I hitched the traces, breasted her up and all like that. Lines snapped in on em just nice. I crawled up on the wagon and wrapped my hands in them lines. I knowed I had to put my weight to them lines to hold em—I had a young mule there, never been hitched to a wagon before. I got up there, I told Elihu to pull the twist off her—I had em held, I thought, and I did have em. Said, "Pull the twist off."

When he pulled the twist off that young mule just stood there.
And I said, "Come up."

She raised up and made a lunge just as hard as she could; but
them bits on her, brand new bridle, and them lines, brand new heavy
leather lines—she settled back down.

That older mule there, she was ready to go; she knowed what
her job was. She couldn't move, though—she did start off; I kept
workin my lines and tellin em, "Come up"; the old mule made one
or two moves off, that young mule just stretched out on the ground
like a dog. The older mule couldn't drag her off. I kept a coaxin her
and the young mule took a notion in a jiffy to get up and when she
got up she got up jumpin. I was swingin along with her, checkin
her at every step. I worked them lines—let em loose and pulled up
on em, let em loose and pulled up—and that Lu mule just teached
that younger mule the way.

I drove on home in the mist and rain, and by the time I got
five miles from my daddy I decided I'd better get my brother Peter
to help me some. I was buildin a barn on the old Bannister place
that fall—fully intendin to leave Mr. Reeve and had traded with
Mr. Lemuel Tucker to rent the old Bannister place; had to rebuild
the barn to fit my stock before I moved there. So I didn't quit drivin
till I got to my daddy's down on Sitimachas Creek. I pulled in there
—my wagon body had tightened up, caught a lot of water in the
bed and the water was runnin from the back end to the front end,
from the front end to the back end, whichever way the low end of
the wagon was—goin down a slant the water come over my feet and
when I went up the least grade it flowed to the back end. That brand
new wagon body just swelled up and sealed itself and held water
like a tub.

And every once in a while that young mule would pick that
front wheel up off the ground on her side; she'd smack it so heavy
she'd pick it up. That Lu mule, she was steady; she was able and
fat, weighed about eleven hundred pounds and this young mule
weren't that heavy.

All right. Got down to my daddy's that mornin and stopped in
the yard. They mighta heard me when I drove up but they didn't
come out until I called a time or two. My daddy come to the door.
I was standin up in my new wagon—my feet done got soaked—
and I was there after my brother Peter. I called my daddy's attention

and he come to the door and looked out and seed me: standin up in a brand new two-horse wagon, had a pair of pretty mules hitched to it. He didn't know the score, said, "Son, whose team is that?"

I said, "It's mine. My team, my wagon; it's mine."

O, that shot him; somethin he hadn't expected, no doubt.

I said, "Papa, I'm just out of Apafalya with this young mule of mine and this other mule hitched together. And this Lu mule, this older mule, is helpin me to hold this young mule in. I can't get out the wagon to leave em. It'd be too much trouble for me. I could get out and tie em maybe, but it's too much trouble. I wants to stay with em till I get home. I come down here after Peter to help me a day or two."

Peter got right ready; he was about twenty-three years old at that time and my daddy was bossin him still, had him workin there like a chap. My daddy taken my labor until I was twenty-one and I got out. Peter was the last boy of my own dear mother's children; my daddy aimed him home and did keep him there, too. So, Peter got in the wagon with me; went on back up the road and kept drivin till I hit back on the Pottstown road and come on in home.

WHEN I moved away from the Reeve place I had that team to move with. Spring of the year, 1913, before it come time to make the crop, I moved down on the Tucker place—really, it was known as the old Bannister place but Mr. Tucker had got a hold of it someway —down on Sitimachas Creek. I'd go to Apafalya that spring haulin guano—that young mule by that time had done gived up her fight.

And Mr. Ruel Akers, man that had turned me down from livin on his plantation, gived the Shaws a bad name, he was livin on a place between here and Apafalya, call it Highgate, above Two Forks. His house set right at the fork in the road—one road turns and goes toward Beaufort, the other one goes straight on toward Apafalya. And I was haulin guano with a pair of good mules and they was mine, and also that brand new two-horse wagon. Met Mr. Ruel Akers in the road one day. He looked at me and I just kept a drivin. He looked at me and looked at them mules. When I was well past him I looked back and he was still lookin hard. I said to myself, 'You see, I tried to get you to help me and you wouldn't do it. Somebody helped me and I made the best of their help.'

Not hardly a year after he seed me drivin that pair of mules to that brand new wagon, haulin guano, his mind sort of changed. Sent me word to come see him, wanted to trade with me. But I had a greater knowledge of the world at that time. My mind told me: when the devil invites you to a party, tell him you won't dance.

WHEN I first moved up on Miss Hattie Lu Reeve's place, I carried my corn to Clay's mill to have barrels of meal ground. Drivin that one-horse wagon that Mr. Reeve had furnished me the money to buy; good wagon, it wasn't a iron-axle wagon, it was a thimble-skein wagon, built just like the two-horse wagon I eventually traded it in for. I'd leave Mr. Reeve's place and Miss Hattie Lu and go down through Two Forks to the upper end of Highgate and turn there and go right out, in sight of where my brother Peter lives now, drivin way down on Sitimachas Creek to Clay's mill. And I'd be carryin a barrel of corn that I'd shelled myself. And when I come out from the mill, I'd drive right up the road where my daddy was livin at that time. I was a married man but because I was his son I donated him freely. He lived close enough to the mill that when I left the mill with my meal on the wagon in barrels, he could hear my wagon wheels turn and know it was me. I weren't gone from the mill but a few jiffies, about a half a mile from the mill on my route home and I'd drive by my daddy's door. He'd come out to the road and if he didn't have his dishpan in his hand—he'd want that big dishpan full of meal. And he was gettin that off me just like I was a underage chap. Of course, he *asked* for it, and he acted like he appreciated it, and in fact of the business, he needed it to keep up his family. Had a whole bunch of chaps and that woman he had for a wife was my stepmother. And he weren't workin hard enough to support em; needed my help right on.

All right. I'd stop there and give him anywhere from a peck of meal to a half a bushel at a time. I done that. Out of my wagon out the barrels, chunked it to him. And at that time I had three children and my wife, and he was comin out—had done left em way over here on Miss Hattie Lu Reeve's place, taken a circle route to Clay's mill, and he'd meet me out on the road to get meal.

And before he ended up, sometime he'd send TJ, sometime he'd send Bob—ary one of my half-brothers—way on down to my house of a Sunday mornin. "Brother Nate"—they called me "Brother"—

"Papa says send him a half of a forty-eight-pound sack of flour and a half a shoulder of meat."

Done quit gettin meal now, I didn't go as often. So my daddy would send one of his chaps to my house for flour and meat and I'd give it to him right on. Killin hogs every fall for my family and he knowed I had it. And he kept sendin his chaps—

One Sunday mornin the boys come there and I was away from home—they always come on Sunday mornin; wouldn't but one come at one time, Bob or TJ, his two oldest boys by his third wife, the woman he married after my mother died. Bob or TJ comin down on Miss Reeve's place callin for half a shoulder of meat, half a forty-eight-pound sack of flour—didn't never ask for no ham. So one Sunday mornin I was off on a walk and when I come to the house the boy had been there on his bicycle—and stayed until I come. Hannah had asked him concernin what he come for. He gived her no satisfaction at all; lookin for me, I was their daddy's son. And just usin her like this: ignore her and not tellin her what he wanted. He had to see me. I knowed my daddy was givin him orders not to tell her what he wanted. Just explain the mess to me and don't tell Hannah nothin.

So when I come home the boy was there and Hannah told me —didn't tell me right before him—she asked him what was he wantin and what was he after and he wouldn't tell her nothin. That just flew in my mind: Hannah was my wife and I wouldn't see her slighted noway under God's sun. She'd exacted of him and asked —she didn't worry him to make him talk. She knew by what he said—"I want to see Brother Nate"—what the trouble was. In place of tellin her what he come for he give her a blast of air. I flew hot as the devil—that was my lawful wife and if they couldn't explain their business to her, it appeared to me they just didn't recognize her. He wanted to get somethin on the fly, my daddy did, and jumpin all over my wife to get it. I told her, "From now on out, if they can't tell you what they come here at, let em go."

My daddy was diggin at me and he didn't want her to know nothin about it. But I considered in my heart and mind that she had just as much right to be told by them what they come there after as I did. That was my wife; she didn't have no crooks in her that they shouldn't recognize her enough to tell her what they was after. I fretted over such treatment as that. She was the same as me—flesh, blood; that woman was a whole person.

ONE time my daddy come to see me through the week. No doubt he wanted somethin at that time, but he didn't mention it. I been donatin him just as free as the water run when he come to me. He weren't workin much—my daddy never did labor like a man ought to in the defense of his family; he didn't do it when I was there at home a boy under him. He didn't recognize his affairs and his business enough to keep his family in what they needed. He was pickin at me and I was holdin him up to a great extent. When I was livin with Mr. Curtis he didn't come at me for food and I knowed his family suffered for many things, but old Nate done married out at that time and had a family to support and was only workin on halves with Mr. Curtis. I moved from there down on Mr. Gus Ames' place and my daddy didn't come at me then. But soon as I moved up on Miss Hattie Lu Reeve's place and commenced a climbin up in this world—I was rentin then, had good stock and a brand new wagon —he started his boys at me for half a forty-eight-pound sack of flour and a half a shoulder of meat. They'd tie it to their old bicycles and ride out with it. And the day my daddy come over hisself, one day through the week, I was in the field plowin. And when I come to the house my daddy was there. He didn't mention he wanted anything—if he wanted anything he'd go back home and send them boys, he wouldn't be bothered with it; he'd send them boys on a Sunday and Sunday only.

When I took my mule out the field and got to the house, there was my daddy, one day through the week. We talked a little bit outdoors and my wife announced dinner. I said, "Well, Papa, let's go in and eat dinner."

I taken my daddy in there and we set down at the table, bathed and got cleaned up and set down to eat dinner. Well, I knowed I couldn't afford and get satisfied at it to set up there and neglect my work—and my daddy woulda done it if I'd a done it. After we et dinner we set up there and went to talkin bout somethin or other; we walked out in the yard and kept a talkin—killin my time and I needed to be in the field. And the words he spoke to me was definitely against my desires. I was a workin man—while we was out there I heard the clock strike for one o'clock—Bam! That attracted my attention. I told my daddy—I was breakin up the conversation, I had to get in the field. I didn't have time to set around and jaw with him; I knowed who he was, he would stay there all evenin if nobody moved him. I knowed his disposition, how he transacted— Walked out the house after dinner, me and my daddy walkin around the yard, talkin, and I heard that eight-day clock strike one o'clock. I told my daddy, "Well, Papa, I appreciate you comin around, talkin with you, but I got to go to the field now, the hour's come. I got to quit"—lettin him know, strictly—"and get in the field. I don't have time to talk all evenin."

I knowed I had to move quick; it'd been right down his alley to tie me down talkin. And I didn't have that kind of time to throw off.

I told him, "Uh-oh, Papa, it's my field time, one o'clock. I got to get away from here; I got to get in the field."

Here's what he said when I told him that—honorable before God; and there's nothin honorable before God but the truth. He raced up to me, "Son, you works too hard."

That fretted me, them words. Me knowin my duty for my family's sake and wantin to comply with my duty.

"Son, you works too hard."

I was dutiful to my labor, I had to put it out. I didn't want to come up behind with nothin in my field if I could help it. And he wanted me to stay and talk, give *him* my attention. That stuck him when I told him I had to quit and get in the field, right on.

"Son, you works too hard, you works too hard."

Not thinkin how I was holdin him up, givin him everything he asked for. How could I satisfy him if I didn't work for what I gived him? I just raised up at him when he spoke them words.

I said, "Papa, I come here to work out. I didn't come in this world to rust out. If I need anything done in my field I ought to be there if time will admit it, on time. I got to work. I'm born to work. I can't sit around and jaw and talk and kill my time with you or nobody else. My hour has come to get in the field."

My words was gettin through to him. He seed I meant to leave him. It was my duty. I couldn't set up and lose a half a day's time or just as long as a person wanted me to talk with him and it weren't nothin to my gain—it was losin! Fool with somebody that never had done what he ought to done, and I knowed it.

I thought very deep at his past operations; go to the field it was all right, if he didn't it was all right. Well, that aint the way to make no crop. That's why I chopped him off like I did. I just got right busy and went on to the field. And I told him at the last words, I said, "Bye, bye, Papa. I'll be plowin right over yonder in the field. Come out to the field if you want to, why don't you? I'll be plowin right straight across over yonder."

I had no reasons to believe he'd come to the field.

I said, "You can see me from the house. If you want to talk with me or bid me goodbye, come on over to the field where I'm at."

I was goin to be out there at work. Weren't much chance I would lose many minutes more. Whenever I went to the field I went to work.

So I caught my mule and hit it to the field, left him there. I said, "You can stay here." I gived him the privilege of comin to the field, knowin that I was goin to keep a drivin. "You can stay here and talk with Hannah and the babies."

I had three little old children at that time: Calvin was my oldest one, first child to come in this world that I was the father of; Rachel was next, she was born on Mr. Ames' place; and Vernon. Hannah was pregnant when I moved off of Mr. Ames' place up on Mrs. Reeve's place and Vernon was born there.

I said, "It's your pleasure whatever you do, but I'm goin to the field."

I don't know when my daddy left my house that day. I was workin out yonder toward the north end of my farm and he never did come out there. And he never did in his lifetime notice my crop, never did walk over it with me.

WHILE we was livin on Mrs. Reeve's place, my wife's baby brother —she didn't have but one brother and three sisters: Lily, Lena, and Mattie—that boy got throwed in Beaufort jail. He was accused of burnin up a church buildin but he got cleared of it. The ones that had him arrested couldn't prove he done it. Little Waldo Ramsey— his name was Waldo but he was "little" on account of him bein his daddy's son. He was twenty-one or twenty-two years old at the time; might have been as high as twenty-three.

He was married too then. His first wife was a girl named Leola Hawkins, Joe Hawkins' oldest daughter. And old man Joe Hawkins—this church was supposed to be on his premises but he didn't have it paid for. The church set about a half a mile from where I was livin, over toward the back side of Miss Hattie Lu's farm. One night it burnt up. The buildin weren't much account, weren't no fine place at all, just a old buildin, never had been painted, but they held meetin there—called the place Manassas.

And this boy was livin with his wife way down here in the piney woods on a man by the name of John Walker's place. Old man Joe Hawkins didn't like the boy nohow. And when that old buildin burnt down old man Joe Hawkins jumped up and laid it on little Waldo, which was his son-in-law. High Sheriff of Tukabahchee County come down and arrested the boy, carried him to Beaufort jail. Me and the boy's daddy went up there on a buggy together— hitched my mule and his mule and went up to Beaufort, me and old man Waldo Ramsey; got up there and we hired a lawyer to clear the boy. Day the trial come up, Hawkins and his crowd didn't have no witnesses to prove the boy done it. It was just a malice affair. The prosecutor went up there and he didn't have a bit of help under the sun. The judge just throwed that thing out; the boy come clear.

Hawkins stayed against the boy but for what cause I really don't know. And the boy, after he come clear, he went back to his wife—her daddy wanted to break that up, wanted to separate em, just kept a diggin at him. He was a preacher too—he built that church on his own premises where he could boss it—but he had hell in him. He weren't no God-sent minister, just somethin that called hisself a preacher. I read his pedigrees a heap of ways.

So, rocked along, he kept a diggin at this boy. He didn't realize that people had their eyes on him: what was he diggin at that boy for? And the boy and that gal couldn't get along good—probably it was brought about by her father—and it was said that they had a argument and the boy give her a little scratch somewhere on the wrist, nothin more than that. Joe Hawkins jumped up, big man, rode out and sent the sheriff at the boy again and arrested him. Swore out a warrant—and this time put him in the Tuskegee jail.

Well, at that time, I was fixin to move down on the Tucker place on Sitimachas Creek off of Mrs. Reeve's place. So I was buildin a barn down there, preparin a place for my stock—I put four stables under that roof—workin down there every day, goin out from Mrs. Reeve's place in the fall of the year, 1913. I was buildin that barn on the creek when I heard the news—they jumped up and put little Waldo in jail again about that scratch on his wife's wrist; put him in jail in Tuskegee, headquarters for Macon County. He was already livin down there in Macon County when they accused him of burnin up that church buildin.

Didn't stay on Mrs. Reeve's place but three years and he got put in jail twice durin that time. Second time, his daddy went down alone—I'd gone over to *my* daddy's and got my brother Peter to stay with me and help me, what he could, two or three days. That mornin, I went first to Apafalya to swap that one-horse wagon for a brand new two-horse Welbuilt wagon; that one-horse wagon didn't have no blemish against it, been lightly used—I picked up my brother Peter and carried him on to my house. And durin of that day's trip, old man Waldo Ramsey went to Tuskegee to see about his boy.

Next mornin, me and my brother was aimin to go to work on my barn down on Sitimachas. But I didn't feel right about it until I'd a heard what the outcome of little Waldo's case was. Told my wife, that mornin, "Darlin, Pa went to Tuskegee yesterday to see about Buddy"—little Waldo's people called him Buddy—"and I aint heard from him what the situation is. I believe I'll run over there"—didn't live no more than a mile apart—"and see whether he got him out of jail or not." I was under the impression—didn't nobody tell me but I thought if he went down there to see about the boy, he probably woulda got him out.

So I said, "Now you and Peter and the little fellas, you all just go ahead and eat. I'll be back just as soon as I can run over there and back."

I took off. Trotted on over there that mornin and I met old lady Molly comin out—their house set off the road way out in a oak grove, in a level place, on their own fifty acres of land—so I met Hannah's mother comin out from the house. I didn't ask her where she was goin but they had some neighbors there, old Price Mac-Farland's family, right up the road. I met her, said, "Good mornin, Ma."

"Good mornin, son."

I said, "Well, Ma, you all well and up this mornin?"

She said, "Yes, Nate, we all doin very well."

She asked about Hannah and the children. I told her, "They's all right. I just left from up there and come over here quick as I could get here this mornin to see what Pa done about gettin Buddy out of jail."

She said, "Nate, he weren't able to do it. Ramsey—" she called her husband Ramsey; his name was Waldo Ramsey—"Nate, Ramsey didn't get him. Just went down there and talked with him and he didn't get him. I'm afraid Ramsey goin to let my child stay there—"

He was the boy's own dear daddy. But he was one of these old kind of fellows, he weren't fast to jump up and do a thing; he'd take his time and eventually he'd do it if he ever did it at all.

"I'm afraid," she remarked to me, "I'm afraid that Ramsey goin to let my child be sent off. He didn't get him yesterday. He just went down there and talked with him and I'm afraid he goin to let him be sent off."

She let into cryin. And when she let into cryin about him bein in Tuskegee jail and his daddy didn't get him out the day before I went over there that mornin, I said, "Ma, aint no use to cry about it; it aint goin to happen that way. Don't worry. If I'd a went down there yesterday I'd a got him. And furthermore, I'm goin today and get him."

She said, "Nate, you reckon you can get my child out of jail?"

I said, "Of course I can; it just takes a little money. And I'm goin to get him. Quit worryin. I'm goin to have him here at your house before the sun goes down as a satisfaction to you."

She made a great moderation. She said, "If you get my child out of jail I'll make him stay with you as long as you want."

I said, "You don't have to do that, Ma. He's grown. Your authority over him to make him do such things is over with. If he don't want to do it, you can't make him do it."

She said, "I'll make him stay with you—" repeated it two or three times.

O, she was so glad to hear my talk. She didn't know like I knowed—it didn't take nothin but a little money to move him.

I said, "I'll go back home now. Ma, I'm busy workin down on Sitimachas Creek every day, and I aint got time to loose up on my job because I got to move down there, made a trade for the old Bannister place to move down on it. But you just go ahead and rest satisfied. I'll get him here today. I aint goin to *try*, I'm goin to get him and bring him home."

She become hopeful off my talk. I knowed what I could do—with money. I knew I had the money to move him; I didn't have to beg nobody.

Went right on back home quick as I could, told my wife, "Darlin, your brother Waldo, only brother you got in the world, he's settin down in Tuskegee jail and your daddy weren't able to get him out. I'm goin down to spring him. I promised your mother I would get him and bring him back to her house before dark. I'll set down now and eat what little breakfast I want, then catch my mule out and hitch her to the buggy"—I had that young mule in the lot had never had a bridle on and I was goin to catch my older mule, which was well broke—"and while I'm doin that, you get me out forty dollars from the trunk."

I decided it would take maybe forty or fifty dollars to spring the boy. Time I et my breakfast, caught that mule out, brushed her off, harnessed her and hitched her to the buggy, my wife walked up to me and handed me that forty dollars. I crawled in my buggy and went up by this boy's baby sister's husband, Clarence Reed, and picked him up for company. After he got on the buggy with me I didn't stop drivin till I got in Tuskegee. I told Clarence I was ridin in defense of the boy and I was goin down to get him.

Went on down there, got off my buggy and walked into the courthouse. I didn't know nothin bout no law but I knowed to have some money if I were goin to get that boy; I knowed that money would speak to get him. I walked in the courthouse—Clarence was foolin around there in town someway—went right straight to the probate judge.

"Good mornin, Mr. Judge."

"Good mornin."

I said, "Mr. Judge, your honor, I'm huntin a boy by the name of Waldo Ramsey that's here in jail."

I went on and explained his troubles to him. The boy's wife's daddy and her together put him in there—he had put a scar on her wrist but it didn't amount to nothin. This girl's daddy had already proved hisself to be against the boy—he had put him in the Beaufort jail one time. The boy was livin in Macon County at the time with a fellow named John Walker; there was three of them Walker boys: John Walker, Alvin Walker, and Dan Walker. Dan Walker was dead at that time.

I went on down there blue about it—addressed him nice as I could. I told him I come after the boy and if money would buy him out I was ready to pay it.

So he said, "Yes, your money will do it."

And he wrote me out a script to the clerk of the court and he left it up to the clerk to tell me the price—that was his business. Quite natural, I believe they done talked it over between em and if they didn't talk it over, why, you take a crowd of laws, every man knows his business. I took that script from the probate judge and went straight to the clerk of the court and consulted with him, showed him the script from the probate judge. When he seed who that script was from he set down and questioned me some. And I asked him, "What will it cost me to get the boy out?"

He said, "It'll cost you thirty-six dollars and ten cents."

I said, "Well, I want him, please, sir. I got the money to pay you."

He said, "You have?"

I told him, "Yes sir, I can meet your price."

Had forty dollars in my pocket or maybe a little over with what I already had in my pocket before my wife gived me money out of the trunk.

He wrote me a note after he asked me was I ready to pay it.

I said, "Yes sir, any time I can get my boy."

Then he wrote me out a paper givin information to the jailer. Told me to go out there—fellow by the name of Bert Calhoun was the sheriff at that time. Clerk said, "You go out and give this to the jailer, you'll find him out there somewhere."

I walked out on the steps of the courthouse and looked over the city—had the money still in my pocket, I was just totin notes. I walked out on the steps of the courthouse and looked every whichway. And I was lucky to spy the sheriff standin bout a half a block from the steps, in a old long overcoat near about touchin the ground. Standin there smokin a cigar—Sheriff Bert Calhoun. I walked on right quick to him before he moved.

"Good mornin, Mr. Sheriff."

"Good mornin."

I said, "I have a note here for you from the clerk of the court."

I pulled it out and handed it to him. He stood there and read it. He said, "Uh-huh, what you want is this man out of jail, Waldo Ramsey."

I said, "Yes sir, that's the man, Mr. Sheriff."

He said, "I'll get him for you in a few minutes."

And he took off down the block right in front of a line of stores—I knowed the town well—and he went down the street so far, to about the middle of the second block and he went right in a store door. I looked at that and I said to myself, 'Now you goin in that store there and kill a whole lot of time'—I didn't know where the jail was, all to my surprise about it—'and I'm kind of in a hurry; I want to get back home quick as I can, work on my barn. No tellin how long you'll be in there before you come out.'

He disappeared through that store door. I didn't know it, but goin through that store was the straightest way to the jail. I didn't know nothin bout no jailhouse—I'd never been in jail in the whole of my life.

I turned around after a thought or so and walked back to them courthouse steps; walked up, stood on top, and looked all over town; but I continued to watch the door where he went in. I stood there a good while lookin for him to come out and bring the boy, if that was the way he was supposed to get him. And in a few minutes' time, out come the jailer, the sheriff—I recognized him when he hopped out the door in that long overcoat. I kept a watchin that door, in preference to anything else, to see if that boy was comin, or how it was goin to work. And in just a jiffy or two after the sheriff come out the door to that store, here come the boy, right behind him. I looked and I was satisfied then. Time that boy got to me—he lagged behind the jailer all the way—sheriff got to the courthouse, he just come on up the steps, walked right by me and into his office. And when little Waldo started up the steps—I was standin on the top step lookin down at him—boy walked up there with his little bundle under his arm followin the jailer, that sheriff. I know the sheriff directed him if he had anything in that jail cell to get it out. He walked up there, come up to the next to last step. And he looked in my face. Talk about a boy jumpin and grabbin me— after he seed who I was he jumped up and grabbed me, he did, and howdyed with me and told me these words: "Nate, the sheriff come down there and got me out of jail. I don't know what they goin to do with me—"

I was feelin his sympathy. I said, "They aint goin to do nothin with you. I'm goin to carry you home"—if them weren't my exact words I aint a colored man— "They aint goin to do nothin. No use anticipatin what they goin to do; they aint goin to do nothin. I come at you this mornin—your mother was cryin at me, your father come down here yesterday and couldn't get you, didn't get you and I went over there this mornin to find out about you. I didn't wait a day, I didn't wait a minute till I got in shape and come down here to get you. It was on my mind. All right. Come on in here to the clerk of the court. That's as far as you goin; I'm goin to carry you home."

Walked in there to the clerk of the court; clerk said, "Well, you got your man. You ready to pay his claim off?"

I said, "Yes sir." And I spanked his money down—thirty-six dollars and ten cents. I turned and told the boy, "Let's go, your mother's at home cryin for you this mornin."

Got about ten steps from the clerk's door, he called me, said, "Say, come back. You aint got no papers on him. You can get papers on him and if you and him can't agree, if he don't treat you right about you gettin him out of jail, you aint got nothin to do but return him."

I said, "I don't want that. I don't want no papers between me and the boy."

He looked at me and said, "O, you must know your man."

I said, "Yes sir, I do know him; he's my brother-in-law. Don't need no papers on him"—how if I got him out and he disobeyed my orders I could turn him back—"I trusts the boy; them papers won't improve him."

Well, we walked out to the buggy and Clarence Reed, this boy's brother-in-law, who married his baby sister, was there. We crawled on that buggy, all three of us; I looked around at the boy and said, "Buddy, you had any breakfast?"

He said, "Yes, Nate, I've had breakfast but you aint never been in jail and know how jail fare is. Sometime you got a appetite to eat and sometime you aint. You aint never witnessed that. So, I aint hungry and don't worry me about it."

I said, "That's all right. Is there anything you want to eat?"

He broke down then. Told me he wanted a sandwich, a hot dog. He said, "I drinked a little coffee this mornin but I aint et nothin."

I said, "Get in the buggy and set right there till I come back. Don't move. Stay in the buggy with your brother-in-law. I'll get you somethin to eat if you aint et nothin."

I went on across town to the hot dog department and got him two hot dogs. Carried em back and handed em up to him on the buggy. Went right on around and untied my mule, put my tie halter in the back of the buggy, one of these big grass tie halters with snaps. Unsnapped it, got it clear from the mule's mouth, put it in the back of the buggy and—home bound!

Drove right on back—crossed into Tukabahchee County and dropped Clarence Reed off at his house, carried little Waldo home with me. Got there and I told him, "Now, Buddy, me and Peter, my brother here, we goin down on Sitimachas Creek to work on a barn I'm buildin on the old Bannister place. We're due to be movin there soon and I got to get the barn done. You just carry yourself right straight home now to your mother and father and stay with em long as you please. Let em know that you're out of jail and clear. You got nobody to look back at but me. If you treat me right, that's all I ask."

He went on his way, and me and my brother went another route down to the Bannister place on Sitimachas. And when we got back home that evenin, me and Peter, little Waldo was settin up in my house; done went over to his mother and father, showed hisself to em. I walked in there that night, I said, "Buddy, you didn't tarry with your mother and father this evenin. When we left here together you went on over there and we went on to work on the Bannister place, and here you is now sittin back here. You didn't stay over there long enough."

He said, "Well, Nate"—he got up—"well, Nate, reason I didn't, I knew that Sweet and the children was here by theirselves and you down on the creek workin on your barn—and also, I thought my comin back here would give us a chance to talk over how I'm goin to pay you. I mean to satisfy you."

I said, "Yeah, but you weren't obliged to come back that quick. You coulda waited till tomorrow. Although, like it is, there's no harm done. But I meant for you to stay over there and talk to your mother and father and stay all night if it was necessary to please em."

He said, "Well, I decided weren't no use to that. I come back here to be with Sweet and the little children until you come. Now I want to consult with you about how you want to accept your payment. I can work at a public job somewhere and get it up and give it to you. Or, the thing I wants, let me stay with you a year and give me a crop on halves. I'll pay you that way."

I told him, "That's all right, by your method. I'm not settlin on you to get it no certain way. If that's what you want, I'll agree with you on it. You can pay me back that way."

When we agreed how he was to work to pay me, I didn't know what his full mind was. He said he weren't intendin to go back with his wife. He knowed who put him in jail—her and her daddy. But they had a child at that time, a little old boy. And quite naturally, little Waldo wanted to see the boy some. He kept up with the chap, too, as a father, but he stayed away from his wife.

That boy went on—and I had that young mule there, that Mattie mule; I wanted to break her myself. So I put him to plowin my older mule, the one that was broke when I bought her. Doggone good mule too, that Lu mule. Had a little age on her but she got up and got in any place I wanted her. I put him to plowin Lu and I give him a crop on halves—I rented that plantation from Mr. Tucker, the old Bannister place, and I had plenty of land to give him a crop. Mr. Reeve continued to furnish me the first year I worked with Mr. Tucker; gived me cash money and out of that I gived the boy what he needed.

He didn't go back with his wife that year; he come on and stayed with me and his sister Hannah. I had another house rented there on Tucker's place—it come with the land—but I didn't let him move in there. He didn't need to because he done made up his mind to quit this woman and he didn't need a whole house for hisself. So we took him direct in the house with us. And he didn't move no house goods in there at all. He just come there and stayed. Here's the way we worked that: my wife had a pretty good education and she kept check on what he got. She washed for him, ironed for him, what was needed to be ironed. Fed him right at the table with us—and a reasonable price was figured down against him for all these washins, ironins, cookin for him. And when he called to me for a little money, I'd give him that—didn't hold back on him noway. And Hannah was keepin the books against him, her brother. She didn't definitely charge him—it was against my rulins to charge him for everything.

And when he got through the gap and satisfied us far as he could go—paid up his expenses, paid up gettin him out of jail, when he got that done out of the crop he made under my administration, he was yet owin me twelve dollars. I give it to him, that twelve dollars he couldn't pay.

And after he got clear of me he decided to take that Hawkins girl back. At that period of time, her daddy and all of her relatives had left this country and moved to Middletown, Ohio. Her mother was dead and her father had remarried to a woman by the name of Irene Todd. Leola Hawkins, who was Leola Ramsey after little Waldo married her, she wanted to follow her father and sister and brother to the northern country—only one brother, called him Son Hawkins. And she plotted with some fellow that had a car, at Waldo's absence—little Waldo hadn't left us complete but he was trekkin back at her and she didn't want to be bothered with him— he believed he could convince her back with him. Well, her and this other fellow made a plot. And one day he carried her on his Ford car and slipped her to the train, her and that little old baby boy that her and Waldo had. She just cleaned up when she done that— hit it to Middletown, Ohio, and the balance of her family. Little Waldo never did see her no more.

He jumped up and married again; married a young woman that had never been married. She was a Goodrich, his second wife, she lived over close to Apafalya; Amon Goodrich was her father. She was a slender-built, tall, dark-skinned woman. Leola, his first wife, Hawkins' daughter, she was a ginger-cake colored woman.

This second woman he married, he got on better with her to a great extent. But after so long they separated and he fell right back on his people; and went ahead, after him and this woman parted, and he married another woman. She was a Fox, old man George Fox's daughter.

Three times he married, and him and his second wife, Amon Goodrich's girl, they didn't have nary a child livin when they separated; had one born but it died. And him and this Fox girl never did have nary a child together; she had a child already when they married, a little old girl. Little Waldo's son by his first wife, he recognized his daddy enough to come back here several times and visit with his daddy's people, includin Hannah, little Waldo's sister. And he fell heir to old man Waldo's old home place after the death of little Waldo. He aint been back to this country, to my knowin, since the death of his auntie, since Hannah died.

Little Waldo's first wife was a Hawkins; she's dead. His second wife was a Goodrich—I aint never heard talk about her bein dead or alive. His third wife was a Fox, and she was his wife when *he* died.

II

I wanted to stretch out where I could get more land to work, and Miss Hattie Lu and Mr. Reeve—they had a little girl child but he weren't the father of it. Miss Hattie Lu had the chap before they married. And this girl had married and moved up there on the place with her husband. So I couldn't get more land than I had. They wanted to keep me there but on the amount of land they wanted, and it was too little for me. Then, too, me and Mrs. Reeve's son-in-law didn't agree much with each other. When he moved up on the place he wanted to take it over and boss me too. Well, you know blood's thicker than water, and Miss Hattie Lu was goin to let him have his way. I decided I'd pull out and I was pullin out in time, too.

I looked ahead and figured my best route. Moved down on Sitimachas Creek on the old Bannister place. And there, regardless to my dealins with Mr. Tucker, I begin to prosper good and heavy. I had learned a rule for my life workin with Mr. Reeve—I could make it anywhere by workin and tendin my own business. I was able to advance myself because I never made under five bales of cotton—made five bales the first year I rented from the Reeves; next year I made six; next year I made eight—with one mule and no help to speak of. Cotton picked up the second and third years to between fifteen and twenty cents, along in there. It was a big difference in the price since I started farmin for myself. I was under the impression that the government was takin hold of the market—1912, 1913. The second year I quit workin halves and took my business in my own hands, cotton floated up to a higher level.

But things went bad the year I moved down on the creek. Cotton fell to a nickel a pound, 1914. A man couldn't pay nothin much on his old debts and nothin at all on his new ones. I disremember just exactly what I paid Mr. Reeve on the money he furnished me that year—he stuck by me, furnished me cash money the first year I dealt with Mr. Tucker—but I didn't pay him off. And I owed him a little over two hundred dollars after I sold my cotton and paid him what I could. And in addition to that, I owed Mr. Harry Black a hundred and thirty dollars for fertilize that I'd used the last year I worked on Mrs. Reeve's place. He was a guano salesman, lived out in the country above Tuskegee; and every year I lived with Mr. Reeve I bought my guano from him. 1913, I carried my guano debt over to my next crop; it weren't unusual to do that in this country and he agreed. But when cotton fell to a nickel I couldn't pay nothin hardly. And, to tell the truth, I didn't make the cotton I had been makin on the Reeve place. So I owed money for fertilize that applied to a bigger crop than I was makin now.

That was boll weevil time, the boll weevil was in circulation. He had just come in a year or two before then—these white folks down here told the colored people if you don't pick them cotton squares off the ground and destroy them boll weevils, we'll quit furnishin you. Told em that—puttin the blame on the colored man for the boll weevil comin in this country. Well, that was a shame. Couldn't nobody pay on his debts when the weevil et up his crop. The boll weevil cut in my cotton to a certain extent, but at that time it was mainly the low price that injured my chances. If I had got the price, I could have paid a heap more on my debts although I was makin less cotton.

I was runnin two plows—myself and my brother-in-law, little Waldo Ramsey, my wife's brother. But when cotton fell to the bottom both our crops combined couldn't pay what I owed. I did manage to pay Mr. Black thirty dollars; owed him a hundred and thirty dollars and I paid him thirty and that hundred runned over for five years before I could pay it.

THAT first year I moved on the Bannister place, Mr. Reeve died— died that fall, while I was gatherin my crop. What did Miss Hattie Lu do when he died? She come to me and told me, "Nate, Mr. Reeve's gone now; he aint with us no more. We want to arrange to get in all of his estate, get it all together."

I agreed with her.

She said, "Now what you owed Mr. Reeve"—I couldn't pay him on account of cotton goin down, and then too that was my first year on that rocky place, my crop weren't quite what it had been; boll weevil seed to that also—"and whoever else owes him, like you do"—everybody doin business with the man owed him, you know—

"we will, if it suits you, name somebody to take up your debt with Mr. Reeve."

And she named Mr. Tucker as the man to take up my debt, at ninety percent on the dollar. They knocked off ten percent to get Mr. Reeve's business closed in. Miss Hattie Lu told me, "Nate, Cousin Lemuel Tucker"—Miss Hattie Lu and Mr. Tucker was cousins someway—"he'll take up your debt, what you owe Mr. Reeve. And you only entitled to pay Cousin Lemuel ninety cents on the dollar. That ten cents, we knocked it off, that's our laws. You just pay ninety cents on the dollar to Mr. Reeve's estate; pay it to Cousin Lemuel, he taken up your debt."

I didn't know nothin against Mr. Tucker to make me contrary to the idea, so I told her, "Let him take it up." But the amount that I owed Mr. Reeve, I couldn't pay Mr. Tucker nothin on it that year. And I had that guano debt besides. Mr. Reeve transacted his business like this: he'd furnish you money to buy groceries and anything else you needed except fertilize; he wouldn't give you a penny for fertilize. You could buy fertilize from whoever you pleased but you had to arrange to pay the dealer out of your crop. I got along well under Mr. Reeve's system as long as cotton was bringin anything. But when cotton fell, that's when the trouble come.

So Miss Hattie Lu consulted with Mr. Tucker and he took my debt over. And he come down to my house on the creek one day, told me, "Nate, I took over your debt and paid Miss Hattie Lu the money you owed her dear husband's estate. I settled your account in full. Now you just pay me what you owed Mr. Reeve."

I said, "Mr. Tucker, you didn't have to pay the whole debt, you only had to pay ninety percent on the balance. The knock-off wasn't given to you."

He jumped up when I told him that. "Did she tell you that? She's mighty darn smart to tell you all that."

Right there was where I caught him. Miss Hattie Lu had put me in the light.

He said, "The thing for you to do is pay me what you owed Mr. Reeve."

She told me to pay ninety cents on the dollar and he wanted the whole thing, what he didn't have to pay.

I said, "Mr. Tucker, she told me that ten cents weren't given to you; it's their loss, just their loss. Yes sir, she told me in a straight way; I'm entitled to pay you only ninety cents on the dollar and the dime goes loose."

He said, "The thing for you to do is pay me what you owed Mr. Reeve; that's the thing for you to do."

I said, "Do you think it's right to charge me for somethin you didn't have to pay?"

He said nothin. But I had no political pull; that was my flaw. I said, "All right, Mr. Tucker, go ahead. I'll see you later."

Well, he took up Mr. Reeve's debt and made himself ten cents on the other man's dollar. I had the brains to see how that transaction was runnin over me, but I had no voice on account of my color—and never had any with most men, only had a voice with some.

I had bargained to buy the old place, the Bannister place, but I got so deep in debt by Tucker takin up what I owed Mr. Reeve at his death, havin to reach back and pay off the whole claim—I couldn't make the payments on the place and it fell back into Mr. Tucker's hands. I stayed on there, rentin, and Mr. Tucker kept the title to the place.

That barn I built on the premises, it didn't cost him a penny, not one penny. I put four stables to the barn. In fact of the business, the old barn was there but at the present time that I took a hold of the place, there wasn't but two stables in it. And I went ahead and tore the old barn out practically, braced it and sturdied it up and took out the old log supports—it was a old log barn—and built it up in a frame way. I bought lumber to make the change and when I quit workin on the barn I had four good stables when there weren't but two when I started. My brother helped me some but mostly I done it by myself, and well done it too. I nailed two by fours to the upright logs, braced em, then sawed out doors and even covered that barn. In other words, I rebuilt that barn to meet my standards. I had went in the name of buyin the property so the expenses come on me—he didn't allow me nothin on improvements. And when I become so deep I couldn't buy the place, he inherited my labor in that barn.

I had just bought a horse at that time and I had that pair of mules and I prepared that barn to hold all them stock. Every place I wanted a stable I cut out and done it with planks—them old logs been decayed. And when I wound up I had four stables, needed em. Mr. Reeve furnished me money to build that barn and Mr. Tucker got that out of me on top of the barn.

So I decided, I was owin Tucker, I didn't know really what I was goin to do, at one time it struck my mind to just sell what I had and pay Tucker up. And I took a notion I'd sell my Mattie mule—everybody wanted her and I had another mule and a horse at that time. But Tucker had done mortgaged that mule and all of my personal property at that time and all the property of all his hands; he runned us up all together on a joint note. So I let Mr. Tucker know that I was intendin to sell that mule. I didn't mean to take just any kind of deal for her. She was one of the lightest mules, in weight, that I ever owned but she weighed right at a thousand pounds. She was a thoroughgoin mule, just right for a plow mule, single or double. And when it come around to sellin her, I hung up, of course, to an extent.

Tucker wanted to sell the mule hisself, claimed he had a right to sell her on account of that mortgage he held. So he brought a white man to my house one day to look at the mule. I led em out to the pasture—didn't know the white man on sight. Drove the mule up, let him look at her. We was out there in the pasture at the edge of a big pine thicket, big enough pines to saw for lumber. White man looked the mule over. I didn't say a word. When he asked about the mule he asked just like he was askin Tucker—but I done the answerin.

He said, "Well, she's a nice mule all right, but she's too light for what I want her for."

He'd done asked what I'd take for the mule, had I made up my mind if I was goin to sell her and what did I want for her. Well, I gived a hundred and eighty-five dollars and then done broke her and she become quiet. My wife just thought the world of that mule and she named her Mattie.

"Take two hundred dollars to move her."

He looked and he looked; he decided she was too light for that much money—and she was just as pretty as a peeled onion.

They begin to walk away, him and Tucker, after he made his excuse. Tucker didn't care—I knowed his theory—he didn't want to see the man turn the mule down, just so it didn't undercut *his*

price. I knowed he had a opinion of it but his opinion was too
light. So as they started walkin off I just throwed it into em like
this: "Well, you think she's too light for you?"

"Yes, too light for that much money."

I'd a raised the devil if Tucker had went on and tried to sell
that mule to him anyhow, cut my price. I said, "You needn't go on
off over the hill somewhere and come back, it won't do you no good.
It'll take two hundred dollars to move her; I won't take a penny
less. If you don't want her, just go on, don't come back."

That white man never did come back. He went on out of there,
Mr. Tucker tellin him, "Uh-uh-uh-uh, O yes, that's a dandy good
mule, worth all of two hundred dollars."

MR. TUCKER had a special place he sent his hands to trade; weren't
his store, just some of his friend people there in Apafalya that sold
groceries. All the hands that Tucker had out in the country here,
right in between Two Forks and Pottstown—some of these people
was on *his* places and some of em was on places he had rented for
em. He'd rent places from other white men and sub-rent em to his
niggers or let em work on halves, and he stood for em.

Weren't no use to kick against his orders, we, all of us on his
places, was forced to trade where he sent us. I don't mean that he'd
drive a man like a dog or a hog, but if the poor fellow wanted a
home and he fit him up, that man traded where he was sent. It
was just a way of controllin the nigger, his money and hisself.
Sometime a colored man would kick against the proposition but
very seldom.

Prices weren't no higher at the store he'd send us than the
average other places in town. But, you understand, this was a friend
to him, he goes in there and gives him all of his trade, makes arrangements with him for his hands to come there and get groceries,
monthly or anytime they wanted em. And he'd go to the bank, draw
money—he had every bit of our stuff mortgaged by his own rulins;
he knowed what all we had and mortgaged it to stand a security
for the money he was gettin. And he'd take that mortgage money
and traipse around the stores—kept a doin that every year. That's
how he'd run his business. We'd trade where he told us to trade and
he'd pay it up once a month with the money he got from mortgagin
our stuff.

But there weren't no great sight of groceries got at a store by me because at that time I raised my meat and lard, corn, vegetables —we was a family of people that all we bought at the store was coffee, flour, sugar, salt. So it weren't no burden on me to trade at Tucker's choice of a store because I didn't trade much.

I'D be askin all along for five long years and every fall I'd come up just a little deeper—1914, 1915, 1916, 1917, 1918—I'd go to Mr. Tucker for a settlement and he'd tell me, "Well, you lackin so much and so much of comin out—" For five long years I was fallin behind dealin with that man. Up until the fifth year I dropped into town to pay him: "Well, what are you holdin against me now, Mr. Tucker?"

"You owe me five hundred dollars, Nate."

Done got all of my crops for five years and I still owed him five hundred dollars. That was his tune. Five hundred dollars and one penny. I labored under that debt—I'm tellin what God's pleased with—lingered five long years and he was gettin every string I had to give.

So, the fifth year I lived with him, he left his plantations up here and went down below Montgomery to boss a big farm business for some rich folks. And he traveled back up here every week to see what his men was doin. Get on his car and get out from down there and come up here every weekend. In them days he didn't have nothin but a little old Ford car—hadn't got up to buyin Chevrolets, Buicks, and so on. He come up here every weekend on that little old Ford; lookin around, seein how we was gettin along, men that he was standin for—me, Wilson Rowe, Leroy Roberts, Silas Todd. Come to see if we had anything he could get any money out of.

He was travelin around amongst his hands one day in the fall and he come to my house. He had already told me I owed him five hundred dollars and one cent. So he come down there one evenin in the mist and rain. He lived out here in the piney woods between Pottstown and Apafalya and I lived back close to Sitimachas Creek, somethin like two miles from him. And I was in the house with my family when he come.

I had done ginned and baled and hauled back home and throwed in the yard three bales of cotton. He come up there and he seed that. Whoooooo—he had a knack of scratchin his leg and spittin when he talked; that was his way of doin. So he come in my house and he got to scratchin his leg and cryin bout how he needed money: "Uh-uh-uh-uh, by George, Nate, I see you got three bales of cotton in the yard and I'm up here for some money, I need it for my business affairs. And I see you got this cotton ginned off and layin out here."

I said, "Yes sir."

"Uh-uh-uh-uh, by George, I'm just in bad shape for money, I can't tell you how bad I need it. Load your cotton up and bring it out to Apafalya and sell it and get me up some money."

I loaded that cotton, went on out there that evenin and sold it. Well, many people say it, "A good thing follows a bad one, a bad thing follows a good one." Any trap set somewhere goin to break loose after a while.

Well, the government had done jumped back into the cotton business at that time— I knowed I owed him, I just loaded up them three bales of cotton. My little boys was big enough to push some so I set skids alongside the wagon and rolled them three bales up there on the flat-body, hitched my mules to the wagon and pulled it into Apafalya. Them three bales of cotton knocked the bark off the whole tree: I collected, I got a check for five hundred and sixty dollars out of them three bales of cotton—if I'm not tellin the truth, I'm the biggest liar ever spoke. Cotton was up around forty cents or a little better—that was in wartime; hit the war and cotton brought a little over forty cents a pound. Five years before that, I moved onto the Tucker place and made my first crop, cotton was down to five cents. Now it was bringin forty on account of that war.

Had that check in my hand from the man that bought my cotton, I walked on to the bank. Mr. Tucker was there waitin on me. I said, "Mr. Tucker, what was that you told me that I owed you?"

"Uh-uh-uh-uh, let me figure—"

Whirled around there and went through a little alley to where generally there was a little old table of some kind—you go into a bank, they got nice fixins there for you to write on. Well, he run over there to that little old table and he figured. Whirled around to me again and he come out with this: five hundred dollars and one penny. "If you pay me the five hundred I'll knock the penny off."

Mr. Grace standin right there, CD Grace, the banker, president of the bank. He standin there listenin at us. I just issued my check to him; it called for five hundred and sixty-nine dollars and somethin cents. I said, "Take out that five hundred dollars, Mr. Grace, and give me the balance."

Got out of them bales of cotton, five hundred and sixty-nine dollars, some-odd cents. Mr. Tucker got five hundred of it, Mr. Grace gived me the balance. I just stuck that money in my inside coat pocket. I happened to have on my coat that day—it was cold and rainy.

I said, "Now, Mr. Grace, I want my note."

I was payin Mr. Tucker all I owed him, but that weren't killin the bird, understand. Mr. Tucker went to scratchin his leg, "Uh-uh-uh-uh, Nate, I don't know whether you can get your note or not until I pay my bills."

There was a fraud in that but Mr. Grace overruled.

"I-I-I don't know whether you can get your note or not."

That was killin to me. Because if he didn't pay what he owed, they'd come to me for it. We were under that joint note business, all of his hands and the man himself. He was the only one that could draw money on it but we were all responsible for what he owed. He took a joint note on everything we had—Leroy Roberts, Wilson Rowe, Silas Todd, and me. I signed the note but I didn't know what I was signin when I signed; he didn't tell us what it was but a note. I've always heard that it was illegal to force a man to sign a note without readin it to him, tellin him what he's signin— I've heard that. Just fooled us to do it. Had us come in to the bank there one at a time to sign and had a different paper for each of us, but it was all for the same note.

A joint note is a bad note; you might say it's a clearin-house note. I caught how it could damage a man—if that note messes me up it's goin to mess you up too, goin to mess up everyone that's signed to it. And if you didn't understand it, they just took advantage of your ignorance. What man would freely of himself sign such a note? If you and I both sign this note and you can't make your payment, they goin to take it out of me. My stuff is subject to your transaction, your stuff is subject to my transaction—that's a bad note. Some of my color and some of the white people too talked to me bout it afterwards. Told me, "Nate, didn't you know no better than that? That's a joint note. They goin to work you until they get everything you got."

I said, "I didn't know it at the time I signed. Mr. Tucker pulled the blinds over my eyes and I believe it's illegal."

But illegal or legal, don't make no difference—any way we fix it goes for the nigger.

So I kept a lookin at Mr. Grace. And he was lookin at me and lookin at Mr. Tucker and he acted undecided for a minute. Then he said, "Yes, Lemuel, he can get his note. He done paid you all he owed you; he can get it."

"Uh-uh-uh-uh, by George, give it to him." O, he scratched his leg, "Give it to him."

Mr. Grace marked that note up and handed it to me. I put it in my inside coat pocket along with the balance of the money I got from my cotton. Right there and then it struck my heart and mind: 'You'll never get another note on me, never under Christ's kingdom.'

Mr. Grace turned me loose from that joint note business and I walked on out the bank.

THAT next spring he sent me word to meet him out in Apafalya, he got word to all his other hands and one of em come to me and told me—Silas Todd, he was livin my closest neighbor. Silas got Mr. Tucker's word and he come to my house one day. He called himself a cousin to me; said, "Cousin Nate, Mr. Lemuel said for us all to meet in Apafalya Saturday and sign up for our year's supply. And we aint got nothin to do but sign our notes."

Every spring as long as that joint note was goin on—it went on five years with me—the week Mr. Tucker wanted us to sign, on a certain Saturday, he'd notify us not later than the middle of the week. That would be in February, when notes was openin up and the farmin people was gettin their business straightened out for the new crop.

So, here come Silas Todd tellin me, "Mr. Tucker said for us all to meet him at the bank Saturday."

Good God, I had just paid him up and got through with him that previous fall—high-priced cotton pulled the kinks out of me. And when Silas gived me Tucker's word, I just shooed it off, wouldn't let it take my head. I acted careless about it and short and Silas smiled; then he broke out and laughed: "You don't want to go. You aint goin, is you?"

"I don't know what I'll do. I have to study it."

I wouldn't tell Silas definitely I wasn't goin; told him, "I don't know what I'll do. I'm undecided."

I failed to go. I wouldn't go sign no note. I was ignorant out of the knowledge of knowin what a joint note meant until I paid Mr. Tucker and saw for myself everything that was on that note.

First business I had after I got the order to come out to the bank and sign that note, I went to Apafalya—that was my tradin town. One Monday I got on my buggy and drove out to Apafalya and just as I got inside the suburbs of town I seed a little old Ford car come a flyin, meetin me, comin up the road. I never had a thought it was him. And when he got close to me I could see it *was* him. Mr. Tucker looked and seed it was me. He drove by me a little piece before he checked that little old Ford up out of the road and jumped out. I looked back and I stopped too. He left that little old Ford car and come trottin back to my buggy. When he got to me he said, "Uh-uh-uh-uh"—he talked thataway—"uh-uh-uh-uh, Nate, uh-uh-uh, I see you didn't come down Saturday and sign the note. You know—uh-uh, you goin downtown now, aint you?"

I said, "Yes, I'm goin down there."

"Well, you aint got nothin to do but just go straight into the bank and sign."

Mr. Tucker was weedin a bad row for satisfaction then.

I said, "Mr. Tucker, I don't reckon I'll sign no notes this time."

He commenced a scratchin his leg. "Uh-uh, what's the trouble? What's the trouble?"

I said, "Well—" I'd sworn to God and man, in all of my thoughts, when I got that note that Mr. Grace just gived me anyhow, that was the last one. I wouldn't be tied up no suchaway as that again. Mr. Tucker gived me trouble about it but it was nothin that a colored man didn't expect. Long trouble. I had done paid him the money I owed Mr. Reeve and everything. Then I didn't owe nobody nothin but him and Mr. Harry Black. And I paid him every penny he had comin, then I went and paid Mr. Harry Black, too. All right. He couldn't get me to sign at all.

"No sir, I aint signin."

"Well, what's your objection? What's your objection? What you goin to do?"

I said, "Well—"

He said, "You know you aint able to help yourself."

I said, "I don't know that, Mr. Tucker. But it's a matter that I paid you every penny I owed you last fall down there at the bank. I got straight with you at last. I think it would really be better for me now to suffer for some things than to tie myself up in a situation such as that any more. I aint goin to sign no note. Be honest with you, I aint goin to sign. I'm goin to live the best I can, the hard way. Furthermore, I see my way clear that I can go part of the way and then very well live off the fat of my gut."

He said, "You better just go ahead and sign that note because you know you're goin to need—"

I said, "I don't doubt what I'll need but I can do without some, too."

"Uh-uh-uh-uh, by George, I see what you mean now. You goin to fool right around here until May and then you goin to cry for help."

I said, "Well, if I do, there's plenty of time to sign a note in May if it gets up in May and I need money. You can sign a note any time of year."

He seed he couldn't do nothin with me—I was set.

"And I aint signin no note this time at all; no way, shape, form, or fashion."

Jumped back, beggin me. I said, "No, Mr. Tucker, there aint no use. I aint signin no notes. I've made up my mind. I'd rather do without somethin and suffer for it than to get in your debt and be as long payin it as I was before."

Passed him up and he went on and got back in his car, went on home or somewhere and I went on down to Apafalya and done what I wanted to do, every way but sign that note.

All right. Lingered, lingered, lingered—he come back home and he told the rest of the hands, "Uh-uh-uh-uh, by George, old Nate is actin a fool this time. I can't get him to sign no note or do noway. Just actin a fool and he'll pay a fool's pay."

I said, when I seed him again, "If you want me to move, Mr. Tucker, I'll move. It's gettin mighty late in the year to move. You couldn't rent that place to nobody if I move off it. And I'll move before I'll sign any note, I'll just move, let you have your place."

He wouldn't kick at me then. I said to myself, 'Well, now I don't owe you nothin and I've set out to manage my own business.'

And I kept my word: I went several years, all through the year and nothin I had had no mortgage against it. I hauled lumber for the Graham-Pike Lumber Company after my crop was laid by. They paid me enough that I supported my family—my mules got to where they didn't want to eat no corn raised at home, they et so much sweet feed and number one timothy hay and oats; they got to where they wouldn't eat my corn and I had plenty of it.

WHEN I got my note after a five-year run of bein in his debt and I wouldn't sign no other, Mr. Tucker run to every guano dealer there was in Apafalya—he knowed em all—and told em not to let me have no guano. I didn't know he done it until I went into Mr. Bishop's store one day that spring to buy my guano. I thought I'd recognize Mr. Bishop and get my guano where I'd been gettin it. I was my own man, doin business wherever I pleased.

That man turned me down just like I was a dog.

I said, "Mr. Bishop, I been buyin guano from you through Mr. Tucker for several years. Now I paid Mr. Tucker every penny I owed him and I don't owe nobody but what I can pay on it. I don't owe Mr. Tucker a thing. And I thought that by bein straight"—had got enough to get myself straight—"I can just buy my guano myself."

He looked at me, "I wouldn't sell you a bit. Go ahead and buy through Mr. Tucker like you been doin."

I just turned around and walked out. All those white folks there was throwin their weight for one another—I hate to speak as much as I do, in a way, I hate it; wish it hadn't a never happened —Mr. Tucker runned around there and forbidded em all of sellin to me. I couldn't get my guano from Mr. Jack Bishop and I seed I was bein headed somewhere I hadn't planned to go. I left Mr. Bishop and knowin that Mr. Russell was a guano dealer, I walked right straight up the street and went in his store. He was a big shot man, had piles of money. Laid the same larceny on me.

Told him, "I don't owe nobody anythin but what I can pay. I'm clear otherwise. If I could buy guano from you I'd appreciate it, Mr. Russell. I'd go ahead and make my crop and I could easily pay you. I don't owe nobody nothin and I'm only buyin groceries on a light scale. I know my circumstances well—the notes I've made until now I've paid. Haven't had no trouble with nobody that way."

Mr. Russell stood there and listened at me. I told him my background—he said, "Uh-uh-uh-uh-uh-uh, I wouldn't sell you a bit."

Them's the words *he* told me—he stuttered when he talked. "I wouldn't sell you a bit."

I was comin to see in my mind that Tucker had me barred; he done posted my name and guano dealers wouldn't sell to me—tryin to drive me back to him. I didn't like bein geehawsed about that way and objected to. The days I owed Mr. Tucker I labored until I paid him and then I was clear. I was supposed to be a free man to buy from whoever I pleased that would deal with me. But I was knocked clean back just like a dog; couldn't get nothin from nobody. Friendship business amongst the white folks drivin me to one man, the man I'd throwed off me. Well, I seed Mr. Tucker there in Apafalya that evenin and I walked up to him—I was aimin to talk to him bout my fertilize for that year. I said, "Mr. Tucker, it appears to me that I can't buy no guano at all this year, nobody will sell me a bit. You have a hand in that mess, surely. What I want to know is this: what are you goin to do about my fertilize?"

"Uh-uh-uh-uh, by George, you went over to the bank and signed that note?"

I said, "No sir, I aint signed it today and I aint goin to sign."

Told him again. He said, "I aint goin to let you have no guano less'n you sign that note."

I kept a tellin him, "Well, I'll just move. If I can't get no guano I'll move, I'll get off your place. I'm barred by every guano dealer I been to. Mr. Bishop denied me, Mr. Russell denied me—they are the main guano dealers in town."

Told me, "Go on over there and sign that note and you can get all the guano you want."

Told him, "No, I won't sign no note."

Well, Mr. Harry Black would come into town on Saturdays to conduct his business and I knowed where to find him. He was a guano dealer—lived out in the country; didn't have no store operation—and durin the years I lived with Mr. Reeve I bought my guano from him. I was free to buy my guano anywhere I wanted then; in fact of the business, under Mr. Reeve's administration you had to trade for guano thoroughly on your own.

I just politely walked up to Mr. Black and laid my plight to him. I said, "Mr. Black, Mr. Tucker got me barred on fertilize. Won't none of em furnish me no guano. Mr. Bishop first and then

Mr. Russell, nary one of them men will sell me a bit. Turned me down straight."

He looked at me, said, "The hell they won't. Goddamnit, I'm goin to see to it— Go on back home and Monday mornin, when you get up, hitch your mules to your wagon and come on down here to Apafalya to the carbox and get all the damn guano you want. I'm goin to show em. They can't do you that way."

I knows a heap and I considers things, too. He was just a different type of man. He was a white man that recognized *all* men.

Mr. Black gived me them strong words. But he hesitated in the doin of it. He said, "Go back to Mr. Tucker *one more time*. Then if he don't let you have it—"

Told me what he'd do if Tucker didn't give me satisfaction. So I went back to Mr. Tucker and I said, "Mr. Tucker, what are you goin to do about lettin me have some guano? You goin to let me have it or not?"

I was sure of myself then. Mr. Black done told me if he objected me again, take my wagon to the carbox Monday mornin and get all the damn guano I wanted. All right. I went back to Mr. Tucker and he seed I weren't desperate no more.

I said, "Mr. Tucker, I'm not tellin you what I'll do if you don't let me have guano, but it won't leave me in no hard position."

He fell out of the box when I told him that. I was my own man; I'd found somebody that would deal with me.

"Uh-uh-uh-uh, by George, go on over there and tell Mr. Bishop I told you to tell him to sell you your guano."

It suited me better to buy my guano from Mr. Bishop and it suited Mr. Black, too. He decided—in business, people have these thoughts—he'd buck them other white men if they was stuck down definitely on me and weren't goin to let me have no guano at all. He fretted with the problem—"Go back to Mr. Tucker one more time—" and he treated me like a gentleman and got his satisfaction out of the deal, too. Mr. Tucker cleared the way for me to get my guano and Mr. Black stayed out of my business. He didn't say he was afraid to let me have it; told me, "Come and get it." But the way the thing worked out that weren't necessary. He just protected hisself and me too.

Mr. Black wasn't goin to let Mr. Tucker bar me from gettin guano after the way Mr. Tucker done treated *him*. Durin the years that joint note mess was runnin, I owed Mr. Black a hundred dollars for guano I'd used on the Reeve place. The first year Mr. Tucker had a hold of me, I met Mr. Black in Apafalya one day, right about the time I was ready to start my crop.

I said, "Mr. Black, I paid you last fall thirty dollars, all that I could pay you for guano. I know I owe you justice—one hundred dollars more. Mr. Tucker has got my business in charge now, what little I got, and I just can't pay you. Thing I'm goin to do is give you a note"—but not thinkin that Tucker would keep Mr. Black roped off like he done—"I'll give you a note that I owes you one hundred cash dollars for fertilize."

He told me, "No, Nate, a note from you wouldn't do me no good because Tucker done got your business in hand. I don't expect you'll soon have the money to pay me."

I said, "Yes sir, I don't doubt what you say, Mr. Black, but I'm goin to give you a note anyhow showin that I owe you until I can pay."

Fall of the year come, first year Mr. Tucker took me over, I couldn't pay Mr. Black a dime. Well, at planting time next spring I offered to give him another note. He told me, "Nate, you didn't pay me nothin, but I understand the matter."

I said, "Yes sir, I'm glad you do. Tucker's between us. Hit or miss, Mr. Black, I'll keep you with a note showin that I owe you."

He was a quiet man, dealt with me quiet. Said, "Your note aint worth a damn, Nate. You aint goin to be able to pay me until Tucker gets out of the way, no matter how long that is. As long as Tucker standin in the gap you aint goin to be able to pay me nothin. No, I wouldn't have a note from you."

I said, "Mr. Black, it'd show that I owes you."

He said, "Yeah, but owin me it makes no difference what it shows. If you can't pay it, you can't pay it."

Left it like that. One day I went into town, met Mr. Black again. He said, "Nate—"

I said, "Yes sir."

He said, "I got a question to ask you."

We stepped off to the side and talked. He said, "Well, my question is this, that I want to ask you." Looked right in my face. Said, "If I die before you pay me, will you pay what you owe me to my children?"

He had grown children, married children at that time. I gladly told him, "Yes sir, Mr. Black, I'll pay it because I know I justly owe you that hundred dollars. I'll pay your children if you happen to die before I pay you."

He said, "That's all, Nate, I wanted your word."

Rocked along there five years and when I did wind up with Mr. Black—he come to see me when I paid off Mr. Tucker; Mr. Tucker put him on me. Five hundred and sixty-nine dollars I got out of three bales of cotton and I paid Mr. Tucker five hundred dollars of it. That left me sixty-nine dollars and some-odd cents. Mr. Tucker jumped up then and got the word to Mr. Black that I done paid him up on all I owed him, clear. Told him—Mr. Black told me about it—told him, "Now's your time come. Nate's got more cotton in the field and he can pay you now."

One day Mr. Black drove his horse and buggy—had a big black mare that he drove to that buggy—come down to my house on Sitimachas Creek. Drove down to the edge of the yard and stopped and I went out to meet him.

He said, "Nate—"

I said, "Mr. Black, I been lookin out for you. I wanted to tell you that I paid Mr. Tucker up on everything I owed him and now you next. You goin to get your money. Ah, yes, you goin to get your money."

He said, "Nate, I didn't drive down here huntin no money; I just drove down here to show myself to you and to let you know what Lemuel done. You done paid him and soon as he got his money he reported it to me. But I didn't come here after your money. I'm goin to leave it up to you and I believe you'll pay me. And I'll just wait until you *can* pay me."

I said, "Well, Mr. Black—"

He said, "I thinks but little of Tucker the way he treated you and the way he treated me. He was the chunk in the way until now. And if he hadn't a done like he did, you woulda paid me, I believe you would."

I offered to give him the balance of the money I got out of them three bales of cotton—he wouldn't have it. Told me, "Nate, I aint worried. I believe you'll pay me and have no diddlin around about it."

I said, "Mr. Black, you just look for it. I'll be down there to your home this comin Wednesday and bring you your money."

I knowed I could take another half a bale of cotton to the gin —cotton was bringin that high wartime price—and I could pay him then. And in the wind-up of the deal I was the most deceived fellow you ever saw. I hurried up and ginned that half a bale of cotton and made a little under a hundred dollars. Went to him Wednesday to my word—Mr. Black is dead now; that's a good white man gone. I'm goin to hold em up if they done right; if they done wrong, I aint scared to tell it—Wednesday come, I told my wife, "Well, I've got to go now and give Mr. Black his money. He wouldn't have what I had here when he come a few days ago. Left that in case I'd a got in a tight, I'd a had a little money. And I promised to go down there today and take him his hundred dollars."

Hitched one of my mules to the buggy, jumped in there, and drove out to Mr. Harry Black. He lived out in the country on the west side of Apafalya on a pretty straight line between Apafalya and Tuskegee. Didn't have to go into Apafalya to get there. Got down there and I called to him. His wife come to the door. She said, "He's gone to Tuskegee and I'm lookin for him any minute."

I told her, "Yes'm. I come here to pay Mr. Black what I owe him. Miz Black, I'll just hitch my mule out here and wait till he comes."

After awhile, I looked down the road and here come Mr. Black, drivin that big black mare and she was fat as a pig. He drove up to the yard and one of his boys come out of the house and took that horse and buggy over. Mr. Black walked right up toward me and I walked part of the way up to him.

I said, "Hello, Mr. Black, I'm here with your money."

He said, "All right, Nate."

I run my hand in my pocket and counted it out to him—one hundred dollars.

He looked it over; he was satisfied. Now what did he do? Somethin I wasn't lookin for! When I counted that hundred dollars into that white man's hand he looked at me, said, "Now hold out your hand—"

I couldn't imagine hard as I tried what he meant by tellin me to hold out my hand.

He said, "Hold out your hand. Hold out your hand."

Counted fifty dollars of that money back in my hand, half of what I'd just paid him. And said, "Now, Nate, I know you've had a hard time. Take that money and go on back home and buy your wife and children some shoes and clothes, as far as it will go with that money. Nate, don't spend it for nothin else."

When I got home with that fifty dollars I gived it to my wife and told her what Mr. Black told me. And that's what it went for —shoes and clothes, clothes and shoes.

I was registered for army service durin the war but I had too many children for em—that's what caused em to lay off. Some of the white folks got around and worked to hold me out; they thought it would be better for the state of Alabama me stayin with my wife and children than me goin off and leavin em to beg on the state.

I didn't definitely know who it was in war in them times. And it wasn't clear to me what that war was all about. But after the battle is fought and the victory is won—I'm forced to say it—it all goes over to the whites. What did they do for the niggers after all these foreign wars? The colored man goin over there fightin, the white man goin over there fightin, well, the white man holds his ground over here when he comes back, he's the same; nigger come back, he aint recognized more than a dog. In other words, it's the same for him, too, as it was before he went. What did they do to the niggers after this first world war? Meet em at these stations where they was gettin off, comin back into the United States, and cut the buttons and armaments off of their clothes, make em get out of them clothes, make em pull them uniforms off and if they didn't have another suit of clothes—quite naturally, if they was colored men they was poor and they might not a had a thread of clothes in the world but them uniforms—make em walk in their underwear. I know it was done, I heard too much of it from the ones that come back to this country even. You a damn nigger right on, didn't give you no credit for what you done.

I've had white people tell me, "This is white man's country, white man's country." They don't sing that to the colored man when it comes to war. Then it's all *our* country, go fight for the country. Go over there and risk his life for the country and come back, he aint a bit more thought of than he was before he left.

But the war was good to me because it meant scarce cotton; and scarce cotton, high price. Cotton reached forty cents and it held up for several years. It fell off war prices by the time I moved off of the Tucker place in 1923. It fell to twenty-five cents and a little less and it kept on fallin and cotton never brought as much any year after that as it had brought the year before. Speculators run that thing and they run it in their own favor and against the farmers until the government took hold of it. Every time cotton dropped it hurt the farmer. Had to pay as much rent, had to pay as much for guano, but didn't get as much for his crop. The price just fell out of my hands—never was really in my hands or in any of these white folks' hands in this country that I knowed.

ONE day I told my wife, "Darlin, I'm goin to Apafalya to get me a load of cotton seed hulls for my cows and some meal."

She said, "Darlin, you goin to town, I want you to get Rachel and Calvin some shoes"—they was the two oldest.

Told her, "All right. I'll do that."

She didn't know what number they wore but here's what she done: she went and took the measure of their foots and told me to get em shoes just a little longer than the measure from the heel to the toe. Well, I was fully determined to do it—and that was some of my first trouble.

I drove into Apafalya, hitched my mules, and walked into Mr. Sadler's store to get some shoes for the children first thing; then I was goin to drive on down to the carbox at the depot and load me a load of hulls and meal. Had my cotton bodies on my wagon—

I went on into Mr. Sadler's store and there was a big crowd in there. The store was full of white people and two or three colored people to my knowin. And there was a crippled fellow in there by the name of Henry Chase—Mr. Sadler had him hired for a clerk, and several more, maybe three or four more clerks was in there and some was women clerks. I walked in the store and a white lady come up to me and asked me, "Can I wait on you?"

I told her, "Yes, ma'am, I wants a couple of pair of shoes for my children."

And she took the measures and went on to the west side of the store and I went on around there behind her. She got a ladder, set it up, and she clumb that ladder and me standin off below her. There was a openin between the counters—and I was standin down there, just out of the way of the little swing-door and she was searchin from the front of that store nearly down to where I was.

And this Chase fellow, he was kind of a rough fellow and it was known—a heap of his people there in town didn't like him. So she was busy huntin my shoes and she'd climb that ladder and take down shoes, measurin em, and she'd set em back up if they wouldn't do, didn't come up to that straw measure. And she was just rattlin around there, up the ladder and down it, and this here Chase fellow was standin off watchin. After a while he come around there, showin his hatred, showin what he was made of, that's all it was. And there was a old broke down—it had been cut in two at the bottom—a old, tough brogan shoe sittin there on the counter, a sample, you know. And he walked through there by me to get behind that counter where she was. I was standin on the outside waitin on her patiently, weren't sayin nothin. And he didn't like that white lady waitin on me, that just set him afire—I knowed it was that; I'd never had no dealins with him, no trouble with him noway—and he remarked, "You been in here the longest—" right in my face.

I said, "No sir, I haven't been in here but just a little while."

The white lady spoke up too; said, "No, he hasn't been here very long. I'm tryin to find him some shoes."

He said, "You been in here the longest, you too hard to suit."

I said, "No sir, all I'm tryin to do is buy me some shoes to match the measure for my children's foots."

She said, "No, he hasn't been here but a short while."

Good God, when she said that he grabbed that old shoe up— he didn't like her to speak up for me—grabbed that shoe up and hit at my head with it. I blocked his lick off. Well, when I blocked his lick off—he'd a hit me side the head with that old shoe, or on the face; no doubt he woulda cut me up—he throwed that shoe down. He seed he couldn't hit me with it, I was goin to block him off. He dropped that shoe back down on the counter and out from between there he come and run down to the low end of the store. And Mr. Sadler kept shovels, hoes, plow tools, and every kind of thing down there, on the low end, back end of the store. Chase runned down there and picked him up one of these long-handled shovels and he whirled around and come back—he just showed that he was goin to split me down with that shovel. He come back—he begin to get close to me and I sort of turned myself to him one-sided.

I said, "Don't you hit me with that shovel"—told him to his head, didn't bite my tongue—"don't you hit me with that shovel."

He wouldn't say nothin. Just stood there and looked at me, wouldn't move up on me. Kept that shovel drawed, lookin at me, lookin at me, lookin at me. I just dared him to hit me with that shovel—I never told him what I'd do and what I wouldn't. Well, he stood there and let into cussin. He disregarded that white lady, just stood there with that shovel on him, cussin me, lookin like all he wanted was a chance. I'd a turned my head and he'd a hit me, looked like from the way he acted.

All right. We got up a loud talk and all the people in the store noticed it. After a while, a fellow by the name of Howard Crabtree —old Dr. Crabtree was a horse doctor and this was his son—runned up there and started his big mouth. And this cripple man Chase tellin me all the time, "Get out of here, you black bastard. Get out of here." Tryin to run me out the store and I hadn't done a thing to him.

And this Crabtree, he runned up, "Naw, he aint goin to hit you, but goddamnit, get out of here like he tells you."

I said, "Both of you make me get out. Both of you make me get out."

Couldn't move me. The white lady had done disbanded and got away from there. I stood my ground when this here Howard Crabtree runned up and taken Chase's part. I said, "I aint gettin nowhere. Both of you make me get out."

Chase runned back and put the shovel where he got it from and down the aisle on the far side of the store he went. And there was a ring of guns there, breech-loaders. I kept my eyes on him, watchin him. I weren't goin nowhere. The white lady went on back to huntin my shoes after Chase left from there—he come out from the back of the store and went on down to where that ring of guns was, sittin right in the front as you go in the door. And he grabbed up one of them single barrel breech-loaders—that's when a white man befriended me and several more done so until I left town. There was a white gentleman clerkin in there, Mr. Tom Sherman—I seed this here Henry Chase grab that gun and break it down, run his hand in his pocket and take out a shell and put it in there. Totin shells in his pocket so if anything happened that he needed to shoot somebody—picked up a gun and broke it down and unbreeched it and run his hand in his pocket, pulled out a shell and stuck it in there, then breeched it back up and commenced a lookin for a clear openin to shoot at me. I just considered it for a bluff—he weren't goin to shoot me there in that man's store, surely. And I watched him close, he jumpin around lookin, first one way then the other, holdin that gun in his hands, lookin. And Mr. Tom Sherman just quit his business when he seed Chase drop a shell in that gun, walked right on up to him and snatched the gun away. Chase didn't resist Mr. Sherman—that was a heavy-built man. Mr. Sherman took that gun out of his hands, unbreeched it, took that shell out of it, set the gun back in the ring and stood there by that ring of guns. Out the store Chase went.

Well, by that time, the white lady done got my shoes. I turned around and paid her for em. She wrapped em nice and I took the shoes and went on out the back door—it was handy; I come in the back door and I went back out it. I didn't go down the front. Chase'd gone out of there and I didn't want no trouble with him.

So, out the back door I went and I turned to the left and walked on out in the middle of the street, goin to my wagon. And when I got out to where I could see clear, Aunt Betsey Culver, Uncle Jim Culver's second wife, was sittin in the street on a buggy. Uncle Jim was over there by Sadler's store, he seed all that happened there. I walked up to the buggy and howdyed with my auntie—didn't talk about that trouble neither. I just set my shoes in the foot of the buggy and was standin there talkin with her. And after a while I happened to look down the street and here come that cripple Chase fellow—he was a young fellow too, and he walked in kind of a hoppin way, one leg drawed back—and the police was with him, old man Bob Leech, settle-aged white man. They was lookin for me and they come up to me quick. Chase pointed at me and said, "That's him, standin right yonder; that's him, standin there at that buggy."

Old man Leech walked up to me, looked at me, looked me over. And by me standin kind of sideways at Chase in the store, he done went and told the police that I acted just like I had a pistol in my pocket. Well, he never did see my hand. I had on a big heavy overcoat that day, just what the weather called for. So, he pointed me out to the police; police walked on up to me but wouldn't come right up to me, not very close.

He said, "Consider yourself under arrest."

I looked at him, said, "Consider myself under arrest for what?"

"Uh, consider yourself under arrest."

I asked him again, "Consider myself under arrest for what?"

"That's all right; that's all right."

Come up to me and patted me, feelin for a gun. I said, "You want to search me"—·I just grabbed that big overcoat and throwed it back— "search me, search me, just as much as you please. Search me."

He got up close enough to run his hands around me, feelin my hip pockets. He didn't find no gun. I had no gun, I didn't tote no gun around thataway. He said—he talked kind of through his nose, funny. And I called him in question about every word he spoke to me. He said, "Well, c'mon go with me."

I said, "Go with you where?"

"Gowanup-t-th-maya-uvtawn."

I couldn't understand him.

"Gowanup-t-th-maya-uvtawn."

I said, "To the mayor of town?"

He talkin thataway and I couldn't hardly understand him, talkin through his nostrils, looked like. I understood him but I just kept him cross-talked. Well, I started not to go—my mind told me, 'Go ahead with him, don't buck him.'

He carried me on down the street and hit the left hand side of town goin in—left my shoes in my uncle's buggy. And I went on. Got down there and went up the stairs—the stairsteps come down to the walkway. The mayor of town was upstairs. And by golly, when I got up there, who was the mayor of town? Doctor Collins! Dr. Collins knowed me well, been knowin me a long time. Walked on into his office and old man Leech, the police, spoke to him. And before he could say anything, Dr. Collins seed who was with him. He said, "Why, hello. What you doin with Shaw up here?"

"Well, him and Henry Chase got into it down there in Sadler's store."

Dr. Collins said, "Um-hmm." Dr. Collins was a pretty heavy-built man himself. He said, "Well, Mr. Leech, where is Chase?"

"He down there in town somewhere, in the streets."

"Um-hmm."

"And they got into it in Sadler's store."

"Mr. Leech, go down there and get Chase and bring him up here."

The old police went down and got Chase, brought him up there. He come up hip-hoppin, hip-hoppin—that's the way he walked, doin just thataway every step he took. Chase said, when he got up there, "Hi, Doc."

Dr. Collins said, "Howdy, Henry."

I was standin there listenin. He said, "Henry, did you and this darky—" he wouldn't say nigger neither; that was a white man, and there was some more of em in this country wouldn't call you nigger.

Dr. Collins said, "Henry, did you and this darky get into it down there in Sadler's store?"

He said, "Yeah." But wouldn't tell nary a thing he done, uncalled for. "He was down there in Sadler's store—" wouldn't tell what I was waitin on or nothin, just told what he wanted Dr. Collins to know—"was down there in Sadler's store and we got into it"—wouldn't tell him what we got into it about—"and I told him to get out of there and he gived me a whole lot of impudent jaw."

Dr. Collins said, "Um-hmm. Who seed that beside you, Henry?"

"Well, Howard Crabtree seed it."

And the whole store seed it but none of em weren't busyin theirselves with it. Mr. Tom Sherman seed it and he went and took that gun away from him. Dr. Collins said, "Um-hmm. Well, go down, Mr. Leech, and get Howard Crabtree and bring him up here."

Chase said, "And he kept his hand behind him like he had a gun in his hip pocket."

Crabtree walked up with his big-talkin self. Dr. Collins said, "Crabtree, did you see this darky and Henry Chase get into it down there in Sadler's store?"

"I did. I did. I seed it every bit."

"Well, Crabtree, would you—"

"He had his hand behind him—" told the same lie Chase told —"had his hand behind him and he kept a tellin Chase not to hit him, better not hit him, and givin up a lot of other impudent jaw."

Dr. Collins said, "Um-hmm. Crabtree, would you swear that he had his hand in his hip pocket?"

"No, no"—he jumped back then—"no, I wouldn't swear he had his hand in his hip pocket, but he looked like he had it in there. I don't know where his hand was, he had on that big overcoat."

"Um-hmm," Dr. Collins said, "Um-hmm."

Dr. Collins knowed me well. Never gived nobody no trouble, tended to my business, let other folks alone, I didn't meddle in things. And at that time I had a good name, right there in Apafalya, I'd been there since I was a little boy up till I was grown and after.

Dr. Collins said, "Well, the little old case don't amount to nothin. I'm just goin to throw it out."

After Crabtree told him he wouldn't swear I had my hand in my hip pocket, Dr. Collins asked me, "Shaw, did you have a pistol?"

I said, "No, Doctor, I aint seed a pistol in I don't know when. I had no pistol."

Chase allowed to him, "He went out the back way; he coulda carried it out there and stashed it."

Well, good devil, just as sure as my Savior's at his restin place today, I didn't have no pistol, never thought about no pistol.

All right. They whirled and left from up there when Dr. Collins said he was just goin to throw the little case out. And when they started out, I started out right behind em. Dr. Collins throwed his finger at me—"Shaw, this way; Shaw, Shaw."

I was lookin back at him and I stopped. He said, "Just be yourself and stay up here a few minutes; that'll give em time to get away from down there, clear em out, then you can go."

I just made myself at home, stood there. After a while, Dr. Collins said, "Well, you can go ahead now. Mess don't amount to nothin nohow, that's the reason I throwed it out."

When I got down the stairsteps onto the walkway, there was Mr. Harry Black, man I had done my guano dealin with, and there was a fellow went around there in Apafalya, heap of folks called him Tersh Hog—that was Mr. Bob Soule, went for a cousin to Cliff Soule. He lived out about a mile from Apafalya and he didn't take no backwater off nobody. If a thing weren't right, he were goin to fix it right. Some of em didn't like him because they had to pass around him, white folks. And I seed him walk the streets right there in Apafalya with his pistol in his—just like a law, only he'd carry his pistol in his coat pocket, and that handle was hangin out over the pocket. Didn't nobody give Mr. Bob Soule no trouble in Apafalya and nowheres else he went. So, Mr. Bob Soule was standin there at them steps when I come down, and Mr. Harry Black and Mr. Ed Hardy—I knowed them definitely and there was a couple more of em, bout five altogether standin there when I come down. They said, "Hello, Nate. Hello, Nate."

I stopped and spoke to em polite and they was polite to me. Well, Uncle Jim Culver had done stood there too at the bottom of the steps while this trial business was goin on and he heard them white men speak this: "If that nigger comes down from up there with any charges against him, we goin to paint this damn place red."

I didn't know—I didn't hear em say it. Uncle Jim told me, "They was standin there for a purpose. I done stood here and listened at em. Said, 'If that nigger comes down from up there with any charges against him, we goin to paint this damn place red.' "

All of em knowed me well: I'd traded with Mr. Harry Black and Mr. Ed Hardy and they had passed confidence with me. And Mr. Bob Soule, he loved justice. When I walked down amongst em, all of em, I knowed em, looked in their faces, standin huddled there where the stairway hit the walkway. They was satisfied. They left there when I left.

Uncle Jim added his advice: "Things are hot here, son. Now you go on up the street and get your mules and wagon and turn around and go on back home."

I said to myself, 'The devil will happen before I do that.'

And he said, "Don't come back, don't come back through town. Go on home. Take your mules and go on home now."

I went on up there and pulled my mules back and hitched the traces and untied em from the post they was hitched to—both of em hitched to the same post and them inside traces dropped—set up on my wagon and went just as straight, just as dead straight right back down through Apafalya as I could go. Uncle Jim was standin there and he told some fellow, "There that boy goin right back through town and I told him to get his mules and wagon and go on back home."

But I was game as a peacock. I just went straight to his buggy and got my shoes out and carried em to my wagon, hitched my mules back, crawled up in the wagon over them high bodies, right down dead through town I went. And when I got down close to where the railroad runned under that bridge there in Apafalya I turned to my left and went on down to the depot. Loaded my hulls and meal—and when I left, I had a straight way right out from there up the back streets of town toward home.

One day after that, Uncle Jim got at me bout goin back down through town. I told him, "I aint no rabbit, Uncle Jim. When a man's mistreated thataway and he got friends and they proves it, he don't need to be scared. Of course, it's a dangerous situation and if I'd a been guilty of anything, why, I'd a took low."

There was a old colored fellow down at the door at Sadler's store the whole time this ruckus was goin on inside. Mighta been inside himself at the start but he runned out if he was; he acted like he runned out. And he stood where he could see me. And do you know he just stood there and beckoned to me that whole time, he beckoned to me to run out. That just roused the whole store up. The old man tickled me. He was a pretty heavy-built old man and he weren't as high—his head, he could have walked under a tall horse and never touched it. Heavy-built old colored man. And he had on one of these old frock-tail coats and it hit him just below the knee and it was cut back like a bug's wings. And he just stood there and bowed and beckoned for me to run out there. And every time he'd bow, that old coat would fly up behind him and when he straightened up it would hit him right back there below the bend in his legs. Tickled me, it tickled me. I thought it was the funniest thing I ever saw. He was scared for me and wanted me to run out of there. I didn't run nowhere. I stood just like I'm standin today—when I know I'm right and I aint harmin nobody and nothin else, I'll give you trouble if you try to move me.

HENRY CHASE's daddy kept a hardware store—Mr. Henry Chase. The boy was named after his daddy; only child Mr. Chase had as ever I heard of. I bought a lot of stuff from old man Henry Chase— he always gived me a straight deal. I bought my two-horse plow from him; I bought a Oliver Goober from him, iron-beam plow; and I bought my middle-buster plow, but that middle-buster's wings wore off and I just dogged it out. So I bought them three plows from old man Henry Chase. And durin of the years when I was haulin lumber for the Graham-Pike Lumber Company I bought a cook stove from him; it was called to be a Wetter's range and I carried it home to my wife. Cost me a little more than fifty dollars. And I bought a brand new dinin safe to hold dishware; that thing cost me thirteen dollars. I bought a rubber tire buggy from Mr. Henry Chase, had him to order that buggy on my word, special-built buggy, a Dixie buggy. I gived him a hundred and eighty-seven dollars and a half for that special-built buggy. Mr. Lester Watson, he had buggies and wagons to sell but I didn't want none of his buggies because they was nothin but red painted buggies and this here one I bought from Mr. Chase, it was between a black and a blue color buggy all over. And I bought a pair of heavy mule bridles, fancy everyday bridles made out of good leather, highest priced bridle in the house—O, I spent a lot at his hardware store. And them stores where they kept shoes and dry goods and so on, buyin for my children. Bought a sewin machine for my wife and also she bought a record player, cost sixty-somethin dollars at the time. Even our Bible, it's only now beginnin to get frail, I bought *it* when I was haulin lumber.

At the time I was tradin with Mr. Chase his son weren't in that store, little Henry Chase; I didn't expect to meet up with him there. So one evenin, I'd gone down to the lumberyard, planin mill, and unloaded and I drove back up through town and stopped at the store. And old man Henry Chase weren't in there; young Henry was in there, his son. That was the first time I seed him since him and me got into it down there at Sadler's store and I was surprised to see him. He looked me over—didn't move his head at all, just lookin at me with his eyes. He said, "Shaw"—first words he spoke—"I want some fryin-size chickens; I want some nice fryers. Do you know where you can get me up any? I'll give you a good price if you can get me up six fryers; I want six fryers, nice fryers."

Told him, "Yes, I think I know where I can get em."

He said, "Well, if you have a idea where you can get em, look right around out here to the west side of the store and you'll find some chicken crates."

I went on around there and I found two or three nice chicken crates. Picked up one and set it on the hounds of my wagon, throwed my chain over it to hold it still. And I said, "I'll bring you some fryers when I come back to town."

I was doin good for evil, tryin to. I watched my way through the world and watchin a heap to stay out of trouble, and I couldn't see no tricks in his thoughts. So I went on home with his chicken crates and I told my wife about it. She had some nice fryers and her mother had some nice fryers. I said, "That crippled Chase fellow in Apafalya that I had some trouble with a little while ago, he wants some fryin chickens and he asked me could I get him some. Darlin, you got a lot of fryers here, you want to sell some of em?"

She said, "Well, I can sell some if you think he really intends to buy em."

"Yes," I said, "I think he does." That was a good woman, kind woman, too; she was lookin out for my and her benefit. I said, "Well, I told Henry Chase that I'd bring him six fryers. Tell you what I'm goin to do. I'm goin to give your mother a chance at it too. You catch three of yours and I'll go to your mother"—she generally kept fryers, especially at that season of the year—"and I'll let her put in three, and you all will make out his number, how many he wants, your three and your mother's three."

So, Hannah put in three and her mother put in three—she was glad to do it—and I set them chickens on top of my lumber and drove on to Apafalya and set em off, unloaded my lumber, then put them chickens back on the hounds and drove right on up to Henry Chase's hardware store and delivered em to little Henry Chase. And he told me where he lived, on the street goin out of town toward the Baptist church, white people's church. And he said he lived in a certain house, goin out there on the west side of Apafalya. Wanted me to drive out there and put em off and he paid me nice for em.

So I went on down there to his house and went around to the back door and called. And when I called at the back—he had done come right on down there behind me and when I hitched my mules back and unhitched the traces and tied my lines so they couldn't get away and went around to the back of his house and called, I heard somebody comin across the floor in the hallway—thump, thump, thump, thump, thump. I looked in the door and seed it was him.

"Hi, Nate, glad to see you found me some fryers."

Well, he already knowed that; I done brought them chickens to his daddy's store and he told me to bring em on down and put em off at his house and here he was. He come to the door when I called and acted just like it was news to him. And when I got ready to leave, he told his wife—her name was Celia, John Buchanan's daughter, and he told her, "Celia, this here's the man I been tellin you about. Him and me got into it down at Sadler's store"— wouldn't tell her what we got into it about—"He lacks respect"—he smiled— "but he aint too big to bring us some fryers."

Right to her face. She looked at me and smiled. They both smiled. But I didn't let it worry me; I said, "Well, Mr. Chase and Mrs. Chase, I'm sure these fryers will suit your purpose."

He said, "Yes, Nate, if they don't you'll hear from us." He laughed at that and she just smiled. I got on my wagon, turned them mules out to the road, and hit out for home.

I had people to tell me, "I wouldn't a carried him no chickens."

I said, "I weren't scared of him and I'd favor anybody with kind deeds. He wanted chickens and he promised to pay me nice for em and he did do it. Yeah, I carried em—"

They said, "I wouldn't a carried him no chickens noway."

III

First work I done for the Graham-Pike Lumber Company, Mr. George Pike, who run one of the company's mills, Mr. Ed Pike's brother—had nine big mills in this country and Mr. George Pike run one of those mills right joinin my daddy-in-law's place. And he seen me drivin up there with my mules, good pair of mules, he knowed em, and he come and asked me if I would haul logs for the mill. I bought them mules to farm with—that's strictly what I bought em for—but I meant to patronize that company and to make me somethin workin round them sawmills; I meant to make me a speck if I could and then go back to my farm, quit and go back to my farm.

They started to haulin after the crops was laid by one year and they gived every man a job that had a good pair of mules. White and colored, took em all if they'd work. Had a white snaker and a black snaker; had a white man haulin lumber, had a black man haulin lumber—put anybody to the jobs if they could handle em, if they made em a hand; and if they didn't make em a hand, they'd turn em off.

And Mr. George Pike put me in the woods. As the snaker would snake them logs up to the docks and roll em on the drays, he put me there to steady them logs on the drays—that was my first job —and somebody else snakin. I'd hook them logs up on the docks and help load them drays out as they come to them docks in the woods.

Mr. Ed Pike soon put me to haulin logs. Knowin that I had a good pair of mules that could swing it, it was, "Nate, I want you to haul logs." Hauled logs to the mills two or three days, boss man Ed Pike told me, "Soon as you catch em up good with logs, go on to haulin lumber." They had a yard of lumber with about two hundred and fifty thousand feet, right southeast of my house on the creek. And I started on that haulin regular from the yard to the planin mill in Apafalya. I stuck to that lumber haulin job too; didn't haul logs at all except to catch the mills up when they'd fall behind. Logs was heavier—it was first logs or no lumber, you understand.

Hauled lumber on my wagon up from the creek and out from under them mountains and all and stocked it on top of the hills where the trucks could pick it up. Taken the body off my wagon and set it down somewhere about my house and run a couplin pole in that wagon from the front axle, where it fastened down with a stay-pin, back. Long couplin pole. When a wagon's first bought it's got a short couplin pole just to fit that body; and you can take it out and use a couplin pole to fit the different lengths of lumber you haul —ten-foot lumber the length of that body, twelve-foot lumber, fourteen-foot lumber, sixteen-foot lumber, twenty-foot lumber.

White men drivin them big GMC trucks would pick up them loads of lumber where I left em on the road, done carried em out from under the hills where the sawmills was and hauled it up and out of places them trucks couldn't successfully pull. Them big GMC trucks, had two of em—good God, you might meet em on the road with a load of lumber, looked like a house comin. Mr. Clint Moffat, from Apafalya, he was one of them GMC drivers; Lyman Ridley was the other driver at that time.

I was paid three dollars per thousand feet to haul that lumber up out of hard places and leave it for the trucks. I drawed every week and I commenced a checkin and puttin the weekly amounts together and I drawed as high as two hundred and twenty-five dollars a month, haulin lumber, just me and my mules and wagon. I put up eight months haulin a year at that figure, or near that. It was a lot of money but I had one breakdown with a mule—I gived two hundred and fifty dollars for her. And I was supportin my family—I had a wife and a houseful of children. And I bought that rubber tire buggy from Mr. Henry Chase in Apafalya, and house furnitures. Well, all that et up my money. I hauled lumber for Mr. Ed Pike, Graham-Pike Lumber Company, from Christmas to Christmas for four long years and for parts of other years. And I hauled from two different yards, where there was anywhere from two hundred and fifty thousand to three hundred thousand feet of lumber at each of em at one time. Cut the timber back to where it was a long ways to haul it to the yard and they'd move the mill. So they had lumberyards over this whole country, from the Tukabahchee River clean back to Apafalya; lumber, lumber, lumber, all bought up by the Graham-Pike Lumber Company.

I loved that work. I always was a man that liked workin in the free air. If the sun got too hot I'd set down if I wanted to. Nobody to tell me not to. And if it was rainin, well, he didn't want you to load it and haul it in there wet. After it'd stay in the yard where it'd be sawed and stacked and dried out, he'd have it hauled to the planer in Apafalya for dressin and shippin. And if that lumber was good lumber, it was a pleasure to load—it'd load smooth and it had a nice scent. It waked you up to haul that lumber.

I hauled lumber—I wanted to come in possession of somethin that would profit me but I never did settle my mind on no certain thing. I wanted to boss my own affairs; but I never did let it hit me to want to be a big man, ownin this, that, and the other. I was workin for a livin and I wanted to get to the stand to help myself, regardless to what I accumulated and regardless to what I lost. I wanted to have more privileges, back myself up without havin to beg my way. I was a worker; this whole country knowed me for my work.

One Saturday evenin I was late gettin in to Apafalya with my load. There was always a man in the company office to tell me where to put the lumber. I knowed after I caught on—each grade of lumber to its place. They had a shed covered several acres and in there was lumber on top of lumber, stacked up accordin to the length.

Walked in late that evenin, bout first dark, and there was a heavy-set white gentleman in the office there talkin with Mr. Ed Pike. Mr. Ed turned from him and spoke to me, told me, "Well, Nate, I aint got enough cash without a right smart number of pennies in the deal to pay you. It's too late to go to the bank, it's shut. If it wasn't I'd give you a check. I've got enough money here if you'll accept pennies."

"That's all right, Mr. Ed. Come along with your pennies if you desire. I aint goin to back off." I would always pay my bills around when I drawed my money, if I owed any there around the town. I said, "It's perfectly all right, Mr. Ed, let your pennies roll."

He got busy and counted me a handful of pennies, then paid me the bills. White man standin there lookin. When Mr. Ed gived me them pennies, this white man said, "Ahhhh, you'll be all set for the crap game tonight."

Mr. Ed said, "Uh-uh, uh-uh, not this darky. What he works and makes he carries it home to his wife and children."

Mr. Ed took him up before he could get the words out of his mouth. I don't know who that white man was, meddlin and throwin off on me because it looked like I was a *Negro*. But I didn't let it worry me, I couldn't: it was too common, too common. I just went on my way.

Somedays I'd get ready and unload there at the planer in Apafalya, I'd drive around up through town, fasten my mules to where that they couldn't pull off, go in the store there—Mr. Richard Tucker's store, Lemuel Tucker's uncle—go in there and get me a nice lunch to eat, some sort of canned goods and cheese; but whatever I'd buy, things that suited my taste best, I'd call for enough for my wife and children, and of evenins when I'd go in with my last load of lumber, I'd be thinkin of them at home, where they'd be eatin plenty, which was home grub—they weren't sufferin for nothin —I'd hurry up through town, if I didn't buy it while I was there at day dinner and keep a check on it, take care of it to bring it home, I'd go up there then and call for two or three times the amount to what I would eat, same stuff, put it on the wagon and carry it home to my family. I was a fool about it. I'd buy cheese and other nice tasty things; I wouldn't buy less'n a pound, pound and a half of good cheese—I was born and raised lovin cheese. I loved sardines. Cheese, sardines—I'd carry em home to my family for a special delight. When I'd get home with that cheese, it'd done greased the paper wrapper through and through. Real cheese, crumbly cheese, cheese with a hole through the center, sharp cheese, mild cheese.

I hauled lumber for the Graham-Pike Lumber Company, worked at the sawmill some, and I had to quit. I had a good team and I was rentin a place to farm and I had to do somethin about it. I couldn't buy mules and stand em in the lot and me workin at the sawmill. I had to put them mules to plowin. I told the boss man at the mill, Mr. George Pike—now his brother Ed was the head of the whole thing, but Mr. George Pike and Mr. Jim Pike, Mr. Ed's brothers, they was runnin the mills. And I told Mr. George on Saturday as we was knockin off, at dusk, "Mr. George, I'm sorry to tell you, but I just have to quit and go home and start my plows. I'm forced to quit. I got a place rented that I'm livin on and I got a pair of mules there and I have to go to plowin them mules; they standin in the lot on me since haulin slacked off. And they'll stand there as long as I let em stand and aint carryin on plowin and farm work. I'm sorry I have to quit, I hate to quit, God knows I do, but I can't keep both jobs. My boys is too little to manage the farm."

He put in and prevailed with me, begged me not to quit,

promised to raise my wages—they was well pleased at my labor. I'd work anywhere they put me—haul logs, haul lumber—done more of that job than any other—work at the sawmill. We was sawin on Mr. Oneal's place at the time.

"Well, Mr. George, I hate it, but I'm between two straits. I got to quit. I got my mules standin yonder in the lot and me public workin. My children can't handle them mules and I got to raise a crop on that land."

I had my business cut and dried for farmin; I couldn't do that sawmill job and my farmin both successfully. I'd just as well to sell both my mules outright at that point and take what I could get for em. I had good money tied up in them mules and I couldn't let em stand in the lot and not plow em. And I absolutely had my heart in farmin. I knowed that what little lookin out I had done on the farm brought me up to them high-priced mules and I didn't know definitely at that time bout what the sawmills would bring me. I had it planned at home to make a livin and that's where I decided was my best hope. And so I told him I was goin back to my farm. And he told me to my head—I knowed it was a joke; I had sense enough to know jokes when I heard em—"Nate, you think because you got a damn good pair of mules you goin to come back and haul lumber when the lumber gets dry enough to haul."

I looked at him and laughed.

He said, "Well, I aint goin to let you haul a bit."

I knowed that if he didn't let me haul I was goin to live right on. Mighta been tight or mighta been good, I knowed I was goin to live. Sawmill work weren't goin to keep me eatin. But he was just jokin with me—and besides, he weren't the boss. They done found out what there was to me. So I went on and quit, went on back to my farm.

NEW ground, just as soon as you get done gatherin your crop, at your leisure time break that new ground up; if you get a chance, maybe break it twice—the more you break it the better it will work when it comes time to make your crop.

But before you break your land, you better go ahead, knowin that spring is comin after winter—you got to cut and saw you up enough wood and haul it up and cord it to do you that crop season comin, so you'll have no trouble and no outside work to take you from your crop. That's one thing you got out the way; you got your wood prepared even before you start breakin your land.

New ground, you must tear it up before Christmas. The average way to do it, put you on a scooter, diamond-point scooter or a bull-tongue scooter—you got to use a small plow in there amongst them stumps. If you plow deep you'll stall that mule workin new ground that way, owin to the size of the mule and his weight—you can fix any of them plows in a way that a animal just can't hardly pull em. If he pulls em he aint goin to last pullin em. New land, fresh land, it aint been plowed of recent years, you can break two to three acres a day as well as it's due to be broke with one plow and a good animal.

Any boy that's big enough to plow can break new ground or he can plow in old land where it's clear of stumps. But I didn't put my chaps in rough places and look for my work to be done; I hung around there and helped. Some jobs I'd do em by myself, let the boys hang around there enough to see how it was done.

When I was a boy comin along, and I seen plenty of it after I got grown, a man would get out there and take a hickory club about the length of a good long walkin stick, somethin that'll stand, and beat them cotton stalks down, along in January. Walk on his feet across his land, and if he aint got a stalk cutter, take that seasoned hickory stick or seasoned oak stick, somethin stout that won't break easy, walk them rows, just gradually walkin steady, and beat down two rows at once. Them stalks done got dry and brittle in winter, and doggone it, if he can't eat em up and cut em low as his ankle to the ground. But the best way to get them stalks is to take a stalk cutter, hitch a pair of mules to it, and drive all over that field—there's a seat up there for you to sit on—that stalk cutter just eatin up them stalks. Pick your chances when them stalks is dry and in just two or three days you'll cut your stalks, cuttin stalks with a cotton-stalk cutter on a two-horse farm.

Now you got your stalks cut down, or if it's new ground that you done broke up once or twice in the fall, you ready to make your crop. Catch a seasonable time when the ground's in good shape to plow, as early as you can—don't plow it wet. There's a time to all things; you mustn't plow your land wet, wait until it gets in the right attitude to plow. Sometimes it don't make no difference when you plow; big rains will pack it back just as hard as it ever was. You got trouble on your hands then, you got to re-plow it.

I plowed, in plowin my mules, I'd take my two-horse plow, jump in there right after Christmas, take my stalk cutter, hitch my mules to it, and cut my stalks just as soon as they was dry enough that they'd break good. When that was done, I'd go on and get my wood all in for my year's cookin; then get my land broke with my two-horse plow—I've tried it all sorts of ways. Sometimes I'd break my land maybe two or three weeks, a month before I got ready to plant. I'd go back, that land was just like it never been plowed. It showed it'd been plowed, but doggone it, it was packed again tight as wax. Some years I broke my land early—that gived the vegetation and the cotton stalks a chance to rot up some; and the land would pack back or not pack back, accordin to conditions I couldn't control.

I don't say breakin your land and gettin it ready in January is the only way. You got plenty of time, you on time if you have it prepared by the first of April. But if you don't, you better hustle like the diggers to get it ready or you'll make a feeble crop. Jump in there the first of April and you might have a little you want to rebreak or even a patch that aint been broke, but the majority is ready for plantin. The best way, if you don't want to lose a corn crop, regardless to the cotton, if you want to make a cotton crop and corn crop too, successfully, you get out there and hustle and watch the time, be on time the first time because sometimes you might have to plant that crop over; you don't know. If you can't be on time—you must use your time, a heap of times, when God gives it to you. God's a man, you can't start His time, you can't stop it. Some folks don't use the time God gives em; that's why they're liable to come up defeated.

You done got that land broke and prepared. Your last preparin before your plantin come along is this: you take a middle-bustin plow—that land broke, in good shape—that's a plow that carries two wings, throwin dirt each way, makes you a nice bed. Take your middle-bustin plow and go over your land and lay it off. Whatever width you want your rows, if you a plow hand and knowin what to do about it, you can make your cotton rows three and a half—that's the average cotton row—three and a half foot wide. And it's owin to the land; if it's rich land you better not crowd it up there too close. Rich land, well-prepared land, sure-enough good land, better

not lay your rows down under four foot, four-foot rows; if it's thin
land you can close them rows down to three foot. Rich land, grows
a big weed, you usin a whole lot of fertilize, that'll make that cotton
get up and get.

You a mule farmer, runnin plows, walkin behind em and doin
your own plowin, if you make a big crop or a little crop, you have
everything set by April to get your seed in the ground. You can go
ahead and plant your cotton first if you want to; you can plant
your corn first. As a rule, if a man is fitted up for farmin, he's got
a good cotton-seed planter. I've owned two different kinds of
planters. I've owned what they call a rake planter and I've owned
what was a one-armed planter, one arm just worked off the side of
the seed box droppin the seeds. But this rake planter has two arms
to it and a box that'd hold a pailful of seed to start off. You don't
have to put down many seeds to a row to get a stand if the weather's
suitable. And it'd just drop them seeds right along regular, them
two arms runnin.

I'd always run my planter myself—any particular job you
want to get a decent stand you put a careful hand at it—and one
of my boys maybe, if he was big enough to work at it, he'd take a
spring-toothed harrow—it's a tool that you walk behind just like a
plow stock and it carries a whole line of teeth, one mule pullin it;
it aint no trouble for one mule to pull. You can catch hold to it and
lay them teeth clean back on each side so it sits in the shape of a
V; and everything them teeth catches on that bed it'll shed off like
a comb. I've seed people take a old heavy slab of oak and bore a
auger hole through it and drive a heel-bolt in there and put it on
a scooter plow stock to use in place of a harrow. If it's smooth land
that slab will drag the bed off level.

That planter, rake planter or some other grade of planter,
hitch a mule to it right behind your harrow. That rake planter has
a spoon bout as wide as my two fingers that runs into the ground
just ahead of them seeds and them seeds feedin out right behind
that spoon. Don't just go out there in that field with that planter
and let it wiggle and woggle every sort of way. If you do, your stuff
aint goin to come up to no sort of line. Notice your business, know
how to go at it—I always tried to grow straight lines of crops and
if I didn't succeed it was just because I put the wrong boy to handle
the plantin if I didn't care to do it myself. Plant all over your field,
plowin with a pair of mules, one knockin off the bed and one pullin

the planter, plant ten acres in two days or less—if you get out there and work and go on time.

You take a guano distributor that you walk behind, just like a plow stock only it's got a big box to it, and get on that bed with one mule and put out your guano before you put down your seed. And then that knock-off runnin light right behind it, a light knock-off with your harrow. You mustn't let the teeth of that harrow down into the ground where it'll tear that bed up—don't disturb that bed, just knock it off gently.

If you take a notion to put a addition to the growth of your crop and the amount that you make to the acre, you go back there when you scratch around that cotton and chop it—you loosenin up the dirt then—why, take that distributor and put another application of guano around your crop. Them plants goin to get the benefit of that guano when the feed roots spread out. Now the brace root of a cotton plant, what you call the tap root, it goes down there sometimes four foot, huntin moisture. And them feed roots puts out from that tap root, clean across the middles, all around that cotton.

If the weather's just right, you can plant the first days of the week and by the middle of the next week, you got a pretty stand of cotton all over your field. Cotton and weeds all come up together and when they come up the weeds beats the cotton growin. Just as soon as that cotton will bear your cultivators, when it's just bustin the ground, drop your fenders on your mule plow and work that cotton. That fender bolted to your plow beam—it won't allow the dirt to fall in them drills and stop that cotton comin up.

Just as soon as that cotton gets up to a stand, best time to chop it out provided you feel that the cold won't get what you leave there. But you don't always know about that. If you chop it too early, decidin wrong about what the weather's goin to do, you go out there and thin out your crop, that bad weather come and get the balance of it. Or you might chop it wrong if you don't have the experience of it. You'll be diggin out too deep, guano and all, and you'll bruise the plants. But if you chop it out right and the weather don't change on you, it stays mild and in favor of growin, what you leave there will make a good crop.

Dry weather can cut the growth of that cotton to an extent. Too much rain can cause it to overgrow itself. Cotton's a sun weed, cotton's a sun weed. Too much water and it'll grow too fast, sap runs too heavy in the stalk and it'll make more stalk than cotton. Cotton is a kind of sunflower; it just takes so much rain. You can make a good cotton crop a heap of times in a dry summer, owin to how much rain you had in the spring. Anyway, you just runnin a risk farmin; you don't know whether you goin to win or lose. You can bet on it ever so much, but sometimes you lose your bet and if you a poor farmer, you in a hole then. It's a heap like gamblin—you don't know what you goin to win, you don't know what you goin to lose. You take a farmin man out there, he dependin on his cotton and his corn. He don't know till he gather it what he goin to get, if he goin to get enough to come up even. I believe a man can put too much trust in his crop; he'll bet too heavy on it and he's subject to lose. He's takin a desperate risk. How can you get out there and plant any kind of a seed—cotton, corn, peas, tomatoes, vegetable seed of any kind, of the least and the most, what's about *you* to make it sprout and come up? What's about you? You got no power. God got the power. But God has got a part for you to do—He aint goin to come down here and plant nary a seed of no sort for you. God aint goin to come down here and run nary a furrow out there in that field, plow that ground up—He aint goin to do it. He give you wisdom and knowledge to do it. But if you set around and don't do nothin, won't work, you burnt up, you hear? God fixes it so, He's so merciful and kind—you can't sprout no seed, but go to work and tear up that land and plant that seed yourself. God requires you to do it and if you don't, He aint goin to come down here and do it. Still and all, think about it: the power's in the Almighty. You can't make your seed grow! It takes sunshine and water to make vegetables come up—sunshine when He sees fit to send it, water when He sees fit to send it. You get out here and do your part, what He put you here to do, because God aint goin to do your labor, He aint goin to do it.

I've made a crop more or less every year, come too much rain or too much sun. I've had my cotton grow so fast as to grow to a weed. I've picked from many a stalk of cotton that growed so high until it was just a stalk, not many bolls I'd get off it. On the other hand, when the seasons just hit right, I've had stalks of cotton weren't no more than three foot high, just layin down with bolls. It don't take the tallest cotton to make a big crop.

In the year 1912, second crop I ever made on Miss Hattie Lu Reeve's place, good God it come a snap—and my cotton should have been thinned out, by right, but I weren't done choppin it out. And it come a cold day and and it sleeted on my crop. Done that again the next year, sleeted on that cotton in May, 1912, and 1913, too. And that cotton turned yellow as a fox and shedded off every leaf on it, but left the buds. I examined it and it looked terrible—in a day or two when the weather moderated, I examined my little old cotton and seed it was still alive, and them buds, after the sun hit em good, turnin hot after the snap of weather, little old cotton buds just kept livin and commenced a puttin out, flourishin. I just chopped it regular when I seed all that. And when I laid that cotton by, plowed it and put the dirt to it, it still looked weak and yellow. But it wouldn't die, it just kept a comin, kept a comin until it come out and made me that year eight good bales of cotton—1913. That was a high production for a one-horse farm. In them days people didn't make a bale to the acre. I had about eleven or twelve acres under cultivation and it weren't no first class land. But it was smooth land, easy to work.

There's a ought hoe; and then there's a number one and there's a number two—light-bladed hoes. I didn't use these heavy-bladed goose-necked hoes. But I used what it took to chop out a plant with one hoe lick. You got to be a careful hand—cotton is young and tender when you chop it; hit it just a light lick, just a light lick on smooth land. On the average, I'd leave ten inches between the plants, all across my field.

Owin to when it was planted, if it was planted any time after the first days of April on up until the middle of April, that cotton will be bloomin, if you treat it right, the last of May. Dry weather, reasonable dry weather, it takes to make a good crop of cotton. If it sets out to rain a whole lot and that cotton is highly fertilized, it's goin to make more weeds than cotton. But a reasonable good cotton season come along, that cotton will grow on up there and them branches will just roll off with squares. And as them squares grow they'll bloom; keep a growin just a short period of time, it won't be many days after that square comes out that it's bloomin. And when it blooms, it'll bloom today, you see them blooms come out of a mornin, between mornin and dinner your field is just shinin with cotton blooms. Well, they'll go through tomorrow very well. After your cotton blooms out there full bloom, by sometime late tomorrow night, or not over two days, them blooms will fall; and behind em, there's your little boll. When the bloom falls the boll is right behind, and that little boll aint a bit bigger than the tip of your little finger. That boll goin to grow then; won't be many days until it's a great big boll and it keeps growin till it gets fully matured. Cotton will make what it's goin to do in fifteen days; it'll do it or lose it in fifteen days. A stalk of cotton bout three and a half foot high, if everything suited it, that stalk'll produce a hundred bolls, sometimes more than that. It'd be so heavy with bolls until it couldn't stand up.

We hand-picked that cotton, all of it. Five years old, that's big enough to pick many a little handful, and my daddy had me out in the field pickin cotton before that. And I picked until I picked many a hundred pounds for my boy Vernon, for four years after I quit foolin with it myself. When I quit off pickin for Vernon I was able to pick as much as a hundred pounds a day—that was a little help to him. I been able, pickin regular on my own farm, to pick up to three hundred pounds a day. The Bible says, once a man and twice a child—well, it's that way pickin cotton. I picked at the end of my cotton pickin days how much I picked at the start.

I always picked clean cotton, practically clean of trash, no burrs, no whole bolls in it, or I coulda picked a greater weight than I done. Cotton I picked was worth the full price that cotton would bring. That was my native way of pickin cotton. Get that lint just as clean as I could and leave the boll behind, not grab leafs and every other kind of trash.

Gathered that cotton from when it first opened up, around the latter part of August or the first week in September, and right through till it was all gathered. White man get out there and raise a big crop of cotton—when I was a boy and after I was grown, every little Negro chap in the whole country around, as far as he had time to go get em, go get em and put em in his field pickin cotton. And his little crowd, maybe, if he had any chaps, they'd be pickin some on off-hours of school. Come home and go to pickin cotton. But mainly it was nigger children gathered the white man's crop when I come along. And if a chap had in mind that he didn't want to pick this man's cotton—chaps knowed whose cotton it was— mama and papa was sufficient to make him pick it. Carry that child out, some of em, in a white man's field, they'd work his little butt off with a switch if he didn't gather that cotton. You'd find some industrious white people that would work like colored; they was poor people, they'd get out there and pick. But ones that didn't

care so much about stoopin down and pickin cotton, their cotton got
ready—the little nigger chaps wasn't goin to school; scoop em up
like flies and put em in the field.

Picked cotton in a sack—that's how we done it in this country,
and other cotton countries I've heard spoke of. Put a sack on,
long sack, sometimes the sack would be draggin behind you far
enough that a little chap could walk up on the end of it. You'd have
a strap to that sack, cross your chest and over your shoulder,
resemblin to a harness, and the mouth of that sack right under
your arm; you'd pick cotton and just drop it in there. That sack'd
hold a full hundred pounds.

Take that sack and empty it in a big basket, cotton basket.
White man would set it in his field, or a Negro, if it was his field
and he had baskets. I used my own baskets, I made cotton baskets.
Didn't pick my crops no other way but empty the cotton out of the
sack and into the basket, and that relieved my sack, the weight of
it on me, that would take it off, any amount of cotton I had picked
in my sack.

I'd take my wagon to the field after me and my children done
picked several baskets of cotton, stand it there and go to emptyin
that cotton in the wagon. Set them baskets out there to keep a
gatherin. I could nicely weigh my cotton in a basket then throw it
on the wagon. Weighed my cotton right there, as I loaded it. My
wife had good book learnin, she'd take the figures to the house—I
could make figures but I didn't know enough to add em up; give
her the book with the cotton figures on it, she'd add it up and tell
me when I got a bale. That wagon had to move out of the field
then.

On to the barn and empty the cotton in my cotton house, on
the floor—it'd stay dry in there. That cotton house would be sealed
superior to a dwellin house. Come time to make a bale, I'd drive my
wagon up to the door of that house and load it all out, take it to
the gin. Anywhere from, averagely, twelve to fourteen hundred
pounds at a load: loose cotton, seed cotton, ready to go to the gin.
Make a five-hundred-pound bale after ginnin. The rest of the weight
went for seed and trash.

From my first startin off farmin after I married, even workin
on halves, I had to carry my cotton to the gin. And when I got
to where I rented, I'd gin at any gin I wanted to. I had mules able to
do it; hitch them mules to my wagon, take em to the field; take

em from the field to the barn; pull out from the barn to the gin. Drive up under a suction pipe; that suction would pull that lint cotton off the wagon and into them gins and the gins would gin it out—separate the lint from the seed and the seed would fall in a box. Another pipe carried the seed overhead from that box to a seed house out yonder. Didn't have nothin to do but go out there and open up that seed-house box and catch all my seed. Cotton went from the gin machines to a press—all them seeds and whatever trash was picked with that cotton done been ginned out. And a man at the press would work a lever and the press would press the cotton down into a box the shape of a bale so he could bale it off. He'd already have a underbaggin under it and he'd pull the top baggin down and wrap that cotton up, fasten them hooks, and bale it.

It was their job to roll out the bale and load it on your wagon. When the bale was wrapped and the ties was pulled and the press was lifted off the bale, workmen there would get behind it and push it out. If the gin was runnin proper, I might be in and out of that gin operation in less than thirty minutes. I have gone to the gin of a mornin, looked at the situation: the yard would be covered with wagons with loads of cotton, trucks sometime. Before I quit raisin cotton, they'd haul that cotton there on trucks and them trucks might have anywhere from two to three bales—a ton, ton and a half of seed cotton. Well, I'd go in and talk with the ginner; he'd tell me about when my time would come. Take out my mules from my wagon and go home, leave my wagon standin there with my cotton, come back late that evenin or the next day. And I'd better be back on time; if I didn't, several bales would be runned in ahead of me. They observed your turn strictly, for white and colored. It was mighty seldom that anybody would go ahead of your wagon. And while we was waitin our turns, white and colored, we'd talk about our crops and how much more we had at home and how much we done ginned and what the cotton was bringin that year.

I always ginned for cash money, so much a bale. A bale of cotton, it'd cost to put the baggin and ties on it, ginnin and all, anywhere from five to six or seven dollars a bale. Sometimes I'd sell the seeds to the ginner and the seed out of one bale of cotton would pay for ginnin two bales. But I always reserved enough seed for myself to have it for my next crop—very seldom did I buy cotton seed. I tried to have as good a grade of cotton as anybody and I kept my seed as long as I got satisfaction with my cotton at the market.

Right there and then, and aint aimin to sell that cotton, you take that cotton back home and dump it off your wagon. It's used, startin at home—my mother, after the cotton come back from the gin, seed removed and leave the pure lint, I've seen her take a pair of cards, two cards each about as wide as my four fingers, and it's made in the resemblance and in the manner and in the style of a mule brush. And she'd take one in one hand and lay a handful of that cotton on it, take the other card and comb it—that's called cardin batts—then change cards and comb it the other way until she got a nice clear batt of cotton in them brushes. And she'd have a quilt linin stretched out in the house and she'd take that batt of cotton, nice wad of cotton, and lay them batts all over that quilt; she could lay em as thick or thin as she wanted, then spread the next layer of cloth over it and sew the top layer and the bottom layer together around the edge—sewin that cotton in there and pullin it just tight enough to make it flat like she wanted a quilt. And when she sewed as far as she could reach, then she'd roll that quilt, take it loose from the corners of her frames, pull out them nails or small spikes and roll that quilt under, roll it under, just get it far enough, close enough, far as she could reach with her hand sewin. She'd do all around that quilt thataway, from one corner to the other. Had a bed quilt then, warm quilt, plied through with cotton.

They don't do that now worth nothin—that proves how long I been in this world. Buy blankets in stores and they fall apart on your bed, just layin there. I've knowed my wife to make a quilt or two and sell it, one that we didn't need for home use. And she didn't labor noway but what she got the benefit of it and the profit. I always thought like this: if I couldn't make it out there in that field and on some of the other jobs I followed, I weren't goin to make it noway. What I want to follow up behind her and exact her money? Low-down, half-assed scalawag—I wouldn't never a been guilty of such a trick.

All women born and raised up the age of my wife, their mothers knowed about makin quilts and they taught their daughters. But that was the end of the line for quilt makin in this country.

IF you want to sell your cotton at once, you take it to the market, carry it to the Apafalya cotton market and they'll sample it. Cotton buyin man cuts a slug in the side of your bale, reaches in there and pulls the first of it out the way and get him a handful, just clawin in there. He'll look over that sample, grade that cotton—that's his job. What kind of grade do it make? You don't know until he tells you. If it's short staple, the devil, your price is cut on that cotton. Color matters too, and the way it was ginned—some gins cuts up the cotton, ruins the staple.

They had names for the cotton grades—grade this, or grade that or grade the other. Didn't do no good to argue with the man if you didn't agree with the grade. Thing for you to do if he graded your cotton, examined it and gived you a low bid, take it to the next man.

Much of it is a humbug just like everything else, this gradin business. Some of em don't pay you what that cotton's worth a pound. They want long staple, clean cotton: the cleaner and the prettier it is and the nearer it comes to the specification of the staple they lookin for, the more they'll offer you. Generally, it's a top limit to that price and that's what they call the price cotton is bringin that year. If it's forty-cent cotton or six-cent cotton, it don't depend much on *your* cotton. It's a market price and it's set before you ever try to sell your cotton, and it's set probably before you gin your cotton and before you gather it or grow it or even plant your seed.

You take that cotton and carry it around to the cotton buyers. You might walk in that market buildin to a certain cotton buyer and he'll take your sample and look it over, look it over, give it a pull or two and he just might if he's very anxious for cotton, offer you a good price for it. But if he's in no hurry to buy your cotton and he gives you a price you don't like you can go to another buyer.

Heap of em buyin that cotton to speculate; he got plenty of money, wants to make more money, he buyin that cotton for himself and he don't care what company buys it from him. Maybe he might be buyin for a speculatin company, a company what does business in speculation. Or he might be buyin for a company that uses that cotton. Or if he can handle the matter, he buys for two companies.

Niggers' cotton didn't class like a white man's cotton with a heap of em. Used to be, when I was dealin with them folks in Apafalya, some of em you could have called em crooks if you wanted to; they acted in a way to bear that name, definitely. Give a white man more for his cotton than they do you.

I've had white men to meet me on the streets with a cotton sample in my hand, say, "Hello, Nate, you sellin cotton today?" White men, farmers like myself, private men; some of em was poor white men.

I'd tell em, "Yes sir, I'm tryin. I can't look like get what my cotton's worth."

"What you been offered?"

"Well, Mr. So-and-so—"

"O, I see here such-and-such a one offered you so-and-so-and-so—"

Heap of times the scaper that I offered to sell him my cotton had a knack of puttin his bid on the paper that the cotton was wrapped up in. I didn't want him to do that. The next man would see how much this one bid me and he wouldn't go above it.

And so, I'd have my cotton weighed and I'd go up and down the street with my sample. Meet a white man, farmin man like myself, on the street; he'd see what I been offered for my sample—the buyer's marks would be on the wrapper—or I'd tell him. And he'd take that sample, unwrap it, look at it; he'd say, "Nate, I can beat you with your own cotton, I can get more for it than that."

Aint that enough to put your boots on! The same sample. He'd say, "Let me take your sample and go around in your place. I can beat what they offered you."

Take that cotton and go right to the man that had his bid on it and he'd raise it; right behind where I was, had been, and get a better bid on it. I've gived a white man my sample right there on the streets of Apafalya; he'd go off and come back. Sometime he'd say, "Well, Nate, I helped you a little on it but I couldn't help you much."

And sometime he'd get a good raise on it with another fellow out yonder. He'd bring my sample back to me with a bid on it. "Well, Nate, I knowed I could help you on that cotton."

That was happenin all through my farmin years: from the time I stayed on the Curtis place, and when I moved to the Ames place, and when I lived with Mr. Reeve, and when I moved down on

Sitimachas Creek with Mr. Tucker, and when I lived up there at Two Forks on the Stark place, and when I moved down on the Pollard place and stayed there nine years. Colored man's cotton weren't worth as much as a white man's cotton less'n it come to the buyer in the white man's hands. But the colored man's labor—that was worth more to the white man than the labor of his own color because it cost him less and he got just as much for his money.

I wasn't raisin under five and six bales of cotton every year that I stayed on the Bannister place. Raised corn—I kept my corn to feed my stock, met all my expenses with cotton and what I was makin off my lumber haulin job. I didn't never want for no vegetable, what I had I growed em. Okra, anything from okra up and down— collards, tomatoes, red cabbages, hard-headed cabbages, squash, beans, turnips, sweet potatoes, ice potatoes, onions, radishes, cu- cumbers—anything for vegetables. And fruits, fruits for eatin pur- poses and cookin, pies, preserves—apples, peaches, plums, water- melons, cantaloupes, muskmelons. I quit growin muskmelons for one reason: they got to where some years the worms would take to em. They is a different melon to a watermelon. The inside of a muskmelon is yellow like the inside of a cantaloupe—they're good tastin, sweet. Cut em open and scrape the seed out of em, sprinkle if you like a little salt over em. Sometimes I've seen people sprinkle a little black pepper over em too.

I raised many a crop of ice potatoes but you had to keep them ice potatoes sprinkled for bugs, anointed. Just planted enough for family use as long as they'd last. Same with sweet potatoes—I'd store em, put em in a bank. Sometimes I'd have four banks of sweet potatoes, and the seed ones in a kiln to theirselves and the eatin ones to theirselves. Clean out a wide space for whatever number of potatoes I had to bank, accordin to the amount I raised. Cut me out a big circle, made it flatter in the center than at the outer edges, and put me a layer of pine straw in there, then salt my potatoes and pour em in there until I had a big pile. Then I'd cover em sufficient with pine straw and if I thought they needed it, I'd use somethin like pasteboard, apply it around that bank to keep the dirt from runnin on the potatoes, take my shovel and ditch all around them banks, pile the dirt up to the top—just leave a hole enough at the top of the bank for the potatoes to get air. Sometimes I'd even put a tin top, bought tin, over it to keep out the rain. I'd have potatoes then for table purposes way up in the spring of the year. Eventually they'd lose their sweetness and get pethy. Chop em up then and feed em to my stock, mules if it was necessary; but I always had plenty of corn without havin to feed my mules sweet potatoes. But hogs, I'd feed my hogs on em a plenty.

I had my own cows to milk—my children started to milkin on the Bannister place, my oldest boy and oldest daughter and still their mother wasn't milkin. They milked when I couldn't milk. After them children got to be nine years old they helped me regular. I went to the lot and showed em how to milk and they was glad to learn. My wife didn't have to milk no cow; she didn't have to go to the field, I'd drive her out the field.

And I killed all the meat we could use until I killed meat again —from winter to winter. I had a white man walk through my yard— two of em, Mr. Albert Clay and Mr. Craven. I don't know Mr. Craven's given name but that was Mr. Clay's brother-in-law. Come through my yard one Saturday evenin and I had killed three big hogs, me and my little boys, and had em stretched out over the yard after I cut em up.

They walked up to my back yard on the north side of the house —that old house I was livin in was built east and west—and they come up from towards my barn. I was surprised in a way but I didn't let it worry me, people go where they want to and walk anywhere they want to. Mr. Albert Clay and Mr. Craven come up from towards my barn. My barn set west of the house and back behind the barn was my pasture. Well, they come right up cross the back yard—that yard was covered with meat from three big hogs I'd just killed and had the meat put out; it was all of nine hundred pounds of meat. They looked there in that yard and stools, boxes, tables, benches, and everything had planks across em and them planks was lined with meat, just killed and cut out. Dressed, gutted, and cut open but not fully cut up, layin out, ready for salt.

Mr. Craven made a big moderation. "Where'd you get all this meat, Shaw? What are you goin to do with all this meat?"

It was all over the yard, coverin everything in sight. Three great big hogs weighed over three hundred pounds apiece. Had more meat there than you could shake a stick at.

"That's more meat than ever I seed any nigger—" that's the way he said it—"I aint never seed that much meat that no one nigger owned it."

They looked hard, didn't stop lookin. After a while they crept on out of there, still stretchin their eyes at that meat. They didn't like to see a nigger with too much; they didn't like it one bit and it caused em to throw a slang word about a "nigger" havin all this, that, and the other. I didn't make no noise about it. I didn't like that word, but then that word didn't hurt me; it was some action had to be taken to hurt me. I just rested quiet and went on preparin that meat.

So, I begin to insist on the boys—I had a brand new rubber tire buggy, I bought it from Mr. Henry Chase in Apafalya, had him to order it special for me. I told the boys to catch one of the mules out of the barn and hitch him to that rubber tire buggy. I was right ready, I was rushin to get off to town and get me a sack of salt. Told em, "Go to the lot and catch Mattie, brush her off and hitch her to that buggy." Brand new harness at that time, brand new buggy.

I jumped in that buggy and went straight to Apafalya quick as I could without runnin my mule to death. I didn't never call her for nothin but a ordinary trot. She was a good mule, she answered me—I've owned some mules as good as this country ever seed; I've owned as high as four head of stock at once in my barn—that's where my trouble come. Many a year I didn't ask nobody to furnish me nothin. I've seed the time when I was haulin—I got too high, I reckon, and it made a damnation on me. Some of the white folks wanted my hide.

Well, I didn't get two miles and right there at Highgate, Mr. Craven had a son livin up there, called him Doc Craven. He lived on the left of the road right along there before you get to Zion. I looked out and seed Mr. Doc Craven walkin along the road a short distance this side of his house.

He hollered, "Let me ride in there, let me ride in there."

I was goin to Apafalya to get me some salt; I stopped the mule and buggy—and that mule was just as fat as a pig, she just wobbled almost in the harness between the shafts. Mr. Craven climbed in my buggy, raised up and looked around. Said, "God-damn, there aint many white folks got a outfit like this, and no niggers—" throwin that slang just like his daddy done in my yard a few minutes before.

I didn't say a word. I said to myself, 'I didn't haul you up here to hear that shit.' I got him right to his house, stopped and let him off. Well, I thought over his comment and what his daddy had said. One made a moderation at my meat, the other, here he was makin a moderation at my mule and buggy. It just fell in my mind that the Craven family hated to see niggers livin like people.

I carried him home and stopped. I'd picked him up way down the road below his house—don't know what business he had in the road and didn't try to find out. It was none of my business. I just picked him up and pleasured him to a ride on home. At that present time he was livin in a house that I do definitely know it was built for a Negro, built for John Ivey, a nigger. The house was right on the public line; white folks didn't like to see niggers livin right on the front—that was well known amongst the niggers.

Well, I was a Negro of this type: regardless to what people said, regardless to how much I knowed that they was a enemy to me, I just pulled myself along anyhow to the best of my abilities and knowledge. Didn't hold myself back like they wanted me to. So that man that spoke that word about my meat, then I went on up the road and done his son a favor, picked him up and carried him home, cut him out of some of that walkin, and he jumped up and admired my mule and buggy in a way that made it clear he didn't like to see no nigger have a outfit like that—and it would have made him spiteful to see a *white* man with it—happened all one evenin.

TIME I could get my crop planted and laid by, here come Mr. George Pike, goin by Mr. Ed's orders, put some men to haulin lumber. And he come to my house a bustin.

"Nate, the lumber's dry enough to haul. Why don't you put your wagon on the road and go to haulin?"

He changed his song right there. I picked up that pair of mules, hitched em up, and crawled right on the job. They was haulin from a yard of lumber just south of me right joinin my daddy-in-law's plantation, up a big swamp. Mr. Ed gived us three dollars a thousand to haul that lumber in to the planer at Apafalya. Shipped that lumber out of there, every bit of it, shipped it on the railroad. I didn't know where it was goin. That lumber run right out from under the shed where the planin machine was set; had a man standin there feedin it in, and it goin right up in a carbox. And a man, one or two men in that carbox catchin that lumber, drawin it in, stackin it.

Put me in there haulin that lumber; put white men in there with their teams. Put Mr. Horace Tucker in there, Lemuel Tucker's brother, him drivin a pair of mules; and Mr. Horace's son, Estes Tucker, he was big enough to drive. Mr. Horace would come in there, him and Estes drivin a pair of mules apiece to two wagons. Mr. Horace would help load Estes' wagon and his'n too, and him and Estes would take off to that planer. Mr. Ben Stark was in there with a team, haulin, and I don't know who-all else; two or three more white men with their teams in there haulin. I was in there haulin.

When we hauled that first yard in to Apafalya, me in with that white crowd, Mr. Ed was payin us three dollars a thousand— Ooooooo, that just ruined some of the people, that's no lie. I hated to see it, but then if a man bring a thing on himself, why, he just out of luck; I can't help him. They runned in there, soon as they cleaned that yard up—I carried the last load in from that yard. Mr. Horace Tucker and them had done runned in there with their last loads and I was behind em, carryin in my last load, and wanted to find out from Mr. Ed Pike where was the next yard he wanted to haul from. He told em. They jumped up, bein white folks—but they got the wrong hog by the ear when they told Mr. Ed Pike the words that they told him—they told me that they told him when he told em what was the next yard, "We can't haul that yard as cheap as we hauled this other yard." Wanted more money for haulin that yard than they got for the yard they just finished. What did he tell em? I heard definitely what he told em; he didn't tell me but some other parties was standin listenin at the subject. He told em, "Well, I'm runnin my own business. If you can't haul at the price I'm offerin you—now, boys, I'm lettin you all haul, farmers and all, if you got stock sufficient to haul that lumber in to me. I'm goin to pay a reasonable price that you can live on to help the poor class of people and the farmin people, givin you a job after your crop is laid by. I aint obliged to hire you; I'm doin that to help the people of the community. And if you can't haul at my price, go home and put your damn mules in the lot and stay off the job."

That day we went in with our last loads, I didn't question him about it; he just come up and spilled it to me himself, told me,

"Well, Nate, I cut off them white fellows—" told me who-all they was. I hated to hear that. Mr. Horace Tucker was one of the ones he cut off; he always appeared to be a friend of mine. I didn't know his heart but I knowed what he done, how he acted and what he said. I hated to hear Mr. Ed Pike call off them white men's names— told em to go home and put their damn mules in the lot, turned em out. He didn't tell me what he said to em but other parties heard the conversation. Told em he weren't obliged to hire none of em, he was lettin em haul to help em. Well, that was true, in a way, but lumber don't walk to the mill. He stopped em cold from the shoulder then; there weren't no comeback to em.

I went on to the next yard where he directed me. There weren't no white men at that time real eager to go back with him because all the white people that was haulin from that yard where I started haulin from, he done stopped em, sent em home. When I drove up to the planer that mornin the mess was over; them white men had got their walkin papers. Well, I drove up, Mr. Ed come out to meet my wagon. I'd hauled my loads with a smile. Right then I had done set my business, got my crop laid by and turned my mules back to haulin lumber. Now especially he knowed he was goin to need me. He said, "Nate, do you want a regular job haulin lumber and maybe haulin logs sometimes? Do you want a regular job?"

Told him, "Yes sir, I'd be glad to have it."

He said, "All right, tell you what I want you to do. You go over there to that yard of lumber back of Israel Fry, you topload that lumber out. I'm goin to give you a price that you can live at and clear a little money along for other uses or purposes. You go on over there and start to haulin that lumber out. See what you can make out of it at that price. And I'll be out there Tuesday mornin— that'll give you a day's haul over there before I come. And I'll see how you gettin along at it and decide with you whether you can make anything at it or not. If you can't I'll raise your wages."

Monday mornin I hitched them mules of mine up and crawled on over there and got on the job. Hauled all day, I didn't play, hauled all day. And I seed that I *could* make a livin at it and have money to buy extra things at the price he first offered me. I always tried to look out in a way to not want more than I was worth— or less than I was worth. I wanted to get a reasonable price that I could live at for my labor.

Mr. Ed Pike come out there that Tuesday mornin and definitely asked me, "Well, Nate, what have you decided? You think you can make it at that price or not?"

I said, "Mr. Ed, just let the matter rock along, I can live at that."

I had done seed that I could make a livin—and I expect he seed I could too—and I didn't ask him to go up. Right there he liked my opinion, couldn't help but like it. Good times, fair days, with my health and strength, I could make a good livin at his price. I couldn't average top money every month of the year, but what was my place to do? Look out for off times and rainy days.

Soon, after awhile, some of them white men come back to haulin. Mr. Ed took em back at his price. They seed where they was losin money; their stock was standin in the lots at home and they feedin em and weren't makin a penny. Mr. Horace Tucker got back on, and a few more. And he put some colored men to haulin lumber beside me. All of us at the same price, one price for white and colored. Mr. Ed Pike come into this country from North Carolina; he weren't native to the state of Alabama, and that was his system of business.

Mr. Henry Culpepper went to Mr. Ed Pike one day—some of the rest of em come out that way, but weren't no use for me to worry; just go on haulin for the trucks out from them mill places. And Mr. Henry Culpepper went to him—I hated it but I couldn't help it, I didn't ask Mr. Ed for *that*. Mr. Henry Culpepper went to him one day and tried to get a job haulin, on the same job I was haulin, a job he used to have—Mr. Culpepper was in that crowd turned off their jobs. Some of em begged back, begged back. But Mr. Ed wouldn't take him back directly, and he told Mr. Culpepper and he told me—I hated that, Mr. Ed tellin him all that. He told him if he got a job he'd have to come in under me, said, "I got Nate out there haulin and all the business at the present time is in his hands about haulin out for the trucks. You can go and see what you can do with him. Whatever he says about it, that's with you and him. But listen, all your pay on haulin goes to Nate; you'll just have to look up to Nate for your money. I got him out there, he's over the job and you'll have to make it agreeable to him."

Mr. Ed told me these words himself but I wouldn't mention to Mr. Culpepper what Mr. Ed told me. I just turned Mr. Culpepper down to his head. Here's the way he come to me: let him haul a week or two in my place and couldn't I find somethin else to do and give him a chance to haul some. And even told me that he weren't able, out of his crop and so on, to pay his tax without gettin a job as a addition.

I said, "Well, I'm sorry, Mr. Culpepper, but I'm tied up with Mr. Ed Pike; I'm responsible to Mr. Pike to stay on this job. If I stays here there aint no room for nobody else. I got my family to support and my little demands to meet. I'm sorry, but I can't lay off my job a week or two, I can't do it."

I just had to turn him down and I knowed that weren't quite agreeable in this country, a colored man have a job tied down and a white man turned away.

I told him, "Just aint no way in the world I can turn loose my job. I'm sorry for you, Mr. Culpepper, it's nothin in me against you, but it's nothin I can afford to take away from my family if I can help it. I can't do no more for you than feel your sympathy. I'm obliged to stay on my job."

RIGHT at that particular time, I was haulin with as good a pair of mules as this country could afford. They wasn't as big as some mules, but big don't get it all the time; it's how they work and their attitude. I gived Mr. Grimes at the Apafalya mule pen one hundred and eighty-five dollars for that Mattie mule; and I gived Mr. Jeb Birch two hundred dollars for her mate—I called her Calley—and I made my figures this way on that mule. Mr. Birch lived right close to the gin house and I first asked him about that mule that fall when I was haulin cotton. I had thought it over and I was goin to try to buy the mule. I seed Mr. Birch hangin around the gin one day and I asked him, "Mr. Birch, you got a mule that I'd love to own, to match my mule that I already got"—I had two head of stock right at that time but one of em was a rented animal, young horse. I wanted another mule of my own, quit rentin stock.

He said, "Which one of my mules?"

One of em was a blocky mare mule and the other was this Calley mule, I knowed her good. Mr. Freeman North was the man that bought her out the drove and she was pretty tight and he couldn't handle her like he wanted to, so he sold her to Mr. Jeb Birch. I wanted the mule.

I said, "That Calley mule, that bay mule, that's the mule I want if money will buy her."

He said, "O, that mule will cost you two hundred dollars."

Well, I went on. I wasn't against givin that for the mule but I went on and studied over it. She was a nice match for Mattie—and that finally moved me to pay a little more for her than ever I paid before for a mule. It was my business to buy just as cheap as I could and work the mule to the greatest limit without injurin her.

I told my wife one day, "Darlin, I'm goin down to Mr. Birch's, see if I can buy that Calley mule from him my way. I got my limits fixed; if he'll come to my figures I'll buy that mule."

I was pickin cotton at the time. Hitched Mattie to the buggy that evenin late and drove down to Mr. Birch's. He was livin on the Calusa road close to Tucker's crossin. I had a rope in the buggy to carry Calley back if he'd deal with me.

"Hello, Mr. Birch."

"Hello, Nate."

All these white folks knowed my voice; ever they messed with me a little bit they knowed my voice.

"Come out here, Mr. Birch, please, sir, I want to talk with you a little."

Out he come.

"Well, what do you say, Nate?"

"Mr. Birch, I'm down here tonight—you know, you told me, we was talkin on that Calley mule of yours, and you told me it would take two hundred dollars to move her."

Doggone good mule but she weren't as heavy a mule—she wouldn't a weighed but a thousand pounds, she'd make a clear thousand though.

He said, "Yes, that's what I said it'd cost you. She's one of the best ones. Take two hundred dollars to move her."

I said, "Well, Mr. Birch, I aint ready to buy her right now but I'll see you again."

But I was ready for Calley; I wanted to get her.

"What's wrong, Nate, don't you want the Calley mule? How come you in such a hurry to go?"

I said, "Yes, Mr. Birch, I want her and since I see that you want to sell her, and you'll sell her to me, I'll make you an offer."

I made him an offer and he took it up and that was the whole crop to me. It weren't less than two hundred dollars, I told him that, but it weren't the two hundred in one piece.

I said, "Will you sell me that mule for a hundred cash dollars down and the other hundred next fall, clear of any interest?"

He studied it, said, "I'll do that. I'll sell her to you that way."

I said, "All right, sir, if you'll do that and come out to Apafalya in the mornin, meet me at the bank, I'll give you a hundred dollars cash for her and let the other hundred run over till next fall, I'll buy her."

"All right. She's yours."

I runned down to the pasture side of the road where his mules was and caught Calley out. Tied my rope to her halter and led her on home behind my buggy that night. Next mornin I got up and loaded a couple of bales of cotton on my wagon, carried em in to Apafalya and sold em, paid Mr. Birch a hundred cash dollars. Had a note fixed up for another hundred dollars due at my next crop.

I went on back home and went to haulin lumber regularly. I knowed I could get that hundred dollars out of my crop and my lumber haul together. So, Mr. Grace held that note at the bank between me and Mr. Birch, somehow or other. He mighta held it on account of Mr. Birch owin him. I don't know; it weren't none of my business.

All right. One day in the summer I seed Mr. Grace walkin down there by the planer mill with his hands in his galluses, overlookin. Walked on by me where I was unloadin a load of lumber. I happened to think—he got about fifteen feet past me, I walked out and said, "Mr. Grace, let me speak to you a minute, sir, if you please."

He stopped. I said, "Don't you hold a note against that Calley mule of mine for a hundred dollars?"

He said, "Yes, I do."

I said, "Two weeks' time that note will be due—"

He said, "Well, Nate, don't let that worry you. If it runs a little over it'll be a hundred dollars; if it comes under it's a hundred, or if it comes today, it'll be a hundred. But don't you worry bout bein a little late on it, I guarantee you it won't bother you."

I said, "All right, thank you, Mr. Grace"; but I didn't test him on his word. Two weeks' time I walked in that bank with that hundred dollars.

He said, "Nate, where did you get that much money in that time?"

I said, "My labor gets it."

He said, "You don't mean to tell me that you made that money in two weeks' time?"

I said, "Yes sir, I did do it, I scuffled to get it."

Paid him that hundred dollars and got my note. Bought that mule complete then from Mr. Birch by makin the second payment to Mr. Grace. How come it? White man's business throwed me from one of em's hands into the other's, but that hundred dollars was the same regardless to which one I gived it to.

ONE day I was haulin lumber right there close to home, off of Lemuel Tucker's place. Officers come to my house in my absence—

Now Mr. George Pike, he loved whiskey and wine and everything else. He come to my house—at that particular time every year, my wife would make up three or four gallons of wine. Mr. George Pike found it out—she'd make it for me to drink; I liked good wine. Wine won't do you like whiskey if you takes it in small amounts.

Mr. George Pike was runnin one of the mills close to my house. And he caught on some way, askin me bout whiskey and wine and I told him, "Yes sir, I likes wine; my wife got a little wine over there now, she made it for me."

O good God, what'd I tell him that for? You take public workmen, they go for such as that, most of em. He wanted a quart of that wine and I made him a present of it. That just ruined him. Got to where he'd drive to my house huntin wine, Mr. George Pike, Ed Pike's brother. So, he had a knack of comin there late in the evenin —it was good wine, blackberry wine, Hannah made it. They'd go off up the road there from my house and hit the Apafalya road there at Two Forks. They'd go out merryin, hoopin and hollerin—there was another one in the drove, he was related to them Pikes. All of em liked wine, whiskey too. But they never did get a drop of whiskey at my house. But they'd come there just hoggish for wine. And they'd get it and go off up the road, jollyin like drinkers will do. Somebody detected it—people between my house and Two Forks, I believe some of them done it—and they reported to the laws that I was sellin whiskey.

So one day, I was haulin lumber. I weren't over a mile from home. But I never did, even when I was that close, go home between hauls. I'd stay on my job all day, kept feed with me. Feed my mules, kept em eatin. Every time I went to load I'd drop em down somethin to eat and unbreast em, slackin their traces; they'd stand there, eat, while I was loadin my lumber. Heap of times if they wasn't quite done by the time I finished loadin my lumber I'd give em a few more minutes to eat. My mules stayed fat all the time—and when I'd get home at night I'd pour it in to em.

First thing I knowed, two officers come to my house—I weren't there. They wanted to examine around for whiskey. After some of em up that road seed them fellows comin there so regular and goin out merryin, they just figured I was sellin whiskey. But I weren't sellin no whiskey. Come home that evenin and my wife told me about it. Said the officers come there and wanted to search for whiskey. But she convinced em so and got em clean out the notion that they'd find any whiskey. Told em, "Yes sirs, you're welcome. My husband aint here but you welcome to look around, see what you can find. But I assure you, you won't find no whiskey here."

She berated em on the evils of whiskey and she professed to be a Christian woman. They listened at her and as long as they listened she talked. Come to the end of it, they said, "Auntie, we believe you, we believe you."

They called her "Auntie," that was their rulin then. If it was a man, they'd call you "Uncle," "Uncle So-and-so." A young fellow, they'd call him by his name if they knowed it. I didn't worry bout what they called me because I knowed they weren't goin to call me nothin but what they wanted to anyhow. We took that—there's colored people all through this country now, white folks still callin em uncle, auntie. A good crowd of em comes here and calls me "Mister." They can call me "Mister" as much as they please; I know that they don't want to do it and they aint of it, they just passin the time.

So, she thoroughly convinced em away from there. And she kept a beggin em, told em, "I have a smokehouse around here in the back. Go around there and I'll give you the key. Unlock the door and see what you can find."

One of em went on around the house and went to the smoke-house at the south end of the house, in the back yard. And the other one walked through the dwellin house, come in the front, walked clean on through the dinin room and out the back, didn't stop. By that time his friend was unlockin the smokehouse door. Went in there and looked around, come out and locked the door and come to her there on the back step and gived her the key and left out from there. Aint been back there no more long as I stayed there.

WHEN I first went down on Sitimachas Creek where I was livin when I was doin most of that lumber haulin, I had three head of stock. And right down there before I moved away from there I lost one of the best mules in the whole country, that Mattie mule. White man come up to me, said, "Well, Nate, I'm sorry for you. You hit it hard, lost one of the nicer mules that the country could afford. What you goin to do now?"

Fellow by the name of Max Meade, little Max Meade's daddy's brother, asked me that question. He was a pretty heavy-built white man and, O, he played like he was sorry for me. I was just a poor colored man, I told him, "I don't know what I'll do. May just stop; may just cut me out from this lumber haulin." Didn't give him no satisfaction bout what I was aimin to do.

I lost that Mattie mule in March, round about the last of the month. I had had her clipped and right soon I got caught in a hail storm and a cold blusty rain. That drawed her up considerable. Some mules wouldn't stand for you to clip em and some of em would. Just ease them clippers over em and clip em all over clean. Shorten their hair and they'd look like—that Mattie mule I had clipped looked like a peeled onion. If it's a long-haired mule, keep her clipped for the summer—don't clip her but once and that's in the spring of the year. But you shouldn't do that and let a cold snap catch em. That's what I done and how come I lost her.

Had my sister's boy, Davey, he was older than any of my boys, and my oldest boy, Calvin, on a second wagon that day. Hitched my plow horses to that borrowed wagon and them boys carried between seven and eight hundred feet of lumber behind them horses. And I was along with em with a thousand feet of lumber— that was my regular haul, a thousand feet. Drove in there at the planer mill in Apafalya and unloaded them two wagons, me and the boys, and got on the road back home. And out from Apafalya about a mile, right there at Jerusalem Cemetery, that bad weather hit us. That Mattie mule drawed up and turned one-sided, no hair on her hardly, fresh-clipped; well, we drove right regular on in home.

Never hurt that Calley mule of mine because she was a short-haired mule and I didn't have her clipped, didn't need it. And them horses, weather didn't hurt em at all. Drove em on home and I took that Mattie mule and throwed a heavy blanket over her back and fastened it under her neck and I led her in the warm stable. But in spite of the world that mule got chilled through.

She took bronchial pneumonia and I lost her. It was awful. Dr. Crabtree from Apafalya, he come out and looked at her. I called for him on a Wednesday mornin—I was livin five miles out from town. He came out on his car, said, "Where is that sick mule you got here, Shaw?"

"Doctor, she's down there in the barn."

We went down there together and he examined her.

"Shaw," he said, "that's a mighty nice mule to be in that condition."

I said, "What's the matter with her, Doc?"

"She got bronchial pneumonia."

That was the second mule I ever bought and the first one I bought that had never had a bridle on her—I broke her myself. And when I lost that mule I had had her for eleven long years. Was as good a mule as ever I owned and I've owned some good mules.

Mr. Hoyt Thompson, man that run a mill for the Graham-Pike Lumber Company, off down here in a scope of pine thickets and swamps near my house, he furnished me his mule to hitch with my Calley mule and I drug that Mattie mule off one day, bout a quarter mile from my house over a hill right at Sitimachas Creek to what they called the old Thompson Ford, and put her down under that hill where she'd roll into the creek. I hated that. I said to myself, 'If it just hadn't been rainin when I drug that mule off, I'd a went over there and labored and dug a hole beside of her in a way that in diggin she'd a rolled in there and I'd a buried that mule.' But it was rainin and I didn't do it.

I went right on then and bought another mule from Mr. Duncan Walls in Apafalya. At that time Mr. Grimes weren't there no more, man that I'd bought that Mattie mule from. He'd done went to live in Opelika and Mr. Duncan Walls was runnin the mule pen.

That Calley mule of mine made a dandy mate to Mattie. Had a pair of good mules then, nice a mules as you wanted to see for farm purposes; that's what I bought em for, farm purposes. Calley woulda weighed thoroughly a thousand pounds or a little more; but it weren't the size of the mule that impressed me, it was the *vim* of the mules I had. That Mattie mule didn't even weigh a thousand pounds fully. But she'd drag her part of a thousand feet of lumber out from under any reasonable hill.

Huntin a new mate for Calley.

"Hello, Mr. Walls."

"Hello, Nate."

"Am I correct, sir, in thinkin that you are in the mule business?"

"Yes, Nate, I have been but I sold out; I aint got a mule here for sale. I got one, but I reserved her for my own self. She'll weigh about a thousand fifty, somethin along like that, maybe she might weigh eleven hundred. Big mule. But I reserved her. I got one of Noah Root's boys hired here to work a little crop for me and I reserved this mule for him to plow. I don't expect you'd want her nohow. First, she'd cost you two hundred and fifty dollars and next, I don't expect you'd want her because Noah Root's boy let her run away twice since he been a workin her here. He let her run away with a guano distributor, tore that up; then she run away with a one-horse wagon and wrecked it. I don't expect you'd want a mule like that."

I said, "Good God, Mr. Walls—"

"You wouldn't want her nohow, Nate."

I had employment for the mule and I was makin money—

"She'll cost you two hundred and fifty dollars."

I said, "Two hundred and fifty?"

He said, "Yes, yes, I got to keep her; I need her and she's the only one I got."

"And you wouldn't sell her?"

"O, no, yes, I'd sell her if a man would pay me what she's worth."

I said, "Is she a mare mule?" I didn't never buy a horse mule —I didn't have nothin for a horse mule to do. All the mules ever I bought was mare mules.

"Yes, she's a mare mule but I don't expect she'd suit you since she's runned away twice with Noah Root's boy."

I wanted to see the mule regardless to the price and regardless to her temper he was tellin me about. I said, "Well, I got to have a mule someway, Mr. Walls, if I can get one. Where is this mule of yours we talkin about? You got her here anywhere close?"

He said, "O, yes, she's down there in the barn."

I said, "Let's go see her."

He was comin on out from his work anyhow, makin it back toward his house up at the road where I had my mule and one of Hoyt Thompson's mules hitched together that day. I'd carried a load of lumber out to the planer, Saturday evenin, and got to Mr. Walls on time to see what he had in the way of a mule. I knowed I had to buy one.

Went on to the house and turned down to the stable. The mule walked out, big heifer of a mule, and the hair on her tail weren't no longer than a little chap's fingers. She had a barbed tail—she was a big mule and the hair on her tail had been barbed off by her bein in the drove and the young mules catchin and pullin one another by the tails.

I said, "So this is the mule you say will cost me two hundred and fifty."

"Yes, that's the only price will get her, Nate. I wouldn't take less than that."

I said, "Well, put a halter on her. I want her."

"You just goin to buy her anyhow!"

I said, "You say you'll take two hundred and fifty dollars for her. You don't want to sell her but you'll take two hundred and fifty for her." I knowed what good stock was. "Put a halter on her."

He said, "Catch the mule there, son"—speakin to Noah Root's boy—"and put a rope in her halter."

Took her out to where I had my other mule and Mr. Hoyt Thompson's mule, standin out there in Mr. Walls' grove with the traces around em, the lines tied back to the couplin pole so they couldn't go nowhere.

I said, "Well, come on up to the bank, Mr. Walls, and get your money."

I tied a long rope to the halter of that barbed-tail mule and tied the other end to the back of my wagon and led her away from there. Mr. Walls come up to the bank by and by and got his money.

I delivered Mr. Thompson's mule to Mr. Fred Touchett, white gentleman that was sawin for Mr. Thompson. And I cleaned out my stable where I had kept that Mattie mule until she died. Named the new mule Dela and Dela was a big mule beside my other mules

I'd had. In fact of the business, she was enough mule to overbear that Calley mule. Rocked along and in a few days I worked Calley and Dela together. Dela was so much heavier than Calley was— and I had lumbered Calley and Mattie together several years and they made it nice, gaited together. But Dela overbet that Calley mule. She was younger, she was heavier—the way she'd reach out and step with her head up, she just overbet Calley too quick. I seed Calley wouldn't gait with her. So I went back to Mr. Duncan Walls that fall and I gived Calley and one of my horses for a black mule named Mary. Right there I matched Dela to a T. Hitched them pretty mules to my wagon, the fools run away with me before I got home.

IV

I raised Davey—that was my sister's son, twelve years old when she died and I took the boy. My sister Sadie, my own dear blood sister. My mother was the mother of both we children. When Sadie died she left three little boy children—Davey, Tommy, and Henry. She had them chaps by her first husband. And when he died, the father of them children, she married a fellow up there at Litabixee and he was noted, more people noted than one, he was a drag-behind fellow, slow, messin with whiskey along through his days. And he got her in a family way and he half-treated her. So she gived birth to a baby and it left her in bad shape. And he didn't take care of her. And the baby died. And in a few days after the baby died, she died.

I was livin on Tucker's place at that time, hadn't moved from there, and my brother Peter come over to my house one day and told me, "Brother, the only sister we got is dead. Sadie's dead. I was notified about it and I come to let you know."

I just got in a hurry and took that mule out of the field, went on to the house, me and him—bout three quarters of a mile to the house. I was down on Sitimachas Creek plowin on the bottoms. I took that mule out and carried her on to the house with my brother and put her up to feed while I was dressin, gettin ready to travel. When I got ready I caught that mule out and hitched her to the buggy and me and my brother went on to his house and gived him a chance to fix hisself up. And when we drove into Litabixee that evenin it was a little after sundown. And this husband of her'n weren't there, he weren't at home. There was a old lady stayin there with my dead sister—he didn't carry her to no undertaker or nothin like that.

We drove in there and two of my big uncles—one of em was heavier than I was and the other was still a big man, heavy-built— I had notified them and they got on their buggies, them and their wives, Uncle Grant Culver and his wife got on their buggy, Uncle Jim Culver and his wife got on their buggy, and all went up to Litabixee with me and my brother Peter. My sister's own dear uncles just like they was my and Peter's uncles.

All of em was quiet men. We assembled around there, but this here husband of her'n weren't there. That old lady was there. In the night after dark he come pokin in. He had just mis- and half-treated my sister, that's what he done; he didn't take no care of her at all, not while she was livin and not while she was dead. She just died for attention. I said to him when he come in—had a fire out in the yard that night, me and my uncles, our uncles, my and my brother's uncles and my dead sister's uncles.

So this fellow come a walkin up in the night. We howdyed with him, he howdyed with us—draggy-talkin fellow, you could look at him and tell there weren't nothin to him much. I didn't come to argue with him, I come to put some questions to him.

I said—Ernest Hines was his name—I said, "Brother Ernest, how long had Sadie been sick?"

"O, she hadn't been sick very long."

I said, "How come you didn't warn us and notify us before she died?"

"I didn't think, Brother Nate, she was that sick."

I took it all, never said nothin; I kept askin my questions.

I said, "Well, Brother Ernest, Elam Baptist Church out there a mile the other side of Apafalya, that was her membership and that's where our mother is buried at. Where are you aimin to have your wife buried? I'd be very glad if she could be taken to her home church where her dear mother is buried, our dear mother. Tell me what you think about that."

"Well, Brother Nate, she's in such bad shape I don't think it would do to haul her that far."

I still wouldn't say nothin. Got done tellin all that and I allowed him his pleasure about it. Then I asked him, I said, "Well—" talkin to a sorry man, too—"Well, if you think that's too far to haul her on account of her condition, she must be in bad condition."

"Yeah, I think she is in too bad a condition to haul that far."

I said, "Well, where are you plannin to bury her at? Where do you want her buried?"

"I thought, Brother Nate, we'd bury her up here at Pilgrim's Rest."

I quit talkin with him; I wouldn't contrary him. Up there at Pilgrim's Rest, that weren't two miles from his house.

And said, "We want to bury her as early as possible tomorrow."

We spent the night there and stayed up, worried around my dead sister Sadie. That next mornin, by nine o'clock we were hustlin to the graveyard with her body. Went up the road to a little church just above his house and we turned to the left and come back in there back of Litabixee, west of Litabixee. Quickly buried her and returned right back to the house, all of us, me and my brother and our two uncles and their wives, returned back to the house. She had died and left three little boys and they was raggedy as a can of kraut. No clothes to wear, no mother and no father—it struck deep, it struck deep in me. Took em every one away from there that day, the three of em—Davey, the oldest one, he's dead now, died in Prattville down here in Montgomery County, he was the oldest; Tommy was the next oldest; Henry was the youngest, the baby boy. He lives out yonder on the road straight from here to Apafalya, now. Tommy stays in Florida, been in Florida about twenty years.

When I brought them out of Litabixee that mornin—I told him, I consulted with him bout everything. I said, "Well, Brother Ernest—" when I got back, all of us, from the cemetery and hitched our mules there at the house, I said, "Well, Brother Ernest, I got a little talk in regards to these little boys my sister died and left. I want to get your consent about it. I'm goin to treat you right. I got a plan that I want to lay to you about the condition of these three little boys"— the oldest one was twelve years old, Davey—"Let's step aside and talk about it a little. I've considered and thought over some things about them and I'm goin to consult with you and see how you feel about it."

"All right, Brother Nate."

I said, "Your wife is dead and gone. These little boys here was her other husband's children. But I'm goin to consult with you as you is their stepfather and they aint big enough and old enough to help themselves. I'll tell you what's on my mind. You aint the father of these little boys. And you got three or four here yourself, and your children and her children is mixed here by you and her bein married. And I don't think that you are calculated to take care of your children and her children too. And they all on you. You got no wife and it's just you and these children in the house here, you've got em all. You're overloaded and she's gone. Now I'm goin to lighten your burden if you'll accept. Don't you think it would be profitable for me to take her little children, her three little boys and take em home with me? That'll lighten your burden on this children business."

He looked at me. I said, "How will that suit you? It'll help you. You're not their father. It would be very bad, it would look bad for me to ignore these little boys of my sister's; their daddy's dead and now their mother's dead. These children are not a drop of kin to you. That's one reason I want to take em off you, take em home with me."

He said, "Well, Brother Nate, it was Sadie's request for me to keep em."

Right there it brought about hard words. I said, "Keep em for what? There's the railroad right out in front of your door, Western Railroad; you can't stay here at all times and keep these children from ramblin and rovin, some of em just might get killed out there by a train. And probably there's other dangers. The best thing, I think, is for me to take em and take em home with me. And to treat you right, that's why I'm consultin the matter with you. I want it took care of. Sadie's request aint no good in this case. She's dead and gone and she's left two brothers here, which is these little boys' uncles. And there's *my* uncles, two big men of em here, all of us connected to these children. They are these little boys' great-uncles. Me and my brother here are their own dear uncles. What are you goin to do about it now? Sadie's dead and gone and her little children is left at the mercies of the world. And I don't think that you can take care of em as they should be."

He said, "Well, it was her request."

I got mad then; he stuck to it. "It was her request for me to keep em."

I said, "Brother Ernest, if you keep em you keep em over my dead body."

I walked off. If he'd a kept em he would have butchered em up;

them children would have suffered, surely. Maybe some of em
would have got killed; out of the three some of em would have got
killed. He didn't take care of his own children. And he didn't take
care of his wife. He was just a sluggard. Tell you what happened
to him after Sadie died. In a year or two, two or three years after
she died, he messed with whiskey. He went off, but thank God he
didn't go off and leave them little children. I brought em away from
there that day. And two or three years after that, he had to crawl
home one night. He was on the west side—accordin to how I got
the news—he was on the west side of his home and he crawled
through a cotton patch or out of a cotton patch and somebody
knocked him in the head. And he died. Never did get over it. People
in that settlement didn't talk much, but I heard, strictly, that he
was a whiskey-head, and he bootlegged whiskey, too. But I come
into the knowledge to know, before he died, there wasn't much to
him but somethin to butcher up a woman and children.

He dropped his head. That old woman that was stayin there
with my sister was standin by the door—that old house didn't have
no veranda to it—she was standin in the door and she heard my
talk. I had never looked to see her standin in the door listenin to
the conversation, and before I knowed anything she spoke up,
"Ernest!"

He looked around and I did too; seed that old woman standin
in the door callin him.

"Come here, son." It weren't his mother, just a old woman that
knowed him. "Come here, son."

He went on to the door and she busted open just like this:
when he got to the doorsteps, he looked up at her and she said, "Son,
why don't you let that man have them children? You done heard
him what he said. How come you won't let him have em?"

She knowed it would better his condition, if it could be bettered,
for me to take them children. That was takin em off her hands,
maybe. And she done heard me tell him if he kept em he kept em
over my dead body. I was angry then.

I heard her say, beggin him, "Son, why don't you let that man
have them children? You heard him what he said. He's goin to
make trouble for you if you don't."

I was standin still listenin. When she said that I begin to move.
It was a short time till I done what I wanted to do and was aimin
to do. When I heard her say that I begin to stir around in the yard.

He come right back to me, told me, "Well, Brother Nate, I'll let you have em."

He wasn't their daddy and he half-treated his own children, so what could I expect from him? And he messed up my sister's health; didn't stand by her as a husband.

I told him, "You were well to have said that earlier; it would have saved all the words and arguin. Saved it. You were just as well to have said that at the start. Now, if these three little boys has got any clothes in the house, I'll thank you kindly to get em together. I'm goin to carry em—" wasn't nothin else there for me—"I'm goin to carry em—" I never did look back there for none of her little furniture because they had nothin in the house like a family ought to. I said, "Get their little clothes up what they got."

He went back there and told that old woman, "Get em up!"

And when the clothes come out of there they come out in a little old sack about as big as a small pillow slip. I took em up, put em in the buggy, got the little children ready quick as I could—I taken the oldest one on the buggy with me, Davey. And Uncle Jim and Uncle Grant put the other two fellas, one of em in one buggy and the other in the other, and rolled away from there.

When we got down here, way out here this side of Apafalya, the road forks and my home was still continuin on the Pottstown road, and the branch-off goin toward Clay's mill down there was where my daddy lived. And I happened to be lucky to meet my daddy right at that fork that mornin. Met him, stopped and consulted the matter.

I said, "Papa, we went to the death of Sadie, me and Peter and Uncle Jim and Uncle Grant and their wives—was all that went. We seed her buried this mornin, a little after nine o'clock; buried her quick. I picked up her three little boys and brought em this far with me. I'm in route home with em now. Bein as you is the granddaddy and I am their uncle—" he didn't go to the death of his daughter at all. His wife was sick, he said, and he couldn't leave her, TJ's mother—I said, "Papa, you is the granddaddy for these little boys and I am their uncle. I'm goin to leave it up to you how we'll divide em, if you want em; if you don't want nary one of em or can't keep em, I'll keep all three of em."

He considered and he said these words and that's the way we stood.

"Well, son, I'm perfectly willin to take some of em. I'll tell you what I'll do. Bein'st that you got a house full of children and nobody to wait on them children but their mother, and none of em aint big enough to help her with the rest of em—I got three or four large girls in my house can wait on em. And bein'st as it's thataway, I'll take the two least ones, Tommy and Henry, and let you keep the oldest one, Davey. He's twelve years old and maybe he might be a little help to you. And that would keep a crowd off of your wife— if you aint got no children big enough to help her."

I said, "That suits me, Papa, but remember one thing: these little boys aint got no mother and father. I'm only their uncle; me and my brother Peter over here is uncles for these three little boys" —we didn't put nary a one off at Peter's—"and you is their grand-daddy. Let's handle em like this: don't get the two little boys, the youngest ones, off at your house and the oldest one be at my house and we hold these little boys apart and won't bring em to see one another. I'll bring the little boy that I keep, the oldest one, around to your home amongst the other two. And you forward the others to my house and let em grow up knowin that they are brothers. Don't keep em separated in a way that they'll forget about one another. Don't do that, Papa."

He said, "I won't, son, I won't."

Well, we went on and on thataway and them little boys stayed in remembrance of one another. I took Davey and he was just twelve years old. My wife and I treated him just like he was our own child. And my children and him got along just like one, just like one. I got along with Davey just like he was my chap and they got along with one another just like all of em was sisters and brothers.

ME and Tucker fell out but there weren't no fuss. I just picked up and moved right into a house on Mr. Ben Stark's plantation up at a little place they call Two Forks. It was a better house than the house I moved out of on Mr. Tucker's place. It was a old house but it was a warm house, partly a board house built out of plank and partly a log house.

Four children come with me: Calvin, Rachel, Vernon, and Francis; them was my children. And Davey made five. Mattie Jane come next, and the balance of my children after her, all them children was born on the Pollard place. When I moved to the Stark place, Vernon was big enough to help me farm. He didn't plow but

he was big enough to help me other ways. He had plowed some before I moved up there at Two Forks, but he started to plowin a regular turn after I moved away from there. Moved up there in 1923 and moved off in 1924. Stayed to make one crop and then I bought into my own place, the Pollard place, where that I lived until the state of Alabama removed me to the penitentiary.

There's some of the places I used to move to, I didn't pick em as a man would do under free choice because I wasn't allowed, I couldn't live anywhere I wanted to—white people didn't want a nigger livin anywhere he could prosper too fast. Where I could get a place to my likin, that's where I moved.

I was living right on the highway front when I lived at Two Forks. And a white man there—I had some words and a cuss and frolic with him. He lived just above me on the same road and I passed by his house goin to my house. And he was livin on a place he had bought there joinin this place that I lived on. That was all smooth land country, better land than Tucker's land—you could work it, plow it anywhere. And I had a little less than a small three-horse farm rented there. I gived two hundred and fifty dollars rent —come out of my cotton and corn, but mostly out of my cotton.

I went down there in the fall after I rented the place, not thinkin nothin, and you or no other person wouldn't have thought nothin about that. Before I moved there, but after I rented it, I went over and sowed me a few bushels of oats and bought me some brand new barbed wire and wired them oats up, not thinkin they was goin to be destroyed. Sowed my oats and wired em up out on some of the cultivatable land. And this white man that was livin joinin me, just a wire fence between his plantation and mine, he had a devilish yearlin—that's where the trouble come. He had more cows than that yearlin but he couldn't keep that yearlin from rovin out of his pasture or he didn't try, I don't know which. But I know that yearlin got in my oats and grazed em when he got ready and he ruint em too. He's in there every day he wanted to go. Got through the wire, got in some way. I kept a warnin the man—his name was Toby Culpepper. I kept a tellin Mr. Culpepper, I said, "Mr. Culpepper, your yearlin is just ruinin my oats."

But it didn't do no good. I kept a tellin him that and his yearlin kept a grazin my oats when he got ready. And at last, one day, my boys was in the field plowin and they looked yonder and seed that yearlin in my oats; they was plowin down below and kind of south

of the oat patch. I was at the house and the boys come up there and told me, "Papa, that yearlin is over there in your oats again."

All my talkin to the man didn't amount to nothin. That yearlin just throwed my oats back—eatin up a good grazin pasture before them oats ever started to head, just cleaned my oats up. Well, I just went on to the barn and got a rope, went on over to where the boys was plowin after they notified me, went right on back to their plowin. And there was another fellow there that I had sub-rented part of this place to, colored fellow by the name of Hamp Rowe, just had a wife and one child, and I rented Hamp a small plot of land to have him some corn. The place was in my hands complete and I could do with it what I pleased that year as far as right, if I didn't hurt the place no way. So, Hamp was down there at his house plowin. I went by and told him I wanted him to help me catch a yearlin in my oats. I called his attention to it—he was plowin, had a nice horse and he was plowin his horse there on the ground I had rented to him. He just took that horse loose; he said, "All right, Mr. Nate—" and he come up with me and my boys and we surrounded that yearlin and caught him. That was a crowd enough to do it— Hamp Rowe and me and my two boys, Vernon and Calvin, and my sister's boy Davey.

I went on up then to the wire fence between the two plantations and the white man was plowin right there—we was all plowin there pretty close together. I got up to the fence and said, "Mr. Culpepper, I caught your yearlin a while ago—" He might have been way on the other end of his row next to his house, reason he didn't know it; or he could have just knowed it and weren't sayin nothin. I said, "Mr. Culpepper, I caught your yearlin in my oats again."

He done declared to me he was goin to keep her out—never did keep her out till that yearlin ruint my oats. She was a half-grown yearlin, or maybe over half-grown. She was a heifer—hadn't never had nary a calf. And he had a chain on her that mornin and she was draggin that chain on her head.

I said, "Your yearlin got in my oats and I caught her this mornin."

He said, "Where is she?"

I said, "You see—" I looked back toward the road—"You see them boys with that yearlin goin up the road to my lot now? Yonder go the boys."

He looked and seed. Here's what he told me—hadn't never paid

a nickel for his yearlin ruinin my oats. Just lingered along till she ruint em. He told me when I showed him the boys carryin her to the lot—I put a rope on her head and told the boys to lead her—said, "Well, I'll just go on over there and get her, that's all."

I didn't object. And he hadn't paid me nothin and he promised to keep her out of my oats and didn't do it. I was satisfied he was just goin to try to bull me over. He hitched his mules to one of the wire fence posts with the bridle rein and untied one of the lines and drawed it out of the traces and folded it up. Then he jumped over that wire fence and he was goin to get her. He took straight off cross my field. I just went on with him, never said a word, just let him go on over there and get her like he said. But there was a little somethin else that I considered was goin to take place—

He went on around my house to the back yard, went straight to the lot. He never said nothin to me except he was goin to my lot to fetch his yearlin. And he unchained my gate and walked in and chained it behind him as if to say he didn't want her to run out of the lot, he was goin to stay there till he caught her. I didn't tell him I'd help him; I didn't tell him I wouldn't. I was just watchin his motions. In fact of the business, I kind of followed in behind him, unchained that gate and walked in there and sat down on the roots of a big old hickory tree. I set there and looked at him. He chased that yearlin around the lot a little bit and he got a rope on her; then he stood behind her and started comin toward the gate.

I said, "What you goin to do, Mr. Culpepper? You just goin to carry on anyhow and not say anything bout payin me for the destruction? Just goin to drive her out and carry on? And she done ruint my oats; been grazin on em ever since she got big enough to graze." I flew hot. I said, "You can't bring her out here, you aint offered me a penny. I will release the yearlin if you give me a dollar for catchin her—takin time and losin time to catch her. If you give me a dollar you can have her. If you don't you can't."

He stopped and looked at me. He got mad then. Said, "You don't aim to let me have her then without I pay you?"

I said, "No sir, you got to pay me a dollar for catchin her out of my oats."

He said, "Well, I'm comin—" There was a little old grist mill—I was livin right at the fork in the road and Mr. Rivers was runnin a little old grist mill out below me—and Mr. Culpepper said, "I got to come back to the mill this evenin, after dinner, and I'll just bring

one of my boys here with me, as I got to come to the mill. And I'll
bring you a dollar then."

I said, "I'll appreciate it. Your yearlin done ruint my oats, et
em up and tramped em to where they won't never do me no good;
they won't be worth cuttin. Turned my crop to a grazin patch."

He got mad but he pulled his rope off that yearlin and walked
to the gate and unfastened it, went on just like he come there,
straight back through my yard and around the house, then walked
on across the field. I walked along behind him goin back down to
the field where my boys was plowin. And he turned around to me
and here's the words he said, and I made a curse over em when he
said that—you take white folks in them days and way further back
as I had learnt, never did want colored folks to live up on the front
in the public view. He said to me, "That's the way it goes with fellas
like you. You don't have no business livin up here on the highway."

Got mad because I wouldn't let him have his yearlin. "That's
the way it goes with fellas like you. You don't have no business up
here on the highway, livin where you livin."

I just told him to his face, "You aint got a damn thing to do
with where I live."

He didn't say no more. Went on back to his plowin. At dinner
he come up there and walked into my lot and done the same thing.
I walked in behind him and set down on that old hickory root and
waited patient until he gived me that dollar. Then I opened the
gate and let him carry his yearlin on home. He gived me that dollar
—he roped the yearlin first, but I was waitin on him. If he hadn't
gived me the dollar I wouldn't have let that yearlin out of my lot;
it'd taken wings to move her.

MY children weren't goin to school worth nothin then. It weren't
their fault, they wanted to go, and it weren't my fault, I wouldn't
have stopped em from goin. That school for colored children up
yonder, it'd run two or three weeks, maybe a month and a half on
the outside, and word would come down from Beaufort, "Cut the
school out; money's gone."

I have been in school business amongst the trustees and the
school officials and the patrons, I've been in it. Durin the time that
I was haulin lumber for the Graham-Pike Lumber Company, we had
a school meetin one night. And all the patrons was to attend—that

was the parents of all the children that went to school. We had to run around here and supplement what money come down to us from Beaufort to start our schools. Mighty little we got from the state government. That money was comin here through white hands and they was half-concerned with keepin colored children *out* of school. I don't know how it was in other states but it was this way in the state of Alabama: the white people's schools would start on due time. And just before they'd allow the niggers to start up their schools, there'd be a delay for some cause that the nigger couldn't affect; they'd wait along and the niggers' schools would open way after. And if we did manage to open our schools, they weren't touchin no white schools, weren't touchin em. Government weak, aint got the money, and they'd give out orders strictly for the colored people to start their schools up—white folks' schools been runnin, no shakes about it. Some way, some how, it was plain; and the nigger couldn't understand how come it runned that way, and if he did understand he couldn't do nothin about it. It hurt the nigger more that way, to come into the knowledge of his fortune and couldn't do nothin about it.

Well, the white folks' schools done started and runned along several weeks, maybe months; it'd just be left to the nigger to set still and wait on the white folks' orders. We was always left to wonder whether we would have any schools or not. White folks' schools runnin; the nigger children was at home. White man could go up there and hire the colored children from their parents if they wanted to, nothin said. Take em off over there on their plantations, work em: poor fellows, at home, cut loose from their books. White man come up there cotton choppin time, in May, nigger chaps already at home sittin down, couldn't go to school, the school was closed down on em, white man walk up there and call for em to work—better let em work for him; don't, they'll get mad with you, and it'll hurt you one way or the other. That chap got to come out of that house, big enough to work, and get in that white man's field, and white folks' schools runnin right along. Takin advantage of the colored race, keepin em by the throat. Them same conditions was in effect durin of my comin along and durin of the raisin up of my children.

So we started to supplement what money the government give us for teachers and we even sent some people to visit the government and ask for more help than what we was gettin. Well, the government promised to increase us, but the money still comin through white folks' hands and it helped them more than it helped we who needed it. White schools was runnin on part of the colored schools' money.

We'd hold meetins and we knowed what we had to do: we just had to supplement our school money to a greater extent if we cared to carry our schools on. Well, there was so many patrons disable— and there's some false-hearted folks amongst every race of folk God got on this earth. My children could have had a good education even under supplement if some of my own color had abided by their race. But the colored man had been mistreated back so far until he just learnt to mistreat hisself. Tell you what they done.

We had a school meetin at a small church one night down on Sitimachas Creek and the head ones of the school organization had taxed us all up ten dollars apiece and every patron family was sup-posed to bring that money in there at that time. I was a big man, you might say, you could say it that way and some of em did, but I was dutiful to my duties. I walked in there that night to school meetin and put down my ten dollars; carried that money to the front table and laid it down. The most of em come up—some of em carried up as low as a quarter—most of em come up with less than five dollars. Now some of em couldn't give more—that quarter took more out of em, in a way, than that ten dollars took out of me. But there was others there that could have afforded to give more than I gived, or as much, but they shied from their duty. One man come up, old man, my neighbor in past days, old Uncle George Fox and old Aunt Mercy, Uncle George's wife; nine years close to me on the Bannister place and there wasn't a clump of earth between my and their children. They got along like peas in a pod. Uncle George Fox got up—he'd been my closest neighbor for nine years, old man, had grandchildren, had great-grandchildren, and he was tryin to do right by his people—Uncle George Fox got up that night in that school meetin, poor old fellow, old man, put down six dollars. And the next nearest to that was a little less.

Fellow by the name of Israel Fry, he was one of the head offi-cials in the plan, supplementin money, gettin ready to try and start up our school—we wanted to get up and cut lumber and build a schoolhouse. I was haulin lumber at that time for the Graham-Pike Lumber Company and I asked Mr. Ed Pike about bein off and he told me, "Nate, take off what time you need for your affairs but come straight back to your job as soon as you are finished." And above that ten dollars I laid down I went and helped saw logs to go to the sawmill—several days' labor cuttin logs in the woods. Goin to use that lumber to build a new schoolhouse, that was the idea. But there was some rascals on that ship and they proved themselves to me. Cut them logs out there ready to haul and I vanished away back on my job. Next news I heard, one of the head officials come up to my house and told me, "Say, Shaw, Israel Fry got hurt; load of logs turned over with him and butchered him up bad."

I rode for Israel Fry to get a doctor; had to ride to more than one doctor to find one that wasn't too busy to look at him, then had to change doctors when they found out how tore up he was. I done it with a smile until I learnt the truth about the situation. One of the school patrons by the name of Eph Todd come to me; I was back on my job, haulin lumber regular every day. He found me drivin a load somewhere and he said, "Shaw, you know Israel Fry done let out a whole lot of that lumber over yonder and he's squandered that money—" the money we had put down on the table at the school meetin, that was in Fry's hands, and he loaned it out to some colored people, squandered it. And there was a white man by the name of Johnny Reeve, went over in the woods there and Fry let him have a whole lot of that schoolhouse lumber, let him have it someway, I never did learn what for. Just as sure as you born to die, Fry lost all that money and gived out the lumber.

Eph Todd told me, "He let Mr. Johnny Reeve, white man, have some of that lumber. And Leroy Roberts went down there and got some of it."

I said, "Do what?"

My money tied up in it. My labor cuttin logs—I had done more than anybody, backin my part of what I was taxed to do; takin time off my job to cut logs; ridin around the country fetchin doctors for Fry and him hurt haulin that lumber off to a white man or maybe for hisself. I got hot as the devil. Told Eph, "Well, I'm goin to break up some of that. I can't pay my money for school affairs and they doin with it thataway. I'm goin over there and get me some of that lumber and haul it away from there."

Next day it was drizzlin rain, drove my mules over there— had a good pair of mules, that Mary and Dela, they was just about the same size, biggest pair of mules ever I owned. Drove em on a scale one day and weighed that pair of mules together: weighed twenty-two hundred and sixty pounds together, over eleven hundred pounds apiece. I always knowed what I had—that first pair of mules, I aint goin to tell the weights of em, they was smaller mules, but I aint never owned a mule that if I hitched her up to a wagon and she couldn't move it, she'd die tryin, if I just held her there and kept a prankin with her, she'd pull every time I called to pull—I hitched Mary and Dela to my wagon and drove em over to the school house site one Thursday mornin and all the heavy lumber was gone. Wasn't nothin there but some foundation blocks and two-by-fours, two-by-sixes. They had bought that property from a white man by the name of Tom Meade to build a schoolhouse on, but they runned away with the money and the lumber too. Done away with it before they done anything else. Some of em didn't pay no money hardly and they weren't there helpin cut them logs. I put my ten dollars down free as water. And all they showed was their faces. Malcolm Todd gived less than six dollars and that was a man, at that time, if he'd a gived twice that it wouldn't a hurt him. Old Uncle George Fox, oldest man at the meetin, put six dollars down. And I put ten down, what they asked for, then slipped behind my back sellin the lumber and doin away with the money that was supposed to go for our children's benefit.

I was lackin a dollar and seventy-five cents of gettin that ten dollars back, too. I drove that pair of mules over there and I loaded whatever lumber I could find. I didn't want to get over a thousand feet and strain-halt my mules, I just wanted to take enough to make back that ten dollars. Loaded that lumber on my wagon—two-by-fours, all two-by-fours—pulled it out on home about two miles and set it down in my yard. Saturday mornin I reloaded that cut lumber and pulled it into the planin mill at Apafalya. Mr. Ed Pike was there. I said, "Mr. Ed, I got a load of two-by-fours here. Would you buy it?"

He said, "Yeah, I'll buy all the lumber you can bring me. If you haulin my lumber I'll take it and if you haulin for somebody else I'll take it."

He walked around the wagon, asked me—they had reached a point of trustin me to where they wouldn't count my lumber when I'd drive it in there less'n I insisted on it. Just, "How much you got, Nate?" "So-many and so-many, such-and-such a length"—one-by-twelves, one-by-tens, one-by-fours, one-by-eights—"got on so-many and so-many of em." I learnt what it took to make—I aint got no education but I learnt by practice what it took to make a thousand feet of all grades.

So I told Mr. Ed Pike what I had on my wagon that morning and he figured out the price—eight dollars and a quarter. Walked right in the back to the office part and he gived me a check. I carried it on to the bank and cashed it. Aint nobody said nothin to me about it this mornin and that was the year of '23.

Didn't nobody talk about buildin no schoolhouse after that. We moved the school then to a church over there called Little Bethany. Had to supplement it right along. I made a set of benches for that school, schoolhouse benches, long benches, took em on my wagon and carried em up there. They didn't need em all so I brought one of em back to my house and set it under a ten by ten hip-roofed shelter to the north side of my well.

All of my children learnt a little somethin: my two girls in Chattanooga got a lot out of school. But I had some hard-headed boys: Eugene, that's my boy in Ohio, my fourth son, and Calvin, my oldest boy over here in Tuskegee, and Vernon—them's three of my boys; my other children all got more out of school than they did. My youngest daughter got the most of all and my oldest daughter got a little better than most. That was one of the sweetest young ones—

1923, I got what the boll weevil let me have—six bales. Boll weevil et up the best part of my crop. Didn't use no poison at that time, just pickin up squares. All you could do was keep them boll weevils from hatchin out and goin back up on that cotton. Couldn't kill em.

The boll weevil come into this country in the teens, between 1910 and 1920. Didn't know about a boll weevil when I was a boy comin up. They blowed in here from the western countries. People was bothered with the boll weevil way out there in the state of Texas and other states out there before we was here. And when the boll weevil hit this country, people was fully ignorant of their ways and what to do for em. Many white employers, when they discovered them boll weevils here, they'd tell their hands out on their plantations—some of em didn't have plantations, had land rented in their possession and put a farmin man out there; he was goin to gain that way by rentin land and puttin a man out there to work it; he goin to beat the nigger out of enough to more than pay the rent on it. And the white man didn't mind rentin land for a good farmer. That rent weren't enough to hurt him; he'd sub-rent it to the fellow that goin to work it or put him out there on halves. Didn't matter how a nigger workin a crop, if he worked it it's called his until it was picked out and ginned and then it was the white man's crop. Nigger delivered that cotton baled up to the white man—so they'd tell you, come out to the field to tell you or ask you when you'd go to the store, "How's your crop gettin along?" knowin the boll weevil's eatin away as he's talkin. Somebody totin news to him every day bout which of his farmers is pickin up the squares and which ones aint.

"You seen any squares fallin on the ground?"

Sometimes you'd say, "Yes sir, my crop's losin squares."

He'd tell you what it was. Well, maybe you done found out. He'd tell you, "Pick them squares up off the ground, keep em picked up; boll weevil's in them squares. If you don't, I can't furnish you, if you aint goin to keep them squares up off the ground."

Boss man worryin bout his farmers heavy in debt, if he ever goin to see that money. Mr. Lemuel Tucker, when I was livin down there on Sitimachas Creek, he come to me, "You better pick them squares up, Nate, or you won't be able to pay me this year."

Don't he know that I'm goin to fight the boll weevil? But fight him for my benefit. He goin to reap the reward of my labor too, but it aint for him that I'm laborin. All the time it's for myself. Any man under God's sun that's got anything industrious about him, you don't have to make him work—he goin to work. But Tucker didn't trust me to that. If a white man had anything booked against you, well, you could just expect him to ride up and hang around you to see that you worked, especially when the boll weevil come into this country. To a great extent, I was gived about as little trouble about such as that as any man. I didn't sit down and wait till the boss man seed my sorry acts in his field. I worked. I worked.

Me and my children picked up squares sometimes by the bucketsful. They'd go out to the field with little sacks or just anything to hold them squares and when they'd come in they'd have enough squares to fill up two baskets. I was industrious enough to do somethin about the boll weevil without bein driven to it. Picked up them squares and destroyed em, destroyed the weevil eggs. Sometimes, fool around there and see a old weevil himself.

I've gived my children many pennies and nickels for pickin up squares. But fact of the business, pickin up squares and burnin em—it weren't worth nothin. Boll weevil'd eat as much as he pleased. Consequently, they come to find out pickin up them squares weren't worth a dime. It was impossible to get all them squares and the ones you couldn't get was enough to ruin your crop. Say like today your cotton is illuminated with squares; come up a big rain maybe tonight, washin them squares out of the fields. Them boll weevils hatches in the woods, gets up and come right back in the field. You couldn't keep your fields clean—boll weevil schemin to eat your crop faster than you workin to get him out.

My daddy didn't know what a boll weevil was in his day. The boll weevil come in this country after I was grown and married and had three or four children. I was scared of him to an extent. I soon learnt he'd destroy a cotton crop. Yes, all God's dangers aint a white man. When the boll weevil starts in your cotton and go to depositin his eggs in them squares, that's when he'll kill you. Them eggs hatch out there in so many days, up come a young boll weevil. It don't take em but a short period of time to raise up enough out there in your field, in the spring after your cotton gets up—in a few days, one weevil's got a court of young uns hatchin. He goin to stay right in there till he's developed enough to come out of that little square, little pod; taint long, taint long, and when he comes out of there he cuts a little hole to come out. Pull the little leaves that's over that little square, pull em back out the way and get to the natural little pod itself. Pull that pod open and there's a little boll weevil and he don't come out of there till he get developed, and then he do that hole cuttin. Cut a hole and come out of there, little sneakin devil, you look at him—he's a young fellow, looks green colored and sappy. Aint but a few days when he comes out of that square—aint but a few days stayin in there, and when he comes out of there—

I've pulled them squares open and caught em in all their stages of life: found the old egg in there, and I've found him just hatched out and he's right white like a worm, just a little spot in there, that's him; and if he's a little older he looks green-colored and sappy; and after he gets grown he's a old ashy-colored rascal, his wings is gray like ash. I've known him from the first to the last. I've picked him up and looked at him close. He's just a insect, but really, he's unusual to me. I can't thoroughly understand the nature of a boll weevil. He's a kind of insect that he'll develop in different colors right quick. He'll grow up to be, if he lives to get old enough —don't take him very long to get old—he'll grow to be as big around as a fly. He's a very short fellow, but he's bigger than a corn weevil. And he'll stick that bill in a cotton pod, then he'll shoot his tail back around there and deposit a egg—that's the way he runs his business. Then he done with that square, he done ruint it, and he hunts him another pod. And he's a very creepin fellow, he gets about, too; he'll ruin a stalk of cotton in a night's time. He crawls along gradually from one square to another; he gets on a limb where it's rolled off with blooms or young squares and he traces his way from one to the next, and he punctures every one of em just about, in a short while. Then he's creepin on, all over that stalk. Maybe he's so numerous sometime you can catch three or four, as high as half a dozen or more, that many off of one stalk of cotton.

If you meddle the boll weevil—you can see, travel amongst your cotton crop, I've done it myself, walked around amongst my cotton and looked, and you can see a boll weevil sometime stickin to a stalk and if you mess with him the least bit, he goin to fall off on the ground. And you watch him, just watch him, don't say a word. And he'll get up—he aint quick about it, but he'll get up from there and fly off, you lookin at him. Common sense teaches a man—how did he get in your cotton farm out there? He got wings, he flies. And you can get a handful of em in your hand, I have had that, and them scoundrels, if you don't bother em, they goin to eventually fly away from there.

When I seed I couldn't defeat the boll weevil by pickin up squares, I carried poison out to the field and took me a crocus sack, one of these thin crocus sacks, put my poison in there enough to poison maybe four or five rows and just walk, walk, walk; shake that sack over the cotton and when I'd look back, heap of times, that dust flyin every whichway and the breeze blowin, that cotton would be white with dust, behind me. Get to the end, turn around and get right on the next row. Sometimes I'd just dust every other row and the dust would carry over the rows I passed. And I'd wear a mouth piece over my mouth—still that poison would get in my lungs and bother me. Now they got tractors fixed with boxes to elevate that poison out, carry poison four rows, six rows at one run.

Old weevil, he can't stand that, he goin to hit it out from there;

maybe, in time, he'll take a notion to come back; you go out with
your poison again. Sometimes, if the cotton's good and you keep
him scared out of there and dusted out as much as you can, the
boll, at that rate, gets too far advanced for him to handle it and
that boll will open with healthy locks. But that's the only way to
beat the devil, run him out the field.

It's like the tale they told on the old sheep. A sheep is a thing
that the nature of a sheep is to be scared of dogs. And—it seems
like a old tale, but old folks have told me in olden days, olden days,
everything could talk. It just might be a tale, I wouldn't know, I
wouldn't swear to it. Well, one day, the old mama sheep carried
her little ones all out of the barn on the ranch to graze. When they
got out there, the little sheep, little lambs, always believed in keepin
up with their mother. And said, one day she carried em out on the
ranch to graze and she got em out there and showed em what to do,
and put em all to grazin, nippin grass. And she turned and went
back to the barn after she had let em out on the ranch and put em
to grazin. And she got off a little piece from em and one of the
little sheep called his mama. Didn't want to graze nohow, wanted to
follow her back to the barn. This little lamb raised up, said, "Mama,
must take the long grass or the short grass?"

"Take it all long," she answered him.

He weren't satisifed. His native wants was to follow his
mama back to the barn. After a while, soon as he got that word out
and his mama started on her way to the barn, the little lamb raised
up again, "Mama, it's rainin."

She told him, "Crop the long grass, crop the long grass."

He was pickin a excuse to leave the ranch and follow her back
to the barn. First excuse was he didn't know which grass to eat;
second excuse was it was rainin; third excuse, "Mama, yonder
come a dog."

"Come on, my child; come on, my child."

He kept throwin excuses to her until when he called the dog,
she didn't like the dog herself—it's a sheep's nature to be scared
of a dog—and she told him, "Come on, my child," and he took off
with her.

So, it's that way with the boll weevil, it appears to my mind. A
boll weevil is goin to take it all long; he'll ruin your crop if there's
barely enough in there. And there's no way he'll leave your field

less'n a man come through there dustin poison. Then they'll take out from there, all ages of boll weevil, but they'll be back when the man leaves and the dust settles.

Old boll weevil, he don't leave the country in the fall. He goes out there in the woods under the pine straw, or he goes under the earth. But I couldn't say definitely where he goes, to save my life and be truthful. I don't know what his full nature is. But come next spring, you plant your crop, he comin in. Everything, every creature in God's world, understands how to try to protect itself. And I believe that scoundrel goes right into the forests and finds his appointed place to wait; spring of the year, he right back in the field, soon as your cotton come up, he right back on it.

God understands his insects here, He knows em well. And everything God created He created for a purpose and everything drops to its callin, and most of the things obeys His rulins better than man do.

THERE'S a kind of old worm or bug, I would say it's a worm, that'll get in your crop and heap of times he'll cut your cotton squares worser than the boll weevil will, he'll cut it all to pieces, he'll cut enough hole in it to kill that pod that's comin to be a bloom. And on top of that, there's another kind of worm—some folks call him a caterpillar. And if it's a field of cotton, these caterpillars is just as thick sometimes as the fingers on your hand. Get in that field when the cotton is green—they don't bother the cotton, they don't bother the boll except to cut every bit of shuck off of that boll. Some folks call em army worms, and they're in that field just broadsided. Maybe your cotton will go on and open when they get through with it, but they'll hurt it so before it gets done makin. Don't leave no leaves on your crop at all, he'll eat em all off, your field will look raggedy as the devil. And when he cleans that field up—skins them leaves off, eats em up, leave your stalks naked and your bolls shinin—if there's a field of cotton yonder cross the road, you can see em all in the ditches and all in the road, crawlin across to get in that field.

The natural old original weevil himself will strike your corn— that's common, to have the corn weevil. They gets in your corn out in the field, when the ear is on the stalk, when the stalk grows to the proper height for the ear to grow and mature. I can read them corn weevils from A to Z. He gets in that corn when it's in roastin ear and he goin to stay there too, all over your field. And when you gather that corn and put it in your barn, he's in there. Bring it out the field and he's in there and he'll eat your corn, every ear he strikes, he'll eat all the insides and the heart of that corn, he'll eat it down to the cob. They inside the shucks when you bring it out the field, just a few of em in a load of corn, a few of em in a few ears, when you put your corn in the crib, they goin to create in there.

You ever heard talk of such a thing as a camelfly? He flies just like a butterfly all over your field, as long as the weather aint too cold for him, and he's layin a passel of eggs on that corn crop— some folks call him a butterfly but he aint nothin like these big old spotted-winged butterflies that trembles in the air all over your garden; he trembles, he flies, but he's just a little old devil and he puts down his eggs—that's the corn weevil man. The corn weevil, when he's eatin your corn, he don't do much flyin, but he do fly if you stir him up. Heap of times you meddle with your corn and you set them little old camelflies just flyin out of it; well, that's the fellow, out in the field, that creates them corn weevils. And when you put that corn in the crib, blessed God, you open the door to your crib and meddle with that corn awhile, and you'll see em flyin up and out. They in there depositin eggs in your corn; consequently, that corn will become full of these little old black weevils.

There's no other insect bothers your corn worth talkin about except these old roastin ear worms; and that roastin ear worm don't deposit his own eggs. They comes from these old devilish flies that drops these foreign eggs in your corn when it's in roastin ears. You can shuck a heap of corn out in the field, or in a roastin ear patch, and you'll see a old worm done cut his trail all around in there. They're never in the butt end next to the stalk; they lurks in the free end of that ear of corn, and you shuck it, there's a old worm or two in there. Knock him out and he hasn't defected that ear of corn too thoroughly, he just worked on the end, and you get that roastin ear in a position to have fried corn. And when you get that ear of corn cleaned up for table use, and scrapes the tops of all them grains of corn off in your pan, and scrape the juice and goody out of it, you throw that cob down. Most of we farmers drop the cobs in a vessel and put em in the hog pen; if you got a fattenin hog in the pen and them cobs is green and tender, he'll eat up every one of em. It's good for hogs.

Who sent the corn weevil here? And who sent the boll weevil
and all sort of pesters, who put em here? Who created the heaven
and earth and everything therein? God put all these pesters and insects here. As bad a old thing as a snake, God put him here; and
He put them things here—maybe, I wouldn't accuse God of nothin
wrong—to trouble people. Folks in this world needs pesterin to
wake em up to their limit. And to my best opinion, God put the
different weevils here and the weevils does their duty. Some things
may do more than God put em here to do—that's the human, he do
more things than God put him here to do. But God thought so much
of this human race He created humans in His image and His own
likeness, and still they're the worst things God got on this earth
to one another. God knew you'd do it but He gived you a chance,
He put you here, He put His holy righteous words here for you to
read and look over; and if you can't read God's words you still can
believe some things. He thought so much of you He gived you
knowledge He didn't give the other animals. And He gived you a
soul to save, He made you responsible to that knowledge: a man
is responsible, a woman is responsible, for the acts of their flesh
and blood and the thoughts on their minds.

I can't hate God's pesters, definitely, because they doin what
God put em here to do. The boll weevil, he's a smart bird, sure as
you born. And he's here for a purpose. Who knows that purpose?
And who is it human that can say for sure he knows his own purpose? He got all the wisdom and knowledge God give him and God
even sufferin him to get a book learnin and like that—and what
the boll weevil can do to me aint half so bad to what a' man might
do. I can go to my field and shake a poison dust on my crop and
the boll weevil will sail away. But how can I sling a man off my
back?

1923, them old boll weevils stayed in my cotton until they ruint it.
I didn't make but six good heavy bales and it weren't bringin twenty
cents. About twelve and a half and fifteen cents. And it got lower
than that, fell to half of that, lower than any man believed it could
fall in the years to come.

Just before I got ready to move away from Two Forks—I hope
God will be with me—Mr. Stark tried to get me to destroy the
house. He had it insured; told me, "Nate, your time is up on this

place and you movin elsewhere. I want you to destroy this house when you leave."

He tried to put me up to burnin the buildin down before I left. He had jumped up and sold the place just about the time he found out I was goin to move. And he wanted me to burn down the dwellin house *after* he sold it. You see, he could collect on the insurance until the other man moved onto the place. It was sold all right, but he still had possession. And if I destroyed that house—

He laid plans for me how to destroy the buildin myself; just thought I'd be fool enough to jump into it and do it. I didn't say I would do it and I didn't say I wouldn't do it.

He said, "Now here's the way for you to do it. When you get started movin out, don't take everything; leave some of your throwed off stuff in there. Then destroy the house on the last round, destroy it."

I would have been the biggest rascal and the biggest fool, workin against myself, as ever there was if I'd a listened to him. And he got on me a number of times before I moved. He said, "You aint never done what we was talkin about."

I said, "No sir, I aint done it."

Still didn't tell him I was goin to do it and didn't tell him I wasn't. And I haven't done it this mornin. I estimated the matter in my judgment this way: you never know what'll happen in a heap of cases until it happens. I considered I was a poor colored man and he had done went ahead and sold the place to another white man, fellow by the name of Jim Horn, who come out of the hills up yonder and had never lived down in this part on smooth land. Mr. Horn's dead now but his son got that place today, right there at Two Forks.

So, Mr. Stark told me he'd give me three hundred dollars to burn down the dwellin house and the close-by outbuildins. He'd jumped up and rented me the place, I moved there, and before I could get my crop gathered he sold it. He didn't tell me he was goin to sell it until after he sold it and then he put his proposition to me. Well, that worried me less than this: there was two things on that place that I reserved and called him in question about, that belonged to me. I had in the fall before I moved up there sowed me them oats that Mr. Culpepper's yearlin done ruint, and bought me some brand new barbed wire and wired em up. And when Mr. Stark sold the place I come up to him, said, "Well, did you reserve my new barbed wire around them oats? You didn't sell that with the place, did you?"

"No," he said, "your wire, I reserved that."

I said, "And that harness house of mine—" nice little harness house sittin outside of the barn. I'd built it on the Tucker place down on Sitimachas Creek. And when I moved from down there, I coupled my wagon out long enough that I could put me on some of the Graham-Pike heavy lumber and drive up there and turn that harness house over on that lumber, between the wheels—moved it up to the Stark place, put it down, blocked it up there. It weren't nailed to the place at all, just blocked it up and leveled it. It was as much as six foot high and four foot deep and I could handle it easy on my wagon. Hauled it up there and put it down on the same blocks I had it on down there on the Tucker place.

I asked Mr. Stark about it. He told me, "No, nothin you has aint included in the place. You can take your harness house with you."

When I got ready to move, I went over in the field and took my barbed wire down and rolled it up, carried it to the house so it'd be there, and I loaded it up in movin. And that harness house was the first thing I moved. Went out there one mornin, coupled that wagon out long enough—just like I been haulin lumber— coupled it out long enough to haul sixteen-foot lumber and then put that sixteen-foot stuff on it to hold that house up good and stout. Me and my boys pushed the house up on it. Carried it about a mile and a quarter or not over a mile and a half to the Pollard place, where I was movin to. I didn't never tie it down to no place and it was a nice-built harness house, light enough that me and my boys could handle it.

Mr. Jim Horn was game enough—one day he come there lookin around and he forbidded me—he'd heard somethin about that harness house; maybe Mr. Stark might have told him, but he meant to keep that house there. So his boy come there one day and he said, "Nate, Daddy says don't move that harness house out there."

I said, "What you say?"

"Daddy says don't move that harness house."

I said, "Well, I'm goin to move it."

He said, "You better not; Daddy done sent you word by me tellin you not to move it."

First thing I jumped up and moved when I got ready to move. I moved that harness house and everything else I had away from there. And I didn't disfigure the place; I couldn't afford to do that.

So, I met this Horn in the road one mornin as I was comin out of Apafalya, goin to a lumberyard way back out over in them hills. He met me, said, "Nate, I'll just give you—" I was bull-headed as the devil; I didn't bear no thoughts of not movin what I knowed was definitely mine, and it weren't nailed to the place. They mighta used to have a law, but I didn't know anything about no such law— but if you left and moved off a place, you couldn't draw out nails and move a thing if it's nailed to a place. Anything that aint tied down that you could load up without knockin nails out of it, why, that's your privilege.

So he said, "I'll give you until tomorrow night to get that harness house back up there."

I looked at him, said, "Mr. Horn, that harness house is mine. I built it before I moved on the old place you bought and it weren't never nailed to the place. It's my right, as I know it, to take it with me if I please." Told my mules, "Come up," and went about my business.

I never picked that house up again once I set it down on the Pollard place. And burn down them buildins for Mr. Stark—I wouldn't a done that for no man. No tellin what he might have slipped around and done to me if I'd a destroyed em. When a person takes a notion to do devilment, the devil incarnate can't stop him. If that white man would destroy his own house, have me do it, what would he do to me? He liable to collect his insurance then turn me in to keep from payin me anythin— Please Lord, take care of me. If they knowed I was accusin em of such as that some of em would be hot with me today.

V

I moved on the Pollard place and become entangled with Mr. Lester Watson. And in the wind-up of it, big trouble come off—a shootin frolic in '32.

I never had worked none of the land when I agreed to buy. I'd seed the plantation in passin—old colored man by the name of Amos Pollard owned that place when I was a boy and his wife, old

Uncle Amos Pollard's wife Becky; they lived there and Uncle Amos owned it and it went in his name. And one day, my daddy, when I was a small boy—I was big enough to go two or three miles by myself walkin, and old Uncle Amos Pollard was a blacksmith and he kept a little old shop on his place. My daddy would give me plows to tote—at that period of time my daddy didn't live hardly two miles from old Uncle Amos Pollard, on further up Sitimachas Creek. He'd tell me, "Go over to Uncle Amos and tell him to sharpen my plows for me."

I'd take them plows, three or four, four or five scooter plows and go over there for him to sharpen em for my daddy. Quite natural, I hate to say it, it just busts in my mind—my daddy weren't doin much with no plow, but he'd want sharp plows ready if he decided to do somethin. I'd take them plows and carry em— and one mornin, I walked up to Uncle Amos's house about nine o'clock. Bein a boy, I didn't look around at the condition of the land. It was sort of hilly around there but that was all I could tell. I went over there that mornin with a turn of plows and Aunt Becky —and there was another old lady stayed with em, her name was Susan; they was both old ladies and Uncle Amos was a old man, but he was still plowin, workin a little crop, workin in his shop.

I got there that mornin and weren't nobody at the house. Well, I discovered Aunt Becky and that other old lady out there in the field on the north side of the house—it was hilly back there some— burnin brush on some fresh land that had just been cleared up and they was rakin with their rakes and pilin brush and cleanin it off for Uncle Amos, seemed like. I went on out there in the field where they was. I walked up to the two old ladies—and it appeared plain that there had been many big log heaps burnt up there on that fresh land they was cleanin up. I looked around and I asked Aunt Becky, "Aunt Becky, where is Uncle Amos?"

She said, "Honey, Uncle Amos is way down yonder in the low field close to Sitimachas Creek."

She showed me whichaway to go. I listened at her—done left my plows up there at the house. And all them old big log heaps round there on the new ground was burnt down to ashes. Me bein a little old boy, I didn't know, looked like them log heaps had been burnt for several days. So, Aunt Becky told me where Uncle Amos was, I thanked her and fixed to get on my way and go to him. And I went hustlin through one of them old burnt up log heaps, lookin

down to see the ashes scoot up between my toes and the dust
settle on the bottom of my pants legs. When I knowed anything I
was just a jumpin and a hollerin and a runnin—some of them hot
coals was stuck to the bottom of my feet.

Aunt Becky run to me, "Honey, honey, honey, I'm sorry."

But Aunt Becky weren't to blame; it was the way I was transactin myself, not knowin no better. Them log heaps had burnt
clean down to nothin but ashes and still some hot coals under there,
and that shocked me. But I hopped and went on and Aunt Becky
took off to the house like a old lady would and got some ointment
and rubbed it on the bottom of my feet. My feet had a fire-crust on
em—O, Lord, it just set my whole body afire. But I scuffled on to
where Uncle Amos was, just about a half a mile from where that
happened. I went there and told him what my daddy wanted—
he couldn't sharpen them plows that day but he told me he would
do it, asked me where did I leave em and so on.

So I hobbled on back home. I been knowin that place ever
since them days, like to had my feet burnt off down there. The first
man I knowed after the death of Uncle Amos—I was growin up
then in the world—the place laid out for a while after Aunt Becky
and Uncle Amos died. Then Mr. Morris Wiley bought it, white man.
I don't know who-all definitely and what twistin up happened between the death of Uncle Amos and the time that Mr. Morris Wiley
bought the place, but that was the first man I knowed to live there
after the death of em. I don't know who he bought it from—they
had no children to go to for it. And Mr. Morris Wiley, when I got old
enough to know anything, he bought it and built a pretty good
house there, weatherboarded it and sealed up one room. And the
house on the place when he bought it, the old house Aunt Becky
and Uncle Amos had lived in, it was a pretty big old house but it
was a log house. And Mr. Morris Wiley built him a big roomy house
with plank and he built it in a L-fashion; bedroom, dinin room,
and kitchen went off from the livin room in a L.

Well, he stayed there and farmed several years and he never
did make no success of it and he whirled up and moved away from
there. Somehow or other the land fell into Mr. Watson's hands and
the Federal Land Bank in New Orleans, both. And Mr. Max Meade,
young white man, old man Tom Meade's son—old man Ralph
Meade was the father of Tom Meade, and Joe Meade and Max Meade
and Millard Meade was Tom Meade's boys—and Max Meade bought

the place. Little Max Meade they called him. He was a poor white fellow and he never did, him and his wife never did have nary a child as long as they lived together. He married Miss Cordy Vail's daughter, called her Esther. So, he got on this old Pollard place after Mr. Morris Wiley got off. He got on it through Mr. Watson and the Federal Land Bank, he bought it and he couldn't handle it, didn't have no children, no help or nothin, and he hashed around and done the best he could and he had to give up. And he talked with me about it, got me to take it over. He didn't tell me bout the condition of the land—man goin to sell you a place he aint goin to give you no odds and ends, he goin to get it off on you if he can. Well, I never had plowed it a day in my life but I knowed it, I thought I knowed it—but I never had the least idea it was as rough and as poor as it was. I just decided—I had good stock, tools, and my boys was gettin to be big enough to be a help to me, and he mentioned the place to me, told Mr. Watson and all, got it lined up and I took it over from him and commenced a buyin it.

The place went for sixteen hundred dollars and they was supposed to give me several years to pay it in full. I'd send a check in the mail to the Federal Land Bank in New Orleans, sixty-some-odd dollars a year. And sixty-some-odd dollars to Watson, I was payin him along. He didn't like that. He seed where he was cut off from me. I only had to keep up with the land debt with him—he didn't have no mortgages on my stuff for nothin. But he wanted it all and everything I had.

He lingered along for a year or two, then he undermined me and didn't tell me he done it. He got in with the federal land people someway and he got full possession of the Pollard place. I didn't have no political pull and I couldn't do nothin about it. I was still goin in the name of buyin the place but now I was buyin from him complete. When I didn't geehawse like he thought I ought to, he took the place over, blotted my name out with the federal government. To this day I don't know how he did it. I expect he offered to pay my part to them and they agreed; taken my part out of my hands and payin the federal government, then made me pay him what I was payin them—they turned it all in his hands. They got their money for the place from him and he had me over a barrel.

I was in good shape when I got dealin with Mr. Watson. Time for him, he thought, to come in dealin with me. When the time rolled around for me to buy the old Pollard place I had a pair of good horses and a pair of good mules, raised my own food for my stock, and at that time I had a little blacksmith shop. I didn't have no notions, no dreams, of doin no work for no outsiders when I set it up. I done that for my own benefit because at that time I was runnin them four head of stock and the price for blacksmithin was quite high so I decided I'd try to do it. And as it worked out, I shod my own mules; shod mules for Mr. Jack Knowland, man my daddy hired me out to in 1904—now he come to me to have his mules shod. And I made a right smart little bit of money, unexpected, shoddin stock for other people.

I bought my blacksmith tools from Mr. Hinton Wheeler; he had been usin em but he didn't know too much about em and he didn't like the work. So he sold me his anvil, vise, and blower. I burnt up several pieces of iron learnin how to use them tools, but it weren't much I burnt up, a few little old slivers that got hot quicker than I thought. I'd stand there and blow the fire—it fired *me* up to make a fire so hot. I enjoyed it and soon I become expert at the job. Workin over them coals, buildin up my fire, keepin it goin and regulatin it—

Blacksmiths used to say, and a heap of other folks: "It's hard to set a scrape to do nice work." Most anybody can beat out a scooter and draw it to a point and sharpen it, but when you start settin them scrapes and sharpenin em, that's a rough job. I done a bit of it after I started that blacksmith work. And I had more of it to do than I thought I would when I moved on the Pollard place.

THE old place contained somewhere around eighty acres and after I worked it awhile I found it was rough as pig iron and if I made any crop—O, I made a little stuff there but I didn't make nothin like I was due to make with the force I had and the stock. It was rough and rocky land—round rocks the size of your fist to littler and the size of your fist to bigger. You just couldn't make it on that land by itself. Of course, Watson didn't care about the land, he cared about the type of man that worked it, whether it was a man that worked hard to have good mules and cows and hogs, a wagon and a buggy. And to tell the truth—one word brings up another— none of em didn't care usually nothin for you just as long as you made a crop, nary a man ever I worked with. There was Mr. Curtis, put me on the poorest land he had; I didn't make chicken shit. And

as the boys said at the time—they laughed about it a whole lot—
that old land was so poor until it would grunt sproutin peas. Well,
I moved down with Mr. Gus Ames and it was the same thing,
really; put me on the sorriest land he had. It just absolutely didn't
do me no benefit. And when I moved away from there to the Reeve
place, I commenced a makin out better for myself. I got a hold of
my business there—but his son-in-law was takin over the land; he
was a young fella and when he moved up there he wanted to boss
the whole place. That didn't suit me. And I moved then off down on
the creek on the old Bannister place under Mr. Tucker's administration. It was rough as the devil and then them hills, too. Good God,
it was ill to work a man or a mule there. Well, I moved from there
to the Stark place, at Two Forks, and the boll weevil took over my
farm. I didn't make but six bales of cotton that year. I moved on
back then to the Pollard place, just backtracked along the same
road and stopped and settled down where I could buy my own land.
When I got there I fell out again—didn't know the old place was
so rough. Couldn't make no corn worth a boot and had to work
like a devil there to make a little cotton—made that between the
rocks. When I discovered that, I just come out and went to rentin
me some smooth land in the piney woods. I was livin on the Pollard
place but I had to rent other land to make enough. I worked Miss
Cordy Vail's land, clean land; I worked it on halves and I made six
bales of cotton on four acres. That weren't no triflin crop in them
days. And on Mr. Thurman Groves' place where I had fifteen acres
rented, fourteen or fifteen, his land weren't so strong but it was
easy to work, I made six bales of cotton there too. Cotton was down
then to about twelve cents so it taken a heavy crop to prosper a
man. And so, down on Mr. Groves' place I made six good bales of
cotton; six on Miss Cordy Vail's four acres—and I worked some of
my father-in-law's place. That Pollard place was joinin my father-
in-law's place. But if I'd a depended on that Pollard place I'd a been
just out of luck. Still, I made seven bales of cotton there and I
was improvin the cultivatable land all along.

I was with my daddy-in-law the night he died. I was haulin lumber
for the Graham-Pike Lumber Company and when night come I'd
go over there and stay with him through his sickness. Well, my
mother-in-law, soon as he died, she put all the business of their

little old place in my hands. They had a little piece of land that they quickly bought after they married, so they told me. It weren't too long after the surrender that they bought that land. I attended to it dutifully, payin tax on it and everything until I was put in prison. Then my wife and Vernon taken it over and kept up the taxes. And right after old man Waldo Ramsey died, several of these white people that knowed about the place wanted to buy it from me. They commenced a runnin at me quick. But I told em, "No, I won't sell. I'm the caretaker of the business part of the place and if anybody is goin to profit by it let it be the Ramsey children."

Some of the Ramsey children jumped up and wanted to sell the place to get their part out of it. My wife kicked against it—she didn't want to sell her mammy and daddy's home place. So I studied a way to keep any of em from sellin. If they'd all consented I mighta sold it if I could have gotten what it was worth. Well, white people didn't offer me but four hundred dollars for it and my wife didn't want to sell her part of it. Still the other children kept a naggin and a naggin bout sellin it, dividin up the money. I said to myself, 'I'm just goin to give it to em in equal parts.'

So, I had it counted off and every one of em got ten acres apiece—Hannah got ten acres, Mattie got ten acres, little Waldo got ten acres, Lena got ten acres, and Lily got ten acres. I had a deed drawed up for each of em for their ten acres. I knowed that would hitch a knot rope—didn't nobody want to buy just a piece of the property. When the white people come back to me tryin to buy it, I told em, "Well, the place is divided up in ten-acre plots. And if any of the children wants to sell theirs, if you want to buy ten acres of it, that's all you can get—ten acres from one child."

"O, we don't want just ten acres, we want the whole place."

I said, "Well, the place aint mine to sell. It's divided up and my wife won't sell her part at all. But if any of em wants to sell their part, why, that's all right."

"No, we want the whole place, we don't want no ten acres."

So that stopped em. The land is standin together today.

Four years after old man Waldo died, his wife married again, and she died. And before she died, the home house burnt up, the house that she married in the first time and raised up her children. And she asked me, "Nate, you got good mules and you know your way around saws and hammers and other tools. Will you build my house back?"

I told her, "Yes, I'll do it."

She said, "I'll tell you what to do. You go to that sawmill where they're runnin that saw back on this place and reserve enough timber to put the house up."

I reserved the lumber that was needed to build the house back and the balance that was cut brought seventy-five dollars. I taken that money and carried it to my mother-in-law. I'd told her after old man Waldo died—fact of the business, I taken my children and what children of hers, what girls come to help me and the boy, and gathered the crop he left that year. And I sold it off—every time I'd gin a bale of cotton and sell it, I'd bring her the money. I told her, "Ma, I'm goin to give you the receipts I got for this crop so there won't be no confusion bout how much it brought."

She said, "Nate, child, I don't want no papers, I know you aint goin to beat me out of a nickel. I aint worried about it."

I said, "Well, Ma, I'm goin to try to do straight so nobody can't come up and say that I took over here and consumed all my daddy-in-law's stuff."

She said, "No, Nate, let em talk. I know you aint doin it; you too honest to do such a trick as that."

I said, "Well, you just keep these papers. Let your children, they got a book learnin, let em look over em, see what the stuff brought."

She took em, too, but I can't say that she ever looked at em or had anybody else to look at em neither.

I went on, and the timber that it taken to put the house up, I hauled it to Mr. Ed Pike's planin mill in Apafalya and had it dressed for construction. Mr. Levi Wheeler, carpenter, he come there and helped me lay the foundation and put up the studs. Then I cut all the plates, all the rafters, and boxed the house up, sealed the floor and the overhead. The stove room was a pretty good-sized room, twelve by sixteen. I never did put a partition in there, so you could use the stove and dinin room parts all together. And just before I finished the house, old lady Molly Ramsey died.

I hauled lumber until the mill shut down. They just cut this country out of wood, cut this country out of wood. I laid with em to the end, too. People come here from all parts of Alabama and people come out of Georgia too, durin of the operation of the mill. I've known six mules and three two-horse wagons to come out of the state of Georgia, work for the Graham-Pike Lumber Company, haulin lumber, and stuck at it as much as a year. Fellow by the name of Ball, white man, brought two colored fellows over here and a pair of mules to each man, and put his son, one of his big boys, to a pair of mules. Put em all over here haulin lumber, three wagons, six mules—and talk about beatin mules and brutally treatin em, it was goin on regular with that crowd.

I was haulin lumber out from up close to a place they call Jerome, some folks used to call it Gem Stone, way out there between Apafalya and Crane's Ford, near Newcastle. One mornin I was later gettin to the yard than they was, and they had done got in there and loaded and left before I got loaded, and when I come on out cross Sitimachas and got in there between Sitimachas and Elam Church, goin to Apafalya, right there on top of a big hill stood two of old man Ball's wagons, and the third wagon bout halfway up. Them wagons was all loaded too heavy, long hauls to make, bout a ten mile haul from the yard to the mill. I never would pull a load of lumber right from the mill into Apafalya with more—or less— than a thousand feet. My mules managed it like a top, a thousand feet of dry lumber. A little old triflin pair of mules could make it with that, and when I'd get on them long hills, I wouldn't say nothin to my mules until I did this: that brake lever there to them hind wheels, I kept it hooked right by my seat. I'd pull my mules bout halfway up them long hills then reach for the rope to that lever, snatch it, you'd hear the lever drop in its slot, Plop. I'd tell my mules, "Aaaaaaaaaaaayyyyyuuuuuummmmmmmm, rrrrrrrrmmmm-mmmmmmmmmmmm."

Got them wheels locked, them mules stopped still, just layin in the collar, restin.

Well, when I drove up behind that Georgia crowd and caught em there on that hill, fightin and beatin them mules, that there white fellow—of course, it was his daddy's mules, he'd handle em any way he wanted; and handle them colored fellows' mules any way he wanted. Quite natural, he had dominion over all them mules. And when I got on that long hill, two of them wagons had made it to the top but one pair of mules had run backwards until they run the back wagon in a ditch and give up complete, wouldn't make a trial at it. That white fellow took him a club of some sort and he beat them mules that didn't make that hill, he beat em over the head and nostrils. I stopped my wagon, got off and walked up there and looked at him. And he done beat one of them mules till it was bleedin at the mouth.

I said, "Don't do that. It's wrong to treat him thataway."

I had feelin and sympathy for dumb brutes. I said, "Take em out, I'll pull your wagon out; take them mules loose."

I knowed what I could do. I'd been doin folks—when they'd overload their mules, goin up steep grades and not lettin em rest. O, I couldn't stand to see it. I went on back down the road there to the foot of the hill where my team was standin, took em loose from my wagon, sidetracked em, took em loose and went up there and hitched em to that white man's wagon and pulled him out. My mules just walked up that hill like babies.

I been blessed in my life, I was sure-shod, sure-shod. In all the years I hauled lumber for the Graham-Pike Lumber Company I never did break even a wagon wheel down. Never had no wagon trouble but a wear-out. I wore out one wagon and bought a new one, kept a rollin. When a wagon come up condemned with me it just wore out.

Mr. Ed Pike and Mr. Duncan Walls was the only men in Apafalya that sold that number one timothy hay—Mr. Ed kept it at the planin mill for his hands. And it was such a choice hay for stock to eat. Best hay ever I heard of or fed my stock on in the whole of my life, number one timothy hay. Stock loved that hay—them people out in the country where they was raisin that hay and shippin it about, they took care of it and made first class hay out of it by handlin it right and cuttin it just at the right time. You never found no rotten mess amongst that hay. Well, my mules dearly loved it. They'd eat it just as soon as they'd eat that high-grade sweet feed. And they got to where they wouldn't eat corn raised on my farm, so I bought it for em regular.

I went to Apafalya one day to buy a load of that hay. Mr. Pike didn't have none at the time and I wanted a ton too because I had my horses at home plowin and I wanted hay for them just like my mules et. As long as the Graham-Pike Lumber Company stayed in this country I kept a pair of good mules on the job and a pair of horses at home with my boys, plowin.

So I asked Mr. Walls, "Mr. Walls, you got any hay on hand? I want a ton for my stock."

He said, "Nate, I aint got a bit, but I got a carload comin."

I said, "If I can get a ton of it, Mr. Walls, just take my name down and your money's ready when the hay come."

His hay come and he dropped me a card. I hitched my mules to my wagon and taken that oldest boy of mine with me to pick up that hay. He was big enough to help me considerably at that time. Had a good two-horse wagon with a new bed on it and that dandy pair of mules. Mr. Ed Pike weighed them mules, I went to his gin one day and he put em on the scale together. Mr. Pike was runnin a gin there at Apafalya too. When the woods was all cut out and the lumber operation begin to cease off, he bought a gin house out and opened up his own gin there in town. And when he quit ginnin he stayed on there awhile. I had to crawl off that lumber haulin by it gettin lighter and I decided I'd better ease and put my best attention back to the farm.

So I loaded the hay that mornin, just stacked it pretty right there in town and roped it down good to where it wouldn't have fell if my mules hadn't run away with me.

I drove out with that ton of hay and got to the graveyard on the west side of Apafalya—the white people has a church there they call Jerusalem Church, Primitive Baptist denomination. And just as I got there even with the front end of the graveyard I met up with a colored fellow on a Ford car. I knowed him well; his name was Hiram Frond. And I looked up the road there at Jerusalem cemetery and I seed Hiram Frond drivin toward me, eatin up the road. My mules stopped still, I couldn't budge em. One of em was a black mule and the other was a bay-colored mule. And that black mule pitched a fit there. She just stretched out on the ground and I was settin so high on top of them twenty-six bales of hay, ton of hay, until I didn't have no purchase to hold them mules like I should have. And that Mary mule just squatted down, stretched out her front feet and buried her head between em. That fool mule—she was a big mule, fat and round, she just patted the ground. I'd been handlin them mules and I thought I could manage em in any situation but I was mistaken. I ought to have considered I was in a devil of a place to hold em. If I'd a swung down on em, my force would have pushed that hay out from under me.

I told Hiram Frond—he sidetracked his car. I was in the road and he pulled over next to the ditch and the ditch was just deep enough to shake up a wagon whenever a wagon wheel dropped in there. He stopped sharp and when he stopped I tried to quiet the mule down and get her up. She had done squatted, stretched out in the middle of the road. Well, that other mule, that unnerved her. But I got em quiet and I thought I'd make it. I beckoned for Hiram Frond to come on. He started to move off and my black mule just stayed flat out on the road. And he drove on with a wheel in the ditch, tryin to ease by. That doggone Mary mule kept her eye on the nose of that Ford and I just kept beckonin to him to go on by, and he drove on by just as easy as he could. Soon as he done that, that mule jumped up and when she first moved off she moved off jumpin. Well, the other mule couldn't do a thing; both mules weighed about the same and it seemed like nary one of em had a advantage over the other. And it frustrated that Dela mule and she got to stampedin too. They put out to runnin and when they runned off, Hiram Frond stopped to look back at me. Them mules run a piece, then whirled around to the left and when they done that, the wagon dipped down in that little sink and bounced and bounced and just the time they pulled the wagon out of there they was headin, looked like, right for that cemetery gate. I couldn't hold em and the hay commenced a givin way. It was roped but it weren't roped substantious to be up as high as it was.

I raised up and jumped off and when I jumped off I fell right against one of them blackjack trees—big blackjack grove of trees there—I fell clear against the roots of it. I was so high on that hay, when I hit the ground I couldn't handle myself, couldn't hold up myself. Down I went, my right shoulder hard against the roots of the blackjack tree. I held them lines and they drug me away from that tree and when I looked and knowed anything I was just rollin and wallowin right up under that front wheel. I flung them lines away. Them mules draggin me and pullin that wagon too, just like a sand-sifter runnin. And when I turned em loose they got right sure enough. Looked like they was headed straight for the cemetery gate and they gradually turned. And when they turned, makin it back to the road that I just come up along, I looked up on the wagon and Calvin was sittin up there. I commenced a beckonin him to jump off, beckonin him to jump off. And he raised up and jumped.

And the road—there was a wire fence beside the road and it run around and around goin, it looked like, out to Mr. Tom Sherman's house set way out in the field, big, old-timey house. The mules jumped back in the road and they looked like they was headed for home then, done made the turn away from the cemetery. Headed for home. And I run out there. I didn't think I was hurt, it was all so quick done. And there was a big oak tree standin in the V of the road where a little road turned off the main line and went on down to Mr. Tom Sherman. And I beat them mules to that V and stood there and throwed up my hands and got em excited—they didn't know what to do then. And they run—I wouldn't let em go toward Mr. Tom Sherman and I wouldn't let em go up the road on the route home. I run out there and cut em off ary way they tried to go, zig-zagged em, and when they run, got to this fork, I was right there. And I run em into that oak tree. That tongue—brand new wagon bed—that tongue hit that oak tree—BOOM—one of the mules on one side of the tree and the other mule on the other side. Old oak tree was five foot around. That wagon just shot up on em and tripped em. The traces were hitched and they couldn't do nothin. I run up there and grabbed em both and got em quieted down, commenced a talkin to em and quieted em down. And my boy, Calvin, he run up there and I said, "Son, catch hold to the hind wheels and roll em off the lines."

My lines was down there but didn't break my lines, just busted the tongue clean out of the hounds, and the end of it next to the wagon where it went into the hounds joinin the back axle to the front axle dropped to the ground. Calvin caught the wheels and rolled em—weren't but thirteen bales of hay, half the load I carried out of Apafalya, left up on that wagon. My mules done throwed off the balance of em. Some of that hay fell clean off into Mr. Sherman's field there at the side of the road.

And I looked around there in a jiffy or two and here come Mr. Tom Sherman, who lived out in that field, in the naked openin out there, and Mr. Melville Tucker, Mr. Lemuel Tucker's brother; he lived just up the road on the other side of the church, on the right, goin toward home. I looked around and seed Mr. Tucker and Mr. Sherman both. And them two white men begged me to go to the doctor.

Mr. Sherman said, "Nate, we thought you was killed but we're glad you're not no worse than you are—"

Both of em lookin at me and accordin to what they seed, they told me they knowed I was hurt.

I begged off of em. I said, "Mr. Sherman, Mr. Tucker, I appreciate you all's kindness toward me. I'm happy to have your sympathy. But I aint hurt—"

I didn't *feel* hurt but my collarbone was knocked down. I couldn't raise up my right hand.

And so, they said, "Nate, go to the doctor. We know you're hurt."

I said, "Mr. Tucker—" He had a good wagon, two-horse wagon hisself, and it was a Owensboro. The tongue from his wagon didn't exactly fit in the hounds of my wagon but it'd fit. I said, "Mr. Tucker, I'm goin home. I kindly thank you two white gentlemen for having sympathy for me. But I aint hurt bad and I'm goin home. Could I borrow your wagon tongue and put it in my wagon till I come back this evenin?"

I was dependin on gettin Mr. Tom Russell's—white man lived close to me, he had a Owensboro wagon and my mind thought right quick: get Mr. Tucker's wagon tongue and go home and unload that hay and come back with Mr. Russell's wagon and give Mr. Tucker back his tongue. And that's what I done.

I told Calvin to come around and unbreast them mules. Then I said, "Now, son, go and pick them lines up and straighten em out and bring em to me."

He done it. But the mules rared back like pretty boys. They wanted to get away when they realized they was loose from that wagon—that tongue was on the ground. I couldn't have held em if they'd a started with me, I couldn't a done nothin but what I did do. They knowed me. I coaxed em and talked to em kind and petted em down and they halfway forgot they was loose.

Well, Calvin runned up there to Mr. Tucker's house and pulled the pin out of his tongue and pulled the tongue out of his wagon and brought it to me right quick. We put it in my wagon then for a tongue and I went and hitched them mules back to it, held them lines and drove around back to the hay that was spilled around both sides of the road and some of it on the road too—and tried to load what I could get my hands on right there close.

And Calvin said, "Papa, let it alone. I'll put it on the wagon."

He put on two or three bales and I told him I was goin to help him, I could use my hands. And I went to help him raise up as light a thing as a bale of hay and I couldn't do it. I just didn't have no power at all. Well, he had me to get out of the way then and he put on the hay by himself. But I just had half my load on then. I decided to go on home, carry what hay I had on the wagon home and come back that evenin to get the balance. And so I got in the wagon and sat down, not feelin too bad, and I wound up my lines short as I could so I could pull the mules down if they started, I thought.

I said, "Now son, you get in there and sit right beside them brakes and if they start karoin,* makin any move about runnin, just throw them brakes over, snap that rope, and throw them brakes over."

He had to do that two or three times before we got home. Them mules was still nervous—and I had about four miles to drive. So Calvin set there and when they started to karoin or freshened up like they wanted to run again, he dropped them brakes over. That throwed pressure on em, and I had them lines. Got on home—I hurt so bad then—when they got home they was quiet, no cars runnin around. So I drove the mules on down to the lot, stopped the wagon, and told my boys to unload it—I let them boys handle them mules around the house or they could plow em, but I wouldn't trust em on the road with em because I knowed them mules would kill them boys if they took a notion.

My wife had a nice dinner fixed that day—always killed all the meat I wanted. We kept plenty of meat and lard to do us from Christmas to Christmas, four and five cans of lard, these fifty- and sixty-pound cans. We didn't have to look but to what we produced ourselves. After our fresh meat would give down, why, I'd go to the store and buy a little freshness; but my main livin come out of the hog pen, come out of the cow lot.

FOR as long as an even month, I could pull my shirt off some, maybe, but most times I couldn't. My wife or one of my boys would have to pull it off for me to lay down at night. I never did look around at my girls at all; it weren't their job to strip their daddy, but my wife or boys could do it. And mornins when I'd get up, Hannah would bathe me with liniment and she'd bathe me twice a day, chest and shoulders and all. Mornins I could get my overalls on but they always had to put my shirt on for me.

* Misbehaving; "carrying on."

And so I lingered that way for a month and I got to where every mornin I'd try to see if I could use that arm and I'd raise it up just so far, and I had to ease it back down, lay it in my lap. And I kept on and tried myself every mornin until I could raise my arm to the top of my head with the fingers straightened up.

Well, I overcome it, I sure did and it left me with only one effect: all of my born days, after I got big enough to chunk rocks, I could draw back and throw a rock with all force, but that hay spill cut that throwin off. Ever since that day I can't—I can undercut but I can't draw back and throw. If I don't throw underhand I might just as well drop the rock because I aint got no power drawin back.

I couldn't do no heavy work right away but I didn't quit travelin; had a pair of good horses and that pair of nice mules. Both of them horses was quiet but one of em was too fast for God's sake, she was too fast for me to be foolin with her—she was a mare, young mare. Never bought but one horse in my life after I started raisin up a family, the rest I bought was mares. I always liked a she-thing along a animal line. Old horses, old mules, is stubborn, biggest majority of em. I never did own a horse mule. But at that time I had that Mac horse—lingered along and the Lord was with me, my wife taken special care of me, anything I wanted done them boys would do it. If I took a notion to go to town or anywheres else, I'd tell em, "Boys, go to the lot and catch Mac, clean him off and curry him, harness him, hitch him to the buggy for me."

I'd get in there and take them lines in one hand and drive anywhere I wanted to.

When I first started to plowin after that, I give away so in my bad shoulder I just had to lean over the plow handles to keep from fallin out. Leaned over and braced myself with one hand as good as I could and this shoulder was givin way. One mornin I was plowin double, had them mules out; they started off that mornin, fightin cotton stalks, and Lord they was walkin. I couldn't keep up with their pace. The old land was rough too, and that plowin just cut me down. I stopped. I had drove that plow about fifty yards out from my barn and it was just one foot up and the other one down, one foot up and the other one down. I told my mules, spoke to em like this: "Whooooop! Whooooooop!" I didn't say, "Whoa" or "Come up," I talked to em in my own language and they caught it. They slowed down nearly to a stop and I lifted the point of that plow out the ground and turned them mules around. Out the field I carried em.

WELL, I commenced a prosperin then and got over it. I said to myself and told my wife and children, "I'm goin ahead now to see the doctor and get him to exempt me from public duty."

I hitched up my mules to the wagon and drove on out to the doctor on the road between Apafalya and Tuskegee. He examined me thoroughly, said, "Well, Nate, you say it don't hurt you now?"

Told him, "No sir. I've about got over it all right."

He said, "Well, I'll tell you. If you'd a come to me when that first happened I could have exempted you from public duty. Now you just stayed away from me and got well yourself. You able to work."

I had to put in so many days a year workin on the public roads. Weren't no asphalt roads through here then. Weren't no asphalt roads clean into Apafalya or Opelika. Called out every man in the county, white and colored, had to work the roads about eight days a year. Paid you nothin—you could pay *them* and get out of workin, pay the street tax. Everybody had to work or pay; didn't make no difference how much land you owned or if you didn't own none, when you come of age, come old enough for road age, you had to work the roads without pay or pay the tax. If you didn't have a mule or hog or nothin, when you got the right age to work the roads you worked or paid. Quite naturally, if you had nothin you was more likely to work than pay because you wouldn't have no money to pay with. Well, the white folks didn't work like the colored. Now the white ones, many a white one worked the road but if he was able to pay the five dollars he worked nothin. Work or pay. I become able to pay the five dollars and I quit. Didn't work no roads at all after that. I wouldn't work eight days for the devil where I could get out of it for five dollars.

When the doctor told me he couldn't exempt me, I was right close to the limit and I just went on and claimed my age to be too old and jumped the roads. Had to work the roads from eighteen years old until forty and only one year did I fail to work *and* fail to pay. 1906, I weren't married, my daddy had me hired to Mr. Jim Barbour in Apafalya. And I'd walk into town every Monday mornin and when the week was out I'd walk back home. And I'd walk right by Mr. Joe Hooker, foreman of the roads, white gentleman. Mr. Hooker never said "umph" to me bout workin the roads that year. I don't know whether Mr. Barbour paid the street tax under my name or if they just didn't bother you if you was hired out to a white man. But they didn't bother me at all that year. I worked for Mr. Jim Barbour and I stayed inside the corporation. Heap of times when I'd be goin on to Apafalya, Mr. Hooker would be crossin the road goin to feed his stock. His barn set on the far side of the road.

"Good mornin, Nate."

"Good mornin, Mr. Hooker."

Right on I'd go and he never called me for public duty.

Diggin ditches, gradin the sides of the roads, smoothin out. Used a shovel or a pick, shovel or a pick, and they'd have a mule and a plow on the roads—when I started workin the roads they had a mule plow plowin up the soft dirt for folks to throw in the road holes. And we'd rake out and clean out the ditches. Well, they went from that to road machines and from that to asphalt roads. They had a colored fellow drivin that road machine when it first come in; his name was Clint Kirkland. He was the only fellow that could drive that machine. And a white man learnt how to do it and turned Clint off the job. And they went to payin the white man more than what they'd been payin Clint. See, they paid the man that worked the machine, paid him and paid the road foreman too. And they didn't like for no colored man to operate no machine, pay or no pay. Colored man was good to work a mule or a horse, or give him a shovel or a rake. But give the white man the machine. Machines come in before I quit workin the roads and before the machines come in, white and colored did the same job. That was all back yonder when I was a young fellow from a boy up to grown. Then the machines come in and this colored man worked it awhile, then this white man come along and got that machine out from him. Clint Kirkland was drivin but this white man had a family to support and at that time Clint Kirkland didn't have nobody but Clint Kirkland. And they took him off the road machine and gived it to this white man.

I done reached out and got as high as four head of stock and a two-horse wagon and a rubber tire buggy. I was prosperin and when I married I didn't have decent clothes to wear, had nothin. But I never did have no view ahead that caused me to work as hard as I done. I did have it in view to support my family, keep em in shoes, clothes, groceries—and to accumulate what I could accordin to what I was makin at the time. Often, somethin to buy, I'd want it if I *could* buy it, but I wouldn't dote on it if I didn't have the money. I bought a brand new Ford car when I was haulin lumber. As colored people started to buyin cars, I started right along in there not very many months behind the first colored car buyer.

One Sunday I was over here to a church, way out between Sitimachas Creek and Beaufort, called it Sylvan Grove Church. I was up there for services. And my mother-in-law was livin up there after the death of her first husband and I kept up with the old lady, I'd do her favors, I knowed it was my duty. I never slighted my mother-in-law, I never slighted my daddy-in-law in his lifetime. Well, after he was dead about four years, she married an old colored man by the name of Joe Louis, lived right there close to that church. I thought well of the old man but he was too old for me to put trust all the way through to take care of the old lady, and I dearly loved her as a mother-in-law. I'd drive up there every week sometimes to see about her.

I drove my car up there enough, but when my wife and children took a notion that they wanted to go somewhere for pleasure, I never did set down or object—wanted to go visitin, wanted to go to church—I wanted to go up in them hills, see about her mother; the old lady was definitely lookin for me at any time. So I'd tell my wife and children—my oldest son could drive, Calvin Thomas—"You all take the car, go on about your business. Mac and that rubber tire buggy is down there at the barn yet, waitin on me. You all take the car and go ahead."

So, when my wife and children would hitch up to the car, go where they wanted to, I'd clean up and get ready, travel to Sylvan Grove meetin, and also my wife's mother lived close to the church with old man Joe Louis. Hitched that Mac horse to that rubber tire buggy one Sunday, before I ever bought that Ford car, and I hit the road through Pottstown and on in to Sylvan Grove Church, fully intendin to stop for services, then drive over to my mother-in-law's. Nobody in that buggy but me—my wife didn't visit her mother as regular as I did; we had a crowd of children and she always believed in pleasurin the children unless somethin was the matter with her mother that she had to go. And she'd tell me, "Tell Mama how I is, and tell her that I'll come as soon as I can."

Got up there at Sylvan Grove one Sunday and a fellow said to be a cousin of mine by the name of Elijah Giddings was there at meetin. We men would stand out and huddle or set out and talk. Here's the subject come up: we got to talkin about cars and I thought but little of that, in a way, because I knowed how the conversation would run.

I told em, "Yes, I'm thinkin of buyin me a car, get me a new Ford. Thinkin about it; I haven't done it yet but it's my thorough aim—my boys, anyway, they done got big enough to go and correspond girls and I think I'll just buy me a new Ford to please them. I can make it all right with a car and the stock I got and my rubber tire buggy. So I think I'll get me a car."

And our colored race is a curious race of people. Don't want you to have nothin less'n he got it too—that's what I call a begrudgeful heart and a heap of em is that way. So, I said, "I think I'll get me a car, new Ford."

Elijah looked at me and said in the presence of them other fellows, "Yeah, all of us will know when you get a car."

I wouldn't say nothin out the way to him.

"All of us will know when you get a car."

He just thinkin I was talkin bout somethin that I was as far from, the way he expressed it to me, as the east from the west. Well, in a few days I bought a Ford car and drove it up there, drove it right across the yard. When I got ready to leave, after service broke, I cranked that car up and drove it back across the church yard and my cousin Elijah Giddings was standin there lookin. He wouldn't turn his head hardly. When I drove through the crowd—soon as service was over they just crowded out in the yard, all in the way. And I got in that Ford and cranked it up, started off, easy, and blowed my whistle for em to get back and let me through.

Elijah Giddings never did lose no time with me from that day until he died.

That was steppin up higher than some—but I was a workin man, whatever I had it come to me through my labor, and the work weren't hurtin me. I didn't mind jumpin out and rollin in the defense of my family, if it was for groceries or a way for them to ride and go and enjoy themselves. I was just as proud of that car as anything I had—in a way. I didn't love it. And I weren't the only one that had a car there at church that day. But I was the only one that had a new car, spankin new Ford. I'd always been a poor man, but I was scramblin. I didn't buy that car to try and get bigger than nobody else, I didn't buy it to show myself rich—I weren't rich; I bought it to serve my family and I knowed I was entitled to anything I wanted if I had the means to get it. There's a heap of my race didn't believe their color should have a car, believed what the white man wanted em to believe. And I'm thankful to my God I have had as much outside property—leavin off ownin land—I've had nice buggies, nice wagons, nice a mules as any white man drove.

My boys, after they got big enough to drive cars, they come to me—they drove the car more than I did for their pleasure; that was most of the reason why I bought the car. After they got big enough to help me work, I found out, they'd talk it to me, they'd be glad if I bought a car so they could enjoy life some. So I went on and bought a brand new Ford car. And it got to where, after two years, them boys wanted me to change it and get a Chevrolet—a little higher grade of car.

I bought that Ford from Collier Motor Company in Tuskegee. Mr. Ed Pike was a agent for em and he got on his car and carried me and my oldest boy to Tuskegee and represented me to the motor company. Told the head boss, "Nate Shaw here wants a car. Fix it up for him and let him have it."

And he told em what was needed to tell em for them to sell a car to me. Well, I gived the head boss ninety dollars down payment and he had the mechanics to fix up the car. When it was ready, we got on the car and I put my oldest boy to drivin, Calvin; he understood it. He drove that car out from there and before we got to Apafalya—we wasn't over three or four miles out of Tuskegee and I detected that left hind wheel, every once in a while—cling-aling-aling-aling-aling—just kept a drivin, I listened at it definitely. I said, "There's somethin wrong with it."

Drove it right to Mr. Ed Pike's garage there in Apafalya—he had a garage too at that time; planer mill, gin house, and garage—and he come on out of his office and told one of the men that worked for him, young white fellow by the name of Mike Holt, said, "Mike, come out here and pull the left hind wheel of Nate's car off."

Mr. Holt come out there and jacked up the car, pulled the left hind wheel off—found it didn't have no brake-shoe in there. Mr. Holt said, "Mr. Ed, this car aint got no brake-shoe in that wheel."

"Put it back on, Mike."

Got in and drove right on back to Tuskegee—Mr. Ed told me, "You tell the head man there that I say for him to have that wheel pulled off and see what the trouble is. I know what it is and I want him to see it for himself."

Told the head man about it. He called them two fellows that put the car up that mornin; said, "Pull that left hind wheel off this car and see what the trouble is in there."

They pulled the wheel off and found just what they should have found and knowed at the start, but how come they hadn't put no brake-shoe in it, I don't know. One of em looked at the other and laughed, said, "You done that. You done that."

"No, I didn't. You done it."

"No, I didn't. You done it."

So they got up on that car and when that car left there the second time it was jam up, had all the tachments to it. Never did hear that racket no more.

And when we go back to Apafalya, I told Calvin, "Well, son, your time is out now. I'm goin to drive it from here home."

I stopped the car in the yard, settin under the steerin wheel myself. Got out, fooled around there awhile. My wife and the little children what was in the house at the time come runnin out soon as we turned off the road—not all the children was yet borned— Two of the boys, Vernon and Davey, was workin down here on the Tukabahchee River that mornin.

After a while, Mr. Lemuel Tucker come walkin up the road. I thought about that: what in the world was he doin walkin? Come from down close to the place where I moved from, comin from down the road. He stretched his eyes when he got to my well—the well was close to the road—and he looked in my yard and seed a brand new Ford car there, somethin he'd never seed before. He didn't never walk up to the car but he come in the yard. He looked at it, said, "Uh-uh-uh-uh, by George, Nate, I see you got in the car business."

Told him, "Yes sir. I went to Tuskegee today and bought one."

"Well, you better—"

He started to say, "you better mind what you doin now," that was what he meant to say but he caught hisself and changed it.

"You bett—uh-uh-uh-uh"— scratchin his leg and talkin—"you always managed every proposition you went against."

I could tell from the breath he was breathin what he meant

to say but he decided not to tamper with me and went on his way. I jumped on that car that evenin right by myself and I drove it back to the highway there at Two Forks and come on then to Pottstown and from Pottstown on down by the river where they'd been cuttin and haulin logs out of the woods. Went down there and got my boys on that Ford and right back home I come.

SHOW you how I learned to drive a car. My half-brother, Bob Shaw, TJ's own dear brother, had a Ford car just about the time the first colored folks was reachin out for cars. And he come to my house one day and me and my three boys, Calvin, Vernon—they was my own dear boys—and Davey, my sister's boy, we all got on Bob's Ford and went up to the fair in Opelika. We stayed there till about one o'clock in the mornin and then we left out from there and come all the way from Opelika to Apafalya and drove about halfway out of the little old town to the corporation limit and Bob sidetracked the car and stopped it. I had never drove a car. Told me to get under the steerin wheel and drive. And when I did that—he was a kind of a giddy fellow, just looked like he didn't know how to transact right, but he could drive that Ford. So, I just crawled under that steerin wheel—them little old Fords was geared in the floor. Had nothin to do but crank it up and when you'd mash the clutch in, it'd move off. And you'd hold it and get off a piece, take your foot off the clutch then and if necessary add a little gas to it—that's all there was to a Ford car.

So, I commenced a drivin Bob's Ford and when we come on out there close to where I'd lived in '23—used to be a vault factory there where Mr. Neil Barrow built vaults—and right there just about a half mile from the old Stark place, I turned to the right, headin north. And I done drove that car all the way out from Apafalya and never had a minute's trouble. Bob was slouchin on the front seat, next to me, just like he was asleep, and my boys was on the back seat. And when I turned to the right, there at the vault factory, I had to go up a little slant—now that's where the devil come up. Mr. Barrow's house set down below and his yard set up above and the road turned off at his house and went right up by his barn in route to my house. Made that turn and Bob jumped up— it was just a little old Ford, weren't no high-powered thing nohow, and I weren't playin the gears. It was just Cadillackin along, takin that little grade just as nice—he jumped up there and hollered, "What's the matter? What's the matter?"

I was givin the car time to take the grade, didn't change no gear. You could put it in low but it was movin fine and just about got over that rise. Bob jumped up, my half-brother, and he hollered and grabbed the steerin wheel. And when he grabbed that steerin wheel that car jumped up a bank four foot high—you know, it had some speed and up the bank that car went. That was a mess-up for no cause in the world. We had to get out of the car then; didn't hurt nobody but the fender got hung under a barbed wire fence. We pushed the car back on the road and he got under the steerin wheel and went on. I got mad because heaven knows I weren't makin no mistakes. And he jumped up there and throwed a fit and caused a accident. Didn't hit no car; weren't no cars on the road but that one that night.

I told him, "Bob, you know well as you know you're livin, I done drove that car out of the corporation of Apafalya and hadn't had a lick of trouble and drove some windin roads and bad hills comin through there by Highgate before we hit the level piney wood country. And between Apafalya and the place where we had a wreck"—barbed wire scratched the fender but the car was already scratched up—"the car never did give me no trouble until you throwed a fit."

He seed I was too hot to argue with. He was the kind of fellow that sometimes he'd be too sure of himself and other times he wouldn't be sure enough. He didn't say a word.

I learnt to drive a car that night and in under a year's time I went on to Tuskegee and bought me a brand new one. I just figured it was a inducement for my boys that I could afford. Drove that little old Ford about two years and the boys wanted me to change it for a Chevrolet. So, one mornin I went on back to the Collier Motor Company and changed that '26 Ford for a '28 Chevrolet sedan and gived six hundred and twenty-five dollars to boot. Right there I let it lick me, took a beatin on that deal. The difference between them two cars cost me more than the Ford did new, and the Ford was in pretty good shape when I traded it. Of course, I had to have that little old Ford looked after when it was necessary, some little deficiencies went wrong with it but nothin desperate. My boys just wanted a little faster and a little nicer car. And I was aimin to please my boys, get em the car they wanted and keep it in my yard for them to use, less'n they couldn't find satisfaction at home.

Two or three days' time, I deducts back to buy this Ford that I traded for that Chevrolet back. Got there and that car was gone— I always tried to realize and consider when I was takin too much expense on myself and I let them boys drive that Chevrolet to the log woods two or three times across the river at Calusa and out towards Unity. I decided that was too much car for me to be lettin em drive to the sawmill. They drove it two or three times—that was as much as I could stand. And that Chevrolet, when you'd drive it in the shed where that Ford had parked, the bumper still stuck out. It had bumpers in front and bumpers behind, sedan style. I could drive that Ford in that shed out of sight and shut the door. But I had to adjust the matter to get the Chevrolet in there—add more to the station and set the door back. Quickly come to my attention, 'That's the wrong car for you to let the boys drive to the sawmill.'

So I took off back down to Tuskegee to buy that Ford back and it was gone. Well, I went on then to another dealer, fellow by the name of Leon Montgomery. I knowed his daddy and mother well. His mother was a stepdaughter of Mr. Gus Ames. And Mr. George Montgomery, Leon's daddy, married her. I went up to Leon Montgomery and he fixed me up with another '26 Ford. It weren't nearly the car that that first Ford was. Still I kept that Chevy, I didn't swap it—had two cars then. And the boys drove the Ford but it didn't stand up like that Ford I swapped. Sometimes both of them cars would be on the road and I wouldn't be on nary one of em. One boy goin one way and one goin the other and—see, there was three of them boys goin round amongst the girls at that time—Calvin, my oldest, Vernon next, and Davey, he was older than any of my boys. I never did object to them drivin them cars if they was goin to somebody's home. But I forbidded em of haulin crowds, pickin up all sorts of loafin boys and haulin em, hurrahin. I said, "But if you get you some girls and want to enjoy yourselves, that's all right. But I don't want you pickin up these old loafin boys. I aint goin to have it."

I took that Chevrolet out of the woods and after a while the boys took a notion they wanted me to change that second Ford and get another one. Calvin come up to me in the yard one mornin and he begin to consult with me—Davey and Vernon was back down at the barn and Calvin was speakin for all of em. Told me, "Papa, we want you to change that '26 Ford off for us. We seen another car, closed Ford, over there at Calusa and we wants *it*. We want you to take this one over there and change it for us."

They was cuttin logs down here on the river at that time, workin for the benefit of their family and themselves. I thought a little and said, "All right, son, if you and the boys is sure you want it"—that crowd in Calusa was sellin cars then, new ones and all— "I'll take it down there when I get a chance."

"Yes, Papa, we don't want you to stop now and do it. When it gets too wet to work outside, some day, that'll be soon enough to change it."

My wife was standin at the door listenin at us, tryin to catch on to what it was. When the boy left me and went on to the lot where Vernon and Davey was, she come out the door and called me. She said, "Darlin, what was Calvin nuzzlin you so close for this mornin?"

I looked around; it was her spoke, I knowed it was her. I said, "O, he just wants me to change that Ford off and get em a closed Ford with a glass department."

She said, "Are you goin to do it?"

I said, "Yeah, I'm goin to change it for em."

She said, "Uh-huh, you just pay attention to these boys and get em everything they want, if you can reach it. After a while we won't have nothin here but cars."

I said, "Them's my boys, and they're your boys. I'm their daddy. They do whatever I tell em to do without a grumble. They lookin to me and I'm goin to pleasure em just as long as I can. Now, you got anything to do there in the house?"

She said, "Yeah, I got a plenty to do in the house, and I got a plenty to do out here too, watchin you and the boys full up our yard with cars."

I laughed and I told her, "Well, my boys wants to live in this world—your boys; this is the only world they can do their livin in."

They was big enough to work and pay for what they got, and weren't disapprovin at that. They was log cuttin kids—Calvin, Vernon, and Davey. Calvin and Davey cut logs as regular as the day come. Payday, they'd bring me the money or check, whatever, and I'd put part of it into home affairs and give them part. Me and Vernon was at home makin the crops. And after he got big enough

I reduced him of farmin, to an extent, and he went on to the woods. Francis, he come of age big enough to work in the field and Eugene could help a little and the girls could help, but not very much; not very much did I exact from my girls in the field.

VI

While I was livin on the Pollard place, I rented a few acres from Mr. Lemuel Tucker and put my boys on it and let them make a crop theirselves. Mr. Tucker agreed to furnish me fertilize and fifty dollars—weren't no groceries and nothin else in the deal; land rent and fertilize and fifty dollars was all I allowed him. I gived my boys a mule and told em go to it. Well, Mr. Tucker gived me the land right on, but he got so weak he couldn't furnish me nary a bit of money. I could donate to my boys enough little change along to keep em goin. And was feedin em right at the table where they had always et. That carried em through; they went on and made the crop.

Them boys toed the mark; they done what I told em even-up. One time I got on my car and went to Fort Payne, Alabama, to the death of one of my uncles. I was gone Monday, Tuesday, and Wednesday before I could land back home. My boys was home plowin and workin in the crop and when I arrived everything was as jam-up—they was still in the field. I drove in there early that Wednesday evenin and that house just emptied out; my wife and children run out to the car and covered me, kissin and huggin, glad to see me. I'd never been away from em more than one day or one night in their lives before that. I asked my wife and the girl children, "Where is the boys?"

I couldn't see em nowhere in the field around the house there. She said, "The boys got through over yonder on the old place"— that was her mother and father's old home place, workin that, too —and said, "they said they was goin on down on the Meade place " that's where I'd rented from Lemuel Tucker—"goin down on the Meade place, found out that stuff needed plowin and they down there now, plowin."

I was always satisfied with my boys, the work they done. They knowed their daddy didn't leave his home less'n he had to. I didn't get on the car, run up and down the road to frolic. And they was dutiful boys in my absence. Sometimes they would be plowin in one field and I'd be over yonder in another field by myself and I was just as well satisfied with their work as I could be with mine. And when I let my boys loose on that rented land, they made me ten good heavy bales of cotton. That was my Calvin and Davey, my sister's boy.

MR. TUCKER had a big poultry yard, these old white-legged chickens, and he was sellin eggs—doin every way he could to make a dollar. Had his hands on places up near Apafalya, had hands back down in here. And when they commenced a pullin him across the coals, he commenced a hollerin. One day he come by my house talkin bout his chickens and eggs and how much he was gettin out of that poultry yard.

I said, "Well, Mr. Lemuel, it's none of my business but like I see things gettin now, somebody goin to fall out the bottom. It's got to where these people can't stand in this country for nobody to have nothin but what they got to have it too. The land and country through here and everywhere I go, it's a poultry business, a poultry business. Watch out! None of you won't get no good out of it after a while. Everybody goin into one kind of business, I reckon nobody won't get nothin good out of it."

He jumped up when I told him that.

"Uh-uh-uh-uh, by George, you just got to know your onions."

Them's the very words he told me. Well, I told him the business was goin to weaken. Next news I heard, he was haulin eggs to the market by the bucket, one or two little bucketsful. Well, that weren't profitin him enough to buy gas. Next news I heard, he got into it with Mr. Grace at the bank and Mr. Grace tore him all to pieces.

Nothin never goes over the devil's back but what's goin to latch on to his belly—business went bad for Mr. Tucker. Before it was over they cleaned him out. He used to stand good at the bank—went down to Mr. Grace and wanted to borrow money to take a big trip. He owed Mr. Grace at that time twenty-five hundred dollars, which is two thousand five hundred. So he went up to Mr. Grace to borrow money so he could take a trip to California. Did he get that money? Did I give it to him? Did I let him borrow it? Mr. Grace turned him down, told him, "Tucker, you owe me twenty-five hundred dollars, hear? If you'll pay me that and get straight with me, I'll let you have it."

And that stuck Mr. Tucker with true force. He got mad as a wood hammer and he went to Montgomery—he had a lot of dairy cows and he went to Montgomery and mortgaged them fine dairy cows he had. Right there he sold hisself down the river. Mr. Grace wouldn't let him have the money—that was sung all over the country amongst white and colored too—went to Montgomery, got the money anyhow, mortgaged his cows to get it, took his big trip to California. And when he come back, he went in the bank there in Apafalya and Mr. Grace just let down to him. Told him, "Well, Tucker—" that was the pressure time, too—"Tucker, I'm gettin tight and I need the money you owe me." And he insisted on him to pay it. "I just have to have the money, Tucker."

When he took that trip to California, by his way and actions it made a new man out of him. He come back to Apafalya and he killed himself dead there, in a way. He didn't kill himself, understand, but he killed his influence. He went around the streets there —and I knowed some of the fellas, colored fellas, Tucker runnin up shakin hands with em and familiar with em. Told em how he had such a good time and such good treatment from colored people on his trip and all—O, he just courted my color. There was one special fellow, by the name of Caleb Moss. He owned a good deal of land down there between Sinking Creek and Apafalya, colored fellow, owned one or two nice places. He could go to Apafalya and get anything he wanted, or anywheres else he was known. He was recognized. Of course, they'd a tied him up hand and foot if they got a chance at him quick as they would anybody. So, when Mr. Tucker went out to California and come back, O, he was just changed so bad and he was just whoopin about it. And right there in Apafalya he runned up on Caleb Moss and good God, he just went up and grabbed him by the hand, shook hands with him, other white folks lookin on—and this is true facts. Some of em said, "I wonder what's the matter with Tucker. He's goin around here shakin hands with niggers. Must be losin his mind."

Throwin off on him because he was doin somethin that they wouldn't do and didn't like for any white man to do it.

One night he come up to my house. I was settin inside and a car drove out there in front of my door. I got up and went to the door and it was Mr. Lemuel Tucker. I walked out to the car—didn't know what he wanted—and when I walked out there he let into talkin. Well, the weather was quite ill that night—it was in winter time—and he said, "Get in, get in, Nate, and sit down. Get in out of the cold and shut the door."

I got in there and set down and he just preached me up a sermon. I didn't know it was in him. Told me bout his trip to California. He went over there to see his son Rex Tucker, that was his name, his oldest son. I don't think he ever had over a couple of boys. And his other ones, if he had any more, they was younger than Rex. I knowed Rex well. And Rex told his daddy to come visit him in California. He was out there makin a big man of himself, handlin a big trade there or big concern someway. All right. Mr. Tucker went off to see him and when he come back home off his trip he come by my house one night on his car and called me out for a long talk. And he told me these words: he was awful familiar with me, tellin me about what a big time he'd had on the train and how the colored people, the colored porters on the train treated him and just made him welcome to anything and set him up. "O, Nate, they was nice to me, I'll just tell you."

He was braggin down to the brick. He said, "Now you don't say nothin bout this—" They know their color is treatin you wrong but the most they'll do is whisper it to you. He said—he was so tore up and stirred up until he told me, "Don't say nothin bout what I'm sayin. This country lacks for *honestry*. It lacks for *honestry*. They don't recognize people—"

I said to myself, 'Good thing you went off somewhere and found out something.'

Next time I saw Mr. Tucker, I went down to his house and paid him the land rent what I owed him for the place I'd rented for my boys. It was a pretty cold day and he told me to come on in the house to the fire. I walked in, set down, and he talked: he laid his troubles to me and all. Told me he went in the bank there to Mr. Grace and Mr. Grace let down on him for that twenty-five hundred dollars. Then wouldn't nobody take it up but Mr. Alf Grinstead, man supposed to have more money than any one man in Apafalya. Mr. Grinstead walked right on into the bank and paid the debt off for him; then he took his business over and took title to all his property. When they wound up with him, in a few days— he told me, I didn't see it, but I know they got it all—three big trailer trucks come out from Montgomery and loaded all them dairy cows and pulled em out of this country. Mr. Tucker had to make his wife guardzine* over what he had. Still they took his land, took everything he had but his home place, the house he lived in and the farm it was on. Didn't take that. But he had a lot of places he had bought and they took all them, he lost em all. Even had to sell them chickens out for cash.

So he told me there that day in his house, "Well, Nate, I hit it harder than I ever expected. I done somethin I didn't want to do and thought I'd never have to do it"— O, if he didn't bellow; he bellowed!—"I had to mortgage my home place"—Mr. Grinstead done took a hold and got everything in his hands. And sittin there talkin with him, I could see he was miserable, all out of shape. When he returned from California he had to pay up, get a man to pay up all he owed. He thought he was goin to get a chance to go through like he'd always been doin.

And while I was sittin there talkin with him, he took off his shoes, tan shoes, brand new pair of high-top shoes, and he offered to sell em to me. They was just too hard for him, I reckon. So I looked at em and I said, "Mr. Tucker, I got a pair of Sunday shoes to wear at home. I aint able to buy your shoes. I'll just go ahead, as I got shoes, and let them do."

I didn't buy them shoes; I didn't intend to buy em when he showed em to me. I didn't need no shoes at that time in particular. I had to put money in things that was needed and things I didn't need right at the present I did without. Mr. Tucker just wanted to get shed of them shoes and get all the money he could. Took em right off his feet—that's the last time I remember ever seein him. When he got his business straightened up, he moved Mr. Morris Wiley into his house. Mr. Wiley was a man that worked a little crop.

Well, Mr. Tucker's wife picked him up a little bit and backed him up into a boardin house in Auburn and he hung on there a good while. Next news I heard he was dead.

MR. LEMUEL TUCKER, Mr. Horace Tucker, and Mr. Melville Tucker was brothers. I don't know whether Mr. Lemuel went to his brothers when he needed money or not. But I will say this: people won't

* Legal guardian; executor.

jump back on their close relationships for money, usually; they'll go to somebody else. Even if it'll ruin em, they'll go to somebody else. Don't want to press them relationships as hard as a money loan will press em. Won't nothin press em no harder.

Mr. Sam Tucker was father to them three Tucker boys and was the father to some more children. I helped him one time to move his family to Apafalya. Took my wagon and mules—now, I didn't help him move his house goods, but all his out plunder that I could get to, even fence rails; pulled up his house fence and carried them fence rails into Apafalya. They was good rails, hard wood, old-timey fence rails, all of em was pine rails, and he wouldn't leave em on the place after he moved. And what he done with them fence rails, I don't know, but I hauled em into Apafalya. And he moved on the inside of the city limits. He sold his place out in the country to Mr. Lucius Little, white man. He got kind of old and he was supposed to have plenty of money to take care of his lifetime, and so he talked hisself into movin to town. But he felt very hurt for movin—that's what caused him to kill hisself. He just lost out, made a mistake, and he grieved hisself to death, then he killed hisself.

I went to Apafalya one day after I'd helped move him there. And I was in the bank that mornin, had some small business to look after. And Mr. Smith run the bank, Merchants and Farmers Bank, that's the kind of bank it was. Mr. Sam Tucker walked in and spoke to Mr. Smith, then he spoke to me. Stood around there a little and he commenced a worryin, looked like, talkin bout his place he had, he had had, out in the country. He'd been doin fine until he done wrong and sold it. And it was worryin him—I heard a heap of people talk about it too, white people. He said, "I was livin out in the country where I was doin well, and if I'd a just kept my place—that's the thing I oughta done. Kept my place and got Nate here and moved him there on my place with me. I'd a had somebody that woulda worked if I'd a had a good man like Nate, and I'd just be happy and comfortable. I'd a been a hundred percent better off if I'd a just kept it and moved Nate on the place and let him work it."

He didn't like town a bit, he found that out. He had done got to where he couldn't make a crop hisself and he figured he was just as well to be in town. He didn't need the money he got for his place—that weren't why he moved. He had money enough to take care of him and his wife and baby. O good Lord, it carried him down. He was a sick, sick, sick man off his trade. And he tried to buy the place back but the wife of the man that had bought it from him, Lucius Little's wife told him, "You'll never get this place back." The place was right on the Calusa and Apafalya highway and it was a good house on the property. Mr. Tucker built that house hisself and moved into it—him and his wife and had one little girl. And he told his wife, after they moved to Apafalya and he just lost his mind just about—you know he lost his mind when he killed hisself—and he asked his wife to let him kill the baby, then kill her, and then kill hisself. She wouldn't agree to that noway, so he went on by hisself down to a little feed house he had built there below his house in town. And had a lot of corn feed in there, hulls and meal. Got his pistol out the house one day and went down in that feed house and over to the backside of that feed and shot his brains out.

His wife heard the gunfire and it unnerved her. She stampeded and begin to run around and look and all, and she couldn't see him nowhere. She looked around the house sufficient and her mind told her to go down to that feed house. And when she went down there and went in she found him dead. And he showed signs of where he had crawled over them cotton seed hulls and scattered the feed around.

I had only one man to come to me and try to get me to move on his place; white man, he was a native of Macon County and he tried his best to fool me and bait me up to move off of the Pollard place down there on his plantation at Sinking Creek, close to Tuskegee settlement. And he made three trips to see me to my knownst. Somebody'd recommended me to him. I figured him out when he run and made so many trips—and he wouldn't a had to back me up to nothin but land to work, that's all. I had plenty of good stock and plenty of everything I needed to make a crop. Had my own little blacksmith shop, what it took to sharpen a plow, sharpen a scrape, or anything.

I felt at all times that there was somethin peculiar about him —he was the wrong man for me to mess with. And when he first started to come at me he brought a colored man with him. I never did try to know the colored man, I just paid attention to him and his talk. And he proclaimed to have some other business up there to see after; what it was he never did announce to me, but he let me know enough he was seein after some other business in that settlement.

And I eventually told some of the colored people about that man comin up there. Met up with a fellow one day that knowed him. Told me, "Good that you didn't pay no attention to that man. He was just after what you had. If you'd a moved down there on his place, left from where you was and moved down there and settled down with what you got, it'd been his'n then. He only wants you if you got good stock, tools. That man is known, no matter what you carry on his place, it's his'n then."

I said, "I thought he was that kind of man."

He said, "Yes, he don't care how you got your stuff, he don't care nothin bout that; you move there you leave it there when you leave."

RIGHT at that period of time, Mr. Hoover got to be President, hollerin, "Keep the dollar out the niggers' hands." These white folks down here sang that like singin birds. "Keep the dollar out the niggers' hands."

I didn't hear Hoover say it but it was told to me he did and the white people repeated it. I do know that it was tight as the devil under his administration. He just sat down on us. The white folks in this country was goin in that direction anyways—nigger couldn't have any of their money to make a start with, no way to make somethin for hisself unless he started with his own money. The idea—"keep the dollar out the niggers' hands"—these white folks went rock bottom with that. Afraid a nigger might do somethin if he got the money in his own hands, do as he please; might hold on to it if he wanted to hold it, might spend it accordin to his pleasure. The white people was afraid—I'll say this: they was afraid the money would make the nigger act too much like his own man. Nigger has a mind to do what's best for hisself, same as a white man. If he had some money, he just might do it.

I heard a white gentleman walkin the streets of Apafalya and playin with his baby and talkin—one of the Russell boys. Weren't no kin as I knowed of to Mr. Ed Russell, who turned me down on fertilize one year; he was of a different set of Russells. One day I was walkin on the streets of Apafalya and I heard him laughin and talkin to another white man—he had his little chap with him and he was playin with the chap and braggin on him. He told that other white man—and a crowd of em heard him, *I* heard him, there on the street—"You ask my child about the President, that little fella will tell you: who do we want to vote for—'Hooooover, Hooooover, Hooooover—'" They just made a song of that. I looked at the little child as the white people got him to hollerin on Hoover, Hoover, Hoover, and I said to myself, 'They must want Mr. Hoover pretty bad for the child to be singin a song such as that.'

They said Mr. Hoover was goin to cause the womenfolks to wear bag and sack dresses; and sacks was guano sacks, made out of good, old, tough, heavy material. He was goin to put them to wearin guano sack dresses and all like that. And they hollered out, them that was singin for Hoover—and that was the key to the whole proposition: "Keep the dollar out the niggers' hands. Keep the dollar out the niggers' hands."

DURIN President Hoover's administration, cotton fell to about five and six cents. My best idea for that, and not only *my* idea: it appeared that people was producin more cotton than was needed and that just knocked the bottom off the price. Any year that cotton went down they claimed they was overstocked with it. And whenever it picked up, they claimed they was gettin more calls and more cotton was needed.

Cotton first fell, to my knowin, back in 1914. Then the war boosted the price up to forty cents and I wiped out my debts. Cotton commenced a slidin right after the war until it leveled off at twelve and a half and fifteen cents. Still I supported my family and had everything a poor man needed to make a livin. I was public workin to help my farmin—hauled lumber for the Graham-Pike Lumber Company in Apafalya. I had good stock, a good two-horse wagon, a rubber tire buggy, automobiles. And I drove a bargain with a white man to take over his payments on a farm, the Pollard farm, where Mr. Lester Watson was half interested. Then he got the whole thing out from under the Federal Land Bank and I had to pay him the balance. Cotton knocked off again and that put a lot of we farmers in a hole.

I come up to my house one day—I was out checkin on my fences—
and my wife told me there was a card in the mailbox tellin me to
come to the bank in Apafalya and sign papers on my place. I said,
"If I go, any way I go, you goin with me." See, she had book learnin
and she could read and write. So I told her, "Well, we'll go to
Apafalya this evenin, right after dark."

She was right down with me. Sometimes she'd say, "Darlin,
you know what's best to do. But you can't decide *what* to do until
you knows every side of the proposition. And bein that you can't
read and write, it's profitable for us all for you to make me your
partner."

I told her, one day, and many a time, "I'm married to you. And
I think my best business should be in your hands. If anybody knows
the ins and outs of it, you the one to know. But so far as workin
in the field, I aint never had a high opinion of that and I intend
to always be that way. Your business is at the house, mine's out in
the field."

She was a girl that her mother would put all her business in
her hands—her mother couldn't read and write. You could drop
any sort of paper in front of Hannah and she could pick it up and
read it like a top. She was pretty far advanced in education. She
wasn't a graduate but she understood anything and could talk it off,
too. She was, in a way of speakin, the *eyes* and I was the mouth-
piece.

So, when I went there to sign them papers, I told her, "You goin
with me."

I wanted her to read them papers to me; I knowed they
weren't goin to do it. All I had to do was sign, but I wanted to know
what I was signin.

Watson had taken over the place from the federal government
and it was him I had to sign with. My wife and I jumped in the car
and went right on to Apafalya. Got there and walked in—weren't
nobody there in the bank but Mr. Grace and Mr. Watson. O good
God, the doors flew right open and I broke out; I couldn't help it,
I got red hot. I was signin—called it signin papers on that place.
I knowed what I was signin before I signed; that's what brought
the devil up.

"Hi, hello, Nate."

"Hello, Nate."

"How do you do, Mr. Watson, Mr. Grace."

Said, "Well, you come here to sign your papers, didn't you?"

I said, "Yes sirs, that's why I'm here."

Pushed it through the window for me to sign. My wife was standin right there and I just handed it to her. That's when I found out the devil was in the concern; that kept crossin my mind all the time and that kept me, to a great extent, from signin any notes at all with Watson.

Hannah turned away, stepped off a step or two, whipped that paper right over in a jiffy. She come back with it and touched me on my arm. I listened to her. She said, "Darlin, that paper covers everything you got: your mules, wagon, all your tools and your cows and hogs and everything you got's on that paper."

Good God, when she told me that I hollered. I just pushed the paper back to em through the bars. I said, "I won't sign that paper, noway under the sun it could be fixed like it is."

I'd expected to come there that night and sign papers on the land—Watson knowed what I had—not reach out and take my mules, my wagon, my hogs, my cows, on that paper. And if I'd a signed it like they was preparin me to do, I could have lost it all. Just be late payin on the land and they would take everything I had. I had sense enough through my wife to see what they was tryin to do to me. Wooooooooo, I meant to buck it.

I said, "Aint that land sufficient to stand for itself and not none of my personal property on it? I can't carry it nowhere."

Tried to saddle everything I had. Right there I burst like a butterbean in the sun. I wouldn't sign that note for Jesus Christ. I just stuck that paper back through them bars—I knowed the type of him. I felt a fire in my heart; told my wife, "Let's go."

If I couldn't do better I was goin to move away from there. Soon as I told my wife, "Let's go," and got nearly to the door, "Come back, come back, Nate, we can change the paper; come back, come back, we can change it."

I just say now I was a fool—I went back. They changed that paper to suit me and I signed it. It just spoke for the land then. So I signed to buy the place from Mr. Watson and if I couldn't make the payments all they could do was take it back.

Watson was a man, he was fixin a mortgage on my stuff without askin me any odds about it, just fixin it like he wanted. All I had to do, walk up and sign it. I kicked like a mule kickin a stable door down, I didn't hide, I kicked it bald-headed, right before him and the banker, CD Grace, there in the bank. Broke that thing up, too. But Watson continued to dig at me.

I was aimin to live through this world, till death, without lettin a man handicap me that way, and much as I had around, *it* paid for, let a man come up and handicap me with a little old rocky-assed rough place, take a mortgage on everything I had for the land when I sensibly knowed that the land was able to stand for itself—weren't nothin but a rock pile nohow; then wanted to take advantage of my ignorance—he thought I was ignorant to that, but he soon found out at the pop of a finger, I weren't ignorant to *that*. Right then I had over a thousand dollars' worth of property: mules, hogs, cows, wagons, two automobiles—close to two thousand dollars' worth. Tryin to ignore me and discount me enough to fix a mortgage on all that just for a rock pile.

So they changed the paper. The new paper just covered the land and nothin else I had. But the devil is busy; you may get him off his track but he's goin to get where he wants to go some other way. That night they had to change the paper to get me to sign, but it wasn't the last time they tried to tie me up. I was full aware to what they was aimin to do.

I was dealin with the bank in Apafalya then, but this banker seemed to want to turn me loose and let his friend Watson disable me. When I failed to be geehawsed in that note signin business, I decided they would just try to put me over in Watson's hands another way. But they couldn't do it. I lingered along and made good crops for several years, and I noticed every time I'd go to the bank Watson was there. And he didn't have all that much business at the bank.

I wanted to keep dealin with the bank because there you draw the money for your supplies and when you paid that back and the interest on it, you was clear and loose. Better to deal with the bank, better by a hundred percent; you knowed what you was gettin in the first place. You deal with one of these men out here in the country or with a moneyed man in town somewhere, other than the bank, you burnt up. So, after the papers was fixed up on that old place, I went right back to the bank the next year—Mr. Grace turned me down. He turned me down. I didn't like that. I said, "Well, Mr. Grace—"

He said, "You're partners in business now with Mr. Watson. I'll just let you and him run it, him and you; you don't need the bank's help."

I said, way down in me, 'No, I won't deal with Watson.' And in kind words I asked Mr. Grace to recognize me and let me deal on with him. I knowed that from what I made on my cotton I could pay Mr. Watson on that land right along. Mr. Grace kicked at helpin me but I begged him in these words. I said, "Mr. Grace, I been dealin with you and I've always paid you and I knowed what I was payin when I paid it. I'd just feel at a loss if you turn me loose and don't help me to what I need to be helped. If I can't get it out of you it leaves me lost. Please, sir, carry me on."

He carried me on one year. That fall, as usual, I walked in the bank one day to pay Mr. Grace and I paid him square and fair to the last penny the note called for. Mr. Watson was standin there lookin on at the transaction. I thought that was so audacious. Mr. Grace went to get my note—he got the note to give me, Mr. Watson standin right there. "Give me that. Give me that."

Mr. Grace looked at me and looked at Mr. Watson—stood there on a study like before he gived it to ary one of us. Mr. Watson continued, said, "Give it to me."

Ooooooooo, I felt like fallin out, but I couldn't help myself. I knowed though, definitely, he had no more business with that note than he had with a hog in his pocket. God knows if it didn't give me the blues. I was standin there waitin on my note; Mr. Grace was slow to give it to me. He looked at Mr. Watson and looked at me. After a while he just hauled off and handed it to Mr. Watson. I thought that was a helluva come-off. The note I just paid the bank, paid Mr. Grace, and he handed it to Mr. Watson. O, it hurt me so bad—the note weren't any good to the man, he couldn't collect a dime on it. I didn't owe nothin on the note and I didn't owe *him* nothin. What good was it to him? That showed me what he wanted from me—his plans was naked as a baby. I didn't need no more indication about it.

MY daddy died while I was livin on the Pollard place. Now I think it was really about '28 when he died because when I bought that '26 Ford I hauled him around right smart for several years; in fact, every time he said he wanted to go to the doctor I'd go and carry him.

I don't know his troubles but he was a man that had married four times. His first wife was Matilda Todd, so said, told me about it many a time, old man Sam Todd's daughter. Him and her had one chap, and the boy died. She was one of these high-strung women, the way he told it, and I reckon he told some truth about it. She was a hot-shot, Matilda Todd. Her and him had one child and that child died before they thoroughly separated. Then he jumped up and married my mother; her name was Liza Culver. She died— I was big enough to know the month and the year when my dear mother died—she died just before I was nine years old. So then he married Maggie Reed, which was my first wife's auntie. Her and old man Waldo Ramsey had the same mother. Well, when she died I was married at that time, had several children myself. And when I married I left from anywhere around the settlement where my daddy lived. Went on away from there and stayed away. I picked up my shotgun—I had a single barrel breech-loader—and— there aint no use to talk about the clothes, I didn't have no fittin clothes; just did have some worse-fit clothes to stand up and be married in.

So, my daddy lingered along, I was married and had several children. Then he married again. The old man was gettin mighty feeble then. I talked to him about it. He got to runnin around with this last woman he married—he had a old horse and buggy; he'd lost all his property at that time but for a old horse and buggy. He was rarin around to marry, I knew he was, but he was too old to be marryin that woman, and I told him about it.

He come to my house one Sunday mornin early and spent part of the day. And we went in the house, sat down, got to talkin, and I seed a pistol in his pocket. I said, "Papa, what are you doin totin that thing?"

"I keeps it for protection, son."

But, you know, in his way of transactin, he was his worst enemy. Well, I talked it off with him, told him I didn't see no cause for him to carry his pistol up and down the road on his buggy with him—he might knock it and shoot hisself, old as he was. So, my little boys done went and fed his horse and he set there a while and et dinner with us that Sunday; then he set there awhile in the evenin before he left. And I think to the best of my knowledge when I seen my daddy again he done married that woman. And so when he got ready to leave, Calvin and Davey went and caught his horse out and hitched him up. My daddy crawled in the buggy and the old horse went backin on off.

So, I was haulin lumber for the Graham-Pike Lumber Company and I met him on the road one day. I'd been to the planin mill in Apafalya with a load of lumber and I was on the route back out of town. And good God, I met my daddy goin to town.

He said, "Well—"

I was hotheaded then about the situation. I knowed he was too old to marry this woman he'd been runnin around with. And he met me, stopped for a talk.

"Well, son, I got you another mama."

I looked at him, said, "You aint got me no other mama, Papa. You aint got me no other mama. You had me a stepmother and she's gone. That's the last. I won't recognize no more."

This woman he married was a pretty rough woman. I knowed it, knowed it from a chap up. Her name was Bonnie Tubbs. She'd been married about twice before herself. Didn't have a child in the world. Lonnie Tubbs was her first husband and another fellow, I knowed him too, had been her husband. And she quit him and after she quit him he died. Then my daddy went and married her. I knowed he was marryin a rough cat. And that was his last marriage. Well, lingered along and she threatened to quit him—she was a rough woman from the start, been used to runnin over men. My daddy met his match when he married Bonnie Tubbs. And some sort of disagreement come up between em—I never did trace it up. I knew she weren't goin to stay with him. So she got hotheaded, moved out and left him. Then he jumped up and moved—

I was right at grown when my daddy commenced a buyin the place he moved away *from*. After I had growed to the years of maturity, I felt that I had to look out for myself and I was really scufflin to get away from my daddy. I couldn't afford to pay too much attention to his affairs then. I was just about my own man right at the time my daddy bought a place—time for me to go. Bought that place from Mr. Charley Todd, son of old man Clem Todd, who owned a territory of land, several hundred acres, in his lifetime. Old man Clem Todd was a one-legged man. He would drive his horse and tote his crutches across the front of his saddle. I knowed him well. Heap of times he'd come up to my daddy's house—he rode a old dark red-colored horse; never did keep his horse fat but he kept him in livin order. He'd ride that horse to my daddy's house, seein after the business between my daddy and himself. And he had funny eyes; he'd chew his tobacco, roll his eyes, and look at my daddy, talk to him. He'd be sittin on his horse talkin to my daddy.

"Hayes, so-and-so-and-so-and-so."

I was a little old boy, standin around—I was big enough, my daddy had me to work after I got big enough to work and I never gived him no trouble bout workin. My daddy kept me in the field just as regular as he wanted to. Sometimes my daddy would be out in the woods huntin when Mr. Clem Todd would ride up there.

"Where's Hayes?"

He knowed. He knowed my daddy was a hunter.

After old man Clem died, Charley Todd, his son—there was three of them boys: Mr. Billy Todd was the oldest one, he was married, he married a Bond lady; and Mr. Meek Todd, the second son, I don't know who he married; and Charley Todd was the baby son, baby child of the family. And this Charley Todd, after the death of his daddy, he bought this small place for my daddy and my daddy was supposed to pay him for it. My daddy bought that place through Mr. Charley Todd; it was a Wheeler place, right there joinin the Todd plantation, and Mr. Charley Todd had become guardzine over it some way. I don't know all the transactions because I stepped out, but my daddy had a mess of children there livin with him that he could put to work to pay for the place. And my daddy just kept hashin along, scrubbin along some sort of way. But to go down to truthful facts about it, I don't think my daddy ever paid Mr. Charley Todd in full; but he paid on it like the devil and finally he couldn't pay no more and Mr. Charley Todd took it back. My daddy lost TJ's mother at that period of time when he was buyin that place. And he jumped up—he was a hot-tailed old man; he was the daddy of many a chap, inside his married life and outside—and he married Bonnie Tubbs. And he got distracted on that woman and he let his business slide. The next news I heard, that little place was fully in Mr. Charley Todd's hands.

So, he got shed of that place—and that was the end of his marriage. He woulda stayed with that woman if she woulda stuck with him, but she weren't a woman of that type. She was more than he could handle. But before him and her married *he* was ill to all of his wives, far as I knowed. He was ill to my mother, he was ill to TJ's mother—that's all I ever stayed under my daddy, durin the time he was married to my mother and my stepmother. He was ill to em. And he weren't ill to em neither bout talk; I've seen him beat my mother up scandalous when I was little. It didn't take nothin to start him—God have got all sorts of people in this world, don't you know; think over it. He got low-down ones, he got people here that won't treat theirselves right much less you. The only man or woman that's blessed in this world—the Bible says, best that I can understand it, "Suffer little children to come unto Him because they are such as the kingdom of heaven." Devil don't work out in children—God's good to all from the start—but they follows the route their parents walk and they lost, a heap of em.

My daddy had a mean temper in him and all like that, quick, but he never would fight nobody that I knowed of, he wouldn't fight em. Of course, his wives who he could run over, he roughed em up. But his last wife didn't give him a chance. Bonnie Tubbs went on about her business when she found out who he was—and she was the devil herself, too, before he married her. We children and everybody that knowed him and had any sympathy for my daddy, didn't want him to marry that woman. But he went on and married her. He ought to have considered: if you marry in this world, what do you marry for? Do you marry to better your condition or do you marry to turn out to be a slum? And always into it and can't agree with your wife and your wife can't agree with you. God don't want that: He wants peace and pleasure on this earth. We ought to consider when we marry what we marry for. Not just marry a woman to linger between her legs—there's more to a married life than that, there's more profitable things to it than that. Now I loved women; when I was young I loved em for more than to just linger between their legs—and I knowed when I got old enough and took a notion to marry and wanted to marry, I considered that my marriage weren't goin to be what most folks cracked it up to be, mine was goin to be a lifetime journey.

But they don't do that today, and they didn't do it yesterday. I could call several marriages right through this country here: the man just took his old hat and walked out, or the woman, she didn't waste no time sayin goodbye. No more left to them marriages. Well, what do I want to mess myself up thataway for? A man can't prosper here by hisself; he can't get ahead less'n he stays around and holds on to what he has. I want a woman that wants to stay with me until I die or I'll stay with her until she dies—let death part us.

When my daddy died he died without a wife. I visited him, I hauled him to the doctors, and the evenin he died—he died just a little before first dark—where was I at? Sittin down in a chair and me only, right by his head. He was lyin there on the bed and I was sittin there with a peach tree brush, keepin the flies off of him when he died.

I got the word one evenin—he was livin out there in Apafalya on the back streets and his two little grandsons was livin in the house with him, Sadie's boys: when she died I taken the oldest one, Davey, and my daddy taken the two youngest ones. And also, one of his daughters was livin in the house, child he had by TJ's mother, one of TJ's sisters, Amy; her name was Amy. And Amy had one or two children at that time herself. Well, that whole crowd stayed in the house with my daddy out yonder on the back streets.

One evenin I was down on the back of the Pollard place with one of my boys—the older boys was sawin logs down on the river. And this boy, I kept him at home that year on the farm with me; he was big enough to plow good. So we was down on the little old backside of the plantation one day and I said, "Frank"—Francis, he lives in Philadelphia today—"Frank, we better try to save a little of that fodder down on the creek."

Well, he was right with me. We got down there and we went to pullin fodder. And first thing I knowed, I looked back up through the corn patch down close to the little creek and here come Tommy, my sister's boy, the biggest boy that was out at Apafalya livin with my daddy. I thought mighty quick somethin must be wrong. Tommy come on up to me; he said, "Uncle Nate, Papa—" he called his granddaddy "Papa," since he took them two little boys—"Papa is sick, somethin the matter with him. Amy cooked some greens yesterday for him and he et some of them greens and some of em he never did swallow good. They in his mouth now and he's layin there on the bed and some of them greens is comin out of his mouth. He won't speak, he can't say nothin, look like. He's low sick. I come, Uncle, to let you know."

I just laid everything aside and went on back to the house. Didn't change my clothes—I was in a hurry. Cranked up that Ford car and hit the road right to Apafalya. I parked my car in my daddy's yard, got out, and went in the house. I looked at him. He was in the shape Tommy said he was. I looked at him and I called him several times. And if he answered, that little old Ford car answered. Just layin there catchin his breath. Well, the flies was mighty bad but I wouldn't move, I was goin to stick right there with him. And every once in a while I called him; never did answer me. Flies was bad after him, his head and mouth. I walked out the house and there was a peach tree settin out there. I just cut me off a peach tree branch bout long as my arm. Went back in and took my seat right by his head, watchin him, brushin them flies off him. He was just layin there breathin, very slow. Every once in a while I'd say, "Papa, Papa." Long as I called him, several times, if he answered that peach tree branch answered. And I watched him close: he got weaker and weaker, he was just absolutely dyin, that's all. I stayed there until the last, set right there and kept the flies off him until the last breath went out of his body. I felt him and I seed he was gone. I tried my best to get him to answer me and there was nothin I could do.

The last time he was at my house, he come there on a Sunday evenin. I sent one of my boys at him on that Ford car. He come into my house and set around there—I had very bad feelins at the time, I begin to feel that he was weak. He et a little bite of breakfast, next mornin, that Monday mornin, but he didn't eat much. And his oldest daughter by TJ's mother, TJ's sister, Lorna, she lived right up the road at that time. Ralph Courteney and her stayed up there on Mr. Mosley's place. So, my daddy got up from the table that Monday mornin and said, "Son, I wants to go to Lorna."

I said, "Well, Papa, I'll take you or I'll send you by Calvin."

So he got ready that mornin after mornin things was off and he et breakfast. He got his stuff ready—and he come out of the room, one of the bedrooms where the fireplace was, and come on through and come on into the dinin room and walked by me and stopped and talked with me a minute or two—and it was shown to me that mornin that was close time for him, my old daddy, and

he might have felt it too. Calvin had the car out and was ready
to carry him to Ralph's and Lorna's. And he walked out there very
stooped that mornin, walkin slow. I walked on out the door with
him. And the last words he told me in this world—he looked at me.
said, "Son, pray! Pray! Pray, boy, pray!"

I told him, "Papa, I will. I will."

I didn't go for a Christian man at that time with my Savior; I
was just a sinner man. I'd been pretendin to pray for a long time
but pretendin don't convince God. You got to give God this heart of
yours and talk to Him in earnest. Well, I taken quite exception to
what my daddy said, and I thought, 'What could he mean?' The
Lord was a stranger to him as far as I knowed, but of course, he
weren't no stranger to the Lord. He went on out, I went on out the
door with him, pokin along. Got on the car and Calvin brought him
right over to his daughter's and put him off there and come back.
That was on Monday. And blessed God, Wednesday evenin I got the
message—he was in bad shape—and I rushed there.

Had his funeral at Elam Church. We got his body in the
church and the preacher got up there explainin all about the death
of him. And the preacher told all my daddy's children that was
there to straighten up and not live a sinner life—my wife jumped
up. I was a sinner man, I was her husband; she jumped up and
clapped her hands and said, "Lord, you got so many here that aint
of Christ. O, you got so many."

That hit me like hotcakes because I knowed I was amongst
the many and I was her husband. It hurt me, but it hurt her more
than it hurt me.

Now I didn't have a mother or father livin in the whole world.
I was on my own, lookin out for myself. I'd been lookin out for
myself for a long time, too. I learnt that under my daddy's administration, had to. And when they buried him I was thinkin bout
myself and how I come up under him and what times we children
had had in his house.

THE night my daddy died, I stayed there the balance of the night,
studyin and plannin on how to take a hold, run around and see
about all of his connections. I got back home that mornin and
first thing I done when I drove in the yard, I stretched my eyes
toward the barn and I seed my boys down there with a yearlin

hangin up. My wife walked out and told me— We was milkin a couple of cows and I had a Guernsey cow there that strictly belonged to my wife. I bought that cow from a colored fellow by the name of Warren Todd. She was a good cow, Guernsey cow, I give Warren Todd fifty dollars for that cow—my wife gived me the money and I bought the cow, it was her cow then. I had other cows there but she wanted a good milk type to furnish milk and butter. I just figured it was mine to take care of and use but if ever the cow was sold or anything happened to it, it was her cow. She was a large cow, a heavy milker. Vernon went with me over to Warren Todd the mornin I bought that cow; lived out there between me and Apafalya on what they called the Joe Grimes place.

So, when my daddy died, I rushed back home from Apafalya that mornin and when I drove in there around the back yard to the car shed, two-car shed—had two cars at that time—my wife come outdoors and I said to her when she got to where I could see her, "What's the matter at the lot?"

She said, "Darlin, Fanny killed my heifer this mornin—" that was the cow, Fanny; she said, "The boys milked this mornin and they turned Fanny out knowin that she was ill, and my heifer—" She had a nice heifer there, it weren't Fanny's calf, neither; it was a heifer from another one of my cows. So, my wife told me there in the yard that mornin: Fanny was ill. She walked out of the lot and this heifer was standin out a piece beside the fence. Soon as Fanny walked out there—she had short horns, a short-horned cow—she walked right up to that heifer and all at once before the heifer thought, Fanny lunged into her side and busted a hole right behind that heifer's leg, right front leg; when she horned that heifer she busted the hide and went through. One of the boys had just turned Fanny out and he was standin there lookin at it. He went and runned her away. But this heifer stood there and trembled and walked off and fell. My wife told me all about it quick as she could tell me. The boys had to kill that heifer. They seed she couldn't make it after Fanny done hooked her in there somewhere close to the heart. They got around her after they seed they had to kill her—that heifer happened to be fat and pretty, and when I got there they had that heifer hangin up, done near bout got her skinned. I went on down to the lot and helped em finish the job. Then I took my saw and sawed her down, then I sawed her half in two. Well, I treated that meat and hung it up, sold a little of it but kept the biggest part of three quarters, both front quarters and one of the hind quarters. Other hind quarter, I prepared a place in the back of my car and quick as I could I took off back to Apafalya with one of them hind pieces in there, carried it to Mr. Ed Pike. He jumped on it and bought the whole hind quarter; weighed it and gived me from fifteen to twenty cents a pound for it. That was the steak part—I figured I could sell the hind quarter better than I could any part of the front. I didn't need all that beef for my private use. And what I reserved for myself I had to cure the biggest part of it: hung it up, salted it, put a small fire underneath that meat and my wife put pepper in the fire—flies couldn't stand it. That beef lasted—there was twelve of us in the family at that period of time: nine children of our own plus my sister's child made ten, me and my wife made twelve.

I stayed on the Pollard place as long as I did—I had a pretty good old house there, best house that ever I lived in. And what held me there was this and only this: I had plenty of good stock and makin a good livin by rentin other folks' land, smooth land, clear enough of rocks so you could work it good. I went out in the piney woods and worked some on Miss Cordy Vail's place, and some on Mr. Thurman Groves' place—made good crops every year, regardless to the price they was bringin, and that weren't much. And by lingerin along and not havin no serious trouble noway, and havin plenty of good land to work by rentin other places, I was doin as well as any poor colored man could do in this country.

I considered many a scheme to profit my farmin in the limits of what a farmer could do. Hit or miss, it gived me great pleasure to try out myself.

I started off raisin hogs—had a hog pasture down in the swamp west of the barn. I had raised hogs down there on the Bannister place, didn't have but one sow. And when I moved to the Stark place at Two Forks, I cut down on my hogs, broke up my hog raisin. But when I moved back toward where I'd come from, to the Pollard place, I opened up then raisin more hogs than ever I had before. I didn't haul no hogs over the country for sale or allow people from all over the country to come to my house and buy em. I didn't supply the settlement with hogs. I raised em for meat purposes in particular and just sold a few along.

I gived Mr. Claude Wilcox there in Pottstown five dollars for a full-blooded Dew Rock Jersey hog, young shoat. And I taken him home and reserved him—I bought him for a stock hog, put him amongst my other hogs and raised em up; he was the father to several litters of pigs—and when I bought the shoat, I didn't keep him many days until he got out. One mornin I went to the pen to feed my hogs and that shoat was out and gone. I couldn't imagine to save my life where he had got to and I hated it. Well, I tracked that hog down through the field and hit the pasture, north from the barn and the hog lot, then I couldn't track him no more. Well, I wandered on my way across the pasture lookin for him—I didn't see him, and by that time I had got over towards the back end of the pasture where I could see the other field between the woods and the creek. I looked and I looked and I looked, stood there that mornin and I looked, wonderin where he was and how he was. I went on in the direction of the field between Sitimachas and the pasture and I looked. And as God would have it, I kept a lookin and after a while, way down, straight across that field toward the creck, I discovered the little red devil. He was just trottin right regular—dip-dip-dip-dip-dip-dip-dip-dip—just like a little old pig or hog would do, comin right straight back toward the house. I thought to myself, 'Uh-huh, you comin back the same way you went.' And that's what he was doin, too. I hurried up and got away from where I was standin— I figured that he was goin to stay on his track, trackin hisself back. A animal is a curious thing, you can take a animal the darkest night that ever was—I've tested that about road mules—you take a cow or hog or mule, if he roams off the darkest night that was and stays off, let him crook his route or however he may go, he knows direct the way back; if he comes back he comes right by the way he went; comes back by the scent, he knows.

I decided that shoat was comin right straight back, so I stood and watched him until he got as close to me as forty yards and I just eased off from where I was straight on off of his route. I didn't never let him know I seed him neither. And he went just as straight back to that hog pen as he could go and me lookin at him.

Then I made other arrangements about keepin him. I didn't know, when I found him out and gone, if I'd ever see him again. But I hunted him until I laid my eyes on him and I watched him run his course back eventually to the hog lot. Then I confined him. I made a fool out of that hog, too. It's easy to make a hog, the fool hog lose his mind about you, he'll follow you to the jumpin off place and attempt to jump in behind you, if you was to jump off. I was so afraid that hog would get away. I had other hogs and I hoped he would stay around there on account of them but I didn't put confidence in that only.

I doped that hog with my urine. I went and I fed that hog and I sprinkled lightly—I didn't know if my urine would set altogether with him or not, but I knowed a little wouldn't hurt him. I gived him slops to eat, drink, sprinkled my urine on it; if that didn't get him, glory! It sure tamed him. I fooled with that hog just enough that way and that hog, I couldn't keep him out from under my feet. I wouldn't keep the hog up and confine him very long, I wanted him to have a outlet and a plenty to eat so he'd grow, because I was intendin to make a stock hog out of him and did do it. I commenced feedin him on my urine and in a day or two, two or three days I turned him out. Doggone it, I ruined that shoat. I don't care where I was, if he seed me he comin to me, around the house or in the field—if I was *in* the house, anybody drove up called me, if that shoat was anywhere about the house where he could see me, when I hit the ground off of them steps, here he come. I'd go on maybe to that fellow who called my attention, start talkin with him, up come that pig, crawl in there between my legs, bump me and lay down—and me standin there talkin with that person. Well, people commenced a noticin it: "Say, Nate, how come that hog walk up to you, just lay down and go to sleep right there between your legs? How come it?"

I'd say, "He's a pet, just a pet pig. He got a mind like a dog."

Well, I got tired of that. And that shoat got up some size and I put him in the pen then with them hogs on the swamp. I kept two or three hogs down there—he didn't like goin off with em, but he couldn't help it. I had to stop him from runnin up between my legs like he done—people took to noticin it, wanted to know how come it. I never did tell em definitely how I created him that way.

I raised my own honey when I was livin on the Pollard place. I had several stands of bees settin out in the open, down on the south side of the barn close to my fattenin hog's pen and my main hog lot. Mostly these bees I had was this Italian bee, big yellow bee. I also had these little old black bees, call him the swamp bee. He's a smarter bee than a Italian bee: if you watch, in robbin em, you gets more honey—all of em starts workin at the same time, but a black bee will fill up quicker than a Italian bee. But the black bee is smart to sting you too if you don't handle em right or if you scared of em. They'll cover you more so than a Italian. Italian bee is a quieter bee than a black bee, swamp bee; that's a ill little devil.

I raised my honey for home purposes. My daddy used to raise em and I caught on to how he done it. He kept his bees in the peach orchard when I was growin up on the old Todd place down on Sitimachas Creek. Had some good trees in that orchard; weren't none of his trees bought trees and set out, but it was old-fashioned fruit and he had a big orchard. And he had his hog pen where he fattened his hogs down in that orchard too. And one day—there was a apple tree at that hog pen that bore real apples; that tree loaded up every year. And we children would slip over there and pull them apples, sometimes against my daddy's orders. And them bees was down there in that peach orchard just below that hog pen. That main apple tree and that peach orchard stood right close to the pen, on the east side of it. My daddy's bee groves—we'd go down there at that apple tree and sometime them bees was operatin so close to it until we'd have to be shy around there to keep from gettin stung. Well, my brother Peter, only brother I got in the world, whole brother, one day me and him went down there pullin apples off that tree. And two or three of them bees got on us. Peter took off down through that orchard, just a runnin and a jumpin and a hol- lerin, "Ahhy-ahhy-ahhy-ahhy-ahhy," and fell down—I laughed— and his nose and face plowed into the dirt. I laughed about that a long time. But I was cautioned there about handlin myself around bees. I married, and I never did take a interest in a bee, raisin and havin em myself, until I lived on the Pollard place.

I worked them bees several years and they got to stingin my stock and all—I kept my fattenin hogs under a big tree, close enough for that tree to cast a shade over them and my bees. My stock couldn't get right up to the bees but got to where some of em would sit right close to the wire fence, and that'd be sufficient to flustrate the bees. After a while I seed em take off runnin—bees got on em. And just before I went to prison, just a year before, I quit foolin with bees. They was aggravatin my stock and they'd aggravate you if you messed up too close to em.

I was a milk peddler; drove to Calusa once a week, every week with milk, butter—nice homemade butter; sometimes syrup, eggs, carried em around amongst the people to their houses and sold em. Done that several years. Sometimes they'd be standin out there lookin for me. They come to expect me and I was a regular supplier— chickens, eggs, milk, butter, syrup; vegetables, too. I raised a fruit crop and a vegetable crop and usually I'd raise a over-production. I'd give my neighbors some and reserve a little to sell. Winter, I'd load up stove wood, cut, cured, and dried, put them cotton bodies on my wagon, fill them bodies up, carry my load to Calusa, sell it in person. I never did love a sellin job but I could get somethin out of it and it weren't takin away from my family, so I done it.

I was a *cotton* farmer; I was lookin for my money to come out of that cotton. I was as much able, as far as my physical health, to raise a *little* cotton as a big farmer was to raise a heap. And I got stout as a consequence of my labor. I was always pretty prosperous for this country and for the kind of work I done. I went on to the Pollard place with plenty that was paid for when I moved there, and I thought I was buyin my own land, at last.

IF I could have made a livin raisin vegetables and corn crops, water-melons and such as that, I'd a let cotton alone. But I just couldn't realize it. I tried to sell watermelons after I started rentin, livin on Miss Hattie Lu Reeve's place. I carried several loads out for sale, carried one load to Apafalya—couldn't get enough out of it to pay me for my trouble. I'd a been better off settin down makin a basket. It was too weak a way to travel and everybody sellin watermelons. And they had a little rule—the white people cut the colored people clean out of sellin fruits and vegetables. Colored man could get shed of his stuff but who would get the benefit of it? Nice beans in the spring of the year, tomatoes and many different articles; he'd go to sell it and they'd offer him a low price, too low to make a profit. They'd buy from the white man, at these markets, and give him just a little more for his stuff, no great big price but just enough to take him in and cut the colored man out.

I have got a little money out of big crops of peas, old unknown peas, speckled peas; I never did raise no white crowder peas enough to do no good but for home use. But unknown peas, speckled peas, and a pea they call a iron pea, that was the heaviest weight pea ever I used. A few of them iron peas would outweigh a pile of any other kind of pea. It was a small pea and it weren't a pea for human use—a stock pea, strictly. And I have raised and sold several bushels of them peas for a white man that runned a store in Apafalya.

Dropped them peas between the corn in spring, and the last furrows around that corn covered them peas. Go out there and drop a gang of peas of a mornin and had to go right on and plow around that much corn that the peas was dropped in before I done anything else to keep the partridges from pickin them peas out. A drove of partridges will follow a row and eat up every pea. I'd go out a heap of times before breakfast, get in a hurry, carry my sack of peas out and drop them peas to a certain distance and mark my place with a sign, how far my peas went, on the last row. Go back to the barn and catch my mule out and get in that field and get busy runnin that last furrow around that corn to cover them peas before the birds got to travelin too much. Cover my peas, and I've made peas on top of peas. They'd stand right there in that corn and make, grow. Sometimes the vines would get so rank in there before that corn was made, until I'd go through pullin fodder off my corn to feed my mules—that eventually run out, this fodder pullin; I'd go and buy me hay to feed my mules on for roughage and let the fodder burn up on the stalk—soon as that corn fodder burnt up, or even if I pulled that fodder, them peas could get sunshine and air. Good God, come fall of the year you have to gather your corn, maybe you just had to gather them peas out of there to keep from runnin over em with your wagon and tearin em up; gather your peas first, then go back and gather your corn. Haul them peas out the field and pile em up in a certain part of the barn house or another outhouse specially built for vegetables and such. Somebody over yonder in the settlement would have a pea thrash; get him to come there and bring that pea thrash on his truck or wagon and set it down. Take them peas up by the basketful, tote em out of that house, that man there throw em up on his pea thrash and thrash them peas out. And under that pea thrash where they come out, put a trough to catch em. Thrash the last pea I had in there and when he'd get done I'd have anywhere from fifteen to twenty, twenty-five to thirty bushels of peas. That man had nothin to do but move his thrash out and load it, leave me with my peas. He'd take peas for his toll,

take peas. Set my peas in sacks, back in the house them peas went.
Time come that I could get em out, I'd carry em to Mr. Earl Hollander in Apafalya. He'd buy the last one of em, pay anywhere from
two to three dollars a bushel. And there's not much expense to
growin peas, you don't have to work em—unknown peas, speckled
peas, iron peas. Them unknown peas and iron peas would make
your peas. Now speckled peas would do very well but they didn't
make as much to the acre as iron peas. Them iron peas was the top
peas of all. They was a little old kind of clay-colored pea.

I made ax handles for Mr. Hollander when I was a boy. First
pair of shoes I remember gettin, I made ax handles enough and
carried em out there to Mr. Earl Hollander in Apafalya and sold em,
and I bought me a pair of Sunday shoes, called em Fireside kid-skin
shoes. I was about fifteen years old—go to the woods and cut a
piece of hickory down, good-sized tree, straight, clear of knots; take
it home, split it up, take it to the draw place and draw ax handle
lengths with the draw knife—put it in the draw horse, draw it off,
and dress it down to a certain size, then set down and take my
pocket knife and nicely whittle it off, get it right direct in ax handle
shape. Then take me a piece of glass and scrape it down slick and
pretty; take a piece of sandpaper and sandpaper it up—ax handle
as good as you ever stuck in a ax.

My daddy put me to makin baskets and he collected and
pocketed all the money. But when it come to ax handles, he would
let me set down and make ax handles at my leisure, take em out to
Mr. Earl Hollander and sell em, at a cheap price, too, ten cents for
a handle. One Saturday I carried enough ax handles out there, homemade good handles, and got me a pair of Fireside kid-skin shoes;
and I paid for a little old trunk to hold my clothes, off of ax
handles.

ONE day I taken Hannah on the car and a pretty good lot of vegetables and we drove down to Tuskegee. I was haulin lumber for
Graham-Pike Lumber Company at that time and I notified the boss
man at the planin machine and I got off for the day. And we carried down a load of greens—there was a place out in the open and
cool, over there at that Normal School, where you could lay out
your vegetables to sell. So we went down there one time—well,
there was so many crowded out there with vegetables every which-

way, our sale wasn't good. Where there's too many people followin
the deal down on the same method you is, somebody aint goin to
have success at it, and the biggest majority will fail. Take Lemuel
Tucker and his eggs— Well, that was the first time and the last
time I tried to sell my vegetables that way. And I have met the time
when I had so many vegetables they have gone to waste.

And fruits, ground fruits and tree fruits, many a year I produced more than my family could use and get rid of, nearly. I've
raised two different kinds of peaches by my own settin out; raised
pecans by my own settin out—on these places I bargained to buy.
Didn't plant no fruit trees, nut trees, where I knowed I was goin to
rent or work on halves. I had pecan trees on the Pollard place. They
was practically young when I left there, but we did get some pecans
off them. I set out scions, bought scions, as many as six or eight
pecan scions and set em out. And I had on the Pollard place, right
there to the northwest side of my car shed, a bought plum tree that
was out of the bud; I set *it* out. Raised these great big purple plums,
and that tree bore more plums than a little. And I've often thought
about it—my boys done away with that plum tree after they was
runned off of that place; our labor, our time, our hearts' feelins
put out on it. Every year the limbs of that tree would just lean over
with plums. That tree growed up high as the house. O, it was a
beautiful tree, right to the northwest side of my car shed, two-car
shed; had that '26 Ford and that '28 Chevrolet stationed close to
that plum tree.

VII

I was climbin up in the world like a boy climbin a tree. And I fell just
as easy, too.

I was livin on Mr. Watson's place, buyin from him since he
took full control from the Federal Land Bank, and Mr. Grace just
went ahead and drifted my business over to Mr. Watson's hands.
And in that, I learnt that the banker had a disposition to help this
man Watson dig at me. That was in '31. And when Mr. Watson
got a little toehold, he told me, "Bring me the cotton this fall, bring
me the cotton."

When he told me that I got disheartened. I didn't want him
messin with me—still, I didn't let him take a mortgage on anything

I owned. I was my own man, had been for many years, and God knows I weren't goin to turn the calendar back on myself.

I always sold all of my cotton myself but one year, 1907, the first year I worked for Mr. Curtis; brought him my cotton to sell by his orders. I seen my daddy sell his own cotton; and sometimes the white man would sell it. And if my daddy owed him any money, he had no choice but to let him sell it. Mighty seldom my daddy ever got anything out of a cotton crop. Many times the white man wouldn't tell my daddy nothin bout the price he got for that cotton; weren't no use for him to tell him nothin, weren't no way to dispute him.

I was shy of Mr. Watson, I didn't want no business with him at all. But eventually, he pulled at me so hard I decided I'd trade with him a little. I got about fifteen or twenty bushels of corn from him. How come did I get that corn? Well, my plow horses would eat it, but my mules wouldn't eat no corn at that time; they didn't eat nothin but sweet feed. But my plow stock, regular plow stock, would eat corn. And I fell a little shy of corn that year; didn't need much and I went to Mr. Watson to get it—just givin him enough of my business, I hoped, to keep him off of me. But it didn't do no good. And that corn he let me have, he took it away from somebody else, I knowed that, but I couldn't do nothin about it.

That's all I traded in Mr. Watson's store except for a few things, spring of the year. Startin late up toward July and August I quit goin in there at all; wouldn't go in there for a pinch of salt. I didn't owe him but forty or fifty dollars and I had plenty of cotton to pay all of my debts—and cotton was bringin a low price, too. He had done taken my business over with the Federal Land Bank and I just thought: weren't no use of me cryin, I had enough cotton to pay him what I would have paid the Federal Land Bank and all I owed him at the store, too.

He wanted more than that. Kept trying every year, practically, to get a mortgage on my stuff, but he didn't get it. That poisoned him. Sure as you born, he picked at me all the time. But he couldn't move me. We was on a seesaw and a zigzag, but I just shed him off as best I could by not goin his way. Along them times I wasn't botherin with any of the white people too much because I was makin it on my own. I was buyin guano from whoever I wanted and I wasn't buyin it from him.

So I carried him three good bales of cotton. He was out of his store and gone when I got there. His clerks was in there but they couldn't tell me nothin, and I didn't particularly ask them. Carried the cotton to the warehouse, had it weighed, left it there in Mr. Watson's name, by Nate Shaw. A few days after that I went back to town to see him about it, see about a settlement for what little I owed him and get my business reconciled. Jumped up and told me —I asked him for a settlement—"Aw, there aint no use of that, Nate, there aint no use of that." Walked away from me.

I seed if he couldn't do me one way he was goin to do me another. He wouldn't give me no settlement, wouldn't recognize that I'd paid him. He just ignored me and talked his big talk. He read just exactly his pedigrees that I knew and felt in my heart and had heard a whole lot about. Denied me altogether. And that three bales of cotton would have overpaid him, I know; it wouldn't a stopped at no forty- or fifty-dollar debt. It was bringin a price enough, even at five cents—that would have brought over seventy-five dollars. Don't you see? Don't you see? Five hundred-pound-weight bales—I weren't a straight fool, I knowed I paid him more in the cotton than I owed him. Wouldn't go to his book here he had me charged, tell me what the cotton brought definitely, just took the cotton and went on.

But in '32 I wound up with all of em. I went on to the government and the government furnished me. The news was out through the settlement—the federal people was in Beaufort puttin out for the farmers.

I told my wife one mornin—I'd made up my mind that I was through with Watson, I was burnt up. And I said, "Darlin, I'm goin to Apafalya this mornin to take care of some business at the depot. And after that, I don't know if it will be today or tomorrow, I fully intend to go to Beaufort to see the federal people."

I drove my car to town and parked it. He had done meddled me there before about havin a closed Chevrolet car, '28 Chevrolet; done walked up to my car and looked it over, had the assurance to tell me, "I see how come you can't pay your debts—" just doggin at me—"I see how come you can't pay your debts, sittin in a closed model car."

I said, "Mr. Watson, what have I ever owed you and didn't pay you?"

He said, "You just a fool Negro," and he walked on off. He had it in for me. He knew I had good stock and I was a good worker and all like that. He just aimed to use his power and break me down; he'd been doin to people that way before then.

All right. That day I drove into town on my Chevrolet and parked it as soon as I got there. I walked on down the street and looked ahead of me and there was Watson standin there with his foot propped against the bank—bank was just below his store and the drugstore was between his store and the bank. Fellow by the name of Mose Todd, was supposed to be a little relation to me—I seed it was him Mr. Watson was standin there talkin to. I walked on by and got a little below em, just in hearin distance, and I stopped to hear their conversation. Mr. Watson considered me to be one of *his* Negroes too, and that gave me good encouragement to stop and sidle around and listen at him. I aint said a word that mornin to nobody. Just held my breath and looked at him and listened. Mose was standin there on the walkway with his head down and it looked like he was tryin to beg Watson to do somethin. I heard Mr. Watson tell Mose Todd, "No, I aint puttin out a dollar this year. I aint puttin out a thing. All of my men has got their own stock, they got their land to work, they got corn enough to feed their stock, and I aint puttin out a dollar. They all in shape to make a crop. And I'm goin to let em go and go ahead; I aint puttin out nothin."

I thought to myself right quick, 'You aint goin to put out nothin, how do you expect for em to make it? I know them people needs fertilize if nothin else, and you not puttin out a dollar. That's mighty bad—farmers can't get no furnishin at all out of you. They come to depend on you and now you leavin em to theirselves. I know what you goin to do; you goin to look for what they make this fall. You goin to do it, I know, you goin to look to take it and aint furnished em nothin.'

And just as sure as you born, if he had a claim against em they couldn't transact with nobody else. They was his niggers and he could do with em like he wanted to and nobody else wouldn't fool with em. I figured this, and I might have been a fool to think it, me being a colored fellow and knowin the rules of the state of Alabama, partly, if I didn't know em all: if you furnishes nothin, right and justice should say it's nothin you get. If you don't carry me on and help me, the law ought to take care of me and give me how much time I need to pay you whatever I owe you. Cotton was down then, too, wavin about at the bottom, five and six cents.

I standin there catchin it, wouldn't say a word. I hadn't even whispered to Mr. Watson, and wouldn't do it, just stood there until I caught all I could catch. And I understood, reasonably, that they was talkin bout Mose's business, and Mose had been one of Watson's customers for years. Now Watson was turnin him away. He just definitely told Mose to his head, right before me—I didn't question him because I had my route picked out. I was aimin to go to Beaufort to see if I could get furnished by the federal government, branch line. I just set out to move my little concerns out of his reach. O, he went down on Mose that mornin; told him what he were goin to do and what he weren't.

I just eventually walked on off and went on to the depot where I'd started to go. Seed after my little matters down there and I turned around and went right straight back up through town. Watson and Mose Todd both, when I looked up the street, was gone. Well, it didn't matter a continental with me where they was gone, I weren't takin hold with him no more for nothin. I had a right to get loose from him and he didn't have no sort of papers against me—that's what I was dotin on. His first step in business with me, he proved he just wanted to wind me up and get a mortgage on every bit of my personal property and take it over with the land, and if I crooked my little finger or wanted to leave, I'd lose everything I had, leave it right there. He woulda had a mortgage on it and I couldn't a moved it. Do you reckon I was goin to be fool enough to stand around and let him do that? I did have a little goat-sense and I was goin to stick him up right when I left him and wind up with him.

So, I kept movin till I got on my car and I come on home. Next day, with the full consent of my mind what to do, I crawled on my car —there was Leroy Roberts, Virgil Jones, and Sam MacFarland wanted to go to Beaufort with me on the same occasion to get in with the federal loan deal. Virgil and Leroy was Watson's niggers too, I know they was. So, me and them three fellows went on to Beaufort that mornin and when we got to Pottstown on route—it was cold that mornin and the boys took a notion they wanted to stop for some smokin tobacco. We stopped there and they disappeared into one of the stores and I walked on in to Mr. Billy Thompson's

store—he sold dry goods there and run a little druggist business
too—and I went on around to the back room where the heater was.
And Mr. V. Basil, white gentleman, was sittin by the stove crosslegged. The whole community knowed Mr. Basil, coloreds and whites.

I said, "Good mornin, Mr. Basil."

"Hello, Nate."

We talked and from one thing to another he put in talkin bout
how the times was for furnishin people—the pressure was on. I
stood there and warmed, talked with Mr. Basil. He was a man that
wore a mustache so long you could almost tie it around the back
of his neck, Mr. V. Basil. Stood there and talked with him awhile
bout the hard times, men puttin out money on farmers and couldn't
get it back, farmers weren't able to pay their debts and he, too, he
was goin to quit, he weren't goin to let his farmers have nothin,
wouldn't put out nothin. He talked Mr. Watson's talk that mornin—
I listened at him.

I said, "Well, Mr. Basil"—in a friendly way—"you a moneyed
man, why don't you help the boys this time around? All of em has
stuck by their word in the past"—I weren't talkin at him for nothin
for myself, I wouldn't fool with him. I said, "Why don't you help
the boys? You got plenty of money—" with a smile on my face.

He said, "Hell, yes, Nate. I got plenty damn money. And I got
plenty damn sense with it."

I laughed.

He said, "What kind of fool would a man be— No, I aint goin
to keep puttin out my money until they drain me and get the last
dollar I have, foolin around here farmin, and I can't get it back.
No, I aint goin to do it."

He went rock bottom against puttin out his money. I said to
myself, 'I don't want your money. I'm just feelin out your mind on
the subject.'

The boys got ready to go. I got on my car, cranked it up, and
we pulled out. When we got to Beaufort, all we boys, they took us
in the office there one by one—didn't meet us all there standin at
once—and one by one let us put in our complaints and what we
wanted and all. All of em went in before me and when they come
out they told me they went through all right, got agreement to be
helped. I was the last man in before the federal people to talk to
em—all white people, businessmen, no colored folks in it; only
way a colored person was in there, he went in there to be furnished.

So I told em my circumstances: didn't owe anybody anything. I was clear and I knowed it, told em straight. Well, I had done paid what I owed the devil—Watson—and got wound up with him, unbeknownst to him so he made out. I thought I had the privilege then to do business with anybody I wanted to because I had done cleared myself up and I knew Watson didn't have no mortgage on nothin I had. And I knowed I stood a better chance with the government than I did with any of these folks here, absolutely. I wouldn't turn around to look at one of em if the government was beckonin me to come in with them. *They* knowed it too, and they didn't like for the government to come into this country and meddle with their hands.

Well, they just gladly fixed me up. The federal government took me over and furnished me that year, 1932. Less interest, less interest on the loan money with them than with anybody I ever knowed. Altogether a different proposition.

They told me, "Look out in your mailbox on such-and-such a day and you'll find a check there for you to buy your fertilize. And after that, you can draw your other checks, all that you need to make your crop."

That certain date I went out to my mailbox and the check was there. I took that check and I come over here to Calusa with my wife to have it cashed. And when they cashed it for me they asked me if I wanted to leave it there in the bank. I said, "No, sir, I don't want to leave nary a penny. That's my fertilize money and I need it."

Went right on back home and in a day or two I got Mr. Horace Tucker to take his truck with a long trailer to it and when he stopped drivin we was in Union Springs. Drove right up to the guano factory in that little old city and bought all the guano I needed and loaded it on Mr. Horace's truck—the company did, the hands there workin—and carried it on home. Couldn't get me no soda there, soda was scarce, and the next day Mr. Horace carried me to Opelika on that truck—same man, same truck. He weren't gettin nothin for hisself, he went for me. Of course, I paid him, didn't expect but to pay him for them trips, drivin that trailer truck and haulin my fertilize. Well, couldn't get no soda at Opelika but I got some ammonia chemical to answer in place of it. Mr. Horace Tucker—wasn't a nicer white man for accommodatin you in the whole settlement.

The second government check was my supply check; it come several weeks later and I used the money strictly for groceries—and that was flour, sugar, and coffee, but for no meat and lard, I didn't need that, raised my meat and lard at home.

I went on and made my crop that year, '32. Didn't go to Apafalya nary a time for nothin. And after crops was laid by I hauled a little lumber, spot haulin, no regular operation. I got home one evenin—night—I was workin right close to my home then, and my wife told me, "Darlin, Mr. Watson come through here today."

I said, "He did?"

She said, "Yes."

I said, "Did he stop?"

She said, "No, he never did quit drivin, just drivin along slow and lookin every whichway."

All right. That was on a Thursday. He went right on back to Apafalya after he drove around the men what had been dealin with him and he printed up some cards and sent em around, one to me, one to Leroy Roberts, one to Virgil Jones—we was *his* men. Said on the card, "Those who consider that they are my customers, come out to Apafalya Saturday evenin and get em some beef."

My wife asked me, "Darlin, is you goin to go to Apafalya like the note say?"

I said, "If I do, I'll walk on my hands."

Weren't nothin to that note but a sham. He just wanted us to come out there so he could question us about how we was doin our business. The other boys done as they pleased along them lines, they was all grown. I never did ask Virgil Jones did he go get that beef, and I never did ask Leroy Roberts; it weren't none of my concern. But I know what Nate Shaw done. I weren't hungry for none of his beef, and I never would get so hungry that I couldn't get somethin to eat other ways. I wouldn't be fool enough to go out there huntin no beef if I were down to my last piece of bread. My children will tell you, any of em, they never knowed what it was to get hungry and couldn't get somethin to eat.

THE panic was on that year—cotton was cheap, had done hit the bottom. And when the wind-up come, the government gived me a date to comply and bring my cotton to the warehouse that the government rented here in Calusa. You could sell your cotton yourself and pay the government cash or pool your cotton in the government's name at the warehouse, just so much cotton as they told you, accordin to the price they figured. The order come to me to pool so many hundred pounds of lint cotton.

As the panic was on, the government was lenient and kind to their customers. And that poolin, that would give the cotton a chance to go up—but I'm satisfied that I paid to store that cotton out of the amount of cotton they called for. I didn't worry bout the cotton goin up or down no more that year once I turned my cotton loose. The government was just takin a chance of gettin what I owed out of it.

That fall, I come up to the requirement. The bales of cotton that I pooled weighed a little over what they asked for. I went on, after I put the cotton in the warehouse in the name of the government—so much lint, so many bales weighin so-and-so—went back home and I finished gatherin my crop. My wife got a bale of cotton weighed five hundred and sixty-five pounds. Me and my children worked to make it on my wife's mother's and father's place. Gathered that cotton, ginned it, had that big bale belonged to my wife and three bales I had for myself that I held back after carryin the government three bales. I took up one of them bales one mornin, the lightest bale I had, me and my boys put it on the wagon and I told em to carry it to the market and sell it and bring back the money—they done it, just like Papa said do. I gived every nickel of that money to my wife to use to buy the children and herself some shoes and clothes as far as it would go. It weren't no great sum of money—cotton only brought five cents that year, as little as it ever brought in my lifetime.

All right. I took them other two bales of mine and headed em up to the door of my cotton house, weatherboarded cotton house I'd built when I moved on the place, rolled that cotton in there and stood it up. Took my wife's bale and stood it up beside my two bales—they was lighter bales than her'n. I locked the door. Left em there and that's where they was standin when I was put in the penitentiary.

FROM the first bale of cotton to the last one, that Vernon of mine—he got big enough to handle my mules on the road, my second son, he'd try anything he seed his daddy try. Got my first bale of cotton on the wagon one mornin, said, "Vernon, come on and go to the gin with me; me and you will go to the gin today."

Went on down there to Tucker's crossroads to the gin, walked
in there and made arrangements about ginnin my cotton, had that
bale of cotton ginned, went on back home, and I never did haul
another bale of cotton to the gin that fall myself. Next bale of cotton,
Vernon hauled it to the gin—first time I'd ever trusted him complete,
he was grown then. "Vernon, time to go to the gin now, we got a
bale of cotton. Take it to the gin." He hitched them mules to that
wagon and pulled off. Them mules was game as the devil, but he
managed it and he done it gladly.

My mules at that time was named Mary and Dela; Mary was
a black mule and Dela was what you might call a bay-colored mule.
Both of em was heavy mules, big enough for farm use, road use,
anywhere you put em. That Mary mule was the devil on hinges, no
doubt. I didn't dread sendin Vernon off with her and Dela though,
because I knowed if there was any chance in the world they could
be handled, Vernon would handle em. Sometimes he'd go to the
gin and be late comin back. I'd walk out the house, go out to the
road and look up the road see if I could see him. And when that boy
come in sight with them mules and that bale of cotton sittin up in
the wagon behind him, that Mary mule would have her head in the
air, her heels up in the corner next to the double-tree. I could see
the devil was in her. I'd stand there, heap of times, Vernon'd hit the
yard, I'd say, "Old Mary is good and hot, aint she, son?" "Yes, Papa,
she's been cuttin a fool ever since we left for the gin." She didn't
stand a automobile—any way she heard one comin behind her, she'd
stampede like the devil, dodge from it and lean off and then, after
it passed, she'd break to run. She was the most devilish mule ever
I had but she was as good a workin mule as ever was hitched up.
But that way she had, you had to watch chances to live behind
Mary. She'd spill you, tear up the wagon, and do everything else
if that bay mule, old Dela, would second her; that's all it took. But
Vernon was able to hold her and talk to her—it took a heap of talk,
holdin didn't do no good a heap of times. Come along in front of the
house with her head throwed out in the air and go through to the
back yard between the car shed and the house goin to the barn. O,
she was a piss-ripper. Vernon held her in though—he went with me
the first bale I hauled to the gin in '32, made my arrangements bout
ginnin not only the bale I brought that day, but for up until my
last bale that year, whether I was to be there or not. Vernon was on
the wagon haulin it himself when the last bale was hauled. And

that Mary mule would come in there every time just like a tiger. I hated her ways but I had faith enough in Vernon to believe he'd stay with her.

THERE was a white gentleman by the name of Leonard Wilcox— his sister lives right up there at Pottstown today, she married Mr. Grady Rudd for her second husband; and that was her brother runnin all over the country, singin, "Watson say he goin to take all Nate Shaw got this fall and all Virgil Jones—he goin to take everything they got."

Well, he was tellin it around for several weeks and at that time he never did tell me directly about it. And I wondered how come he went tellin it to other colored fellows. I reckon he was tellin whites too, "Watson say he goin to take all old Nate Shaw got this fall and old Virgil Jones."

Well, one day this white man come by my house, right after gatherin time, and he hadn't never told me nothin about it, skippin me, tellin it to everybody in the whole settlement around, just singin it. I was out there by my well and my well was close to the road and I looked down the road and here he come, Mr. Leonard Wilcox. Come on up to me and stopped. Here's his song with me: "Watson say he goin to take all you got this fall, and all old Virgil Jones got."

I looked at him and I said, "He did?"

Said, "Yeah. Take all you and old Virgil Jones got this fall."

I said, "Well, there's a law for that and the law obliges the likes of him as well as me. I aint goin to hide. When he starts, it's goin to be trouble."

A heap of families, while I was livin on the Tucker place down on Sitimachas, was leavin goin north. Some of my neighbors even picked up and left. The boll weevil was sendin a lot of em out, no doubt. I knowed several men went north, some with their families and some without; they sent for their families when they got to where they was goin. More went besides what I knowed of, from all parts of this southern country. They was dissatisfied with the way of life here in the south—and when I was livin on the Pollard place it come pretty wide open to me and touched the hem of my garment. But my family was prosperin right here, I didn't pay no attention to leavin. I wanted to stay and work for better conditions. I knowed I was in a bad way of life here but I didn't intend to get out—*that* never come in my mind. I thought somehow, some way, I'd overcome it. I was a farmin man at that time and I knowed more about this country than I knowed about the northern states. I've always been man enough to stick up for my family, and love them, and try to support em, and I just thought definitely I could keep it up. In other words, I was determined to try.

And durin of the pressure years, a union begin to operate in this country, called it the Sharecroppers Union—that was a nice name, I thought—and my first knowin about this union, this organization, that riot come off at Crane's Ford in '31.* I looked deep in that thing, too—I heard more than I seed and I taken that in consideration. And I knowed what was goin on was a turnabout on the southern man, white and colored; it was somethin unusual. And I heard about it bein a organization for the poor class of people —that's just what I wanted to get into, too; I wanted to know the secrets of it enough that I could become in the knowledge of it. Now I heard talk about trucks comin into this country deliverin guns to the colored people but I decided all that was talk, tryin to accuse the niggers of gettin into somethin here that maybe they weren't— and maybe they were. But didn't no trucks haul no guns to nobody. Colored people hadn't been armed up for nothin; it was told like that just to agitate the thing further. Of course, some of these colored folks in here had some good guns—you know a Winchester rifle is a pretty good gun itself. But they didn't have nothin above that. It weren't nothin that nobody sent in here for em to use, just their own stuff.

Well, they killed a man up there, colored fellow; his name was Adam Cole. And they tell me—I didn't see it but I heard lots about it and I never did hear nothin about it that backed me off— Kurt Beall, the High Sheriff for Tukabahchee County, got shot in the stomach. He run up there to break up this meetin business amongst the colored people and someone in that crowd shot him. That kind of broke him up from runnin in places like that.

And these white folks woke up and stretched themselves and commenced a runnin around meddlin with niggers about this organization. And it's a close thing today. One old man—and he was

* See Appendix.

as big a skunk as ever sneaked in the woods—old man Mac Sloane, come up to me one day—he didn't come to my home, he met me on the outside—old man Mac Sloane come to me hot as a stove iron, "Nate, do you belong to that mess they carryin on in this country?"

I just cut him off short. I didn't belong to it at that time, but I was eager to join and I was aimin to join, just hadn't got the right opportunity.

"No, I don't belong to nothin."

Mac Sloane, white man, said, "You stay out of it. That damn thing will get you killed. You stay out of it. These niggers runnin around here carryin on some kind of meetin—you better stay out of it."

I said to myself, 'You a fool if you think you can keep me from joinin.' I went right on and joined it, just as quick as the next meetin come. Runnin around and givin me orders—he suspected I might be the kind of man to belong to such a organization; put the finger on me before I ever joined. And he done just the thing to push me into it—gived me orders not to join.

The teachers of this organization begin to drive through this country—they couldn't let what they was doin be known. One of em was a colored fella; I disremember his name but he did tell us his name. He wanted us to organize and he was with us a whole lot of time, holdin meetins with us—that was part of his job. We colored farmers would meet and the first thing we had to do was join the organization. And it was said, we didn't want no bad men in it at all, no weak-hearted fellows that would be liable to give the thing away. It was secret with them all that joined it; they knowed to keep their mouths shut and meet the meetins. And this teacher said—don't know where his home was; he had a different way of talkin than we did—"I call em stool pigeons if they broadcast the news about what's happenin." And said, if a nigger, like myself, went and let out any secrets to the white folks about the organization, the word was, "Do away with him."

Had the meetins at our houses or anywhere we could have em where we could keep a look and a watch-out that nobody was comin in on us. Small meetins, sometimes there'd be a dozen, sometimes there'd be more, sometimes there'd be less—niggers was scared, niggers was scared, that's tellin the truth. White folks in this country didn't allow niggers to have no organization, no secret meetins. They kept up with you and watched you, didn't allow you to associate in a crowd, unless it was your family or your church. It just worked in a way that the nigger wasn't allowed to have nothin but church services and, O, they liked to see you goin to church, too. Sometimes white people would come into the Negro church and set there and listen at the meetin. Of course, it weren't nothin but a church service goin on. But if a nigger walked into a white church, he'd just be driven out, if they didn't kill him. But if a Negro was a servant for white people, then they'd carry him to church with em, accept him to come in and take a seat on the back seat and listen at the white people. But if you was a independent Negro you better stay away from there. But if you was a white man's dear flunky, doin what he said do, or even on the woman's side, if they was maids for the white people, well thought of, they'd take em out to their home churches, dupe em up in a way. They knowed they weren't goin to cause no trouble—and if they did, they'd just been knocked out of the box and called in close question. But they never did act disorderly; just set there and listened at the white folks' meetin quiet as a lamb. And when the white folks would come in the colored churches, good God, the niggers would get busy givin em first class seats—if there was any in that buildin the white folks got em. They was white people; they classed theirselves over the colored and the colored people never did do nothin but dance to what the white people said and thought. White people was their bosses and their controllers and the colored people went along with it. White men, white women—I been there—go in colored churches and be seated. Nigger aint got nothin to do but run around there and give em the nicest seats.

FIRST thing the organization wanted for the colored people was the privilege to have a organization. That's one of the best things they ever could fight for and get on foot. From my boy days comin along, ever since I been in God's world, I've never had no rights, no voice in nothin that the white man didn't want me to have—even been cut out of education, book learnin, been deprived of that. How could I favor such rulins as have been the past?

The teacher would send out literatures and these literatures would get around in colored folks' boxes and they got so bold they went to puttin em in white folks' boxes. I couldn't definitely say what them literatures said—I aint a readin man—but they said enough that the big white men didn't like it at all. Malcolm Todd, who married my wife's oldest sister, he heard a white man say, "The Lord is bringin down the world, the Lord is bringin down the world."

Well, it was many conditions that called for such a organization as *that*. Niggers had to get back and get back quick when the white man spoke. Had to be humble and submissive under em. My color needed a protection so long, so long. You couldn't get a nigger to poke his head out in them days for nothin—scared, and—I looked at it from another angle and that was the worst thing that could ever hit my attention. We had too many colored people that if they knowed anything was goin on amongst their own color, any sort of plot at all, they'd turn it in to the white people. No use to try gettin together to do somethin bout the conditions we was livin under because somebody would run and stick his head under the white man's shirttail, and that was that. I call em Uncle Toms. They'll prowl into the niggers' business to get the dope and carry it to the white folks. Uncle Tom's a devil of a man; he's a enemy to his race.

Niggers was scared to run their business together, buy their fertilize together, sell their cotton together, because the white man —the average colored man was workin on the white man's place, and if he weren't on the white man's place he had to cooperate with the white man to get furnished and so on. And the white man held the final rule over the Negro—"Bring the cotton to me." I heard it; it was told to others and it was told to me.

Conditions has been outrageous every way that you can think against the colored race of people. Didn't allow em to do this, didn't allow em to do that, didn't allow em to do the other. Knowin and comin into the knowledge of what was goin on and how it was goin on in the United States as far as I knowed, which was the state of Alabama as far as I knowed, Tukabahchee County—I knew that it was a weak time amongst the colored people. They couldn't demand nothin; they was subject to lose what they had if they demanded any more.

Good God, there wasn't but few privileges that we was allowed. If you was flesh and blood and human and you tended to want to help and support your friends in the community, and make somethin of yourself—white folks didn't allow you that privilege. But we had the privilege of workin for the white man—he who had the chance had better do it; get yourself together and get over yonder in Mr. So-and-so's field or anywhere else he told you and do what he tell you to do. And when pay time come he'd pay you what he wanted to, and in many cases it'd be less than what he'd pay a white man. And some work, like pickin cotton in the fields, white folks didn't fill a basket—most of em. That was niggers' work. And if a poor white man got out there and picked cotton, he was pickin cotton like a nigger. Colored man just been a dog for this country for years and years. White man didn't ask you how you felt about what he wanted to do; he'd just go ahead and do it and you had to fall under his rulins. And bein in his home country, he been allowed to do as he please by the capital of the United States.

I heard talk when I was a boy of how the colored people come to America. Now the talk that I heard might not be exactly how it was but I have no reason to argue with the words. It all comes down to this: the colored people was transferred here from Africa just like you transfer a drove of stock. White man gathered em up in the distant countries; they didn't have no knowledge of where they was goin, they had to move by orders, had no idea of where they was goin. Passed em across the water in some form or fashion and they was put over in this country and sold just like you'd go out here and sell a hog, a horse, a cow, just so. They was black people—all of em was dark at that time—but they wasn't recognized as people. They had no say-so, they had no choice noway. Well, after they got over here—I has a hard time keepin myself together when I thinks about it—they was put under the possession of marsters and mistresses, just like your beast comes under the possession of you when you buy it. Had no voice, no privilege, only had to go by orders every way.

    And whoever come to be bought by such-and-such a one, why, they was his. And when he wanted he'd sell em and swap em. And I was told that in the time the colored was under bondage—niggers as they called em, right quick—they was divided out like this: one white man that bought a drove would give his children so many colored folks apiece, just like he'd give em a hog, make his children a present of em just like that.

    And the nigger was handicapped to death. He had to go by orders, he had to come by orders; when he knocked off he knocked off by orders. And the only way the nigger come out from under that marster, he was sold to some other man. That big fellow out yonder with so many colored people, he noticed this man's crowd, he knowed what he had, and all of em knowed what they had—it was a business proposition. So some of em would take a fancy to some of that man's slaves over yonder; look around, walk around, and take a fancy to em. More than likely, if I wanted, I'd buy that woman or that man from that marster over yonder. And if that marster had a nice lookin, healthy colored man, I'd give him a pile of money for that big Negro, carry him home and put him with my crowd and produce a mess of young-uns like hisself. They didn't like so much the little scrawny colored people, weren't able to work much. If the marster caught a little, bitty, scrawny nigger foolin round amongst his women, there'd be no holdin up on the whippin he'd get. They wanted these big healthy fellows, big healthy women; they wanted to create a race of people to suit em.

If there was any way in the world that I could buy the one I wanted, well, I wouldn't have to ask the nigger nothin, I'd talk—this marster over here would talk to that marster over yonder about you. And if he could buy you he'd buy you, if the man would sell. Just like you was a cow or a mule, he'd buy you out the drove. You had no choice. I realize what that meant. I might belong to you and you might have a woman over here too that was my wife. Or I stayed with her if it was your request for me to stay with that woman; but if it wasn't, I couldn't—for breedin purposes. And you got the privilege of sellin me away from my wife, if the boss man over yonder wanted me or if you just needed the money; it was in your power to sell me. I had no choice, weren't allowed no choice. I'd have to get gone from that woman, made no difference if I loved her or not. You know it's nature for men to love women, and for women to love men; they loved each other in them days, too. And they just abused nature by sellin me. "You got to do what I say, you aint no more than the mule you plow, in my sight. You belong to me, you aint nothin but my property." It just points right to that, you look at it. I'm just your property. I got a wife here, I love her. You see fit to move me, that marster man over yonder wants to buy me—that runs deep with me, I can't forget it. It was like that too, or maybe worser. A heap of things you hear and you aint experienced it, you can't feel it like you experienced it.

I belong to you. You got me livin here. Got plenty of others livin here too, them's your servants. That boss man over yonder, marster of his crowd over yonder somewhere, he look over the situation and see me; maybe he like my looks, he like my ways, regardless to what I think, you can do with me as you please. He come to you and make you an offer to buy me. Well, you realize that I'm your mainline servant, you'll price me high to him and he gets me, he got to pay a price just like he was payin for a mule or a horse or a hog—I has no choice, I has no voice or nothin, I'm just handicapped to death and I got to go where old marster puts me. Marster sees fit to sell me, he goin to sell me and pocket up a pile of money off me.

They told me that good able-bodied Negroes and Negroes with good health sold for a pretty penny. I might be a carpenter, I might be a blacksmith, or I might just work in the field. You'd sell me accordin to what I was worth to you. That man over yonder buys me, I'd cost him somethin.

And the owners of these colored people would fall out with one another about em. That was their livin: they had it all figured out how much a certain colored man or colored woman cost em to buy and raise and how much they would make off of that nigger as long as they owned him. It run that way for years, they tell me, it run that way for years. A time of brutish acts, brutish acts.

The old boss man, the old marster, disregarded the nigger, disrecognized him in everything, but he slipped under the covers at the colored women, and here's how that was done: poor colored women, slaves in them days, didn't know nothin but to do what they was told to do, bow for the marster. Old marster, he'd wait his chance and when his wife would leave home for pleasure or enjoyment or anything—he might cause her to be away from home —and they had housemaids and they was always the best lookin colored women, the most obedient colored women—they run for that today. Old marster, old missus, maybe both of em would pick out one of the nigger women that looked like she'd suit em. They'd put her in the house as a maid to cook, iron, wash, take care of the house, keep it decent and clean—just pick out the nicest one and give her a job in the house to keep that house cleaned up and cook food for their table; in other words, a housewoman. Old missus would go anywhere she wanted to go and leave that colored woman there. Old marster would slip around, he wanted to get to that colored woman. And he'd wait till it was quiet and all, until his wife left home—she gone, he'd sneak around there, make that colored woman lay down on the bed for him, pop it to her much as he wanted to. She had to lay down for him, poor woman; didn't, no tellin what would happen. She belonged to him but he wanted to keep his doins outside of his wife, wouldn't fool with that woman long as his wife was there; he knowed that would cause trouble.

That's the way it was cut out and that's the way it was done and I've lived amongst the very people it was done to, enough to tell it close. I've dug up the root and branch of it. And I can say they wanted to be free, have their rights as they was created by God above. God gived the colored man and gived the colored woman some knowledge and it was knowledge enough to know they wasn't free. I have lived in bondage myself, just like bondage, and I can say they wanted to be free.

I was able when I was just ten or twelve years old to understand how they was treatin the colored folks in this country. I used to say—I criticized it and had every thought as I could have against such as that when I was a boy. I used to say—but I come down off that and just keep my mouth shut. I used to say, "I won't stand to rest the way they treatin colored folks in this country, I won't stand it." And I showed it to em, too, when I got grown, I showed it to em. I give em what they wanted when I was a boy, but somehow or other I got to where I couldn't keep that spirit in me, I had to do somethin.

I wasn't over ten or twelve years old until I begin to come into the knowledge of more different things wrong than I can really tell. They'd overpower you every way—meet colored folks in the road, young colored boys when I was a boy, beat em up, whip em up, make em get in the field and go to work. I knowed too darn well they weren't payin em nothin hardly. These people in this country, that was right down their alley. Done that—called it vagrancy. It was just like slavery, God knows it weren't a bit of difference. In place of ever changin and gettin better, it was gettin worser and worser as I come up in this world.

THE way I caught it and the way I can explain it accordin to my best ideas, this here organization was workin to bring us out of bad places where we stood at that time and been standin since the colored people has remembrance. They didn't say to us how this was goin to happen—we didn't have time to work up a plan; only I felt it, I could feel it was somethin good. It was goin to rise us out of these old slum conditions which that we had been undergoin since slavery times, bring a clearer life to live, push the white man back.

I heard this spoke by the officials, the people that was advertisin this union: they was tired of the rich man gettin richer and the poor man gettin poorer. They seed it was a freeze-out. Tired, tired of that way of life. That's the way I looked into it, and the rest of em, some of em looked at it that way too. And we put these thoughts in our literatures. I didn't never put out none myself; if I'd a done put em out I couldn't a read em. But we had some in our home when I was arrested—they never was sharp enough to get em, but they got so many others. And it's all got lost today. My people was treated in such a way that they done good to save their lives by the help that helped em. Couldn't save no literatures.

The first teacher attracted the attention of several of us by his talkin bout the future comin. He told us, and we agreed, the future days follows the present. And if we didn't do somethin for ourselves today, tomorrow wouldn't be no different. But you know, people is people in this world. You can show em a thing that means a benefit to em and they'll run off; can't see where today might end and tomorrow begin. They held the meetins all right, but they was shy like rats. And what was they lookin for? They was keepin their eyes open for stool pigeons and giveaways; that throwed a check in the business. It showed that they—we—didn't have no confidence in each other.

Well, we was taught at our meetins that when trouble comes, stand up for one another. Whatever we was goin to do, whatever that was, we was goin to do it together. And by colored people in this country havin any kind of sense that was profitable at all, they joined this organization. I was eager for it, eager.

I paid a small dues when I joined, nothin to hurt me, not more than a few cents. Somebody had to take care of the teacher. He was helpin us, that was his job, and we had to look out for him. I don't know whether he had a wife and children or where they was if he did have, but *he* had to live. He was comin regular and holdin meetins—he had more knowledge and authority than we had and from his words I went out and talked it over with folks. I went to several places, even out the other side of Apafalya, and informed some people I knew about the organization. Some of em went in, too, by my descriptions. I told em it was a good thing in favor of the colored race and it was so far a over-average help—as far as I was taught I told em what the organization was goin to do. The organization would back you up and fight your battles with you, do this and do that and do the other, as far as I was taught by the travelin man.

I recommended it thoroughly to particular ones I knowed—some of em was too scared to join and some of em was too scared not to join; they didn't want to be left alone when push come to shove. I recommended it to my brother Peter, but he never did join it. He was livin on Mr. Watson's individual place at that time, about a mile and a half from me on the Crane's Ford road toward Apafalya. He got along with Mr. Watson by givin him what he made— Mr. Watson got it all, that's the truth to it. My brother Peter was easy and hush-mouthed and he just settled down to that. He made up his mind that he weren't goin to have anything, and after that, why, nothin could hurt him. He's my own dear brother he said he was discouraged of this organization but I knowed he was afraid.

Here's the rule of our colored people in this country, that I growed up in the knowledge of: they'll dote on a thing, they'll like it, still a heap stays shy of it. They knowed that their heads was liable to be cracked, if nothin else, about belongin to somethin that the white man didn't allow em to belong to. All of em was willin to it in their minds, but they was shy in their acts. It's just like the old man and the bear. When the bear was comin in the house, he warned his wife about it—we colored people, some of us is like that today—the old man jumped up and run up in the loft where the bear couldn't get him. The old woman, when the bear walked in, she grabbed the fire iron and she labored with the bear until she killed him. And when she killed him, then the old man come down from the loft, sayin, "Old lady, aint *we* brave, aint *we* brave. We killed that bear. We killed that bear." And hadn't done nothin but killed hisself runnin. He'll talk a whole lot but he's too scared to take a hold.

IN a few weeks' time it come off, it come off. Mr. Watson sent the deputy sheriff to Virgil Jones' to attach his stock and bring it away from there. Virgil had got word of the plot and he come to warn me and several other men of the organization. I knowed I was goin to be next because my name was ringin in it as loud as Virgil Jones' was. Virgil come and told me about it on a Saturday evenin. That next Monday mornin I fixed myself up and walked over there, bout a mile from where I was livin. My wife's baby sister was livin on a little plantation right near there, her and her husband. I went over by their house that mornin and went on out across the road to Virgil Jones'. Got there and good God I run into a crowd, and Virgil Logan, deputy sheriff, was there fixin to attach up everything. I just walked up like somebody walkin about, that's the way I played it.

Several of us met there too, but we had no plan strictly about what we was goin to do. Leroy Roberts and two or three more of em come there early and left before I got there. Well, the devil started his work that mornin. I asked Mr. Logan, the deputy sheriff, I knowed him; he lived right over here at Pottstown at that time and he was a Tukabahchee deputy for the state of Alabama—I asked Mr. Logan kindly, talkin to all of em, "What's the matter here? What's this all about?"

The deputy said, "I'm goin to take all old Virgil Jones got this mornin."

Well, I knowed doggone well accordin to the quotation I was goin to be next. He just startin on Virgil Jones first. I stretched my eyes and said, "Mr. Logan, please sir, don't take what he got. He's got a wife and children and if you take all his stuff you'll leave his folks hungry. He aint got a dime left to support em if you take what he's got."

I begged him not to do it, begged him. "You'll dispossess him of bein able to feed his family."

Our teacher, the man that put out this organization in this part of the country, he told us to act humble, be straight; his teachin, to not go at a thing too rapid and forcible. Be quiet, whatever we do, let it work in a way of virtue. They got a song to this effect, did have years ago: "Low is the way to the bright new world, let the heaven light shine on me." Low is the way, humble and low is the way for me. That's what I tried to give Logan, too. I tried to go by the union's orders.

"Please, sir, don't take it. Go to the ones that authorized you to take his stuff, if you please, sir, and tell em to give him a chance. He'll work to pay what he owes em."

I knowed it was Watson gived him orders what to do, or Beall, the High Sheriff Kurt Beall, he was backin it up.

The deputy said, "I got orders to take it and I'll be damned—"

I asked him humble and begged him not to do it. "Go back to the ones that gived you orders to do this and tell em the circumstances. He aint able to support his family. Aint got a dime to support his family."

He said, "I got orders to take it and I'll be damned if I aint goin to take it."

Well, that brought up a whole lot of hard words then. I just politely told him he weren't goin to do it, he weren't goin to do it. "Well, if you take it, I'll be damned if you don't take it over my dead body. Go ahead and take it."

He got hot. After a while I seed Cecil Pickett go in the lot with bridles in his hands to catch Virgil Jones' mules. That was a colored fellow had no sense; white folks could get him to do anything they wanted him to do. He come over there that mornin on the deputy sheriff's car. He was one of Logan's superintendin Negroes and he didn't know no better than to come over with Logan and help take what Virgil Jones had—that was the white folks' rule: when they got ready to do anything, didn't matter what it was, they'd carry a nigger with em. O, they could get some nigger to follow em to hell and back. I feel angry over that today—

I told Cece Pickett that mornin, goin to the gate with bridles in his hands—I don't know where he got them bridles but he had em, goin in that lot to catch them mules. Lookin right at him. He walked up to the lot gate, unlatched it and walked in. I didn't see the mules but I reckoned they was in the stable. I said, "What are you goin in there for?"

Mr. Logan said, "He's goin in there to catch them mules. That's what he's goin for."

I said, "You just as well to come out. Catch no mules there this mornin, till a further investigation."

Kept a walkin—I said, "Well, you can go ahead and catch em but you won't get em out of that lot; go catch em, go on."

When I told Cece Pickett that he stopped. Looked at me and he looked at Logan, looked at me and looked at Logan.

I said, "Go ahead and catch em, if you that game. I'll be damned if you won't ever bring em out of that gate."

Somebody got to stand up. If we don't we niggers in this

country are easy prey. Nigger had anything a white man wanted, the white man took it; made no difference how the cut might have come, he took it.

Mr. Logan seed I meant it—I was crowin so strong and I was fixin to start a shootin frolic then.

"Come out, Cece," Logan said, "Come on back, Cece. Let em alone. Come out."

Then the deputy walked up to me and said, "You done said enough already for me to be done killed you."

I said, "Well, if you want to kill me, I'm right before you. Kill me, kill me. Aint nothin between us but the air. Kill me."

I didn't change my disposition at all; if my orders hadn't a been listened to, the devil woulda took place sooner than it did.

A nigger by the name of Eph Todd seed me lowerin the scrape on Logan and he runned up on me from behind and grabbed a hold of me. Good God, I throwed a fit because it popped in my mind that quick—I heard many a time in my life that a man will meddle you when another man is fixin to kill you; he'll come up and grab you, maybe hold you for the other to kill you. I looked around and cussed him out and he left there. The deputy sheriff looked at me —I kept my eyes on him—and he walked away, just saunterin along.

One come and found the water was hot—Virgil Logan. He told the crowd that mornin, shyin away from em, "I'll just go and get Kurt Beall; he'll come down there and kill the last damn one of you. You know how he is"—well, all the niggers knowed that Mr. Kurt Beall was a bad fellow—"When he comes in he comes in shootin."

I told him, "Go ahead and get him—" every man there heard it—"Go ahead and get Mr. Beall, I'll be here when he comes."

He left then. Drove away in his automobile and took Cece Pickett with him. Went to Beaufort and delivered the message to the High Sheriff, Kurt Beall.

After he left, I went in Virgil Jones' house one time to see who was in there, and there was four, five, or six settin in there and they was so quiet. Virgil Jones was there, but his wife and children was long gone, I don't know where they was. Sam MacFarland was there. Boss Hatch was there—they never did catch Boss Hatch neither. And there was some more of em. I stood there and looked at em and I could see they was scared. I went right back out the door where I could keep my eyes open, just keep a watchin for them officers to drive in. After a while, about twelve thirty or one o'clock—I know it was early after dinner—I looked down the road and I seed that car comin. Well, I knowed that was the same car that left there that mornin. And I called the boys, "Hey, fellas, come on out, come on out"—I know they heard me—"Yonder they come, yonder come the officers."

Good God almighty, when I told em that, next thing I heard em runnin out of that house, hittin it to the swamps, just cleanin up from there. I reckon some of em peeped out the door or a window and seed them officers. So, stampedin, stampedin, stampedin out of there and they was still runnin scared when I come out of prison.

I just stood right on and I was standin alone. I seed there was weak spots in them men and there was bad acts comin up, but I didn't run a step. I stood there and they all runned out of there like rats runnin out of a woodpile, and all of em that run, run out the back. I didn't let that worry me; I just taken it for granted and let em go. I didn't think about gettin shot and I didn't think about not gettin shot. I thought this: a organization is a organization and if I don't mean nothin by joinin I ought to keep my ass out of it. But if I'm sworn to stand up for all the poor colored farmers—and poor white farmers if they'd takin a notion to join—I've got to do it. Weren't no use under God's sun to treat colored people like we'd been treated here in the state of Alabama. Work hard and look how they do you. Look how they done my daddy in his time and look how Mr. Watson tried to do me. Dug at me and dug at me, couldn't handle me, then he made me bring him the cotton. I carried it to him—I was workin for a easy way out—didn't carry him all of it but I carried him more than enough to pay him what I owed him. Still he dug at me and he dug at his other niggers too. Virgil Jones —he was in the organization, he was solid in bein with us, but when the showdown come he run like the rest of em. Some of em is yet standin with a watery mouth, ready when times are made better by those that's men enough and women enough to stand up, when the thing ever comes into effect; they goin to run up then and accept the good of it and they won't give you a bit more credit for riskin your life than they would a rabbit.

Virgil Jones was a friend to me. He was rentin his farm—he weren't buyin it and he weren't rentin it from Mr. Watson; Mr.

Watson didn't own that place. But Mr. Watson was dealin with him,
furnishin him—had been—that's what I understood. And he
claimed that Virgil owed him money. I don't know how much Virgil
owed him or if he owed him at all, but that weren't the issue with
me. I was forced that year to face what was happenin—

So, them officers runned that car up out there to the road
comin to that house, and that house stood a good little piece off of
the public road. Four of em come back there that evenin. I was
outdoors, walkin around, watchin for em to come. Virgil Logan
done dashed off and went and got what he could but he didn't get
Kurt Beall. He wouldn't come there; he'd done got shot at that rip-it
at Crane's Ford and he was shy, he wouldn't come down there. And
after all this trouble was over, blessed God if a white man didn't
shoot Sheriff Beall down and kill him. Since then, since then.
There was a ruckus up there above Beaufort between a man and his
wife and he sent his deputies to cool the water and they couldn't do
nothin. He decided he'd go up there and do it. And they tell it—
and there's good evidence to back it—soon as he got there the white
man killed him.

Well, I didn't care if Kurt Beall come back and I didn't care
if he didn't. Who came back with Logan? Lew Badger from Hamilton, just up above Beaufort; Byron Ward, Kurt Beall's deputy from
Beaufort; and a old fellow by the name of Platt, I never did see him
before but I knowed of him. And of course, Virgil Logan come back
with em. They stopped that car and jumped out of it and come right
straight toward the front of the house in a fast walk—they weren't
trottin but they was walkin as fast as they could walk. I stood there
and looked at em till they got up to me. And when they hit the edge
of the yard, Virgil Logan pointed his finger and said, "There stands
Nate Shaw. That's him right there."

He just kept a walkin; him and Lew Badger went on around
the house. Platt and Ward come straight to me. I noticed that Platt
had a automatic shotgun—I could see about four inches of the
barrel; he'd pulled the stock of it under a big brown weather coat.
Platt walked right up to me. Ward went to the doorsteps and just
laid down nearly, peepin in the house to see who was in there, me
watchin Platt and watchin Ward too. They surrounded that house
then and Platt walked up just about five paces from me and
stopped; that's as close as he come. And he stood there, flashin his
eyes over me, keepin his gun pointed on me. Right at that present

time I was the only fellow out there. All the rest of em done run away and gone to the swamps and woods where the sheriffs couldn't see em.

Everything was so quiet there—Mr. Platt stood and looked at me, looked at me; wouldn't say a word, wouldn't say "umph," wouldn't even grunt. Looked at me from my head to my foot. Stood there for the longest and kept that gun presented right to me. Well, I was just as impudent as I could be—he didn't know it though. He'd run up against somebody that weren't scared. If they didn't want me to do nothin to em they oughta just stayed away from there or killed me at the start, on first sight, because I was goin to try em, sure as I was alive.

I reckon Platt was lookin for a crooked move someway. I was standin there with my hands in my pockets, just so. Only my finger was on the trigger of my pistol and the pistol was in my hand. I'd carried that .32 Smith and Wesson there with me that mornin and concealed it from view. I had on a pair of Big-8 overalls, brand new, and the pockets was deep. And I had on a white cowboy hat and my jumper—that's the way I was dressed. And a pair of Red Wing boots about knee high. I was beginnin to get prepared for winter—it was already December, before Christmas, December of '32. I don't know what date it was but I know it was on a Monday.

Well, everything got quiet and Mr. Logan and Mr. Badger was around there lookin in the back of the house. And Mr. Ward was busy at the doorstep there, just a few steps from where me and Mr. Platt was—Mr. Platt weren't sayin a word, he just lookin me over.

After awhile—I stood there just as long as I wanted to and I decided I'd go back in the house and get out from amongst em, and if nothin else, see if the house was clean—which it was, clean out, didn't a man show up in my sight but Mr. Platt. I weren't goin to stand right up there and look at him shoot me so I turned and walked off from him, started on into the house. And Mr. Ward was there at the doorstep. He just raised up and fastened his hand to my arm. I was a pretty good man then, I was young—I aint dead yet, thank the Lord—soon as he grabbed that arm, I just loosed up what I was holdin in my pocket and come out with a naked hand. Then I snapped him up to me and gived him a jolt and a fling—off he went like a leech. I never offered to hit him, I just flung him loose from my arm. Nobody hadn't said nothin to me, not a word.

All right. I started on again into the house, right on. Took one or two steps—BOOM—Mr. Platt throwed his gun on me. I didn't stop, the game didn't fall for him. BOOM BOOM—shot me two more times before I could get in the door. Blood commenced a flyin —I never did quit walkin. He filled my hind end up from the bend of my legs to my hips with shot. I walked on in the door, stopped right in the hallway and looked back. He was standin right close to a big old oak tree right in line with the door. Run my hand in my pocket, snatched out my .32 Smith and Wesson and I commenced a shootin at Platt. Good God he jumped behind that tree soon as that pistol fired; he jumped like lightnin. My mind told me: just keep shootin the tree, just keep shootin and maybe he'll get scared and run; you'll have a chance at him then. But as the devil would have it, the more I shot the tighter he drawed up behind that tree until I quit shootin. I seed his head poke around the tree—that tree saved him—and he seed what I was doin: good God almighty, I was reloadin and before I could reload my gun, them two sheriffs round the house, Mr. Logan and Mr. Badger, pulled out across the corn field headin to the road. Them two that had come to me, Mr. Platt and Mr. Ward, all I seed was their backs runnin. Every one of them officers outrun the devil away from there. I don't know how many people they might have thought was in that house, but that .32 Smith and Wesson was barkin too much for em to stand. They didn't see where the shots was comin from—nobody but Mr. Platt knowed that.

They hitched up to their ass-wagon and took off. And five minutes after that man shot me three times—I was standin in the door lookin out—my feet was just sloshin in blood. Now if that aint the truth the truth aint never been told. I was just burnt up with shot. Wonder they hadn't shot my secrets out.

I come out the door with my pistol shot clean out and I seed Sam MacFarland layin to the left there, bleedin at the mouth. I couldn't say to save my life where Sam come from. I walked up to him, looked at him—I was sorry, I hated that. He went for a little kin to me, Sam MacFarland did. And they tell me that Mr. Mac Sloane come there—grand rascal, he didn't live long hisself—and stomped Sam MacFarland's head. I done gone home then and gone to the doctor. And some of em told it that that nigger Cece Pickett shot Sam, but I never seed Cece come back there with them white men that evenin.

I walked on away from the house and went down to the south side of the barn where there was four or five fellows standin; had done runned up out of the swamps and they was armed. And the officers' car was out there side of the road and them officers had done runned to it. And when they seed that crowd of niggers at the barn throw up their guns they jumped in the car. Boss Hatch, chunky-built, dark complexioned fellow, he had a Winchester and he couldn't operate it. Little Waldo Ramsey—he was there—he told him, "Give it to me." Boss Hatch handed it to him. Little Waldo took that rifle and he shook it up, juiced it, changed the sight, dropped on his knees and throwed that rifle up on that car. I was standin there, just as bloody as a hog, lookin right at him. He cut down on that car, knocked the glass out and injured the stock of one of them deputies' rifles—so they said in court.

I walked on home after I was shot, and time I walked in the yard I seed my wife run out of the house. Vernon had done reported conditions to her and stirred her all up. I didn't know Vernon had been nowhere about. Virgil Jones' house set way back off the road but there was another house, Sam MacFarland's house, settin right beside the road. Well, Vernon was up there by *that* house lookin down on that shootin business. He didn't come down there though.

I walked on in home just shot all to pieces in my seat. Vernon and Hannah taken me on my Chevrolet car, and a fellow by the name of Ambrose Butler, one of the Butler boys, got on that car with us as a friend and a protection, and when Vernon stopped drivin, the casins on them car wheels was touchin the hospital steps, Tuskegee hospital. It was called to be sixteen miles from my house to Tuskegee. Hannah went in there and got a entrance for me and they sent a stretcher out—two men with a stretcher come out to the car. I asked em, "What you all doin bringin that out here for?"

Said, "Brought it to get you."

I said, "If you just sort of help me out of this car I can walk in there myself. You don't have to tote me."

They helped me out—my wife and son helped me out and I walked in there. Doctors put me on the table and commenced a pickin shot out of me, and some more come in the room there and asked me how come I got shot and so on. But you got to keep some things to yourself, my judgment told me. Be careful, not tell everything. I didn't tell em it was the organization act because I couldn't afford to tell that to people I didn't know. I told em it was a riot, just a riot between the blacks and the whites.

So they treated me—they had to treat me—but they wouldn't keep me there that night, a man of their own color. Scared the white folks would come after me and find me there and maybe tear the place up or accuse em of helpin me. It was their duty to doctor me and they did, they did, but they wouldn't keep me. They didn't tell me where to go, they didn't tell me where not to go, just leave that hospital that night. So I left. I couldn't stay there without authority.

My wife carried me away from there and on down deeper in Macon County, anglin southwest out of Tuskegee over in Quitman's Flats, to her cousin's, and I stayed there that night. Her and Vernon went on back home and run into a shootin frolic and a whole lot of devilment when they got there that night. A riot crowd come to my home and shot all over my people and around em, shot with shotguns and rifles. One shot hit one of my little girls in the jaw—Leah Ann; it weren't no bad wound, it didn't leave a mark. But it scared her and scared em all to death.

Tuesday evenin that mob crowd caught Vernon and told him if he didn't tell em where I was they'd kill him. Some of em wanted to carry him off from the house—and there was a old well out there, I spect that well was forty foot deep. Of course, I had throwed many a old dead chicken in it—that well'd been dry as long as I knowed about it. No doubt, if he hadn't told em just where I was, why, they'd a got him out there and seed that old well and throwed him in there. They'd a done it. I aint got no confidence in these folks.

They had heard that my wife and Vernon had gone to carry me somewhere but they didn't know where. Somebody told that secret. And when they got back home—that night, the night before they caught Vernon and forced him to tell em where I was, my wife runned into her brother somewhere or other and she told *him* where I was. And he come tearin down to me—I hated it—he come in there a late hour of the night. I asked him, "Where'd you come from?"

He said, "I come from up there at home."

I said, "You have no business comin down here. They goin to catch you too in it. They goin to come here at me. They goin to

rally and raise the devil and shoot folks and kill em till they find
me. Now you here too."

He had a breech-loader in his hands and I said, "What you
goin to do with that gun? They goin to hurt you if they find you
here with that."

I couldn't move him. He wouldn't leave his brother-in-law and
he wouldn't get shed of that gun.

So, Tuesday evenin, bout two o'clock, the white men come
runnin there to my wife's cousin huntin me up where Vernon said
they left me, him and my wife, his mother, left me. Folks' house
I was hidin at—this woman was a cousin to my wife and also to
little Waldo; she was a married woman but her husband weren't
at home.

And so, when I heard the cars rollin up to the house—that boy
coulda got away if he'd a done it. They didn't know definitely he'd
been at Virgil Jones' house that mornin because he was off in the
swamps and he could have stayed out of it after that. Now them
Tukabahchee deputies *might* have knowed he was there, but them
men that come after me from Tuskegee that evenin didn't know it.

I said, "Here they come." I knowed it was them. "They rollin
in here after me."

Little Waldo jumped up and runned out the house on the far
side—he was too game, he didn't use his sense. I begged him not
to go, I begged him to leave his gun in the house but he run out
and they killed him, good as killed him. I told him to stash hisself
off in the woods and get away. He oughta knowed with them officers runnin down on him he'd be just like a rabbit, but he wouldn't
consider that. And they weren't after him; they didn't know he was
down there with me. And blessed God, when he went out of that
house, he went out shootin and took off on a run. They just throwed
their rifles on him—old Bert Calhoun, he'd been sheriff at Tuskegee for years. He was in there helpin shoot him down. And Cliff
Soule, he was head man at that time; he done defeated Bert Calhoun for sheriff and I couldn't swear that he done the shootin—
but Bert Calhoun and some other Tuskegee white men, they shot at
little Waldo until—I heard the shots, I was in the house. Soon as
the bullets ceased, the guns ceased shootin, here come Mr. Soule
in the house to get me. Found me there sittin up in a chair. Mr.
Cliff Soule—I had been a friend to him when he lived out here close
to me in the country. He had his boy haulin lumber for the Graham-

Pike Lumber Company and many a day I helped his boy out with
his daddy's mules. Harvey Soule was the boy and when I got into
trouble his father wanted to kill me, Cliff Soule. Many a time I took
my mules loose from my wagon—and it was known, good God,
my mules never did fall back from a load—and I had Harvey Soule
to take his mules loose and get em out the way and I'd bring my
mules to his wagon and pull it out from where his mules done
backed up and run it into a ditch with a load of lumber on it. Tell
him, "Move your mules—" He had a nice lookin black-colored mule,
she was blocky-built, heavy; and a old long-legged sorrel mule, good
lookin mule, between a sorrel and a red. If he took a notion he
wouldn't pull—he'd get out there in the road, stop and stall and he
wouldn't pull the hat off your head. And I'd hitch my mules to Mr.
Soule's wagon and call em. Doggone it, that mule would come out
of that ditch. Done it every time. Now his daddy come to kill me.
I knowed that regardless to what you done, some of these white
folks would just receive your labor and your kind favors and soon
as you stepped aside and done somethin they didn't like, they'd be
ready to destroy you. Cliff Soule was one of them kind.

Come in there, "Uh-huh, here he is. Get up and get out of
here."

I got up and walked out. And I had to pick up little Waldo
and lay him in the back of the sheriff's car on the floor. Carried him
on to Tuskegee and put him in jail, and he shot up like he was.
And where they shot him, I looked at it: one bullet hit the side of
his head and just split the skin. Next place they shot a hole in him,
just between the top of his shoulder and his heart. And the next
place he was shot was through the wrist. They shot at him with
rifles just like they was takin a walk, shot at him till they shot him
down. I was listenin at the rifles cryin behind that boy.

When they come there to arrest me, they made Vernon get on
the car with em and bring em directly to me. He was sittin in the
sheriff's car when they loaded me and little Waldo in there. Vernon
waited for his chance to talk with me and he said, "Papa, if I
hadn't told em where you was they would have killed me. They
said they would."

I said, "You done right, son, you done right. Tell em where
I'm at every time and save yourself. I'd rather go down than for
them to harm any of my boys."

WE left out from Quitman's Flats goin to Tuskegee; got up the road a good ways, Cliff Soule looked around and said, "Nate, I wouldn't a thought that of you. We didn't know that there was such tricks in you. We always taken you to be the leadin darky for Tukabahchee County."

Yeah, I was leadin. I preached many and many a time to my color: don't mess with these white folks in a way to keep trouble built up on your back.

I just listened at him. I knowed it wouldn't do me no good to call up any of my goodness and kindness. I asked him then, "Mr. Soule, what have I done wrong? If it's wrong, worse things than that have happened."

"Well, just shut up; don't tell me nothin."

That put my boots on still tighter and laced em up. I didn't have no voice—and soon as they heard of me bein in a thing like that, why, they was surprised; they thought I'd be a check to hold the other niggers out. But when I wouldn't stand under their whip they arrested me for *bad* crimes—that's the way they termed it, *bad*—fightin a crowd of sheriffs over what was mine and what was my friend's. O, that was terrible. Weren't it terrible?

Wednesday mornin, they called up Beaufort to come down there and get me. Old man Kurt Beall and Ward, his deputy, dropped down there quick and took me and Vernon both. But they didn't take little Waldo—Ooooooo, that boy was crazy about me as if I had been his own dear brother. When the sheriff come around and got me out of Tuskegee jail that boy let into hollerin, "Nate, Nate, Nate, is you goin to leave me? Is you goin to leave me?" It unnerved me and brought tears to my eyes. That was the only brother my wife had. I liked the boy, I loved him—he was the only boy old man Waldo Ramsey and old lady Molly Ramsey ever had, and four girls—Lily, she was married to Malcolm Todd; Lena, she had *been* married; my wife, Hannah; and Mattie, baby child of all, she was married to Clarence Reed.

And he just hollerin and chargin and callin me—but I had to go, you see, they was transportin me. And that was the last time I saw him. Next news I heard, he was dead. The talk got out that they gived him black-bottle—poison—there in jail. I don't know that for a fact but I had just about decided they weren't too good to do it. Didn't no doctors lose no time with him while he was in jail. Left the bullets in him and caused him to die—if they didn't black-bottle him. They carried his body to Birmingham and had a funeral for him up there. The organization done that.

And Virgil Jones, white folks killed him after they done caught me. When I heard about the death of Virgil, Mr. Kurt Beall come around close to the jailhouse that mornin and told the crowd there, "Tell Nate that old Booker Jones—" he called him Booker—"Tell Nate old Booker Jones is dead." Well, I couldn't help that. Virgil was there alive at the house when I left. They shot me and I had to go on then to try to get to a doctor. It was after they found me and put me in jail and carried me from Tuskegee to Beaufort that they killed Virgil. I never did learn how they got him. But Leroy Roberts—he'd been over there at Virgil Jones' house that mornin and when I counted who was there, Leroy done been there and gone. And they caught him on the road somewhere and shot him. Mr. Horace Tucker picked him up and carried him to Leroy's house and the white folks didn't like that at all.

All right. When they landed me and Vernon in Beaufort jail I begin to inquire about the situation and I heard pretty quick that my oldest son, Calvin, was in Wetumpka jail. Called it puttin him in there for safe-keepin. Well, they might have—I couldn't swear that they didn't put him in jail for safe-keepin. Them was my two grown boys at that present time, Calvin and Vernon, and the white folks got both of em.

In a day or two they gived orders to get Calvin out of Wetumpka jail and bring him to Beaufort and put him in jail with us. They was messin up men on account of them knowin that they belonged to that organization—my boys didn't belong to it, still they put em in jail. They didn't stay there but one night after Calvin got there. Mr. Kurt Beall, big man, he come around and questioned me. Was my boys in the organization? Was they at Virgil Jones' house the mornin I got shot? I told him, "No, my boys had nothin to do with it, no way, shape, form, or fashion." Some of em runned around and told that Calvin, the mornin I left home and went over to Virgil Jones' place, he run up there to Two Forks, buyin shells, on my car—they put every lie to it they could. Shit! I didn't have no breech-loader that day that I wanted to be bothered with. I had my pistol, that 32 Smith and Wesson in my pocket, and that was all.

So, Mr. Kurt Beall turned them boys out of jail way after dark that night. And told em when he released em, "Go on back home and go to work—" I listened at him—"Go on back home and go to work." And them boys had to foot it clean on down here cross Sitimachas Creek, fifteen miles or more, home to their mother and their small sisters and brothers.

VIII

Calvin sloped away from home to get out of danger. My sister's son, Davey, who I raised up, *he* left. And when they got done leavin, that left four boys there—Vernon, Francis, Eugene, and Garvan, the knee baby, youngest boy I had.

It didn't surprise me a bit how that worked out. I'd caught Calvin's weakness before this trouble ever come off. I called Calvin to me one day. I said, "Calvin, I want you to hitch Mary and Dela to the wagon—" Vernon was there but Calvin was the oldest boy and I was tellin him to do the job. I said, "Catch Mary and Dela out and hitch em to the wagon—" I knowed he was a little shy of them mules but I thought he could manage em. I said, "Hitch Mary and Dela to the wagon, go out to Apafalya, and tell Mr. Tucker—" Mr. Richard Tucker, uncle of Lemuel Tucker, he runned a store there and I was familiar with him, traded with him cash and credit—"tell Mr. Tucker to send the such-and-such I told him I wanted. Hitch Mary and Dela to the wagon, go out there and get it."

Tryin to learn my boys, as long as they were stayin in the house with me; when they got big enough to do these things I'd put em at it.

He looked at me just this way. Said, "Papa, I'd rather you let Vern—" he called Vernon "Vern"—"I'd rather you let Vern do that."

Right there my feathers fell. How did they fall? This way: oldest boy I had and scared to take them mules to the wagon and go to Apafalya to a store there and tell a man a thing. He was as much able as Vernon was but he backed off it with them words.

I called, "Vernon."

"Sir."

"Come here."

I didn't mention Calvin to him. Calvin was standin where he could hear me; I didn't mention his name. I seed he dreaded them mules. In fact of the business, he was with me when them mules run away with me haulin a load of hay home from Apafalya; he was up there on top of that hay. It struck my mind that he got chicken-hearted from that affair. So I called Vernon over after I couldn't get him. He didn't say he was scared, just said, "Papa, you let Vern do that." He'd been in that wreck with me, but he didn't happen to get hurt. Still, he come out of it scared of them mules.

I called Vernon. Vernon knowed exactly how them mules was, much as I did. But I never had trusted em off with him on the road because I didn't want em to act up with him. I knowed my boys didn't understand thoroughly how to handle mules. After all, a mule in the field is not a mule on the road. When you put em out on the road they takes liberties with you. But I knowed that Vernon seed enough of em and knowed enough of em that he could handle em if I gave him a chance. Vernon was stouter than Calvin was anyhow. He growed up fast and was a good man all of his life until this sugar struck him—

And so, I told him, "Can you take Mary and Dela—" I *asked* him—"can you take them mules and hitch em to the wagon, go to Apafalya and get such-and-such from Mr. Tucker?"

Soon as I put the question to him he shot back, "Yes sir!"

That was the difference in my boys. Caught them mules out, hitched em to the wagon, and went on, too. He got excited when I gave him the privilege; but Calvin, he got scared. He was a good boy though, he always done what I told him if he weren't too scared to do it.

So he left home and went on over to the Little Texas beat —way back out there somewhere in the neighborhood of twenty miles the other side of Tuskegee. And he aint been back here since except to visit his people. He got scared, but I won't say he didn't have good reason to be scared. After they let him and Vernon out of jail he told his mother he was leavin and he left. It weren't no easy life to be Nate Shaw's oldest boy, and that's how he was known.

That boy Davey, he got scared and left here and made a bad record of life. He skipped the family—he had been gone before that come off, down in Jackson, Alabama, followin up the sawmill business with one of the Pike gentlemen. He'd frolic around down there until he got sick someway and sooner or later he'd come home. And another thing—I hated it but there was nothin I could do about it after he got grown. Fellow by the name of Sam Jones was his daddy; he married my sister and I didn't like him when he married her; that was her first husband, father to this boy Davey. He was a whiskey-head; he just loved whiskey and would get drunk and neglect hisself, *least* of all hisself. And both of his boys do that trick today, that's livin. Davey's dead.

Davey come home one Sunday, all out of shape. He become disabled to work down there in Jackson, Alabama, and he lingered and lingered and lingered and never did write and let us know it. So when he got to where he could sort of travel, he got on a train and come to Apafalya. And he met up with some boys there that knowed him and he knowed them and he got em take him on a car and bring him out home that Sunday evenin. I was off in the pasture walkin around and when I come back to the house my wife told me who it was. She met me at the back door of the house, the kitchen door—the house I lived in on the Pollard place was built north and south, the main parts of it, and the kitchen door, as I come up to it from out of the pasture, looked to the north. Time I got close enough for her to speak to me she said, "Darlin, Davey's in the house."

I said, "He is?"

She said, "Yes, and he's sick. You just ought to look at him. He look just like a skeleton."

And he always had been fleshy, short and chunky-built. I hated to hear that. I just walked on in the door, turned and went into the room where he was. I looked at him. He was sittin down at the fireplace. It weren't cold enough for a fire and there weren't no fire in the fireplace, but he was sittin up there. I walked up to him; he jumped up, grabbed me by the hand, shook hands with me, looked at me and I looked in his face. I said, "Boy, what in the world is the matter with you? You done fell off to skin and bone. What happened to you?"

He said, "I don't know, Uncle." Made me shed tears. "I don't know, Uncle, but I been down for several weeks, disabled to do anything."

I said, "Um-hmm."

My sister's child, oldest child, and I raised him up from twelve years old. My wife was just as good to him as she was to her own dear children; fed him out of the same spoon in every way.

I looked at him, said, "You been sick a long time, now you aint nothin but skin and bones. You knowed where me and your Aunt Hannah was, didn't you?"

"Yes sir, I knowed where you all was. And I wanted to come home before now but I couldn't."

I said, "In other words, you knowed where home was too. Umhmm. You knowed home. Boy, I'm sorry for you. And I'm goin to do somethin bout your condition if I can."

That Sunday evenin, late, I said to Calvin—I had a good Ford car, T-model car—"Calvin, I aint got time to go. Monday mornin I want you to get in that car and take Davey to Dr. Thompson in Tuskegee and tell him that I say to examine Davey and fix him medicine accordin to his complaint that will do him good, please sir, for me."

Calvin taken Davey on the car and carried him to Tuskegee and back. And when they come back, Calvin taken me out around the car shed and told me directly what Dr. Thompson said: "Papa, Dr. Thompson didn't tell me nothin to tell you about Davey bein serious with no certain complaint. He just examined him after I gived him your name and told him what you said and he told me, when this bottle of medicine that he gived Davey, when that's out, come back. And he said for you to come back with him."

Well, I done by the doctor's orders. I carried Davey to Tuskegee next time myself. Dr. Thompson fixed him up some more medicine and I paid him for it; paid him for the first bottle that he fixed for him when Calvin carried him there. The doctor's practice done good; Davey commenced pickin right up. And I didn't allow the boy—that was fall of the year—I didn't allow him to do nothin in the field. I told him good and plain, "Boy, you stay in the house and do whatever your Aunt Hannah tell you to do. This field work, pickin cotton and so on that we got to do, it aint for you to do this time." At that time we was usin a wood stove. I told him, "You'll find the stove wood already split up and ready to throw in; you bring stove wood in for her and draw water." He had strength enough to do them jobs around the house, and if he didn't, the work would give him the strength.

And so, it picked him up clearly. He stayed at my house—his house, if he wanted it to be—he stayed until he got straightened up and could go. He went by my orders, stayed out of the field, just stayed at the house and helped his Aunt Hannah out there. He got to be Davey again. He'd just been run down, wore out, might say from exposin hisself. He was in shape where he needed some help and I stuck it to him. All right. When the riot come up he got scared and hit it out from there, went on back to Jackson, Alabama. Well, Calvin gone, Davey gone—that left Vernon to bag the whole thing.

TJ, my half-brother—my daddy was daddy to him; I've worked for many a meal TJ have et, through my daddy—he weren't a member of that organization but he faced up to the riot crowd and helped my family out. He stuck to em like a man of heart. TJ and Ben Ramsey —that was my wife's first cousin; his daddy and my wife's daddy was brothers—TJ and Ben Ramsey and some more help got together and moved my wife and children away from the Pollard place. That turned the place over to Mr. Watson, but he didn't get my stuff, not a bit of it. TJ was livin at the time on Mr. Will Culpepper's place. And Mr. Culpepper let TJ move em all into the house with him. He was a good white man, went for a Christian man.

I had on the Pollard place, outside of my hogs, cows—had three or four milk cows. My wife had one cow there, a big Guernsey cow, one of the best milk types that people have. My oldest son, Calvin, he had a couple of head there that he'd bought with the money that I gived him out of the crop. But what I had there: my cows, my hogs— had eight or nine head of hogs, shoats—white people didn't get nary a cow, didn't get nary a hog. And saved my mules and wagon, saved my automobile. Even moved the stove out of there but left behind the chimney pipe. TJ got up there and carried my people down on his vehicles, then carried my stuff for them to have what they needed to make a livin.

The barn that I used on the Pollard place, it weren't no good when I moved there. I jumped up and done it the same way I done Tucker's barn. Old log barn and it was rottenin down. I cleared them logs out of there, sawed em out and put up my studs against the logs to hold the buildin where it was, then built a four-stable depart-ment in that barn. I taken that place in the name of buyin it from the federal land people in New Orleans. Then when Watson swung it over in his hands I discovered I was no longer buyin the place from the federal people but from him. So, I done built that barn for his benefit, in a way of speakin. When the showdown come and I was arrested on account of bein a member of this organization, and my family was runned off of that place, that barn I counted amongst my losses.

And I had a cotton house there. It was built east and west and I put my cotton, till I'd haul it out to the gin, I'd put it in the east end of the house; put my cotton seed in the west end. You couldn't see in there; it was built tight as a barn—I mean a good barn too. And I had a lock on the door at all times. And I had, when I wound up sellin my cotton and carryin Mr. Watson three bales, I had three bales left in there, already ginned and baled. All right. When the riot crowd come to get what I had—I had my tools in there and they stole two things: my oat cradle—I reaped my oats myself—somebody got that, had a good cradle; and they took my horseshoe nippers, what I cut horse feet with. But that was all I missed from there in the way of tools. Didn't get my blacksmith shop; my family took that away. And that cotton seed house had a lot of seed in there and them three bales of cotton, my wife's bale, heavy bale, and my two bales.

What happened to that cotton when they made my people move out from up there? TJ had a little old pickup, little old T-model Ford and he'd made a pickup out of it; he went up there and loaded them three bales of cotton and brought em away from there, put em down where my wife and children was waitin. They held on to that cotton, hopin that the price would rise and they could get more for it than sellin it on the spot. My two bales and her bale—I always gived Hannah every penny that her bale brought, clear of fertilize and everything; I didn't charge her for fertilize, just fertilized it like I did my crop.

And durin of the time I was put in jail, after I done pooled that cotton for the government, the government sent me papers and she received em. And she come to me one day to jail and told me about my business. She said, "Darlin, the government has sent you a paper statin and showin that the cotton lacked thirteen dollars of payin your debt." Government had that cotton pooled but the price didn't climb high enough for me to make the debt. And today, I still owe the government that thirteen dollars accordin to their papers.

THEY arrested me in December, 1932; put me in jail in Beaufort. And in three days' time, here come the International Labor Defense people, two of em, white people—I disremember their names. I don't know where they come from but I knowed they come out of the northern states; I was well apprised they was northern men. They was concerned for this union, but I can't say definitely how they was connected. They come in to talk with me and they didn't ask none of them other fellows no questions—there was several other members of that organization in jail at that time—I noticed it, they just laid all their questions to me. They was friends to me—I could tell that by the way the sheriff treated em; he didn't like em at all, tried to hamper em from talkin to me. I told em what they wanted to know and they left there and said they'd be back, but they never did come back. I reckon they was obligated somewhere else.

And the next day or two, in come Lawyer Stein. First time I ever seed him. He was a well-built white man, pretty heavy, but not so tall. I don't know whether Mr. Stein was a member of the organization, but he was in the work of it. And he come to that jail there in Beaufort and he wanted to see Nate Shaw. The jailer turned me out in the hall for him to talk with me. We talked, we talked, we talked—he told me, "Shaw, I been all around the country here. I been where the riot taken place, I been to Tuskegee, found out all about you goin to the hospital and everything after that, I been to your wife's cousin's house in Macon County—"

And he begin to ask me questions then: was all these things that he done already learnt about the situation true facts? He been pretty well posted and seed everything for hisself before he come to Beaufort to talk to me. But there was somethin yet he didn't know.

"How many men was there at Virgil Jones' house when the carload of sheriffs arrived?"

I told him, "There was about six or seven, along there thataway."

White folks wanted to get that thing proved—Lawyer Stein led me into the lights enough to let me know that the sheriffs wanted to make out it was a straight-out mob crowd of niggers that run over em. Of course, weren't nobody there but me at the time all that shootin took place.

He said, "Shaw, that big oak tree standin in front of that door, it's full of bullets. Who done that?"

"I done it." Weren't tellin him no lie neither.

He said, "What was you shootin at?"

I said, "I was shootin at one of them officers by the name of

Platt. The reason that tree is full of bullets as you say it is, when he shot me three times, I got in the door and I shot back at him. First time I shot, he jumped behind that tree. I just kept a shootin—"

He said, "Just keep that to yourself. Don't mention that to nobody."

I understood him, I reckon I did. That man Platt tried to kill me and if I'd a got a chance I'd a returned the favor.

"Keep that to yourself."

I gave Lawyer Stein all the particulars. Every time he come there—he come to the jail every three weeks from then on for five months, until my trial. Come there, I'd look out, somebody comin there to see me. The jailer would tell me, "Here's Mr. So-and-so to see you." They didn't have a bit more use for him than they did a dog. "Here's that man that comes to see you, he's out here again." I knowed who it was. Walked out to Mr. Stein and I answered every question he'd ask me. He come there and told me one time, "Shaw—" he didn't call me Nate, called me Shaw—"Shaw, you the best man we got, we goin to stick with you. We may can't pull you out of it though; their laws down here is *their* laws—we got that throwed up against us. We may can't pull you out of it but we goin to stick with you."

O, they hated his guts. One day Mr. Stein walked in and called for me. The old jailer unlocked the door for me to walk out and he thought he'd try Mr. Stein a bit. In place of goin on about his business he stood there and wouldn't leave us alone. Mr. Stein didn't pay no attention to him definitely till he looked up, got ready to talk to me and there the jailer standin—weren't goin to move less'n he was told to move. Lawyer Stein told him, "You can go ahead. I come here to talk to Shaw. You aint Shaw. This here's Shaw. You can go ahead." He lit away from there with them words. Then Mr. Stein could talk to me like he wanted to. And he'd always praise me and boost my spirits: "We goin to stick with you Shaw, got to. You the best man we have."

I'd call some of the rest of em's names. He'd say, "Well, they aint with us no more." Talkin bout Leroy Roberts and such as that. They defeated it, see; they what you might call defeated their union. While they was in jail there with me they abused the organization. The officers of the state of Alabama up there at Beaufort, they listened at em, too. Them niggers just abominated theirselves for ever joinin the organization—they ditched it right there.

All right. Lawyer Stein stuck to me. And when he come there he'd ask me every time, "Shaw, is they been knockin you here?"

I'd tell him, "No, sir, they aint offered to hit me."

He'd say, "They better not, they better not. If they hit you and I find out, I'll run em."

AFTER the International Labor Defense come in there, four big white men from Apafalya come to see me. And they pulled at me to get my property in their hands before my trial. But I turned em flat as a griddlecake. Here come Mr. Watson, the main man that was goin to take what I had. He brought the banker with him, Mr. Grace, who had been furnishin me for several years; and when he seed that Mr. Watson was diggin to get me under his thumb, he helped push me under there. Mr. Watson, Mr. Grace, Mr. Maynard Curtis, Mr. Charley Flint—four of em, I knowed em every one, been used to em. I was born and raised up close to Mr. Flint. Charley Flint was a brother to Jim Flint, he was the baby boy of the family. And I used to work with Mr. Curtis, first two years after I come out from under my daddy's administration. Worked on halves with him 1907 and 1908. Now all them men come up there that mornin to see me, lookin me over; come in there with Mr. Watson, he led em in there.

I walked out—they unlocked the jail door for me to walk out and talk with em. All of em spoke plain to me.

"Hello, Nate."

"Hello, Nate."

"Hello, Nate."

"Hello, Nate."

I was mad as the devil. I told em all, "Good mornin." "Good mornin, Mr. Watson, Mr. Grace, Mr. Flint, Mr. Curtis."

They allowed to me—Mr. Watson said—"Nate, we sorry to see you here."

I said, "Yes, but I'm here."

Then he put in on me bout—"Nate, we come up here this mornin—I come up here to get you to sign this paper out here on the desk."

I said, "What sort of note do you have for me to sign?"

"O, no note, it's just a paper."

I said, "What good do it do to sign a paper? What is it for?"

"O, it don't amount to nothin, just a paper."

See, I couldn't read and write.

"Don't amount to nothin, just a paper. You can just come out here to the desk and sign it."

I said, "No sir. I aint signin no paper no way, shape, form, or fashion. I don't care how it's fixed. I ain't signin no paper."

I was sharp enough to know it was a mortgage paper, that's what it was. And he didn't have no claim at all against nothin I had and I weren't signin nothin. He begged me, he begged me— Mr. Flint, Mr. Curtis, Mr. Grace wouldn't say a word.

I said, "I aint signin no paper, Mr. Watson, for nothin, noway, with nobody. And for nobody. I aint signin no paper." And I kept askin, "What sort of paper is it? Won't you tell me what sort of paper it is?"

"O, it's just a paper, it don't amount to nothin."

I said, "Well, I aint signin, I aint signin."

I had sense enough to know what it was but I wanted him to say it.

"It don't amount to nothin."

I said, "Well, you aint got no mortgage on nothin I got and you know it."

"O, yes I has, Nate, yes I has."

I said, "When did I give you a mortgage on anything that's mine? When did I do it?"

He wouldn't speak to me noway.

I said, "You got no mortgage on nothin I've got."

And do you know, they wouldn't dispute my word, nobody said nothin. Mr. Grace knowed it was true and he wouldn't part his lips.

I said, "What did you do for me there one year, what did you do for me?" This was relatin to Mr. Grace then, what I was goin to speak. "What did you do for me? That's the only mortgage ever you had in your hand against me, and it weren't your mortgage. The last mortgage paper I gived anybody, it was gived to Mr. Grace there in the bank and you had nothin to do with it. When I paid that mortgage off—" O, if I didn't bellow like a poor little calf—"when I paid that mortgage off to Mr. Grace, you told him, you were standin there in the bank that day, you told Mr. Grace to give you that mortgage paper and he gived it to you, too. What good did it do you? It weren't made to you, and he gived it to you."

Mr. Grace wouldn't have no words in it at all—I was just pokin it to em.

"What good did it do you? It weren't your mortgage paper, it weren't made in your name, it was made to Mr. Grace."

He dropped his head when I shoveled that corn to him. I just told him to the last, "You got no mortgage on nothin I has and never has had."

Well, he jumped up then and told me if I wouldn't sign no note, "How bout lettin me have that big pair of mules of yours and the wagon and enough corn to feed em?"

I knowed if he got that he'd take everything. I didn't give him a chance even to tell me what he'd give me for that stuff. I weren't goin to agree for him to take a nail. I said, "You got no mortgage on nothin I've got, Mr. Watson, and you know it. Stay out from there and let it alone. What's there I left it with my wife and children and it's mine. I aint there to control it, but—"

He said, "You just as well to let em go. That there pair of mules, that big pair of mules you drive, they goin to kill them boys."

I said, "Let em kill em, let em kill em."

He said, "You know you never would let nobody drive them mules but your own self."

I said, "Well, they can drive em now. My boys has got as much strength—I got some boys there that's men as good as I am. If they fool around and let them mules kill em, it'll just be some more colored people killed."

"Well, they goin to do it. You know them mules is dangerous."

He knowed I had a pair of mules that didn't hesitate and was able to do whatever I put em to. They *was* dangerous, I knowed that, but my boys I considered grown and could handle em. If anything come up and they couldn't handle them mules, why, sell em to some other man that could and give the money to their mother as it was their duty to do.

Asked me twice more to let him have them mules. I said, "Just stay out from there and let everything alone; you aint got no mortgage on nothin there. Furthermore, I carried you three bales of cotton on my debt; that overpaid you right there. But what did you tell me when I asked you for a settlement? What did you tell me?"

O, if I didn't kick like a Texas mule.

After awhile he seed he couldn't move me and he said these words, "Well, let's go. I can't do nothin with him." And as they started out, the High Sheriff Kurt Beall jumped out from behind the office door. I didn't know he was there, didn't know he was listenin.

I didn't know who had unlocked the jail door for me to come out and talk with them white men because he vanished right quick. I reckon he done that for a point.

He run up to me and looked me right dead in the face, squallin like a panther, "Aint he got a mortgage on that stuff? Aint he got a mortgage on that stuff?"

I said, "No, he got no mortgage on it."

"Well, you just as well to let him have it. I'm goin down there and get all you got and bring it up here and put it before the court-house to sell."

I said, "You go ahead and do it if you think you can come out of there, go on."

O, he jumped just as high—he was a heavy-built man, kind of pot-bellied, he'd a weighed fully two hundred pounds—he jumped just as high as he could jump and stomped on the floor and hollered, "Get back in jail you sonofabitch."

That was the end of it. Them white men cleared out of there. Mr. Grace, Mr. Curtis, Mr. Flint—never said "umph." Mr. Watson runned right on down here on Mr. Will Culpepper's place and tried to con my wife out of them mules and wagon, corn and stuff. *She* weren't on no note with him, she'd never signed no notes with me, never signed her name next to my name—he didn't have no note anyhow.

She come to jail to see me and not knowin that Watson done been down there worryin her, I told her, "Mr. Watson come here and tried to get me to sign a note and I wouldn't do it. Then he wanted the mules and wagon and enough corn to feed em. And I wouldn't agree to that. What I got is there with you and our children —you all. Don't sign no notes noway against em."

She told me, "Well, he already come to me, too, and he wanted me to let him have the mules and wagon and corn, but I turned him down. I told him what we had there was yours. And if he was of a mind to take it, he'd take it at his own risk."

I said, "Yes, that's the best stuff you have. That's for your livin, for my boys to have somethin to plow and food to feed em on."

She said, "He come there pleadin for em but I turned him down flat. Then he flew up from there and left."

Just actin a rascal all the way though. Now he's layin in the grave.

I left my family in good shape to start on livin without me. TJ moved my people in the house with his people on Mr. Will Culpepper's place. Then what did Mr. Culpepper do? He seeked around and rented the old Courteney place for my people and put em down there time enough to make a crop. Mr. Grace owned the Courteney place at that time. How come it? One of the triflin boys, triflin and low-down, too, managed to lose that place and Mr. Grace soon latched on to it. I don't know how much it was, I wouldn't swear to it, but it was about sixty or eighty acres. Them people that had owned the place, old man Miles Courteney and old lady Sophia Courteney—they had a houseful of children. And soon as they died, one in the bunch called Preston, this Preston Courteney went over to the bank in Apafalya and borrowed money on the place and never asked them other children how they felt about it. Used that money to buy cars and trucks and fool it off. Naturally, Mr. Grace let him have it and eventually Preston couldn't meet his payment and Mr. Grace took the place over. And when he took the place over, the community tried to get Preston to redeem the place back. He done runned over his brothers and sisters and done as he pleased. And he never was able to make it up to em. And there weren't but one child that bought back a interest in that place and she lives today somewhere in the northern states. Her name is Tillie. And there's Ethan Courteney, Hoke Courteney, and another one, kind of a humpbacked one in the crowd, Ralph Courteney, and Preston Courteney makes four boys. And the girl in the northern states, she married one of the Kirkland boys, and Will Wiley married one, and Willy Floyd Todd married one—that was three girls to my knowin.

Anyway, soon as the parents died, this Preston—whiskey drinker, gambler, and everything that he oughtn't be, everything but what he ought to been—he jumped up and gived Mr. Grace a mortgage on that place and turned around and lost it. And could have redeemed the place—the word got out after he lost the place how much he would have had to pay; it weren't much, maybe fourteen, fifteen, or sixteen dollars.

First, my family come to TJ's, on Mr. Will Culpepper's place. Second, moved down on the Courteney place, Grace place. Stayed there two years before movin out. I never seed nary crop they made there; it was all out of my hands then.

I was put in a place that all the facts of my life come to me—in jail. And I was very miserable over it. But I never would give up; I didn't give up my thoughts and I didn't give up prayin. Well, in my past days from the time that I was big enough to consider and realize people callin theirselves Christians and seekin religion, long in my teens of years, from then up until I found salvation for my soul, I called myself prayin. But there's a certain attitude that you got to drop in before God will even hear your prayers. So I prayed and prayed and prayed, called myself prayin but my prayers weren't truly from my heart. I was lookin all along at the ways of this world and enjoyin the benefits of this world but I was just a rank sinner myself, hadn't become in the knowledge of God. I used to, when I was travelin through the world, God blessin me along the line all the time—I realize now that He were God even while I didn't acknowledge Him, and beside Him there aint no God. And He's a man that can open doors that no man can shut. He can close doors that no man can open. Any person that have never received the love of Jesus in his soul, he can't imagine it until it hits him. When it hits you, you'll know it. There's a great undiscussible change takes place with you, somethin that never had before. And on the twenty-eighth day of April, 1933—I was placed and bound down in Beaufort jail, couldn't help myself, couldn't do nothin but laugh and cry and talk and study over my troubles. O, I tell you, it was bluesy times. Right there I was converted; right there I received the love of Jesus.

I come down then, I got touched then, when I got in trouble. No one to help me but my friends, I kept sight on them. Looked like the biggest part of the world was against me. I never did get scared for myself, I just didn't want to be there. I never worried over what they was goin to do to me. I could see that they personalized this convulsion on me—but that made me merry, in a way. I done what was right: white man takin everything Virgil Jones had, then goin to start on me—I weren't goin to let him do it without a fight. And had nothin ever shook me—when they shot me it didn't shake me, when they arrested me it didn't shake me. But it shook me to see my friends was but few. I studied over it—

The devil told me some years before I was arrested and throwed in jail—I knowed it weren't nothin but the devil—I had entered into my forties, and I was forty-seven years old when I was put in

jail, I seed a birthday in Beaufort jail. And so, I was on my job one
day, whatever I was doin, and the devil told me, "You aint goin to get
no religion, you done got too old." Just revealed that to me. But I
paid it no attention. I was prosperin, makin my way through the
world at a good clip. Had everything in reason a poor colored man
could have—and then some. Well, when I got in jail and all my
troubles come down on me, bein away from my family and they
havin a hard time without me, I strictly saw the way the thing was
goin on. My preliminary trial which I was supposed to have—they
fought that down, made a mess of it and quit it, didn't give me no
preliminary trial. Well, that was a judgment against me. These
people here that knew me was so bitterly against me until they
wouldn't discuss my case, dropped it until my full trial come along.
I was in trouble then. What did I have to look forward to? Lawyer
Stein come and told me, "Shaw, I'm goin to stick with you but I may
can't clear you—" All right. He knew the thing, the way it was
goin. Said, "We can't overrule their laws here in every respect, but
we goin to stick with you." He was right there, consolatin me all
he could.

The twenty-eighth day of April it was. That mornin I got up
—there was some terrible fellows in jail there with me, they had a
pick at me. They didn't never jump on me; if they had, no tellin
what I'd done. Now the boys that was in there for bein of that
organization, they didn't bother me, didn't trouble me. But some of
them other hellions in there had a pick at me. I don't believe anybody put em up to it; they was just hellish fellows, meddlin with
me for what I done. They knowed I was in that riot and they had
no respect for it. Really, they had no respect for theirselves so they
picked at *me*. I done something that they wouldn't a done—stood
up for myself. O, they was against that, numbers of em. The least
word about it and they'd fly, scared to death. That was a great disconsolation to me. Talk about what I was in there for—and all the
time it was somethin for the benefit of them.

The mornin I was converted, I was walkin around there in the
jailhouse fixin to shave. And I couldn't satisfy myself to save my
life—walkin around, leapin everywhere, in a trance. I couldn't rest
nowhere—they lookin at me. And all of a sudden, God stepped in
my soul. Talk about hollerin and rejoicin, I just caught fire. My mind
cleared up. I got so happy—I didn't realize where I was at. I lost
sight on this world to a great extent. And the Master commenced a

talkin to me just like a natural man. I heard these words plain—I dote on it, dote on my friends, too—the Lord spoke to me that mornin, said, "Follow me and trust me for my holy righteous word." I just gone wild then, feelin a change. "Follow me and trust me for my holy righteous word." The devil don't talk that way. And said, "The devil in hell can't do you no harm." Good God almighty, I just felt like I could have flown out the top of that jail. I commenced a shoutin bout the Lord, how good and kind and merciful He was. Freed my soul from sin. I was a raw piece of plunder that mornin in jail. God heard me and answered my prayers. Some of the worst fellows in there looked at me but they couldn't stand it, had to turn away, and their faces looked just as sad—I had took over the jailhouse, couldn't help it. You could—except what I was carryin on—you could almost heard a pin fall on that jailhouse floor. They come just as silent as stone.

All right. I couldn't read and write but Leroy Roberts was in there—it just condemned him, it just et him up the way I was actin—I had Leroy—he was writin to my people at that time for me, and when I ceased down and quit I had Leroy write a letter to my wife and I had him tell her that God had answered my lonely calls. I had seeked my soul's salvation and found it. And she come bustin in there when she got that letter just as quick as she could come. I told her my condition, not just talkin, but I had found Jesus. And Leroy Roberts told her, when she come, said, "Mrs. Shaw, if there's ever been a man converted, Nate's one of em." She felt so good about that—she was cryin, she was so happy. She was a woman—she was a Christian girl when I married her and I was a sinner boy.

Well, they had my trial and put me in prison. The Lord blessed my soul and set me in a position to endure it.

THERE was a white gentleman in prison in some part of California at the time I was waitin for my trial, wrote me a letter wishin me well—was all he could do, you know—feelin my sympathy and tellin me how *he* got into it: had a union out there and he belonged to it and tried to get other folks to join. Moneyed people of the state of California didn't like that and throwed him in prison—that was his troubles. Told me that the high people of that country fought his union. Well, I reckon near bout all of em fought it all they could; a thing of this kind is ever dangerous to em.

The letter was sent to my wife and she brought it to me. The man that wrote it called himself Tom Mooney,* out of the state of California. I didn't inquisite after who he was definitely and ask no words about him because I was so agitated at the time. But I figured it like this: the workers of this organization knowed which ones was in prison and them that could read and write, they tried to show their feelins to the others.

I sure taken him to be a friend to me. He just wrote in a way to let me know straight that he was tied up in the same thoughts and acts as I was. I taken that to mean that my name was known for what I was into and what this work was about—newspapers carried my name to distant states. And the beauty part about it, for me—I stuck there and stickin there today. I stuck there so good and tight, and this white gentleman that wrote to me, he had confidence in me that I would. You take such work as this: from the beginnin up until this minute, I believe in it and I see good of it, I see more good of it than I really can explain. And I believe in stickin to a thing that's right until whenever my eyes is closed in death.

FIVE months I stayed in Beaufort jail. After the International Defense people left, they was supposed to give me a preliminary trial, but they fooled around and it never come up. Some of the northern people ridin in my defense demanded they give it to me. But this is southern country down here, this is the state of Alabama. They didn't have enough pull to get me that preliminary trial. Nobody to my knowins started that trial—but I was so badly aroused at that time I couldn't discover everything that was happenin to me unless somebody enlightened me. It appeared to me that several Beaufort people got up there and delayed the case, set it for another date and overruled Lawyer Stein and kept him overruled.

Old Kurt Beall—he was as bad as anybody, a little worse maybe —he told the boys and told that deputy sheriff Ward, when they crossed us up and threw out the hearing, "I reckon them sonofabitches see now," as good as said, "See, they can't run things down

* Socialist trade union organizer sentenced to die for his alleged part in exploding a bomb that killed ten people and injured forty more at a San Francisco Preparedness Day Parade, July 22, 1916. His sentence was later commuted and he was pardoned on January 7, 1939.

here." There was a heap more said behind my back, I'm satisfied of that, but I seed and heard a heap besides.

Well, the day that Lawyer Stein come for the main trial, two white ladies was with him and each of them ladies had a briefcase. They all set down there at a table in the front of the courtroom, a little to one side, and I could see Lawyer Stein just writin it all down.

I couldn't tell who was in the courtroom and who wasn't. I didn't even see if Mr. Watson come to my trial. But I do know this: they wouldn't allow Mr. Horace Tucker in there. He tried to come in the buildin but they made him go on out again, get away from there. He'd been known—he took Leroy Roberts, after Leroy was shot down, he picked Leroy up and carried him home. So they didn't allow him in the courthouse; they didn't want the public to know that some of their color took any stock in helpin the niggers out.

Well, my brother Peter come, he was up there, and TJ. My wife was there, some of my uncles and aunts, and my cousins too.

They brought me to trial—I can't speak about all of it. How come? Because I didn't know what they was doin myself. But they kept the thing upset there enough, durin of my trial, to have a fight in there, nearly. Lawyer Stein got hot at the officers that come up to testify, and the judge got hot at him, then he got hot at the judge. And the judge, old man, got agitated some more and rapped his hammer on the table, just beat it with that thing. Old Judge Bolin, from LeMoyne—he was a settled-aged man. I was forty-seven years old then; he weren't twice that but he almost was.

Tom Heflin* was the head man in there amongst the prosecution. He made a big talk against me, tried to prove I'd committed a crime—assault and raisin the devil when they come down there to take what we had. But I never did think it under God's kingdom—I knowed we colored people wasn't allowed no secret organization, but the idea of takin what a man has, and him not owin nothin, and causin his wife and children to suffer, then takin him away—that thing looked bogus to me. Keep that nigger in jail and at the end, make that woman and them children stay there on that place and

---

* Alabama representative to Congress, 1904–21; United States Senator, 1921–31. Known as "Cotton Tom" for his unstinting support of southern cotton interests. Noted also for his white supremacist and anti-Catholic sentiments. His refusal to support the 1928 Democratic candidate for President, Alfred E. Smith, a Catholic, led to his own defeat in the Alabama senatorial contest of 1930.

farm, and some big man takin everything they produce—I've seen that done under several cases—just tie em to the land, nigger's wife and children, give em a home there but take everything else. White man made hisself a law for that and his word was stronger even than the law because *he* made the law. The sheriff come on a white man's place messin with the colored folks he got workin on it, that man would call the sheriff's hand in a minute. "That's *my* nigger—" I've heard it said myself; sheriff had to go by the landlord's orders, landlord had power over the sheriff and he'd talk his big talk in defense of that nigger. How come it? Because that's *his* nigger, he weren't goin to see him mistreated because that nigger was just like his property. "Let him alone, I'll be responsible for him. I'll come up there at such-and-such a time and straighten it out." He'd go up there and pay that nigger out of trouble, leave that nigger at home at work. O, there was many a glad Negro because he was under the white man thataway. And in some cases the nigger had to stay then on that white man's place and do what he said do; and if he didn't, the white man would turn him back to the law. Nigger got caught in the spokes of the wheel any way it rolled. So I stood up against this southern way of life. Can you call that a crime? Can *I* call it a crime?

Mr. Stein, Lawyer Stein, he got up to plead my case. First thing, he questioned the backgrounds of the deal.

"Do you know anything against Nate Shaw that would keep you from givin him a fair trial?"

"No, we don't know nothin against him. We goin to give him a fair trial."

"Well, has he ever been arrested before?"

I hadn't done nothin for em to arrest me—didn't do nothin then, neither; that's the way I sum it up. Holdin up for myself, that's all.

"No, he aint never been arrested."

Lawyer Stein asked em every question he could ask; he wanted justice for me.

"O, we goin to give him justice." That's what they said. "He never has done nothin till this time."

Well, you know, if a man got a good record—right there they heard enough out of Lawyer Stein to know I'd never been in trouble noway with the law, I oughta been gived some consideration. But they gived me nothin.

All right. They kept up the devil there and every once in a while somebody'd holler and they'd jump up and haul that person out of there.

This here man that shot me, they called for him, Mr. Platt. And some of em said, "O, he's out there in the street somewhere." Judge Bolin told the sheriff, "Go get him."

Those two white ladies from the north that was sent to be with Mr. Stein, they was sittin there with him, writin and figurin out what was goin on. I was sittin close to em, kind of on the side part of the front, and I could see every man comin up to make a talk. So, brought Platt in there—they didn't know nothin to hurt me, had no malice in em against me—they pleaded that when Lawyer Stein asked em. But when that Platt come in, they asked him this question—I don't know who asked him, the old judge or old Heflin, one of them heavy laws asked him, "Mr. Platt—" When he come in the courthouse door he wouldn't come on down there to the judge's stand; just stopped up there bout halfway to the judge's stand from the door. They asked him that question before he stopped walkin. "Mr. Platt, did you shoot Nate Shaw?"

Here's what he said. "I tried my damnedest—" shot me three times in the back—"I tried my damnedest." Whirled around, right on back out the door he went.

Just asked him *did* he shoot me; didn't ask him how come he shot me or where he shot me. And they didn't ask me bout no shootin; they wanted other facts from me. They wanted to know how many was there at Virgil Jones' house that day. I told em what I wanted em to know and what Mr. Stein told me to tell em if they asked me. To tell the truth, there was a crowd there to start, but when they discovered the law goin off and gettin another crowd of laws, they pulled out from there and run like rabbits. And when the officers come up they seed nobody but me. And I didn't move out of my tracks. But they didn't ask me for that at my trial—they wanted me to tell em how many was there. I told em, "About five or six, somethin like that." They wanted to hear bout more than that, so they asked me again. If I'd a told em a crowd was there, they'd a went to askin bout all of em's names. That woulda throwed em to huntin everybody up that I called. I never had had no case in court before but Lawyer Stein warned me what to tell em, said, "If they ask you how many was there that day, don't tell em there was a crowd there; just tell em four or five, five or six, somethin like that."

What more did they ask me? Not much, not much. They didn't mention the union. They talked about that as much as they wanted outside the courtroom, but inside, it weren't spoken of. They all knowed what it was, and that it *might* have been involved, but they didn't want to consider that *their* niggers would have anything to do with a union. They wanted that thing to perish—so they didn't ask me. Just a matter of a nigger done got into trouble tryin to destroy their way of life.

TRIAL didn't last but one day. Started one mornin in May and it was over when they took a notion some hour before dark; quit it and left the thing open. And the next day, mornin, didn't have nothin to do but put the sentence on me. Jury come in to the courtroom first thing that mornin and pronounced me guilty. They'd separated me from the other boys when it come to the trial, but we all stood up there together at the sentencin—me, Leroy Roberts, Ches Todd, Wat Smith. And they tried Sam Todd and Willy Turpin, but they was tried after we was put in prison. Them officers took down a bunch of names at Virgil Jones' house that mornin, but there's numbers of em didn't meet that trial—

Judge Bolin called me up to the stand and gived me twelve to fifteen years in the state penitentiary on good behavior. He sung to me some that I'd been misled—he didn't say who misled me, just that I was misled. That "misled" didn't strike my shirttail—but they made that shot touch me; didn't shoot me with no bullets, shot me with shot, they made *that* touch me. But nothin they said didn't touch me because I knowed that was their interpretation and wasn't no more right in it than in their laws and rulins. They had we colored people muzzled down here in this country and didn't allow us no break for nothin. So, when old Judge Bolin put the sentence on me—twelve to fifteen years on good behavior—he didn't put so much on none of the rest of the boys, none of em; didn't give em over seven years. That was Leroy Roberts, Ches Todd, and Wat Smith. Of course, none of em didn't talk to that deputy sheriff like I did, I was the leader in that—that's why they stuck so much time on me. When the thing was sounded out, I was the head, and they put all the time on me they could, they doubled it up on me. It appeared I was standin for the whole organization.

And then, what hurt so bad, Lawyer Stein appealed my trial —done carried me on and put me in the penitentiary and when that appeal time come, I was carried back to Beaufort. That same old judge overruled it again. Lawyer Stein took up the case. He didn't beg, didn't beg; he told em straight: they done mishandled my preliminary trial down to where they done knocked it out altogether. Then they didn't do right by me durin my main trial, didn't allow my defense to ask the questions and hear the answers they was due to be allowed—that was a shame. But the judge wouldn't admit that. Lawyer Stein told him, "Judge Bolin, you know so-and-so-and-so, you know so-and-so-and-so—" "I don't remember—" I was lookin right at the judge—"I don't remember—" Couldn't get him to remember nothin. Throwed the case out. That was my education right there—

The nigger was disrecognized; the white man in this country had everything fixed and mapped out. Didn't allow no niggers to stand arm and arm together. The rule worked just like it had always worked: they was against me definitely just like they was against those Scottsboro boys. And in the present time durin of the two cases—against the Scottsboro boys and against me—the Negro stood a light show; he wasn't allowed the full extent of his oath. And for what cause? The white man could get all out of the nigger that he wanted to know about before goin to the courts. They already had the dope they wanted on me and they didn't ask me for my story. The nigger's voice just wasn't substantious to stand up for hisself. The trials was just a sham, just a sham, both of em. I might tell em everything just like it was but they'd kick against me in court, in regards to my color, unless it come up this way: now a nigger could go in court and testify against his own color in favor of the white man, and his word was took. But when it come to speakin out in his own defense, nigger weren't heard in court. White folks is white folks, niggers is niggers, and a nigger's word never has went worth a penny unless some white man backed it up and told the same thing that the nigger told and was willin to stand up for the nigger. But if another white man spoke against the nigger and against the white man that was supportin him, why, they'd call that first white man "nigger-lover" and they wouldn't believe a word he said.

Take the Scottsboro boys: them girls, some of em, that reported them boys, changed their song. Them Negroes never bothered us, they said—I heard it that the words was spoke in law, one or two of them white girls, one in particular I know, she denied it to the last that them Negro boys didn't have nothin to do with her. And one of em got up and testified that they did. Well, that was just agitatin the thing against the nigger right on. And this'n that told it that the Negroes never had nothin to do with us noway, they didn't believe her; they went by what the other one said, that the niggers did meddle em. The average white man of this country wanted to believe her story—and it reached for miles and miles away, accordin to my knowledge.

Heywood Patterson, Andrew Wright—was two of them Scottsboro boys, and there was six or seven others. And I was told that people from all across the waters sent letters in here forbiddin em of destroyin them boys. They sent letters on top of letters in favor of them boys. One lawyer come down here and outlawed their trial, got two of them boys, at that period, and carried em away from here with him as he went. I heard that. But that Heywood Patterson, they held him a long time. They got down to just Heywood Patterson, holdin him here. But last count I heard, didn't do em no good, Heywood Patterson escaped.*

* On March 31, 1931, nine black youths were indicted for allegedly raping two white girls on a train between Chattanooga, Tennessee, and Paint Rock, Alabama. They were tried in Scottsboro, county seat of Jackson County, Alabama, some ninety miles northeast of Birmingham. Despite testimony of doctors who examined the girls and declared that no rape had occurred, the nine young men were convicted, and eight were sentenced to die. Appeals, reversals, and retrials continued through 1937. After the initial trial, the International Labor Defense took over the defense of the youths. Twice the United States Supreme Court reversed lower court convictions, the first time (Powell v. Alabama, 1932) on the grounds that the defendants had not been permitted adequate counsel; the second time (Norris v. Alabama, 1935) on the grounds of improper jury selection. Eventually, four of the nine were convicted: one was sentenced to die (commuted to "life") and three were given seventy-five- to ninety-nine-year sentences. Indictments against the other five were dropped, though one was convicted and sentenced to twenty years for assaulting an officer in an escape attempt. All those imprisoned were later released on parole except one, Heywood Patterson. But, as Nate Shaw learned, prison couldn't hold him and he escaped in 1948.

LAWYER STEIN stuck with me to the last. He even come to see me after they put me in the penitentiary. He made the trip over there one Sunday—that was the last time I seed him. Last time he seed me—outside of hearin about me and I'm satisfied he heard —he didn't come to the penitentiary but one time and he come down there and told me when he got ready to go, "Well, Shaw, I'm obliged to hit the train back home. I have to go now. I'm goin to tell the ILD people in Montgomery to look after you here. So be good. Just go by their orders and make out the best you can. I'm goin to stick with you, too. But I can't stay no longer, I got to go."

Now what he done, I couldn't swear to it, and what he didn't do, I couldn't swear to it. But I know by the fact that they never did give me no trouble at all through prison that he done something. And the ILD sent me five dollars a month the whole time that I was in prison. And they was helpin my wife, too. That's what the organization believed in—takin care of a man's family when he's pulled away from em. It's scandalous the way they done we colored people down here along that line. When they'd take a colored man away from his home his folks would go to the devil. Take a colored man away from his home, put him in jail or the penitentiary, they'd jump back and put his folks to work—the white people would, moneyed people.

PUT me in Beaufort jail less'n a week till Christmas, 1932, and I had a birthday there in jail, on the twenty-eighth day of December. And they carried me out of there in May, 1933, to prison. Well, durin the time that Vernon and his mother come to see me and see about me I gived Vernon my laws and orders—he didn't seem to panic and flicker and he was the only child I knowed of was threatened to be killed. I told him, "Now I'm away and will be away for twelve years, twelve to fifteen years. I've got nothin to depend on but the people that's for me and God above. I'm leavin you all at the mercy of the world. They aint goin to bother you now, I don't reckon, I hope they don't. You all's got a chance to make it. Vernon, you are not the oldest boy in the family, you are second. But now you have to take the place of the first. Stick to your mother and your little underage sisters and brothers and take care of em the best you can; stick to em until your daddy gets back."

He done it, he done it. He got married right after they carried me to Spignor and he brought his wife into his mother's house. And my wife treated his wife just like she was her own dear daughter.

So, I just give up my hold on the family then—I seed that they had messed me up all they could. And I told Vernon, it was my rulins and I held it out to him, "Regardless to circumstances, as long as God lets you live, stay with your mother and the rest of the children."

PRISON

WHEN the roadrider that went around to the county prison departments pickin up criminals to carry em into Kilby—the day he drove his truck up to the Beaufort jailhouse to pick up me and Leroy Roberts and Ches Todd and Wat Smith, when we walked out to climb on the truck, Mr. Kurt Beall told that road-rider, "Them four sonofabitches ought to be dead."

The old man said, "Yeaaah." But he didn't tarry and jaw with that big sheriff. Loaded us up and pulled out. Way that evenin, late, he drove all up in the upper part of the state pickin up prisoners. Alabama stands up as high as Fort Payne and he drove up thataway, though he didn't go so far. Took us on a roundabout trip and when he wound up he unloaded us at Kilby, head prison camp for the state of Alabama.

We rested over there Thursday night, Friday—Friday they lost no time with us—Friday night; Saturday they classed us up. Wanted to know what sort of occupation we was fit for. Called us into a office there one at a time and asked us what we could do, what we been doin: "What was you doin on the outside? What was your job? Farmer? Public worker? What was you?"

I knowed what all them boys was doin before they got to the

penitentiary; they was nothin but farmers—me a farmer, Leroy Roberts a farmer, Ches Todd a farmer, and Wat Smith a farmer. Never knowed nothin but to farm, that's all they ever knowed, and me too. All right. They classed me and Leroy Roberts and Ches Todd up for the farm at Spignor. And Wat Smith, they was a little undecided about him, they was watchin him—there was a point to that, I think, but there's some points you don't never understand. I knowed Wat well. He was a farmer and he'd always worked on halves and he done most of his workin on halves for Mr. Lucius Little. Didn't live far from me. Well, they sent Wat Smith to Atmore prison, road camp. He stayed down there thirteen months or less— I heard this before they transferred me to Wilcox County—and they found Wat Smith at the bottom of a well. Poor fellow, they announced he had some amount of money in his pocket, near a hundred dollars—he'd been seen with that much money—and he was found in that well dead and his money was gone. They claimed some old half-crazy nigger robbed him and killed him. Well, I don't dispute that, but who told him to do it? I learnt this much: they had some sort of grudge against Wat Smith before he was arrested. He had some enemies in the country for some cause—I never did learn what it was about and I also never come to know how come he had a hundred dollars in his pocket—and I just decided that they followed him to prison someway. And when they got him in a place that he couldn't help hisself, they bumped him off.

THEY had at Spignor a great territory where they was raisin cotton and vegetables—I knowed everything a poor colored farmer could know about them crops. Had plow mules in the barn, and horses; had hogs in the pen. And had cells for us to live in—long wood houses painted on the outside, double buildins separated by halls. Them cell buildins held a hundred and sixty men apiece; mighta had more than that too, but I heard em say that them cells was *able* to hold a hundred and sixty men. And every bed was a double bed, a bed underneath and a bed overhead, didn't take up no more room than a single bed. Old iron beds, upright beds. They locked them cell doors at night and kept lights, electric lights, swingin over you all night long. I weren't used to that. I'd lived in the country all my life and I was used to sleepin in the dark.

They was all colored prisoners in there with me, but they had a right smart whites in some of the other cells. Kept the races strictly to theirselves and O, good God, they had white prisoners some and it looked like a lot when I'd see em all together, but they had enough more colored prisoners than they had white. And at that time, they didn't work them whites out in the field—had the colored in the field and the whites at the cotton mill or stayin behind in the cells, superintendin and cleanin up for the whites that was out.

They had me choppin cotton under a field guard—white, white, white man. The state had him hired over we prisoners. And the cotton we raised went to the state and the state sold it. I stayed there long enough to see one crop ginned at the state gin right there on the premises. The prison yard was covered with cotton. I couldn't tell how many bales they made but they runned several plow squads and dozens of field hands. And they didn't leave a weed in the field, them fields was picked clean. Weren't no tractors then and I don't know that the prison department now got no tractors—they want you to labor there. But if they has changed their rulins and they usin tractors over there now, no one tractor could cultivate that field.

Every bit of the food we et come off of that farm. That farm was doin better, accordin to the yield, really, than the farms out here at home. And the prisoners was eatin better, in a way, than folks was on the outside. They gived us fried eggs, good biscuits, syrup, meat, cake, cheese, vegetables—you couldn't kick about the food.

But it was hell to anybody there that couldn't stand prison ways and wouldn't obey. I stayed twelve years in prison and there never was the weight of a pocket knife laid on me. I never did ask for no favors but they'd grant me many a privilege. But I don't give em no credit when it comes down to right and justice; in my deep thoughts I don't give the prison department and the state of Alabama no credit for the way I went through prison. I give credit to those people in the northern states that was standin up for me.

I always stood good under my boss man at Spignor—never did dog me. They had more boss men—field bosses—for that whole passel of different squads than you could shake a stick at. All them boss men at Spignor knowed what I was sent up for but they all pretended to like me. One of em *did* like me—called him Captain Evans. He ruled a squad of hoe hands and I heard him tell another white man, "These Tukabahchee boys is good hands, good hands."

It weren't left with that boss man out in the field, it was up to the deputy warden and the head warden, who he had in his squad. Them boss men couldn't get out there and change no men; they had to work with what the warden give em. And they had to produce. If a boss man got stuck with a squad of lazy hands, it looked bad for him. They all had their own ways to get a man to work: some of em made rough talk, rough acts—but the colored man was used to havin the white man lookin over his shoulder all the time; that was the main way of life in this country since slavery days. They never had to step on my tail to get me to work. I was my own man before they put me in prison; I didn't work under white men but four years and I got out. Worked for Mr. Curtis two years, worked for Mr. Ames two years, then I quit. Bossed my own business after that. I was just one of them colored fellows that worked like a slave to get out from under this workin on halves. And when I done it I commenced a drivin my own mules and wagons up and down the road, drivin automobiles in time. I knowed how to work. And I tried to be my own man in prison—I worked!

My name had rung so until the man that issued out mail every day at dinner, mail call—I walked up when he called my name one evenin. He looked at me, said, "Your name Nate Shaw?"

Told him, "Yes sir."

"I'm goin to kill you."

What he said that for, I couldn't definitely pick it out; it was a matter, probably, of him carryin somebody else's hatred for me. Surely *he* had no reason to hate me. He weren't the warden and he weren't the deputy; he stayed in that office and handed out mail. He was a free man, must have been. But he didn't stay there long after I got there. They transferred him away from there some way or other, and it was a kind of hush-mouthed thing. So I never learnt what he was all about.

I just decided they was tryin me, see what was in me, and I played a nice hand with em. One day Captain Evans was ridin his horse along with his squad in the field and I was in that squad. Had us choppin cotton. And I noticed him sittin on that horse with his pocket knife, whittlin on a stick, but I paid him no attention. After a while he called me: "Nate."

"Yes sir, Captain." Looked up in his face, on his horse.

He said, "I dropped my pocket knife out there—" let it be a

evil trick or let it be a accident, he said, "I dropped my pocket knife
out there. Yonder it lay, right yonder."

Well, he was as far from that knife as he was from me. I
wondered to myself, how did he drop that pocket knife way out
there and him sittin here on his horse? I believe he pitched it out
there when I wasn't watchin. I was steady choppin cotton.

He said, "Hand it to me," and he pointed his finger at it.

I thought to myself, that was mighty queer. I tried to glean
his meaning: he lettin me get that knife in my hand for some purpose he had in his mind. I might pick up the knife and try to use
it on him, or grab it and run. But I weren't that kind of fool, I didn't
have that kind of principle in me. I went and picked the knife up
and it was wide open. Put the blade end in my hand and handed
him the handle, in place of handin him the blade. I could have
jugged him with it, just a little easy trick, but it'd been too bad for
me to do that.

Captain Evans, Homer Evans was his name. I just turned the
blade in my hand and gived him the handle. He thanked me kindly
and I went right on back and picked up my hoe, went on choppin
cotton. No evil acts in the matter.

ALL of them boss men at Spignor rode horses, kept their weapons
up there with em, from a pocket knife to a shotgun layin across
the horn of that saddle. And they weren't shy to use em.

They had a pick at a prisoner in my squad one day, some
trouble come up against him. And the deputy warden come out to
the field to talk over the trouble with the boss man. And after a
while they called this fellow out from amongst the other men to
come up and explain his side of the trouble and give over to em,
the officials, the man that was carryin the squad and the deputy
warden. They got to talkin at him and he listened a bit, then he
just started walkin off from the field, leavin the squad—one of
these block-headed contrary fellows; turned and walked away from
em while they was talkin to him. Made out like they wasn't there.
The boss man told him, "Stop!" But he just kept a walkin.

This man, he had stole a radio and they put him in prison for
it and they called him Radio. Heap of times, you in prison for a
certain thing and they mark you, they know you by what you done,
throw it up at you.

"Stop, Radio, stop!"

He didn't stop. The boss man took up his shotgun and shot at Radio, but he shot in the air over his head. The nigger got scared then and he stopped. Next thing, they removed him from the squad.

That was the first shootin took place in the squad around me. I just stood still, I didn't move. But when this boss man over this hoe squad out there said, "Stop," the fellows in the squad commenced a scatterin and the officials bid them all to stand still. "We aint goin to shoot you." And didn't do it neither. Them prisoners huddled down then like partridges in a drove, the ones that they wasn't after. They caught their man when Radio give up to em and whatever they was after him for, they settled it.

They shot another fellow, sprinkled him good. He was a rude rascal, pretty heavy-built, dark complexioned. And he had been buckin their orders for some time. And the deputy warden come out to the field to investigate the matter. And if he couldn't cool down everything quiet, it would go before the head warden. So he called this prisoner to him to explain hisself. And *he,* too, just took off out of that field, walkin away, peaceable, cowlike. The boss man didn't wait long with him. "Stop—" and he shot, shot *at* him, sprinkled him good. He never did break to run, just walkin.

Well, they transferred him out of Spignor and he got killed, too, after he got transferred. He kept on with his disobedience till he went down. And also, before he got killed he lost one of his legs. Well, I don't know how come for him to lose his leg, from shootin or a accident someway. He just couldn't get by in prison: you must obey orders or you can't get by; you'll die before they'll set you free.

I had sympathy for him but I seed he was bringin it on hisself. You must first think and realize that you in a bad place, if you guilty of your crime or not guilty. The main thing to do in prison is be good, obey orders to get *out* of prison. If you don't, you aint treatin your own self right. You in a place that you got no way of helpin yourself, under the laws of the state of Alabama, where I was born and raised. You may be picked up and put in prison and you haven't committed no crime, but if a panel of jurors stand up in court and decide you guilty, you goin to suffer. If you aint guilty but they decide you is, you goin to suffer. I think of my daddy's words —he had a whole lot of good in him and good logic. He done wrong things—I don't say he committed no crimes, I never did know him to commit a crime. And he had his own theories and he always said, "When you in Rome, you got to take Rome's fare." Well, that's very truthful, because you got no way of helpin yourself when you land in prison. You got to obey orders if you think anything of yourself because you got your hands in the wolf's mouth then. You got to live the life they demand and work out of it. If you go by orders, you'll protect yourself. Care and think everything as you should for your own life.

I didn't stay at Spignor hardly thirteen months and my wife come to see me every month. She'd come right on to the prison department gate and by who she was they'd let her in. I'd come out of my cell—it'd be on a Sunday—I'd come out and talk with her, see her, touch her. Now there at Spignor, they had a settin room for us to meet; officer standin there with his eyes on us all the time. All right. When they sent me to Wetumpka, I could take my wife— she could come right in the cell and sit down and talk to me, if she had a mind to. I didn't stay but a little over a year at Spignor until they transferred me to Wilcox County, road camp, and I didn't stay there but eight months until they transferred me to Wetumpka prison. And there I made the rest of my sentence; stayed there ten years and that was less than twenty miles from my home.

Spignor weren't over twenty-five or thirty miles from my home. And just before they transferred me—they had made Leroy Roberts a cell attendant, took him out of the field. Had him workin as a hoe hand like me until he commenced a complainin—he had a old case of Parkinson's disease and they was shootin him up regular for it. His blood was bad, that's all I could tell. Leroy was a kind of sleepy-headed fellow; he'd set down anywhere and be sleepin in five minutes, in the raw daytime. He'd set up at the dinin room table many a time at Spignor and go to sleep. And so the officials got to noticin that—they didn't never accuse him of makin believe— and they took him out of the field and made him a cell attendant. There weren't no work to that at all. And by the time they transferred me, I was the last fellow out of Tukabahchee County to stay in the field. My job weren't nothin but a hoe job and a water toter. And when the crop was laid by they put me to openin up ditches and cuttin briars off of ditch banks—kept me workin every day at somethin that had to be done, or didn't have to be done, had me doin it just the same. I didn't put up no mealy-mouth, they weren't workin my guts out. Somebody was standin at the barn door the way they handled me and I had sense enough to know it. I fell on my feet when they dropped me in prison and I stood straight, too, for twelve long years—

So Leroy Roberts come out of the field, and soon Ches Todd did too. I was born and raised up knowin them two. Leroy was fully as old as I was or a little older. And Ches weren't as old as ary one of us. They was first cousins, Ches and Leroy, sister and brother's children.

I'd go to the cell where Leroy was every evenin when we'd check out of the field and I'd say, "Well, Leroy, how you gettin along today? How you feelin?"

Here's what he told me one night—that hurt me, too. I didn't want to hear him talk that way but I couldn't help it.

"Leroy, how you feelin this evenin, old boy? How you comin along?"

He never did tell me he was feelin good. He'd always have his hand to his hip and half-hoppin.

"Don't feel good."

Last time I asked him, just before they transferred me—"I don't feel good, Shaw, I want to get out of this damn place. I'm goin to send—" O, God, that hurt me—"I'm goin to send for Mr. Watson to come and get me."

I didn't say a word because I knowed there weren't no help for it. I learnt his nature before we ever left home and was put in prison, and his nature was this: he always thought he was a little bigger than what he was. Leroy Roberts had cut my hair many a time—he was a pretty good barber and he'd been cuttin my hair and cuttin hair for lots of folks for years. All of a sudden he become too big for the job; he fell out with the hair-cuttin trade right then. He weren't no rich man and he weren't no big man, really, but he had at that time a brand new buggy and a young mule. And he was livin, at that particular time, with Mr. Lemuel Tucker right on Mr. Tucker's place. Leroy's house set right on the Pottstown road just below Mr. Tucker's house. And I was over there one Sunday wantin a haircut. I set there and set there ever so long. He was Leroy Roberts, he weren't no more than that. But he wouldn't cut my hair. His wife knowed me as well as she knowed any other man in the settlement—he had a good wife; her name was Bella. She was

a Cole before Leroy married her. So I set there and set there and she
asked Leroy after a while, said, "Lee"—she called him Lee—"how
come you don't cut Mr. Shaw's hair? He's waitin on you." He didn't
give her much ground. "I aint cuttin his hair no more; I aint cuttin
nobody's hair no more, that's all there is to it." I never did go to
him for no haircut again. It's nothin he knowed against me to keep
him from cuttin my hair, nothin under God's sun. He just thought
he had come to be more than what he was and took hisself to be a
big man. And when this here trouble come up, he went over to
Virgil Jones' house that mornin and when he seed what was brewin
he hauled it back home. And the mob crowd found him on the road
and they shot him up. And if it hadn't a been for Mr. Horace Tucker
—there's no tellin where Mr. Horace was when he heard that
shootin, but he come along on the road and seed Leroy, picked
him up and carried him home.

So, Leroy told me he was goin to send for Mr. Watson. All
right. I went on, had to go where they transferred me. And
eventually they turned Leroy loose to Mr. Watson. Watson got him
out and carried him home. Leroy was livin, at the time he was arrested, on his daddy's plantation, some eighty acres of land. And
Mr. Watson had got wound up in his affairs someway. At the death
of old man Booker Roberts, Leroy's daddy, the place become Leroy's
for him to finish payin on it and it was his. But it didn't stay his
long when he come out of prison. Watson took that land and runned
him away from there. Let him keep a little old mule, young mule—
Leroy had two little mules at that time; he never did have no big
heavy mules—and he got to keep only one of em. Watson eased
along with him and let him start a crop, then he pushed him off
and hired somebody else to work the crop and gather it.

Now, Leroy had two or three boys and, quite naturally, when he
called for Watson to come to the penitentiary and get him out, why,
that throwed his whole family under Watson's administration. And
they all suffered for it. Lost the old home place— Leroy allowed
em to parole him to his enemy. And his enemy he was and that
was proof, if he needed any more proof than he already had.

Ches Todd was pullin that way too, and Sam Todd—Ches
and Sam was brothers; they put Sam in prison after they put me
and Leroy and Ches and Wat Smith in there. But he didn't stay
long, accordin to the news I heard, and when he left out from there
Ches went with him. I was the only Tukabahchee man that stuck

out his sentence, and I was given more time than any of em. I don't know definitely what they gave Wat Smith, but it was a short sentence. That didn't do him no good because he was killed before his time was up.

So they sent me to Wilcox County, road camp, and they classed me up there for a landscaper. Workin out in the swamps and woods and decoratin the roads and sharpenin axes for the squad—mostly I was a ax sharpener and a water toter. I never did go out on the grade. They had me doin all them other jobs but didn't have me to gradin the roads.

These road camps is rough places. One night, old Captain Castle, head warden—he was mean as a snake—he gived orders for that road gang to take over the cell that was lived in by the prisoners that done other work, like me. Well, that stuck me up: I didn't want to do it, I don't know why he said do it, but I never bucked him at all. So they taken over our cell and we went in their cell and before I knowed anything I was covered with lice, these old crab lice that gets all in your privates and searches all over your hairy parts. They aint bad about your head though, crab lice— I went in there just as clean as a baby and in just about a week's time, somethin was bitin me all over and I let into scratchin. I took showers every day but that wouldn't get em off. Them lice gets on you and hides in your bed clothes. You can wash yourself as good as you please and you go back to bed at night, them things gets on you again. Finally, I went up yonder at medicine call and the colored fellow up there fixed me some medicine that knocked them lice sky high off me.

Crab lice is as nasty a lice as ever gets on you. And they bigger than these little old body lice—I seed them body lice before I ever went to prison, when I was a boy comin up. They got in my daddy's home once. Some fellow way up yonder somewhere about ten miles from here, not more than that, right where I was born and raised—stayed right there in hollerin distance till I was twenty-one; my daddy lived there on the Todd place. So I learnt of them body lice—Mr. Lionel Clay, at the time I was a little boy, he had a well dug at his house. And he had two colored fellows to come from Opelika to dig his well—well diggers wasn't plentiful then, had to send out of the settlement to get em. And one of them fel-

lows, they called him a Milliken. He was a settle-aged man and he
gived his name as Ike Milliken. And my mother and father lived
right there close to the Clays, just the other side of the creek. Mr.
Lionel Clay runned the big mill there, and my daddy lived up the
road a little piece from the bridge over the creek, above the mill.
Well, my people visited with the Clays and knowed em—all like
that. And they wanted my daddy to board them fellows from
Opelika. My daddy done it. Got lice in our house then, them there
old body lice. Weren't no crab lice. My mother just taken out all
the bed pieces and cleaned em up severely, and some of em, old
things, she burnt em up and got rid of em. That destroyed the lice
and the lice eggs. But it acquainted me with a terrible creature
and it weren't the only creature I come to know that tried to eat
the poor colored man up alive.

THE only time in twelve years my wife missed comin to see me was
when they kept me there at that road camp in Wilcox County. She
begged me on her letters the whole eight months to let her come
down there but I wouldn't never consent for her to do it because it
was too crooked a roundabout route—that was ninety-six miles
southwest of Montgomery and she way up here forty-somethin miles
above Montgomery; time she'd get into Montgomery and get
straightened out on the route to Wilcox County, strange country,
white folks' country, she mighta got deadlocked along the way. And
I thought to myself, 'I know my Chevrolet car has done so much
travelin for farm purposes and pleasure purposes, it ought to be
gettin weak.' I just didn't want them to take that trip on that car
thinkin it was in that condition. O, they drove that car, and Vernon
he was the head man over it and him bein a young fellow, he was
rough on drivin. I didn't put much trust—so I wouldn't let em
come down to Wilcox County on that car, afraid it would give out
and leave em in the road somewhere. I'd write her back and tell
her—I'd get some one of the trustable boys to write a letter; that's
the way I done, all through prison—I'd tell her, "Gettin along, gettin
along all right." And here was my theory, and I weren't fooled
neither, though I didn't know, in truth, how the thing would work
out. I'd write and tell her, "I don't think I'll be down here long."
And so, eight months, only eight months in the deal, eight months
in the twelve years of prison that I didn't allow her to come. And

it was on account of I dreaded for her to take that trip, knowin that her and Vernon would come by theirselves and leave the balance of the family behind. It never does well for a whole family to leave home less'n they obliged to.

THERE was a colored fellow there at Wilcox County sentenced up from Brantley, Alabama. He was a nice talkin young fellow— heavy, chunky-built—he looked about twenty-two or twenty-three years old. Called this colored boy Shakey. He liked me and he loved to talk with me—called me Uncle Nate. And he got to talkin with me one day about makin baskets and what sort of trades did I know. I told him, "I makes baskets and I runs a blacksmith shop and there's a few other things I know how to do, but basketmakin is a special labor with me. I can make any kind of basket, most you want to see—fish basket, feed basket, clothes basket, market basket, cotton basket, any sort of basket in reason."

He said, "Uncle Nate, is that the truth you tellin me?"

I said, "Yes, I can make em."

He went right on and didn't stop until he told Captain Springer, man that worked over us, told him about it. That was a pretty nice white man; he was a Springer, out of Montgomery. He was spare-built, small, and when he walked he sort of toted his head sideways. He come to me, said, "Nate, can you make baskets like I been hearin bout you?"

Told him, "Yes sir, Captain, make you any kind of basket you want."

"Make fish baskets?"

"Yes sir, I make fish baskets; been makin fish baskets off and on every year, all my life, after I got big enough to work white oak."

He said, "Nate, if you makes fish baskets, I want you to make me one. But don't let this old warden here know you makin it for me. He's hell—" old man Frank Castle, he was a cat, too; made them boss men jump—"I'll tell you how to do it"—I was a water boy then, mainly—"I'll put another fellow on your job till you make me a fish basket. You just go out"—the whole state premises was wired up there—"just anywhere on the inside of this wire you can find some white oak, cut yourself what you need and make me a fish basket. You know that great big old pine log down there on the side of the road where you go out the big gate to the public road?"

I said, "Yes sir, I've seen that old pine log there."

Old pine log was seven feet high, what was left of that tree. You could sit down behind it, couldn't nobody see you.

He said, "You get your white oak and sit down there; split it out, do like you want to do it and make me a fish basket. If you'll do that I'll give you all the fish you can eat." Them was his words. And said, "You stay down there. I'll come down there to you once or twice and see how you doin. How long will it take you to make it?"

I said, "O, I can make it in a couple of days."

It would take a couple of days if I wanted it to, or I could do it in one day. But let him put another fellow to totin water and I'll see how I feel settin off and workin white oak. I'd just be off— but I sure stayed where he sent me, I didn't ramble. When they gived me a break thataway or anything happen in my favor, then I'd be submissive—behave and go by orders that's profitable to me. And not let em know I'm enjoyin myself too much. Might order me that way again. They liked to give orders, a heap of times not for nothin but the givin of em.

So I said, "I know where's some white oak right now. I seed it the other day, over there at the mule lot."

He said, "Well, you go on to where it's at and cut yourself some and make me a fish basket. I'll give you all the fish you can eat."

I went right on off that mornin—mule lot was about a half a mile from the camp—took me a ax and went on. Cut that white oak down, took it on my shoulder and went on down into the swamp until I got to that big pine log. I stayed there two days foolin with that white oak and I made Captain Springer a fish basket about as wide around as my waist or a little wider. I don't do this, usually, but it's easier if it's done: cut a hole in the side of the basket and fix a way to have a little door. He wanted me to put a door to it. My baskets would always catch fish but I never preferred havin a door to empty em. But Lord, I've caught them baskets full of fish up to the muzzle, many a time. I'm a fisherman—

So, he didn't want old Frank Castle to know about it. And I kept it out of his sight. One time durin them two days Captain Springer visited me—never did come there but once and he seed I

was gettin along, made hisself satisfied and went on his way. And
he told me, "When you finish it, just leave it layin behind that log."
Place was wired up, couldn't nobody get in there without climbin
over that high wire fence.

The evenin I got it done I went and told him. He said, "All
right Nate, I'll go by and get it."

And the next evenin, he got a call from Montgomery to come
home at once—his wife was sick. He told us, "Well, boys, I got a
call to come home tomorrow"—that was on a Thursday—"my wife
is sick and I got to get off. You all be good fellows till I get back."

And he told me, alone, "Nate—" There's a fellow that drove
a big state truck with a squad of hands every mornin; went over
to a place they called Balkins' bridge. The driver's name was Vargas,
white man, and he carried a colored squad there at Wilcox County
camp. There was a creek by that bridge and what happened? Mr.
Springer said, "Nate, I'm fixin to get off home now. That basket
you made me—" I'd finished that basket on Wednesday evenin.
Down below the camp and out from the tool house, you could ease
through a big pecan orchard and go down there to that old pine
log, where that basket was. And Thursday evenin, Captain Springer
said, "You go down there and get that basket, bring it up here,
and put it in the tool house out there by the water tank."

I went down there and got that basket and brought it out—
wouldn't shoulder it, just toted it along by the cuff and put it in
that tool house. Friday mornin, Captain Springer come to me, said,
"Nate, you get that basket out of the tool house and put it on
Mr. Vargas's truck. He goin to carry it to Balkins' bridge and put it
in the creek for me. I got to go home—"

I went on out to the tool house and got that basket, put it on
Captain Vargas's truck. The old warden hadn't seen me, didn't know
nothin about it. And this little man Captain Springer, he took off for
Montgomery. Captain Vargas's truck went right on to Balkins' bridge.
And Captain Vargas put that basket in the water that day for
Captain Springer. Sunday evenin, early, Captain Springer come back
from Montgomery. And Monday—always a long trailer truck would
leave the camp every day of the week and carry them hands of
Captain Vargas dinner to Balkins' bridge. I don't know what the
devil they was doin down there, less'n they was repairin the bridge
with prisoners. So, just about one o'clock, Captain Springer's
squad turned off the road to go to work, landscapin, and I went on

further down the roadway, goin to a spring. And just as I fixed to
turn off, that dinner truck come tearin up the road, headin back
to camp, carryin the dinner vessels. That was on a Monday; the
basket had been put in the creek on Friday mornin—I've put
baskets in Sitimachas Creek, like today, and go back the day after
tomorrow, they just be full of catfish. I've never caught, in all of
my days, as much as fifty pounds of fish with hook and line; my
hold was a basket.

So, I was a water boy. Met the dinner truck comin in, deliverin
the dishes and things. Truck passed by I seed a crocus sack sittin
up there on the bed. I didn't think at all about what it was. And I
looked down the road and I seed that truck stopped where Captain
Springer's squad was workin, and didn't tarry long to put that
crocus sack off. Captain Springer called me, called me twice. I
stopped and looked around—I hadn't got into the swamp yet off
the road.

"Nate, Nate, come here. Come here, Nate."

I set my bucket down side the road and went a runnin back
down there. When I got up to him, I seed that big crocus sack
settin down in the road, what that truck had just put off. Captain
Springer said, "Nate, look in that sack and see what your fish basket
done."

It was a surprise to him, but I had confidence in my work.
There was two catfish in that sack about as long as from my elbow
to the tips of my fingers, each about a foot and a half long. And
there was two cats in there just about a foot long. And there was a
cat in there—I'm not goin to tell about the weight, there was nothin
said about the weight, but there was a catfish in there that
measured six inches across the top of his head. That catfish woulda
weighed twenty-odd pounds—showin me what my basket had done
for him.

He told me, "Nate, take these fish back to camp and clean em.
Tell the cooks up there"—men cooks—"tell em that I said they
should give you a bucket and salt to salt em down after you dress
em."

I went on up there to the back of the dinin room and told the
two cooks what Captain Springer said. They gived me buckets,
gived me salt—just fixed everything clear for me to clean em.
After awhile, I looked around there, just as I set my buckets down
and filled em with water, here come old Captain Castle, old warden.

He walked up there to the kitchen department, poked his head around: "What are you doin here with all this damn mess back of my dinin room? Where'd these damn fish come from?"

I said, "Captain Springer told me to bring em here and clean em, sir."

"Goddamnit, get em up from here and take em down yonder to the wash house."

Well, there was two buckets of water and all them fish there for me to skin and clean and everything—my knives, pliers. I had to get em together and needed time to move. He come right back at me, "Get them goddamn things out from here and get em over yonder to that wash house."

I looked up at him, I said, "I reckon you'll give me time."

Didn't say another word. Them three white men that was workin over the prisoners there didn't like him. Well, he had never bothered me until then, and he commenced a doggin me, cussin over me so.

I picked up them fish and carried em to the wash house. Then I took my pliers and skinned every one of em, little, big, and all. And when I got through dressin em, it took a couple of common foot tubs to hold em. I asked Mr. Springer, "Captain, do you want me to save the heads too?"

"No, I don't care nothin bout the heads."

So I gived all five of them heads to the wash house men—two little heads, two big heads, and that overgrown head. And they told me they had all they could eat and liked to not eat that much—off of fish heads now, and when I caught fish at home I throwed the heads away.

So that evenin I cleaned the fish I went back and told Captain Springer how the warden talked to me about it. He said, "I don't expect no more of him. He's a damned old sonofabitch, anyhow."

Well, Captain Castle wouldn't let em cook them fish for supper —he was contrary as the devil; he wouldn't let em cook them fish for supper and they was nice, fresh fish. Wouldn't let em cook em for breakfast that next mornin; wouldn't let em cook em for dinner —waited till the *next* mornin, let em cook em then. And they was as good a fish as ever I et in my life. Fed everybody at that camp. When they did fry them fish for breakfast, Captain Springer—see, them white men that was workin over them prisoners, they et there too. Boarded there, and there was four or five of em and none of em had no use for old man Frank Castle. They just stayed on at that road camp workin for the state—the state was payin em. All right. Captain Springer sent me a small waiter bout as big as a plate, just piled it up with fish, fried fish, catfish. Talk about eatin fish! I was used to that, too, because I caught fish that way for my people when I was at home. I told Captain Springer when I got a chance, "Captain Springer, you overdone it. I couldn't eat all the fish you sent my way. I gived some to the other boys and it was all they could do to eat it."

He laughed and talked with me like free men will do. Told me in my ear, "Wasn't they nice fish, though, wasn't they nice fish?"

Well, they trucked me out of Wilcox County and assigned me to Wetumpka, women's prison, and I made some fish baskets there. Took em out and put em in the Coosa River. But somebody stole em and I didn't catch a fish for ten years.

ONE day there at Wilcox County, road camp, a fellow died—they called him Blue, dark, dark colored fellow, a young fellow too. I helped to bury him. Took men out from Captain Springer's squad and Captain MacGinnes's—the dog man, he looked after the dogs and kept a squad. They used dogs to track them prisoners down if they runned and he was the dog man. I didn't know the man before and I knowed too much about him when I become acquainted with his heart by watchin him close that day.

So, this fellow died; they called him Blue and he died. They set his body out by the wash house for a day or better and one mornin, Captain Springer and this fellow MacGinnes, they taken some men out of each one of em's squad, mixed em up and sent em off on a Reo truck, brand new Reo truck, and we hauled that fellow about ten miles. And we got him out at a old cemetery, a brief place, and we buried him.

And looked like we never was goin to get to that cemetery. And when we got there—it was a long ways off the highway, somethin like two or three miles back—them boss men gived them prisoners orders to jump in at a certain place there and dig that grave. Well, they hammer-hacked and they hammer-hacked but it didn't take all day. Captain Springer carried me because I was his water boy; I didn't have to dig nary a lick, just toted water to the boys—and that wasn't very much needed—and standin around lookin at em.

Captain MacGinnes was givin the orders. Captain Springer, he was a pretty nice little white fellow, he was standin about, smokin his pipe and lookin at the boys diggin the grave. And him and Captain MacGinnes talked a great deal. And I was there lookin on.

Captain MacGinnes told them boys diggin the grave, "Don't stop until you get it way down." Wouldn't hardly stop at six foot deep. "Put him on down there, dig him on down, dig him on down so he can't come back." He went on ridiculous—"so he can't come back."

I never seed a person buried so deep in my life. Them boys went on down and Captain MacGinnes stood over em, cussin all the time. Well, when they got the grave dug, he jumped up and helped let Blue down in there. Captain Springer was just standin lookin on. And Captain MacGinnes went on ridiculous and scandalous. After awhile, Captain Springer told Captain MacGinnes, "I see that Nate don't like this way of buryin a man." Well, I wouldn't like it to save my life, but what did I have to do with it? Captain Springer spoke them words for me—and blessed God, Captain MacGinnes got a hold of the rope and helped let Blue down. Me standin there lookin. He got in there and helped let him down. He looked at me, wouldn't say nothin. And I didn't say a word to him. I was under Captain Springer, not Captain MacGinnes.

I got to where I don't love to go to buryins nohow, because when I was a boy comin along way back yonder years ago, I seed em put the corpse in a box, in a coffin, and I seed a many a one put in a homemade coffin, set it in the ground, put a few planks over it and throw the dirt in there on it. Well, that always seemed to me like throwin a person's body away. I disliked it and I've seen some buried that way since these vaults has become stylish—to bury a person in a vault. And I'm so afraid every time I go to a burial that I'll see em bury em that old fashioned way. I just got to where I hated that so bad I didn't want to go to no more burials.

THAT Wilcox County road camp was a new prison outlet. They sent twenty-five men there from every camp that already had a crowd of men, to make up a number there. I was one of the twenty-five men sent from Spignor to Wilcox County. Then they transferred me to Wetumpka. That was a straight women's prison but they kept men there for plowin. About twenty-odd men is as much as they kept—one plow squad, all colored men. And all the colored men, practically, was plowin. They had some white men there—flunkies and carpenters and shop boys.

Harry Payne, head warden from Kilby prison, come to Wilcox County hisself to pick out a crew for Wetumpka. Captain Castle had every prisoner in his charge to line up out there in the yard. The line stretched several hundred feet and I was about at the center. Captain Payne overlooked all these men ahead of me and hit me the first man—you know, the looks of some people suits other people. I was almost fifty years old at that time, but I was fit: I weren't too stout and I was hard as bone. He come to me and looked me over. Asked my name and I told him; asked me how long I'd been in prison, I told him. Didn't ask me what I was there for—he mighta knowed after he got my name but I didn't say nothin bout that.

Well, he went on to take all the names that it took to please him—took the names of twenty-five men for plow hands at Wetumpka. I was the first man he called and I purred like a cat when he called me. Wetumpka prison was close to my home, nine miles closer than Spignor, first prison they sent me to, and Spignor weren't far.

I could have plowed every day but I learnt when I got to Wetumpka they weren't after me for plowin, they had younger men to put behind the plow. I weren't nothin but a water boy there for three years and a basketmaker after that. I toted two small buckets —just one squad of men I had to tote water for—nary a bucket weren't no bigger than a house bucket.

I couldn't have asked for better quarters. The buildins was tighter, warmer, than any house ever I lived in. I stayed in two buildins in ten years—stayed in one buildin there until all the other buildins around it burned down. Numbers of buildins, numbers; didn't all get burned at the same time, but one after the other. They had two big barns while I was there and them barns burnt down too; both of em burnt down on the day shift. I was night watchin them barns at the time—

When they transferred we men to Wetumpka, they was buildin another prison department for the women up on the Hamilton road and when that was completed, they moved the women up there, bout three quarters of a mile from the old camp. Well, at that time there weren't over two or three buildins left in that yard. And they moved we colored men out of our old quarters on what they called TB hill and put us down there in the buildin where the white women had stayed—that was a straight wood buildin, lined with glass lights all around. The buildin that the colored women had stayed in down there was mostly brick. I never stayed in a brick buildin in my life, but I fancy in my mind that a brick buildin is a more substantious buildin and has a chance to be warmer than a wood buildin. But the main difference in them buildins, I presume —you couldn't tear up a brick buildin like you could a wood buildin, no way, you couldn't tear out the walls. And the colored women, they found out, was more liable to do such a thing than the white.

They mixed no colored men up with white women—that would have been unconstitutional; mixed no white men up with white women; mixed no colored men up with colored women. But the most definite part about it, they didn't mix up the colors at all, except for the colored prisoners to have a white boss. Had no colored bosses, none whatever.

I quickly found out that them officers would believe what I said, by the way I conducted myself. And I commenced tellin stories for the boys, my fellow prisoners, recommendin em to the officers. Stayed straight myself, gived em no trouble, made a record that after several years I could come home on weekend parole or go any- wheres else—they wouldn't have to lose a minute by me.

Didn't make no difference what happened out in that field or nowhere they knowed that I was around. To my surprise, they'd tell me to come into the office and they would ask me about some incident that been reported to em, and I caught on that I could cool the water. "Nate." "Yes sir, Captain." "Where was you when so-and- so-and-so, when that was goin on?" "I was there, Captain, I was there." "Well, did So-and-so do so-and-so-and-so?" Question me as far as they wanted to question me; and they tried me several different times, several different ways, and I come up with the truth. And the truth I told em never hurt nobody—that was my purpose.

One day, I told the boss man out in the field that I needed a new bucket. I said, "Captain, I need a bucket that won't leak. One of the buckets I'm totin has done got a hole in it and I can't get from where I get my water out to the boys in the field without losin half of it. The other bucket's standin up good. But that one bucket, it don't do no good to tote it; I need another one, Captain."

He said, "The deputy warden will give you a bucket, Nate, ask him."

I walked in the office the next mornin—the head warden's office and the deputy warden's office was joinin. And who was the deputy warden? Captain Homer Evans, first man I ever done a day's work under in the field at Spignor—when they transferred me from Wilcox County to Wetumpka, he was there as the deputy warden. I learnt that Captain Evans done married Captain Harry Payne's sister, the head warden at Kilby, 's sister.

I walked into the front of the hallway, stopped and said, "Captain Evans."

"What is it, Nate?"

He knowed my voice, he had me cased good. I told him what I wanted. So he jumped out the back door and went down in the women's yard where the supply house was, got the bucket, brought it back, handed it to me—the head warden was sittin in his office listenin to everything we said. His office door was open but I didn't know he was in there.

I said, "Thank you for the bucket, Captain."

Captain Carter—Captain Henry Carter from Scottsboro, head warden—he heard me thank Captain Evans and just as I turned and started out, he called me, "Nate."

"Yes sir, Captain."

"Go ahead out and go down there to some of them shrubberies below the door and stop a minute or two. I want to talk with you this mornin."

Told him, "Yes sir."

Walked on out the door with the new bucket in my hand, wonderin what did Captain Carter want with me. But I knowed it weren't nothin about me because I hadn't done shit. Come to find out he wanted to speak to me bout a old man named Jube who was sentenced up there from Eufala.

So I walked out there and stopped at a high shrubbery bush a little higher than my head. After a while, Captain Carter come to the doorstep and stepped down, turned and come right to me. He said, "Nate, what I want to talk with you about is that old man Jube that works out there in the squad. You out there with him every day and you know what's goin on out there, or ought to know."

I said, "Yes sir, Captain, I'm out there every day, right with em."

Workin at that time in what they called the body labor field.

He said, "What I want to know: what sort of man is that old man Jube that works out in the squad?" He appeared to be a older man than I was, and I was surprised, really, that they kept him there at all. "What do he do out there wrong all the time enough to be reported to the office? The boss man in the field done reported him three times for a whippin. I aint whipped him yet. Now I decided I'd ask you—"

I looked at him, said, "Captain Carter, you right, I'm out there all the time and see and hear what goes on. And I aint seed no disorderly acts out of old man Jube, not a bit. I know he's dutiful to what the boss man out there tells him to do. And I'm totin water to him every day, every time he wants it, like I do to the other boys. Yes, sir, quite natural, I should know and I do know the ins and outs out there."

He said, "Nate, I know you know, that's the reason I asked you."

I said, "Captain, I can't tell you nothin against old man Jube; it's just a sham business, these complaints. Captain, he's a good man. Whenever the boss man tells him anything, he's up and gone doin it. There's no stubbornness in old man Jube. But Captain, old man Jube's a old man. He can't jump and squat like them young boys out there, but he do get up and move when the boss man tell him. I don't see nothin he do, at all, to be reported for a whippin."

He said, "Well, Nate, there's some folks goes around here talkin, he wears his clothes slouchy, in a slouchy way, all hangin down, and he uses cloth strings over his shoulders for galluses."

I said, "Captain, there's a cause for that and I can tell it to you. I heard old man Jube ask Captain Evans one evenin, right recently, at the clothes department, for a pair of used suspenders"— call em galluses in this country—"Captain Evans told him—I was listenin right at him when he told him—they was out of suspenders and he couldn't give him none. That's how come he's wearin them strings across his shoulders. I don't believe it calls for a whippin."

Captain Carter considered all that. He said, "But they talks about him wearin his clothes too big and hangin under his feet."

I said, "Well, Captain, they're hangin down on account of he don't have nothin but strings up there."

It went against prison rulins to wear your clothes slouchy. You had to have your clothes upon you correct; of course, it had no bearin on makin a ugly person pretty, but it was a way of showin respect and they demanded it.

I said, "Well, Captain, old man Jube can't help it. When he goes to the clothes house and comes back, them clothes hangin down on him too long for him, or somethin of the kind, too short for him, they just aint his clothes. Sometimes the boys runs out of a suit of clothes of their own wear. And the wash house people will give him anything they have around, just for him to have somethin to wear. It's the other fellows' clothes he's wearin."

Captain Carter considered that.

I told him, "Captain, I do know the circumstances and I know that old man Jube is innocent of any kind of misdemeanor, innocent of disrespectin the boss man, he's innocent. But Captain—" I knowed how to talk in the defense of a man and how to swing a outcome in his favor. I said, "Captain, if you see fit to whip old man Jube, whip him, there's no help for it; if you don't see fit to whip him, please sir, don't whip him."

He said, "Nate, I aint whipped old man Jube yet and I aint goin to whip him."

My word went straight. I didn't have to tell em no big lies and I didn't never disagree with em exactly, tell em, "It weren't like you say." I just applied their words in a little different direction and they'd believe it, like they'd said it themselves.

I'd learnt about old man Jube before I ever talked with the warden. One mornin I was totin water—I'd water the boys, sometimes I'd stand in one place, if there was enough of em to stand for, two or three or four come along in the same breadth plowin, I'd stop and water em all. Weren't no rule that one drinks at a time and the others had to stand and wait, just keep a drivin until I could get to em. Three or four or five could stop right together. Then if another little few is plowin, not comin in the same direction as the others, I'd go over in that crowd and water them. That's what I had to do. So, in that, I walked up to old man Jube one mornin, poor old fellow. I called him Brother Jube; he called me Brother Nate. He was a settle-aged colored man and he claimed to be a Christian. So, Jube stood there drinkin water, didn't drink much. He said,

"Brother Nate, I got a question to ask you and somethin to do for me, if you'll do it." I didn't know nothin bout the field boss reportin him for a whippin. He told me, "They have got me reported for a whippin; now this makes the third time that I been reported."

He didn't know what they'd reported him for. That was the first time I come in the knowledge of it.

He said, "I want you to talk to the warden for me—"

I had quickly learnt that I didn't have to run and report things to the warden for myself, much less anybody else. But he would ask me questions bout a thing when the time come for him to ask me. I wanted to talk to the warden in defense of the prisoners, but I'd just better not do it less'n the warden asked me. I was liable to get a blessin out, talk about whippin me, might have. I told old man Jube that mornin, "Brother Jube, I can't do that. I can talk to the warden and the deputy, but I have to let them call my attention to a thing." That's the truth, too, state of Alabama, that's the rulin when you're in prison here. I said, "Brother Jube, I aint got no authority to carry no reports in to the wardens in your favor or against you. That's somethin I can't do; I aint that heavy here."

He said, "O, Brother Nate, don't tell me that. I know these folks will believe anything you tell em."

I said, "I aint heavy with em at all, Brother Jube, and don't book it thataway."

He said, "Well, I know how heavy you is. They believe what you tell em. You the only man in this squad they'll believe what you say."

I hated he'd found out all that, I hated it. He shook his head. I said, "Brother Jube, I'll tell you, Captain Carter aint goin to whip you. Go ahead and do just like you been doin, you'll come out clear."

I headed him off and tried to pacify him. The next mornin— this thing run three mornins—when I got out to the field with that water, I walked right up to him and said, "Brother Jube, did they whip you last night?"

He said, "No, Brother Nate, they said though they goin to whip me."

I said, "Yeah, you told me yesterday mornin they goin to whip you and you scared about it. But what happened? They didn't whip you and they aint goin to whip you."

Third mornin, I needed a new bucket and I went to see the deputy warden about it. And when I did that the warden called me in question about old man Jube. I told him the facts about this thing and begged him almost with tears in my eyes—I knowed it was definitely wrong to whip that old man. It'd been definitely wrong to whip a white man, if he was clear as old man Jube was. Some smart dude just meddled him and put somethin on him.

I just rejoiced over the outcome. I went right on to the field, uplifted in my mind. I walked up to old man Jube that mornin, stopped to give him a drink. "Well, Brother Jube," I said, "I got good news for you this mornin. Captain Carter tackled me a while ago concernin your troubles out here and I talked to him in your favor."

Whooooooo, that old man like to shouted, he was so glad.

I said, "Captain Carter told me to my head that he hadn't whipped you yet and he weren't goin to do it." Lord, that old man never did have a minute more trouble.

I'd waved, and in bein wavy I taken care of old man Jube; what I told on him didn't hurt him and also, Warden Carter was satisfied. The way I worked it, I kept the bucket balanced.

SEE, I was a water boy, I'd hit the highways—and the state had a field way down on the Coosa River, called it the river bottom farm. They planted corn down there, strictly corn. One day I left out from that field, took my buckets and headed to the spring. This spring was way down on the river, but close to the highway, between Wetumpka and Montgomery. And there was a trail comin from that highway to that spring, and that spring was under a gulf. I walked up to that spring and I was surprised to find two white gentlemen—travelin people can find most anything they want. They looked like Jews or of the Irish nation of people; they wasn't like *this* nation of people. I knowed them men done come from a long way; each of em had a big luggage on his back bound with a protection from the rain.

I hadn't seen a footman—when I was a boy, comin up, durin of my mother's lifetime and after, I'd see and meet travelers comin through this country, white people. And they'd sit down at the table and eat with us. Spring of the year, poor white people travelin through this country and they'd stop at my daddy's house, politely ask my daddy if he could spare a bit of food, and my daddy would give em what he had. Done it so many times. He'd have my mother fix em as nice a meal—sometimes it'd be fish, my daddy caught fish; they'd sit there and they'd enjoy that fish. Sometimes it was fried ham, chicken; sometimes they'd like fried eggs. Heap of em couldn't pay and my daddy didn't ask em for money. And some of em was raggedy, too. I remember once, a settle-aged white gentleman come through there, taken dinner with us, my mother fed him; and he had a young woman with him. He never did make no alarm bout who she was and my parents didn't ask because it was none of their business; didn't know whether she was his wife or daughter, or neither. He was travelin with her, and walkin, at that—all of these people would be walkin, all of em. They'd tell my daddy sometimes they was headed for Florida, or might be they was headed to the northern states.

So, there was two of em standin at the spring that mornin, eatin and talkin to one another. I walked up and spoke to em, they spoke to me. And that was President election time, the election had just passed, and they got to talkin—I reckon they had some hot coffee; they had a thermos and a small cup, talkin and enjoyin theirselves around that spring. I walked up and spoke to em—they didn't offer me nothin to eat. I never did tell em I was a prisoner and they couldn't tell from my clothes that I was. In fact of the business, you take travelin people out of the northern states, they don't know how the state dresses prisoners here.

They looked at me as though I'd understand the subject of their talk and what it was all about; but I was a man with no education and a prisoner at that. I've always held myself in a position though, tried to, to catch on to things, and lots I've caught on to in this life. So they got to talkin about the President and one said, "Well, President Roosevelt got it, President Roosevelt got it. The people didn't want him but they had to go back and get him." President Roosevelt, if I aint wrong, he served three or four terms; he was in there and they couldn't get him out. And them was the words the white gentlemen spoke: "The people didn't want him"—they talked as though *they* wanted him—"but they had to go back and get him." And was laughin and tellin me that with a smile.

I didn't say nothin, I just looked at em; but I showed em that

I admired em for tellin me that. I liked the quotations I had heard of him, President Roosevelt; that was one President I liked—of course, I didn't vote, never voted in my life. But I felt that President Roosevelt, he was different to a heap of Presidents that I have watched along through life. The government stepped into this farm business under his administration more than they ever had before. And that was better for the poor colored man than anything that had been done for him until then.

That NR and A, that was Roosevelt's, they had just then begin to operate in this country. I heard a white man say one day—he was a prisoner too, there at Wetumpka—when the news reached out— see, I couldn't read; if I could I'd a knowed for myself, if they hadn't a kept such books as reveals these words out of my hands, if I coulda read em I coulda found out. But they had a knack of keepin certain books out of some of them colored readers' hands, wouldn't show em up, only for whites, looked like, even a old book to read. So, I couldn't read and I wouldn't a knowed if I'd seed the book—but there was a movement in this country went in the name of the NR and A. And I heard a white man say—pretty heavy-built white man, walkin around there in the prison yard—"That NR and A is out now, and I'm so glad I don't know what to do."

I looked at him. He had little enough sense to think they was whippin em down. I walked up and told him this and he hushed his mouth: I said, "Well, maybe there won't be no more NR and A, but it'll be something else." I didn't tell him who and what and how, though—I didn't know.

Right there at Wetumpka prison I was wide open as a goober hull to several things. But I had to back off my rights, didn't make no difference how it went; I was a poor colored man, I had to abide by the consequences, I had to accept what went on and what was done. I had long since come in the knowledge of right from wrong and how certain classes and certain colors was mugged down—

One day I was down there about the office of the women's prison, I went up to the gate—the gate practically stood unlocked but there was a man right up over your head, in a shack, watchin you at all times. That day the shack man got up and unlocked the gate—had it locked then for some cause. Corner shack was right up over that gate and around at the northwest corner of the yard was another shack. Right yonder was the northeast corner, and another shack up there—shacks built above each of them corners—right over here was the southeast corner—white men sittin up there with shotguns. That yard was walled up there almost too high for you to peep over, then a barb wire fence was concreted in that wall, then net wire from there up, clipped over towards the yard—devil of a fence.

So, that old shack man, just as I got ten yards from the gate, goin on to the walkway straight east and west, he let into talkin to this man at the northwest shack. I heard the first words he said and I stopped and acted crazy to catch it all: "Our southern senators is havin a hard time in Washington now—"

I said to myself, 'Um-hmm, no wonder they havin a hard time'—I knowed how these southern senators would go up there to Washington, D.C., and recommend these states, dupe em up up there—'they ought to have a hard time.' I'd done caught on to their way; they'd go up there and tell a lie about how they was gettin along in this country, class it up like they wanted it; but them people in Washington, D.C., had come in the knowledge of their lies and they was givin em the devil and jackin em up and questionin em close about conditions down here. Of course, I couldn't tell what all they was askin em, but I imagined—

There was one at that time, from the state of Alabama, went up there and told all his fancy lies. They was questionin him and he'd answer, "O, everything is just fine, colored is pleased at the way of goin," and so on. Well they didn't believe him definitely, Congress smelt a mouse in his testimony. So he gets back here and gets one of his best equipped niggers, sends him up there. And the nigger went up there and plastered it up for the state of Alabama, tellin how great it was down here. The nigger, whoever he was, he weren't nothin but a pimp, and he scared to talk anyway except the way the white man wanted him to talk. White man well dressed that nigger before he started him up to Washington, put him up to all that shitty talk. The thing quit goin so hot against em then.

I was in prison at that time, off bein of that organization. Roosevelt was the President and the NR and A was travelin through this country, helpin the colored man and the poor man to ease out of their condition. I was all for the good they was doin, all for a turnabout in this southern way of life. I told em all through prison that I was a union man, told em so, wouldn't bite my tongue. Didn't tell em what sort of union, definitely, but them white folks knowed, them officials, what sort of union it was. I didn't expose that union noway. They mighta done me like they done Wat Smith once they learnt what they wanted to from me.

II

After stayin there at Wetumpka several years, I begin wearin my own clothes, citizen clothes. I come home on Christmas parole one year and it was unusually cold. And I had two big heavy yarn shirts at home. My wife told me, "Darlin, you reckon you could wear these yarn shirts in prison to keep you warm in the daytime?"

I said, "Yes, I ought to carry em back with me."

She said, "Well, if I was you I would. They'll keep your body warm, good heavy wool shirts, yarn shirts."

Carried them shirts back to prison—never said nothin bout it to the warden at all, just carried em on over there. And there was a old crooked white man there, boss man, called him JB Knox, heavy-bodied fellow, he'd a weighed way over two hundred. Walked around there amongst the prisoners talkin his big talk, tryin to scare em. Roared at em—had a heavy voice. He done it often, and this here happened on a Sunday mornin. I was sittin off by myself, just sittin in the cell. And this old Captain Knox would torment all the other boys, then he'd come to me. Looked at me—here's what he said and he weren't obliged to say it: "You is one of these easy Negroes."

I looked at him, said, "I don't bother nobody, that's right; and you aint goin to get me to bother you."

He backed away from me and we had no more words at that time. So, when I come off my Christmas parole with them two big yarn shirts, he seed me wearin em around—I'd just started off wearin my citizen clothes. He come to the breakfast table one mornin and looked at me. Said, "I see you got on a big heavy yarn shirt there. You pull that shirt off and give it to me. I aint heard nothin this mornin bout you bein allowed to wear clothes such as that. And until I do, you give it to me or I'll pull it off you myself."

I pulled it off and gived it to him.

"You got ary other one?"

Told him, "Yes sir, I got another one."

Made me bring that one to him, too. I went and got them shirts back right away. Didn't waste no time with him, went to see Captain Carter, the warden—he went for a Christian man and I believe he was. I said, "Captain Carter, on my trip home on Christmas parole, when I come back I brought me two big yarn shirts to wear em around here and keep the cold out of my bones. But Captain Knox didn't like the way they looked on me and took em away. Made me pull one of em off and give it to him, then made me bring him the other."

He said, "What did he do with em?"

I said, "I reckon he put em up somewhere." I didn't see him put ary one of em on hisself. I don't believe they'd a fit him neither.

"Well, you tell him I said to give you them shirts back." That's all he said.

I went on to Captain Knox, told him, "Captain Knox, Captain Carter told me to tell you to give me my shirts. And I'm waitin on you to give em back to me."

He said, "He did? You are?"

I said, "Yes sir."

He said, "Sendin a prisoner to give *me* a order?" He looked at me and made a noise in his throat. Then he went and got them shirts and gived em back to me.

When he come in the cell the next Sunday mornin, he come around me and made that same noise like he was about to say somethin to me. I think he meant to tell me what he thought about the deal, but he couldn't get the words out of his mouth. And he was a big talkin man.

One year again, I come home on Christmas parole. And my northern friends would always send me a great big box of fancy candy, three layers to the box, for a Christmas present—outside of they was sendin me five dollars a month, every month. And on top of that box of candy would be a fruit cake. They'd send it directly to the prison office at Wetumpka—well, that year I come home before I got my box of Christmas candy. And I got back—I thought I'd get it when I got back, and did get the box. But Captain Knox had done got that box of candy first, some way or other, and brought it up to his house.

Now this old Captain Knox had a wife—that man had more

bad luck than a little, I don't know how come but he did. He had a
wife and two little girls, and he had done checked my box of candy
out of the office and brought it up to his house and issued the candy
out to his little girls. At last he come out one day to give me the box.
I looked into it and seed one whole layer was gone and a few pieces
out of the second layer. I spoke to him about it. "That's the way it
was when I opened it."

Well, I didn't have no words with him over that fancy candy.
I weren't livin on candy and my mind told me he just wanted me
to say somethin so he could come down on me—that was his way
of acts there in the prison, amongst the prisoners. He had such ill
luck in the outside world, he just come in there and taken it out
on us.

Durin the time he stayed there, his wife fell in the fire. He
had two big coal burnin fireplaces and two big chimneys risin above
the top of his house. And his wife fell in the fire and got burnt seriously. Well, that gnawed on him. And he went on across the river
and rented one of the Pickerel people's houses and moved in there.
And he wouldn't pay no rent, and he wouldn't pay—old man lived
on the Montgomery road, old man Bob Rule, him and his wife and
had one child. And he had a little old gas tank there in front of his
little old store. And this here Captain Knox traded there until he
got fifteen dollars' worth of gas and wouldn't pay it. And Mrs. Rule
and the boy Mark, Mark Rule, Mrs. Rule and old man Bob Rule's
son—they was goin to see Knox regular to collect their money.
He never would have it or he just never would pay it. And he
wouldn't pay no house rent to the Pickerel lady neither, and went
dressed up every day, big man, had a nice Chevrolet car—bought
a brand new one while he stayed there at Wetumpka. And he locked
up the house one day and went off on a vacation, took them two
little girls and his wife. When he come back the house had a attachment on the door. He had to pay his rent before they'd even unlock
it. O, if he didn't cut up then! He cut up and riled around about it
and demeaned them Pickerel people. But he paid his bill and they
opened the door just enough for him and his family to clean their
stuff out of there—made him get out of that house. Had to sleep in
that Chevrolet, the whole family, until they could find another place
to rent. And durin of the time he was drivin through the country
lookin for a place, the state cut him off. He come to the prison office

one mornin and Captain Carter told him they didn't want him there
—the state done paid him his last. I never heard no more about him
after that.

NIGGER named John, two-fingered man, he was sent up to Wetumpka from Kilby—that weren't nothin but a slaughter pen, strop
men till the last breath gone from em, then they commenced settin
em in the lectric chair. So this two-fingered Negro, called him John
Barbour, every finger was off of his right hand but the little finger
and the thumb. No tellin how long it'd been that way. I never did
hear him tell *how* it was done. Well, they checked him in there at
night—carry a prisoner anywhere they wanted, day or night, get
him up and carry him to a different place—and the next mornin,
the deputy warden checked him out in the field under this man
Captain Locke that was over the field hands. And I was a water
boy—

That night when we checked in our cells, after we et supper
and got quiet, directly after we all set down, laughin and talkin
some of em was—I was a man that when I was in prison I set off
to myself, practically, less'n I was talkin to somebody that I knowed
and had knowed; I kept to myself and stayed quiet. And this new
man, John, was sittin way back over against the wall on the far side
from the door, and I was sittin kind of anglin from him toward the
end of the cell. And that low-down fool—I wouldn't a dreamt of
such a thing if he hadn't spoke, but you can't never tell where the
devil's at. I was sittin up there by myself and he sittin over there
with his low-down self—all of us was in there, just sittin like old
men sits, and weren't nobody very old in there. I was the oldest that
I knowed of and I was in my fifties.

All of a sudden this nigger John throwed his finger at me, said,
"Old man, you aint no good, you aint no good."

Just thataway. Lord, if that didn't attract my attention.

I said, "You talkin bout me?"

He said, "Yes, you. You aint no good."

I said, "Friend, what have I done to you? What have I *ever* done
to you? You just done your first day's work here today and you done
found a fault in me, somethin that these other boys aint never said
to me or knowed. We get along good here, we don't—who do you
take me to be? You take me to be a snitcher? You aint caught nothin

wrong of me and I definitely knows it. Why do you have it in you to talk to me like you is? You come out from Kilby where there's a lot of taletellin and rough acts amongst the prisoners, and you come here takin this place to be like that? That don't go on here. And if you take me to be a snitcher and you runnin your tongue on me because I'm a water boy, you just as well to crawl off of that horse. I'm no snitcher and these boys here knows me better than that. You take Joe Jefferson here, Pete Sparks, Billy Joe Spooner, Tom Martin—ask them how it rolls with me." The cell was quiet as a rock pile. I said, "All right, if you take it like that, go accordin to the way you think. You can come over here and jump on me if you want to. Come on, don't stop. You come on over here if you want to and jump on me."

All them boys was settin there with their heads down, listenin at the subject. This nigger wouldn't get up, he wouldn't do nothin but talk his big talk and he set down durin that. Well, the argument died down and everything become quiet.

And so, next mornin, Captain Evans come up there and checked us out with Captain Malcolm Locke, the man that carried us to the field. Straight down the road to the barn, them that was plow hands had to catch the mules out and go to plowin. I branched off bout halfway between the buildin we stayed in and the office, went off to Captain Locke's house—I was a milk boy for him and a flunky around the house. If there was anything to do there, I'd look after it for him. And he trusted me to a great extent. Me and him would go possum huntin at night, many a night, there in prison. He gived me a gun more than one time and I'd go off to myself rabbit huntin. Captain Locke, field man over me—I was his water boy. And he had a brother, I heard him say, carried a squad at Spignor and he had killed two men. Captain Locke cried about that to me.

So that mornin we checked out after that big bluffy quarrel, the boys went on to the barn with Captain Locke and caught the mules out, went on to the field. Got on out there and this here John, the boys told him—some of em told me they told him that in the lot, before they even got out to the field, catchin mules they told him—it was Joe Jefferson and Billy Joe Spooner told John Barbour, "Fellow, if you'd a jumped on that old man that you was talkin to last night, we'd eat you up, we'd eat you up"—they went down on him and gived him the devil about it—"The best thing for you to do is never bother him no more." They built up on his back that mornin.

When I got in the field to give em water, Billy Joe Spooner was the first man I watered. He said, "Papa Nate, the devil been to play out here this mornin."

I said, "Billy Joe, what's the matter? What caused it?"

Said, "Some of em told Captain Locke—"

I never did ask Billy Joe who told the boss man what happened in the cell, it could have been one of several in the crowd. Captain Locke found out about it and he called that John Barbour up. All of em stood and listened when Captain Locke told him, "Uh-huh, I hear you and Nate got into it and you wanted to jump on him last night in the cell." And from that word on, Billy Joe told me, Captain Locke cussed him like he'd cuss a dog. And he had a great big old hickory walkin stick, up at the end it had a handle hold and it sloped on down gradually. It was hard and seasoned and they told me that Captain Locke threatened, "If I hear talk about you messin with Nate again, I'll beat the cow-walkin hell out of you."

So, after all of it was over, I was good and hot still, the way that nigger talked to me that night and I knowed I was innocent of doin any evil against any of them boys in camp. I went around givin em all water that mornin, time I got around to him—he dropped his head and asked me to pardon him. I said, "Well, friend, I'm very sorry that you talked to me like you did; and them boys that stays with me and you, they knows I'm no peacebreaker, no fussmaker, no snitcher. Them boys takes me to be a friend to em. All I ask you, take me for what I am. You was wrong; I hate that anybody look at me in suchaway as that. And I know that you know I didn't report you this mornin."

They soon transferred his ass away from there. Sent him to Wilcox County, road camp, and he kept up a uproar there. One night a fellow got him down and stabbed him—these is true facts and I aint sayin it because he talked rough to me and insulted me; he couldn't hurt me with his mouth—so some fellow stabbed him with a dirk and cut him all in his thighs and it took close attention to save his life. So they transferred him again, right out of there. And I heard before I got out of prison, he died, died in prison. Last I'd heard before that he couldn't walk; that dirk done poisoned his legs and the poison spread, the way they told it, to his whole body. Well, that ruint him; he just caused his death by his way of life.

CAPTAIN LOCKE would stand and talk with me bout many a subject, just like I'd been a white man. We was standin by a fire one cold mornin, way out here this side of Wetumpka; he had his squad out there and I was a water boy. The squad was all out in the pine thickets cuttin timber, four-foot wood pieces for them big prison ovens. And they was cuttin at that time on a colored man's territory right close to a colored people's church and school in New Style community. We was standin there by the fire talkin and he said to me, "Nate, they electrocuted two Negroes at Kilby last night."

He always read the news and heard the quotations. I looked at him and said, "Captain, what's that all about?"

He said, "Well, rapin a white woman."

I dropped my head.

He said, "It's hard to testify the facts about it."

I weren't goin to betray myself by talkin against the white race of people. I said, "As many colored women as there is in the country, they'd be wrong to do that, they ought to go to their own color with that game. Furthermore, a man aint got no right to overpower no woman, run over her thataway about her nature, regardless to her color. But tell me, Captain, did they really do like they was accused of doin?"

"Aw hell, Nate"—dropped his head when he spoke—"I'll tell you the way that goes. Niggers and white women has been doin that for the longest and runnin together. Whenever a white woman, if she been foolin with a nigger, as soon as she finds out that she's in a little danger of bein found out, she goin to jump up and squall and holler. Nigger's burnt up then"—I knew it and I let him speak —"They goes with em until they gets tired of em or somebody walks down on em, then they squeal. Been doin it for years." Talkin that subject to me—he knowed it well, he knowed how such things as that run.

I come to find out that Captain Locke would take them colored gals out from the prison department—and there was nothin to a white man but to do that. When they'd check them colored women out there for farm work—choppin cotton and hoein cotton and rakin out ditches—this fellow Locke would take a chance with some of em. The way they runned it there, if there was any way in the world for the plow squad to get out of field work by havin other jobs like cuttin that cord wood, why, the colored men was put between the low handles and that farm labor was put on the colored women. The white women there at Wetumpka didn't go out in the field to work at all; they'd work in the garden squad right there at the prison department—that's as far as they'd trust a white woman. Anything to do out in the field, put the colored women to it. Well, that gived this man Captain Malcolm Locke a chance to be amongst em. Whenever he announced to the warden what he wanted done out in the field, right soon you'd see that prison truck come out from there with a load of colored women. And them colored women belonged to Captain Noyes' squad—Captain Noyes and Captain Locke was buddies, Captain Noyes was a older man than Captain Locke.

Well, I heard the subject whispered under the cover. Captain Locke at that time had a colored man in his squad that would holler and raise the devil when he discovered anything like that. That was a brave nigger, in his way, and a bit of a fool. Captain Locke soon found out what this fellow was singin and had him transferred out of the squad and away from Wetumpka. But commenced a little secret talk around—Captain Locke was runnin with them colored women. And in that, rolled along and rolled along until the deputy warden caught it; no doubt it was sung around there by some loud enough for all to hear. I was goin around totin water, hush-mouthed —I could hear it.

So, Captain Locke fooled around and let Captain Evans catch his crookedness—I never did see Captain Evans have too much talk with ary a colored woman. And it got to where Captain Evans wouldn't take Captain Locke's word for hog slops. He'd take a colored man's word before he'd take his.

By me bein a man out in the field when Captain Locke would order Captain Noyes' squad to be out there, many a day I'd tote water hand in hand with them colored women. The water girls in that crowd, me and them went to and fro. Well, that was a fixed thing between Captain Noyes and Captain Locke. They caucused out in the field one day and they agreed, "Let Nate tote water with them girls, right along with em, hand and hand." So they put me at it and me and them water girls went into the swamps, into the woods, to the

springs at every field place we worked at. How come they put me
with them girls? Them colored girls would go out, they said, and
they had a knack of free men meetin em out at them springs, so
them two officers put me out there to watch over em. They gived
me orders to keep my eyes on em. Said, "Nate, we goin to hold you
responsible for what wrongness goes on. If any free men—" Them
colored men in the squad had to stay busy, they couldn't run out
with em, but I was a water boy and I was supposed to report it if
any free men come along to tamper with them colored women at
the springs. But if there was ary a free man out in them bushes,
Christ aint a Christian.

There'd be two water gals totin water for that squad of women
and only me totin for the men. And I toted two reasonable-sized
buckets; didn't bother me to tote em at all. Many a time me and
them girls had been to the spring over yonder and we'd come out
on route to the field, Captain Locke would meet us. I toted his water
in a long flask, separate from the water for the squad. I'd fill up
that bottle, screw the lead down on it, hook the neck wire over the
side of one of my buckets. My buckets bein smaller than the girls'
was, I'd give one of em one of my light buckets—each of em carried
only one bucket, but it was heavier than ary one of mine—and I'd
tote her heavy bucket and one of my light buckets. And with Captain
Locke's bottle, the wire of it, over the mouth of that light bucket,
that made it sort of equal up with the girl's bucket, in the weight.
I had sympathy for them gals because they was my color—of course,
I'd a done it for white women just thataway, but I didn't tote no
water with them white girls.

Many a time we'd meet Captain Locke. I'd look ahead and see
him comin on his horse, makin his rounds through the fields. He'd
say, "Nate, I really need some water." Set that girl's bucket, heavy
bucket, down, and take the light bucket with his jar hangin to it,
hand it up to him on his horse. Never did forbid me from totin the
heavier buckets for them women. In that regard he was a decent
man.

So, lingered along, lingered along, no troubles comin out of
the fields, nowhere we went. And at that present time we was
travelin down to a two-hundred-acre field, across the river bridge
and through the heart of Wetumpka city—called it the river bottoms field. Had a place there on the prison side of the river, called

it the body labor field. Had a place southeast, called the Whitman field. Had a place, before you crossed the river, called the river bend. O, we worked a territory, we prisoners did; four different fields we worked in.

ONE day Captain Locke had his squad of colored men down on the river cuttin cord wood. And right about twelve o'clock, I went out to a house where there was a well of water—I was totin water for the squad. I got to the well and was drawin the water, I looked around and here come Captain Carter and Captain Evans drivin up. They soon stopped their car before they got to where I was, got out and started walkin out through a open place on the way into the woods to Captain Locke and the squad. Seemed like Captain Evans was stickin everything against Captain Locke he could—I caught that from many angles, the weakness between Captain Evans and Captain Locke. I started walkin back to the squad with my buckets and Captain Carter and Captain Evans walked out to meet me. Well, we talked there for a minute and Captain Evans asked me, "Nate, how is everything goin on out here?"

I said, "Everything apparently seem to be goin on all right, Captain."

But he proved to me in the subject that they didn't have no use for Captain Locke. They walked back towards the squad and left me halfway between the squad and the well. I heard the conversation between em as they walked away. Captain Carter told Captain Evans, "Well, Nate aint goin to tell you nothin bout what goes on out here less'n you ask him directly."

What did Captain Evans want to learn from me that day? Them wardens questioned some of the other fellows about Captain Locke but I didn't catch what they wanted at that time. I was a little hanky at Captain Locke myself since I'd heard about him runnin at a certain colored woman. That didn't go well with me.

The more dope they got on Captain Locke, the further and further out it put him—till he were gone. Lingered along, lingered along, first political pull that come up, it was very pleasin to Captain Evans to get shed of Captain Locke. He transferred the shit out of that white man. Captain Locke done spoke too close with some of the colored men—I knowed that from my own experience—and he runned with them colored women. They sent him to where there weren't no women, and well do I know it. Sent him to Four Spots, county camp, over men strictly.

I had milked cows two or three years for Malcolm Locke and after they sent him away from there I commenced milkin for Captain Noyes—had two nice milk cows. And Captain Noyes let Captain Carter have one of his cows for milk purposes. Captain Carter put me to milkin for him, and the cow was with calf, and as usual, most anybody that knows about milk cows, if the cow gets with calf, why, you milk her right on; it's very necessary to.

I milked animals there at Wetumpka for four different white men: milked a goat for Captain Oliver Cook, doctor put him on goat milk and he went and got him a milk goat and I milked it; milked cows for Captain Locke, milked cows for Captain Noyes, then milked a cow for Captain Carter, one of Captain Noyes' milk cows. Anything had milk, I was the milker for it. If one man got dispossessed of his milk animal, that other one, if he had anything to milk, he'd put me to milkin for him.

Well, I noticed while I was milkin for Captain Carter that Captain Noyes was runnin around there every few mornins to the back of the prison department where I milked at to check on that cow. I'd found out the cow was with calf, I could see the calf kickin her after it got far enough advanced in the cow. So, one mornin I caught Captain Noyes there, dutifully checkin on that cow. She was near bout ready to birth the calf, the way it kicked in her, I'd watched it —I'd watched my cows, I knowed the nature of em when it come to breedin calves. So, I hailed Captain Noyes, "Good mornin, Captain."

"Good mornin, Nate."

"Well, you lookin after your cow, the condition of her? Her time's about ready—"

He said, "Yes, I noticed that several days ago."

I said, "I thought you might be goin around to test her out, see what sort of calf she goin to have, a heifer calf or a bull calf."

He looked at me strange, "I don't know nothin bout such as that. I don't know what it's goin to be when it comes, and nobody else knows, nobody can tell."

O, he was pickin in the right row then to get his hundred. I said, "Well, Captain Noyes, I can tell you what sort of calf she goin to have if you want to know."

I done watched that cow, found out; it worked just like I told him, too. I said, "I thought that's what you was lookin for. I can tell you now what sort of calf she goin to have. It's goin to be a bull calf."

He just stretched his eyes and repeated to me, "Aint nobody can tell about that."

I told him, "I can."

Off he went. I watched the cow close then to see when was the calf comin. I couldn't tell about the day it was goin to come but I seed it was a bull calf she was carryin. And he commenced a watchin definitely too. One mornin he beat me around there, and when he got to the lot, the cow'd come in. He told me hisself when I got up there, "Well, that cow done come in."

I said, "She is?"

"Yes."

"What sort of calf she got, Captain?"

"I don't know, I don't know."

Now I knowed when he seed that cow had a calf he fooled around there long enough to tell what sort of calf it was. He had to get away from around there, go back and check out his squad, had his usual squad of colored women checked out to him. So he went on back around to the office and before he got out of sight good I seed it was a bull calf. I said to myself, 'Um-hmm, you seed what that calf was but you didn't want to acknowledge it to me; you knowed that I was goin to find it out.' It deceived him so bad to believe that nobody couldn't tell nothin bout that—and I told him. And just like I told him, the calf come, a bull calf. I had helped my cows when I was at home free before I ever thought about a penitentiary—I have went and followed my cows up and I have watched and experienced and studied over the condition of a cow, and whatever side I seed that cow kickin, most of the time, if it's a bull calf, he lays to the right side in his mother; if it's a heifer calf she lays to the left. You watch that cow, when she gets far enough advanced for that calf to kick in her side, and he starts that, she starts, the calf gets far enough developed in its mammy's womb, it'll prove to you, if you watch, what side a bull calf kick on and what side a heifer calf kick on. Quite natural, when a cow breeds and gets a calf in her sack, some few times it lays in a way that you can't exactly tell, but if it's layin to her side, either side, you can tell what it is: a heifer calf lays to the left and a bull calf lays to the right.

Put Captain Oliver Cook there in Captain Malcolm Locke's place at Wetumpka. He was a older man than Captain Locke and his wife was a much younger woman than he was. He had been married before and this lady he had for a wife was his second wife; didn't have nary a child by her in the world. But he had a grandbaby there in the house and it was just a baby too, small enough to tote in your arms. That was his and his first wife's son's baby, and Captain Cook and his second wife was raisin the chap.

Fall of the year, first fall he was there, Captain Cook put me to makin syrup. I stood—and a pan was put in my possession on a furnace to boil down the cane. I'd produced many a gallon of sorghum syrup when I was raisin my children—growed sugar cane too. Made barrels of syrup, that old native sugar cane syrup, pure syrup; I was born and raised up eatin syrup. My daddy raised sugar cane every year he farmed—white men never did take his syrup. He didn't make no overproduction of syrup, he just made it for home use, and sometimes he'd make fifty and sixty gallons.

I runned off several pans of syrup at the prison department. And that pan was as long as a common wagon bottom. Fire that furnace under that pan and the syrup starts to cookin; your job, if you is over that pan and you is the maker, you just stand there and take them dippers—them dippers is several feet long and as wide as my two hands, holes in em to strain the skimmins, keep them skimmins floated to the back end of the pan to keep em from cookin and evaporatin in that syrup. Watch it, know when it's done, know when it aint done—that's your job. The most of your job, help out the syrup, keep it from scorchin, it boilin up there and blubberin all the time. Watch them skimmins, keep em raked back, float em back.

Home, I always hired my syrup made; paid a toll in so much syrup. Had a furnace on the Pollard place down in the pasture, hauled my cane— One year, some old hogs was hangin around there where the man was makin my syrup—I stood by that pan when he was makin it and I caught on to where I could make it. But I never did own a syrup mill. I'd cut down the cane, strip it, haul it to the man's mill out there close by the furnace. Well, got done makin syrup and throwed all the skimmins in a barrel, but I was so busy with my syrup I neglected them hogs, didn't keep em runned off like I oughta done. I got all my syrup out of there and hauled it to my house and a few days after that, I went back out there and seed that these old devilish hogs had upset my barrel and got drunk off them skimmins. Weren't my hogs, other folks' hogs. My hogs was up in the hog pasture. I'd toted a few skimmins up there and poured em out for them. But these wanderin hogs overfilled their-selves, took blind and staggered off. It didn't kill em, but it made em drunk as a cooter.

THEY put me to makin syrup two seasons at Wetumpka. And at that time there come to be nobody over the men prisoners but Captain Oliver Cook and the head warden lady herself. How come that was all that was there? Who woulda guessed it would come to that?

It had risen up a disagreement amongst the officials and it was personalized. White men, officers, was comin there from them other prison departments and havin intercourse with them white women prisoners—they come from Kilby all the way to Wetumpka, and they was comin from Spignor. It went up to the governor's office in Montgomery, all such conditions as that. And they cleaned it up. Why, one white gentleman there—he was actin deputy warden at the time; Captain Evans was away for some cause—and his wife was watchin him close as the state was watchin and she caught him one night with a certain white woman, prisoner, and she had a pistol in her hand. And they say she would have killed him—he was sort of a raw-boned white man—if it hadn't a been for one of the other prisoner women anticipatin her before she could do it. So they scattered that mess out, got shed of the warden, Captain Henry Carter, and the deputy warden, Captain Homer Evans, and when they got through scatterin, weren't nobody there but Captain Oliver Cook and Miss Phoebe Burnside. Miss Phoebe Burnside was the head warden and Captain Oliver Cook was the boss man over the men.

THERE was a white lady boarded with Miss Phoebe Burnside and worked in Montgomery. And them two white ladies would go off on joy trips and pleasure trips at night, usually on a Saturday. Miss

Phoebe Burnside would come after me—didn't make no difference what I was doin, she wanted me to stay at her house that night. Of course, she'd lock up the house but there was a nice servant house for me to stay in. And she had two servants, a cook and a butler boy. A woman by the name of Ella was her cook and Conrad Ball was her butler boy. They was trustees and the warden would let them off for a Saturday sometimes. And when she let em off, if her and that white lady was goin off on their pleasure trips—suppers and dances—she'd come to me: "Nate."

"Yes, ma'am, missus."

"I want you to stay at the house tonight."

"Yes, ma'am, missus."

I'd go up there and walk around that house some, overlook everything, go back to the servant house and set up in there. Sometimes I'd go up there and I'd be gettin in just as soon as they'd be goin off, first dark. They'd get in Miss Phoebe Burnside's Buick automobile and they'd get gone. Late that night they'd come in, I'd be there—that's the way I was used. The place was on the Wetumpka road on the route to Montgomery, below the prison department. I had all chances to run and get away from there but that never struck my head.

I safely could say, them white people at Wetumpka treated me better than any of their color have treated me on the outside. They didn't scorn me and cuss over me and provoke me; they didn't overpower me. I knowed they had the power but they had sense enough and heart enough to check it. But every landlord ever I had dealins with tried to euchre me, puttin unnecessary figures against me—Mr. Tucker made me pay up what I owed Mr. Reeve, and that debt was pulled over with ten percent on the dollar knocked off. He told me to my head, "The thing for you to do is pay me what you owed him." Well, he got the whole figure from me, and all down the line —Mr. Watson, the last mite of dealins I had with him, it weren't over fifty dollars' worth and what did he tell me? "Bring me the cotton this fall, bring me the cotton." I carried him three bales of cotton, more than what I owed him, surely, and did he give me a settlement? Did he give me a settlement? And before that he gived me a note to sign on that Pollard place and I wouldn't sign—callin for all my mules, hogs, cows, wagons, and all my personal property

—he strapped it on. This is a fact: I was travelin through the world, different places, when I was in prison; wherever they sent me I went, had to go. But I had no trouble, seriously. And didn't nobody try to dupe me: I was already in a trap, you might say, caught in a wire trap. Outside, they raised figures against me in place of wire.

And I venture to say this: them prison officials just knew what was behind me and who was watchin me all the time and they just as well to back their legs and be milked. They took my word, they trusted me; asked em for anythin, they granted it—I was recognized more in prison than I was recognized out here, sure as you born to die. Some of em thought I didn't have sense enough to realize what it was all about, I know they did, but I had my cap on every day I stayed in prison. I knowed the meanin of their acts, I knowed the causes for the way I was treated. I knowed that the penny had always kept the wedge hid. I become to have friends in foreign countries and I knowed that they was workin for me, and what I was of and what I stood for. I rared like a mule in a stable; but what crazy person wouldn't rear when he seed the man fixin to take everything he had and he knowed he didn't owe him nothin? Who is it that wouldn't rear?

I didn't have a thing on my mind but workin to get back home to my wife and children. They offered me a parole as much as three times and it sorely tempted me but I turned em down. That Montgomery crowd would come up to talk with me from the parole department, tell me they'd give me a parole if I'd accept their offer —leave the country and move to Birmingham. And asked me all about the very work of the organization: What did I expect when I joined? How did I feel about it now? One white woman tried—it tickled me in a way; there was two white women and two white men —that was the parole board—come up there and labored with me one day. O, I was a hard nut to crack; they couldn't do it.

They walked in the main administration buildin there at Wetumpka, taken their seats and they commenced a questionin me. I was settin there right across from em. They first set in on me about this affair—that woke em up, every one of em. What did it mean? And how come I joined? And what was it goin to do? Told em I didn't know nothin bout none of that at all, no way, shape, form, or fashion; wouldn't comment on it. One of them white women got mad. She questioned me backwards and forwards, couldn't get nothin out of me. And had done let me know that they come up there to parole me if I'd cooperate with em and give em a lot of talk. Wanted to parole me but didn't want me to come back home—go on over to Birmingham. Told me, "Them folks over there in that settlement in Tukabahchee County, they don't want to see you again." They branched off on that, and then they come back to the mainline questions. They wanted to find out everything about my experience in the organization in order that they'd know, if I'd accepted a parole and taken their word and went on off in some other country in place of comin home, would I start somethin up over there. They looked at all that. Well, they couldn't do nothin with me no way, couldn't get the answers out of me they wanted, couldn't get me to accept their parole, leave my country and go to the city.

And just before they broke it up, this white lady got mad. I'd fooled around there until I cross-talked her down. I didn't care for her kind of parole; I weren't goin nowhere but back home—that was my thorough intention. She seed all through the subject that she couldn't move me—and them white men was sittin up there laughin at her. She got hot with me then. They was takin notice to the way she was talkin with me and weren't gettin nothin. She told me, "You one of these smart Negroes. Go ahead and make your maximum sentence."

I told her, "Yes'm, missus, that's what I'm goin to do anyhow, make my maximum sentence and be a clear man when I get out. I wants to go home to my wife and children and back to the country I come from. If you can't do that for me, you can keep me bound down in prison. I wants to live and abide by a way that I can be free like folks is free. And I don't mean nobody no trouble—if they don't give me no trouble."

Wooooooo, she got hot, hot, hot. I'd tied her up, gone backwards on her, made a game of her questions. Goin into all the details —they knowed I was in it, probably knowed most everything I knowed, only wanted to hear it from me. Mighta got some literatures out of my house in the roundup—if I'd a been there somebody woulda got more than literatures. I just got mad all over and I couldn't help myself, just to see how hard I was pulled at and approached about my leanins. They wanted me to fall on my knees, cry out and spill my guts. Well, I just soured on em. I held back my feelins and cross-talked em, turned em against one another—

had them white men laughin at that white lady. Had the lady dig at me for what the men couldn't get. And I kept em *all* down. "Go ahead and make your maximum sentence; you're one of these smart Negroes." She couldn't draw me up to what she wanted. Never did tell em what they wanted to hear. I just abided by the consequences; went right back down the road to my cellhouse and didn't let em catch me at no bad acts noway. I made a record there—never was nothin laid on me with a threat to whip me. I went through prison just as quiet as a plank of wood.

What I wanted to tell em I told em; what I didn't want to tell em I didn't tell em. And I never did want to tell em nothin bout this organization. They wasn't about to be told by me. While I was there in prison, from the first day to the last, didn't nobody pick my guts about it as hard as that white woman. And when she finished, she knowed just as much as she knowed before she asked me.

MANY a mornin I'd go to the field, tote water, and off my water hours I'd go to the woods and swamps, cut me some white oak, put it on the wagon to carry home. And when Miss Phoebe Burnside become warden, she took me out of the field completely. Put me down at the barn and the blacksmith shop on the Coosa River, keepin watch on the state's property. Hog pasture went right to the bank of the river, kept plenty of hogs there. I was a watchman and overlooker for them hogs.

Naturally, I spent a lot of time around the blacksmith shop. But I didn't have to sharpen no plows or shod no mules—I could do it but I didn't have it to do, it weren't put on me.

Well, Captain Oliver Cook taken sick and had to go to the hospital and they put Captain Lew Hurley in his place over the boys in the field. He come off of bein over a women's squad and they took his women and divided em out under them other boss men. And at that period of time, there was a white lady workin in the prison department and she wanted me to build her a chicken coop. So I was in the yard near the blacksmith shop at this old women's prison, nailin and fixin that white lady a chicken coop, wire chicken coop, and I heard a horse come up in the yard; that horse hit that asphalt—blok-ablok-ablok-ablok-ablok-ablok-ablok—I quit and raised up. I knowed it was a state horse because other horses didn't come in there, nothin but state horses—had a old gang of mules there and

one saddle horse. I quit workin, quit nailin; had my saws and other
tools there where I was makin that chicken coop. And that horse
come right down on me. I seed it was Mr. Lew Hurley on that horse.

"Nate."

I said, "Yes sir."

Now he oughta knowed that I was busy and I weren't no shop
man—

"Get them boys some sharp plows over yonder. Them boys'
plows is all dull. And get em over there at once."

Soon as he said that I just quit listenin and bowed down to
my work. I didn't carry no plows nowhere. He whirled around on
that horse and went back. I reckon he was lookin for them plows
to come regardless to what I said or done. But he didn't see no
plows then.

Well, the farm superintendent come in there that evenin after
Mr. Lew Hurley had done went back to the plow boys. I didn't know
he was there—Captain Albert Morehead—and he went on over in
the field where Captain Hurley was. Captain Hurley raised sand
when he didn't see no plows come and he reported me to the farm
superintendent. Told him—some of the boys listened at him and
some of em, one or two of em, one of em was my right-hand friend
—that was a little old chunky-built fellow sentenced up from Birmingham, by the name of Willy Akers. So he told me that night
when the boys checked in from the field—Willy Akers overheard
what Captain Hurley told Captain Morehead; told him, "I went over
to camp to get some plows and I told Nate Shaw to bring em out
here and he wouldn't do it"—Willy Akers listened at him— "You
oughta put his damn ass in the field. He's just sittin over there at
that camp and he don't do a damn thing, just sittin."

Willy Akers told me that—he heard him, he was one of the
plow hands. I asked him, "What did Captain Morehead tell him
then?"

He said, "Captain Morehead didn't pay him no attention far as
raisin a big talk; he just passed him up."

That raised my hackles. I said, "Well, I aint too good to go back
to the field—"

Willy Akers looked at me, said, "You done put your days in
the field, Uncle Nate. You don't have to put out no more."

"I know it," I said, "if I understands the warden's orders. And
if Lew Hurley tries to make me break them orders or tries to break

em hisself, he just might find *his* ass in the road. He already violated the rules here some time ago—" That was before Miss Phoebe Burnside become warden. One of them colored gals broke to run one day in the field and he shot at her. And that was strictly against orders. He had to plead for his job after that. I learnt all about it: he told the warden he didn't shoot to hurt her, he just shot to scare her. He didn't hit her but you wasn't allowed to shoot noway around them women, to shoot em or to shoot to scare em neither.

Willy Akers knowed that history.

"No, I aint goin back to the field. I'm goin to stay where the warden put me until I go free. Lew Hurley is one boss man this colored man aint goin to recognize."

MORNINS them boys would hitch up the mules—boss man'd check em out—all get ready for the field. I'd be walkin around at the blacksmith shop and the barn and the pasture. But if I took a notion I'd go off and cut me some white oak. Evenin, I'd get me a ax and sharpen it, prepare it for the next mornin. Mornin come, I might catch the boys and go on to the field, carry that ax with me, and I knowed what I was goin to do when I got to that field—I'd reach down in the wagon, grab my ax, and jump off. Go right on to the woods, swamps, wherever I went, tell the boys, "I'll see you all." Tell such-and-such a one, the wagon driver, "Stop over on that road a piece on your way back, please; and if you find any white oak piled up there, bring it to the blacksmith shop."

I hung around the blacksmith shop where I could see what come in and what went out. Saturdays, when the boss man would come up out of the field with the boys, from work, he'd watch and see that the boys ungeared them mules and put em up and he'd turn his saddle over to the lot man; it was the lot man's job to put feed out, ready for him. Boss man would come on back around by the blacksmith shop, goin to the office, I'd go out and stop him: "Captain."

"What is it, Nate?"

"I needs a wagon and a pair of mules this evenin."

"Nate, you better go around and tell the lot man; you know how it is, he turns them mules to pasture at one o'clock every Saturday. Tell him whatever mules you wants this evenin, tell him not to turn em out, turn the rest of em out but keep them two you want in the lot."

I'd get right up, go around there and tell the lot man—sometimes it'd be a white man, sometimes it'd be a colored man—tell him, "Such-and-such a pair of mules, I want to use em this evenin and I done asked for em, granted to me. Don't turn em out—I'm goin to use em to the wagon."

I was liable to drive them mules three miles or more from camp, huntin white oak. Take that wagon and a pair of mules at one o'clock, drive off from the barn up to the back of the shop, stop and get my ax and lay it in the wagon—hit the road. If I was out and black dark comin in, they never did hunt Nate Shaw up. I'd just be late comin back to the shop with a load of white oak from some woods, somewhere or other.

And sometimes I'd take one of the prisoner boys with me, one of the field workers that wanted to breathe on the outside for a-while. It stuck me to see them boys locked in like they was and sufferin to go out; if they'd let em out every once in awhile they'd a been glad to come back. I'd go to the office and tell the warden, "Such-and-such a one wants to go with me and I believe you can trust him."

"All right, Nate, but you're responsible for him. You can take him with you but bring him back. If you can't bring him back, you just have to get on the wagon and hustle on back here, let it be known."

I'd say, "I appreciate it, sir."

There was two different fellows there at camp, two especially, one or the other would always want to go with me, ride out on the wagon into the country. Never did carry off one that acted like he wanted to run. Many a Saturday night, that wagon'd roll back there and I'm holdin the lines and one of them fellows was with me. Come back late hours, after dark, drive that wagon on around there to that blacksmith shop and take out from it; carry them mules on to the lot and put em up.

HAD a great big old tree beside the blacksmith shop; I'd set under there and make my baskets. That hackle tree would throw shade like a cloud—biggest hackle tree I ever seed in my life. I'd sell my baskets to anybody that wanted em—I never did have to carry a basket off of the camp grounds to sell it. Them boss men that worked there over the prison department, night watchmen and so on, they'd have me to make em baskets, bottom chairs, and the next mornin when their time come to crank up their cars and go home, they'd load up what they bought from me or had me to work on their chairs. And that advertised my work clean up in Coosa County. I just didn't have enough time to do all the work that come in for me after that.

People would come to the prison—one white man come soon one mornin, told the warden, "I heard that you have a man here that bottoms chairs, makes baskets, and so on."

Warden said, "Yes, I got a man here of that type."

"Well, I'd like him to bottom some chairs for me and make me some baskets."

Warden listened at him and listened at him. He got his story told and the warden said, "Yes, but you see him about it. And whatever he promises you, he'll do it. And when he makes your baskets and bottoms your chairs, don't you come in here and pay it off— you pay it to him. We allows him that privilege here."

Well, the white man wanted to know where he could find me at. Warden told him, "I dont know where he's at. He goes down there by the blacksmith shop"—told him how to get there—"and if he aint there, go on down to the barn, right around the corner of the prison department here. Nate Shaw—he'll do what you want done, and when he does it, you pay him."

So he come out of there lookin for me. The field man hadn't got his boys straightened out to go to the field yet. And them boys that plowed was all around the shop there waitin on the field boss to come around and get em to go to the field. I was at the edge of the bunch standin around at the blacksmith shop—great big level yard and the blacksmith shop set right in the midst of that openin. Them boys was in a huddle, standin there laughin and talkin and I happened to be standin over on the far side—I weren't exactly amongst em. And I seed that white man walk up—I knowed there weren't no worry bout him botherin nobody because he looked like a farmin man, and a strange white man to what I ever seed come around. He walked right up to them boys, looked at em and said, "Which one of you fellows is Nate Shaw?"

I was lookin at him. Some of the boys told him, "That's him, right over yonder."

He waded on through the crowd and come up to me. Said, "Nate—is your name Nate?"

I said, "Yes sir, this is Nate Shaw, what's left of him." As I grew older in this world and less than I was when I was sure enough at my best, I'd tell em, "This is Nate Shaw, what's left of him." And every time I'd tell it, I'd remind myself what I used to be.

He said, "Nate, I come down to see the warden and talk with him this mornin about you makin me some baskets and bottom me some chairs. And she told me where I could find you. Maybe you might be around here"—he told me what the warden told him—"if you wasn't around here she couldn't tell me where you was. I'm glad to run up with you."

Told him, "Yes sir."

And he told me everything the warden said. I liked to laugh when he was tellin me all that—he couldn't hold it in—but I hardly cracked a smile. I thought quick: he might think I was feelin *big* that I was allowed the privilege to sell my own baskets. And I didn't want to think that about myself.

He said, "Now I want so-many and so-many baskets and I got so-many and so-many chairs to bottom."

Wasn't many at all; bout two or three baskets and two or three chairs he wanted bottomed. I looked at him, said, "Well, I'll do all that. Did you bring your chairs with you?"

He said, "No, no, I didn't bring nothin. I just come to see if I could get it done."

I said, "Well, if you didn't bring the chairs, you bring em to me when you can. I'll bottom them first, then make your baskets."

He left me and went back, whatever way, I didn't see; I was around there at the blacksmith shop and from there to the barn. And by twelve o'clock—he was livin way up in Coosa County—and before dinner come he had them chairs there at the shop. I bottomed em for him, then I made his baskets. He paid me good money—and I was a prisoner. Charged him a dollar apiece for them baskets and I charged him for them chairs dependin on how long I worked on em.

I enjoyed that money, but in this way: most of it I gave my wife for the support of my family. And I gave her, while they kept

me there at Wetumpka, six to eight dollars and as high as fifteen
dollars a visit. It weren't what I could have gived her if I was free
—the labor of a free man always brings more than the labor of a
prisoner—but what I did give her, it enabled me to think better
of myself. I knowed why I was where I was, I could think clear
through that, but I was lost to my family and they was lost to me.
All the money I could give em couldn't balance that.

III

When TJ and Ben Ramsey from the settlement down in here
went up and got my people away from where they was when I was
arrested, they moved em to the Culpepper place, right in the house
with TJ, piled em up in there with him. All right. When they left
there they come down on the Grace place, Courteney place you
might say. And when they left there they moved out on Warren
Jenks' place, right this side of the crossroads out here. And when
they left there they moved over on the Leeds place out on the
Beaufort road, goin through there by Lavender's bridge. And they
was livin on the Leeds place over yonder when I come free. I didn't
keep no track of just exactly how many years they lived at all these
places but I do know where they went from one place to the other.
And when they was livin on the Jenks place I begin to visit em on
Christmas parole and soon, on weekend parole.

My wife would come to prison and tell me bout every move
they made. Vernon moved my family—he taken over that job from
me. Him and his mother, they would consult each other about it
and make the move. And whatever part of my native family was
still with their mother, they'd move with em.

I had three children grown when I was arrested, their own men
and woman, two boys—I don't count my sister's boy—Calvin and
Vernon, and one girl, Rachel. Calvin was the oldest; Rachel was
well past eighteen years old—girl considered grown at eighteen,
she could walk off and marry if she wanted to. Vernon, the youngest one of them three children, he was just past twenty-one years
old. And he was the boss of all the farmin; I turned it over in his
hands when I was put in jail and looked into the future, seed I was
headin to the penitentiary. Francis was the next boy grown after
Vernon, and Vernon, Francis, Eugene, and Garvan was the four

boys left there with their mother. Garvan was too little to work; Eugene was just big enough to start off.

Calvin Thomas, my oldest boy, he married in a year or less time after they pulled me out of my family. I reckon that he was already engaged to marry when I was arrested; hadn't said a word about it to his mother or father but I could tell in the way he was correspondin a certain girl that he intended to marry her.

And so, I'd come home to the Leeds place on weekend parole —home was where my family was. I'd drop in there on a Saturday, bout the middle of the evenin—I seed they was makin heavy crops, good crops. The government weren't furnishin em no more; they fell back on white people that would help em. Rocked along and eventually Vernon got in business with Mr. Van Kirkland between here and Beanville. He runs a store there at a place they call Tukabahchee City; it aint a city, really, just a crossroads and a shoppin place. Mr. Van Kirkland took Vernon over as far as furnishin; Vernon bore a good recommendation as a workin boy—and his daddy was known to be a workin man.

So, when I'd come home, I'd bring my wife some money off of what I was allowed to make for myself in prison. I'd come home or she'd come to Wetumpka—I had just a little over ten years hung to me when I got to Wetumpka, out of twelve. I come home in '45, and before I come home a free man, I'd come home on visits; and whenever I'd come home I'd put some money in my wife's hands.

She asked me one day, said, "Darlin, where do you get this money to give me when I come to you or when you come home? You aint no gambler and no thief noway and no rogue. Where do you get it?"

I smiled and said, "Be honest with you and tell you. The Lord provides many things but He don't provide money. I'm on my old job, makin baskets and bottomin chairs. I realize you and the children is at home by yourselves. I'm not there to help do nothin. I just have to take your word for what you need and how you gettin along—"

But I could see for myself they weren't sufferin at home for nothin—only for their father, and my wife, her husband. She was worried at all times for me, but I weren't havin no hard way to go —just a matter of bein away from her and the children. That was hard on my mind but prison didn't touch my body. I grew older, that's all, by twelve years. And durin that time, Hannah's health

begin to go bad. She begin to complain bout her health when she'd
come over there to see me and when I'd come home. Just enough
for me to have a doubt that she was well.

HANNAH come to prison one day and told me—she had three
things she'd call me: she'd call me by my natural name sometimes
if she wanted to ask me something, but her usual way of callin me
was "darlin"—she called me "darlin" that day—or "boy." Mighty
seldom she called me Nate. And never called me Shaw. I called
her "gal" or "darlin," I seldom called her Hannah. She was a Ramsey
girl when I married her, Hannah Ramsey. Me and her stayed
husband and wife and would have stayed longer if the Lord hadn't
taken her, forty long years—and that weren't enough for me.

So, she come to me in prison one day, told me, "Darlin, we
lost Dela—"

That was the best mule I had; she weren't no better workin
mule than the other one, but she was more agreeable. She didn't
want you to hit her with the line, she didn't want you to squall at
her. And she was the best quality mule—

Well, I blamed Vernon for that; it aint a woman's job to dic-
tate on stock and outside stuff if there's a man to do it. I sure hated
it but it couldn't be helped. My wife told me—I just dropped my
head and thought over it, soon forgot about it; weren't no use for
me to worry about it. She said, "We lost Dela the other day. Vernon
put her and Mary in the field—" Now that mule had got attached
to that stuff and took a bellyache once before—butterbean vines
and them old butterbean hulls, and they frostbitten too. A mule
will eat em and it'll kill him. A mule don't belch up nothin and
chew it over like a cow. When that mule chews up and swallows,
it's goin out the other end.

So, Vernon put that mule in the pasture—they lost Dela on
the Jenks place. White man since bought the land from Warren
Jenks, turned around and sold it to another set of white people, by
the name of Bailey, Bailey people. One Bailey bought one side of
the road and the other Bailey bought the other side. And this Bailey
that bought the side my people used to live on, he died and left it
in the hands of his wife and two boys. Both of them boys married
out and one of em livin in that house now, the home house, house

that controls the place. So, when my wife and children was livin there, Vernon turned them mules out in the pasture, Mary and Dela; and there was a garden beside of that road at that time, from the house runnin down to the crossroads. And the fence along that road runned around the outgrounds of the pasture to the lot. That garden was separated from the pasture by a less substantious barb wire fence. Them mules of mine was good quality mules but that wouldn't keep em from tryin to get out of a pasture that got a fence around it—take away the fence and maybe they wouldn't want to leave the pasture. And so, Vernon put em in the pasture and that Dela mule, my wife told me, she went around there and she was hard to keep away from that garden regardless to the wire fence. Fooled around and she et them butterbean vines and them old frostbitten butterbean hulls. A butterbean hull has got a point to em and they'll clog a animal. She et all she wanted and it killed her dead as a nail.

VERNON and Eugene, when farm labor would cease down, cut logs for Mr. Jim Pike for several years. And in that, they carried down my '28 Chevrolet car. Drivin to the sawmill and rippin up and down the road huntin gals—Vernon married, Francis married; well, as long as the boys was runnin after their gals on my car, drivin to the sawmill and takin all them long trips to see me— drove that sedan car down. And when they done that, there was a white man come over there and wanted to buy—that motor never did give up, but the upholstery went bad—white man tried to buy that motor. But I told my wife when she come to see me, "No, don't sell the motor out of my car. I might could do somethin with it when I gets home."

She told me the car run until the last, but it got so raggedy and other parts begin to fall out of it and break down.

I said, "Just keep that car. I be home and I might want to make me a wood saw, might hang me a wood saw to that motor."

And when they come to see me after that, they was drivin on a different car—car that Vernon and my wife had bought. And *it* was a Chevrolet. This here car I left em with was a sedan but the one that they come to see me on was just a common two-door car at that. And they owned two different cars before I could come home in the twelve years' time. They had a way to come, always, and nary a car never stopped along the road.

Got to where I begin goin home regular to the Pottstown beat, twice a month on weekends. Good God, what more could it take to satisfy me than that? Miss Phoebe Burnside told me, "Nate, you got a A first class record. You never have gived no trouble here in anybody's remembrance. When you want to go home, you aint got to ask me to let you go. Just tell me *where* you goin and hit the road and get gone."

Well, in my comins home, weekends and Christmas, quite natural, I taken a interest in the farm business. I weren't there regular enough to dominate it, and I looked and I listened at more than I spoke up for. So, I come home one Christmas after Dela died eatin them things, and Vernon had sowed some oats up there in the field. I plowed Mary some, helped him plow them oats. Mary was thin then. But I couldn't exactly fall all the way out with the boys about her condition—I knowed the mule was gettin a little age on her, but I had sense enough to know a mule's age aint goin to make her fall off. But why I kept cool about that mule lookin like she was lookin when I come home that Christmas—she was just a grand rascal, she wouldn't try to take care of herself—I had kept her fat; she weighed a little over eleven hundred pounds once, and she was heavy enough to try and pull things her way with them boys. But she was rippin and a rarin at all times, as scared of a car as I'd be standin naked before a bear and nothin to hit him with. She'd drag you off if a car come along close to her.

Soon after I come back to prison off the Leeds place, Mary died, my poor Mary. That man Watson had told me to give him the mules—told me right there in Beaufort jail—give him the mules because them mules was goin to kill my boys. But my boys done killed my mules, they did, by the way they treated em. If I'd a been at home, that old mule woulda been fat, and that first mule, that Dela mule, she wouldn't a roamed out by no butterbean patch. If I'd a been at home and livin—I'm yet livin, and them mules' bones is somewhere layin on the dead hill white.

WHEN I went off to prison I was a able-bodied man, my wife was a able-bodied woman, and we lost nearly all our nature activity. I taken it pretty hard at the start; but after several years, I begin to

come home on parole, weekends. And that was every other week.
And when I weren't comin home, she was comin to where I was.
And I made a record that they allowed us to get together to do anything we wanted, nobody around us. Not in the cell—had special
outhouses for just such purposes. Right there at Wetumpka, I
stayed there a little over ten long years and durin most of those
years wasn't a time she come to me but what we couldn't—we
could even get out—of course, I never did make it a practice of
carryin my wife out in the woods, but there was places, outhouses.
They weren't no prepared houses for nature affairs but I could
look after that. Every Sunday that I wanted to, I'd take my bed up,
roll up my mattress and carry it to one of them houses. Hannah'd
come visit me, why, we'd have a clean place to go—

With me, and I expect with them other prisoners, it had a
great bearin on my married life. I had my pleasure, my wife had
her pleasure, didn't have to seek our pleasure nowheres else. We
was livin—whenever she come to see me, we had a privilege of actin
like husband and wife. And they allowed others the privilege. But
them that was sentenced up there from the far counties and
their wives couldn't come regular, didn't have the means, they
suffered.

Nature-privilege weren't gived to us, exactly, by the officers
at the prison. These places was available, though, and they wouldn't
try to keep the prisoners out of em. But nothin said, they left it up
to you. Everybody understood what nature was and they didn't try
to buck it. Only, you couldn't mess with them prisoner women;
they bucked that like the devil. But the prisoner women could have
their men folks come in there.

My wife told me many a time after I come out of prison,
"Darlin, I believe that I'd a gived birth to another heir if you hadn't
a been off like you was." And she come close, no doubt, even with
my bein off. But she changed lives while I was gone and it weren't
possible after that.

I've told Josie, this woman I got for a wife now, I've said, "That
is one of the greatest privileges God ever gived, for a man to have
pleasure with a woman and a woman to have pleasure with a
man." You take me today, I done got on them borders, I don't worry
my wife like I done before—I say *worry*, it weren't no worry, but I
just can't handle myself like I could when I was young. And she'll
get to where she'll pass it up, won't worry herself about it.

THERE was nothin under God's sun, as far as earthly things, that suited me better in this world than gettin back to my wife. I was scared many a day that I was goin to hear talk of her bein serious sick someway and I knowed that woulda tore me all to pieces. I'd been away from home so long—I kept my wife and children on my mind at all times, practically. And my wife was comin to me and I could see that her health was leavin her for some cause, I didn't know.

And I was givin her so much money right along. She said, "I'm goin to save some of this money so you'll have some"—she'd a done it too—"when you come home."

I said, "I aint givin you this money to lay up and save for me. It troubles me how you all are gettin along. I'm givin you this money for the every day."

She said, "Well, there's one thing, darlin, I want you to do. Don't let the children know that you're givin me money. I don't want em to know it. Them two youngest children in the house, Garvan and Louise, if they knowed you was givin me money, I couldn't keep a nickel."

I told her, "Well, I aint goin to tell em."

Now I didn't feel at all like she meant any harm by not lettin the children know it—but there was a hereafter that could arise. I was watchin her health then and the matter struck my mind that she might just set down and die right at once, the way she was complainin. Told me she felt weak and tired most of the time. She'd never been sickly but now she was goin to the doctor a whole lot. But the doctor never did tell her what was wrong with her. Don't know as he knowed what it was until it matured.

The thought come to me like this: if she would happen to drop off and die—now I was livin under the impression that I just didn't know how it would go, but I didn't have much confidence after she started to complain that she would live too long. And if she happened to die or anything serious would happen that she couldn't speak up for me—you mustn't take chances like that. So, at that particular time I studied over the matter. I had care and respect for my wife, doin all I could for her and obeyin her to a point. Thought come to me: 'Well, you givin her money a little enough to help her. Supposin she was to die and you off over here in prison? You go bustin home quick as you can and get to tellin these children what you'd been doin—the death of her causes you to explain these things, what you done as a benefit to her, bein your wife and a mother to your children. Some of em might just jump up and tell you, "Well, Papa, we didn't know nothin about it; Mama didn't say you was givin her nothin," and might consider the thing to be a lie, that you just runnin up sayin that because you stand condemned at the death of her because you never gived her nothin while she lived.' It was revealed to me, one way or the other, I was goin to miss my wife.

You don't know nobody's heart; you just know your own heart and that's all. But the main point was, I wanted my children to know what I was doin. So I come home one Tuesday in the week—how come I come home on a Tuesday? Captain Oliver Cook was goin to Beaufort to pick up some of the warden's furniture that she'd put up there when she come out from her home to the prison department. Miss Phoebe Burnside, the warden I went free from under—she was born and raised up there at a little place between Wetumpka and Clanton on out toward Birmingham on the Birmingham road, called Marbury. But she'd lived last at Beaufort before she taken the job as warden at Wetumpka prison. Truck driver was goin to carry the boss man up there and he was goin to tote her furnitures back to Wetumpka. Boss man come to me and said, "Nate, do you want to go home tomorrow?" He quickly told me what they was goin through there for. Said, "If you want to, you'll get a chance to spend awhile with your people."

So the next mornin, I got on that state truck and got off at Beanville where the road we was on met the road goin up to my folks; and kept them on a straight route toward Beaufort. And I'd made a nice basket for the boy that run off to Tuskegee, Calvin; he'd come home every once in a while and let em know how he was. And I made him a nice basket and brought it home that Tuesday mornin when I dropped in unexpected to em. Got there directly after they et breakfast, walked in the yard, stood there a few minutes talkin with my wife and the little children, Louise and Garvan. I asked my wife, "What's become of Eugene?"

She said, "He gone down there to Vernon's."

Vernon lived right below, in callin distance, him and his wife. He'd rented a place convenient close around his mother. Well, I'd had breakfast before daylight at Wetumpka and I decided I'd just

go down to Vernon's too, spend a little time there. I looked at my
wife close—and I walked on down there amongst my boys with all
these studies on my mind about her condition. My mind kept tellin
me to tell my big boys about the situation and what I was givin
their mother. I didn't tell nobody what I thought—but a heap of
things that you take in when somethin strikes you, it's not a fact
yet, it's only a impression, maybe trouble in it and it's a warnin.
And I was well warned of her death. It dwelled in me.

So, Vernon and Eugene was in the back yard at Vernon's place,
close by the woodpile when I first seed em. I come through the
house and spoke to Vernon's wife and his two little girls. Then I
went right on out to where my boys was. I howdyed with em and I
said, "Boys, I got a secret to tell you—" I didn't want no mistakes
and no lies, I didn't want no disbelievin. Vernon and Eugene was
grown at that time. Vernon was good and grown; he come of age
in '32, on the thirtieth day of May.

I said, "Boys, now don't worry your mama about this and don't
let her know that I told you. What I got to tell you—up until this
mornin, I have given your mother a hundred and fifty cash dollars
since I been at Wetumpka. And I expect to give her money as long
as I'm in prison—" Vernon didn't say a word from the beginnin to
the last, he just stood there listenin. I said, "Up until this mornin
I have given her a hundred and fifty cash dollars right out of my
pocket above buyin things over there at Wetumpka and totin em
home to her. And I want you all to know it, you all are grown boys.
But Garvan and Louise, they are underage chaps and they might
not let your mother keep a nickel of it if they knew. Now I don't
want you to confuse her bout how she spends her money or where
she gets it. And don't scold her for throwin money away—she
aint. That's money I gived her to help you all along if necessary
and help herself."

Eugene spoke. He said, "Papa, I been thinkin somethin; now
I know it. I been wonderin—sometimes Mama gets in a tight for
money and she asks me or Vernon, whichever she wants, she asks
us if we got any. And we say, 'We'll let you have it any time.' And
we watch—I have, I have watched definitely and when the time
comes that she promised to pay this money back to us, we know for
certain the money she gives us aint the money we let her have. And
in that, I got to watchin and wantin to learn how did she get any

money to pay back what she got from us. I wondered how that was, and she aint able to work and don't work to get it."

I said, "Yes, son, that's where she's gettin her money—" outside of what the organization was sendin her. I said, "I know you two boys won't try and get it from her just because you know I'm givin it to her and you know she's got it."

Vernon aint parted his lips; he aint parted his lips.

I got my word in then and I was satisfied. I went back to Beanville that evenin to meet the state truck. Boss man told me to meet him there about four o'clock—I aint seed that prison truck this mornin. I didn't know what the trouble was; I just went on back home. I told Eugene, "Well, I don't know what's the matter with that truck I come here on. My time is out. I went over to Beanville and waited before the hour come and until a long time after, and I aint seed em. Son, there's been a change in plans. I want you to carry me back—"

He took me on the car and carried me to Wetumpka safe and sound and I got off. Night come, I went to sleep. Next mornin, I went out and found the boss man at home, Captain Oliver Cook. He said, "I'll tell you Nate, we had some trouble with the truck and got belated. And when we got back, we heard that you done been here and reported in. I'm happy for your sake that you done that, Nate, I'm happy for you."

Mr. Cook went for a Christian-hearted man. He *had* to be happy for me.

I said, "Well, sir, my sentence is nearly up, twelve long years, and I'll be goin home a free man, thoroughly free. That's the day I'm lookin to. Yesterday don't count with me; today don't count, in a way of speakin. So, yes sir, I come back here when I was supposed to regardless to what avoided you from gettin back. I depends on myself to act just suchaway."

FRANCIS left for Philadelphia just before I got out of prison. That was the first boy I had to leave this southern country, and it didn't surprise me that his mind were so inclined. He always was a curious child—he weren't meddlesome, he just would stay at a thing until he learnt all there was to it and he weren't afraid about what he didn't know.

He come to see me one Sunday and he brought his mother with him. He told me, "Papa, I thought I'd come to see you here in prison before I left this country. I'm leavin in a few days, though when I'm gone I'm comin back along. Maybe at that time you'd have done served all your time and I'll find you livin back home with Mama."

And he offered me some money. I told him, "There aint no use in you givin me no money, son. I appreciate it, I appreciate your offer. But you goin to the northern states and I feel your sympathy as a father. Someway I'll stay in touch with you. You leavin your mother well, and I'll hear from you if you live. And I hope you'll get along good in your travels. There aint no use for you to give me no money. I'm makin a little money nearly every day I stay here in prison."

My wife said this: she set there and looked at Francis and looked at me, said, "Darlin, why don't you take the money? He wants you to have it—it'll make him feel better about leavin."

I didn't want to take it. He were fixin to travel and I told him, "Son, I don't want your money. And I don't mean to show you disrespect by not takin it. But your money don't tickle me. You been a good son to your daddy and a good son to your mother; that's all that washes with me. Take your money and spend it on your travels; that will suit me better than to give it to me."

Told me, "Papa, I'm leavin—" Him and his wife had separated —married while I was in the penitentiary, separated while I was in the penitentiary. Had five children when they separated; him and his wife stayed together until they had two girls and three boys, and the oldest boy is named after me, Nate Shaw. He's in the north and all of his brothers is in the north, and one of the girls stays in Atlanta.

Francis had got his wife in a family way before he married her, then he didn't want her—and if he done it, he aint the only one ever done it. My wife told me, she come to prison one Sunday, said, "Francis is married. This girl he married, her mother insisted on him to marry her."

I knowed the girl's parents—Junius Gresham, Cora Gresham. Junius was quiet, he didn't have much to say, he weren't a fussy man. And this boy of mine, my wife told me, this gal he was goin to see of Gresham's was goin to be confined and it was Francis's baby. And the old lady begin to chew the bit about it. Francis looked like he was sort of flackin off from the girl. And my wife tellin him all the time, "Go ahead and marry Amelia, go ahead and marry Amelia." Went on and married her. But he had it in him someway that he didn't want Amelia, he wanted a girl by the name of Irene. And that's the girl he got now—went on and married again. Been married twice—Amelia, that's his first wife, stayed with her long enough to have five children. Then they separated and he married again. He kept fishin back here until he got this other woman that he was goin with before he married Amelia. She jumped up to Philadelphia one year—it weren't long after he left here, neither—and he married her.

Once, when I was comin home from prison on weekend parole, I caught the bus in Wetumpka, as usual, and I noticed, on the route home, the bus stopped over there at Two Forks and picked up Amelia. We howdyed and shook hands and she "Papa Nate this" and "Papa Nate that" and "Papa Nate the other"—and they was separated then. And from that day till this, Amelia aint told me how come Francis and her parted, and Francis aint told me.

ONE year I come home on Christmas parole, fully intendin to go into the church, be baptized. I'd become in the knowledge of Jesus in Beaufort jail—God spoke to my dyin soul and been standin there ever since, standin right there in that gap ever since. God spoke to me and *redeemed* my soul—surely that helped me through prison.

The Bible tells you, you got to take on the full arm of faith— that's the reason for baptizin. So I gived myself in to the church, Pottstown Baptist Church, where my wife and what children was home at that time belonged. And the preacher accepted me. When I got there that day, some of the head ones, deacons, already knowed that I wanted to join—my wife had told em what I was comin home especially for. Got ready to testify and the preacher come down amongst the congregation and talked with me. Everything seemed plumb agreeable and satisfactory.

I stood up before em and gived em my testimony, told em all about what taken place with me and how it taken place. And I told it with a earnest heart: "I was prosperin along in this world very well. But I was just like a hog goin from one tree to another, eatin the acorns off the ground and never lookin up to see where

was they fallin from. Then I fell"—they knowed all that *about* me
but they didn't know what it *meant* to me—"and I hit the bottom
in Beaufort jail. That's where Jesus answered my lonely calls and
parted me from my sins. The Bible says you must lay off your
mortal ways and put on immortality—accept of God in your soul
and live it. I won't tell a lie on God—He freed me from my sins.
He put the finishin touch on me. I am a true born child by the
blood of the Lord and Savior Jesus Christ. I aint goin to let you
catch me drinkin; I aint goin to let you catch me gamblin; I aint
goin to let you catch me walkin the road and tellin lies, runnin
after women worse than a hog'll run at a pot of slops. O, you can
enjoy yourself; it's not a wrong thing to do, but carry it on in a
decent way. If you are a man, God put you here to love woman.
Your mother was a woman, my mother was a woman—and He put
woman here to love man; He did. He put you here, He put man and
woman here on this earth to create and enjoy one another. If God
hadn't intended that He wouldn't a put us here so close together.
But He didn't put you here to run after every woman you see, or
woman, after every man. Let us act like a nation of people should
act."

   Preacher said to me, "Brother Shaw"—after he got my testimony—"I'll recognize you and take you in as a member of Pottstown
Baptist Church." Then he opened up to the congregation—the house
was full that day—"Brother Shaw, I'll baptize you accordin to your
convictions. But Church, you all know this aint no time for baptizin"—that was in December, just before Christmas—"you all
know it."

   Didn't nobody "amen" him at all. I wanted to be baptized then
and there and they thought I should be too. They wouldn't "amen"
him, wouldn't say, "that's right" or nothin. I seed I couldn't put in no
plea; he done put it before the body of the church. And when they
wouldn't agree with him, he took it in his own hands and refused me.
Well, that brought on a commotion but it didn't move him.

   So I went on back to prison without bein baptized, thinkin to
myself, 'What kind of church is it that won't baptize a man when he's
ready to be baptized?' It was left between God and me when I come
up defeated at church. I lingered there at Wetumpka a year, un-
satisfied. First openin I got was the next Christmas, just several
months before I come home free. That time I was baptized. The
church, some way or other, had done got shed of this man and called

em another preacher. I just walked in, I did, and gived in to him. He accepted my membership and he told me, "Well, Brother Shaw, I'll baptize you—" and set the day before he quit talkin. And that was just before thc day come for me to go back to prison.

We met over there at Teaks' Church, Methodist church— weren't no way to baptize a person up there at Pottstown. They always went down to the little creek to baptize, right below Teaks'. Little old bridge crosses that creek goin towards Calusa. Right there I was baptized. I felt so good—last of December—cold—the deacons led me down in the water and I stepped in up to my waist. I was wearin a blue-colored robe over my Sunday clothes—a good pair of pants, good shoes. The deacons led me down to the preacher, who was waitin on me in the water. He took my hand and led me down the rest of the way. And he baptized me. Caught me by the back of my head with one hand, and his other hand on my breast, he laid me back down in the water and pushed me under. Then he spoke over me.

That's the way the Missionary Baptists baptizes you. Now you take a certain denomination of these Methodist folks, they sprinkle the top of your head. Well, my wife and children belonged to the Pottstown Baptist Church and that's just exactly where I went and wanted to go and the way I wanted to be baptized.

When the preacher pulled me up out of the water, the deacons was there to catch my hands and lead me up. I felt, when I hit the air—and it was early winter when I stepped up out of that water —I felt just like somebody done poured a kettle of warm water over me. I weren't cold a bit. And I commenced a shakin hands all around and laughin and goin mad for joy.

REVELATION

I T was April and the land was all broke but the boys wasn't quite through plantin. They had all of twenty acres—a two-horse farm, maybe a little more for two horses to plow. The field close to the house had about ten acres in cotton, then about five acres in the far field from the house, which totaled about fifteen acres in cotton. And the balance of the land in corn—had good corn, a big corn crop. Raised that corn to feed the stock. My wife had a big iron-gray mare; she'd a weighed around eleven hundred pounds and she had a colt. And the two young boys, Garvan and Eugene, had a mule apiece. One of em had a little old horse mule and the other one had a mare mule. I plowed Garvan's mule, that mare mule, and he plowed Eugene's mule and Eugene plowed that big mare—first year. And the land we plowed belonged to Mr. Leeds; it went by the name of the Leeds place.

I come out of prison in April '45. They gave me several dollars when they turned me out of there, but they didn't give me as much as thirty dollars. And they gave me a suit of clothes—it weren't nothin that I would ever buy for myself, just somethin that looked a little better than a pair of overalls. I stayed there long enough to wear out a heap of clothes—

And I toted a Elgin watch every day I lived through prison. High-priced watch, as good a grade of watch as was made in them days; bought that watch in Proctor's Druggery in Apafalya, way back when I was haulin lumber for the Graham-Pike Lumber Company. And I toted it in my overall bosom—had a long cheap chain, I gived five dollars for the chain that was slung to it. And Sundays, I'd keep it in my pants pocket. And I toted that watch—and the droppin it, and gettin it wet and breakin the crystal off it—twenty-seven long years. And eventually, the last time I dropped it, I unbalanced the jewels in it and that finished it with me. Still, I'd wind it up and listen at it and it'd go to tickin; them wheels was tilted, tryin their best to run, but they give out.

A white man at Wetumpka seed me windin that watch and tried his best to buy it from me. Told me, "Somebody goin to steal that watch." I said, "Well, if they steal it, I'll be lookin at em." And I thought to myself, 'If you want a watch like this one, you is better able to buy it than I was.' And I told him, "If I take a notion to get shed of it, I'll let you have it."

I went all through prison and I never had but one dollar stole from me. When they payin you fifteen cents a day, a dollar is a lot of money. But I could sell a basket for a dollar, so it weren't no more than a day of my labor. That's all the money was stole from me—not countin the years of my life I gived to the state of Alabama; they was stole from me, in a way of speakin. But them prisoners was busy lookin after all their fifteen cents; couldn't do nothin bout the years.

I served my sentence out, didn't owe the state another day of my life. I had warned Vernon and his mother what day to come at me, and they come and got me. That mornin I prepared for em, gettin all my prison duties cleared off of me. Along about twelve o'clock I wound up my last work there and I got busy takin a bath. I went to my cell where I'd stayed every night and rounded up all my clothes —seein that I had everything of mine I was goin to take with me. I pulled out my locker box from under my bed—I had a passable Sunday suit in there, slippers, socks, hat, a summer change of underwear, my watch—

They was in there by one o'clock, not later than one thirty. Soon as Vernon and my wife drove up, they passed Captain Oliver Cook's wife on the veranda of the administration buildin. Hannah got out of the car and stayed back talkin with her and Vernon come on to get me. Weren't nobody in that cellhouse but me; the rest of em was in the field. I was in the room yet bathin when I heard Vernon come up the steps of that buildin—I knowed his footsteps, I didn't have to look and see it was him, I could hear him. He pushed the door open and I looked in his face. "Papa," he said, "Papa, it's time—"

Quickly got ready; and my wife, when I walked out, she was settin there talkin with Mrs. Cook. Got in the car—them prisoner boys hated to see me leave, they hated it. Some of em called me "daddy," *their* daddy. There was a heap of em in there that never knowed their fathers; heap of em that never knowed their mothers.

Went home just as straight as a bee could go. Vernon didn't stop drivin until we landed on the Leeds place over yonder. Vernon weren't livin there at that time, he had moved out. He knowed I was comin home and him and his wife and their two little girls found a place for themselves. He had married a half-white woman who was born and raised in here below Apafalya. Her mother was darker than I am and I never did learn who was her father. She went in the name of her mother's people, they raised her. She was a Sherman, Millie Sherman. And she's got a brother just the same color she is. Then she's got two brothers just a little darker, on the colored side of the color. She's a quiet woman, always has been far as I knowed of her, since Vernon married her.

Vernon weren't in the house with his mother but he was the head man of the family while they was livin on the Leeds place. He had rented it from Mr. Leeds. And when I come home, Eugene was in there and he was married. And Garvan was there, the baby boy, and he soon married after I arrived. And Rosa Louise was the baby of all, she was there, all except bein off at school at Tuskegee. Them three children was in the house with their mother. Vernon had moved out and left Eugene there and Garvan; Garvan was big enough and old enough to plow and he was plowin.

Calvin, oldest child in the crowd, he was livin over close to Tuskegee in the Little Texas beat. That was a colored section, strictly, and he was makin out pretty well, farmin at the time. Rachel, my next child, was married and out. She'd married Ralph Jenks, son of Warren Jenks, and they was gettin along so bad I had some of the white people in the settlement advise me to put the law on him. Mattie Jane, my second girl, she married Thomas

Galloway; he was a good fellow, farmin man, and they was livin close by in the settlement. Leah Ann, my third girl, she was married to Justin Ames and livin in Chattanooga. She was the first girl in the family to leave the state of Alabama; and she left here about the same time Francis left for Philadelphia. She was underage when she married and just about grown when she left. Justin Ames runs a crane at the iron factory, that's his job, been workin there for years. He's got a little lot there in Chattanooga, paid for, and him and Leah Ann aint got nary a child in the world and aint never had one.

I went on to the balance of my family and fell in there. But all the best stuff I had had was gone. I figured when they put me in the penitentiary that my big pair of mules would be sufficient to take care of all the business—all the work they could do. They kept em through trouble and tribulations and they just managed, when they'd lose one, to buy another. When Dela died, they bought a mule from some of the Wilcox people, a gray mule, somethin I never did own, a gray mule. They worked him awhile and I don't know whether they swapped him off or sold him, but I don't think that mule died. And the next news, they bought a mare, a horse, but she didn't want to work. So they got shed of her and went and bought a great big iron-gray mare. The boys was gettin nearly grown and they kept a buyin —when I got home, Vernon had a pair of mules of his own. And they bought two more little old mules, rabbit mules big enough to plow. That made three mules and two horses they bought for family use and two mules reserved for Vernon. Nary one of them family horses would work to a two-horse wagon. And that first horse they bought wouldn't do no sort of work. When I fell in there, them younger boys had a mule apiece; bought em from a white man by the name of Lovett. And my wife had that big iron-gray mare—that mare woulda weighed twelve hundred pounds, she was a big one. Her feet, had the biggest feet—she was as good a plow horse as any animal ever I plowed, as good as my mules.

My wife turned the mare over to me—that was mine. Didn't none of the boys object and I don't reckon she would have gived me the mare like she done if it weren't her'n to give. That was all I had then when I come back home. Them boys was scared to hitch her to the wagon, two-horse wagon. I told em, "She's a big heavy mare and I can see you all is shy of her. If I stay here, she goin to work to that wagon. I'm goin to put her where I want her and she goin to work there."

So I hitched her to the wagon—Vernon helped me hitch her up—and she worked around pretty well, but she tried to run. I held her back like a stockmaster should and she soon ceased down enough to make a good farm animal.

EUGENE and Garvan had everything cut and planned and goin on when I got there. They had the biggest part of the crop planted, of cotton. And I helped em plant about five acres more of cotton and about five or six acres of corn. Vernon done stepped out to clear the way for me to come in and had his business all to hisself. That gived me a openin and I just went in there under my boys' rulins. And we all worked through then.

All right. It was very little that boy cleared that year—Eugene. Cotton weren't bringin over twenty-five cents, but he did make enough to pay off all his debts. He was dealin—him and Vernon both was dealin at that time with Mr. Van Kirkland, here at Tukabahchee City. And after the crop was made in '45, Eugene divided up what was cleared between us—him and Garvan and me and their mother.

Next crop, in '46, when Eugene got that crop gathered and off his hands, paid all his debts and divided what little was left between us, we didn't get twenty-five dollars apiece. But I just accepted it. When Eugene got that crop put over, he farmed no more. And he quit clear—paid all his expenses off of that cotton and we gathered the corn—had a nice lot of corn, too. He just moved on away after that, out of the house, him and his wife. They didn't move far; in fact, somewhere in the settlement, and he stayed awhile. Then he moved off closer to Sitimachas Creek and while he was livin there he worked some at Calusa and some in the fields for other people. But he was just bidin his time. Weren't no more farmin in his future, he told me. And the next year—we was still on the Leeds place—he quit workin in the field complete, for nobody. He bundled up and left this country, went to Ohio. And when he left, before he left, I tried to get him to come over with me even just to plant some corn to go to meal, to support his family while he was public workin. So he helped me plant a few acres but he wouldn't even watch it grow. He left his half of the corn in the field and went off freely.

He had told me to sell his mule. Said he didn't have nowhere to put the mule, livin around the country like he was in rented houses. And before he left I sold his mule and gived him the money. It was a little mule and stock was cheap. Sold it to a white gentleman by the name of Horace Kinney, for sixty dollars. Eugene took the money with a smile. It seemed like he wanted to get out of farmin pretty bad, but I never did dispute him on that.

Now Garvan, he stuck right in there. His mother had gived him her mare's colt and he had that little old mule to make a team. He took a notion he didn't want that mule, little Lovett mule, and he sold it and went and bought him a good heavy mule—she'd a weighed eleven hundred pounds. Put that money from the little mule into the big mule and paid the difference in cash—a hundred and fifty dollars. And he plowed that mule one year, '47, and the boll weevil et his cotton crop up. He had a nice patch of cotton, too, accordin to the weed and how he cleaned out his rows; that cotton ought to have made him at least six bales. The boll weevil didn't leave him but a little over a bale. He just quit complete and throwed up his hands. Told me, "Papa, I aint goin to plow no more. I'm breakin up farmin. I'm goin to Calusa and get me a job and I'm goin to follow it. I aint plantin no more cotton, no more corn—not a thing that grows in the earth. So I won't be needin my mule. Can you handle her, Papa? Would she be any advantage to you?"

I said, "Why, sure she would, son. If that big mule of your'n gets gone, that'd stop my two-horse wagon. I'll keep that mule here if you want me to keep her and I'll have somethin to hitch with that big mare, and haul when I want to haul."

He said, "Well, you can keep her then. I know you'll take care of her."

And he quit. He stayed right on in the house with me and his mother but he didn't have no part of no crop and he hardly never looked to the field.

I took that big mule and worked her, 1948. And I hired a boy to help me, named Jules Gresham. Well, Jules—I offered to hire him and he hired hisself to me. Through work time he stayed there in the house with us, but he didn't give satisfaction.

Well, before he come to take a hold of the job, Garvan had a bicycle there and Jules wanted it. And Garvan wanted nine dollars for the bicycle and Jules wanted me to pay Garvan for it. I went ahead and paid Garvan and Jules got the bicycle and carried it right on home. He was livin at his grandma's, old lady Nancy Gresham.

I kept right up with the boy; I told him, "Now Jules, I done bought that bicycle for you. Don't get too deep before your time comes to start work—" We agreed that I was goin to give him thirty-five dollars a month. Well, the little rascal fooled around and he weren't no account. I repented the day I hired him. And when he come to go to work, he had done got a little more from me on his first month's pay. I had to stick right by him and talk to him; told him, "If I give you any more, you'd be done took up a month's labor here and aint started to work."

I put him to plowin Garvan's mule and I plowed the big gray mare that my wife had turned over to me—Lord, I talk and study, that was quite a difference to what I was before I went to the penitentiary. I had mules and anything else I wanted, all in the name of mine. They used them stock and used em till they used em clean out, and as dandy a pair of farm mules as there was in the whole country. Good mules—but I had to come down from that. Still, I worked in a way to hold a level head and had trouble doin it—

So, he sidled around there and he tried out that mule and the mule cooperated, and just as pretty and fat—I kept that mule in good shape. But sometimes I'd see Jules actin ill with the mule. I'd say, "Jules, don't hurry that mule. If you just follow, she'll do a day's work, you'd be done a day's work if you follow."

Well, plowin cotton, I checked Jules' plowin. And one day, I was plowin right with him and I seed he was frettin that mule and she was yelpin and the plow jumped out of the ground and he just slid that plow on top, makin a scratch to the end of the row. Weren't no plowin in that, that plow just plowin the air. I got at him about it and he never would give me back words because he knowed he was wrong. I told him, "I don't want you to hurry, just want you to plow by the mule's time. She knows; give her a chance. She'll plow enough. All you got to do is follow."

So one day, we was plowin in the field together again. Left the end of our rows at the same time, goin to the far end. And that was a long way distant. And there was goin to be one more row to plow when we got back to the startin place. I turned around at the end of my row and started back. Jules weren't keepin up with me. I knowed that mule he was plowin would walk as fast as that mare.

So I stopped the mare and looked back to see what the mule was doin and what the reason was he wasn't keepin up with me. And Jules had done stopped that mule and he standin up between the plow handles. I just stood there and looked at him, stood there and looked at him. After awhile, I seed him peep around that mule to see what I was doin. He just standin there to give me time to catch that extra row when I got to the end. I said, "Jules, drive that mule on to the end, plow on to the end. I know what you stopped and watchin for. You want me to turn back on that row, last row, and plow while you stand up. Plow that mule on till you get to the end!"

He come on to the end then; looked like a sheep killin dog, head down. I said, "Jules, what sort of way you tryin to do me? You standin up peepin at me to get to the end way ahead of you so I'd plow the last row. Well, I'm goin to plow the last row, I'm goin to plow it. You carry that mule and plow to the barn; take that mule out, put her in the lot, and get your hoe and go to hoein the potato patch."

I turned and went on and plowed the last row and when I got to the end he had finished his row and gone. I just drove right straight through to the house. And Jules hadn't got in the tater patch; made out like he'd forgot what I told him. I said, "Jules, you just shoddin off now. I don't know what I'm goin to do with you; I know what it looks like I'm goin to have to do."

I got me a hoe and went on to the tater patch, went to hoein potatoes. Next plowin we had to do was gettin up right in the week commencement come off at Tuskegee. Jules didn't say a word to me bout wantin to go to commencement till we brought the stock out and put em in the lot. He told me that mornin, "Mr. Nate, I never told you nothin bout I goes to commencement every year."

I didn't want to sit down on the boy; I didn't want to dog him. He said, "I want some money, please. I hadn't said nothin to you before; I'd just forgot to and let it go."

I said, "Well, Jules, you oughta told me about all that and you wantin to be off. Now we need to be in the field regular every day." The boy looked pity-mouthed at the ground. I said, "But you can go ahead to commencement."

He said, "I want some money, too."

I looked at him, said, "How much money you want? You done got way above your wages already."

"I want eight dollars."

I said, "Good God, Jules, that's too much money for you to fool and frolic out in a day's time down there. You shoulda told me about it before now and maybe it'd been better on you. But like I'm runnin it with you, you just gettin in debt."

He dropped his head again. I just runned my hand in my pocket —Mr. Van Kirkland was furnishin me money and it weren't takin all he was givin me just for groceries; when I dropped back home I commenced a raisin my meat and lard again, and vegetables. Didn't have to live out of a store like I do now—I runned my hand in my pocket and I gived him eight dollars. I said, "Jules"—the grass was gettin rampant in the field—"Now I'm lookin for you in the mornin. You aint got to break your neck and get here before sunup or nothin, but I'm lookin for you to be here and eat your breakfast at field time."

"Yes, Mr. Nate, I'll be here, I'll be here."

Well, the next day dinner, twelve o'clock come, Jules aint showed up. Me and Rosa Louise, my baby daughter, was in the field choppin cotton and we took out of the field and went to the house, et dinner, and just as quick as I could get back in the field, I was back. I excused myself and went on out to the field and went to work; didn't say nothin to the girl bout hurryin, let her stay on at the house. Every once in a while I'd look over by the house to see was there anybody around there looked like Jules. I aint heard no Jules and I aint seed no Jules and it was evenin and I was out in the field at work— Well, I kept a lookin, kept a lookin, listenin. And way about the middle of the evenin I heard somebody gwin down the road by my house laughin and talkin. I straightened up and looked hard; come to find out it was Jules. And he was with another boy, I don't know what boy it was. And they was laughin and jollyin, kickin up the dirt in the road—never stopped. And he got right even with me—I stood and looked at him good, didn't say nothin. He looked in the field and seed me—"I'll be in soon in the mornin."

I done told him when I let him have that eight dollars I wanted him there that next mornin. He frolicked all that day. Told me he'd be there soon in the mornin. Well, he come in, and it was late in the day before he got there—lost two man days in the field. He made a plea for his job and I took him back.

So, one day we was in the field plowin corn. In that far field second field, we had corn planted there. And Jules was lettin that mule—she was a good plow mule, she'd mind you and smooth steppin; we was wrappin that corn up, last plowin and he lettin that mule walk right down in the single-tree and that mule single-tree rubbin against that corn, bumpin it, breakin it down. Jules aint sayin a word, just goin right on. I got at him about that. Allowed he couldn't help it. I said, "How come you don't talk to the mule and keep her away from scrubbin and layin right up against that corn row, and just breakin my corn down, goin and comin?"

So I got shed of Jules before he could work off what he owed me. He cost me more when he did work than me just payin him for not workin. And he was old enough to do anything a man could do bout plowin, eighteen or twenty years old.

SINCE I come out of prison, I had a white gentleman or two and their wives, would work in the field for me. White folks around here didn't like that. I had two white ladies to pick cotton—I didn't hunt em up, they come to me. Hired a white lady to pick cotton in the fall of the year I let Jules Gresham go. And after a while another white lady joined in. That made two white ladies and one of them white ladies had a grown daughter and she picked cotton too, they all picked together. I tried my best to treat em nice and no smartness out of me. Paid em a good wage, too. And when the crop wound up that fall, one of these white ladies wanted a gallon of good ribbon cane syrup. I let her have it on credit, didn't take nary a penny for it when I gived it to her. She said if she didn't pay me before I planted my next crop she'd chop cotton for me.

And so, when I got ready to chop cotton that next year, she hadn't paid me—she didn't promise definitely to pay cash. And I went to notify her at her home—her and her husband had separated and she was livin on another white man's place. Well, I went over there one mornin to see her and talk with her and get her to help me chop a little cotton. My cotton needed choppin mighty bad—

When I got there that mornin I learnt the score. They hadn't got up. This white man that owned the house that this white lady was livin in—their houses set close together in the same big yard. He had done moved out of the house he rented to her and built him a nicer house and her and her daughter was livin in that old house.

I went out there that mornin and called her several times; couldn't get no answer. Well, I thought to myself: it just wasn't allowed for a man of my race to mess with a white girl or white woman, and I must consider what would happen if somebody told somethin on me—just like playin with the screws on my coffin.

⸱   I looked out there and I seed that white gentleman that owned the place. My mind told me: don't you fool around here too long. Go out there and let him know what you're here for. So I went over and called his attention and I asked him where was the white lady that lived in his other house. I told him I tried to call her and I couldn't get no answer at all—never told him how come I wanted to talk to her. I left her house because I didn't want to be accused of nothin—didn't tell him that neither—weren't nobody there but women folks, white women, and I was a colored man. I was a old colored man at that time, but still I was colored.

He told me, "O, they in there, they asleep in bed but they in there. They'll be out directly."

Well, I stayed on there and talked with him and after a while he looked around and said, "There she is now, comin out the door."

So I walked over there and talked with the white lady out in the open yard. And she told me she was sick, she weren't able to do nothin and she just had the whole load to pull bout supportin herself and her daughter, and right now she's sick and been sick for several days and weren't able to chop no cotton.

I told her, "Yes ma'am, that's all right."

She said, "And I can't get nobody to plow my little patches round here. They sufferin for plowin and there's nobody to plow."

I told her, "Yes ma'am, it's a bad fix you're in."

She said, "I got a husband but he don't do nothin for me."

I said, "Missus, I'm sorry for you."

She said, "No, he don't help me a bit."

They was separated—I'd found that out. I said, "Well, ma'am, I have to go back home. My work is waitin for me and it won't get done without me."

I left her standin in the yard and I haven't laid eyes on the price of that gallon of syrup today. I never did go back there askin for it. Because if I'd a kept a runnin over there, no way of knowin what'd been told on me. A colored man got to be scared to hang around a white lady's house thataway. It's dangerous as the devil.

GARVAN stuck in Calusa good and heavy. The fall of '48 he come to me, said, "Papa, would you be interested in buyin that mule? I aint never goin to need her no more. You can have her if you want her."

He was a young man at that time; he wasn't married but he was fixin to marry. And had quit farmin.

I said, "Yes, I'll buy her."

He said, "Bein it's you, Papa, you can have her for eighty dollars."

I said, "No I can't, neither. I aint goin to buy her for no eighty dollars."

He said, "Well, you can have her for that."

I said, "You know what that mule cost. You worked her one year. And I done worked her one year, free of charge. Now you want me to take her and pay you eighty dollars for her, you willin to let me. I can't do that; that's beatin you too much, boy, by your own figures. I'll buy your mule but not at that price. One hundred dollars is as little as I'll pay you. I know what you paid—me and Vernon went with you when you bought her from Mr. Fred Heap, and she's a nice mule."

She was fat when I got her, kept her fat the year I used her, and when he went to sell her to me he wanted eighty dollars!

I said, "You workin at Calusa and you say you aint goin to farm no more. If you ever farm, by your words to me, it'll be more than you aimin to do. I'll give you a cash hundred dollars for that mule and nothin less."

He said, "No, Papa, you aint got to give me that much."

I said, "Well, you fixin to marry and you need money to start off with. Tell you what I'll do. You want your money now?"

Said, "No, I don't want it now, but just before I marry I'll want it."

I said, "Well, you just go ahead and see me later. When you ready the money will be here."

He went on to Calusa and kept a workin, kept a workin, and the money was layin there, I had it in the house. And he come in one night, home—next mornin he'd have to go back to his job. I said, "Well, boy, let me tell you somethin. Business is business. If I'm goin to buy that mule from you I'm goin to pay you tonight and then let you do what you please with the money and I'll take the mule over in full; she'll be mine."

I runned my hand in my pocket and pulled out my pocketbook, gived him a cash hundred dollars. That cut him clean loose, no papers and nothin more needed on it. He aint never planted a crop since.

RACHEL was livin with Ralph Jenks just about three quarters of a mile west of my place on land that his daddy had gived him when he married her. And he didn't have no care and respect a bit more than a dog for that girl. He just had sense enough to want to marry her and that was all, that was all. The tricks that he done after becomin a husband to my daughter is too bad to discuss. He knowed how to get children by her but that was the biggest thing he seemed to know. He kept up so much devilment, acted sorry in every dealin he was supposed to put over as a man's duty—he was nothin special as a farmer, neither. What farmin he done, he'd lay the plan, my daughter and her children after they got big enough to work had to do the work. Ralph Jenks laid up around Calusa, called hisself workin. And when he drawed his checks, other women enjoyed his labor better than my daughter did.

He was the worst fellow that ever been born, he was terrible. When I come home he was ill to Rachel. And she was my child, she was a good girl but she'd just take anything off of Ralph Jenks— that was his name. But they had some very fine children, nothin but boys: her and Ralph was the mother and father of six boys—there's two in Boston, one in Florida, two in Atlanta, and the one in Birmingham is the sixth boy.

So, when I come home, the first thing I knowed, he liked to knock out one of her eyes—didn't knock it clean out but he gived her a black eye. And I went to see about it. Thomas Galloway, fellow that married my second daughter, Mattie Jane, he come to my house one night and I told him, after I'd heard the news about Ralph beatin my daughter, I said, "Thomas, I want you to carry me over to Ralph Jenks."

And Thomas had heard about it too. He generally kept one of these big two-ton trucks and he come over on that. Well, he was right down with me. And went up by Vernon's and he come on the truck with us. And they was livin on the left side of the road goin back past my house, up on a rise. It's all growed up now—that's where Ralph was livin with Rachel, had her there with him as a wife. And we was goin over there to see about the trouble between em.

Got there that night and we all set down there in the house. Rachel set down there too amongst her little boys. Ralph was sittin right over on the side of the fireplace and Vernon and Thomas was sittin back above Ralph, closer to the door, and I was sittin right along the other side of the fireplace right where I could look into Ralph's face. Rachel was sittin close to Vernon, her own dear brother, but more toward the center of the fireplace.

I was busy, I weren't sayin a word; I was busy watchin everybody's moves and lookin at her, lookin at Rachel right in the face, and lookin at Ralph right in the face. And that's what I went over there for—I was watchin points and everything. I'd heard he done black-eyed her and I looked at her good. She seemed to want to keep her head turned to the left to keep me from seein her. That put her directly in the sight of Vernon and Thomas. And every chance I could get I was lookin at her face. Every chance she could get she'd flick her head around, but every time she turned her head back I seed that one of her eyes was all but looked like knocked out. I just raised up mad as the devil—accordin to the way I heard he was treatin, livin with her, he was just makin a dog of her and he'd eventually killed her. I just pulled off and said, "Sister—" called her "Sister," oldest girl in the family—"Sister, what's the matter with your eye? What's the matter with your eye?"

She said, "That's where Ralph—" now this was the first fracas that I heard of after I come out of prison. She said, "That's where Ralph hit me, Papa."

Good God almighty, when I asked her that question, what did I ask her for? That's what I was after. I got up and told him, "Ralph, what in the world was you studyin at, knockin my child's eye out near bout that way? If it aint out. You just makin a dog of her."

Right then Vernon jumped up and fastened him. Them little old boys commenced a runnin around, "Papa, don't hit him, don't hit him"—them boys called me "Papa"—"Don't hit him, Papa."

I thinked to myself, 'O, I aint goin to just hit him, if necessary I'm goin to beat the hell out of him.'

Vernon jumped up that quick and collared him. Ralph had a

man in his bosom then when Vernon collared him. I standin there lookin at him. Well, I didn't want to slaughter him, I didn't want the boys to beat him up in front of his children. But if it hadn't been for Thomas Galloway grabbin Vernon, Vernon woulda beat the shit out of him right there, in his own house. He'd a cleaned him up. Well, it all got smothered down—Thomas Galloway grabbed Vernon; he weren't quite as heavy as Vernon, he weren't that heavy, but he was big enough to handle him pretty good. He grabbed Vernon and pulled him loose, got em separated. Ralph weren't goin to do nothin but get his face scuttled, foolin with Vernon. I didn't hit a lick, but I urged it on far as it went, I did. I aint goin to tell a lie. I knowed if I'd a tackled Ralph and couldn't handle him, Vernon weren't goin to let him hurt me. Vernon was the strongest man there and when he grabbed Ralph, that was a *man* grabbed him, too. Ralph was lighter than Vernon but he was pretty heavy hisself, in reason. And Thomas pulled Ralph on out of the house. He managed to persuade Vernon and all, and held to him, got him out of there. Ralph didn't have a possible chance to do nothin.

So, rocked along, rocked along, and he didn't quit his devilment. Next news I heard—he kept a old piece of car around there all the time, and he took Rachel on that old car one night and carried her down the road, come out here to the crossroads—been a road through there for the longest, but for the last lately they asphalted it—and he turned off and went on down there by Newcastle, then turned to the left and hit another road goin over to where Will Tuttle lives now. And he got down there in them swamps and he got him off—*she* said—he got him off a small limb and he beat her down, down there in the dark on the road. Well, when she got able, she come up to my house, told me about it and all. And he got away with that because she begged me—

Next time he cranked his old car up and went off—and he got a sister lives in Tuskegee; went off down there and Rachel went with him. And when they left Tuskegee that evenin, in place of comin back toward home, he come on out from Tuskegee on the Apafalya road and he hit Apafalya—and durin the comin through there from Tuskegee to Apafalya he bought him—she said, he got it—he bought him a pint of whiskey, full pint of whiskey. Then he hit the road through Apafalya and come out this side of town where the road turns and goes on out by Elam Church, went by Elam Church and carried her on off over there on what they call the old

Pine place, just a desert where there weren't no buildins or nothin but a big scope of woods. And he drove out—woods on both sides of the road and on one side was Elam Church, church I was born and raised up goin to, old home church; drove on through there by Elam until he hit them big woods between Elam and Sitimachas Creek. And he drove over in there and stopped on one side of the road or the other. Made her pull off everything she had on but her underwear, and he beat her down over there. Again! Beat her down. And when he went to crank his old car—Lord, if I'd a been there I don't expect I'd a quit shootin until I'd emptied every bullet out of my pistol, if I'd a just walked down on him—well, when he beat her up all he wanted to and he got ready to crank his old car up and come out, old car wouldn't run, wouldn't crank and run for him. He had to come on back out of them big woods over there between Sitimachas and Elam Church, and had to come out *walkin*, and her with him, beat up, beat up. And they runned up into a fellow by the name of Ambrose Lane. I knowed old man Frank Lane and all of his boys well. And Ambrose Lane was married to a woman named Heather Reeve, old man Madison Reeve's daughter. So Ambrose took em on his car and he noticed that Rachel was all beat up, weren't havin nothin to say, just like a dog, humble as a dog. Ambrose brought em home and when they got there, Ralph lingered around out back and Rachel took off for my house. And she was beat up so until Hannah and Mattie Jane, who was livin up there at that time in the house with me and her mother, they got around Rachel and got her to lay down and they greased her body all over practically. And she begged em, Rachel begged em—I was out and gone— to not tell Papa nothin about it and I didn't know about it for a while.

Well, next time he beat her up—and every time he'd beat her up that way, dog her, and just beat her eyes out nearly, when she'd get sort of straightened up in a few days, she'd go back to him. Well, that embarrassed Vernon. He decided if she was just goin to keep runnin back to Ralph, and he just goin to kill her, he weren't goin to have anything to do with it. But I hung in there; I'd a killed somebody or been killed before I'd a stood it.

So, the last time he beat her up, we heard about that. And one Sunday, me and Hannah come down there, right where Rachel's livin now, in the same house, only that Garvan, my baby boy, has overhauled that house and made it livable. But it was just a old weatherboarded shack at the time. And also the road people moved it back from where it stood when they asphalted the road. So, we come down there one Sunday—we was on our way to see one of the Hildreth ladies who was doin poorly; she was subject to be poorly and now she's dead and been dead a year and a half. We was on route to see her and we stopped at Ralph and Rachel's. She settin there all beat up—he was there too. Wouldn't nobody mention nothin. Rachel'd got to where she weren't goin to tell me nothin about it.

And before that was over, the next day, on Monday, the officers got on his tail. And it was colored folks, I believe, that called em out. And he discovered that they was comin for him and he commenced a dodgin around the settlement, keepin out of their sight. Had some friends protectin him, hidin him. He kept runnin and he outsmarted them officers, he kept hid and squandered. And at the wind-up of it, of him gettin away from here, up there at Vernon's I runned into them officers travelin backwards and forwards, huntin him. I told em all that I knowed at the time and I reckon they already knowed what I told em. The white people of the community knowed what he was doin, too—they told me they couldn't locate him nowhere. And we'd decided he'd just about slipped out and gone. I told em, "Well, Mr. Officers, I don't know where he's at. But if ever I locate him, if he's around me and I locate him, I'll warn you all."

And after he sloped off—he been back here two or three times and he went there to see her one time and he got messin around with her and she hit him, Rachel hit him in the face. And he aint been back since. He stays up in Michigan country today, Detroit, Michigan. So, if ever I'd a located him, been nobody between us, I'd a put him straddle-legged.

MATTIE JANE was livin up the road with Thomas Galloway. Now Thomas loved Mattie Jane and he proved it, and he didn't beat her and knock her up. They married while I was in the penitentiary. And Mattie Jane, she was a girl like this: she'd never be so flip—of course, none of my children weren't flip, and she was steady and agreeable but she weren't too strong. And her and Thomas had two chaps, a girl—she stays in Brooklyn, New York—and a boy named Thomas, after his daddy.

Tell the truth, Thomas loved whiskey—the daddy. And accordin to all reports, he had two brothers loved whiskey too. All of em was old man Galloway's children. Old man Galloway married one of the Byrd girls that owned the place they lived on. All the Byrds is dead, practically, and the place has fell to some of the grand-heirs. Well, Fourth of July, 1947, Thomas come to me in the field where I was layin by a patch of corn. Fourth of July come on a Friday that year—so he come to me and before I knowed anything he was right at me. He'd been plowin right above me on the Byrd place and he'd let me have the use of some land over there just below his field and I was over there layin by some corn. We talked awhile, passin time—and Saturday mornin, he come right back down there where I was. I hadn't quite got done on the Fourth, so Saturday mornin I was right there again, plowin, runnin out corn rows. And I looked around, there was Thomas. And Thomas was mighty accommodatin to me. He said, "Pa Nate—" that's what he called me—"Pa Nate, you seem to be layin by your corn. How bout—I got some scrapes up there larger than yours—"

I told him, "My scrape is big enough. This here'n's all right; don't worry yourself about it."

He spoke to me before about that; he believed I'd do better with a larger scrape, but I'd rather use the scrape I had than go borrow one. Weren't nothin my scrape couldn't do. I told him, "It's all right, Thomas—" but I hated to keep a turnin him down, so I said, "Well, if your scrape was out here I'd try it."

He said, "I'll go right down to the house and get it and bring it down here."

He went and brought me two of em, and I knocked my scrape off and tried one of his. Well, it was doin the same work, in a way, that my scrape done, but just to accommodate him and show him I appreciated his kindness, I kept a plowin with that scrape of his and he taken the other one and carried it over to the far end of the field so he would have it to go on home with.

When we got to the end I stopped my plow and he said, "Well, Pa Nate, Daddy's sick and I want to go down there and see how he is today."

I said, "Yes, Thomas, go see about your daddy, how he's gettin along. Keep up with your daddy in his sickness."

And he took his scrape and I took my plow and he left and went on home. I fell into my next row with his other scrape. I indulged him. So I went on and finished my corn rows, then I picked up my other scrape that I'd brought out to the field and carried my horse, plow, and all across the swamp and on to home.

Thomas went on home—Mattie Jane said—and he went to visit his daddy that day and he died before he left from there. Had two brothers livin down there—I don't know definitely whether he ever got to his daddy's or not. And all three of them boys was grown —Thomas, Huck, and Walt, all. Well, Thomas died before his daddy died. He got down there and them boys, Huck and Walt both, liked whiskey and home-brew and all such a mess as that. And Thomas liked it hisself. He got down there and he taken sick. But before he died he talked to my wife—she thought a lot of Thomas; that was her daughter, my and her daughter he married. And when Thomas got down, Huck come a runnin up from State Street down there and notified Hannah. She fixed right up and went over to Thomas's and got Mattie Jane and they took off down there. When they got there, Thomas was low—his stomach done swelled up enough to bust. Hannah sent word to me about it. And someway, somehow, Huck and Walt took Thomas to Calusa Hospital and tried to get him in there, but they wouldn't hear to it, wouldn't let him in. All of us was aware that Thomas was in bad shape—stomach done swelled up like a cow bag. And he claimed he drinked a little home-brew down in State Street, after he got there. He owned to my wife, and to his wife, that he drinked just a little, but it didn't take but a little to get him in the shape he was. And it was supposed, by people talkin, that the stuff he drinked was poison. Them boys had been goin around there, Huck and Walt or Walt or Huck—I don't know whether both of em was in it or just one, but some fellow accused em of churnin out this home-brew there, been doin it. So they gived Thomas some and he just drinked a swallow, he said, but it messed him up. And he told Mattie Jane and Hannah that when he went down to Coalhouse hill—used to have a big coalhouse there, goin into Beanville—weren't no bad hill, just a long slope of a hill, and Thomas said a pain struck him durin him walkin down that hill before he ever got to State Street. He wasn't, accordin to his own words, he wasn't just right hisself. And he was goin to see his daddy when a pain struck him on route. Well, he just went on and he got down there and drinked some of that home-brew and it killed him.

Them Galloway boys didn't stand good enough for them people at the hospital to hear at their larceny and take Thomas in. And then, too, he was colored. They taken colored people in that hospital but they didn't hurry none about it. So, late that evenin, quick as Vernon could get a chance, he took off down there and just picked Thomas right up and carried him to the hospital and weren't no words said. They took him in right there and he died. Died Sunday mornin—a while after sunup Thomas was dead.

Mattie Jane stayed on at Thomas's and her home and me and my wife visited her and looked after her. And she come to our home and stayed some, backwards and forwards until the crop was gathered that fall. I went right on over there and superintended, gathered what little crop Thomas died and left there, and soon as we got that done, I went over there with my wagon and moved Mattie Jane right back in the house with me and her mother, on the Leeds place. They had one little girl when he died, Eva Lu, and in six months' time after the death of her husband, Mattie Jane gived birth to a little boy and she named him Thomas, after the father.

Well, Eva Lu growed along, growed along, and Thomas was a good big boy when Eva Lu finished her schoolin over at State Street and located herself up there in Brooklyn, New York, where Vernon's daughters was. Then this boy got big enough, Eva Lu's brother, and Mattie Jane let him go up there where the girl was. And in about a year or less time, Mattie Jane went up there—followed in her children's footsteps, and she's livin with her daughter today. Eva Lu married a man from across the water somewhere—he weren't a native of the northern states. Colored fellow, and I taken him for a foreigner. I seed him myself, the year I went to Philadelphia and stayed a week with Francis; then, the next week, I landed on over in Brooklyn, New York.

II

I was down to a one-horse farm. Vernon worked a big field right in front of the house, and then there was another field to the north, and then a field back here west—well, I worked them two fields. Vernon didn't stay up the road but two years, and he moved right back down on Mr. Leeds' place where I was.

Mr. Leeds was a white fellow that lived in Phenix City, close to the river dividin Phenix City and Columbus, Georgia. I got on the car with Vernon one day, drove there and Vernon consulted with him bout their business. I met Mr. Leeds and far as I ever knowed of him, he seemed to be a right fair and clever man.

So, Mr. Leeds built Vernon a house on the same plantation that I was livin on. Vernon moved in there and me and his mother stayed on in the old house. And he was workin at Calusa at that time and he hired a hand to work his part of the place and I worked the rest I was controllin my own affairs but I had to come strictly under the government's orders.

When I come out of prison, I went under the allotment. The government allowed you to plant so much acreage in cotton. And all over that—they kept you checked after you planted; they gived you orders to plant so much and after you planted your crop, regardless to what condition it was—how pretty it was didn't help—if you had over the amount they allowed you to have, you had to plow it under. I had to plow—sometimes I'd plow up a little corner. The government rider made it convenient for me, plowed up the sorriest, down to specification.

They left it to you to plant whatever you wanted to on the rest of your land. I looked at it this way: it might be a discrimination on the poor farmer to cut down on *his* crop, but the government was helpin the poor colored people more than anybody else. It was the best thing ever was done until then—to allow the government to rule over this crop business. Let the government fix the acres and control the prices, let em set the interest rates. It's just a better deal for the colored race all the way through than to let these people here preside, the Watsons and the Graces and the other moneyed men.

The government done stepped in and forbidded these white people of sellin the cotton off their place if a nigger made it. Good God that skunked em—allowin folks to sell their own crop. And the government rulin was this: it matters not whose place you workin on and how you workin—jumped in there and slapped that seal on—if you make that cotton on a white man's place, you sell that cotton too; white man couldn't sell it, even if you workin on down to halves. Used to be in this country, if a colored man was farmin on a white man's place the white man would sell it, specially if he was workin on halves, specially. The government stopped that thing, cut it off smack. They didn't like that here, these white folks, but they had to bear it.

Negro workin on halves with the white man, the government
was issuin checks to both of em, a check to the white man and a
check to the Negro, both of em receivin checks for takin the white
man's land *out* of cultivation. Under government rulins. But it
started off, they'd send both of them checks to the white man, and
the white man was takin it all and puttin it in his pocket. The
government found it out and called the thing in question and after
bonin the white man about it someway, they just finally quit and
sent the nigger his check and the white man his. Made a division
then. White man didn't like for the government to pay the nigger
for either farmin on his land or *not* farmin. O, good God, they
swore and kicked against that like a mule kickin in a stable. There's
one white lady in this settlement said, "The very idea of a Negro
drawin money on our land!" She didn't like it at all. But I never did
learn what white woman that was. Nigger tell you a thing, heap of
times he won't tell you who it come from cause he's scared.

The government started these issues while I was in prison and
they was makin a separate division in the checks when I come out.
And there's white people tried to defeat the new rulins by pasturin
their land for cattle, prohibitin the poor nigger from workin that
land in crops. Just drivin the Negro back, let him root pig and die
poor. Pasturin this land and the Negro and poor white man ought
to be workin it for their support, but the big white man cuddled up
over it just because he got a deed.

The news come to me right out of Tuskegee and I'm satisfied
it's true. White man had been hirin colored folks to keep his land
shrubbed off so it'd grow grass for his cattle. And he was so eager
to make money he quit hirin the niggers to keep that land clean;
went out there and throwed poison on every livin plant but the
grass. By God, they tell me he killed his cattle by that act. Quit hirin
the nigger, wanted to keep the nigger down, freeze him out any way
he could.

One white man, fellow by the name of Levi Wheeler, I knowed
him like I know the fingers on my hand, he told a cousin of mine
one day— Now, this was pretty soon after I got grown and married,
but the history of it carries into today. My daddy lived on the old
Wheeler place, old man Frank Wheeler; there was several of them
old Wheeler boys—Doc Wheeler, Henry Wheeler, Cyrus Wheeler,
Frank Wheeler—all them was old man Judge Wheeler's sons. And

this Cyrus Wheeler had two girls and two boys—Mitchell Wheeler and Levi Wheeler, them was the boys; Iris Wheeler and Blanche Wheeler was the girls. I knowed em all, knowed em after they got grown. Them girls married and went away from here south, I don't know where they went. And Mitchell Wheeler married old man Tom Ward's daughter, and Levi married old man Hamp Lovelace's daughter. Now Levi Wheeler is dead, Mitchell Wheeler is dead, and the girls maybe is dead; them girls never did stay about in this country after they got grown, but Mitchell and Levi did. Mitchell never did own no land after his daddy died and left him a home. He fooled around and sold that out and moved to town, him and his wife, this Ward girl. Levi lived on in the country with the Lovelaces, who Levi married in the family of. Hamp Lovelace lived on a road out from Apafalya goin into Crane's Ford and Newcastle. And after so many years, Levi bought him a pretty large place right there at Zion Church, between here and Apafalya, and he built him a nice home and he died. One of his boys is livin right there today and farmin.

And Levi told a cousin of mine one day—Malcolm Todd was the man he told—he was a mighty big talker; I knowed him well as I knowed any white man. Got to talkin bout first one thing then another—northern people, the government; and told him, "Well, if the north sends down any money or anything usable here, the white people gets all they want and if there's anything left, then the niggers can get some." And it carried on just like he said until recent days. That was a ugly act.

Got to where one white man was accused about it, caught him —the government had started sendin groceries out to certain places for em to be handed out. Caught one white man around here sellin his niggers that stuff. They was workin on halves with him and the colored was talkin bout it: didn't let his niggers go get the groceries —he had that thing fixed. Anything that was handed out, why, nigger go to the field, go to plowin, white man go to Tuskegee or anywhere they was givin it out and get it for his niggers, bring it home and sell em the groceries they was supposed to be gettin free, accordin to the government's rulins. They never did jail this one white man about it or arrest him, but he had to dance up to it. Some of em, even up here at Pottstown, they'll resack that stuff, resack it and sell it to the niggers.

ONE white man—the government's orders and rulins was to quit workin these colored children on their farms when they oughta been in school. Government sent a man around the country watchin for colored children workin in the white man's field. And one day, there in the neighborhood of Tuskegee, one of the watchmen passed and he seed a squad pickin cotton across the field and he noticed there was several colored in it—he was sharp, he knew it, accordin to the way I heard it. He got out of his vehicle and walked off across the field goin to this crowd of colored pickin cotton—a few whites in it, but mostly it was colored. And he watchin, travelin toward em, he seed all them colored chaps quit pickin and hit it for the swamps. He smelt a rat—but he went right on till he got to the white man that was out there bossin that crowd. Questioned him bout seein that squad of children runnin to the swamps and the woods. Asked him who was they? He seed who it was, a lot of colored. The white man cried it was his children, but this man knew he didn't have that many children and them colored, too; he just lyin to him. So he gived him a good talk—that's the way the news come to me; I was very eager to find out anything I could and when I found out things like that it gived me pleasure. He warned that white man against such as that. He gived him enough to let him know he didn't believe they was his children—he knowed a gang of em was colored children. Said he told him, when he got done talkin with him, "Don't let that happen no more; you'll catch it if you do." That put a scare on him and he ceased at it.

I looks deeply through all this and it comes to my mind: this organization I joined in '32 was so stout, it was able to hold up in them times for conditions that the government is puttin on today.

The white man, when I first come free, he was tryin to keep the government hid from the colored man and the colored man hid from the government. I know; I'd go to them government talks and hear them riders talk. I didn't have no book learnin but I knowed from my life that them government men meant well for the farmin class of people. And they'd hold these meetins through this country, and right here at Calusa; and they'd ask sometimes when the meetins would meet—they called men workin on halves and every way into that, ones that knowed about the meetins would, but they'd leave the colored fellow out, try to keep him out of the knowledge of them meetins, or tell him, "There aint no use in you goin; it aint for you." And the government man would set there and ask em, "Where is the colored brethren?" They'd state, the white ones, farmers, about their business and so on, and they'd state enough about the colored man for the government rider to know that there was colored people in this business too, and sometimes he never could see em, wanted to know how come they didn't come around and so on. He knowed the nigger was held back—I went, TJ went, and some others, but the biggest part of the colored people done what the white man wanted em to do, and that was not to attend no government meetins with white folks. I don't say all the white folks wanted to keep the colored out, and I do believe, honestly, that some of the white people would have fell right in with the colored. But there was enough of em didn't want the colored there, and the poor colored man, quite natural, he didn't think it was his place to go.

They talked at them meetins bout how to farm and how to get the most out of your land. And they gived instructions and told you what you had to do to comply with the government's orders. Well, that was all very necessary to know if you was a man that wanted to handle your own affairs. And I always was a man of that type.

THE year of '48 I worked, and Vernon helpin me, and Garvan a little bit, up on their place up yonder on Sitimachas Creek. That was my wife's daddy's place, in his lifetime, and when he died, I took it over as far as payin taxes on it and keepin it up, until I was put in prison. Then Vernon lingered with it—my wife had ten acres. Her sister Lena jumped up and decided she'd sell her part. And Hannah paid her a hundred dollars for it and that gived her twenty acres to her name. She had it paid for when I come out of prison, had the deeds and everything. And when she died in '50, that throwed my children twenty of the fifty acres. And that boy that was killed at Quitman's Flats in '32, his wife died and her part fell on Vernon—bypassed her boy because he didn't want it; he's livin in the northern states.

They aint farmin none of that land—just sellin timber off it. But they used to farm it before it become more profitable to leave it alone. Now, every time the timber grow up—Vernon have sold the timber off that place twice since I been back home. And it come to twenty-two hundred dollars' worth of timber he's sold there since he been in charge. There's a white gentleman lives between here and Beaufort, out by Lavender's bridge—sawmill man. He runs a sawmill all through this country and works colored fellows. And told it down in here once, he did, he could live without it. He's a man that loant the state money—that's how much he has. Loant the state of Alabama some money. And he told it, said, "I can live without it. I'm just runnin this sawmill to give my boys a job." Well, he's the man that bought all that timber from Vernon.

One of these days, if he can get justice, Vernon will own all fifty acres. And by hokus, what have I got? What have I got? Nothin! I took care of it just as long as I was able and when I was put off in prison Vernon had to take it over then or else lose the whole thing. Well, them last two parts—Lily made Vernon guardzine of her ten acres. That's the oldest girl in the business, Lily Ramsey. She married a cousin of mine, Malcolm Todd, and when he died she moved somewhere up in Georgia with her son. And she got old, had to go to the old folks' home and she died. And now, Hannah's baby sister, the last one in that entire family—Mattie—is layin a corpse in Birmingham. That's the last one of that set of Ramseys, Molly and Waldo Ramsey's children, the baby girl of the family I married in. She was my sister-in-law, my children's own dear auntie, the last of the children of their grandmother and grandfather.

Some years ago, when I first went to prison, her and her husband moved out from here. They got scared and shiked* out —all the connections and kin people and all. Left this country and went to Birmingham, never did make another crop. Clarence Reed was her husband. He weren't at Virgil Jones' house that mornin in December and the mob crowd never did hunt him up as far as I knowed, but he was a member of that organization. And what did Clarence do? Me and him married two sisters, the two youngest girls in the bunch. My wife was older than his: he married the baby girl. And the day that I stood up at Virgil Jones' house, Clarence Reed got in the road and walked to Crane's Ford to the headquarters of this organization—*walked*, walked up there, so I was told. You could get a hearin there and call for help. I couldn't read and write but the ones that could read and write knowed right

* To go away quickly and quietly in fear or shame.

where to go in Crane's Ford and get a message sent off to the people of New York behind this organization. Clarence Reed understood that part of the proposition.

I never did see him no more after the evenin that I got shot until I got out of prison. I went to Birmingham to see him and his wife, talk with em and visit, and that was the last I knowed of him until I heard he was dead. Didn't see him when I was in prison, he wouldn't come there, didn't come for the whole twelve years. But the evenin I got into it, Clarence was the man that got in the road somehow and went to Crane's Ford. Told about the trouble down here; notified the heads of this organization and they come down to investigate the matter. Clarence Reed was the man and he moved right on; durin the time I first landed in prison he left here.

And he was a man this way: he was a good fellow and he knowed how to work in the field but he had ways like a woman. Him and Mattie never did have nary a child. They married when I was livin up on Miss Reeve's place, and directly after I come home free from prison he died up there in Birmingham. And they brought him from up there down here and buried him. Now his wife's dead. And my children, three of em, Vernon and Rachel and Garvan, and their uncle TJ, went up there—but there's no understandin yet where they goin to bury her. This girl was the baby of all, girls and boys, she was the baby of all. They said she died durin the night; didn't nobody know when she died, just went away—that's the statement that reached here. Died quiet as a lamb. There was some talk amongst the neighbors, people of the community that knowed her from when she lived in these parts, that they goin to bring her body here but you can't count on that. I told Josie, my wife—Josie knowed Mattie well—"It's my best opinion they goin to put her up there somewhere." Little Waldo is buried up there, her brother, only boy in the family of children. Mattie ought to have knowed, as long as she been in Birmingham, where he's buried at. If she didn't tell nobody and leave no record of it, they just might bring her back here.

VERNON bought his own plantation, sixty-one acres, in 1948. That was as good a place as you can find anywhere around here—smooth land, productive land. He agreed to give Mr. Harmon Silver, a white man, three thousand dollars for it.

Fall of the year, and all durin of the year, I was busy runnin backwards and forwards from the Leeds place to Vernon's place, buildin a six-room house up there. Vernon moved into the home house that was on that property when he bought it—he stayed just one year down on the Leeds place in that house Mr. Leeds had built for him—and I built right out on the edge of the field south of him. Vernon and Garvan, and also Eugene helped before he left from here goin to Ohio. All three of them boys lent in and went up yonder on their mother's daddy's old place and cut logs. Trucked them logs into Beanville and sawed em for so much of the lumber. And we hired Preston Courteney, a makeshift carpenter, the boy that squandered the Courteney place after his parents died, and lost it to Mr. Grace—he come over there and laid the foundation. And I come from the Leeds place that fall just about every day, except gatherin my little corn crop; had a little cotton too, but didn't none of it work and upset me enough that I couldn't hustle from pillar to post, hustle over there in the mornin and hustle home at night. Drove my two-horse wagon—my boys turned that loose back to me—I left em with more than that. And I drove that big gray mare to it that my wife had gived me when I got back, and the mule I bought from Garvan after he quit his crop.

After Preston Courteney got that foundation down, I boxed that house up all around, just stack-boxed it. Then took sealin and sealed up the overheads, all but one room out of six, sealed em up. Garvan due to be there helpin but he was at Calusa at work. And when we got ready to Sheetrock it, I done the biggest part of that by myself. Preston Courteney had promised to help every day on his off time—nigger worked at Calusa too, and when he come off his job he'd jump on his car and just loll all over the country; had a new car and he'd ride every whichaway. And me there knockin every day by myself, boxin up, sealin the overheads and all. And at the windup, Preston come there and him and Vernon climbed on the house and I handed up tin and they covered it. I never did like it havin as flat a roof as it had, but I just went on. After so long a time, we wired up the house and put lights in there—that was the first electricity we used. They'd had them big lectric lights at prison, on every buildin—on the cells, on the barn, on the blacksmith shop—so by the time we put lights in our house, it weren't somethin new to me. Didn't worry about it; it was just somethin to pacify the country, the people in the country. But I'd lived with it for years.

MATTIE JANE stayed in the new house with me and her mother. We had put our arms around her when her husband died and moved her in the house with us, her and her little girl—over yonder on the Leeds place. And when we moved over here on Vernon's place, she had a little old boy baby and he was the very spirit of his daddy, just as much like him as two peas out of one hull.

So, Mattie Jane had a finger in that house; Garvan had a finger in it; I had a finger in it; my wife had a finger in it before she died—of course, my wife's was the same as mine. And Lord God, if I didn't lose corn—comin over here and neglectin my crop that fall puttin up that house. I pulled my corn and dropped it on the ground, and workin on that house so regular, my corn laid on the ground and sprouted in the pile; lost it. And when I moved into the house I built, I didn't have no more than enough corn to get by with, to feed my stock and make a crop with that first year.

I jumped in after I moved down there and right about the middle of the place I cleared up a big swamp for Vernon's pasture. He had some cows, milkers of his own when he moved there, but he commenced a messin around with beef cattle then, Black Angus. He had a Hereford or two amongst em but he was dotin on them Black Angus.

The piece I farmed I was rentin from Vernon, but he wouldn't be heavy on me; he about halfway gived the house to me. I just took a hold on the land while he was workin at Calusa. But there was a flaw in the deal—that place was washin away, that cultivatable land was washin away. I went on down there and picked me out a part that I wanted—he told me, just any part that I wanted, go to it—and doggone it, when the rains washed across that field the water rose knee-deep. I jumped up, I did, and Vernon workin at Calusa, and evenins a heap of times he'd come out to the field where I was when he come off his job and he'd look over the situation. I told him, "Well, son, this land here is washin away; it got to be somethin done about it."

He looked at it and said, "Yeah, Papa, but I'm workin at Calusa, got to go to Calusa every day."

I said, "Well, son, you got to do somethin about it. You'd be done bought a desert soon." That was a fact. I said, "Son, hit or miss, I'm goin to stop it, and I'm goin to stop it this year, too."

He was drawin rent on the place the first year he bought it. TJ and Ben Ramsey rented several acres apiece from him and the most they planted on it was corn. And they planted peas between the corn, scandalous. Had the best of the place, and they even rented some they didn't work and that part just laid out. They was already havin to work their land at home and they wanted a heavy crop that year so they jumped up and planted a gang of corn in there and filled it up with peas. Made peas there to walk on, so many peas. And that corn growed close as my toes. Biggest lot of corn stalks I ever seed in my life less'n it was on bottom land.

I told Vernon, "Tell you what I'm goin to do. I'm goin to get in there and cut them corn stalks, cut em down with a hoe, and then I'm goin back, I'm just goin to pick up every corn stalk in reach of them ditches where the terraces is broke and the land washin away, I'm goin to fill up them ditches partly, as good as I can, and then I'm goin to pile em in on them terraces and stomp em down. And then I'm goin to take my scoop—" I had a scoop, that big mare to pull it—"I'm goin to take my scoop and scoop off dirt from where it can spare it, gradually, and I'm goin to dump it on them corn stalks in them terraces and in them washes, and I'm goin to weight it down. This fall, I'm goin to hitch the wagon and go out to the woods and pine forests and cut a whole lot of pine limbs and brush—this fall and winter—and I'm goin to haul them to the field by the load, as much as it takes. I'm goin to put the small stuff in them ditches and when I get to the terraces I'm goin to put in limbs and everything and stomp it down."

He said, "Papa, you can't stop it with them corn stalks, especially in one year."

I said, "Well, son, we'll see about that."

I had a heap to work practically everywhere I went to try to save my crop from water washin across it, terraces breakin. I knowed what it took to fix em. Built terraces on the Pollard place; already had terraces but they had been upset and bummed up in a way until the waters had cut ditches through em. That Pollard place was bad on terraces; it was hilly, terraces wouldn't hold.

So, I cut them corn stalks and stomped em down in them washes, just stomped em and piled em up, kept a pilin until I made a hump there at them cut through places. And I went on a plowin. Never did a bit more water go down across that field. I cut it off right then.

Of course, them corn stalks begin to cave and give in some by the last of the year. So I piled more pine limbs and pine brush on the terraces and I'd always stick the growth part of the brush up the hill, and that'd hold em. That place don't wash today—Vernon got it in pasture now. I believe I saved that land, caught it when there was still land to save.

Then turned around and there was a new ground, just across the hollow from this land, and that field contained at least ten or twelve acres until it got down to a swamp. Some of the timber in that swamp woulda squared up six inches. Took my ax and cleared it out; took my gray mare and that mule I bought from Garvan, hitched em to my wagon and hauled them logs out from there and up to the house for wood. And just across that swamp was another new ground, four or five acres covered with sweet gum stumps—O, if I haven't worked since I been in this world and a heap of it since I been out of the penitentiary—I took my mattock and shovel and ax and went out in that new ground where you couldn't hardly see nothin but stumps. Couldn't drive a plow twenty feet without takin up the roots of them sweet gum stumps, then twenty feet more and hangin up again.

I told Vernon, "I'm goin to take them stumps up out of that field, goin to get em."

One day he come from Calusa work and he looked over way across that field from the house, way back toward the backside of his plantation; he said, "Papa, what's all that shinin out yonder, all that dirt piled up; look like hogs been rootin it up?"

I said, "That's where I'm takin up them stumps."

I'd gone to work and taken up eleven two-horse wagonloads of stumps. Now, takin up old sweet gum stumps, and loadin em, and haulin em out the field, they raggedy and rooty, tear up a heap of ground gettin em up—digged em up, had to dig em up, shovel back the dirt to get at them roots, take my ax down close, clean out around that hole, go down and cut em every one. Well, them stumps, it didn't take many of em to make a wagonload. Hauled em to the house and piled em on the woodpile and let em dry out there. And the next winter, I took my ax and cut the long roots off them stumps, took them pieces in the house and used em in the fire.

Some of them stumps, I'd turned em out in the woods, them that was too big to haul; but I hauled eleven two-horse wagonloads to the house. Talk about work—

Some of em predicted, some of my color who was weak, if I must say so, as goat shit—they figured I done the worst thing I could have ever done, joinin that organization. I had colored people to tell me to my face—and what was it but talkin in the white folks' favor—"You done wrong; you had no business doin what you done." Some of these same people run their tongues against me: "O, Nate Shaw won't be no count when he comes out of prison; they goin to work him to death and he aint goin to be able to do a thing." But I figured it this way: it wasn't a matter they cared so much for me—of course, they didn't care a lick—they didn't want to be chased around here theirselves. They jumped sky high away from that union and if I was punished, ruint, you might say, that'd turn a heap of good folks away from the very idea of the union.

The truth of it, I done less work in prison than I ever done outside. I didn't do a hard year's labor in twelve, not a year. I done more work in pullin out them stumps than I done all the years I was in prison. I'd a been sittin on top of the world if I hadn't had no more work to do after I come back home than I had in prison. But how come I had such a easy time in prison? How come? It was what was behind me, I put it all to that; it was them that was standin for me and God above.

THERE'S a secret in this union somewhere and I aint never understood it. They talked to me about it, that this union come from across the waters, and they called it a "soviet" union. It was said to me by some of the white folks at my trial. I don't know what that means—they didn't say and I'm not a readin man, I been kept back from the knowledge of a heap of things. This colored man that was workin in this field, who started out this union in this country, he never did tell where he come from, he never gived it in my presence. But wherever he come from, and wherever the union come from, if it started up in the United States or started up across the water, he never did tell what native he was. But I realize that a poor little cat like me is handicapped from findin out all the secrets of this world. Little cats like me will never know who started it and how it started and where it started—

It was a thing that I never did thoroughly understand and get the backgrounds of it, but I was man enough to favor its methods.

My head and heart had been well loaded about the condition and
the welfare of the poor—I couldn't stand it no more. I jumped in
that organization and my name rings in it today. I haven't apolo-
gized to my Savior for joinin; it was workin for right. A man
had to do it.

Time passed off me in prison, it just passed off. I come out—
I was fifty-nine years old when I come out—and in three years'
time I built a house, and the next year I cleaned up a pasture for
Vernon, filled in his terraces and saved the land, cut out them old
sweet gum stumps so you could drive a plow steady and not hang
yourself up every way you stepped and tumble over the plow
handles. And some of em looked at me in the field and didn't want
to believe what they seed. "He'll kill hisself if he keeps that up; it
aint goin to come to nothin noway." Well, part of Vernon's sixty-
one acres is in pasture today and he farms the balance hisself. And
it was Nate Shaw saved that land, and it was Nate Shaw joined the
organization, and it was Nate Shaw went to prison, stayed twelve
long years—I'll tell that—and he come out fit for hard work, lookin
for it, just like he went in.

I didn't have nobody to help me plow and that big mare that my
wife reserved for me when I come home, she was all I needed and
all I could afford to keep. I could work the mule and the mare all
right breakin land and plowin double, but after that I'd have to
stand em in the lot and feed em. That mare was able, so I just sold
that mule I'd bought from Garvan to a colored fellow named James
Butler. And just what I gived Garvan for that mule, I sold it to him
—one hundred cash dollars. And him and the woman he stayed
with—he weren't married to her—and her mother, the Byrd family
from over on the Calusa road, jumped on a car one day and went
to Beaufort. And there was a white lady up there furnishin em
and she gived em the money for James to buy that mule. James
didn't give it to me, but that woman did, the mother of the woman
he was livin with.

So all I had was that mare to work—she'd belonged to my wife
and when I come home my wife just told me that mare was her'n
and she just turned that mare over to me and I took her over. As
good a plow animal as ever I plowed. She'd pull a Oliver Goober
just as easy as I'd eat a buttered biscuit. She weighed about eleven

hundred, that mare did; she was blocky-built, had great big feet. She just didn't want to work to a two-horse wagon.

Vernon had got a hold of that mare after I commenced a losin my stock—I couldn't help that though, I weren't there to see it. My wife told me when she come to see me in prison, "Darlin, that old mare gived Vernon a pretty little mule."

I told her to tell Vernon—he could work like the devil but he had no experience of a young mule—and told him to his own face, "Take care of your little old mule, your colt; whatever you do, don't start to workin her too young."

Went right on and put her to my two-horse wagon, too young, and strain-halted her. She commenced a draggin one of her hind legs. I told my wife, "I told him and cautioned him: he never had nothin to do with a young mule in his life. All the stock he ever worked I bought em able to work or else I broke em. He don't know nothin bout breakin a young mule and workin her to keep from hurtin her."

Cut that young mule down. She come on and growed and made a good heavy mule before she got done—she weighed about a thousand pounds—but she never did get quiet like a mule.

I went down with my wife to the Holiness Church one Sunday to hear the preachin. And after the main part of the meetin was over, they standin around talkin, church crowd, I told Hannah, "I believe I'll walk over to Will Wiley's awhile—" not knowin his thoughts and what he had in him—"walk over there awhile and talk with him. I been knowin him a long time and it's so many years since I've seen him. He goes for a Christian man—I believe I'll go over and talk with him some. He lives close by and convenient."

So I just got out in the road and walked on over there—old acquaintance, weren't goin over there to talk on no special thing, just showin myself to him and talk easy talk. So many of em said I never would get back home; or if I did, I wouldn't be no account. Undoubtedly, they looked for me to go down in prison.

I didn't think that Will Wiley was my enemy in my young days or he was my friend, but I found out that Sunday that he had hated to see me have anythin like I did have once in life. I scuffled to try and take care of what I had, too, in the defense of my family. Put me in prison because I wouldn't fall over and just let a man sweep the ground where I stood— And Will Wiley, he was glad for a man like me to get in trouble, glad for it.

Used to, when I was a younger man, carry my family to Elam Church, to meetin, every first Sunday. And I'd always drive in past Will Wiley, put my mules in the shade. Come in there on my two-horse wagon—he'd be sometime walkin about there amongst the crowd. He was a caretaker for the church, lookin out to keep everythin quiet. And I'd drive up there and he pointin out and givin orders where to drive to and park your wagon or your buggy. And I thought a heap of my mules, a heap of my buggies and wagons— I had all that at that time. Never did have a double buggy to run my folks on; I run from a single buggy, just carry one or two or three, to a two-horse wagon. Carry my wife and children to church and stop along the road and pick up people, or even carry folks from my settlement, my neighbors, to church on my wagon. I had somethin that was able to pull em; my mules didn't have to hump up their backs and get in a knot to pull. They was good mules, strong mules, and they listened to me. So, I'd drive in there and Will Wiley sometimes be settin in a chair on the outside, in the grove round the north side of the church. My mules would trot along jovially if I called on em but I didn't trot my mules in a runnin race. I took care of em—God knows I did, too, thankful to God. I kept leather halters for both of them mules in the back end of that wagon where they couldn't fall out, and the mules' dinner would be in there too. Oats—oats a heap of times that I raised on my farm and cut em myself. Be layin in the back end of that wagon bottled up. Corn layin in there for em; whatever it took to keep em up, I fed em. Pull in the yard there and slip the bridle off, put it under my wagon in the shade. I didn't allow my leather harness to lay out in the sun. Careful bout everything. Put them halters on them mules, grass tie halters, strap em across the back of their necks and around to the ring underneath, lead em off to a swingin limb where I could reach it and pull it down and tie them tie halters behind that limb sufficient to hold em. Go on about my business—

My mules was used to eatin at dinner times, used to eatin every feedin time—mornin, dinner, and night. And they was used to bein kept from their ribs shinin—you couldn't see their ribs. If they wasn't as fat as they could be, they had plenty of good heavy flesh on em. Bout twelve o'clock them mules would ask for this feed. They'd look around anywhere they was; they knowed me—

any animal knows his master; he may not know the name of him and what he go for, but he knows that's the man that feed him. They know, they got sense just like people; they got their kind of sense and people got theirs. Them mules looked to see me, bout twelve o'clock and I hadn't fed em—"agh-agh-agh-agh-agh-agh-agh-agh-agh—" I'd look around and they standin lookin right at me with their heads up—"agh-agh-agh-agh-agh-agh-agh-agh—" Sometimes they'd bray, squall out, "Eeeeeeeeeeeeeeeeeeaaaaaaaaaawwwwww, hagh-ah-hagh-ah-hagh-ah-hagh-ah-hagh-ah—" That animal needs feedin. There's two causes for a animal squallin—he needs feedin or he's missin his mate. Them animals knowed me and they was askin for their dinner or breakfast or supper. Anywhere, at home in the lot, or if you have em out on duties, they know when feedin time come.

This man Will Wiley would set and watch me, wouldn't say nothin. My wife would go in the church and take her seat with the children, and all the rest of the church that was outside in the yard would go in. Sometimes I'd go in and sometimes I'd stand out by the door—it was accordin to how the church was crowded. And, too, I'd think about how roguish some folks is that go to church, they go just for devilment, they don't go there to hear the service and I was well aware of that. I'd stand where I could keep my eyes on my wagon and that team of mules. I knowed how some of em was. They'd even take your feed out of your wagon, slip it out if they could and give it to their stock. So, sometimes I'd go in the church and sometimes I'd stand out by the door—and I wouldn't be standin alone; many a man would be out there checkin on his property.

Now, years later, I walked over to Will Wiley's house after service and walked in—he invited me in—set down, commenced a talkin on different subjects. He jumped up and poked it in my face that I worshipped what I used to have, I worshipped my property. That was as big a lie as he could have told—I worshipped my mules and wagon and what I had, I worshipped it all. God knows I never did worship what I had.

He said, "You worshipped them big mules and whatever all you had you worshipped—" declarin them mules and what I had was my God. Well, God says don't put no God ahead of Him and don't worship nothin you have before God. *But*, God requires me to feed my stock, He does; they're dumb brutes. Care for em and not mistreat em.

I got right out with Wiley bout that. I didn't insult him—he insulted me, but I never made better out of worse; when I got a chance I got up and bid him goodbye and walked out.

I didn't leave right off, I set there awhile. Looked at him and studied him, thought over what he said. I had had, in my younger days, a little more around me for workin and laborin hard for it, and I seed how he felt about that. I had owned in my past life as good a mules as walked the roads, and as big a farm mules that ever pulled a plow, and he hated me for it. Told me I worshipped em— just because I drove em right, kept em fat and pretty and put a good harness on em, never did race em. All my stock had to do was move when I'd say, "Come up." Pull my lines—well, all my stock always obeyed me thataway. I had some of em move with me, when they'd move they'd run away like to kill me, too. But they wasn't accountable for that.

There's men that seed me drivin them mules and appreciated em for what they was worth. One man got so high, he told me— man that I met in the road one day haulin cross-ties; had two little old small mules and he haulin cross-ties at the Apafalya right-away to the railroad. He gived my mules a year or more before he just had to stop and question me about em. I noticed he'd watch them mules—he'd pass right by me till I got to where I'd turn around on the seat, I'd see him just steady lookin back. And he done thataway until one day he just stopped and asked me whose mules was I drivin. He said, "Well, I noticed, I been drivin and drivin on these roads longer than I can really tell you about. And every once in awhile, sometimes every day, I meet you drivin these mules. And I didn't know but what they was company mules. I noticed I don't never see nobody drivin that pair of mules but you. I wondered whose they was. Is they company mules or yours?"

I told him—I didn't jump up and boast about "they mine, they my mules"; here's what I said. I looked at him and smiled, said, "I reckon they're mine. They stays in my barn day and night whenever I aint workin em. Specially now they stay in there every night and I feed em. I reckon they're mine." That's how I answered his question, told him in a nice way.

So, I was havin a social conversation with this fellow Will Wiley and when he spoke his slander against me, that ruint the talk, what he spoke and the way he spoke it. And I figured that if he had it in him enough to tell me somethin to my face against me, why, he'd tell it to other people if he had a chance. First thing you know, he'd jump up off his nasty behind and go to runnin over the country dislikin you and findin a fault to you where there is no fault. Puttin other people against you off of his lies. And he speaks hard words about you, raises the devil, scandalous. But if he wasn't the devil hisself, he wouldn't be totin news on you. But he don't like you, maybe you got a little somethin more than he got, you in better shape, standin in a good position—and if you get that way in this world, you better be ready to defend yourself against words and bullets, bullets and words.

HANNAH done her housework but she didn't never feel good after we moved over to Vernon's place in '48. Well, '49 she lingered along, still able to do her work. In the year of '50, her sickness set down on her and she taken to bed. Never did get up no more in the year of '50. She lingered—I was right there home with her every day. I'd run out to the field—the girls was there waitin on her —and about the middle of the mornin I'd dash back to see how she was. She'd still be on the bed, hadn't got up since I went out in the mornin. She done give it up then, I felt just like it. I seed she'd got down to where she couldn't help herself; needed one of the children right there with her all the time.

And so, she lingered along, lingered along, and there was no pickin up to her. Called out for the doctor—she went to the doctor a few times before she got down so bad, but not goin like she oughta been.

I weren't fooled when I lost her, because I had taken her ailment more serious than I ever let on. She complained of a hurt in her back, in the kidney, and when she got down, along in the fifth year I been free, she just lost her health completely.

We called Dr. Ginn on a Sunday evenin in August. And he dashed up there from Calusa right quick and examined her. Me and Vernon was out in the yard: Dr. Ginn come out of the house advisin us, "Rush her to the hospital at once, rush her to the hospital at once. She's got cancer at the lungs."

That tore us all to pieces. Well, we rushed her right on into the hospital. It was very sad to me because that was my wife and had been a wife to me since 1906, in the Christmas. She was a lovin wife, absolutely, just as sure as you born. She and I was the mother and father of ten children, and all along when she was birthin them children her health was good. Her mother told me when I married her, before I married her, that she had the hay fever every year, every summer. I went on and married her: I weren't after the fever, I was after the girl. She was eighteen years old when I married her, lackin from December till the twenty-second of February, 1907, of bein nineteen years old.

So, we rushed her to the hospital that Sunday evenin. I was right back there Monday mornin. I walked in her room and my daughter, my and her daughter, Leah Ann was there waitin on her; she come out from Chattanooga to see about her mother. And she went on to the hospital and stayed with her until she died. And so, I went down there Monday mornin just as quick as I could— we was livin on Vernon's place at that time, all of us that stayed at home; and we got a hearin that mornin that she was yet livin, hadn't died. So I dashed down there and I walked in the room where she was. She weren't payin much attention to anybody around her —just callin on the Lord all the time, talkin to her God. When I walked in there that mornin I looked at her and I seed verily she was upset some way. I called her—I walked up and spoke to her. She weren't on the bed, she was sittin on a chair back against the wall. She didn't want to lay down; she had laid down long enough to get wore out layin down, and when I walked up to her she just sittin up there and all I could hear, "Jesus . . . Jesus . . . Jesus . . . Jesus . . ." Me or the girl, one—Leah Ann, first girl child we had that ever left this country, went to live in Chattanooga with her husband—one, or both, walked up to her and walked away. She didn't recognize us.

Well, I come on back home when I was forced to come back. Next mornin, that girl got someone to bring her home on a car; hollerin, "Mama's dead, Mama's dead."

I just felt like my very heart was gone. I'd stayed with her forty-odd years, and that was short, short—except bein pulled off and put in prison. I picked her out amongst the girls in this country and it was the easiest thing in the world to do. I loved that gal and she dearly proved she loved me. She stuck right to me every day of her life and done a woman's duty. Weren't a lazy bone in her body and she was strict to herself and truthful to me. Every step she took, to my knowledge, was in my favor. There's a old word that a man don't never miss his water until his well go dry. You got a good husband or a good wife, you know about it when they gone. I'm praisin her now, I'm praisin her for what she was—she was a mother for her children, she was a mother for her children—and when they put me in prison, the whole twelve years, she stayed by her children, she didn't waver. I left em with plenty to carry on with and they worked to keep it while they made their livin. And she'd keep check on what come in and what went out and never did they lack for somethin to eat.

She was a Christian girl when I married her. And she was a woman that wanted to keep as far as her hands and arms could reach, all the surroundins, she wanted to keep it clean. And I kept myself clean as I possibly could. But in past days, I've sneaked about in places, I did, I own to my part of wrongness. Maybe I've had contact with other women, but not many, not many, and I handled the proposition quiet. I liked women, but it was just certain women that I liked. I didn't pitch out there and run at every old woman or gal in the country after I married her—didn't do it before that. And I desperately kept clean of runnin too much to a extreme at other women when I had her. Regardless to all circumstances, I weren't a man to slip around at women and no matter what I said to another woman or what I done, I let my wife come first.

WE quickly picked Hannah up and carried her to the undertakers at Tuskegee. From there we carried her to Pottstown and buried her at Pottstown Baptist Church; that was her membership, had been. I don't know what caused her to do it, but before she died she moved her membership over between here and Apafalya, to a church was a Holiness Church. She never did—I never did hear her say definitely, but it was sung that she wanted me to join over there too. I had done joined Pottstown where she was a member, just before I come out of prison, and she was still at Pottstown when I come out; then she changed. But how come she changed she didn't tell me.

Now to me, a Christian person is but a Christian person, I don't care who it is and I don't care what denomination. If he been newly generated and born by the holy spirit of God, which is the high power, who is the man that rules the heaven and earth, and what He don't rule, it don't exist—that's the mercy man of the world.

It's just a different performance from one church to another. Same God, but they serves Him different; different enough for you to set and look it through, and hear the difference in the sermons that's preached and the songs that's sung. These Holiness people baptizes you just like the Missionary Baptists do, but they calls for rebaptizin. You join their church, you just got to go in there like you never been a member of no church. As far as I'm able to see, that means they don't recognize nobody to be a Christian but their-selves. Well, I think that's wrong. I think you should be allowed to just go and give in to the church that you want to live with in their denomination, give over to em, explain yourself and take your seat. But the Holiness don't allow it. You got to be baptized over again.

They worships there with a whole lot of music. I've had em tell me, "God loves music." Well, God don't care nothin bout your music; it's just your soul. Open it rock bottom to Him, feel His love in your soul—that's sufficient. And then love the light. You can run around here, go from church to church, join every church, just as many different ones as there is trees in the woods; if you aint been newly generated and born again you aint gettin nowhere. If you aint been changed by the high authority above, changed in your soul and changed in the life you live, you a long way from the will of God. It's just like I told Mr. Miller Wilcox, white man; spoke the word in his store one day. I just politely come out and told him: "I love everybody, for God's sake. I don't love em for my purposes and my sake. I love em for God's sake. I love my race, men and women, colored I love em. I love white men, white women, and everybody under God's sun, to please God. That's my whole heart. Treat em right if they treat me right. Try to treat em right if they don't treat me right. But if you don't want to treat me right, don't treat me noway. Because I won't back off from the trouble you give me."

III

She died in August and I had a crop to take care of that year. I made six bales of cotton by myself; I just hired some choppin done. A white gentleman and his wife and his wife's sister come to me—poor people—and they wanted to work. And all in that family called me Mr. Shaw. It was "Mr. Shaw this" and "Mr. Shaw that"—I felt a little embarrassed about it. They come from this country and still they called me "Mister." I felt that if their color, their race, heard em call me Mr. Shaw, they'd hate *me* for it. The wife's sister was a little girl and she was big enough to chop cotton but she practically stayed at the house tendin to her sister's children while her sister and her sister's husband would work for me. And that girl would call me Mr. Shaw in spite of the world. I told her one day, "Girl, you be careful bout callin me 'Mister.' You'll lose friends by that. Call me Nate, my name is Nate Shaw, you call me that—Nate."

Wouldn't do it. She called me Mr. Shaw till the last day she worked for me. And she come over there and told me one day, "Mr. Shaw, Sister says to send her a watermelon." Me and her went out to the watermelon patch and I pulled her a nice watermelon from the vine and gived it to her. She taken it home to her sister and her sister's husband. And right there I tried—but I couldn't break that child from callin me Mr. Shaw. And she was just about a missus-sized girl.

You know, a heap of em do that now. I don't say a word. Treat em with respect and go on my way. They'll call me Mr. Shaw right before their wives, men do, and their wives. But I know how desperate them that won't call me "Mister" have been against their own color that do. I'd rather they call me Nate, just go on and call me Nate: it sounds better in my ear. But I don't worry bout nothin they call me; they doin all the worryin bout that now. I don't think I'm so much. They didn't used to call me nothin but Nate, Nate Shaw. I don't need no honorin; just treat me right and go on, don't bother me. That's what I want.

MATTIE JANE done the housework and the cookin after Hannah died. Rosa Louise stayed a short while after the death of her mother, then she went to Chattanooga to stay with Leah Ann. Leah Ann was married to Justin Ames and Justin wanted some-body to stay there with his wife until he come out of army service. And Hannah had consented for Louise to go up there before she died. And it wound up, Louise had a baby up there and stayed on.

After Hannah died I made three crops and I married again. Had a crop in '50 when she died; '51 I pitched another crop; '52 I made a crop there; '53 I made a crop there; '54 I made a crop—'53 and '54, Josie, my wife now, helped me chop and gather them crops. The government was fixin the price on cotton regular then. Cotton brought somethin like twenty-five cents and any time you get above twenty cents a pound, you can live, at the amount of cotton people make. I was workin on land that produced better than a half a bale to the acre with common fertilize. Generally planted from twelve to fourteen acres, and a big corn crop. I made corn to walk on every year.

Durin my years as a single man, I plowed that gray mare I taken over when I come home. Before my wife died, she claimed that big iron-gray mare was her'n, that was her'n. Them boys didn't dispute her because they knowed they was losin her. I'd a tore em all to pieces, I'd a messed em up if they'd a kicked against what she said. Tell the truth, me and the children didn't agree good bout nothin since I come out of prison. I'd been away from em so long and they had the ropes in their hands and seemed like they wanted to hold on to em after I appeared.

My youngest boy, Garvan, he cut up like the devil one day— I didn't want to hurt him, that was my child. He was just about grown when I got out of prison, runnin around courtin, correspondin gals, and it wasn't long before he married. So, one day, come up a little disagreement and he jumped up and wanted to fight me—I didn't pay him no attention. His mother was quick to worry herself down for no cause. And I knowed, if I'd a knocked him down with my fist, jumped on him, stomped him and kicked him—I aint got a child but what I coulda fought him, and there's some of em I coulda whipped em. Well, he got mad at the breakfast table bout some words I spoke; come up a quick flustration and his mother come into the room. I got up—I didn't hit him a lick, just walked on through the house and started out the front door and he runned up to me and grabbed me and tried to pull me on out. I didn't hit him, only stood there and mouthed a little at him. He tried to pull me on out and I caught the wall beside the door and held myself back without throwin no strains against him. Hannah was just a cryin and a carryin on. Right then I coulda just turned loose the wall and rapped him against the side of his head and knocked him out—but I weren't goin to do that, bring on a whole lot of trouble, hoopin and hollerin. And he was my child, I couldn't hurt my own child. I just caught the wall—that was the crop. He invited me outdoors—I wouldn't go; his mother woulda had a fit if

I butchered him up. Well, I stood on her feelins; she was already complainin and was under the weather. Right then a cancer had her. And I didn't want to aggravate her. So, Garvan couldn't do nothin with me, he couldn't pull me out the house and he give up.

I worked that mare over on the Leeds place three years. Then I moved over on Vernon's place in '48 and made five crops with that mare until I sold her to Cece Rowe, colored fellow; just practically gived her to him for forty dollars. She was a good animal but I didn't want her no more. She'd plow—we snaked logs up yonder on Vernon's place with that mare; she was heavy and she was agreeable. But when you hitched her to the wagon, you had to be the driver; she'd run away from you the minute you let up. She tried, when I hitched her with a mule, she tried like the devil to run away from me. I said to myself, "That aint goin to help you; you goin to work to that wagon when I want you to."

So I went and sold Cece Rowe that mare for forty dollars just to get her away from me—horses was cheap, I just tried to get a little out of her and be shed of her. And I was lucky to get what I got.

Went on and bought me a mule and I kept that mule until I sold her last winter. Bought her from a white gentleman up the other side of Lavender's bridge, goin toward Beaufort. I'd heard that Mr. John Culpepper had a mule for sale. Went up there and looked at the mule one Sunday—doggone it, I runned into what I wanted then. Vernon took me on his truck and carried me up there. On route we stopped at Miss Mandy Rudd's store at the Pottstown crossroads and there was a little boy runned out of the store. Vernon knowed him, said, "That's Mr. John Culpepper's grandchild. His daddy is Mr. Culpepper's son-in-law."

Vernon got out and asked the little boy, "Is your papa in the store?"

He said, "No, Daddy's gone over yonder to the racetrack."

"Well, is your mother in there?"

Said, "Yeah, Mama's in the store."

Vernon went in there and talked to her—that was Mr. John Culpepper's daughter. He told her, "My daddy wants to buy a mule and he heard that your father had a mule for sale. I decided I'd

stop—I seed your little boy out there in front of the store and I
just come in here to ask you about it. Does your father have a mule
for sale for sure? We heard that he do."

She said, "Yes, Papa got a mule to sell, she's a nice mule too.
Papa got a mule, surely."

Vernon got back on the car and we didn't quit drivin till we
got to Mr. Culpepper's house, just off the main line several miles on
the Beaufort side of Lavender's bridge. We got there and Mr.
Culpepper's wife come out and told us, "He must be down in the
pasture, but he'll be here in a few minutes."

And after awhile he come up. And he had a grown-sized son,
I don't know whether he was of age or not; and me and Vernon
and him and his son went on back down to the pasture; the mule
was in the pasture. Weren't no grass comin up then; she was just
put out in a dry pasture where she had nothin but dead grass to eat.
But the mule was fat as a pig. Walked on down there—she seemed
to be kind and gentle. You start foolin with mules, I aint nobody's
fool. I bought three mules out of the drove myself, my own self,
and I bought as many as two out in the country and I hadn't got
a sorry mule this mornin. And I worked a heap of different mules,
breakin em for people. Mr. Hap Grimes, I broke two or three for
him, way out there close to Apafalya. He put em on me, knowed
they'd be took care of—

So, we walked up to that mule, all of us, and got behind her
to drive her to the lot, one Sunday mornin. I wanted to look her
over good and close. Vernon and Mr. Culpepper and the Culpepper
boy was walkin behind me. And I was between them and the mule,
just watchin her movements every way. She didn't break to run at
all. That mule woulda weighed about eleven hundred pounds, heavy
mule, round as a butterball. She went right straight on to the house
ahead of us, me chasin her like a dog after a rabbit.

Got to the house and Mr. Culpepper told me and Vernon both
how old she was—said she was seven years old and he bought her
from the fellow that bought her out the drove.

I asked him what he wanted for her. He said, "One hundred
and twenty-five dollars."

I thought to myself, 'That's cheap for a mule that look like
that. Cheap.' I wanted to get my hands on her. When I chased
her to the lot that day, I was just hoppin with the rheumatism,

couldn't walk straight, hoppin. But I'd sold my mare and I wanted
to get me a mule so whenever I did get able to plow I'd have a
mule already there. That was my full aim and intention and the
Lord abled me to do it. That rheumatism passed off me like a sudden
spell of weather.

Mr. Culpepper had a horse there and he was workin at Calusa
and nobody there but his son. And he had a brand new tractor there
and that mule and a horse. And he didn't need that mule and that
horse neither; his son was usin that tractor. I said, "Well, Mr.
Culpepper, today is Sunday. I didn't come up here to buy no mule
today, but I wanted to find where I could get one and I'd come back
later, time enough to buy her. Will you give me till this comin
Wednesday to take her off your hands?"

He said, "Yes, I'll keep her."

I said, "Consider, Mr. Culpepper, she's sold."

That Wednesday, Garvan come off his job—he was still livin
with me in that big house on Vernon's place. And he come off
his job with TJ—TJ was workin at the Calusa mill, too. And TJ
brought Garvan right on to me. I was up there at that sawmill where
Cece Rowe used to work when he bought that mare from me. And
I was pilin me out some more lumber there that I was buyin from
the sawmill man and layin it aside to pick it up at a certain time.
I got my lumber straightened out there and jumped on the car
with TJ and Garvan and went on up there to Mr. Culpepper's. Got
up there and he had just come in off of his job at Calusa. Found out
I was there for that mule, went out and caught her. Gived me
her gear—but her gear weren't much account. I pulled out my
pocketbook and gived him his hundred and twenty-five dollars. And
he bridled her and led her out the lot. I gived Garvan the bridle
reins and he took her away from there, walkin; left me and TJ there
on TJ's car. I thanked Mr. Culpepper and we pulled out. Caught up
with Garvan and that mule was just trottin along like a dog. Garvan
was walkin his can off. Every once in a while she'd start a little jig
trot right behind him. Pretty a mule as there was in the whole
country. I felt good, I felt good.

And when we got over here near the crossroads, just about
a mile this side of the crossroads, we met Vernon on his truck,
comin to meet us. And just had passed Garvan with the mule.
Vernon asked us how far was Garvan behind us? We told him,

"He's right up the road apiece. He aint far and he'll soon be here."

Garvan come in sight, right on with the mule. Vernon said, "All right, Papa, you get on my truck now and let Garvan—" TJ done gone on; Vernon wanted me to get on his truck and let Garvan come on with the mule.

I said, "No, Garvan done walked enough—" It was about eight miles from where we got that mule, way up in there the other side of Lavender's bridge.

Vernon allowed, "Papa, just let Garvan bring the mule on. You crippled with rheumatism, let him bring it."

I said, "No, I want to lead her home myself, I'll make it. My body wants to drive on home on your truck, but my mind tells me to walk that mule on home."

We weren't a bit over a mile at that time from Vernon's house. Garvan come walkin up and I said, "Go ahead, son, get in the truck with Vernon. I'll bring the mule on home."

I come on with the mule then and there's a old white gentleman lived just up the road apiece from Vernon—RC Greenwood. And after I passed Mr. Greenwood I hit a little bridge goin through a swamp. I was alone with the mule, hoppin, leadin the mule, hoppin, leadin the mule. We got to that bridge and she swung back, wouldn't come on across to this side. Wouldn't even step on it; looked at it and pulled back. I seed I couldn't move her so I just walked that mule up to Mr. Greenwood's house, told him, "Mr. Greenwood, I got a mule here and I'm on my way home with her and I can't get her to cross that bridge down there. I'll give you a quarter if you'll just walk on down the road with me and the mule and help me get her across."

He looked at me and looked at the mule, said, "All right, Nate, I'm comin with you."

When we got back to the bridge I stepped on to go across and that mule pulled back again. Mr. Greenwood got behind her and just patted his hands on her and hollered: "Eeeeeeeyaaaaaahh, eeeeeeeyaaaaahh." She lit on that bridge and come across. Had no more trouble with her then. Went right on in home, put her in the lot and she stood there several days and it was next Monday come —I brought her home on a Wednesday—I took that mule out and hitched her up. She was the dandiest mule to plow, good a mule as ever I walked behind. She'd give you almost any kind of gait you wanted, too. I called her Kizzie. Changed her name; they'd called her Claude. I kept that mule eighteen years. She held up good and I held up good.

MADE my last good crop on Vernon's place with that mule in '53—made eight heavy bales of cotton, and didn't have nobody helpin me but a little to chop. Worked about ten acres that year and fertilized heavy, so I come out with nearly a bale to the acre. That was my limit; I couldn't plant any more acres and take care of it myself. I aint goin to plant no great territory and let the grass eat up my crop.

Went on after that and made two more crops there, cotton crops, and I made nearly four bales to the crop each year; didn't put but four acres in cotton and I fertilized it heavy. And planted corn on the rest, enough to feed my mule all year round and have some to sell.

The year I made them eight bales of cotton, Vernon hired a hand to work his crop. Vernon didn't have no tractor yet but he had a stompin good pair of mules. And he hired Bob Leech, colored fellow, and gived him forty dollars a month. One day I was plantin —and old man Warren Jenks' place joined Vernon's and there was a young colored fellow workin there on halves. I had one of Warren Jenks' old mules—poor mule, weren't able to do much, I rented him from Warren Jenks and put him with that big gray mare I had and plowed with my two-horse plow, breakin my land. I hadn't got shed of that mare yet, but was just about to and get me a mule before plantin. I kept her just to break that land with. So, one day I was down in the field and had that pair of stock hitched to my two-horse plow and I was breakin land, weren't no foolin around goin on— well, this young fellow workin right below me on Warren Jenks' land—he was a MacDougal—he was plowin right close to the line between the two plantations. And this fellow Vernon had hired was plowin right up above me, had Vernon's mules and supposed to be breakin land with a two-horse plow. I could see him up there but I weren't noticin him much, had no reason to. And this fellow Mac-Dougal come around on a long row next to the wire fence between Jenks' and Vernon's and I heard him hollerin, "Let em go, let em go." And he hollered that two or three times, strong, loud. I looked around and seed it was him hollerin and it excited me to see who

he was talkin to. And I looked up there in the field above me where
Bob Leech was plowin and one of them mules had done hipshodded,
dropped his legs back and stopped to rest. Call that way of standin
"hipshoddin." And the other mule just standin there plain. Bob Leech
settin up there between the plow handles, no tellin how long he
been settin there, and Vernon payin him forty dollars a month.
Settin down on that cross piece between them handles, smokin a
cigarette. Mules, one of em, looked like he just gone to sleep. Mac-
Dougal seed that, no tellin how long MacDougal had been lookin
at him, and he hollered, "Let em go, let em go." Bob Leech settin
right up there in my sight, doin nothin. He hollered back to Mac-
Dougal just this way: "There aint no way in the world, there aint
no way in the world."

Well, when I seed what it was all about—Bob Leech tellin
MacDougal weren't no way in the world to make him keep them
mules goin. You halt a mule like that whenever you please—no tellin
how long them mules was standin still—and you'll break that mule
of his work habits. Vernon come in that evenin from Calusa, off his
job—I taken a very special thought of Leech's act, and that weren't
the first time he done that. He was just a sorry fellow and didn't
want to work, and by him not workin he'd ruin Vernon's stock and
squander Vernon's money—I told Vernon, "He aint doin nothin
but beatin you. He's gettin them mules off in the field by hisself
and he won't do a thing with em. You aint goin to get nothin out of
him and you'll lose a crop if somebody don't watch at him and keep
him goin." He stood and listened at me. I said, "But don't you say
nothin to him about it, he'd know it couldn't a been nobody but me
told you; I was there in the field with him, him plowin off yonder
somewhere and me plowin here."

Vernon already knowed this fellow weren't much good and
I had found it out myself. We had been cuttin down in the pasture
—in addition to these words—it was cold weather still and we
hadn't started to plowin. Vernon sent him off down in the swamps
with me, cuttin. Cold and wet time—got down there one mornin,
me and him, he had a ax and I had a ax, goin down in the swamp
to cut. Well, we was cuttin right close together and every time I'd
look around—when we got there I pulled off my coat and went to
cuttin. It was cold, yes, but it was just nice for that sort of work.
I pulled off my coat and went to slingin that ax. Every time he'd
cut down a sapling or a small tree and trim it up, all between times,

I noticed him goin around humped over and hands between his legs, "It sure is cold; Ooooooo, it's cold." And I had done pulled off my coat and cuttin. It weren't cold enough to stop work or even to complain about it bein cold. I was just as warm as I needed to be— I looked around at him carryin his hands between his legs, walkin along, shimmyin in a kind of drawed up way, "Sure is cold."

I said, "Bob, how come you don't make up here a little fire if you all that cold?"

Good God, that was right down his alley. He made him a fire and he just had to lose too much time with that fire and me cuttin away at the rate the work required. I was cuttin saplings, trimmin em up, pilin the brush; and every time he'd get a tree trimmed up, if he hadn't a stopped all along, he sure stopped then. And that was his constant way about that wood.

Well, when we was plowin in the field that mornin, startin breakin the ground, I thought about how triflin he'd been that day in the swamp. I knowed him—he was a grown man. His daddy lived right there on one of Warren Jenks' places.

So, I told Vernon, "Don't you say nothin to him. I'm tellin you this for you to keep your eyes open. If you's to let him know that I told you these words, he might quit and you'd have a hard time findin somebody to work in his place. There's a way to check his ways. Now here's the settin and it just might work: when you go off to your job every mornin to Calusa, before you go, when you wants a certain piece of work done, tell me about it in place of Bob. When I go to the lot to catch my horse out to go to plowin, I'll tell Bob what to do for you and I'll quit my work even and do that too, with him."

He agreed.

I kept up with my plowin; if I worked I worked, if I set down I set down. I didn't make out like I was workin and set down. If I has anything to do I must do all I can at it; I just feels terrible if I don't. That year I made eight bales of cotton and I cleared a little above six hundred dollars—and plenty of corn to feed a pair of mules and didn't nobody help me plow nary a furrow. Vernon'd tell me what he wanted done and he'd go on to his work at Calusa. I'd go to the lot to catch out, Bob would come and catch out too; I'd say, "Bob, I'm gettin along well enough with my plowin that I can help you today. And Vernon wants me to help you out. We goin to do so-and-so-and-so in Vernon's field today, or if it takes two days. Let's get hitched up here; let's catch out and get hitched up."

That was already cultivatin time. Bob would take one of Vernon's mules out and I'd take out my Kizzie mule, first season I ever walked behind her. Me and Bob both would get out there, plow all day many a day. I'd keep goin myself as much as necessary, look around for Bob and he had to do it, too. After I took hold thataway, it cut him down. He couldn't get off by hisself where he could do nothin, he had to roll on with me. That year Vernon made thirteen bales of cotton—me and Bob together, with my helpin him—and plenty of corn to feed that pair of stock.

If it was choppin cotton, me and Millie, Vernon's wife, and Bob Leech, we all got out there and chopped cotton. Millie was one of these kind: in them days she could work, but she just worked herself until she worked down. A woman can do just so much in the field, work herself to death. Now a man can do too much too, but a woman has children to bear and care for at the house, which the man don't have on him so much, because he got to look after the affairs in the field.

Vernon and Millie had two girls, only children they have in the world, and at that time one of them girls was goin to school in Tuskegee. And Millie'd get out there, Vernon would let her do it—well, that was my son and his wife, I didn't have nothin to do with the way they runned their business. Millie'd work her heart out, looked like almost. Been a wife of mine she wouldn't a done it. On down in the years to come, they'll put out more on her for doctor bills than her help was workin in the fields. Let her run the business at the house and him tend to things in the field, and if he needs any help, hire him somebody. Get that woman out the field!

VERNON had a good pair of mules there of his own that he had accumulated through the condition that I left my folks in. When I got back, every mule I had was dead—I left two mules—and what they had got—mine was gone—was theirs. And after Vernon made that thirteen bales of cotton he bought him a tractor; went out there and sold one of his mules to some of them colored folks up in the hills, some of them Marshes. What come of Vernon's mules but a tractor?

Mules was gettin scarce then. Man get shed of his mule and buy a tractor. Well, how come that? Tractors was in style, you know, and a mule just can't cover the ground a tractor can. The govern-ment was holdin the price of cotton up above twenty cents every year. But, you might say it was holdin the price of cotton *down* under thirty cents. And it just become hard to make a livin on a one-horse farm if cotton was your crop. Of course, it weren't never easy to make a livin at it, but now it become plumb impossible. Your fertilize was high then, and your poisons and your labor if you hired anybody to help you chop or pick. So the ones that stayed in farmin—my boy Vernon over here, and TJ—they commenced a buyin tractors so they could work more land and make a bigger crop to meet their expenses.

But I was a mule farmin man to the last; never did make a crop with a tractor. I did manage to own as much as two cars at once, good stock—I've owned some of the prettiest mules that ever walked the roads. Now there aint none of my children, nary one by name, got a mule.

The year that Vernon started to work in his field with his tractor, he paid off the last nickel he owed on his place. He quit workin at Calusa and took up with his farm again, full time, by hisself. And he had put many a dollar in that land that he'd worked at Calusa for. As low as they was payin in wages at Calusa mill at that time, he saved some of it, in spite of redemption, and got stout enough to accomplish a place. Also, he got some out of his crop above the rent—he made good crops durin the years I was away from there.

WHEN Hannah laid down and shut her eyes in death I was the first man had to get out. They didn't drive me out but I weren't goin to stay there and carry Josie in the house, put her in there with my children. She wasn't their mother and it might have come up a dis-crimination about me livin in the house just like it was mine and puttin another woman in there. So when I married Josie, in '53, out I went over on Mr. Mosley's place in a hole.

I had built that house I moved out of but it was the family house: me and Hannah and Mattie Jane and Garvan—we was all in that house, family house. Not only that house, I put up a nice smokehouse there. I had to bear all that expense and I come out of

there just as naked as my hand. Then after I built that smokehouse
—I had to buy every piece of tin that went to cover it—I built a
shelter for my wagon, two-horse wagon I had possession of. Then,
to make my garden, I went over to Mr. Joe Thompson, man that
sold me the tin, and I bought garden wire and put it around there.
When I moved over on Mosley's place I still gardened at Vernon's
and I farmed there two years after I married Josie. But I lost the
benefit of every house I built—the dwellin house, I gived that up
when I married this outside woman; the smokehouse and the shed.

It was two years after Hannah died before I ever offered to
have a conversation with Josie. But I knowed her well; I knowed
her first husband, Johnny B Todd. He was always said to be kin to
me and he called me Cousin Nate and I called him Cousin Johnny,
but we never did visit one another. Never had my foot in Johnny B's
house from the time he married Josie—only goin to meet em at
church. I didn't have Josie on my mind at all. I just lingered along,
lingered along, married to my first wife and raisin a family. I never
did correspond Josie, never did say nothin to her but "Good mornin."

But I knowed a heap about her background. Her grandmother
and grandfather on her mother's side was Butterfields, Aunt Molly
Butterfield and Uncle Amos Butterfield. They lived northwest of
Apafalya, born and raised there, from slavery time up. And their
daughter was Josie's mother, Mary Butterfield. And Josie's daddy
was a Travis, Simon Travis. He weren't no great big man, but he
was pretty heavy-built. Not so terrible high, neither, ordinary in
height. And he married Mary Butterfield.

This thing's mixed up but it aint mixed up to where you can't
look through it. Peter's wife—my brother Peter—and my wife now,
Josie, is first cousins, own dear first cousins. Josie's mother was a
Butterfield and Peter's wife's daddy was a Butterfield. Peter's wife's
daddy was Josie's mother's brother. Little Amos Butterfield, named
for *his* daddy, and Mary Butterfield was brother and sister. And
Mary Butterfield was a Mary Travis after she married Simon Travis.
And Mary was Josie's mother. And Mary Beth, Josie's daughter by
her first husband, is named for Josie's mother.

Every time I'd go to Apafalya I'd see some of them Butterfields
and some of them Travises. Josie's daddy used to shoe my mules
before I done it myself. He was a noted blacksmith and he worked
for a white gentleman by the name of Shep Meredith right there in
Mr. Meredith's shop. Heap of times I'd go to Apafalya and throw off

a load of lumber down at the planin mill, drive my mules right up there in town and Josie's daddy would shy them for me.

Simon Travis and my daddy knowed one another well, and they didn't live over two miles apart—if it was it wasn't enough to talk about—when this happened: fellow by the name of Hark Todd, he was a friend of my daddy's too, and them three fellows always practically got along good together—Simon Travis, Hark Todd, and Hayes Shaw. They'd visit one another, hunt and talk. Well, one Sunday, my daddy took a notion he'd go down to Hark Todd's. And when he got there Simon Travis was there. So all three of em run up together.

Hark Todd didn't have no wife at all. His wife had died. But my daddy was married to TJ's mother at that period of time and Simon Travis was married to Mary Butterfield. So, settin there at the house and Hark Todd was superintendin around, cookin dinner for his children. No doubt if he'd a cooked a meal they'd a all et, no doubt. They was all old friends, used to travelin together. And Hark Todd had a pistol layin up in the house there, and Simon Travis —let the truth roll; accordin to the circumstances, how the thing went, all of em had been drinkin a little—I don't drink whiskey now, never did do it. My daddy raised me up—I knowed him to buy whiskey and give we children a toddy; he'd pour out a little in a glass, add water to it and put in sugar to sweeten it— Well, no doubt that Sunday they'd been drinkin. And while Hark Todd was cookin dinner, Simon Travis and my daddy was settin by the fire-place—it was in winter, too—talkin, laughin, jawin, you know, and somehow or other Simon Travis got a hold of that pistol, and like men would be that weren't careful about theirselves—I don't know what position my daddy was sittin in, he could have been sittin crosslegged. And Simon Travis got to meddlin with that old pistol and it went off and a bullet hit my daddy's leg right up in his thigh; and it worked around and come up on top of his leg. But the wound was down below—that bullet stretched on through and come up on top of his leg and stopped. Well, that was a great surprise. My daddy said—I think he had a right to say it; they was old friends and nothin between em that I'd ever heard—my daddy called it a accident. And this little old gray horse my daddy used to have—his last workin of that horse was with them Akers, and they cleaned him up and took that horse. My daddy had that little old gray horse at that time. And I could do more with that horse than my daddy could. I could take that horse and work him quiet to a one-horse wagon—my daddy had a brand new one-horse wagon at that time and he lost *it*. I could take that horse, hitch him to that wagon and go anywhere in these woods or any other woods or on the road; that horse never did give me a minute's trouble.

And when that horse come in home late that evenin, who brought him? My daddy was sittin straddled on that horse, in the saddle, and Simon Travis had that horse by the rein, leadin him, bringin my daddy home.

Well, some of the white people wanted my daddy to have Simon Travis arrested. If it woulda come up a lawsuit, why, Simon Travis could have just been out of some money or either prosecuted and sent to the penitentiary. It always appeared like this: if a nigger done anything to another nigger in them days when I was a boy comin along, white man didn't care how it went just so he's gettin the niggers against one another. But if he done anything to a white man, uh-oh, he done wrong then. But if a white man—if they could get niggers scattered and apart, they'd enjoy the results of that. Let niggers keep up a uproar between em and then, if one of em was a good nigger, obedient and do what the white man wanted done, they'd help him out or stand up for him. O, it was a mess. White man rejoicin if he could get the niggers tied up against one another. And old fools, they'd do it, too.

Anything that aint right, it's got to be awful bad for me to pay attention to it. Because I knowed that old rulin and I'd very often see it and I thinked to myself, well, that aint nothin, that's common, that's common—pay it no attention. When the white man would tie up a nigger in this country, why, it was so common I quit noticin it; I knowed it was the rulin and I wouldn't dote on it. I've even seed a Negro that would run and build up a fire on top of another one's back with a white man, by tellin that white man all that nigger's traits. So, if it weren't nothin too bad that happened, I'd pass it up. I've seed so much of that kind of stuff, from the least thing to the greatest, and I'd pass it up.

My daddy's case with Simon Travis—white people didn't care nothin bout my daddy, no more than they cared about Simon Travis —wanted my daddy to have Simon Travis arrested. My daddy told em he weren't goin to do it. It was all accidental. Well, if I get out there, me and my crowd—I'm talkin bout myself now, which is things I've never done—I go out there and lurk with em, and gamblin and drinkin whiskey and keepin up a hoorah and half-feedin our families and me keepin a jug of whiskey or a bottle of whiskey around where I could drink it at all times and stay out of shape, and some of my friends happen to hurt me seriously, I got no business havin em arrested. I'm a fool, surely, for convulsin with em thataway, makin whiskey my hobby—and the white man just waitin for a chance to sunder us.

My daddy had confidence in Simon Travis; he had confidence in Hark Todd; they all had confidence in one another. What is the use of my daddy jumpin up and payin attention to a white man or anybody else and lettin em run him in trouble against his friends? Simon Travis hated that thing, he absolutely hated it. So, my daddy put me on that little gray horse, one day after that happened. He was sittin in the house, weren't workin, weren't doin nothin. And he told me to get on that horse and ride to Simon Travis's and tell him to send him a plug of tobacco. Simon Travis would send my daddy anything in reason—he didn't ask him for unreasonable things. He just sent me to him for a plug of tobacco—that was his way of lettin Simon Travis know he'd thought the thing over and considered it finished. That's all there was to it and all he was goin to make of it.

My daddy sat up in the house and nursed his leg for a long time. That bullet stayed in his leg for two or three years. And how did he git it out?—I'm talkin bout what I know— Sat down one day and pulled his britches leg up, got it out the way of that bullet and that bullet was right along on top of his leg, just under the skin. He caught his leg up and took his pocket knife and split the skin—got that bullet out of there and the wound cured up. And not a word against Simon Travis did he speak.

SIMON TRAVIS and his family was livin down yonder below Apafalya —I was livin nearer to Apafalya in them days than I do now. And I had two first cousins, boys, used to court Josie before she married the first time; two brothers, Tom Shaw and Ronald Shaw, lived right above Apafalya on the Lee place. Their daddy was Lark Shaw, the one that Akers took all he had. I was stayin at Apafalya in the daytime or out in the country, either, workin for Mr. Jim Barbour in his lifetime. And when night'd come, I'd eat my supper there at Mr. Barbour's, then I'd go across the fields and go right over by

Simon Travis's, Josie's daddy's home. Josie was a missus-sized girl at that time and she was old enough to have boy company.

Cousin Lark lived just up the road from the Travises and I'd be goin up there to spend the night where Tom and Ronald was, my first cousins. My mother and their mother were sisters. They had the name Shaw, too, but Lark Shaw was from a different set of Shaws.

Well, these two first cousins of mine sort of disagreed over Josie. Ronald wanted to go with her and Tom wanted to go with her and the way they told it, she didn't care very much for nary one of em. In fact of the business, my wife here now was a kind of say-nothin girl; she was a little shy of menfolks. I knowed it too, and I never did knock around there to see *her,* not before I married the first time. So, two or three nights, I'd eat supper at Mr. Barbour's, then I'd go across the fields and hit the road comin down from Mount Olive Church and headin to the Lee place where Cousin Lark lived; and on route down there I'd stop at where Lester Watson had a house built for Simon Travis.

I always was a young fellow like this: I'd stop and take up time with old people and I bore a good name amongst em. And one of the nights I stopped there, I hailed and he called me in. I walked in and set down and we commenced a talkin on this and that—his wife never would come around less'n she was bringin Simon somethin to eat. And Simon Travis loved whiskey like the devil—never did drink no whiskey with him and he never did drink no whiskey in my presence. So, his wife, of the Butterfield family, she come in there that night and brought a ladle, you might just say a waiter, with two nice custards on it—I don't know whether they was potato custards or egg custards or what. She come in and handed em to him. He took the custards and she turned and left the custards on the plate and left the plate with him, and she went back toward the dinin room. He offered me some. I told him, "No, thank you, Mr. Travis. Just help yourself. I just et supper, come from over by Mr. Barbour where I works at. Just had supper before I left. I'm not hungry a bit so just help yourself." He set there and et up both of them custards, he was a big eater.

Well, durin the time he was eatin em, this here Tom Shaw and Ronald Shaw was hangin at his daughter in the back room. And she was shy of boys in them days, shy; she desired em maybe, but she was a kind of shame-faced girl. When a boy walked in she was out in the other room and gone. So, that night, while Mr. Travis was settin there eatin them custards and I was in there talkin with him—me and him was in a room by ourselves—I seed one of them girls—it might have been Josie; he had three girls at that time and Josie here was the largest one and the oldest one he had. And a few minutes after his wife went back into the dinin room, I seed one of them gals come to the door, peek in at me and her daddy—got gone right quick.

I tells Josie right now, I say, "You used to be shy of men and boys." She says, "Yeah, a heap of times boys come to our house and if I seed em before they seed me I'd run outdoors, go up under the house, keep hid as long as they was there." I say, "That's the rabbit in you." She laughs and says, "Must be, but that rabbit growed out of me."

Tom and Ronald, they'd laugh and talk about her, and it was "who she would" and "who she wouldn't" bout which one had the best time with her. She begin to get used to boys and men and she'd chunk off time with em. And Ronald didn't like for Tom to have the best day with her; Tom didn't like for Ronald to have the best day with her. But I weren't studyin the girl. I was engaged to marry then to the girl I married, my children's mother, and I didn't lose no time with no other girl at all. So, it just lingered, lingered; Tom and Ronald, first one then the other, wanted the best pull at Josie. But she never proved she cared nothin bout ary one of em particularly. When Mr. Ruel Akers cleaned up my cousin Lark, he left from down there and went back up in the Newcastle settlement where he'd moved out from when he moved down here. That put Tom and Ronald out of the picture. Well, Simon Travis's family just extended on.

I come out from Apafalya one day when I was haulin lumber for the Graham-Pike Lumber Company, and I seed this with my own eyes. Josie was married to Johnny B Todd at the time and it was several years before I was put in prison. They was choppin cotton right beside the road. One of them big fields Johnny B Todd worked run right to the highway. And him and Josie was out there choppin cotton. I stopped to talk with Johnny B awhile and look over his crop. They chopped out to the end and was right at the road when I drove up. I stopped my mule and set there on my wagon—never did get off my wagon. Johnny B standin there beside the road where he had done chopped out to—and we talked there several minutes and Josie never did break her gait. When she got to the end—she knowed me too, but I never had had no conversation with her in God's world—she just kept a choppin cotton and when me and Johnny got through talkin and I drove on, Josie done chopped back in that field halfway along a row.

I knew her, knew about her work qualities—she was steady on the job. I knowed nothin about nature ways with her, nothin of the kind. Never did go into the house after they married. I was married and had three children, livin up yonder on Miss Hattie Lu Reeve's place when Josie first married Johnny B. And that's where I was livin when Hannah's baby sister married, too. Mattie and Josie was right close along in age together. Both of em married bout the same year.

And so, after a while I drove on. My mules done stood there, rested a little. Of course, I was sittin in the hot sun. And they was choppin cotton. Josie never broke her gait.

And in the end, she done worked herself to death durin her life with Johnny B Todd. He was a farmer, that's all he knowed to do; and she worked in the field with him like a man so far as hoe work and pickin cotton. She's told me many a time: she used to get on the wagon with him and go two and three miles haulin sawmill slabs for stovewood, helpin him load, helpin him unload. And when she weren't workin with him, the white ladies of the settlement was always runnin around her: "I want you to wash for me today," "I want you to iron," "I want you to sweep my yard." Good God, Josie would wash and iron for white folks all around Apafalya. Any community the colored women live in, the white folks want em to wait on em in different ways, pay em like they wanted to, never ask the colored woman what she charges, give her what they think is right. Josie come under them rulins. She have told me her own self—her mother done it and she used to go around and help her mother wash for white people, and she'd stick her arms in cold water just as deep as a woman had to stick em, washin for white people. And after she married she got down in one of her shoulders —rheumatism and every kind of thing. Well, that was all from exposure. Of course, quite natural, she mighta not wore the clothes that she oughta had and taken cold, but that wadin in cold water, runnin about the settlement washin white folks' clothes—nigger couldn't turn, as they called him, or her, nigger woman couldn't turn without some white person wantin somethin done. All kind of personal jobs that God put us each here to do for ourselves, white folks hire a nigger cheap to do it. Josie come up thataway.

EVERYBODY knowed Josie was a workin woman. And she's a woman likes sports—especially fishin. And she was fishin right there. They was livin close to Sitimachas Creek when they stayed up there by Apafalya; the creek was just back up north of their home. And her and another colored woman, they *stayed* on the creek; soon as she'd be got done with her work, she'd take up her fishin pole and hit it to the creek. Josie would rather go fishin today than eat when she's hungry. She goes fishin now every chance she gets. Somebody come along and goin fishin that she knows, well, she gone. Fishin on the backwaters between here and Beaufort.

I never did care nothin much bout fishin with a hook and line. I always when I stayed close to Sitimachas Creek, soon as I got big enough to have me a basket in the creek—I was born just across Sitimachas on top of a hill. Not no more than a quarter mile from the creek. And I fished the creek with baskets all durin of my boyhood life. And after I married, good God—there's a cotton mill up there at Opelika, they just poured dye in the creek, poison, and killed out the catfish in Sitimachas. You could see the signs of it way down in here, the color of the water—killed them catfish a goin and a comin. It's a pity to kill what people love, it's a pity to kill it out. Well, the government, I think, made a racket behind em. That didn't help, they bummed the creek on the sly. People goin up and down Sitimachas to fish and just find the top of the water covered with nice catfish, poisoned. They ought to put em in the penitentiary about poisonin the earth and the air and the waters, killin the fish in the rivers and the water coasts and all like that. The devil is just loose on earth and the laws is not hard enough on em.

RIGHT after Josie's first husband died, my wife come to see me in prison, one Sunday. She told me, "Darlin, Josie Travis and Johnny B Todd, Cousin Johnny B who died, the only child they had"—she's in Boston now, Mary Beth—"Spencer Ramsey married her."

Spencer's daddy and Hannah was first cousins, but they didn't look like it. She was a yaller woman, direct the color of Josie—the difference in em, in size and looks, Josie's just a heavier-built woman than my first wife was—and Ben Ramsey was dark and his son, Spencer, was dark.

Tell the truth to it, Spencer Ramsey was just a sorry fellow. His first wife had just died over there in that house where TJ livin now; jumped up and went to correspondin Johnny B's wife's daughter. She was young and she married the scoundrel—he used to be a pretty good worker, farmer, but he got jaded and fell off with work.

My wife kept me informed about all that was goin on over there as far as she knowed. So, after Johnny B Todd died, Spencer Ramsey moved into the house with Josie and her daughter, Mary Beth—only child she got in the world livin, the other two dead. Josie had three children, she says, and I reckon she's very truthful about it. Had two little boys; lost em. This here gal was the last child birthed and she's livin today. She got a pretty good book learnin—

Well, Spencer ham-scammed there and run through everything he could get his hands on that Johnny B died and left. That kept Josie all upset—she's told me about it since me and her been married. He'd slip out all of Johnny B's tools and lose em or break em or sell em. Slipped a brand new cross-cut saw out and sold it. Josie found out where the saw was and made the fellow that had it bring it back to her. And he runned through Johnny B's seed cane, that old-fashioned sugar cane. Johnny B raised that, made syrup out of it—there aint ten people out of a hundred but what dearly loves to chew that old-fashioned sugar cane. Well, he stayed there in that house one year, just long enough to run through everything Johnny B had left; then he moved back down here with his wife, and Josie come too. She was followin her child, girl child, the only one livin out of the three. One died, accordin to her quotation, before it ever got old enough to work. And one, the oldest child, a little boy, he was as big as that least little old boy that stays here with us now, and he died. And after that Mary Beth was born and they managed to raise her. All right. When Spencer Ramsey moved into Johnny B Todd's old house he had his first wife's children with him too. And a year later they all moved out of there and come back down here. Spencer didn't own no land, but his daddy, Ben Ramsey, owned forty acres. They was livin there when my wife died in '50 and they was livin there when me and Josie begin correspondin in '52. I was a little slow about marryin again, I had some lonely thoughts about it. And of course, if it'd been left with me, I would never have parted from my first wife.

So, I started comin down there from my house, talkin with Josie, correspondin her. They was all there in the house—Josie and Spencer and Mary Beth and Spencer's children by his first wife and his and Mary Beth's children, four of em, three girls and a boy. And pretty soon they stripped up and moved off the old home place into a bigger house on Mr. Gil Kirkland's place. Well, me and Josie had decided to marry at that time, and one day I went down there to talk with her. I don't know where she was when I got there, but she was washin for white folks regular, off somewhere and due to be home soon. And I was settin there lookin and listenin and Spencer was plowin some right beside the house there in a field for Mr. Gil Kirkland.

People had been talkin that he was goin with another woman then and had Josie's daughter for a wife. And sure enough, Spencer was plowin and this little old woman come around and went out there to where he was. I was settin there, listenin at em; of course, it weren't none of my business, I didn't interfere with em at all, just listenin and lookin out. And he just fair cussed her in every kind of way, Spencer did, and there was a ditch just a few steps beyond the house just before you hit the cultivatable land, and Spencer pushed that woman into that gap. She fell over like a sack of flour but she got right up and walked out of that patch. He didn't hurt her, but not because he didn't try to hurt her, she just wasn't hurt. That revealed to me the kind of man was livin in the house with Josie and her daughter. It weren't too long before Mary Beth quit him and he died.

So, lingered along, lingered along, and I corresponded Josie a little over a year before I married her. I knowed her well, then. The oldest daughter Simon Travis had, him and Mary Butterfield —it's a good idea to consider everything that comes to your remembrance about a family when you go to marry. I knowed her family well and they was well spoken of. And Josie was a woman that there never was no outcries over her principles and character, never was. She was just Josie Todd—first she was Josie Travis—a good woman, hard workin woman. She always stayed clear of men, stayed in clean places. I never did hear talk of no men runnin at Johnny B

Todd's wife, in my other wife's lifetime. She was a widow woman
and I'd never seen or heard nothin wrong about her. She proved to
be a straight, devout woman. And when I walked in I was the only
man that walked in there regular. She gived me her attention and
I gived her mine.

After I went to see Josie and talk with her two or three times
I caught their condition: they was livin almost from hand to mouth.
Them children's mother and their grandmother was all that was
backin em up. Josie worked for em until she was just a big frame
and that was all. And Mary Beth was workin, the best of her time,
right across the river for Mrs. Guy Mahoney. Mrs. Mahoney runned
a hotel there in Calusa and Mary Beth put in several years there.

I told Josie one day, "It appears to me, under the conditions,
as far as I can see, you is sufferin for help. You and Mary Beth havin
a hard time raisin her children, and then has these other children
on you too, which aint no kin to you noway."

She said, "Yes, I has to work in and out."

I just come out and told her, "Well, now, don't stay here and
suffer. I'll help you, as free as the water run; I'll help you, accordin
to our agreement"—we had just got engaged to marry—"Whatever
you get in the need for, if you aint got it, all you got to do is notify
me and I'll help you all I can."

One time she said she had to go buy her some shoes; didn't
have a change of shoes and the shoes she had was worn through
and didn't have the money to get a new pair. I gived her the money
—I was a workin man, farmin, makin baskets. I weren't workin to
get rich.

Well, Mary Beth quit Spencer Ramsey and got engaged to Jim
Foote. It happened all of a sudden—and I'd heard that they was
goin to marry and I come down there to the marriage. Josie spoke,
and she was talkin bout people marryin, and I was standin out in
the yard at that time when I heard Josie speak. She come right close
to the door and they was all rejoicin in there over the marriage and
all and Josie said, "It's goin to be me next." Spoke that right at her
daughter's marriage, "It's goin to be me next." I looked around when
I heard that. And I trembled like a young man will do. She didn't
say nothin about it was me she was goin to marry but that was
already sealed between us. And several months after Mary Beth
married Jim Foote we was married.

I figured, accordin to what I heard, before me and Josie married and after, too, that some of my children didn't approve at me marryin her; had no objections to me marryin but wanted me to marry somebody else. They wanted to meddle and touch things they had no business—Mattie Jane, my second girl, she wanted me to marry a woman over here by the name of Sadie Rowe. Sadie Rowe had been married three times. Her first husband was a Morehead— they tell me a man got a wife and she's got a white liver, she'll kill him in nature affairs; he got to be strong enough in constitution to stand that woman. Well, I knowed this woman done had three husbands and two of em lived with her until they died. And she had two sets of children.

Durin of Morehead's lifetime, I didn't never travel worth anything through this settlement where he was livin with Sadie. My work was other ways, all around and back to Opelika, Tuskegee, Union Springs, Crane's Ford—that was my rangin place. And I didn't know so much about her second husband who stayed in this country; in the meantime of them days I was in prison. And some of em got to talkin after she married her third husband—my first wife told me this, while my family was livin over on the Courteney place. They belonged to the same church, Pottstown Baptist Church, and Sadie would visit her—folks got to talkin bout this third fellow she married, across the river, and my wife said that some of em told him that Sadie had a white liver; she had lost two husbands. In a very few weeks after they told him that, he pulled up and left her, got away from there. And he's dead now, as well as Sadie is.

IT was noticeable to me in my thoughts that some of my children might not appreciate this woman I married. I moved out—didn't wait for nothin, I moved Josie right out to a house to herself, on the Mosley place. Stayed six years in that old house there and it weren't fittin for the devil to live in. It wouldn't rain in there much but it was one of the nastiest places—we moved in there right after Jerry Hatch, poor colored farmer, moved out. Vernon's wife and Mattie Jane and Josie went over there and boiled water in their washpots and scalded that old buildin out. That gived us a clean house to live in but it didn't do nothin against the termites. Even the well went bad; it was passable enough when we moved onto the place by strainin it and all, but it needed cleanin before we moved away.

Didn't get no acres from Mosley, just got the house and the yard. Had a one-horse farm with Vernon, right across the road, as long as I lived on Mr. Mosley's place. Nobody livin there but me and Josie. Her grandchildren would come and go, but nobody livin there but me and her. Mattie Jane stayed over in the family house on Vernon's place where I left her.

Right after I cleared out of there, men commenced a hangin around at Mattie Jane. One fellow from down here at State Street, not only him but there was other fellows come in, and some of em, I detected, wanted to run over her. Mattie Jane told me herself, and there's others would talk it, this fellow from State Street would go up there, and one night, he called her and she failed to open the door for him, she refused him. Well, he took out at her—how some men will do women!—got out of his car and walked around the house, callin her and knockin the house. I heard about it before the rumor spread in the community and I decided, 'Um-hmm, after a-while you'll attempt to knock her door down and go in at her.' I just laid low because Garvan was supposed to be livin in the house with her. He and his wife occupied two rooms of that house, but they stayed down by State Street with her mother and daddy as much as they stayed up there. So this fellow kept a comin up there and weren't nobody there regular enough to protect Mattie Jane and her two little chaps—the world could see that that was her dead husband's little boy baby; called him Thomas, named for his daddy, and not only named, but he's the very spirit of Thomas Galloway, he's just like the twin of his daddy.

One day this fellow drove his car over in my yard on Mosley's place. I walked out—I don't know what he come there for; made a mistake, no doubt. I walked right out into the yard and told him to his head—he didn't get out of his car—"It looks like some trouble wants to start up there by my daughter's and Garvan's. I want to talk with you a little about that"—I was mad as the devil, too—"Up there at that house where my daughter stays who aint got no husband, it's goin to be hell to pay one of these nights." He looked at me. I said, "There's goin to be hell to pay and I want you to know this: there aint nary a boy I got goin to be in it. It's goin to be me —if some of that crap goin on up there like it's been goin on for the last few nights don't cease. Watch your points, sir, watch your points."

He could see in my eye I meant it. Quit comin there altogether, and after that I spoke to Mattie Jane about it. Said, "It must be somethin attractin that fellow up there, but I done gived him his walkin papers. I don't think he'll be havin nothin to do with you no more."

She jumped up and got mad with me, sassed me out. I never did *see* nothin wrong, but as my old daddy used to say, I could tell by a little what a great deal means. Still and all, he runnin up there at her and she barrin the doors against him, didn't want him up there—or did she? And when I told her she'd better stop her part, and talked to her a little too deep about what people would be sayin if he kept a comin up there and what he might do to her—"He liable to come in here and beat you up"—she flew hot at me, told me I was talkin to her like some kind of dog.

I said, "I don't *know* that there's somethin goin on wrong, but I'm warnin you and tellin you the worst could happen."

My whole family come up respectable; but noticin and watchin em through life, I seed that some of em wasn't walkin up to the chalk line—they was varyin a little someway. Then it was time for me to talk to em. But I did not put a bridle on em like my daddy did to me; it wasn't necessary. My children growed up in the world— I never did have to whip em much at all. We talked to our children and they was very eager to obey our rulins. They was well cared for by me and their mother.

Well, she didn't like me anticipatin her and she let me know it. I listened at her, took it in. But I knowed that a bad report would go out after a while if somebody didn't cut that fellow off; I knowed his acts wouldn't do and I thought I'd try to stop him in time.

ONE time I fell out with Vernon but it didn't last long with me. I got plumb hurt to my heart because it didn't seem like I had gived him sufficient cause, or any cause that day to do what he done and say what he said. Me and Josie had been married about a year when this happened. I had my own theory about how it come about, but I had no fact and I has none today.

Now one Sunday we went to Litabixee to a funeral—me and Vernon and Vernon's wife; went to the death of a sister to my dead sister's first husband. This fellow Sam Jones, who married Sadie, it was his sister they was havin a funeral for. We got on Vernon's truck—now this is family business, close, a man talkin bout his son. Some people of a family wants to keep what their folks done hid; I think it ought to come on, whatever it takes, let the tail go with the hide, it'll bring more. And so, we went out by Henry Shaw's, Sadie's boy, first cousin to Vernon. At that time he lived out above Apafalya, on the road between Litabixee and Opelika where the road forks up above a colored church, up in there about a beer joint. Vernon decided he'd drive up there to Henry's because that was the death of Henry's auntie.

And when this happened between me and Vernon later that day, I couldn't tell, but I had a deep thought: while we was there at Henry's that mornin waitin on him to get ready to go with us, I noticed him and Vernon go off around the house to theirselves. Well, when I was in prison, his mother told me that he come home, once or twice, actin out of place and all—he'd been drinkin a bit and she gived him the devil about it. I was surprised him doin that but I never said nothin to him, I just watched him—so, that Sunday, him and Henry went around the house there before we left to the funeral. I don't know what in the devil they was doin, but knowin that he'd drink a little whiskey at that time, had been gettin high off it, I decided that was the case, the reason he later acted like he did. It was a peaceable quiet Sunday. I discovered Vernon and Henry was out somewhere and I went around the house and found em there together, and apparently they was talkin bout some hogs. Yet and still there wasn't no trouble and when Henry got ready we all went on to Litabixee. Well, when we got up there we stayed quite late over in the evenin. And some of the neighbors of that family where that woman was deceased at was around there sellin candy. Me and Vernon mostly set out in the truck; it was kind of slow around there, everything movin in a slow motion, and I got up and went to them parties' house twice and bought some candy. And when I'd come back to the truck I'd offer him some. We'd set there, eat some candy, and we set there peaceable and quiet all day. Well, later over in the evenin, when all of em got done pokin around and got ready to carry the corpse to the cemetery, we followed. Vernon drove his truck through peace and quiet. Now, whiskey's the kind of thing, sometimes it works slow—

So, after the funeral, we got on route home. Come clean on out from Apafalya after leavin Henry off, down that road through Two

Forks and on down through Highgate goin through by Bear Butler's store. Well, comin right along there, just above Tukabahchee City, I looked out on Mr. Floyd Grafton's side. He was one of these cotton acre measurers and he worked a small plantation. Mr. Grafton had a nice patch of early corn and it looked good and tempting. I spoke to Vernon about it, him steady drivin—and when we got on top of a hill there, comin on down to a bridge close to Henry Gresham's house, we was talkin just like people would talk—our last talk was about Mr. Floyd Grafton, nice corn he had and so on—and it come like a shot—I was astonished after the words was spoke. I seed no cause for it in anything I had done that day, and when it happened, I named it to whiskey, whiskey loosenin him up. He raised up there and hollered, "You just aint got no sense!"

Ooooooo, Lord, I didn't look for that. I hadn't said nothin under God's sun that called for that. I was surprised—just like I'd fall out there dead, unexpected by anybody. I looked at him and I had a hundred thoughts. Why did he speak that word to me? I just set in that truck quiet after that. I studied it and studied it—what could he mean by that?

Durin the trip along, he picked up Sid Hardy's wife and her little girl and let her ride. They lived right down that road close to Henry Gresham's. And he picked em up between there and Tukabahchee City. And when we got to the place on the road as far she was goin, Vernon stopped to put her off. I was the first man jumped out the truck. I was hurt and I was mad, too. I couldn't remember nothin that had been spoke between us or nothin I had done to him to cause him to act that way; I couldn't imagine what it was all about. Just a fool act. I just considered he'd been drinkin whiskey and was out of his head. Well, I'm quick, I'll admit that; you mistreat me and it gets all over me like a passion. So, I got out the truck and maybe I mighta spoke somethin when I got out. I was aimin to walk from there on, I weren't goin to ride no further with him talkin that bad talk for no cause in the world. And he was angry at me, too—"You just aint got no sense, you just aint got no sense!"

Well, when I got out the truck—quite natural his wife would take up for him; she made it bad on my side when she come to Josie with it. She told Josie we both cussed at one another when I got off the truck. I mighta done it, but she took pains to let what I done be told. And I hadn't said a word till I jumped out the truck.

Told him he could go ahead—I showed I was mad, I couldn't help
it to save my life—my feelins was hurt. Looked like there was more
put on me than I was guilty of. First thing was the word he spoke
so desperate to me and then, when I got out the truck, he appeared
to have more complaints against me; but I was so hotheaded myself
at that time, I didn't catch what he said. There was some bad words
spoke between me and him and I was keepin up my end—I don't
give up; you got to kill me and I'll stop, but I try my best not to start
up against nobody without a point.

He offered to run the truck over me. I was around the front
of the truck, talkin at him, and he got in a fit up there and threatened to run that truck over me and kill me. I got up a big rock or
two, told him, "Run the truck over me"—standin right in front of
it—"run it, crank it up and come on."

And if he'd a cranked that truck up—he let that motor run
right on and he didn't have a thing to do but turn that truck loose
on me, but noway under God's sun that truck coulda hit me without
—it mighta hit me and runned over me, but I'd a sure busted that
windshield into his and his wife's faces both. So, I dared him—he
offered and it looked like he were goin to do it. Eventually he backed
up and turned from me. I walked home after that. And he told me
when he left me, "You better not come up that road, you better
not—" I was livin over there on Mosley's place at that time, right
across the road from Vernon. That road divided our houses. Well,
damn the road and him too!

I just failed to speak to him any way for a week after that.
But I was his daddy, and I confess to be a Christian man. I just
couldn't hold out walkin around people and not speakin to em.
Wound it up, I was the first one spoke. Told him, "Good mornin."
From that on, the thing quieted down. I ain't said nothin to him
about it from that day to this.

IV

Colored man worked on Mosley's place several years before I
come out of prison. Weren't nobody but him and his wife and he
was sharecroppin. And that white man—Mosley—waited till he
made a crop, good crop—I was told this and I talked with the fellow

got treated this way—and he had to get and get quick, forced out of the country. And when he left he was all beat up and thrashed like a dog.

Fall of the year and this colored man was said to be done paid Mosley all he owed him and his field was yet white with cotton. One day he got on the wagon with Mosley and went down to Beanville to the gin. And Mosley had done got his crowd together and told em where to meet him with this fellow on the wagon. So, when they come back and got right over here, not over a mile, they come to a bridge over a little creek and the white man had his crowd stashed there. Hung out till they come along, him and that colored fellow on the wagon, with a bale of cotton, fresh-ginned. Stopped right there at that bridge and Mosley stood there on the wagon and suffered that crowd to demand that colored fellow out. And they was said to be, most of em, the white man's own dear people—walked up to that wagon, got that colored fellow off and carried him down to the swamps and beat him nearly to death. That was notice to run him off of his crop, and it just white in the field and he done paid the man all he owed him. Beat him up; poor fellow got out of there after they left life enough in him to leave. Some of em said they cut part of his secrets off.

Mosley just drove on home—it was a fixed thing; I'm tellin it like it was laid to me—and he put hired hands in the cotton, picked it out, the balance of the crop. And that colored fellow stole away from here and got down in Montgomery County. And one day after I come home— Vernon and numbers of people right here in this settlement would go down there in Montgomery County and haul hay out off them big hay farms. Vernon particularly loaded up for his cows. So one day we went down there, deep on down in Montgomery County, on down even to Montgomery City, then east back into that hay country. We stopped at a certain big hay farm and the white man there told us he didn't own the place but it was owned by a man that this was the littlest plantation he owned; and good God, said there was twenty-seven hundred acres on that place and that was the least. Well, what man got any business ownin that much land and can't work it hisself? God don't give natural to one man more than to another. How did you come to own that much land? You might come in this world, your mother and father lie down and die, well, you come in possession of what they got, you and the rest of the children, and if it aint but one child he come in possession of all that his father and mother died and left. But if they come by their wealth and their land by swindlin the workin people and they leaves it for you, what are you goin to do with it? I have studied that for many years and I don't know the answer today.

And so, we got a truckload of hay and drove out from down there. And Vernon stopped at a store along the way and that colored fellow happened to be in there. I wouldn't a never expected it. These people up here thought he drove off and died, but he just drove clean out of this county. And he told me out of his own mouth how Mosley had him beat up and nearly killed, runned off his crop and then the white man hired some hands to get in there and pick his cotton, sold it and put the money in his pocket. He was said to be a man of that kind and that was the worst trick he was known to do. The poor colored fellow was half interested in every bit that come out of the field, had done picked enough to pay the man all he owed him. And he was entitled to get what was left but that's the way they done him. And he got down there in Montgomery County and got over his troubles.

That's the way colored people met their lives in this country, livin on a white person's place. White man's money been comin from the colored race—this state, the bosses of it and the moneyed cats, as long as I ever knowed, has been takin the nigger's labor. And if the white man had any trouble with a nigger, or if he was just the type of man that didn't treat a nigger like flesh and blood, he just liable to have him bushwhacked—more liable than not to do it. Colored people has stood—I can't explain it all—far and near, colored people have had a desperate chance in this country.

I got along all right with Mosley, jam-up, because I knowed him. I didn't have no crop with him, not a bit in the world, just doin small jobs for him in the way of payin rent for the old house. That old buildin stood over in a grove where the sun couldn't keep it dried out.

Jerry Hatch, fellow that lived in that house before I did, his wife was afflicted someway and disabled to work. Well, I say she weren't able to work in the field but she'd have a baby every year. Jerry never did have nothin—Mosley gettin his labor, his wife settin

at the house doin nothin, him and his children makin the crops.
And Jerry had a knack, and he done that several times, of movin
away, stayin off a year or two and movin back. And he had a pretty
good-sized boy, crazy-minded boy—Jerry Hatch has got a pretty thin
mind hisself and got triflin acts about him, but he's a good worker
and he stayed with Mr. Mosley, had been stayin with him, moved off
and moved back at the time *this* happened.

I was livin up on Vernon's place. This boy was stayin up there
with his daddy, Jerry Hatch; he was big enough to work and could
work very well. So one day, Mrs. Mosley goes out—as regular as
the days come she had to milk her cows herself, cold or hot, rain
or shine. She milked from one to two cows all the time, Mrs. Mosley
did, from Christmas to Christmas. I'd be around there many a time
after I moved on Mr. Mosley's place, doin little jobs for him he
wanted done, and Mrs. Mosley would be about the lot, soon of the
mornin, just as soon as she'd cook breakfast, she'd take her milk
buckets, go out to the lot to milk. Mr. Mosley and Jason, her husband
and son, they didn't have nothin to do but go in and eat breakfast,
Mrs. Mosley at the lot milkin.

So, one mornin or evenin, whichever, she went to the lot to
milk and it was said she found a note stickin up by the lot somewhere, looked like it was put there on purpose right handy for her
to see it. She took the note—I heard several say that the note weren't
actively wrote; accordin to the quotation of people that read the
note, looked like a chicken stepped in some ink and walked on the
paper. Just a plumb nothin. So, she carried it to the house—I reckon
she read it first—and she gived it to Mr. Mosley. He looked over the
note, and in the windup of it, he called Jerry Hatch's boy—that boy
comes along here sometime, walkin the road just this way: hand
hangin out of control and he just hashin along, just hashin along.
You put him in the cotton patch to pick cotton—talkin bout what I
know now, talkin what I've seed—he's got sense enough to know
how to work a little, but if you put him in a big field of cotton and
it just white as snow, he'll pick all over that field, first one place
then another. He just aint got a good mind.

So, Mr. Mosley called that boy in question about that note. The
note read, so they told me—Mr. Mosley let several people read that
note, and this here Preston Courteney, he let him read the note,
let a Negro into it to try to get all the provation he could against the
boy. Well, a heap of folks said the old note didn't amount to nothin,

never did believe the boy wrote the note. They say it read, "Meet me down in the woods and I'll give you five dollars."

It was well known Jerry's boy couldn't write but Mr. Mosley settled it right down on him anyway. And Mosley hopped on this boy—I was out there in Vernon's field and I couldn't see it for the trees, but he beat the boy unmerciful, Mosley did. I heard the licks —Bam Bam Bam—I didn't know at the time what was goin on. Jerry Hatch aint hit his boy a lick, Mosley done it. And when he wound up with the boy, he sent him off to reformatory school. And the boy stayed away for so long and so long. The white folks got to talkin about it and one white man told me to my head he didn't no more believe that boy wrote that note than he believed he could fly. He told me if he had the power he'd just go on down there and get that boy, if he knowed anything about it more than he did know, he'd just go on and get him.

All right. Jerry Hatch flew up and got gone again and he never has lived close to Mosley since.

One day up there at Vernon's, I got to talkin with a white fellow about it. Vernon didn't like me to tell it—Vernon's a good fellow but he jumps back when anything happens that way. So, I was in his yard when I told this fellow I heard that white man beatin that boy. Vernon told me when that fellow went away, "Papa, you told that fellow more than you oughta told him. You don't know nothin bout what happened."

I said, "No, I don't know nothin about it but the licks I heard; I heard that."

The niggers all begin to throw this man Mosley up, wouldn't nobody work on his place, wouldn't fool with him. That hurt him; he had to take who he could get. Well, there was a white man by the name of Praise Carter, young man, had a wife and one or two little old kids. Praise Carter went up there and made a deal with Mosley —he told me this hisself; he moved up there and Mosley commenced a bossin over him in the field, ordered him to change his plow and set it like he wanted. That was a workin white man too, Praise Carter. He proved it right there on that place. I was stayin there in Mosley's old house at the time.

So, Mosley went out in the field one day and he meddled this fellow Praise Carter. Good God they had a cussin frolic then. Mosley eventually dropped his head and walked away. Praise Carter told me—he hired me to help him pick cotton and I picked for him several days. Praise Carter made eleven heavy bales of cotton on a one-horse farm. Didn't plant no corn— And so, he told me how Mosley done talked to him out in the field, wanted him to change his plow and geehawse like he wanted. Praise Carter wouldn't do it and he forced that man to leave the field to boot. Well, that brought up a great discrimination toward him. Mosley got raw and told him to leave. He seed he couldn't do this white man like he could do a nigger. Praise Carter gathered that crop and got his part of it and moved away from there.

ONE white man come to my house one day and said, "Nate, do you know where I can get a family that can handle a one-horse farm? Maybe a man"—he didn't specify no color—"his wife, maybe two or three kids—"

Well, as God would have it, another white man had done come to see me before this one, said he was huntin a place to live. I told this white fellow, "Yes sir, Mr. So-and-so was here the other day askin me did I know where he could get a place."

He happened to know the man I told him. Said, "Aw, hell, Nate, I don't want no damn white man on my place."

That teached me fair that a white man always wants a nigger in preference to a white man to work on his place. How come that? How come it for God's sake? He don't want no damn white man on his place. He gets a nigger, that's his glory. He can do that nigger just like he wants to and that nigger better not say nothin against his rulins. "Nigger, just go out there and do what I tell you to do, and if I see fit to take all you got, I'll take it and get away with it."

Well, a white man won't take that in this country off another white man. They go right up there toe to toe, and if it's a cussin frolic and a fallin out, why, let it come. So what does the white man do? He fishes around and gets himself a nigger and puts him on his place where he can control him any way he wants to, and that's the crop! Them secrets I know—I go by history. Of course, a man's got to look *ahead* and think and think strong who is his friend and who is his enemy. But you got to have sense enough to learn what you have went through in your past life, Negro. You ought to look back at it as well as forwards. Don't be a plumb rabbit for the world. You know how you been treated: why don't you open up the facts to yourself?

THEY'RE yet callin this white man's country. It stinks in my nostrils every time I think about it. But these big dudes of the white race, they've never showed no care and respect for the poor white man. Well, how come that? They all white, why don't they hang together in every respect? How come they don't hang? One thing's certain and one thing's sure: color don't boot with the big white cats; they only lookin for money. O, it's plain as your hand. The poor white man and the poor black man is sittin in the same saddle today—big dudes done branched em off that way. The control of a man, the controllin power, is in the hands of the rich man. And the rich man is all in favor of the rich man. That class is standin together and the poor white man is out there on the colored list—I've caught that; ways and actions a heap of times speaks louder than words.

I've had the big white ones talk to me against the poor ones; I've had the poor white folks talk to me against the big ones. I know all about the rich white man; what he wants it's wrote all over his face. But I don't know how to take poor white people. There's some of em won't stand a nigger at all; and there's some will go along with him to an extent. But they seemed to have always thought they was a class above the Negro. And what are *they*? What are they? Dough-faces! Raw-gum chewers! There's been many a white man as well as Negro that's been undertrodded. But I just can't loosen up to em; I can't lead em in the lights of nothin. I have to take care. And I can't loosen up to some of my color because if I do lead em in the lights of what I know and what I've found out, when I know anything, every white man in the settlement is against me.

God's got some good people here and He's got some here aint fittin to go to hell, if I must explain. And you don't know none of em's ways unless you watch em. The Bible tells you to watch as well as pray.

MOSLEY weren't able to get nobody on his place, white or colored, and eventually he died. And when he died, his place fell in the hands of his wife and son—just had one boy. This boy, until a few months ago, had a industrious job up there about Opelika. Before old Mosley died, got to where he couldn't get him no hands, he bought him a tractor. This boy drove the tractor for his daddy and made the crops.

Last I heard, he got high enough to buy him another tractor; now he's got two tractors, his daddy's old tractor and the one he bought. And he works a part of the land on his off hours. Vernon works the biggest part of the place—rents it since the daddy been dead.

When the old man died—I'm goin to call myself what they call me—the *niggers* went up to his home where he was layin a corpse, before they carried him to the undertaker, payin respects to his wife and boy. His wife weren't a bad woman, she was just under his yoke all her married life. So, TJ and his wife and me and Josie went up there to look on his body, for God's sake. It weren't our part to slight the man's family for what he done. We colored people was doin everything here, and have always done it, to get along with the white people. And I reckon in many other sections of the land they doin that. We went up there to the death of him after they laid him out. Got on TJ's car one day—we was livin over there on Warren Jenks' place close to TJ's at that time. And this dead man Mosley and TJ had had a little trouble too. TJ never did live with Mosley but both of em lived in this settlement and they knowed each other. And one day Mosley tried to get TJ to take sides with him in a certain matter. He had a colored woman workin on halves with him up on his place. And when it come time to plow up his cotton to meet the government's orders, he wanted to plow up that colored woman's cotton and none of his. And he asked TJ's sympathy about it. TJ just told him he ought to go plow up his own cotton and leave that colored woman alone, and she a poor widow woman. But the white man wanted to switch the government over on her—plow up hers and let his stand and grow. His was a pet patch, he had fertilized it high, and if he lost he wanted that colored woman to lose in place of him. But she couldn't afford to lose and TJ told him that—he was crazy enough to ask TJ's sympathy and he gived TJ the devil when TJ spoke against him right to his head.

All right. We got on the car with TJ and his wife, me and Josie, went up there to view this man's body. And blessed God when we got up there to the house—there was three or four white men sittin out on the veranda, and when we got out of the car and walked in the yard, one of them fellows by the name of Thompson, the head mail rider through here, he wouldn't take time to see if we was headin up to the front door or what. He got up and told us, "Stop! Stop! You all get away from here and go around the back."

Now, it's been the custom and the habit in this country for niggers to go around to the back door of white folks' houses. Some colored folks would go in, where they was workmens for the whites, workin there all the time, they'd go in the front door. But not just *any* Negro.

Josie got sort of fretted over how the white man was conductin us, and she turned around to leave. I had a mind to do that myself, but a death occasion in a family is a serious affair, and for God's sake and for the sake of the dead man's wife I decided to go round the back way. And I convinced Josie to do the same.

Wouldn't let us come in the front door and the man layin in there dead. Why, if I knowed a old dog wanted to go in there and see him I'd let him go in any door he wanted to, watch him in the house and take him to the bed where the corpse is layin; I'd catch hold of him and let him look—if he had sense enough to know what he was lookin at. Told us—he got up off the veranda where he was sittin right where you would come up to the front—"You all go around the back." Wouldn't recognize us as folks. And we was showin sympathy for the family of the dead man. And honorin *him* enough to want to see his body.

So, we went on around the back, all four of us, me and my wife and TJ and his wife, went in the back door and come all the way through the house and into one of the front rooms. We looked at him layin there just as natural—and we passed on out back out the back way, went around and got on TJ's car and left.

Before this man died they sent him to the crazy-house. Stayed there awhile and he come back home, lingered there, got down and died. Some time before they sent him away, he confessed to be a Christian man, a Holiness man, and he joined the Holiness denomination. And, O, he talked to me bout servin the Lord and bein born again—but he eased up from them words and begin to be worried and shook up someway. Just before they sent him away he let into cussin and raisin sand, quit all that godly talk. And when he come home he was quiet. Then he died. I stayed on his place six long years and it was known that sugar wouldn't melt in his mouth. He got to where he couldn't get no colored people to live with him and no white ones neither. I was on his place but he didn't have anything to do with me because I didn't make no crops for him, just livin in the old house.

I made myself satisfied in mind and gived up the cotton plant; didn't grow nothin then but corn. The first year after me and Josie married, I planted less cotton than I ever did plant, come down to four acres. The year just before that I made eight good heavy bales of cotton, right by myself, excusin hirin some choppin. Rachel's little boys, three of em, come there every mornin to help me pick. When I got it all gathered and wound up, I was to the good about six hundred dollars, after my debts was all paid. Well, I married Josie then and I dropped right down to four acres, and that crop, Josie and her baby grand-chap, Mary Jane, done the biggest of the choppin. And in the fall, me and Josie gathered it and I hired it gathered together. I gived Josie fifty dollars out of that crop and then paid what I owed. My expenses wasn't so heavy because I had saved some money from that last big crop I made and put it into this one. Well, I decided I'd make one more crop, so I took four acres on halves with Vernon—he furnished the fertilize and the land, I furnished the labor. I was sharecroppin then, just like I done when I was startin off, just married to my first wife. At the present time I was workin with my son, on his land; that's exactly the way it runned for me. Well, that wound me up with cotton, the year I planted four acres with Vernon, on his place.

I aint planted no cotton since. When I cut down to four acres of cotton I commenced plantin corn to sell. I never did, after that, fail to plant a full one-horse crop, ten to twelve acres in corn. Sold it by the ton, too. Got anywhere from twenty to twenty-five dollars a ton. A heap of it used for stock, and a heap of it used for folks to eat. I'd sell it to Ventosa's mill down here at Tukabahchee City and to Mr. Emmet Wilcox's crush and feed, besides what I'd sell locally for folks to feed their mules on. I sold my sister's baby boy some, Henry Shaw—he goes in the name of Henry Shaw because he was raised by the Shaws but he's a Henry Jones. Lives out between here and Apafalya. I sold him corn, above a ton, once to my knowin.

The year I come down to four acres in cotton, I paid Vernon rent in corn. He needed it because he weren't raisin enough farm products to carry his business through—had cows, too, that needed that corn in winter. I told him, "Come over yonder to the back side of my cotton patch where my corn grows and get you as many loads of corn as it'll take to make my rent." He come over there and loaded up. And I got to keep the cash money I made off them four acres of cotton by payin him with corn. Then I quit foolin with cotton completely and I planted only corn.

I looked at this angle—I was caught between two opinions: new rulins is takin place and old ones is bein done away with. They mostly now buys all this shipped seed—they're treated and they come with a high percentage of weeds and they're high priced as the devil. You just plant em for two or three years out there, make no difference how good the results you gettin out of your cotton, it's workin you to death keepin them cockleburs out. And them cockleburs is in everybody's crop. You got to go to great expenses now to get a big crop made out there; you out of some money. Now they got a grass killin ointment; they got a cocklebur killin thing, weed killer and all. You got to go to all of that mess and keep that tractor goin; if you don't you aint goin to be able to get out of that crop what it cost you. I thought it over and I seed I was left out in the rain. People usin tractors to make a big enough crop to support themselves, and them things costin like they do, and I weren't in the knowledge of handlin a tractor and keepin the breakdowns off it, and not knowin how long I'd be able to just stand on my feet much less drive a tractor, I just walked along with the old mule like I had been and left off tractors till I got thoroughly disabled to handle a tractor. I knowed as much about mule farmin as ary man in this country. But when they brought in tractors, that lost me.

I just wanted to make enough to eat and I knowed that was all I could amount to. I'd got old—but I was able to follow a mule out there and plow, but havin no help, and every year I'd get weaker and weaker. I spotted my chance—and right along about the time I married Josie, the government took over this cotton business to a greater extent than ever before; I jumped out right there. Didn't want to fill out them papers every year, and a whole lot of red tape to it. I can't read and write; Josie can't neither. And if I couldn't conduct my business myself, I weren't goin to have nobody do it for me. Then, too, outside of the labor of me and my wife, I couldn't hire no help at a price to help myself—time for me to quit.

Last cotton I made, I picked it with my own hands and hauled it to the gin, and I sold it directly to the gin folks at Beanville. It didn't amount to enough to carry into Calusa and try to sell it at the market place.

I moved off of Mosley's place in '59, moved all my business up on Warren Jenks' place. I was plantin nothin but corn then—comin down to my last farmin now.

Warren Jenks was a old man, older man than I was, and he owned over two hundred acres in his name and rented it out to colored folks, whatever he didn't divide amongst his children. And they rented some of theirs out. When I moved on the old man's place I agreed to pay him six dollars a acre for the land and six dollars a month for the house. Stayed there ten long years and every year I made a corn crop. Soon as I'd get my corn gathered—he had a drove of cattle and out would go his cows over the field, eatin up my waste—got nothin for that. Sent his cows over in my corn stalks just because it was his land. Payin him six dollars a month for the house in addition to the land rent—that was chokin me but I suffered it. And I suffered his cows to destroy the waste from my crop.

He had enough money to do him his lifetime; he was better off than a heap of white folks. He owned more land than that home place—he owned all this land up and down this road, bought it when he was a younger man. All of my boy days, way up yonder not ten miles from here where I was born and raised, I could hear talk of Warren Jenks, Warren Jenks, Warren Jenks down here. When his daddy died, he inherited a small lot of land—didn't no nigger, in the time his daddy was livin, own no great territory of land through this country. Warren Jenks had a chance—he farmed —land was cheap—and he put his head to a profitable use. Didn't have to pay no rent to nobody for the farm he worked, and with the money he saved on rent he bought more land if ever he could find a white man would sell land to a colored. He inherited a start in this world and used it, didn't throw it away. He had a chance and he added to it; didn't content hisself to stand still, and he become what he was before he died.

His daddy managed to give him a pretty good education someway—I reckon he had to scuffle to do it. And when he come out of school he traveled to Africa. Either the government sent him or he went hisself, to teach farmin, teach this and teach that and teach the other. Stayed over in the far countries four years, to my best understandin. When he come back here he come back with his boots on. He commenced farmin for hisself and buyin up these places. Right smart of the white people respected him—he was independent to em. Didn't have as much as the biggest white men had, he kept hisself under them to protect hisself, but he had enough to paddle his own boat.

He had droves of hands here on halves with him and some that was rentin for cash. When I moved on his place I had possession of the house and nine acres and it was a straight cash deal. And that nine acres, after I worked it two or three years, it was so rough I quit workin on half of it, cut down to four acres of corn. I was gettin on some age and that land was carryin me down.

I had to do a heap of work on that old house and he wouldn't give me a penny toward it; wouldn't do the work hisself on it neither. And it was leakin in there, takin in the water every way. And on a cold day that house weren't no more good than a paper blanket. Wind blowed through the walls and up through the floor—

And I built me a little barn—that barn's standin there today. All he done was furnish me a few pieces of old second-hand tin and a few pieces of second-hand lumber. I bought lumber, bought tin, to complete the job.

He always called me Mr. Shaw; I called him Brother Jenks, my landlord, a man of my color. I went to him one day and said, "Brother Jenks, I need a well of water down there in my yard, I need it a little of the worst. And here's the proposal I'm makin: if you'll dig me a well of water—" We was totin water at that time from TJ's, across the road, and that was too much trouble for my wife. Heap of days I'd be out there in the field plowin and Josie would have to call me to come help her tote water. Well, that would be a hamper to my work. So I told him, "I want you to dig me a well of water in my yard. Me and my wife, we're both age-able, we aint able to tote water—" Weren't a barn or a chicken coop or nothin but a house on that place when we moved there, and I went ahead and built that little barn. My labor, my money—I have always had to back myself up. White men built nothin for me on their places. And now, this colored man—I said, "Brother Jenks, I wants a well of water in my yard, somethin that's never been. If you'll dig me a well of water I'll go fifty-fifty with you. If you dig the well, I'll buy the curbin to go in it. But I'll give you a choice—if you'll buy the curbin, I'll dig the well."

"Uh-uh-uh-uh-uh, Mr. Shaw, I'll take it up with the boys."

His sons. The devil! I said to myself, 'The boys is in the northern states and you here yet controllin the place. You don't have to take nothin up with the boys. You gettin my rent on the place, you settin the figures and overseein the whole operation. And your cows eatin up every year the waste of my crop and you aint doin nothin on the house. And I reckon you don't intend to do nothin; just draw money as long as you live.'

I couldn't get nothin out of him. So I went on that year and had me a well dug, couldn't do without a well no more. Several months after I made my offer he aint done nothin, weren't goin to do nothin, and didn't do nothin.

Roy Willis, colored fellow, lived between here and Tuskegee, I hired him to dig my well—he was a well diggin man. I walked around my yard and I seen a sign that revealed to me the direction of water. Got me a stick and checked off right where I wanted the well dug. I went over to Roy's and said, "Mr. Willis, I'm ready for you to dig my well, any day you can come, if it's today, to start my well."

"All right, Mr. Shaw, I'll be there bout twelve or one o'clock—"

I come on back home and after dinner I was workin out in the yard and I looked out across there field and here come Roy Willis with all he could tote, his well tools on his shoulder. I showed him my mark right where I wanted it dug and he carried that well about three foot deep that evenin. And in two days' time with me drawin up dirt along with the hand he brought to help him, he went down there deep enough and he begin to feel the earth get moister and moister. Time he carried that well down about twenty foot he said, "Well, Mr. Shaw, the walls and banks seem to be solid. Has you got your curbins ready?"

I said, "Well, I haven't spoke for em yet but I'm aimin—"

He said, "You better get em in a hurry because I'm hittin water now."

I quit drawin dirt, hitched up my wagon, and went up to Two Forks, spoke to Mr. Clifford Barrow. He knowed me well. I said, "I come up here, Mr. Barrow, to see if I could get some curbin from you, if you'll let me pay you by the month until I pay you in full."

Told me, "You can have em any way you want em, Nate, cash or credit."

I said, "Roy Willis is diggin my well and this very time we're talkin. I believe about eleven or twelve curbs will get me by." I paid him fifteen dollars down on that amount of curbs, best grade of well curb he sold, had wire reinforcements in em. He had two grown boys there and he had them boys to load them curbs on a long flat trailer truck, one standin on the ground and handin em up to the other one. Eleven curbs, definitely, two-and-a-half-foot curbs; we'd start with them and see how they'd hold up. Got the curbs loaded up and them boys took off on route to my house. Time I got home, they had got every one of them curbs eased off of that truck and they was headin back—met em in the road goin my way, they goin theirs. And I had to go back to Mr. Barrow to get another curb to finish the job. And they took that twelfth curb and put it on the back of my wagon. That was the finishin curb. I had a well then and I could say it was mine, but of course, when I moved away from there I couldn't carry it with me. It's there today and still drawin water. Warren Jenks, before he died, he got the benefit of it.

Some of these *Negroes* here in this country lets their money speak for em, not their color. Warren Jenks, he was just as hungry as the white man was.

I went out and dug a well and when I dug it it cost me—fooled around till that well cleaned me out; diggin it, curbin it, cost me right up close to a hundred dollars. And after that I went off to Philadelphia one year and I come back, the doggone well—it was gettin low with water before we left and when we come back, couldn't get a bucket of water out of it. Dug that well deeper, then I had to pay to clean it out. And by the time I got it all done and usable, it was a good well of water, cold, clear, no wiggletails.

I don't wash my feet with city water. I don't use none for no purpose. City water go right by my door but it don't come into my house. What use for me to let a company put water in my house when God put it here on earth for free? I aint livin in no city. I aint too lazy to step outside and help myself. And that company goin to charge me four dollars and after they gets it here, charge what they please. And the water aint fit for slops.

Here I am out in the country and they runnin water lines through here now just like I was in the city. If I was in the city I might expect to abide by city rulins. But I aint in no city, and I got a well of water that suits me just fine. Don't need nobody to catch my water for me, pay him for it. Out in the country and I'm goin to fall under that yoke too? No, they'll never get me under there, I'll kick at it like a mule kick at a stable door.

WHILE I was livin down on Jenks' place, Francis gived me and his stepmother a trip to the northern states and back home. And we stayed a week at his home in Philadelphia; one Sunday evenin we caught a bus and went on over to Brooklyn, New York, and stayed a week over there with Vernon's daughters, Norma and Binty, which is my granddaughters. When we left out from there—we went in there on a bus and come out on a young colored fellow's car, dodgin them big trucks on the road, big trucks, they travels through in there all the time—I learnt that. The roads was wide and if he didn't fly out of Brooklyn that Sunday mornin, glory!

First trip I ever went north to amount to anything. Now I had been to a place once nearly out of the state of Alabama, and I been to Birmingham. In the times I had a car myself, I drove it to Fort Payne, Alabama, way in there close to Chattanooga, Tennessee. Outside of them trips I never did travel far, except for travelin around them different prison departments, until Francis called me to come to Philadelphia.

I enjoyed life in the city; of course, I was on a trip and I could only observe the life, it weren't *my* life. The rulins and laws is different there accordin to the descriptions I gleaned. I seen white and colored walk right out a colored man's home and walk right in a white one's. Just walkin and talkin and mixin like straws in the wind. I seen colored men that had white wives, white men that had colored wives, and good God, everything was just peaceable and quiet—quieter there than I ever known it here. Still, I didn't let that turn me into a fool. But folks enjoys a hundred percent more freedom up there, white and black, to move about and be with whoever they choose. It aint complete, though, it aint complete, but black and white both is recognized as people, the one aint less—he may have less but *he* aint less—and the other aint more. I watched for that. Now I've always been a man that didn't care anythin for this mixin for myself, but I taken it for a sign that my color is better off there. All I want is to be recognized as people—and it seemed to be goin on in Philadelphia.

My son told me a man is just a man there in Philadelphia.

They don't nigger you around and you don't have to "Mister" anybody on account of his color; don't have to make out like you worship nobody to get along. Colored man could get a job there like anybody else; he could drive as nice a car as anybody else; he could live in as nice a house as his ability allow him. Francis was livin in a big six-room brick home; had about six rooms above ground and a big underground department. He was workin at a storage house where he drove a lifter—that's where he's at today. And the job makes him satisfied. It's mighty seldom he talks about comin back here. He's at home in Philadelphia, his mind is attached to northern ways.

If I lived in the city I wouldn't have no spaces to look out on, no trees in my yard and maybe no yard; no garden and no small crops. But as I stand now in my age, I wouldn't miss it too bad because I can't do nothin with it now. They don't grow the stuff they consume in Philadelphia and many other northern cities, like they do here. But you can't even demand that here—you can't demand the very crops you grow. Get out there on a small farm right here in the state of Alabama, and you produce cotton, you produce corn, vegetables, sugar cane, many other things; that white man whose place you on goin to boss that cotton and everything else you produce —you produces it but you can't demand it, you aint got no political pull whatever under the sun, you got no political rights. And without your political rights you can't demand what you produce. What good for me to work myself to death and somebody else get the benefit of my labor? Then soon as I gets old to where I can't do nothin, don't no white man want to bother with me. Poor colored man, as long as he's a workin man and able to get up and do, and do do it, white folks holdin their hands out for him. But get to where he can't work no more, white folks pulls that hand back.

I've never been able to get out from under a poor man's yoke. I aint over, if that much, ten miles today from where I was born at. Now I'm eighty-five years old, I'm livin in my eighty-sixth year and I've never been out of the state of Alabama to stay over a week in my whole life. I don't love its ways, but Alabama is as good a state as there is in the world. The land will respond to your labor if you are given a chance to work it and a chance to learn *how* to work it. It's the people here is what my trouble is. This land and nothin on this land goin to get up and do me no harm but a person.

I'm a country-raised fellow, all of my born days, and I love the country. But I likes a get-up and a pleasure trip to other parts.

And the trip I was given, to go to Philadelphia and to go from there to the state of New York, that boy of mine up there in the northern states backed it up. Well, I'd a loved to been able to do that myself and I woulda been able if I hadn't been brutally treated in many ways. Today I'd a been able to go anywhere in reason I want to go.

I feel a certain loyalty to the state of Alabama: I was born and raised here and I have sowed my labor into the earth and lived to reap only a part of it, not all that was mine by human right. It's too late for me to realize it now, all that I put into this state. I stays on if it gives em satisfaction for me to leave and I stays on because it's mine.

V

One year there on the Jenks place I done away with three foxes. I started out to the barn one Sunday mornin and just as I stepped out the house, Josie's hens come a flutterin, tryin to walk on their toes and flyin, half-flyin out of the swamps, tryin to get back to the henhouse. I hurried to the lot and got to where I could see a durn fox runnin them chickens right up to the wire fence where the lot meets the pasture. And he runned one particular hen —he couldn't catch but one at a time and that hen gived him such a run he couldn't get none of em. And *she* got away. There stood the fox, lookin through the fence. He seed me and he runned back over cross the holler, got to the edge of the pine thickets and stopped, looked back. I went to the house to get my gun and that scoundrel, when I got back there, was gone.

Well, a fox will catch a chicken sometimes but he can't equal a dog. He kept messin around and I decided I'd trap him over on the little creek that run right below my house. I was trappin for possum regular—there's a bunch of six or seven persimmon trees stood by the creek and every summer they'd bear. Fox and dog and possum like simmons. I decided I'd go down there then; walked up to them simmon trees, the ground was covered with simmons. Said to myself, 'If I set my traps here I might just catch that fox.'

So what I done, I got them traps and got me two pieces of wire enough to go around the bottom of them simmons trees and I run em through the rings on them traps. I figured the fox—and if it weren't a fox, maybe it'd be a possum, one, would piddle around by them traps. I put simmons all out there around em, didn't put nary a one on the plate of them traps.

Next mornin, I goes back over there and had nothin bothered them traps—you take varmints, they don't travel back to the same place every night; they has more feedin grounds than one. So, weren't nothin in ary one of them traps, settin there just like I left em. I went back to the house. Next mornin, I goes over there— had the two traps settin close together where the simmons was most plentiful—somethin jumped up and made a racket, and I looked around and seed it was a great big old gray fox. He couldn't get loose and run, so he set down there just like a dog would on his hind legs. He looked at me and I looked at him—and I just loved to see him in it. I just stepped out there and got me a seasoned limb, long, thick limb, and I broke the small limbs off of it. I walked up there—he still lookin right in my face, watchin my moves. And before he knowed anything I hit him just as hard as I could right the side of his head. Knocked him out. I beat him over the head some—big as a fice dog and he was so fat it was a pity, really, in as good a shape as the hogs I raised. I killed him dead and brought him up to the house and let Josie see him, and she rejoiced over it for the sake of her chickens.

That's one killed.

I went back out there, looked around and seed a great big old possum caught in the other trap. I got him out of that trap and carried him to the house live. You can catch a possum and he'll never bite you if you clamp him in back of the head when he sulls down. If you hurt a possum the least bit he'll fall over and draw up—that's sullin. After awhile he'll get up—his feelins comes back to him and he'll get up but you already got him by the neck and he can't do nothin about it. He'll try to pull off, surely, but hit him with somethin, not enough to break his bones but just enough to make him sull again. Carried that possum to the house live, dressed him and et him.

Some folks say, "I won't eat a possum." But when you cook a possum right, they're good; real meat, tasty enough for anybody to like em. The only reason people won't eat a possum is the idea of a possum—don't want to have nothin to do with em. Just don't tell em what it is and cook it; they'll beat you eatin it. You can't hardly find a person but what he loves hog meat. Practically the best part of the nation—if he don't eat every part of a hog, there's a part about the hog he likes. Aint no difference in a hog and a possum when it comes to the meat. A hog's a thing that'll catch snakes and eat em. And if there's a dead mule or a dead cow drug out into the woods like people used to do with em, a hog will go there and eat until he nearly falls out. A possum will too. I been possum huntin ever since I was a little boy, huntin with my daddy. He used to drag me in the woods far from home at night—sometimes when we'd stop movin I'd stand there and go to noddin; sometimes I'd sit down if I thought my daddy was goin to stay there long enough listenin for his dogs to open up somewhere. One night my daddy heard his dogs strike a track. I had done set down and when I woke up my daddy was gone, and I just could discern a light tremblin way in the woods goin way away from me. I jumped up and took off. I'd run and fall down, jump up and go on. I been huntin ever since then, followin my daddy. He used to have some real dogs, too. He went in the woods with them dogs, weren't but one way he'd come out—overloaded with possums, big ones, too. I was born and raised up eatin wild things—wild turkeys, coons, possums, squirrels, beavers—my daddy trapped them out on Sitimachas—fish, wild ducks—

So, one day after I killed that gray fox and that possum both, I went huntin. I had a good dog, a great big hound I bought from a white man over here in Elmore County, across the river. I liked that dog how he looked. He had three—fellow by the name of Sadler—and I knew him before he brought them dogs to my house. Been raisin dogs several years and said he got tired bein worried with em and just decided he'd sell em out. Well, he brought two dogs there and one bitch, she-dog. That was easily the prettiest bitch that ever I laid my eyes on.

He said that big hound—all of em was big fine hounds, but that biggest of all of em—white man told me, "He aint been trained but he'll run rabbits and things." I was born and raised up amongst dogs by my daddy and I knowed what a dog was when I seed him or what he'd come to be by his looks. So, he said, "He aint trained at all, I wouldn't tell you that he is. He aint nothin but a young fellow—I wouldn't tell you a lie. He'll cost you fifteen dollars if you want him. Them two there, that other dog and that black bitch—" looked like a dog's picture, prettiest thing ever I seed in my life for a dog—"that bitch there and that other dog, they'll cost you some money. I'll sell ary one to you that you want."

I said, "I like this young fellow here you say is untrained."

He said, "Yeah, he aint trained, I done told you bout that. He don't know nothin but runnin rabbits yet. But them other two will get anything practically you put em on."

I said, "I want *him*."

Well, I bought that dog and I'd a had him today but—Ben Ramsey up there right this side of me had some old dogs wouldn't do nothin but eat chickens and lay around. Well, my dog took up with them and got to where he wouldn't hear me when I called him, acted it. So I sold him. I thought a mess of that dog too.

Well, in about a day and a half after I bought him I turned him loose. He was just as friendly with me—he liked his home and he never did go off and try to go back to the man I got him from, never showed a mind to run off at all until he took up with them chicken eatin dogs. I called him Big Boy. That little old boy that stays here now with me and Josie, he thought a mess of that dog too. I noticed in a few days after they started playin together, that boy played a little too rough for the dog, but he wouldn't bite him, wouldn't bite a chap. And I noticed one day that chap started toward the dog, that dog got up and trotted off out the field and lay down somewhere. So I thought one while and I told Josie, that's the reason Big Boy won't stay at home, Alexander was always frolickin with him and he'd hit him with anything he could get his hands on—but he weren't big enough to hurt the dog and make him holler.

Several different white people and two or three colored people just hanked around me regular to get that dog. Told em, "No, he aint for sale, I won't sell him. He got to do somethin bad before I get rid of him. I need him. That's the only kind of dog I keep around me—a big nice hound. I like em; born and raised up—my daddy had em. No, I won't sell him."

Well, before I *had* to sell him, I went off one day over on the little creek near my house, as usual, with my ax to cut some white oak. That big hound trotted right on with me, first ahead of me then off behind—sometime I couldn't see him. He was with me though. And just as I crossed the creek he runned off down a ways pickin up a track. He hit that track several licks, barkin, trailin— I hollered to him once or twice just to let him know I was there yet in the woods. He runned on awhile and his track got cold and he quit it and come trottin right up through the swamp right by me and on up the creek. I popped my finger at him and urged him on, "Go ahead, boy." He went up on the creek a piece and after a while I heard him bark up there. And he barked like he was pretty close on somethin and he commenced a pushin it back on down the creek towards me. He stayed on that track like a desperate man. By the time he come up close to me he got furious at whatever it was he was runnin; I knowed by his commotion that he had done tried to get somethin or had done got it. I just quit workin at my white oak then and broke off to get him. I runned through the briars and muscadine vines and when I got up to him he had done quieted down. Time I come up from below he was runnin around out in a little clear place and smellin all on the ground. I said to myself, 'Doggone it, you done killed a thing or had a skirmish up here someway but now you hushed and I can't even tell where you was at when you made your last furious bark and done got away from the thing you killed, if you killed it.' He didn't act particular like he done caught the thing. But there was a spot where a company had cut logs and just piled em up crossways and every way in there and under that mess he done caught a fox. Hadn't killed the fox dead but he had just about killed him. I stood there and looked at the dog, couldn't see yet what he'd done; just makin hisself contented smellin around there. I said, "Git him!" Just like I'd talk to a man, squalled at him, "Git him! Git him!" He whirled and went over the top of them logs, the dog did, and fell down over in a hole. After a while he grabbed that fox and tussled with him and he come out of there backwards, draggin him over them treetops out of that hole. He pulled that fox up and I could see its tail whip over—I knowed it was a fox. I just kept it to him, "Git him! Git him! Git him!" Got that fox out of there and brought him to me and dropped him at my foot. I looked at the dog and I looked at the fox—after a while I seed the old fox blinkin his eyes, layin there pitiful lookin at me. Couldn't help hisself, he was too near killed, but he could blink his eyes. I jumped on him and hit him a lick with the back of my ax enough to kill him. Went on down through the woods a little piece and cut me a muscadine vine bout as long as one of my pieces of white oak. I gived it a twist or two and tied it around that old fox's neck and drawed it up. Weren't no way for it to come loose. Got my white oak on my shoulder and my ax, took that vine and drug him out from that swamp until I got to the lot gate. I dropped the fox's vine, went on up to the house and told my wife where the old fox was layin—right in front of the lot gate where I turned my stock out into pasture. Josie come out and she was pleased, she was pleased. That old fox wouldn't fox no more.

So, that's two.

The third fox, I got him by myself, the last one. One mornin I went to the lot—Ooooooooo, there was another fat fox. All of em was old gray foxes. A red fox is a runnin rascal; it takes more pursuit to catch him than it do to catch a gray one. So, one mornin I got up and went to the lot, fed my mules—hadn't milked yet. I started back to the house, not thinkin bout no fox, and just as I got up about even with the chicken house I happened to turn my head and look back and there was a old fox trottin out from behind the henhouse, old gray fox. O, he was fat as a brick. I looked at him and I believe he seed me. He never did stop travelin, though, and I walked on, studyin my plan right quick. I was goin to try if there was any way in the world to get in the house and get my gun—

I killed that fox—had no help that mornin; Big Boy done sloped off, he weren't around me nowhere and I fretted that he had hitched his tail to Ben Ramsey's pack—O, these words brings up others and they won't wait: I had to take a dog away from a white man, one of my dogs, once, back when I was livin down on Siti-machas Creek with Mr. Tucker. I got the dog from Ben Ramsey and Ben told me he got him from a white gentleman by the name of Wesley Dowd, back here close to a barroom about ten miles from where I was livin. Ben brought the dog to my house and traded with me—good dog, too, she'd tree possums just like a top. Well, I took my mule out one mornin—only mule I had at that time— and went down on the creek to plow and I turned Queen loose to go with me. She stayed right around there till about ten thirty, eleven o'clock, and every once in a while I would see her cross the bottoms of the field goin into the creek swamps, first one way then another, huntin. And all at once I took a missin to her, couldn't hear her. Well, I just plowed right in up till dinner time, then took out and come to the house. I asked my wife, "You seed that dog come back to the house, old Queen?"

She said, "No darlin, I aint seed her."

I got uneasy then. Ben told me when he gived me the dog that the white man he got the dog from told him to keep her away from down by his place; he had two puppies he had reserved from her and he didn't want her hangin around there because she might trot off somewhere and carry them puppies off, and somebody'd steal em or they'd get killed and he'd be out his puppies then.

I went on and fed my mule; soon as she could get done eatin I had her to the buggy—that was one of the prettiest mules the country could afford, that Mattie mule—and I hitched Mattie to the buggy and first thing I come out from up there on Sitimachas and right to Ben's. He was openin up a new place—Ben Ramsey, poor fellow, he opened up more house seats and cleared more land than any fellow I know of through this country. He was out on new ground up there at his house, burnin brush, burnin off the land. I asked him about the dog. He said, "No, Cousin Nate, I aint seed her"— he was cousin to my wife—"I aint seed her at all. I betcha she gone back down to Wesley Dowd where I got her from. If she is you better hurry down there."

I jumped up when he told me that and drove right down to what they call Sharon's crossroads, took the left fork past where a fellow by the name of Carter runs a store now—he used to work there for Mr. Joe Thompson until he bought Mr. Thompson out— and down to Mr. Wesley Dowd before I quit drivin. It was late Saturday evenin, near night, when I drove up there on my buggy and stopped. Young white man was out at the woodpile cuttin wood. I called his attention, said, "Is this where Mr. Wesley Dowd lives?"

He said, "Yes, right here is where he lives."

I said, "Is he about home?"

Said, "No, Mr. Dowd gone to Calusa this evenin and he haven't come back."

I said, "Well, could you tell me whether you have seen lately a hound bitch that Mr. Dowd traded with Ben Ramsey?"

He said, "Yeah, that dog was here this evenin." You take a old hound bitch, she'll go fifteen miles goin back home, if she gets a chance, to where she was born and raised. And said, "Now, I'll tell you something if you don't say nothin about it at all. The dog was here before Mr. Dowd went off to Calusa, and Malcolm Malone out there wanted that dog and been wantin her for the longest. Mr. Dowd wouldn't let him have her in the first place because Malcolm lives too close to him, he wanted to put the dog away from where she could get at her puppies. But he seen it don't make no difference where he puts her, she goin to come back if she take a notion. So he just decided to give her to Malcolm Malone and that's where she's at now. Malcolm Malone's got that dog. I told Mr. Dowd not to let him have her because she aint been here in several days, and we knowed that Ben had done traded her off to somebody else. I tried my best to get Mr. Dowd to not let Malcolm Malone have that dog. I told him that somebody'd come through here raisin hell about that dog and I tried to get him to keep her here until her owner come for her or he found out definitely who owned her.' He wouldn't do it; he let Malcolm Malone have her. You go out there you'll find the dog. But don't use my name at all."

I said, "Well, I aint raisin no hell but she's mine and I'll be damned if I aint goin to get her."

He said, "Well, that's just with you; just don't use my name."

I didn't betray him but I went on after that dog. Dark when I drove up there, just about gettin dark before I ever left Mr. Dowd's.

"Hello, Mr. Malone."

I knowed Malcolm Malone; knowed more about him than I knowed about Mr. Dowd. He was a sort of hard-boned white man. Gived out a hard "Hello."

I said, "Come out here a minute or two, please, sir, I want to talk with you a little."

He come out to where I was settin on my buggy. I said, "Mr. Malone, I lost a big hound bitch—" I didn't hold back from tellin him where I'd been, but I wouldn't use nobody's name. I said, "I got a big hound bitch from Ben Ramsey a few days ago and she got away this mornin, left me. He got her from Mr. Wesley Dowd. Have you seen anything of her prowlin around you here?"

He said, "Yeah, I got her now." Weren't bootin me at all. "I got her now; I been wantin that bitch a long time but couldn't get her from Dowd. I got her now and I'm goin to keep her."

I had done went and paid taxes on the dog and I thought I had a right to her. I bought her—gived Ben Ramsey a yearlin for that dog; cows was cheap then.

I said, "Well, Mr. Malone, she belongs to me. I done paid Ben Ramsey fair for her—she belongs to me."

"Yeah, but you can't get her now"—talkin his big talk, but he never did cuss me about it. "Aint but one way you could get her— give me a five-dollar bill."

I said, "Well, Mr. Malone, I aint goin to pay you for her"—I was studyin tricks for him then. I seed what I had to do; I said, "It aint right that I done paid for her once, then have to pay for her again. I don't know, I reckon I'll just leave my dog." But I knowed if the law worked I was goin to get her. Weren't goin to have no fuss with him in the dark of night at *his* house. I took a notion I'd drive away then.

Wadkin Todd's boy was on the buggy with me, goin around with me that Saturday night. He's dead and gone now, Wadkin and both his boys is dead. But this Conrad Todd, he was a one-eyed fellow, young fellow, hadn't been long married, he was with me that Saturday evenin. Malcolm Todd, cousin of mine, he was with me at the end.

I said, "Well, Mr. Malone, there aint no way then in the world accordin to your thoughts about the dog and as much as you think of her that I can get her without five dollars."

"No, I been wantin the dog for several years and I wouldn't get shed of her for less than five dollars. When I got her I gived her two big hunks of fat meat to get her started and get her in heat so she can take the dog and raise me some puppies. That's what I got her for and I'm goin to keep her."

I said, "All right, Mr. Malone, I don't know what I'm goin to do about it"— I knowed I wouldn't give him a penny—"I may take a notion to bring you your five dollars, as I aint got it now. I'll be back, sir—"

"Yeah, get me up five dollars and you can get her."

Just before I left there I said, "Mr. Malone, to be sure, I want to see the dog, see it's the right dog I'm huntin and the dog I done paid taxes on. Would you object to me seein her?"

"No, you can see her. She's around here in the back yard in the doghouse."

Got off my buggy, went around there and she was in a small house, just about as high if she stood up as she was. And the door was locked. He unlocked the door, and the dog was in there chained by the neck; chain run to her collar and fastened to the back side of the house to keep her away from the door. I felt like beatin that white man down—I popped my finger—Pop Pop—"Queen! Queen!" She barked and runned right up my breast and whined over me. She knowed the scent of me. I'd had her at my home a few days and she knowed me.

I said, "Yes sir, that's her, that's Queen." A hound dog—I've treasured em, I've watched em, I've experimented on em—a hound bitch, a heap of em is deceitful to an extent: they make out like they think so much of you but if they gets a chance they leave you. But in fact, she wanted to go back to where her puppies was, that's how come she left me. I crawled out the house and Malcolm Malone chained her back to the wall and he come on out too, and locked the door.

Got on my buggy, drove on back home, took my mule out and fed her, went in the house, taken a bath, went to bed. Told my wife all about my rounds. I said, "I seed her but I couldn't get her. Now, darlin, I'm goin to the justice of the peace in the mornin, take out a warrant for her. He live over here west of Pottstown way back toward the backwaters."

His name was Kirkland—I don't know his given name— mighty nice white gentleman. I've knowed a heap of Kirklands and I aint knowed nary a one of em to act off and treat colored folks wrong. So, I went back in that country inquirin for Mr. Kirkland, justice of the peace. Malcolm Todd was with me on the buggy. Drove up to the white man's house and stopped, talked with him about it. It was a little cold that mornin and Mr. Kirkland said, "Come on in the house, you two fellows, and set by the fire."

We went in there and set down by the fire and he turned and set down to one of his desks. And he wrote out some papers and gived one to me. I offered to pay him but he wouldn't have it. He said, "You go down there to Mr. Malone and give him this paper. If he don't release that dog right quick to you, you come right back and notify me; we'll get him and the dog too." The words he spoke.

I drove on down there—early that Sunday mornin, gettin around early—stopped at Malcolm Malone's house and called for him. His wife come to the door, said, "He's not here. He's gone out the other side of Apafalya to his sister's."

I said, "Mrs. Malone, about how long ago was that he left?"

"O, he left early"—never did tell me what time he left—"left just before daylight, goin to his sister's, out the other side of Apafalya."

I said, "Do you know about when he'll be back?" I decided I'd put up around there until the hour he come back; I had a cousin lived right down the road below there.

She said, "No. When he goes off thataway to his sister's, some-times it's way in the night before he comes back."

I said, "Well, Mrs. Malone, I'm the fellow that was here talkin with Mr. Malone about that dog, last night. I'm the owner of that dog."

She said, "O, that dog gone; that dog left here durin the night sometime."

I wouldn't say nothin to insult her. I said, "Mrs. Malone, how did that dog get loose and get out of that buildin with a chain around her neck and it fastened to the wall, and the door to the house was locked?"

"I don't know but she got out of there someway; I don't know."

I said, "Did she get loose chain and all?"

Said, "Yes, she carried that chain with her, snapped it loose."

I said, "Well, if she did must have carried that house with her too; Mr. Malone had her locked up."

I wouldn't talk with her much more, just let her alone. I said, "I declare!" and I drove away. Went on down the road and stopped at Ches Todd's. Took my mule out and gived her her dinner and we set there and talked with Ches until about one or two o'clock. Got up and hitched my mule back to that buggy and drove right back up to Malcolm Malone's. Called him. Weren't nobody there; she was gone then. Before I'd be outdone— I had a cousin lived on down the road from there toward Apafalya, fellow by the name of Ty Haines, married a cousin of mine. I drove on over to Ty Haines'. I said, "Hello there."

Ty answered me. He got up and come out to the buggy to me and Malcolm Todd; Malcolm was still with me and it was approachin dark, been drivin with me since early mornin. I told Cousin Ty what we was there for. When that white lady told me that dog got away chain and all, I just figured her husband got that dog and put her in his buggy or fastened her behind it and escaped into the hills, got out from my way. He was a runnin fox, but I caught him.

Cousin Ty told me, "Cousin Nate, I don't know nothin about the matter at all."

I asked him, "Has you seen Malcolm Malone come through here any time early this mornin or durin the night? Have you heard any buggies comin through here? The way I caught it, he slipped off from his house just before daylight, and the time he could drive two miles with that horse and buggy, you'd a been up too."

He said, "I don't know, Cousin Nate, I aint seed him and I

aint heard nothin about him, no more than what Otis told me—"
That was his oldest son.

I said, "Where is Cousin Otis?"

He said, "He's up there at the house."

I said, "Call him out here."

He come right on out and Cousin Ty said, "Otis, Cousin Nate
wants to talk with you some concernin a dog."

I said, "Cousin Otis, what I want to find out—" Now Ty had
told me that Otis was out early before good daylight and Ty said,
"He'll tell you hisself what he seed."

I said, "Have you seen Malcolm Malone pass here any time
early until up in the mornin?"

He said, "Yeah, Cousin Nate, I seed Malcolm Malone go
through here this mornin."

I said, "As good as you seed him, did you see what he had
around his buggy?"

He said, "Yeah."

I said, "What did he have, as good as you could see?"

He said, "Well, that horse he was drivin was trottin when he
come by here. I happened to look behind his buggy and he had a
big dog tied behind the buggy to the back axle. I don't know whether
it was a dog or a bitch, but it was a big hound, hound dog."

I had the dope then—black and tan hound, he said. I said,
"That's all I wanted. You seed him with that dog tied to the back
of his buggy."

Well, I knowed what dog it was. I said, "Cousin Ty, if we can,
I reckon, me and Cousin Malcolm will just have to spend the night
with you."

"That's all right, Cousin Nate, that's all right; glad to have
you."

My wife and children didn't know where I was; Malcolm's wife
and children didn't know where he was. I didn't make no practice
of leavin my wife and children at night, but she knowed what I was
off for. Of course, she mighta thought that I went off and got hurt
some way. If I had, somebody woulda let her know, because everybody between there and Apafalya, all in below Apafalya where the
dog was, knowed me, knowed her.

So we got up the next mornin, Monday mornin; I drove back
over to Malcolm Malone's—still aint come, still aint come. His
wife was there but he still aint come. All right. I said, "Well, Cousin

Malcolm, I'm goin to catch that dog." Had that warrant from the justice of the peace in my pocket orderin him to deliver that dog. I told Malcolm, "I'm goin to travel till I meet him. Only way I can miss him, if he takes a roundabout route toward Beaufort, then comes down this way on one of them branch roads. But if he stays on this road, and I expect he will, I'll meet him this mornin."

Drove along then in the neighborhood of Apafalya to where Malcolm's mother lived, on that road, Aunt Caroline Todd. Malcolm's daddy was dead at that time, Uncle Joe Todd. Drove up in her yard and stopped—it was cold that mornin. Went around the back of the buggy and pulled out my tie halter and I snapped one snap to the mule's bit and throwed the other one around her neck and snapped it. Hitched her to the hitchin post; she couldn't a broke that to save her life. She was a mule—if a stranger walked up to her she would snort and swing back. And she didn't allow nobody to help me take her out from a buggy or wagon. She'd look at em and snort if they'd go to foolin around with her, unhitchin traces. Had a young fellow one time walk up to me at Elam Baptist Church to help me take her out of the buggy. He had a old parasol and he clamped it between his arms and his body, walked up there and unhitched the traces—that mule lookin back at him. She said, "Haugggggggggggghhhhhhhhhhhhhhhhhhhh." He looked at me, said, "What's the matter with her, Mr. Shaw?" I said, "You just better get away. I hate to tell you that, you might think I don't want you to help me. Clear away from her; if you stay here she's liable to bust out of these shafts before she's took out." She was a cat—I could do anything with her, that Mattie mule of mine. First mule I ever bought out of the drove. Had never had a bridle on her when I bought her. She was a peach for a mule. Kept her eleven years until I lost her—

So, we walked in Malcolm's mother's house and stayed there a long time, warmin, waitin on Mr. Malone to come by. And it's very well we didn't wait no longer than we did. I decided we done got warm enough—we walked out and just as I got my mule untied, I looked up the road and seed Mr. Malone. I knowed his horse and all. I quickly tied that mule back and by the time I got her tied, he was past. He had that old buggy whip out and wavin it over the little old horse, tryin to get her up off the ground. I just took off down the road behind him, hollerin at him. He drove on a couple of hundred feet before I could stop him.

"Hold up, Mr. Malone, hold up, hold up." And wavin my arms at him. I kept runnin behind him doin that and he eventually pulled down on that little old horse and stopped. Small horse but that horse was gettin up. And he had a little girl on the buggy with him; weren't his girl, some of his kinfolks' little girl. I just run around there and said, "Mr. Malone, I got a paper here for you."

Took it out of my inside coat pocket and handed it to him. I was wearin a dress coat, one of my Sunday coats. He took the paper and looked over it. "Who is Mr. Kirkland?"

I said, "Mr. Kirkland is a justice of the peace. That's his name right on that paper."

He said, "Yeah, I see his name, Kirkland, but what about this paper? I can't read it all good."

I said, "Well, you just look at it—" Made out like he couldn't read it—I couldn't read it—and if he could or he couldn't he knowed what it said.

All right. The little girl said, "Let me see it." She took it and read it but she hushed her mouth and wouldn't say nothin.

I said, "Well, however, Mr. Malone, you can understand that paper good enough to let you know what's to it. Furthermore, I'll tell you this much: I was given orders to tell you that whenever I deliver this paper, you must deliver my dog at once, and if you don't, somethin else will have to be done."

He said, "I don't know how I can get that dog now."

I said, "Well, that's your job, Mr. Malone."

He done stashed that dog out somewhere in that country the other side of Apafalya. Might have sold the dog. I said, "If you don't deliver that dog at once like it say for you to do on that paper— I'll give you time to deliver that dog if it's this evenin. I was gived orders to return to the justice of the peace at once if you didn't release the dog."

He got stirred up then. He seed that paper meant to throw that dog off from him. He said, "Meet me up there at Zion at two o'clock this evenin—" I lived only about two miles from Zion.

I said, "I don't see how I can—but I will agree to meet you up there."

He said, "I'll have your dog there at two o'clock but you just keep this thing quiet, hear? Don't let nobody know you served this paper on me."

So, right after dinner time, Wadkin Todd's boy Conrad got on

the buggy with me and we drove to Zion, down on the Calusa–
Apafalya road, right the other side of Two Forks, up there at the
white folks' church. Stopped my mule and buggy, stood there and
waited. I didn't have no further time to lose about the dog. And
two o'clock on the dot, Malcolm Malone come trottin down the
road with that dog tied to the back axle of his buggy. Stopped his
buggy when he got up to me, got out, went around there and untied
the dog. I had a rope of my own to put on her. He said, "I sure did
want a couple of puppies from this bitch. Will you turn her and
raise me a couple of puppies?"

Told him, "We'll see what she bears, Mr. Malone." He'd a been
better off lookin for puppies from a cow—I don't remember ever
seein that white man since. Crawled back on his buggy and drove
away from there.

There's some things can happen between a colored man and
a white man, some of these laws won't hold back off of it. White
man could shoot a colored man and wouldn't be a thing done to
him; but if he taken a colored man's dog, the laws would jump
down his throat.

ONE day, one night, while I was livin on the Jenks place, a white
bunch—you never know how many it was—got on a car and
stopped at Rachel's and shot in the house. She was settin by the
window that night; weren't nobody there but her at the time. And
if she had been settin closer to the window than she was, someway,
they'd a shot her. Shot through the window and into the walls of
that house. Brought up a great flustration—found out who done it,
caught em, and their mothers and fathers runned up and begged
my daughter to not have nothin done about it, and the way it
runned, nothin was done. They was doin that devilment all over
the country here, same crowd, and it brought up great dangers.
And it was understood and known well, they didn't bother nobody
but colored folks.

They come down there to my house one night before they ever
bothered Rachel. I weren't thinkin bout such a thing—and they
throwed a rock up on my veranda. The little house was standin right
beside the road; they stopped on their car and throwed a rock up
there as big as my fist—BOOM—against the house. Then they
took off.

Well, after that, I set out there on that veranda many a night till late hours with my gun across my lap, lookin for em. They never did come back, long as I watched. And so, the insurance man come by one day, fellow by the name of Skinner, from Tuskegee; I had the rock, laid it up and showed it to him, told him bout the dangerous situation in this settlement. I heard over the television just such things was happenin in the northern states. They messed up Chicago in particular at that time. Well, niggers here was scared as the devil bout this rock chunkin, bottle chunkin, shootin in people's houses.

I told him, "I'm goin to shoot, if I don't shoot nothin but the car; if they ever come here again that way I'm goin to be hid around here and when they stop and one of em chunks his rock, my gun goin to fire."

And here's what he told me—I made little of him for that. He was a insurance man, white man, he didn't like my talk and he just went on away from there when he got through with his insurance business. I showed him the rock and told him, "It has to be stopped. One way or another somebody's goin to get killed. This got to be broke up and I'm goin to be in the crowd that breaks it up, too." He standin there listenin at me. I said, "They aint botherin nobody but the colored people. They don't bother the white people at all."

He went on to give me some advice about it, told me I shouldn't make too much out of very little. I told him, "Yes, it's very little to a white man, anything happens to a colored person it's very little, been that way since I can remember. If they'd a been chunkin at white folks' houses thataway there'd a been somethin done about it."

He told me what he'd a done if he coulda caught em. I said, "Yes sir, if you coulda caught em. But you done what the rest of em done—nothin."

He didn't like that talk much. He said, "Well—"

I told him I was goin to shoot the car if I didn't shoot nobody, "Then everybody will know who they is." Right at that particular time, didn't know what crowd it was.

He said, "Well, if you shoot, don't shoot in the car. Shoot over the car."

I said, "Well, if they chunkin rocks *into* houses I'm goin to shoot into the car—if I get the chance. You know if they'd bothered white folks, just taken houses as they come, they'd a caught em in spite of redemption. They couldn't a got away for runnin."

He dropped his head on that.

I boiled to him that mornin—all it had to be was a Negro's house and you'd better keep your head down. You take this road, up the road a little piece it turns and carries you right by Mr. Willy Lee Kirkland's—it's thick-settled through there, white and colored. And there's a old schoolhouse over there in the Byrd settlement— that goes in the name of the Byrd settlement with people that knows—settin to the right of the road after you get up that long hill. And there's a little old block house sets to the left, right on top of that hill; colored gal killed her daddy there bout six or seven years ago, shot him—it's supposed, they said—shot him five times. Well, just beyond that house there's that schoolhouse, and the white crowd went by there one night and shot the windows out and come mighty nigh shootin the woman that was in there, livin there, done took the little old schoolhouse over for a dwellin house, just a man and his wife, colored people. And they shot in the window and shot the window out and come mighty nigh shootin that woman—nothin done about it, nothin. If that was a colored crowd of boys done that to a white people's house, they'd a put em *under* the penitentiary; there's no doubts and no different thoughts to be had about it.

I was born real poor, I had nothin. And what I accumulated in the world, one man worked harder than ary other to take it away from me. And right before he died, Mr. Watson come by my house on the Jenks place. I wasn't there that day—Josie said that another white gentleman drove up there with him; she didn't know who he was. And Mr. Watson inquired about me, but he didn't never get to the point of his comin. But he come there for a purpose of some kind, surely. He didn't just drive out there to *see* me.

I learnt from other people that at that period he'd been goin around to see different ones that had ever had dealins with him in their lives. He even put out a report that he wanted to see one of Simon Travis's boys, said he had somethin to tell him. And he talked to these colored people like he wanted to make some sort of apology. I can't read a man's mind, but it appeared to me like this: he wanted to make an oath and be acknowledged for his past dealins with em—he seed the end of his days comin near. But he never come back to my house and he never put the proposition to me.

This here woman I got now, her daddy, Simon Travis, he used to live with Mr. Watson and he was absolutely skinned by the man —I knowed it. And also, her first husband, Johnny B Todd, he was livin on one of Mr. Watson's places when he died. Worked several years for the man, made good crops too—Watson got it all. So he knowed Josie, had to, as well as he knowed any colored lady.

Accordin to God's words under the ledger of the Bible, his soul cannot be at rest, aint no way for it. He used to have a good time here, but he's catchin hell today. I don't say he's *gone* to hell, definitely; I don't say it with the breath of my body. I just look back at God's words: his soul is required in torment today. I aint goin to tell no lie on Lester Watson; he's dead and gone wherever God and Christ intends for him to be.

He had a wife. I didn't know nothin but this about her—Josie in there knows her well; she have waited on her in her lifetime. He married old man Tom Sherman's daughter; lived with her daddy out yonder close to Apafalya before he married her. And Watson was born and raised right over at a place between Calusa and Apafalya called Ore City. He was a farm-raised man and he moved into town and commenced a pilin up riches off of the farmin class of people.

I heard a illustration against Mr. Watson one day—one of the Bailey family, white people, live over here across Sitimachas Creek, told me, if he was to go to Apafalya to get him a heel-bolt and didn't nobody have one but Lester Watson, he'd catch the train and go on to Montgomery, get him a heel-bolt. Well, was that good logic or bad logic? That white man could talk that mess but I couldn't without bein called in question and cussed out; and if I'd get out of it by bein just cussed out, I was a lucky bird.

SEVERAL white men in the community have come to me since I been out of prison and told me they didn't have nothin to do with that mob crowd that hunted my people them nights and days past. One of em was a fellow by the name of Titus Gilmore; he lives right up there now on the Apafalya–Beaufort highway. We got to talkin bout it once, edgin the subject; never talked no deep talk about it. He told me, "Nate, I weren't in that business. I didn't have nothin to do with it."

I believed him. Titus Gilmore was a man that his daddy-in-law failed and refused to carry him—his daddy-in-law, his wife's daddy —Titus Gilmore had a sick baby and he thought it might die and his daddy-in-law, fellow by the name of Hale Whitney, wouldn't carry him to Apafalya. And Titus Gilmore lived close to me at that time—I was livin on the Pollard place less'n half a mile from the place he was livin on. Poor white man, he told me, "Nate none of em won't carry me. I'd like to get you to carry me to Apafalya so I can call up my brother Robert in Tuskegee, let him know bout my baby bein sick and all."

I just got my car out, took him on, carried him to Apafalya one night. That was the year of '32. I insisted at him to let me stop at Dr. Andrews before he went to call his brother and he agreed. Dr. Andrews was livin way out of the heart of town, on the skirts, up on the Tuskegee road. Titus Gilmore begged him to come out there and see about his baby but he couldn't come. Well, he come back to the car then and asked me would I carry him up to town to the central office. I told him, "Yeah, I'll carry you anywhere you want to go."

We left Dr. Andrews' home and drove up to town to the central office and he called up his brother Robert, and when he got through with his talk he come back out to the car and me and him come on home. And his brother Robert got a doctor there in Tuskegee and come up that night—if he didn't he come the next mornin. He told me later his baby done well after that. I told him, that night, straight, when we got to his house, "Well, Mr. Gilmore, if your baby don't do well and you need my assistance, call on me, I'll go with you. I'll go with you."

He said, "All right, Nate, I'll come to you if I have to."

Well, that man, I know he thought well of me for that act. And he seed me—first time he seed me after I got out of prison, we was in a storehouse in Beanville and he seed me and walked up and shaked hands with me right in a crowd. Didn't care who seed him do it—that baby of his was a grown chap at that time. And he told me, "I weren't in that crowd, Nate. I hated it but there weren't nothin I could do about it but stay out of it."

I carried a bale of cotton to the gin one fall—I hadn't seen Mr. Horace Tucker in several years; that was the first time I seed him since I come out of prison. He was waitin his turn and talkin with some white men—he just left that crowd, walked over and shaked hands with me, glad to see me, acted like, and he stood and talked with me until his time come to gin. Every once in awhile them white men that he left when he come to me would look around, but none of em never did seem to act badly about it at all.

Mr. Estes Tucker, Mr. Horace Tucker's son, carried me on his milk truck one day; he had a dairy and he sold milk and he carried me with him, showin me all of his fixins. He done growed up and as he got older he got to be a heavy-built white man, and I didn't know him by his built and all. And he was a skinny boy growin up—I knowed all them Tucker boys from mighty nigh babies. He told me before I got off his truck, "Well, Nate, come see me, come see me. I don't know where you livin, but don't stay over there and suffer. You been a friend to me when I was a boy, and you was a friend to my daddy, and a friend to his daddy—you've come through this world with all of us; it runs deep, runs deep." Then he made me welcome to anything he had. "Nate," he said, "you got stock, I know, but if you need the use of mine, come and get em, come and get em."

I was workin white oak one day when a young white man come to see me. A colored fellow come there with him by the name of Wade Hennessey. They come together drivin a small pickup truck. And this young white man called me Mr. Shaw—that stirred me up. He said, "Mr. Shaw, you know me—" I didn't know him—"You know me, you knowed Toby Culpepper, didn't you?"

I told him, "Yes, I knowed Mr. Culpepper—" white man had a small plantation joinin the Stark place at Two Forks.

He said, "That's my daddy; I'm his baby. I weren't nothin but a young child when you went to prison, but I was big enough to know you. See, I was the baby boy. My daddy is dead now—" I don't know when he died, the boy didn't tell me that. And he brought up all that had happened to me. I sat and listened at what he said. And he was just as familiar as he could act. Before he left my place—

stayed there talkin a long time—he come up close in the subject, said, "Mr. Shaw, you done right to stand up like you done."

He knowed—I knowed—white folks was just used to takin everything the colored folks had; didn't matter if they owed em or not, just take it, used to takin it. Had to be stopped, had to be stopped—

The Culpepper boy said that three or four different times: "You done right, Mr. Shaw, you done right."

I looked at him and I said, "White man, do you really think I done right?"

"Yes, you done right!"

Just stuck to it and he stayed there ever so long—and when he left he said, "Don't tell nobody that I come to see you."

AND since I done made my sentence and been back home, I heard who a heap of em was in that mob crowd and who they wasn't. None of my neighbors wasn't in it—but it was other folks I knowed.

God says revenge is His—it's under the ledger of the Bible. Every man that I heard talk against me and all the rest of the niggers at that time, every one of em to my knowin is dead and gone. They died like sheep with the rock. The old judge that sentenced me, he didn't live to see me make my sentence. Tom Heflin, man that prosecuted me, he didn't live—my Lord, that opened my eyes; God removed em from this earth. The jury, a heap of them gone. The high sheriff Kurt Beall, he was desperately against me—shot to death by his own color. And them sheriffs that come at me that mornin—Lew Badger's dead, Virgil Logan's dead, Ward's dead, Platt, the man that shot me, he's dead. There's the crowd that come to see me when I was in jail, aint but one of them livin to my knowin, CD Grace, the banker. He come out to see my wife while I was in the penitentiary and he asked her about me and how she was gettin along and before he left there he reached in his pocket and pulled out a quarter and told her to give it to me when she come to see me—twenty-five cents' worth of sympathy. And the rest of that bunch—Curtis is dead, Flint's dead, Watson's dead. God moved em. People ought to live right. They ought to live to inherit the kingdom of heaven after they gone from this world, but they don't give a damn.

There is people that don't count God no more than a dog. Some-

body, I forget who it was, didn't want God to create man. Said if He
created man, man would sin. But God rules: He thought so much of
man He made him in His own image and likeness. The Bible don't
say nothin bout the colored man and the white man, just says man.
With God, man aint but a man. But with the people here, some men
is ruled out, blowed off the map, discarded.

VI

Warren Jenks died while I was livin on his place. Old age carried him away—he was well up in his nineties. And he done got
to where he'd just sit up on the veranda over there at his old home
place and smoke cigars, sit and look out on the road. He had owned,
years ago when his children was comin along, cars and trucks, cars
particular. And he had him a Ford truck at the time he died and he'd
make mistakes in drivin it, but bein his age people had sympathy
for him, didn't nobody run over him; but he'd get his truck in places
sometimes he couldn't get out. Backin into ditches and turnin off
into the swamps when the road went straight or sometimes he'd go
straight when the road turned. It taken other people to get him out
of such situations. Then he died.

I'd lived on the Jenks place bout ten years when Mary Beth told
me and her mother: if we could find a place we could buy, she'd
buy it for us. And that's why I'm here.

White man by the name of Stu Wilcox owned this house.
Vernon carried me over to see him one Sunday. Lived out on the low
line connectin Beanville and the Beaufort highway on what used to
be called the Coalhouse road. Got there and I asked him definitely
would he sell this place—I'd heard he wanted to sell it. He said, "Yes,
I'll sell it."

I said, "What do you want for the lot?"

He said, "I want twenty-five hundred dollars."

Half-acre lot and one buildin on it. He'd bought the place a few
years before when the colored man that lived here come up disabled
to do anything. And when he bought it he had some inside works
put in it and runned a café business here for the colored. And when I
bought it I turned it back into a dwellin house.

You got a tight section of colored people right through here for
a good ways; the colored people—by the land bein owned by the

colored people, they wouldn't sell none to nobody less'n it was a colored. And when this house fell into the hands of a white man —here's the first thing: that house when it was first built, and the fellow it was built for give down, why, it fell back in the carpenter's hands, the man who had it built. Then Mr. Wilcox had a chance to get a hold of it, and he did. He turned around and sold it to a colored fellow and that poor colored fellow had bad luck; he fooled around and got drowned up here in these backwaters. Well, when he left this world his mother come down from Boston, Massachusetts —called her Ruby. Ruby come out of Boston to the death of her son; daddy'd been dead for years. And it was told that she wanted to take over the payments on this place, bein it's her child had money in it. But Wilcox wouldn't let her take it up and the place fell back in his hands. And he kept whatever money the boy had put toward buyin the place before he died. I eventually heard that Wilcox wanted to sell the place again and I taken a interest in buyin it. Ruby had been here and gone about it and she was out of the picture, and Mr. Wilcox had done turned the house into a café. Had people livin in there too, in the bedroom part, that runned the café for him. They moved out of there for me to move in it and we all moved on the same day, on a Sunday, they movin out and me movin in. And they moved right in the house I was movin out of, the colored people that runned the café. As fast as I could move out of Jenks' house and move in here, they was movin out of here and movin in there—just swappin houses. Leslie Meade and his wife—I was goin up a little bit by movin in here and they was goin down; couldn't do no better at the present than move into Jenks' old house.

I went and notified Josie's daughter about the deal. She come right on as quick as she could get here. But I tided it, I tided it. I sold my mule and I sold my cows and everything else I could get my hands on I didn't need: sold my plow stocks, all but one of em; got rid of my little blacksmith shop and most of the other tools of my life.

My cows brought me two hundred and seventy dollars. Both of em was dandy good cows, big bags like good dairy cows. But that first cow had lost part of her bag—if I must say it, that cow lost her bag herself. I sold her yearlin, bull yearlin, and when I sold him out of her sight, she just held that milk tight against her, kept it in her bag, wouldn't let it down, because the calf weren't suckin.

Some milk cows is like that: if you get rid of their suckin calf they goin to snatch up their milk and hold it there. Revengin herself on you, but it's the wrong way for her to do. She suffered many a hard pain in her bag, no tellin—but that's a dumb brute, she didn't know what she was doin when she did her hellish trick. And that other cow, at that time, she had a heifer calf and I sold the calf for eighty-five dollars. So, eighty dollars for that bull yearlin and eighty-five dollars for that heifer—that gived me a piece of change. Then I jumped up and sold that first calf's mother, as she'd messed up and wouldn't let her milk down. I'd go to milk her, mornin and night, every time looked like her bag had as much milk in it after I milked her as before. She was a cow of that type and I couldn't do nothin with her so I wheeled in and sold her to one of the Bailey gentlemen for a hundred cash dollars. I was aimin to keep her and see if I couldn't raise calves from her, if she could get up enough milk just to raise calves; but I soon discovered she weren't goin to do it. I told him, "She's in bad shape, she's lost part of her bag, Mr. Bailey, you can see that; she aint givin no milk out of it and the bag stays filled all the time."

He said, "That don't make no difference; just price her to me. I don't care nothin bout the looks of her bag."

He was intendin to put her on the market for beef purposes and that's what he done, right here in Montgomery.

I said, "Well, say what you think and do what you think, it'll take a smooth hundred dollars to get her."

Runned his hand in his pocket and snatched out a hundred dollars, handed it to me. Rocked along there and carried her home and in a few days he come tearin back wantin to take the other. I said, "No sir, Mr. Bailey, I wouldn't sell her now on no grounds less'n I was forced to. Money won't buy her. She's a good cow, I know it; both of em was good cows up until the other one lost her bag. Now this here is the only one that's givin me any milk, I'm goin to keep her."

He said, "Well, I want her. I'll give you all she's worth, let me make just a little. What'll it take for her?"

I said, "In that case, you can take her if you want to or leave her alone, but it'll take a smooth hundred and seventy-five dollars to get her."

Reached in his pocket and gived me a hundred and seventy-five dollars without battin his eyes. That was the last cow I had. Well, I was gettin up a little money, with what little I'd made on my patches that year. Looked around me and I had a little corn to sell, but I took pains not to sell it until I got rid of that mule.

I sold my blacksmith shop to Mr. Lorne Ray. That white man buys up all this old-timey stuff he can get his hands on, all through this country. The very tools I lived by, he sells em for antiques. He have told me hisself, he gets more for em than he gives me, and the people that buy em don't even use em exactly. He might not get no more out of some of it than he pays me, but take it all around and around, he gets enough more than I got out of him to put back in his pocket than he loses. He gets enough to keep him diggin at these things.

He come to my house one day, "Hello, Uncle Nate"—that's what he calls me—"you got any of this old country stuff people used to use way back yonder?"

Wanted to know about my wife's old dishes in the house and any kind of old style stuff. I said, "I got maybe a few things around here, Mr. Ray. Look around. Here's some old pots that's yet good, not no old broke up pots, but good pots, a good kettle, old things that aint tore up."

He walked around my lot and found him some old pots and kettles that didn't leak. After I bought an electric stove, I just set them things out in my yard. Couldn't use nothin on that stove but these aluminum things; these old-timey pots was too heavy, electric heat wouldn't heat em as fast as wood fire. So, we done away with our old cookin instruments and set em outdoors. Lorne Ray bought it all. Took it away from here and took away my tools—sledge hammer, hand hammer, plow sharpener, anvil, blower. Gived me a frivolous price—but I let it go. Gived me bout half value, hardly half, bout a third value. I'd bought that blower second-handed from Preston Courteney after my blacksmith shop got burned up over on the Leeds place before I come out of prison. I didn't lose my vise but I lost my blower—Vernon was workin in the shop and he was supposed to be the head one, and he let Eugene go in there one day tamperin around and Eugene left the fire in the forge in place of puttin it out, and late that evenin, about night, the buildin caught afire. Burnt up these shop affairs and set a adjoinin outhouse afire and burnt up a ton of natural soda, farm soda; burnt up a brand new wagon body settin round behind the house under a shed, crack brand new one; but it happened that the wagon itself didn't burn. They'd been usin the wagon out away from there and they'd left it out yonder, didn't bring it back to the shed, so it was saved from the fire. Burnt up a brand new cross-cut saw, Simon saw, one of the best grade of saws there was in them days; burnt up a heap of shop tools besides. Burnt up most of my hammers, ruint em; burnt the handles out and when the fire touched the hammers themselves that ruint the tempers—O, it just cleaned me up. Some of it was second-handed stuff but I could have used it all till my finish. Tools like that don't perish like men or beasts—unless you put em to the fire.

Burnt my anvil but it didn't heat it enough to ruin it. That and the rest of my blacksmith tools I bought em from a fellow by the name of Hinton Wheeler. I hired my mules shod awhile but after I begin to own as high as four head of mules I started shoein my stock myself. And eventually, that last pair of mules I bought, them big heifers, when I'd pick up their hind feet—I've never been nothin but a small-weighted man my whole life, I'd pick up them big mules' hind feet and they weighin a little over eleven hundred apiece, them heifers would lay down on me nearly. They didn't mean me no harm, just give over and lay down on me. Well, that broke me up from shoein em; there weren't enough of me for a big mule to lay down on and give over. I could go around and slap my hand on their hips, reach down and get them foots and begin to pull it backwards out from under em—they'd give it up and lay that shoe right across my thigh. I'd trim their foots, clean out their hoofs, and shoe em. But I quit shoein for myself when they begin to lay down on me and in a little while I quit shoein for anybody.

Lorne Ray gived me a pittance to what I'd paid out for my tools and things. All the iron that he could buy, he could sell that easy, and all that other old style stuff—there's people decorates their homes with things that belong to the past. I figured when I sold off this shop material I was gettin on the borders of disable. I didn't need it so I tried to get a little somethin out of it. I just lingered, lingered, lingered, sellin my little stuff off, until I sold the last cow I had and my mule was the last I sold.

I plumb dispossessed myself before I moved into this house. Had to do it, I needed the money to get in here. So I decided I'd better sort of close out. I thinks over it and I know it handicapped me but how come I was to do that? I seed I was growin weaker and older and I couldn't keep up my stock, I couldn't plow a rough grade of land. If I'd a plowed on two or three years longer, I just might have fell out in the field, accordin to my feelins. So I just sold out to where I wouldn't have so much to do. But it don't worry me. As well as I can look through it and explain it—quite natural, it hurts a moneyed man to do away with what he's got and dispossess hisself worse than it do a little old fellow like me. It don't terrify a little fellow's mind: he aint got much, he can brush it off. But good God, what happened to Sam Tucker? He got shed of all his properties and it pulled his eyeballs to watch his stuff pass out of his hands. He just lost his mind completely and killed hisself. But me, I aint never had much but a livin. And I had to work like the devil to get that. So it don't worry me nothin to dispossess myself. I feel like, to an extent, it freed me someway. At that particular time I didn't have nothin but some work tools that I had worked with, and they had worked me. And when I got shed of em I ceased to be a tool myself.

My last bar plow, I let my cousin Zach Culver, up in the hills, I let Zach have it. He come down here and told me, bought him a mule and wanted to know, "Cousin Nate, has you got any plow stocks here you can spare?"

I just told him to take my plow up there and use it, and if I didn't call for it until he wore it out, don't worry. But if I called for it, I wanted the use of it back. He's farmin some, up there in them hills, he got a new mule—he aint farmin no cotton, truck patches and corn is what he's farmin. So, I let Zach have my plow stock and all my good points and I called on him like this: "Cousin Zach, I need some lumber here and it's goin to take a right smart for what I need it for. Has you got any loose lumber layin around your place?" He's on his own place—

He said, "Yeah, Cousin Nate, I had some work done recently and I got some old lumber tore down off of some of the buildins around there, layin there, that I can divide with you."

Went right on home with that plow stock and everything he could load up here that I could spare and come right back with a load of lumber, on a Sunday mornin, too. He didn't wait a bit— that gived me a pretty good start on stuff to build my shed here.

I sold my two-horse wagon when I moved on the Jenks place. All the use that I had for a pair of mules, I had Vernon's mule to work with mine. Kept his mule the best of two years and I fed her and took care of her just like she was mine. She was a stinkin good mule but she was one of these wild rattlers; good God, you go to foolin with her, she'd just go crazy nearly. Whip her and she goin to carry you out of that field with her, or she goin to try. You had to be man enough to keep the lines off her; whippin stirred her up considerably bad. I could holler at her—she wouldn't pay much attention to that. She was quiet herself, quiet like a lamb if I'd be quiet with her. Work anywhere in the world I'd hitch her. And at last Vernon sold her to some colored fellow way up there between here and Beaufort. That put Vernon out of the mule business. And I didn't have but one, and I kept her just as plump as a apple at all times.

I sold that Kizzie mule just before Christmas last year. I held her for a hundred dollars but people commenced a kickin at me, didn't want to give me that—mules has been cheap here in this country for a long time now. She had a little age on her but she had that get up and go in her too. And regardless to her age, I weren't goin to give her away. Stock's a long life liver—you physic your mules and your horses and feed em a plenty, they won't hardly wear out.

When I was in prison over here at Wetumpka, there was a old fellow there by the name of Shug Armstrong—he had once been the warden there. And they had a old mule, called her Dan, old mare mule. And Mr. Armstrong would come by there to visit old Dan. And he'd say, "Old Dan, I bought Dan when I was head warden here, for the state. Dan's thirty-five years old. I know her age." Still alive and just as fat as a pig. But she had old mules' acts and ways. You could plow old Dan out there, plow off a piece and stop and leave her, she'd turn her head around and look at you, watch you clean till you got out of sight, and stand right there till you come back, too. And she had her own gait to the plow. She'd walk right on off but she weren't fast. She showed a disposition to bein old. Mr. Shug Armstrong would say, "You can't tell me nothin bout old Dan, I bought her out of the drove myself. Old Dan's thirty-five years old. I know, I bought her out of the drove thirty-five years ago." She was a black mule and she'd a weighed somewhere in the neighborhood of nine hundred pounds. She weren't no great big mule.

That Kizzie mule of mine was seven years old when I bought her—recommended to be seven years old. She was fat when I got her and she stayed that way. I plowed her every year for sixteen years until I sold her. I asked a hundred dollars for that mule and if I'd a got it I wouldn't a lost but twenty-five dollars and got the best of her labor. I had three or four different white men come to see that mule, turn her down and walk away. Wouldn't meet my price. Colored fellow bought her. One of em had been my half-brother-in-law and TJ's full brother-in-law, fellow by the name of Jesse McCaffrey, lived with his brother Henry McCaffrey on their mother's and father's old home place, the McCaffrey boys. Jesse McCaffrey married my half-sister, which was TJ's whole sister, Judy. So, fooled around and all the white men turned me down and the McCaffrey boys come up and wanted the mule. They told me that they had had a pair of mules but they lost one of em the year before and that left em with just one. And they was glad to buy my mule to match their other'n. I just pulled the bridle off her and give her over to em—cut five dollars on the price. Them boys, colored fellows, both grown men, lived on their mother's and father's old home place, gived me ninety-five dollars for that mule, and she was pretty and slick and fat when I sold her. Then I went and gived em her plow gear, good set—leather collar, good out-haines, a pad for under the collar that I'd just used a year and it didn't have a hole through it noway, good traces—the lines wasn't so hot but I'd plowed with them lines several years.

I didn't work my stock with any sort of old things. Because my mules was more than slaves to me. Mule used to be a thing, before tractors ever come in style, that you couldn't make it without her. She'd make you a livin if you treated her right. That Kizzie mule in particular, you had to be careful with her. Treat her right and you could plow with a string. But she didn't want you to holler at her and go to whippin her with them lines—she'd drag you out of that field, she weren't goin to stand you beatin on her.

I let em have her for ninety-five dollars. Soon as she got gone, several of them white men backtracked and come willin to give me my price. I just told em, "She's gone now. You too late for her, too late."

One white man I had to turn down, I hated to do it. Mr. Claude Wilcox, lives right there now in Pottstown. Durin the time I was in prison, or just before I was sentenced out from jail, there was a great talk against my family by some of the white people right through this country. Mr. Claude Wilcox got wind of it—you won't find no man today that'll run up against Mr. Claude Wilcox, they dread him, they stand off him. He don't take no foolishness. And oo, they was heavily talkin against my family— That lawyer Stein, may God bless him wherever he's at; I hope his soul's restin in Jesus if he's dead. He stopped this thing, got it bated down; they feared him for some cause— And Mr. Claude Wilcox told em, "You just better let Nate Shaw's family alone and have nothin to do with em." And he was a man they knowed didn't take no shit. He was game enough to get up and tell em, "Let Nate Shaw's family alone." I heard it through my wife. She found it out and she come told me in prison.

And he come to me just after I moved here. He heard I had a mule to sell and he told me he had had a good mule, but he put him off in a pasture and he got tangled up in some vines and by not checkin on the mule as he should, when he did find the mule, the mule was caught and couldn't get out and there he died. Evidently, he didn't look after him daily—and he wanted to buy my mule. I said, "I'm sorry, Mr. Wilcox, I done sold him; he's gone."

That's the very man that stuck hisself between the riot crowd and my people; brave man, good man, white man with sympathy.

I was very careful at sellin that mule. I put some stress behind it, told em, "Take care of her. You see the shape she's in, I'd hate to see her go down."

And every time Josie sees em—she goes over by Teaks' Church on the same road where they keeps that mule—she bones em about Kizzie and they tell her, "When that mule dies we goin to have Nate come over here and preach her funeral."

I miss that mule today. I miss her every way—she was a good quality mule too. I could run her into a quagmire waist high and order her to stop and she'd stand right there and wait for death. But the old mule weren't worth nothin; them old cows wasn't worth nothin. I got as good a price as I could get accordin to the age of them beasts.

I was fixin to make a trough for Kizzie when I sold her, or a pipin from the well to the lot. But I never did do it. I just drawed water and poured it in a foot-kit. She never would drink over two kits of water. She would drink out of a big old washin machine— I drove a tight stopper at the bottom where the water'd run out and I'd go there and pour them two foot-kits of water in there and keep that thing cleaned out, and that was her drinkin spot. When I'd get ready to bridle her I'd go out there, reach up the side of the barn door, grab my curry comb and brush, brush her and curry her, harness her and go on to the field. No kicks to come. She done what I asked her to do every way. When I got to where I couldn't put in a day's plowin—before I quit plowin that mule I'd sit down on my plow many a time, she'd stand there—drive her in the shade, sit down, stick my plow down and sit down, she'd stand right there till I started again or took her out. She understood.

First thing I'd do, on the average, every day of my life, after I got my clothes on, dash out and feed them mules. Next thing, if I had to draw water or anything else around the house needed to be done, I'd do it. My wife would get breakfast done and the whole family would set down at the table and eat. Then I was ready to go back to the lot and turn them mules out where they could get water themselves or either I'd draw water at the well. Done it myself and I was very shrewd on them jobs. If my boys fed and watered my mules—maybe some mornin I had some other little thing I wanted to get done real early, first thing. My boys would go to the lot—I could trust em; I always told my boys whenever they'd feed em, "Them mules aint goin to eat no more than they want. Just give em a good feed, plenty."

Sweet feed, oats, sometimes sweet feed and oats mixed, just a certain amount all put in one vessel to make up their feed. Sometimes it was ear corn—never did shell no corn and give em; a mule that's kept in good shape will eat that corn off of them cobs, sometimes he'll leave a few nubs at the end of the ears—mighty seldom my mules would ever eat up the cobs. You get a mule hungry, don't give him enough ear corn, he'll bite the nub end of that corn and eat it. The most of them cobs, my mules left em right there in that trough for me to pick up and throw out when I put out another feed of corn. Fed em three times a day just like I et—them animals, my mules or my horses, I considered the next thing to my family. Fed em mornins early, day dinner when I'd carry em to the barn, nights when I'd put em in the lot. Very seldom that I'd fasten my mules in the stable; unless it was bad weather, I'd leave the door open so when they got done eatin they could walk out in the lot. A mule won't never overeat hisself if he's used to getting plenty to eat. But you'd better not fool with no horses thataway. A horse will overeat his stomach, a horse will outeat a mule—it's nature for em to do it.

You can't trust a horse like you can a mule. A horse is not like a mule and a mule is not like a horse. A horse and a mule has got, as a rule, different ways. When it comes to heavy duties, little mule or big mule, he's kinder and more willin to work than a horse. Of course, any animal that aint willin he's goin to show it to you. That'll be a sorry mule, but it's more in the nature of a horse to act that way. It's known: better to have you a mule out there than a horse because that mule goin to bow when you call him and your business will pick up. If it's a thoroughgoin mule, aint no trouble to get work out of him, he'll bow to anything. Some horses when you hitch em up, they got a lot of fidgetin to do, and some of em just aint goin to work for you to save your life—maybe he'll travel, maybe he'll pull a buggy, but when you put him to plowin, or put him to a two-horse wagon, right there's where you goin to have your trouble with a horse.

Twice a day if I'm plowin, mornin and night, I'd brush and curry my mules. Keep my mules in thrifty condition, keep em lookin like they belonged to somebody and somebody was carin for em. Mule love for you to curry him; he'll stand there just as pretty and enjoy it so good—run that comb over him first one way then the other, backwards and forwards, scrub him good, all over, the fur under his stomach if necessary, and from his head back. Brush the head—mule don't love for you to hit his head much with a curry comb.

When I'd get him curried, hang my curry comb back up on the barn wall—my curry comb had just about gived out at the time I sold that last mule—reach back and get that brush, brush him all over far as I could reach that brush under him; brush his legs down as low as his hocks. Clean that mule up so he'll feel good, then go get his gear and put it on, take him and hitch him to the plow, go to plowin. He feels good to be clean just like a person do.

In plowin, you aint got a thing but a cloth, good heavy cloth made out of duckin, if necessary, across them mules' backs and got hooks on what you call the backhand to hook them traces on each side. Get them traces hitched to the single-tree, and your lines, if you able to have em, set of lines long enough to go to that animal's mouth with that plow stretched out full length, fasten you a new plow line to each side of that mule's mouth, run em back to the plow handles, long enough to make you a loop. And in plowin, you can take that mule and set him close to that plow, or further from it, ownin to how you set your traces to the loggerhead.

If I was goin to a wagon, many a time I'd use strop harness on my mules, with a crupper under their tails, to haul logs. I started off usin britchin on em, them big leather strops behind the back legs and hips, but that wouldn't do to keep them animals cool for haulin lumber. Best thing to do, averagely, for you to haul lumber with your mules, run them leather strops across them mules' hips down to them traces—and that's what you call strop harness. I used em for haulin lumber so my mules wasn't covered up in britchin and leathers, keep em hot. And put brakes on that wagon to hold that wagon off of em goin down hills. I'd load anywhere from a thousand to—wouldn't put on a foot over a thousand if I was under any reasonable hill at all; buck it down, pick up my lines, call up there, "All right, babies, let's get it." You'd see them big heifers fall out then. O, my mules just granted me all the pleasure I needed, to see what I had and how they moved.

Soon as I got my property sold off I moved in this house. I paid Mr. Stu Wilcox four hundred dollars and it's very little I've paid on it since. Mary Beth, Josie's daughter, is backin up the business now. She's got a foreman job in a hospital up there in Boston, Massachusetts, and she claims she's comin down here pretty soon and pay the house off. I can't pay it myself. I can't plow now. I got no income out in the field, no more than a little garden. When I quit plowin I got to where—aint plantin nothin but corn to keep up my fattenin hog, and a little watermelon patch, some potatoes, peas, beans, and so on like that, just piddlin, you might say; it aint nothin to prize me up.

I has one time in life, before I went to prison, I was doin good for myself; part of my labor bein taken but I was climbin up in the world despite it, accumulatin personal property. But it's been a dead drag for me ever since I been put in prison and come out.

Now I has to draw from the government—the government's able to bear it, puttin out their money on me. Well, some of that money I been beat out of. And the government drawin tax to get that money; they aint workin for it. I pleaded and I begged and I runned around everywhere I could go for information to get in touch with the government. Not havin no education, I'd be turned down for some cause. And I runned around till I got to be seventy-nine years old before the government ever gived me anything. All right. I went to Beaufort and put in my complaint. And there was a white lady runnin the head part of the business, by the name of Miss Fogarty. She questioned me close and I told her the truth about my condition. She said, "Well, Nate, I'll see to you bein helped. But can you work ary a bit? Or what do you do to help yourself?"

I told her, "Yes'm, I been farmin all my days up until now and I become disabled to work a crop—I had to cut my crop down to where I can't make a livin at it no more. All I can do is work my little patches. I aint quit plantin a little corn yet to feed my pig on and have a little left to sell in the community. But so far as plantin cotton, that's been over; I aint planted no cotton in several years. But I has a little corn patch, and a garden, three or four acres, that's all I can cover; and I scuffles around and works the best I can. I want to keep plantin my little corn and stuff. I don't want no sort of help that would take that away from me."

Told her I worked white oak and she asked me how much I made from my baskets and I told her. Then she said, "Well, Nate, I'll write you up and your statement will go from here to Montgomery"—that's headquarters for the state of Alabama—"and then it'll leave Montgomery and go to Washington, D.C. And we'll get a hearin from them."

That wound it up there. I went by her word and gived my application a chance to go from Montgomery to Washington, D.C., headquarters for the United States, sure enough. And when I went back to see her, my application had done went and come. She said, "Your application went through just fine. You can have your corn patch and your little truck patches and so on. And you can work white oak. Just so long as there's no cotton in the business."

They started off givin me twenty-nine dollars a month and they just kept inchin up, inchin up. I have to pay lectricity and grocery bill and insurance—I never did ask em to give me more than that twenty-nine dollars, I'm takin yet what they give me. Well, they pulled on up there and now they givin me a hundred and three dollars a month. And when they put out that Medicare I joined that. Now, I aint been sick a minute since I went in and been drawin this relief. The government sends me Medicare cards and promises to pay my doctor bills when they come. I aint got a penny out of that plan today but they aint to blame for that; I just aint been sick.

JOSIE draws a little money from the government and sells candy as a addition to that. White man's candy out of the state of Georgia. This candy costs her four dollars a box and she gets a premium for sellin it or the cash money. Children come out from all over this settlement to our house huntin candy and she sells it to em. They pile in here, sometimes three and four comes in a drove to get candy from Josie—chocolates, Baby Ruths, coconut candy, cookies; just any kind of candy that the man brings and let her have to sell. She generally takes from two to four boxes of candy at one time. Been sellin candy before I married her but she's changed companies. And the children of this settlement been knowin her for many years—she's called to be the candy lady. There's children bought candy from her that's grown and has their own children that come and buy candy from her. She have had a man from a company come right yonder on the Jenks place and wanted her to sell candy for him and she was loaded sellin for another man and she had to turn him down.

These childrens eats any kind of candy, any kind. When she first gets it, they'll pick out all the best lookin, then they has to come back and get the other, and they take it with a smile. Josie credits it sometime, and sometime she has a hard way to go huntin up her dimes—some of these big boys is slow to pay and some of these girls too. These children got pretty good book learnin and Josie stands around and sees em put down on a paper what they owe her, so there won't have to be no argument. Josie don't eat no candy herself; she aint got nothin but hollow teeth.

I can't reach the hill like I used to could but I'm not at a standstill yet. I think about it over and often: if I hadn't got shed of my mule so quick and if I could have got me some smooth land, I could have plowed last year. Wouldn't have hurt me. But I sold my mule, sold my cows and everything. Now I'm eighty-five years old and I don't have a crop in the field, not a crop in the world.

It's been two years since I picked a bit of cotton or chopped out a row. Workin for Vernon and it was this way between us: he'd always pay me but I wouldn't let him pay me as much as he was willin to pay me, bein my child. He so dearly took care of his mother when I was away those twelve years in prison. He went by my orders —and he went by some of his orders too. But he stuck in the house with his mother and his little sisters and brothers. And I feel I owe him a great deal. I wouldn't charge him for my labor like he wanted to pay me. I loved his mother as a wife, I loved her. She stuck by me until the last peas was gone out of the dish—

I learnt that if Vernon could get a thing goin his way when I was in prison—Eugene come here a few weeks ago to see me, come down from Middletown, Ohio, him and his baby boy. And he told me—he didn't tell me no more than I knowed. I didn't know just how the situation runned in my home after I left there, but I figured that some dissatisfaction come about there while I was away. Vernon kept the farm goin and couldn't nobody complain about the job he done. I'd left him with plenty to help hisself till I got back and when he saved my stock and tools from the mob crowd, he had em to work with—didn't have to start from zero. He took care of his family, his daddy's family, in a way that he was more than a brother to his sisters, a brother to his brothers, and a son to his mother and father. But his mother told me that he come home twice to my knowin full of whiskey. And she jacked him up about it. I never trained him up to drink whiskey; that's just a method he picked up. I don't say he was drunk but the whiskey loosened his tongue and he talked in a way he oughtn't a talked over his mother and the other children.

But he observed my rulins and held up for right more than he done wrong. One time, while they was livin on the Courteney place, my wife told Vernon, "If you'll go to Calusa, there's three washins down there—" She was a industrious woman and she wanted to do somethin to help herself. But I'd told her when we married, a-while after we married and commenced a raisin up little chaps, I said, "When you do your washin here at home, and our cookin and other things that's assigned to your hand, you done enough. I aint goin to have none of this here runnin around over the country washin for white folks. You just cut that out from your thoughts."

So, one day she told Vernon, "There's three washins at Calusa I wants to get. If you'll take the car and go down there and get them people's clothes and bring em back here, I'll wash em and carry em back and that'd be a help to us."

Yeah, it'd help—help carry her down, too. She told me plain all about it; come there to prison and told me, "That scamp looked at me when I told him that and what you reckon he told me? He said, 'Mama, Papa never would allow that and you know it. I aint goin to do it.'" Turned her down right there. "'I aint goin down there to get no clothes for you to wash.'" She told me every word he told her. I was so glad of it I didn't know what to do.

So, Eugene got to talkin bout what I had and what I'd left em with and how they got along when I was gone. He said, "Papa, you just don't know what went on when you was in prison. Vernon runned everything his way." And he commenced sheddin tears when he told me. Said, "When you left home, Vernon was the head of everything and he would take me and Garvan—he wouldn't carry us where we wanted to go no time without makin two trips. He'd carry us and put us off where we wanted to go, then he'd pick up his gals and carry them on to beer joints and around"—that stuck me up—"and promised to come back and pick us up where he left us, and we'd have to walk home most of the time. And when *he'd* come home, he wouldn't answer our mother to where he'd been. But we knowed, Papa, we knowed."

That was against my will, that was against my desires: I didn't want to hear he'd treated em nothin like that. Travelin through the country with a frolickin crowd and nobody at home but his mother and her babies. Eugene just thinkin bout how they was treated—that's all he would tell—and he shed tears.

But I have to take his talk lightly to this extent: Vernon didn't mistreat em in a way that amounted to nothin. They had to work under him just like if I'd been over em and, after all, he is their brother. Children don't endure a brother like they do a father. That talk come out of Eugene to me and I'm satisfied it's true. But it aint the last word on the subject. I just figured that if Vernon's pedigree was to come out good and proper like it was, and him forced to be the head one, Eugene would take it for somethin nasty. But I'm just obliged to have two minds about it.

So, I swallowed all that boy told me. "Papa, you didn't know all that."

Told him, "No, I didn't know it, but your mother told me he come in once or twice there with whiskey in him."

Said, "Yes sir, he done that, and we had to do what he said do."

VII

It approaches my mind like this: what is labor? It's a trait of man. God put us all here to work. I know people who used to would work—always there was some of em wouldn't work at all—but since the government been givin em a hand-down, they wouldn't mind the flies off their faces. They'll tell you quick, "I'm drawin, I aint goin to hit a lick with a snake."

You used to could have a field full of hands, but now you can't hardly get one or two in there; it's just out of the question. Aint available no more—they quit it, you can't hire em. Some of em run off and get em a public job; some of em will sit right in the house on their tail or loaf the road, and aint goin to do nothin much nowhere. I've heard em say, my color talkin it: "I wouldn't tell a mule to get up if he was sittin in my lap." But I never heard em say they wouldn't eat the fruits of the earth. He won't plow, he won't chop cotton, he won't pick cotton, but still he's goin to wear these clothes made out of cotton. Everything that's used to sustain life and nurture your well-bein, it comes off a farm of some kind—if it's a little farm if it aint no more than just for family use.

I hear em talk, who I know used to plow and seed em plow: because they has once in days past made crops under the white man's administration and didn't get nothin out of it, he don't want to farm today regardless to what he could make out there; he don't want to plow no mule—that was his bondage and he turnin away from it. He huntin him a public job, leavin the possession and use of the earth to the white man.

You take these public companies, they keeps em laid off these jobs to an extent; the ones that's got em hired turns em loose, out, until way after a while, maybe they call em back, mess em around that way. But a man needs regular work—if he wants to work, it's right, it's honorable for him to work and try to help hisself. But he aint goin to want to work if they liable to turn him loose anytime they please. Work em to death or don't work em enough, that's how they do around here. Cut off that regular work. If I got you hired out there to work on any sort of a public job, I'd be figurin like this: I'm already makin—I'm the boss man, understand—I'm already makin money on that job, if I give you regular work to do and pay you, why, that'd cut me down some. I'm already gettin good anyhow and I'll just lay you off for a few days—they doin that right here, at the cotton mill. I don't know how the people gets along that's laid off thataway. It's like a farmer don't have no land to work or it aint his land he's workin, he just gettin paid by the day, and he don't get the benefit of the crop; just give him enough to keep him goin today till tomorrow.

I'M yet a laborin man, I makes baskets. White folks comes from all parts to get my baskets. One family come, by the name of Hooker, man and his wife, out of West Point, Georgia. Why, if it wasn't for makin baskets and sellin baskets, I wouldn't hardly have no business with white folks at all.

I know some of my color now that tries to dodge whites and shun em, have nothin to do with em. I don't see how they can do it because we're right here amongst em, we got to have some dealins with em. And if you growin cotton, you can't consume that cotton yourself, you got to deal it to the middle man, and there's no nigger cotton buyers. You got to sell it to a white man. And there aint no nigger stores plentiful—there's some about, here and yonder—and there aint a nigger bank that I know of. You just can't avoid white folks and I don't try.

I can't fool with what they want always. What they ask for is out of my line of business. One white gentleman wants me to make him some net hoops—I don't fool with that, I make straight baskets. I use young white oak and makes baskets of different kinds for the public—fish baskets, clothes baskets, baskets to gather corn and peas and so on like that. And I got three chairs with brand new bottoms in my shed. One of em belongs to a colored fellow that lives up by Pottstown Church. I bottomed that chair two weeks ago. He made out like he wanted it—his wife asked my wife if I'd bottom it for em, so I went right on and bottomed it. I bites off just enough to keep me goin, as old as I am. Right now there's a white gentleman

lives between here and Tuskegee, name of McClure, Mr. McClure.
He got a call in here for a little above sixty dollars' worth of baskets.
There's Mr. Lorne Ray, man that bought out my tools and kitchen
material, he buys every basket he can get his hands on. I can't make
em fast enough for the public. I got to keep it cleaned off around
here to make it look like somebody lives here. And then, too, I got
a garden needs hoein and a hog to look after. The Lord keeps me
strong but if I take any more on me than I do, I wouldn't make it.

It works me, it works me, aint no fun in it, it works the stuffin
out of me—goin and gettin white oak, huntin and ramblin all over
the woods, here and yonder. Heat gets me. I get wet with my own
sweat and I give out, hardly able to crawl out of the woods. One
day I set there and after the children left me, I jumped up and
jumped on the worst piece to split in the business. Here's my
thoughts after they left me: I thought I'd just split all of it off and
come on to the house, tote back as much as I needed to get a start
on a basket and come back for the rest on somebody's truck or car.
But before it was over with, I just was lucky to split it open and pick
up one piece of it and come on back to the house.

I taken Josie's grandchaps with me—great-grandchaps, they
stays with us and they wants to go everywhere I go as far as my
travelin is concerned. They stand by me and watch me split the
white oak up. But like chaps will do, they wanted to come back
home before I got my work done. I told em, "Yeah, you all go on
back to the house."

There was three pieces of white oak layin on the ground and
I told em to take two pieces, one take one and the other take one—
that biggest boy can tote a piece as easy as I can. Well, they brought
their two pieces back to the house and I told em I'd be on directly.
And I was already sweaty when they left, workin out there in the
hot sun in the middle of the day; and after they left I got worser.
But still I tried to split that big piece of timber before I carried it
out of the woods. I just plumb give out. By the time I got that biggest
piece of white oak half open, good God I was near doubled over. I
puffed and I panted—I backed off under the bushes and set down
there a long time by myself. And after awhile I decided I'd get up
and finish removin the timber. But after I got up that first time and
went back to splittin, I give out again. I rested myself awhile longer,
got back to it and time I got it split out, I just didn't feel like nothin.
I had to sit down again over there in the woods by myself. The boys

knowed where I was. I kept thinkin that if I didn't get able to get out from them woods, they goin to come back to see about me, which they did. So, I lingered around and lingered around and after a-while my mind told me to get out from there and get right close to the asphalt road so somebody could see me. Well, I just picked up my timber and come staggerin out from there and I made it right close to the asphalt and I had to sit down again. Three or four cars passed and I was sittin right where they could see me, and I knowed some of em did see me—maybe some of em didn't if they didn't turn their heads, but I was sittin right where they could see me. But I couldn't stand up to hail nobody. T'weren't long and I said to myself, 'I believe I'll get up now and try it again.' Stood up then and shouldered that white oak and come on across a fill and walked up a steep hill—it's a steep hill for walkin—and by the time I got up to that woman that lives right yonder in the second house from mine, old lady Fred Brewer's widow, I heard these little old boys hollerin. Well, I got up to this side of the house before I stopped and I just was able to pull that hill totin that piece of white oak. And I looked out in the road, here they come. I was just about to a bush on the left side of the road comin this way where I intended to get clean out from the edge of the road and set down under that bush and cool off—just as I got there these little old boys met me and commenced a hollerin, "Granddaddy, granddaddy."

I said, "Yeah, I'm give out, boys; I'm give out and I aint able to make it to the house. I'm goin to sit down and rest under this bush here. Put my white oak down and rest."

God almighty, when I told em that they hit the road. "We'll be back directly, granddaddy, we'll be back directly."

They took off again and informed Josie where I was and Josie sent that gal that stays with us to my daughter's and she cranked up her car and come right on at me. All them chaps piled in the car with her, Josie in there. I looked up the road and I seed Rachel's car drivin right dead on to where I was settin and watchin—I heard them chaps hollerin in the car and I knowed it was them. Passed by me the first time and turned around in the yard of a house at the bottom of the hill I'd walked up. Come back up the road and parked the car next to where I was. I jumped up, picked up my white oak —it weren't no heavy piece. Rachel took my ax from me and that piece of white oak and stuck em in the trunk of the car and wired the lid down. All of us got in the car then and she brought me right

up to the pine tree in my front yard. She unfastened the lid of her
trunk, took out my ax and that piece of white oak, and brought em
on around back and laid em down. And she stood and cautioned
me a whole lot, as a chap would, and she got on her car and left.
She works down here at Tukabahchee City at a mop factory; and
yesterday evenin after she come off her job she had to come after
me.

That piece of white oak—and them two other pieces the little
boys brought back, they layin here now under the eave of my shed.
And the way I'm goin to run my business they goin to keep me for
awhile. I got to put the brakes on myself. I might get caught in the
woods cuttin down my white oak and fall down, disabled to make
it out of there and nobody knowin exactly where I am. I can't stand
the thought no longer.

People wants baskets on top of baskets and got a whole lot of
orders in here. But there's been a many orders that wasn't filled in
this world. I just won't work myself to death. My eyes is bad now,
too. You take them little boys runnin around here. I can see em
with their sticks in their hands, runnin, see em good. But from here
to the asphalt out yonder, I can't see a man from a mule, only by
the size maybe or the shape and by the fact that you don't see no
mules walkin these roads here nohow.

THESE little old chaps here is Josie's great-grandchildren and we're
raisin em up in place of their natural parents. That big gal here,
Mary Beth took her from one of *her* stepdaughters, Annie Mae
Ramsey, and raised her to where she's at today. Josie did not raise
that gal; she'd keep her some days for Mary Beth but she never did
keep her definitely. And this here brightest little boy is this gal's
brother—both of em is Spencer Ramsey's grandchildren. And now,
Mary Beth's own dear daughter's chap stays here too. Me and Josie
got him just about the time he started to walk. Josie went to Boston
and brought him home with her. Didn't go after him particularly,
but she found out she could get him and she brought him home.
I hired a fellow, drove me to Tuskegee one evenin to meet the bus
to pick her up. And when it come in, there was Josie steppin off with
a baby in her arms. His name is Alexander. He's stayed with us a
little over three years. He's crazy about me now, and tell the truth,
I like these little old chaps just like they was my very own.

These children will have a better time of life than ever been had by my color in history. They're goin and comin as the white children go and come, and right amongst the white children. And somethin I never thought I'd see—school buses travelin every day through the settlement. Change is on, and everything that aint changed goin to be changed—

My boyhood days was my hidin place. I didn't have no right to no education whatever. I was handicapped and handicapped like a dog. When I was deprived of book learnin, right there they had me dead by the throat. I was deaf and dumb, didn't know nothin and weren't given no chance to my rights enough to come in the knowledge of what was right and what was wrong. When I was a little boy comin along—and that runned until way up here when this equal rights movement taken place; that begin to bust these conditions wide open, and many eyes flew open to a great excitement. It's brought light out of darkness. I can just spy the good every day of my life that it's doin—to my first remembrance, here's what was runnin: I was born in 1885. From my birth and I reckon it was before my birth, just such conditions as I've explained was goin on and went on up until recent days. That's well above a hundred years from time to time of the change, well above a hundred years —this is the truth I'm givin; I've kept a record of a heap of things and it gives me a right to speak it—

After I become old enough to travel and go anywhere by myself, I went to them big days, commencement days at Tuskegee in the spring of the year. And I seed Booker Washington—after I was grown and got big enough. I'd heard a lot of talk about Booker Washington, Booker T. Washington. He was a pretty large-bodied man, and he wasn't so high and he wasn't so low, just a average man. But he was a important man, he was a principal there at that school. He was a noted man and he was a man that had quite a bit of influence with the big people in the northern countries, and he was a business man as a white man would be and he controlled and handled that school there at Tuskegee. I seed him and I heard him talk some on them celebration days, and I knowed he was over that school every way. And he'd travel yonder in them northern states and he'd go before them big moneyed men and the officials of the entire United States—he could meet with em and talk with em and he was recognized. They gived that man piles of money to run this school business here in the state of Alabama. But I wouldn't boost Booker Washington today up to everything that was industrious and right. Why? He was a nigger of this state and well known and everything, but here's what his trouble was, to a great extent: he didn't feel for and didn't respect his race of people enough to go rock bottom with em. He leaned too much to the white people that controlled the money—lookin out for what was his worth, that's what he was lookin for. He was a big man, he had authority, he had pull in life, he had a political pull any way he turned and he was pullin for Booker Washington. He wanted his people to do this, that, and the other, but he never did get to the roots of our troubles. He had a lot of friends, he had a lot of courage, but it was all his way. He had a lot of anything a man needed for hisself, but the right main thing, he weren't down with that. Yet and still the veil was over the nigger's eyes. Booker Washington didn't try to pull that veil away like he shoulda done. He should have walked out full-faced with all the courage in the world and realized, 'I was born to die. What use for me to hold everything under the cover if I know it? How come I won't tell it, in favor of my race of people? Why would I not care who sinks just so I swim?' Wrong-spirited. Booker Washington was—quite natural, there's nobody on earth perfect, but Booker Washington was a man got down with his country in the wrong way.

I didn't like conditions but what could I do? I had no voice, had no political pull whatever. They sang that song stoutly to me, too, let me know that the very best that I could do was *labor* and try to labor to a success under their rulins. I done it. You couldn't count no slackness on Nate Shaw about labor.

I worked all that I had to—as far as I can say, the Lord speaks somethin like this: if a thing is necessary to do on a Sunday, do it. Help the ox out of the mire as well on a Sunday as on a Monday. And that very thing have caused me to do a little work on a Sunday. If I was pullin fodder, in fall of the year in gatherin time, I'd pull it to beat the weather, come Sunday or Monday. But I never did go out and pick no cotton on a Sunday. But, pull some fodder on Friday or Saturday and it cured out; well, if I estimated that the rain liable to come, I scurried out there to get that fodder and carry it to the barn. I've done that on a Sunday. That was necessary. It was no harm—

And in all, I had a hard way to go. I had men to turn me down, wouldn't let me have the land I needed to work, wouldn't sell me guano, didn't want to see me with anything. Soon as I got to where I could have somethin for sure and was makin somethin of myself, then they commenced a runnin at me, wantin to make trades with me.

I had business with many a white man and I come out of the little end of the horn with too many of em. When I got in Mr. Watson's hands, he thought he just goin to drive me to what he wanted, which was my destruction. He was goin to take what I had if I owed him; if I didn't owe him he was goin to take it. I'd a died and went home to my Savior before I'd a suffered him to do it. I just carried him three good bales of cotton on about a forty- or fifty-dollar debt—he told me, "Bring me the cotton, bring me the cotton." I didn't have to do it, but I done it. If I had a second chance, I might not do it again—but tryin to avoid a storm by walkin right into it. Give him the cotton and be shed of him. I dumped it off in the warehouse, had it weighed and left it there for him. Then I go back in a few days and ask him for a settlement—"Aint no use of that"; told me just thataway and walked on about his business. He had me then. I done played into his hands. Still, I didn't let that excite me, I stayed cool for nearly a year.

Well, that was common, that was common. There was too many around that was takin the other fellow's labor. And he'd be takin more than one man's labor when he set down with his books. Farewell for some poor man, maybe several poor men.

I never tried to beat nobody out of nothin since I been in this world, never has, but I understands that there's a whole class of people tries to beat the other class of people out of what they has. I've had it put on me; I've seen it put on others, with these eyes. O, it's plain: if every man thoroughly got his rights, there wouldn't be so many rich people in the world—I spied that a long time ago. And I've looked deep in that angle. How can one man get out there and labor for his own way of life and get to be a rich man? Where is his earnins comin from that he's palmin off and stickin it behind? It come out of the poor little farmers and other laborin men. O, it's desperately wrong. There's many a man today aint able to support his family. There's many a man aint able to wear

the clothes that he should wear and accumulate nothin that he
should have, and accomplish nothin that he should do. And who
is the backbone of the world? It's the laborin man, it's the laborin
man. My God, the big man been on him with both foots all these
years and now don't want to get off him. I found out all of that because they tried to take I don't know what all away from me.

I'VE gotten along in this world by studyin the races and knowin
that I was one of the underdogs. I was under many rulins, just
like the other Negro, that I knowed was injurious to man and displeasin to God and still I had to fall back. I got tired of it but no
help did I know; weren't nobody to back me up. I've taken every
kind of insult and went on. In my years past, I'd accommodate
anybody; but I didn't believe in this way of bowin to my knees and
doin what *any* white man said do. Still, I always knowed to give the
white man his time of day or else he's ready to knock me in the head.
I just aint goin to go nobody's way against my own self. First thing
of all—I care for myself and respect myself.

I've joked with white people, in a nice way. I've had to play
dumb sometimes—I knowed not to go too far and let them know
what I knowed, because they taken exception of it too quick. I
had to humble down and play shut-mouthed in many cases to get
along. I've done it all—they didn't know what it was all about, it's
just a plain fact. I've played dumb—maybe a heap of times I knowed
just how come they done such-and-such a trick, but I wouldn't say.
And I could go to em a heap of times for a favor and get it. I could
go to em, even the heavy-pocketed white man, if I couldn't get what
I wanted out of one, I could get it out the other one. They'd have
dealins with you, furnish you what you needed to make a crop, but
you had to come under their rulins. They'd give you a good name if
you was obedient to em, acted nice when you met em and didn't
question em bout what they said they had against you. You begin to
cry about your rights and the mistreatin of you and they'd murder you.

When I jumped up and fought the laws, that ruint me with
the white people in this country. They gived me just as bad a name
as they could give me; talked it around that I was quick-tempered,
I was quick-tempered. The devil you better get quick-tempered or
get some sort of temper when you know you livin in a bad country.

But there's some that wouldn't learn—my brother Peter, he didn't have no trouble with Watson; Simon Travis didn't have no trouble with him that I ever heard; Johnny B Todd, that wife of mine in there, her first husband, he didn't have no trouble with him at all. They just let him run over em and do as he pleased. I can't definitely say how come I growed up to be like I was and they growed up to be them, but I can estimate it: you take a bunch of children out there, sisters and brothers all, they'll grow up with different spirits in em.

My mother died in August and I was lackin from the date she died until the twenty-eighth of December of bein nine years old. And Peter was the baby; he weren't walkin when she died. That puts him near eighty today. I'm five or six years older than he is, I don't know definitely. But I do know that he stayed with my daddy until he was twenty-three years old.

You know you hardly ever find two brothers that operate just alike. There was a great difference in my and his operations; there was a great difference in my and his thoughts about what we wanted to accumulate in this world.

Peter's a good fellow. He got a lot of white friends back up in that settlement where he lives. He don't talk back to em—he got one white gentleman up there that takes a power saw and saws wood and hauls it to him. And here just before Christmas last year he had to go in the hospital at Tuskegee—some of em went down there to see him. He takes better with em than I do because he's been quiet all his life.

I just happen to be one of a different spirit. I've learned many a thing that's profitable to me, and I've learned a heap that aint profitable, but to learn anything at all is a blessin. And I've learned that whatever is in a person, a heap of his conditions is created in him by his life, and for the rest, he's born that way. In many cases I got a quick thought and a quick mind. So definitely, until sometimes I think I harms myself, I acts too quickly. I can't help it though, I was natured that way.

I come into the world with this against me: that if a man comes to take away what I have and he don't have a fair claim against me, I'll die before I stand quiet as a fence post and let him do it. If I die tryin to defend myself, why, let me go. I'm goin to try, definitely.

My own dear boys don't understand why I done what I done. I have never had one of em walk up to me and hold me a hearty conversation in regards to this business. They don't talk with me against it, they don't talk with me in favor of it. But if they do say anything, they show me the weak spots in it. Aint a one of em ever put his arm around me and said, "Papa, I'm proud of you for joinin the union and doin what you done." They don't see that deep in regards to their own selves. They're scared to do it. White folks shot over em, messed with em so bad, in the fall of '32, kept em bluffed down, and they seed what was done to me—it put a mark on em. Well, I don't want no chicken-hearted boys. I want some of em, for God's sake, to show and prove the spit of their daddy.

They done all they could for me after I was put in prison, they stuck with their mother—all of em did except Calvin—but they felt ashamed of what happened. They never caught my meanin— they never asked me. They was just scared to death and ashamed —that's the same thing.

Some of em that don't like the standard I proved in these union affairs tells me I talk too much. Now you take Calvin, Vernon, Garvan, that's three of my boys, my two oldest boys and my youngest boy, none of em have left home today, in a way of speakin; and they don't want nothin said about the past days of this organization. They wish, if they had their way about it, they'd blot all that out so never a word would come up about it no more as long as they live or I live. I caught em caucusin about it, figurin how can they stop their daddy from talkin about it. And they're my children.

Francis, that's my third boy, stays in Philadelphia, and Eugene, that's my fourth boy, stays in Ohio, what they call Middletown, and I've heard less said out of them about it—less said by Eugene than Francis. They lived through them times too. Garvan he's dry, don't say much—I know a person, especially if I raised him—and if he was to say somethin he'd run to consult with Vernon and Calvin. And if I was to please them three boys today—Calvin, Vernon, Garvan—I wouldn't say another word. But if you don't like what I have done, then you are against the man I am today. I aint goin to take no backwater about it. If you don't like me for the way I have lived, get on off in the woods and bushes and shut your mouth and let me go for what I'm worth. And if I come out of my scrapes, all right; if I don't come out, don't let it worry *you*, this is *me*. Don't nobody try to tell me to keep quiet and undo my history. There aint no get-back in me as far as I can reach my arm. And if anything comes up and favors me to knock down and drag out this old "ism" that's been plunderin me and plunderin the colored race of people ever since I got big enough to know, and before that, before that—old mothers and fathers before I come into this world was treated the same, knuckled under. Well, I'm tired of it, I don't want to bear all that. Anything tries to master me I wish to remove it. And I'm willin to slap my shoulder to the wheel if it's ary a pound I can push. And for God's sake don't come up messin with me. If there's any better life for me to live, any more rights that I can enjoy, get out the way and let me enjoy em or let me go down. And if I go down, in the name of the Lord, I'm done with it. Them all that has a mind to stop the wheel rollin by droppin their heads and hidin their faces, that's them. I can't help it but it stirs me from the bottom. I'd fight this mornin for my rights. I'd do it—and for other folks' rights if they'll push along.

I don't call for nobody to run their heads up under a gun, but if you don't rise up in defense of your portion, what good are you? Every nigger in this country that's ever heard about this organization oughta wake up and speak out for it for their own sake. And realize: any business that's transacted for the benefit of you, you ought to risk somethin, you *got* to risk.

I aint got nothin to give my children when I leave this world. I've already gived em—I raised em, and teached em a way of life, and I never did have nothin but some personal property. I aint been able to save a penny. If you find any bank in this country that has a dollar in it I deposited, you more likely to find a apple on a pear tree. I'm willin to vow that I've never had a nickel in the bank in all the history of my life.

I left all I had in Vernon's hands when I was carried off to prison. That gave him a chance to get a foothold and come on up. And what I gived him to start off with—it was gived for the benefit of all of em—it was wore out or destroyed someway, but it had all produced heavy for em. They had full possession and it was enough in the way of personal property for none of em not to suffer. Left it with em premature—that was the moment I gived em whatever I had to give em, left it all to em. I'll have no chance to give em no more.

There's Vernon, only child I got in the world that's farmin. Calvin aint farmin, Francis aint farmin, Eugene aint farmin, Garvan aint farmin—Vernon farmin, makin a success at it, too. With all of his conditions—dropped now and lost part of his health; he got sugar. Somethin goin to kill us all and that sugar's a bad thing—I think he's beatin the other ones. There's all of my boys, start from Garvan, youngest boy I got. He owns a lot and I reckon he's about paid up and everything, and he's got a nice buildin out there. Eugene, he's got a lot in Ohio. He works some but his legs has done failed him. Before he come home the last time he'd got under a doctor on account of his legs, but still he managed to come. I hadn't seen the boy in eight years. Francis, he's got a nice brick house in Philadelphia. There's Calvin, he owns two lots in Tuskegee and a nice new brick home. But a lot won't compare with a small plantation; Vernon's the top of em all. He only owns sixty-one acres but he got about thirty-six head of cattle—I've counted em myself. That's a right smart cattle for a poor fellow got nobody to see after em but him, and then he's farmin too. The reason I say "poor" fellow, he aint got nothin above farmin to work at for his livin and got no way to work more land than he do now. Still and all he's a pretty heavy farmer; he never comes under thirty-odd and up around forty bales of cotton. And he don't think about puttin down less than five to seven hundred pounds of fertilize to the acre. I'm not braggin on him cause he's my child, but he runs about as nice a farm as you will find in this country.

And he done got to where he can handle the money part of the business himself. He gets a little help from his daughters but he don't say so. They stays in Brooklyn, New York—aint but two of em—and they helps him. He got three tractors and two Chevrolet trucks, one of em brand new, and a nice Chevrolet car. Just got em since this movement that's workin today opened things up for him. Vernon didn't have all he has now before these ways and rulins started to change. The boy, he's my child, but he's very careful. He's weedin his way through this world the best he can, and he's yet dealin with white people. Of course, he's dealin with moneyed men and he don't want to offend em.

And, as God would have it, he raised up two of his grandchildren. And out of them three grandchildren that stays with him now, one girl and two boys, ary one of them boys is about as heavy as I am—one of em's heavier than I am, I expect. He get on the tractor he can do anything Vernon can do on it. Well, that's a help to him. And that other one, the least boy, jump on that tractor, break land like a bull. But that oldest boy, jump on that tractor, straddle several rows of cotton and gone, cultivatin or breakin.

If Vernon were to die out, the dog's dead and the hunt's up, that's all. That place will fall to his daughters' hands and just as soon as it come to them, there's nothin doin. No doubt if his equipment and machinery is any account, it'll be dealt off at some price—just as well to do it. No doubt they'll sell the home. They aint comin back here; they is devoted to the northern country. Well, if Vernon drops out of there, what'll become of the land? His wife might just go north, liable to, or go back to some of her people out here the other side of Apafalya. She's got three brothers: two of em stays in Florida, Davis and Charles, one of em's half white, and this here'n over here, the other side of Apafalya, he's colored in full.

My children today is dear in my thoughts and dear towards me. That Francis, his talk is this: he realizes I was his father; he realizes I labored for him and raised him up in the world—that's his talk—when he couldn't help hisself; and how I stood by my children as a father and by their mother as a husband. Francis—and Rachel, oldest girl in the family, she'll talk to me—I don't remember whippin that child but twice in her life; didn't whip her then, just whisked her light. Might say I nettled her.

I don't say that the rest of my children won't talk it, but they aint done it, they never has divulged it up to me that they realizes me as a father, by the way I treated em. Now there's Vernon up there, my child, I love him, with all due respect for him—

I can't say what they thinks but I knows how they acts. And they've all but Vernon lost touch with farmin and some of em has lost touch with me as their father, in a way of speakin. Now I don't expect em to support me, I'm not that kind of man and I don't need *that*, but I'm lookin for em to bear me in their thoughts and feelins. I wish my children peace and good will. I wish the way will be clearer for em than ever in history and to know that I had a part

in makin it clear—that's the grandest of all. I'd appreciate it, if at
the time I'm dead and gone, they know that I did my part for peace
and pleasure and unity. And I did it for them.

I've noticed many things through the past history of my life—
uneducated man that I am—that point to a plan. Time passes and
the generations die. But the condition of the people that's livin today
aint like it was for the people that's gone. And it aint now like it's
goin to be for the people that comes after us. I can't say exactly
what the future way of life will be, but I has a idea. My color, the
colored race of people on earth, goin to shed theirselves of these
slavery ways. But it takes many a trip to the river to get clean.

God knows how this race has been treated. And there's a certain element that's workin to please God and overturn this southern
way of life. How many people is it today that it needs and it requires
to carry out this movement? How many is it knows just what it's
goin to take? It's taken time, untold time, and more time it'll take
before it's finished. Who's to do it? It's the best people of the United
States to do it, in the defense of the uneducated, unknowledged
ones that's livin here in this country. They goin to win! They goin
to win! But it's goin to take a great effort; we ought to realize that.
It won't come easy. Somebody got to move and remove and it may
take—how do I know how many it's goin to take?—I just realize
in my mind, it's goin to take thousands and millions of words,
thousands and millions of steps, to complete this business.

I'd like to live; and if the Lord see fit to able me to stay here and
see it, I'd love to know that the black race had fully shed the veil
from their eyes and the shackles from their feet. And I hope to God
that I won't be one of the slackers that would set down and refuse
to labor to that end.

SOMEDAY I'll be layin in the clay. Mama's already gone, Papa's
got to go someday. I aint scared of dyin; that worries me the least.
I think it over sometimes: 'O, well, I was born to die. They been
dyin ever since I been in this world. I'd love to stay here just as
long as God aims for me to stay, but that's all. I know I got to
go one day, there aint no help for it.' I've never known it said, such
words spoke, that a man can stay here as long as he wants to—
die when he wants to, live long as he wants to. It aint in our hands.

If the people didn't come and go from this world, and it be left up
to us about death, this world would be full of people as a ant bed
with ants.

I'm yet livin, I don't suffer for nothin, the things that I
want a heap of times or could use if I had em, they might be a
damnation to me, I don't know. I used to own cars—aint had the
name of a car since I come out of prison. I'd like to have me a truck
now. I watch these farmin fellows such as my boy up the road, got
two trucks; TJ down there got a truck; Garvan over there got one.
I just count on them trucks to haul my white oak. But you see, they
practically stays busy all the time. Garvan works at Calusa and
then works all over this country here for people. They just won't
let him set still, sendin for him. He's a carpenter, he's a welder—
that boy can do anything you want done. Put in your pipin, connect
it to your house—I reckon that's called a plumber. White folks uses
him all the time.

And so, that sort of cuts me down—he won't spend the time for
me. Will Tuttle down here's got two trucks—of course, some of the
rest of em around here got em, but them's my people. Will Tuttle,
he married my brother's daughter and that throwed him in the
family connection. He hauls a little white oak for me sometime.
But they're farmin now—Will, TJ, Vernon—and I hate to deprive
em of their work. Sometimes they just can't quit.

If I had a good truck I could haul my white oak, haul wood
if I had a fireplace. But if I had a truck today, first thing, I'd work
someway to build me a shed for that truck and let it stand there.
I'd be heartily glad if I could go to the market on my own truck;
haul me some white oak—and maybe I could get me a boy to go
along with me, tote white oak out the woods and stand it aside
the road, just so it was in a clear place where it wouldn't interfere
with the highway, pick up my white oak and drive it home.

And above that, let it go. I craves no riches—money can be
detrimental to your soul. If I did pile up any in the bank I'd draw it
out before I started dotin on it. High-lifin, graftin money, and
changin cars every year—what does God say? He says it's as much
impossible for a rich man—it's under the ledger of the Bible—to
seek the kingdom of heaven as it is for a camel to go through
the eye of a needle. I wants to go to a better home when I leave
here—it's nothin I brought here and nothin I'll carry away. I'm
just out here tappin in the world for my support and workin to carry

the grace of God away from here in my soul. I go for a Christian
man—that was the biggest change come over me in prison. Every
day of my life I has a interview with God. I know of Him. He put
a seal in my breast—bein a thinker and a lover of God, I can't
enumerate what a help it is to me. The day that God suffered me to
walk out and stand up for my rights, I was a sinner man, sinner
man, but I was doin at that present time what was pleasin to Him.
He saw what I done; He heard what I told them officers and I believe He was pleased at it, I can almost say I know it. When they
nabbed me and messed me up, throwed me down in Beaufort jail,
I just felt at a loss. Then my eyes become open to the one that could
help me and do me good. God stepped in and blessed my soul,
saved it from eternal wrath—it made me feel that I could rise and
fly. O, blessed God, it was just a new mornin altogether.

Churches aint goin to save you—churches don't save a man,
don't get that in your head. You got to be truly born again by the
blood of our precious Savior above; that's all goin to save you. You
needn't run around to the different churches and hoop and holler
and clap your hands to get to heaven when you die. Just so you
a believer of Christ, you a blood-bought soldier of God.

God says, "Shun sin as the deadly poison." That makes you
want to treat everybody right, treat em with respect for God's sake.
He didn't put us down here to live like dogs and brutes. God's got
people here in this world that aint goin to do right no way He
approaches em. He knew all that before He created us here. He's all
mighty, all wise God; there's nothin hidden under the cover from
Him. I feel that when He created the heaven and earth He knowed
just exactly how every man and every woman would conduct themselves. He knows all about you. He created you—what I mean by
created, He done a large part. I had a lovin mother once in life; I
didn't come in this world of myself, I was bred. And the Holy Father
above blessed me to come into this world by my mother and father.
Where did I originate? My mother was a Culver and my daddy
was a Shaw. Hadn't a been for them I wouldn't a been here. But
God fixed and planned a way for me. And He's kept His eyes on me
all through my life. God don't tell me to use anger, hatred—that's
of me, I'm goin by what suits me—

I'll make a parable of it: if I catch a white man havin nature-
course with a colored woman, I don't like it. I'm mad as the devil. I
don't want him messin around with my color, he don't want me

messin around with his color. Well, what do God say about this
here chicanery? The niggers hates the white folks, the white folks
hates the niggers—and they're brothers and sisters. So far as the
creatin of us, we're just created with different colors. I don't know
what God's cause was in makin us that way; it aint been revealed to
me. And I don't know that anybody's found out.

He tells me the white is my brother—still I gets angry at it.
God don't throw no chunks about it. He aint goin to come down
here and keep a white man off of a colored woman; He aint goin
to keep no colored man off of a white woman. After a while if that
goes on everybody will look just alike, in a way. Take a certain
length of time and all of em will look just alike, and all of em
won't show to be niggers and won't show to be white folks. You
don't know—you can read till your ears flop but you don't know all
bout what God's goin to do. Maybe when the human race gets
thoroughly mixed, that's the time God goin to call the whole settin
off.

If I'd a just reversed my words and said, "O, all we niggers is just
gettin along fine, and all the poor white folks—we just havin a
ball—" but I aint goin to tell it that way, I can't. No, it's right over
to the other side: they been brutally treated and scorned.

I tries my best to tell people today about this past way of life
but a heap of em don't want to hear me and let me know it to my
face: "We'd rather you talk about somethin else. We wants to forget
what you talkin about."

But I have had my eyes open too long to the facts, and my
ears, what I've heard; and what I have touched with my hands and
what have touched me is a fact. And I treasures what I know and I
so often think about it and how necessary it is to set an example
before God and man. I feel my best sympathy and hold my best
judgment for the poor Negro of my kind and the poor white man.
God knows I won't jump back from tellin what I know. And if
certain ones in this country knowed I've told all this, good God,
they'd be hankin to string me out.

I tell the world: all I wants is protection. I aint stepped back
nary a foot since I joined that union and furthermore, if you don't
slip up and hurt me, you better mind how you walk up on me today.
I stand now where I stood then, with the same thoughts and just

as willin as I started off. I aint huntin no trouble, but I'm flesh and blood and human. Do any man think that I wouldn't take some steps to help myself?

I went on after I come out of prison and bought me another good breech-loader. After that rip-it come off, the white folks runned all over this country takin all the guns they could find away from all the colored people. Even come and took old man Warren Jenks' guns from him. Took three breech-loaders from my house. Wasn't but one of em a stompin good gun and that was my father-in-law's —my mother-in-law gived it to me after the death of him and told me to keep it; she didn't tell me to keep it so long, she told me to *keep* that gun. That was one of the best breech-loaders I ever put up to my face. One of them guns, the plunge in it had done dulled up and got where it wouldn't bust a cap. I bought that gun when I was a young man and it was out of commission when it was taken from me.

They didn't get my short gun. That .32 Smith and Wesson is layin in the house now asleep—and loaded too. I been havin that gun more than fifty years and I takes care of it. I gived a fellow a dog and a little old shoat for it. That thing—on a Monday evenin, in December of '32, that thing squalled like a wildcat. I didn't let up until I emptied all six chambers.

There was a fellow in the crowd there at Virgil Jones' house that day went for a little kin to me, Lynn Cole. This boy is yet livin today in Birmingham. Walked up to me when the shootin had ceased and the sheriffs cleared out; told me, "Let me have your gun, Cousin Nate. Let me have your gun." And, unthoughtable, I handed it to him and I left there and left him with my gun, walked on home.

I heard the next day about the mob crowd ridin the settlement and country over, takin colored folks' guns. I wondered a long time bout what become of my gun. Lynn had got away and went on home with it, and however God would have it—his mother was named Faye, we always called her Cousin Faye Cole. Her husband was dead and him and her was the father and mother of two boys, Greg and Lynn, and a girl named Nellie. She was married at that time, Nellie was, and Greg was married, but Lynn wasn't. Lynn got home and gived that gun to Cousin Faye, his mother. She hid it, hid the devil out of it. And durin of my wife comin to see me in prison —she had been in contact with Cousin Faye. Cousin Faye told her she had my gun and one day she gived it to Hannah and Hannah brought it on home. And she come one Sunday and told me, "Darlin, I got your gun. Cousin Lynn gived it to his mother, Cousin Faye, and Cousin Faye gived it to me. She had your gun."

I been havin that gun more than fifty long years. Now I don't love to just shoot around and be shootin, but I shoots it sometimes just to see if it will yet answer me. I come out my house and stand on the brick doorstep and throw it to the air—I never shoot it straight along. I throw it to the air and ask it for all six shots. Counts em just like a new born baby: YAW YAW YAW YAW YAW YAW.

Nate Shaw died on Monday, November 5, 1973.
He was buried at Pottstown Baptist Church,
Tukabahchee County, Alabama.

APPENDIX

During the early years of the Great Depression, the Communist Party sent organizers to Alabama to build a steelworkers union in Birmingham and a sharecroppers union in the countryside. The cotton system was verging on collapse. Cotton prices had been falling steadily since the end of the First World War, and now, as prices hit bottom, nobody could make a profit. Many poor farmers were uprooted; those who stayed were threatened with the loss of their meager property and means of support.

After crops were planted in the spring of 1931, landlords and merchants in the Crane's Ford area decided to cut off food advances to their tenants and sharecroppers while the cotton ripened in summer. Landlords also reduced day wages for field work.

The *Southern Worker*, a Party newspaper serving the southern states, printed letters from unidentified "farmer correspondents" at Crane's Ford, describing conditions there and asking for help. The Party sent an organizer to form a union local. Black farmers met with him and drew up a list of demands: food advances through "settlement" time; the right to sell their own crops and to plant small gardens for home use; wages for picking cotton to be paid in cash in full; a three-hour midday rest for day workers; a nine-month school year for black children and a free school bus. These demands went beyond measures to meet the current crisis; if met, they would have given poor farmers some control over work conditions and improved their chances in the world through education.

Party strategists believed that fighting for specific demands would prepare black farmers for "self-determination." In the Party's view, the black majorities of black-belt counties shared economic, territorial, and cultural identities; hence, they constituted a "nation." This "nation" would become a reality if the black-belt counties were unified across state lines. Then, in theory, black majorities could enfranchise themselves and vote to decide if they would have an independent political system.

But in 1931, black farmers had to struggle simply to remain on the land. The confrontation at Crane's Ford was a defensive action characteristic of the Sharecroppers Union's (SCU) early history, from 1931 to 1933. Crane's Ford farmers had not yet planned any particular tactics to implement their demands when, on July 15, 1931, their meeting was raided by the high sheriff and his posse. The raid touched off several days of sporadic violence. One farmer was killed and his house burned, and thirty-five blacks were jailed on charges ranging from carrying concealed weapons to assault and conspiracy with intent to murder. They were never brought to trial. By September, all were released, possibly due to lack of evidence and possibly because the cotton needed picking.

But the SCU was effectively suppressed in Crane's Ford. In late fall, 1932, the Party sent a second organizer to Pottstown, some fifteen miles to the south. Nate Shaw describes what happened there. Following the shoot-out between farmers and sheriffs, legal prosecution and vigilante violence curtailed union activity in the area.

Beginning in 1933, the SCU concentrated its efforts in the black belt west of Tukabahchee County. There, organizers saw the large plantations as "factories in the fields." Farm laborers who neither owned nor rented the land were brought by the wagonload and truckload into the fields to chop and pick cotton for wages paid daily, weekly, or monthly. The SCU claimed it had organized several thousand farm laborers, and in 1935 the union led wage strikes with modest success across the Alabama black belt.

Repression was severe, especially in Lowndes County, where whites, outnumbered by blacks seven to one, defended their supremacy with armed force. Seeking protection and additional resources, the SCU turned to New Deal agencies for relief. After

1935, the SCU acted more and more as a liaison between poor farmers and the New Deal.

When, in 1936, the Party called for a "united front" of communist and other "progressive" forces, SCU organizers were already proposing to affiliate with national unions. Tenants, sharecroppers, and wageworkers were each to merge with an older, established union representing its particular needs. By late 1938, SCU tenants and sharecroppers had transferred to the Farmers Union, a national organization modeled on the Grange and the Farmers Alliance of the 1880's and '90's. Wageworkers merged into the Agricultural Workers Union, which was chartered by the American Federation of Labor in 1937 as the Farm Laborers and Cotton Field Workers Union.

Affiliation signaled the SCU's shift from a strategy of "national liberation" of the black belt to positions squarely in the tradition of American agrarian protest. The Farmers Union stressed credit and market problems and lobbied for nationalizing the banks, dismantling monopolies, and reforming the tax structure.

The shift in goals was mainly a shift on paper. Organizers had always responded to farmers' actual needs for self-defense and occupational improvements. Slogans about self-determination of the black belt had little immediate appeal to people fighting to save their livestock or to earn an extra fifty cents a day. Changes in Party strategy, such as the call for a "united front," did influence the SCU's direction and affiliation, but conditions in the field generally determined union tactics.

The SCU's struggle to secure a livelihood for poor farmers was resolved, in part, in the general "solutions" to the Great Depression. By the outbreak of the Second World War, war industries had begun to absorb black and white farmers displaced in the economic crisis; public welfare maintained others who could not or would not leave the land.

INDEX

This index is intended to help the reader locate themes, topics, and events in Nate Shaw's life. As a rule, entries are listed alphabetically, while subentries follow the chronology of the narrative. The Shaw family is an exception. Parents precede children, and children follow one another by order of birth. Nate Shaw has no separate entry.

In selecting characters to be indexed, I was guided primarily by their significance to the cotton system. These characters appear under entries which describe their roles—"banker," "landlords," etc.

Some entries are indexed in greater detail than others, in keeping with their importance to Shaw or to my understanding of his history. "Class" and "race relations" refer to explicit examples or explanations of such. In most entries, I used words that Shaw would have used, or did use.

About the Author

Theodore Rosengarten was born in 1944, in Brooklyn,
New York. He was graduated from Amherst College
in 1966 and received a Ph.D. from Harvard
University in 1975. The next year he moved to
McClellanville, South Carolina, where he lives with
his wife and son. Mr. Rosengarten is currently
studying and writing about plantation society in
the last days of slavery.